AND THE WALLS CAME
TUMBLING DOWN

AND THE WALLS CAME TUMBLING DOWN

Ralph David Abernathy

AN AUTOBIOGRAPHY

1817

HARPER & ROW, PUBLISHERS, New York

Grand Rapids, Philadelphia, St. Louis, San Francisco

London, Singapore, Sydney, Tokyo, Toronto

Designed by Alma Orenstein

Library of Congress Cataloging-in-Publication Data
Abernathy, Ralph, 1926–
   And the walls came tumbling down: an autobiography / Ralph David
Abernathy.—1st ed.
   p. cm.
  ISBN 0-06-016192-2
   1. Abernathy, Ralph, 1926– . 2. Civil rights workers—United
States—Biography. 3. Afro-Americans—Biography. I. Title.
E185.97.A13A3   1989   89-45023
323′.092—dc20
[B]

89 90 91 92 93 AC/RRD 10 9 8 7 6 5 4

To my devoted wife,
Juanita Odessa Jones Abernathy,
without whose love, patience, and strength
my life would have been incomplete

I have much to write to you, but I do not care to set it down
with pen and ink. I hope to see you very soon, and we will talk
face to face. Peace be with you. Our friends send their
greetings. . . . Greet our friends.

3 John 13–15

"JOSHUA FIT DE BATTLE OB JERICHO"

Joshua fit de battle ob Jericho, Jericho, Jericho,
    Joshua fit de battle ob Jericho, An' de walls come tumblin' down.
You may talk about yo' King ob Gideon, You may talk about yo' man ob Saul,
    Dere's none like good de Joshua, At de battle ob Jericho.
Up to de walls ob Jericho; He marched wid spear in han'
    "Go blow dem rams' horns," Joshua cried—"Kase de battle am in my han."
Den de lam' ram sheep horns begin to blow, de trumpets begin to soun',
    Joshua commanded de chillen to shout, An' de walls come tumblin' down.
Joshua fit de battle ob Jericho, Jericho, Jericho,
    Joshua fit de battle ob Jericho, An' de walls come tumblin' down.

Contents

ILLUSTRATIONS FOLLOW PAGE 270.

Introduction

I SUPPOSE IT IS PRESUMPTUOUS for anyone to write an autobiography. When I began to consider the possibility many years ago, I came to the conclusion that most of what I had to tell was a matter of public record; much of the rest consisted of things that every black person had experienced. I had enough to do, after all, without taking the time to write a book about things that people already knew.

But the truth is, after a few years people tend to forget their past; and what everyone once knew becomes a strange and wonderful story to the next generation. I find that idea a little frightening, particularly when I see so many blacks who neither remember nor understand their past. If we are to survive and prosper as a people, we cannot forget who we are or where we came from.

If my personal experience has any value in the 1980s, it is because I grew up in the South of the 1930s and 1940s and because I was part of a great movement that changed the face of American society and made that old way of life obsolete. In fifty years we will all be gone—those who lived under Jim Crow—and when that time comes, I want the American people, white as well as black, to have a record of precisely how it was.

Of course, historians do an excellent job of re-creating the past, but for the most part they do so by superimposing their own abstractions on the concrete particulars of experience. They are great organizers and extrapolators, but all too often they ignore or discard the details of life in order to portray more clearly the truths they recognize.

But I believe everything that happens is valuable and should be preserved, filed away in its proper place, an essential part of the meaning of the universe, which only God can completely understand. And if God remembers every bit and piece of experience, then we oughtn't to be too contemptuous of accounts that tell about everyday life as it was once lived or about the seemingly irrelevant particulars of events that shaped the history of our times.

So I have decided to write this autobiography after all for two reasons: first, to show how life was lived during the era of Jim Crow and, second, to show what it was like to be at the center of the civil rights movement as it operated on a day-by-day basis. If my life has any special meaning, it is because I was both a typical black growing up in the segregated South and because, unlike other typical blacks, I was privileged to be in "command headquarters"—in the earlier years as Martin Luther King's closest friend and "pastor" of the movement, and in later years as its leader.

My childhood was spent in Marengo County, Alabama, where I grew up on a farm, as did most southern blacks until after World War II. During those times we literally "lived off the land," growing most of what we ate, trading for most of the other necessities, and surviving with very little cash to buy the things that an increasingly complicated world required: school books, tuition, automobiles. We were almost completely self-sufficient and therefore we had a larger measure of freedom than did most urban dwellers. Yet we were still prisoners of a system that limited our potential growth and achievement as human beings. So we shared in the institutionalized humiliation common to all our people, and I want to tell about that—perhaps in a way that will surprise many people.

My later years were spent largely on the road, living in motels and private homes, taking to the streets every day, often enough ending up in jail. During this period I was verbally and physically abused, attacked by dogs and fire hoses, gassed, and set upon by screaming mobs. It was only during this lengthy and dangerous era that for the first time we began to understand just what freedom really was and how much it inevitably costs in human sacrifice.

Some portion of this latter story has been told, but there are still dimensions that have been left out of recent accounts, written by white historians or by black observers with a limited vision of what took place. I was there from beginning to end, from the Montgomery bus boycott in the late autumn of 1955 to Memphis in the spring of 1968 to Washington in 1988. No one else experienced it all, so no one else can really tell the whole story from the viewpoint of an eyewitness.

Of course, in one sense the eyewitness is a fallible narrator. He (or she) stands in one place and therefore can't see what is happening along the entire battlefront. If you want to know how the Battle of Gettysburg was won, you can't ask just one soldier or even General Meade. You have to collect a number of reports and sift through them. That's how the historian works.

On the other hand, perhaps you know more about how it felt to be in that battle by following one person's experience of it from beginning to end, even though you don't always know what's happening elsewhere. When people want to know how it felt to fight in the Civil War, they often read the *Red Badge of Courage* by Stephen Crane rather than some formal history, because Crane's story is one man's experience of how it felt to be in battle. I would like my autobiography to be that kind of book—a narrative of how it felt rather than of everything that happened.

Of course, there are other limitations of the eyewitness account. If you tell a story from one person's point of view, then there is always a bias to take into account. Clearly, my narrative of what happened will reflect my own interpretation of the events and the people involved. Other eyewitnesses have likewise reflected different perspectives. As a matter of fact, in reading recent civil rights histories such as *Bearing the Cross* I can almost pick out the sentence when the author stops using one source and starts using another, so obvious is the shifting bias. So I write this less-than-objective account with no more than the usual apologies.

I will say in my defense, however, that with the passage of time I have gained a greater understanding of what went on during those turbulent years. When the Montgomery bus boycott first began, Martin and I were still in our twenties; and while we knew the basic issues involved in the struggle as well as older blacks, we were still relatively inexperienced in the ways of the world, and most of the things we did were in the nature of experiments. When they didn't work, we sat down and tried to figure out why we had failed. When they did work, we often neglected to analyze fully the reasons for the efficacy. Yet over the years I have had a chance to reflect on the past, and for that reason I believe I now understand many things that were puzzling in the 1950s and 1960s. So perhaps it's a good thing I waited to tell my story.

I have told most of it before—in bits and pieces—to those historians, black and white, who have come to me and asked me to recall those times. I have always tried to be generous in relating my recollections; for that reason, some of what you read may sound familiar. But there are some things that I am telling now for the first time, in part because I need to set the record straight, in part because some things can only be told using the first person.

In including some of the things that follow, I have had to agonize, balancing my need to tell a complete and honest story with what I know to be my responsibility to respect the privacy and dignity of the living and the dead. I can only say that I have written nothing in malice and omitted nothing out of cowardice. (Or so I like to believe.)

Finally, I need to give some indication of the way in which I constructed this narrative, giving credit to my sources and to those who helped me put the pieces together, as well as to the editors who provided me with much-needed editorial assistance.

First, my most important source has been my own memory of past events. I now realize that in helping other historians research their works, I have been preparing to write my own account. After all, each time I told a story I remembered more about what had happened, thereby filling in the details of what may have been on the first telling a sketchy and incomplete narrative.

Thus have I been able to render in specific detail incidents that happened twenty-five years ago, because they have never really disappeared from my consciousness. In particular, I would cite my recollections of the first days of the Montgomery boycott and my memory of what happened in Birmingham just before we defied a court order and marched against Bull Connor's dogs and water hoses.

On the other hand, I could obviously not depend on memory alone, particularly since dates and sequences inevitably become blurred after thirty years and more. So I relied on four major types of sources to reinforce my own memory. First, I consulted several important historical accounts, including those of David Garrow (*Bearing the Cross*, New York: William Morrow & Co., 1986) and Taylor Branch (*Parting the Waters*, New York: Simon & Schuster, 1988). In these volumes I was able to verify dates and make certain that I put events in their proper order. In some cases I found the published accounts to be in error; where I was certain that such was the case, I have made note of the fact.

My second major corroborative source has been contemporary newspaper accounts, particularly those of the *New York Times*. Often these descriptions have contained precise phrasing and specific detail that I would otherwise have been able to supply with less accuracy. So I have used them with a little more confidence than I placed in the more recent histories. Newspaper accounts are not nearly as comprehensive or as well organized as history books, but they are certainly more factual.

My third source has been my collection of letters, documents, notes, and photographs to which I have referred in order to refresh my memory. Over the years I have been a pack rat, and my closets and shelves are full of material that I have yet to examine and catalog. But in reconstructing the past, I have found a number of items that have spurred my memory and helped me to be more precise and detailed.

Fourth, I have checked my own recollections against those of my wife, Juanita, and other friends who lived through those years. At times they have been able to remind me of things I had forgotten, and at other times they have been able to correct errors in my own specific recollections.

In consulting these sources, however, I have adhered to one simple rule: If an incident did not square with my own recollections, I left it out of my narrative, no matter how important or how convincing it seemed to be. So what follows is my own account of the past, what I myself remember. I am grateful, however, to these other sources and hereby acknowledge my debt.

In addition to my wife, Juanita—who has been with me from the beginning in planning and executing this project—I would also like to express gratitude to several other people who have also helped immeasurably. My good friend Thomas H. Landess has shared the burden of my research, spending countless hours in the library poring over microfilm in order to check particular points and to find quotations. He has also offered expert editorial advice to which I have paid close attention.

In Daniel Bial of Harper & Row I have had a second skilled editor—experienced, exacting, and patient. He too has made important suggestions and has exacted more from me than I knew I could deliver. For this faith and concern, I am deeply grateful.

I would like to thank my assistant, the Reverend Terry Walker, for his continued help and loyalty in this and in all other undertakings. He too has made important contributions to this volume.

My brothers and sisters, nine of them still alive, have made most valuable contributions to the completion of this manuscript.

I cannot close this without expressing my deep and sincere appreciation to the deacons, trustees, and the entire membership of the historic West Hunter Street Baptist Church, who made the writing of this manuscript much easier because of their love and understanding when their senior pastor needed to be away without explaining his whereabouts. Thanks to all of you, the most beautiful congregation in my estimation. You are truly a great and loving people of God.

Ralph D. Abernathy
April 1989

1

Little David

EW PEOPLE LIVING IN ALABAMA in 1926 could have foreseen that in less than a lifetime segregation would be legally ended and blacks would not only be voting but seeking office in every southern state, even running for president of the United States. Certainly no one in the Hopewell community would have believed such a thing possible, nor would they have believed that the small child born there on March 11 would one day be among those who played a key role in making this social revolution a reality. But my grandmother somehow knew my destiny the moment I came into the world.

Her name was Ellen Bell, and she was a midwife; by general agreement, the best midwife in the county. In fact, she was so widely trusted that she delivered hundreds of children for black and white alike, including those of the white physician who attended the Abernathy family. As it turns out, she died the following September, so I was the last child she delivered. Shortly after I was born she told my mother: "Louivery, I've brought many of your children into the world. In fact, this is the tenth one.

But he's different, strange. I predict that he will be known throughout the world."

Later in life I was told that my father was working in the fields on the afternoon I was born and when he arrived home, my older brothers and sisters crowded around to ask him what I would be called; but he didn't answer immediately. He wanted time, he said, to think about it. Members of our family were not named frivolously, as is sometimes the case in families today. It was a matter to think and pray about; so my father went off by himself and gave careful consideration to what I would be called. Indeed, it wasn't until the next morning that he brought everybody together and announced that my name would be "David."

And everyone called me David for the first twelve years of my life. As a matter of fact, "David" is the name on my birth certificate; and it has never been officially changed. When I was twelve, however, my sister Manerva (whom we called "M. A.") came home from college full of stories about one of her teachers, whom she admired and talked about constantly. His name, as fate would have it, was "Ralph David"; and at some point she began calling me by that name.

Because it meant so much to her, I allowed her to continue the practice, though my family and those people who knew me as a child still call me "David." When I went into the armed forces in 1944, I enlisted as "Ralph David Abernathy," and the name has followed me ever since.

However, after all these years I've had second thoughts, and I now wish I had never consented to the change. In the first place, I had taken a name foreign to my family, one that my father had not given me. Then, too, there is much meaning in a name. If you are given the right name, you start off with certain indefinable but very real advantages.

My father understood this truth when he thought all night before finally deciding to call me "David," after the young shepherd boy who spent his childhood in the fields and then, as a young man, went to battle and killed a giant. Whether or not he foresaw any such life for me, he certainly knew that with all his faults David was one of the great figures of the Bible, a man who knew and loved God. To have been a "David" in my later years

might have occasionally given me additional strength and courage. I do know that as just plain "Ralph" there were times when
I felt inadequate to face the challenges before me, when I could
have used the cunning and skill of a man who slew his ten
thousands and outwitted old King Saul.

In my first years, however, I was still David and remained so
as long as I was under the protection and authority of my parents.
During those times I tried to live up to the promise of my name:
I was the religious boy, always in church or taking care of the
preacher; and I was the shepherd boy as well, tending to the
animals and running errands across the broad fields of my
father's farm. There were no giants in those days, and little in my
life would have hinted at future strife and distant battlefields.

Most of the faces I saw day in and day out belonged to
members of my own family, people who loved me and had my
best interests at heart. In rural Alabama during the twenties and
thirties, blacks and whites alike lived for the most part on farms
owned and operated by a single family; for this reason, close
relatives were not only your blood kin but your fellow workers and
playmates as well, those with whom you spent most of your time
and who most influenced your early life.

So it was typical of the times that the people who most
molded my character were my father, my mother, and my
paternal grandfather, rather than a friend, a teacher, or some
personality in public life. These familiar figures not only told me
every single thing I needed to know in order to survive and
mature, but they also provided me with strong examples to
follow—and in that respect I was extremely fortunate, because
too many children early in life have to face the unpleasant truth
that their parents pay lip service to one set of principles and live
by another. In my case there was never any discrepancy between
what my parents taught me and the way they behaved themselves. They lived up to all expectations and kept all promises.

I suppose my father W. L. Abernathy was the most dominant
figure in my early life. I remember him as a big man, taller than
anyone around him, taller than anyone I had ever seen during

those years. Yet measured by a yard stick he was only about five-foot-seven and therefore of no more than average height with a slim frame. He was stern and righteous, the kind of man other men feared, despite the fact that he never fought or quarreled with anyone. Moral authority, it seemed, added about five or six inches to everyone's perception of his physical stature.

Wherever he was, whatever he was doing, my father always meant business. He was never frivolous or playful, even with his children. His brothers, my uncles, were forever telling jokes, teasing us, entering into all manner of horseplay; but I can never remember my father joining in the fun. When everyone else was playing he would go off by himself and work alone. He was always working, while my uncles took life easy. But they were never as successful as he was, and they never seemed quite as tall.

The Abernathys had always been poor, largely, I suspect, because they were not blessed with a burning desire to work. My paternal grandfather, George Abernathy, had inherited a small farm from which he and his family had wrung a meager living, not because the land was poor but because most of the Aber-nathys had better things to do than plow, plant, and weed. They went to barbecues. They drank a little. They told marvelous stories. Only my father, who never told a story in his life, was single-mindedly devoted to improving his lot.

He was a farmer, as were most people who lived in the South during that time; but unlike some of our neighbors, black and white, we were not struggling to survive on a patch of hard-scrabble land. My father owned approximately five hundred acres of good, black soil that he had bought a few acres at a time, having begun with a wedding gift of a milk cow and a calf.

To get ahead, he did three things: worked as hard as he possibly could; led a severely disciplined and sober life; and married well. My mother was a Bell, and the Bells were known to be relatively prosperous landowners. Grandmother Bell, the woman who delivered me, owned a large farm in the hilly section just north of the place my father had bought, and he would always speak to her as she drove by in her surrey on the way to deliver a baby. Occasionally, she would stop to chat with him, pronouncing fiery judgments on the sinners in the community, or for that matter, on anyone who crossed her. He soon impressed her with his moral earnestness; and when the time came, she was quite pleased to have him as a son-in-law.

Her husband, Noah, died before I was born, but he was remembered by members of the family as patient and submissive, a man well aware of who was boss in his household. I believe my father must have patterned his own behavior toward his mother-in-law on that of Noah, because where she was concerned he was curiously compliant. My oldest sister Ella Louise ("Doll") remembers our grandmother ordering my father to put them to work, which he did promptly and cheerfully, without the slightest protest that she was intruding into his affairs. No one else on either side of the family could have gotten away with such interference; and I don't think it was her three hundred rolling acres so much as the steel in her backbone. In her he recognized a kindred spirit, someone who believed, as he did, in righteousness and self-reliance.

My father always said that land would be the means by which we would rise in the world. He was convinced that the solution to the race problem was economic. He often talked about a time when the bottom rail would rise to the top, when black people would come into their own.

We lived in a six-room house—a long bungalow with huge rooms that my father had paid my uncle Tulfa Bell to build. Uncle Tulfa was a skilled carpenter, and the house was one of the finest and most solidly constructed in the area. In fact, it was so spacious that my paternal grandmother referred to it as "the big white house," probably because she never adjusted to the realization that my father had been more successful than his brothers.

This defensiveness on behalf of her other sons was one of the few flaws in her character, however. From her my father got his religious faith and his commitment to the church. She was a great Christian whose honored task it was to make the communion wine that represented the Blood of Christ and the bread that represented the Body. She did this for most of her life, and when she died she was near one hundred years old. Her name was Manerva, and we called her "Grandma Nervy."

My father, incidentally, was called "Willy" by older members of the family, "Will" by a few white merchants who were his friends, and "W. L. Abernathy" by everyone else. In general, people throughout the surrounding areas knew that he was much better off financially than the average white person who lived in nearby Linden, and for that reason (as well as because of his enormous moral authority) people understood that they were not to bother his wife, his children, his land, or in any way challenge his dignity. They knew that he would pay his bills, that his credit was good, and that whatever he wanted from the bank he could get simply by asking.

He was, after all, a respected farmer in a part of the country where farming was the most respected of all vocations—a way of life as well as a means of making money. Today, of course, farmers need more cash than they did then because today they grow for profit and buy their groceries and other necessities from the supermarket and department stores. But back in those days the farmer took care of his family's needs first, and on the remaining land he raised a crop to take to market.

Consequently, we never wanted for any of life's necessities. Everything I learned about the Great Depression was from a college textbook. We didn't know that people were lining up at soup kitchens in cities all over the country because we raised cattle, hogs, and chickens so we had beef, pork, chicken, eggs, and milk. My father killed thirty to forty hogs a year, and whenever we wanted beef he would kill a calf. We always had hams curing in our smokehouse, and I can remember laborers preferring to be paid in hams rather than in cash because the hams were better than any you could buy.

In the garden we grew corn, beets, tomatoes, black-eyed peas, beans, Irish potatoes, sweet potatoes, squash, okra, collard greens, turnips, mustard greens; and in the orchard we raised peaches, plums, pears, figs, and apples. We had the corn ground to make meal, grits, and "chops" for the chickens; and whatever we lacked in the way of food supplies—like salt, soda, and flour—we bartered for at the general store, which was run by our white neighbor Mr. Robert Jones. Mr. Jones would give us thirty cents a dozen for our eggs if we took payment in trade, but if we wanted cash he would give us only twenty cents a dozen.

Our principal cash crop was cotton. My father was able to produce 100 to 150 bales every year, which provided us with the other necessities of life: clothes, shoes, medicine, and contributions to the church. But there were no frills. With twelve children to support, he made certain that nothing was spent on frivolity and nothing wasted.

I remember as a child being outfitted in my first suit, which—with alterations—was expected to last me for several seasons. Unfortunately, I soon discovered that I was allergic to the wool; I broke out in a rash every time the suit touched my skin. My father was sympathetic but unyielding. There was no money for another suit, so I would have to wear that one for the next few years. And wear it I did, scratching my way through a hundred or more Sundays, dreaming of the time when I would outgrow the suit and be allowed to buy a new one.

Yet there was always money for the church and for education. My father gave much of what he earned to the Hopewell Baptist Church. He donated lumber to build the first Hopewell public grade school, and he also contributed heavily to Linden Academy, a black high school founded by the First Mt. Pleasant District Baptist Association in order to prepare children in our area for college, since there were no public high schools.

On at least one occasion my father's generosity got him in trouble with my mother. On a Sunday morning, our small church was visited by "Professor" G. P. Austin, principal of Linden Academy, who was there to "hit up" the congregation for additional funds, since the school's teachers were in need of a raise. I remember sitting in the rear of the church, squirming in my wool suit, watching my father as he sat upright in the Amen corner while the principal talked about the good work accomplished in the school and the necessity for paying his teachers a living wage. He was certain, he said, that the Hopewell Church would help, because Deacon Abernathy, a trustee of the academy, had already led all others in generosity by giving a thousand dollars. At that moment my mother, sitting across from my father with the deaconesses, suddenly snapped to attention.

"You talk too much," he said to the principal with a weak smile, but the warning had come too late. After church he managed to avoid my mother, but he was trapped at Sunday dinner and there she talked at some length about the pressing needs of the family while my father tried to change the subject.

Yet I don't think she was really angry with him, because she knew that he had given the money not out of a desire to gain recognition but out of a belief in the idea of sacrificial giving and also out of a commitment to the education of his children. Neither he nor my mother had received more than a few years of formal education, and he was convinced that to survive and prosper in a competitive world we would have to go to college.

In fact, he often spoke on this subject at church, when, in his capacity as head deacon, he would address the congregation before the tithes and offerings were received. On these occasions, he would usually begin by commenting on the preacher's sermon and then he would move on to broader social issues, including the matter of race relations, always instructing those present to practice diligence, frugality, and honesty—virtues that he believed would eventually make the difference in the struggle for black dignity. Then he would close with a few words on the importance of education. So it was no surprise on that Sunday morning when "Professor" Austin made his announcement. What was undoubtedly a surprise to everyone, including my mother, was the amount he had donated. One thousand dollars in the 1930s was an enormous sum, particularly for blacks in a small farming community.

He felt, I suppose, that it was important for him to set a good example as well as to offer sound advice. As head deacon for almost forty years, he was the spiritual leader of the entire community; and since the church was composed of our family and its immediate connections, he was also head of the family as well. Hard-working, serious, and abstemious—qualities greatly prized by the rural Baptist church—he was both an example and a reproof to everyone else. The drinkers and gamblers in the congregation feared his gaze more than the preacher's, though he never reprimanded them, either directly or indirectly.

For me he was the nearest thing on earth to God, someone who inspired fear as well as love—and in just about equal parts. He was a stern disciplinarian, one who would use his razor strop at the least hint of rebellion, yet he was affectionate as well; and we never doubted his benevolence toward us, even when he was most severe.

He believed that all human beings were ultimately servants of the Lord, and he saw childhood as a period during which one trained for that service. We all had our tasks, and work was our most important preoccupation. But in addition to regular chores around the house and in the fields, we also served our parents in special tasks.

For example, I was taught at an early age to pinch my father's scalp in a way that somehow pleased him—why, I don't know, since the harder I pinched the more he seemed to enjoy it. In fact, at the end of a hard day's work in the fields he liked nothing better than to sit in a chair, nodding while I pressed the flesh of his scalp between the fingernails of my two thumbs. He would relish this activity for what seemed like hours, and only when his chin fell on his chest would I dare to stop. Then, more often than not, he would jerk his head around, glare at me with sleepy eyes, and say, "What made you stop?" Then I would have to continue until he finally relaxed enough to get up and go to bed.

As I look back on him after more than forty years of life without his day-by-day example, I realize the degree to which he sacrificed his own comforts and pleasures to the greater good of others. He had grown up among fun-loving, hard-living people, yet he deliberately turned his back on laughter and play in order to build a secure life for his family, one that would make them all but invulnerable to the attacks of those whites who, for their own reasons, wanted to abuse black people.

In an era when poverty was the rule rather than the exception, we were provided for; and in a world of racism and Jim Crow, we walked in safety and were treated courteously by whites who knew my father and recognized in his fierce gaze a strength and independence that they either admired or else turned away from in fear and shame.

He gave me many words of advice when I was a child, but one thing he told me stands out above all others, probably because it did not arise out of any specific incident but out of some insight that he must have arrived at in contemplating my character. As we were standing together one day, with no one else around, he turned to me and said, apropos of nothing: "David, if you ever see a good fight, get in it—and win it."

Years later, in Montgomery, Alabama, when I came up against a case of injustice that demanded action on my part, however risky, I suddenly remembered his words, spoken out of a stern and uncompromising love, and I knew what I had to do.

I learned about strength, independence, and moral earnestness from my father, while my mother taught me kindness, love, and gentility. She was the sweetest and most caring person I have ever known; and from the beginning her presence at my side flooded my life with warmth and sunlight. For as long as she lived, I belonged to her, and when she died my youth and innocence died with her.

Her maiden name was Louivery Valentine Bell (she was born on St. Valentine's Day), and she married my father on New Year's Eve in 1905. She bore him twelve children who survived infancy, and I can never recall that they quarreled or raised their voices in anger against one another. As a result of this domestic peace our family was close-knit and loving. The familial harmony that exists today among my brothers and sisters is in large measure a legacy of my mother's.

Not that she submitted without protest to my father's strong hand when she believed he was wrong. But she would never challenge him in front of the children, I suppose because she knew it might undermine his authority in our eyes. But in her quiet, endearing way, she was as strong as he was, something I found out when I was around six years old and entering school for the first time.

Like every younger child in a large family, I lived with

hand-me-downs; I wore them and played with them. But when I went to school I wanted my own books—brand new ones with perfectly white inside covers where I could write my own name without first scratching out the name of my brother. Books were special to me, and my mother understood how I felt.

My father, on the other hand, was more pragmatic. He had housed, fed, and clothed ten of us, with two more coming up; and he saw no reason why he should have to buy more books when there were perfectly legible copies of what I needed stacked up in one of the closets. "You use William's books," he told me. "It's foolishness to waste money on new ones."

I tried to protest, but he simply didn't want to listen. There were other needs, other priorities. He was immovable and my eyes filled with tears.

Then I noticed my mother watching me with anguish on her face; and I was amazed to see her dabbing her eyes with her apron. She was crying because of me! I believe it was the first time in my life that I understood what love really meant, that capacity to feel the suffering of others as if it were your own. I was stunned with the sheer beauty of it, and a little frightened as well. My father wheeled and walked quickly out of the room, on his way to saddle his mule for a ride around the farm. He left behind a room filled with cold air.

Then my mother, without a word to me, charged after him. Through the window I could see her rushing to catch up to him as he walked toward the open field where the mule was grazing. Because I knew that my father's word, like the Good Lord's, was absolutely and eternally true, I turned from the scene and went somewhere to brood.

The next day, when I didn't have the right books, I was scolded by the teacher. I assured her that I would have the books by the next day, though my heart was in despair, because I knew my father all too well. However, when I came in the front door after school I saw them piled in a neat stack on the dining room table: all the books I needed, their jackets untorn and unwrinkled, their pages still white and unsoiled.

I knew immediately who was responsible, and I went into the kitchen to hug my mother. Later, when my father came in from the fields, I thanked him as well, but he merely nodded his head and brushed the matter aside. That afternoon I understood a little more about the world in which I lived than I had that morning.

Like my father, my mother perpetually worked—from the time she got up in the morning until she went to bed at night. Anyone who believes that all labor on a farm takes place in the fields doesn't understand the agrarian enterprise. In this era of frozen foods and TV dinners, we forget that only a few decades ago food had to be enjoyed in season, or else canned or preserved by a laborious process that took days and days in the kitchen, usually at the hottest time of the year. And no one had air conditioning in those days; so with peaches or plums on the stove, it was at least as hot in the kitchen as it was in the fields. And there my mother spent most of her time, making certain that we had enough to eat in the winter, when most of the fruits and vegetables had to come out of a jar. So we never thought of my father alone as the "provider" for the family. My mother, in her own way, was just as much a provider as he was.

She was also as deeply religious as my father, but in an entirely different manner. He was like God the Father to me and to the rest of the family. He knew all the answers to the hard theological questions, and he laid down the law. But my mother was more like God the Holy Spirit—full of hope and joy and love. If my father thought long and hard about his faith, she *felt* hers; and it was her way, finally, that led me to the Lord and to my Christian ministry.

Of course, from the time I knew my name I also knew I was going to be a preacher. The preacher, after all, was the finest and most important person around, someone who was accorded respect wherever he went. But until I was seven I didn't understand precisely what motivated a preacher. Religion—the kind of religion that grabs your soul and won't let go—was something that most children don't experience and are not encouraged to experience. In fact, I had heard my father say many times that "preaching is not a vocation for a boy but for a man." And certainly no one became a preacher until he "got" religion, so as a small child I assumed that religion, like preaching, was for men only.

However, in the summer of my seventh year, an evangelist came to town and held a week-long revival meeting at Hopewell Baptist Church. I can still see and hear him in my imagination: the Reverend L. R. Jackson from Birmingham, a huge man who made sweeping theological statements while grabbing his enormous stomach and cradling it in his arms. Every so often he would let out two or three loud whoops that would start the congregation weeping, moaning, and shouting, all at the same time.

Because I was fascinated with church activities, I went every night, more curious than devout. My mother went with me; and as the preaching and shouting began, I could see that it all had a remarkable effect on her.

Sometimes she cried, sometimes she became suddenly and gloriously happy. Watching her, I felt a little of what she was feeling. I suppose she must have noticed my involvement in her own emotions, because one morning after a night of singing, weeping, and shouting for joy she said to me, "David, why don't you get religion and join the church?"

"How do I do that?" I asked.

"You fast and you pray. You do it all day long, and all night long if necessary, until God speaks to you and tells you that you belong to Him."

I thought about it for a minute.

"I'd have to go without food?"

She nodded.

"Well, couldn't I have my breakfast first and then fast?"

She told me that I could eat breakfast first and then fast if I wanted to, but that the proper way was to eat nothing.

"Could I maybe have one biscuit?"

Again she told me that I could eat whatever I wanted to, but that I was supposed to fast.

So with a deep sigh I walked out the back door, leaving behind me a breakfast of bacon, eggs, grits, and biscuits. I wandered down to one of the fields and climbed up into an old wagon, where I sat and stared at an oak tree at the edge of the woods. I didn't kneel down, though I thought I was probably supposed to; but I did begin to pray as hard as I knew how. And when nothing happened, I kept it up through the long, hot day, uncertain of how God would come to me or *if* He would.

Then, around three o'clock, something occurred. To this day I can't say precisely what happened or how I felt. No voice spoke to me out of the sky. No dove landed on my shoulder. I had no visions. I only know that a sudden peace flooded my soul, and in an instant I was a different human being, changed forever by a Presence that was invisible and inaudible, yet at the same time more real to me than the wagon I was sitting on or the oak tree I was staring at across the field. As young as I was, I knew that God had reached down and touched my life and that after this day he would always be with me.

I sat for a long time, immersed in the peace that surpasses all understanding. Then I jumped down from my perch and started running across the field, full of rising joy. My sins had been forgiven. I had been reborn. I could go back to the house and eat a whole plate of cold biscuits.

That evening when I went to church, I saw Uncle George, my father's oldest brother, standing in the doorway, watching me come. As I scrambled up the steps he broke into a grin and called out: "At three o'clock this afternoon you found God!"

He was a man unlike my father in many respects. Full of jokes and fun, he never tried to be a model of stern sobriety. He took the faith slow and easy; but in his own way he was a deeply religious man. Curiously, he knew the very moment I had been saved, and I can only guess that somehow or other God had told him.

But it was with my mother that I shared my newfound joy. She was the one, after all, who knew that even at the age of seven I was ready for this moment; and from that time forward we were even closer than before, because now all of her other qualities, the things that I loved about her, made sense in a new way.

It is remarkable how different my mother and father were in manner and in outlook. In many ways they were opposites—one stern and rational, the other loving and guided by the heart. Yet they were perfectly complementary, and we children regarded them as exemplary parents, ideally suited to one another. In fact, had I known no one else during those early years, I believe they would have provided all the guidance I needed to prepare me for adulthood.

But in those days, when three-fourths of all Americans lived on farms, "family" meant more than a couple and their children. It meant grandparents, aunts, uncles, and countless cousins, most of them living in the same town or rural area. In such a world, every child knows he is watched with love and concern by literally dozens of people in addition to his parents. I was well aware of the inescapable presence of my kin wherever I went, and I knew that if I misbehaved they would either step in to correct me or else tell my parents about the incident. But if I was hurt or in danger, they were just as quick to come to my rescue or defense.

Such a life had its drawbacks. You lose a certain measure of privacy, something you particularly value as a teenager; and you can never really sin in secret. As a young man in Linden, Alabama, I had the feeling that there was an uncle around every corner, an aunt under every bush. I moved among a hundred eyes and was subject to fifty tongues. So I calculated every move I made.

But I have to admit that as a result of this constant presence of family, I got into less trouble than I might have and made fewer mistakes that I would regret in later life. I also had adults to turn to other than my parents, and at times this was a blessing, particularly when I got a little older and wanted to raise questions about "worldly" subjects. Thus I learned a great deal from these other members of my family, both about the future and about the past.

Indeed, my most important link with the past was provided by my paternal grandfather. Grandpa George exemplified for me not only the history of my family but also of my race for he had been born a slave, and to know him was to come face to face with the paradox of what white men called "the peculiar institution," its shame and its grim glory—for it is that condition out of which virtually all American blacks have come and over which we have finally triumphed.

Let me pause here briefly to say a word about slavery. Nothing I have to offer will be particularly original, but it needs to be stated in explicit terms so no one who reads about my grandfather will be tempted to sentimentalize him or sell him short. He came out of hard times, and his good nature was a quality of character at which he had to work.

The institution of slavery was a tragedy of history, an evil that flourished for a time in the Christian world because people forgot the spirit of the Gospel and selectively used biblical passages to justify their laziness and greed. If you look at Jesus' summary of The Law, in which He said we should love our neighbors as ourselves, then you can see immediately the self-deception that slave traders and slave owners practiced when they first brought black people from the shores of Africa to the West Indies and then to America. No white clergyman, no New England sea captain, no southern planter would have traded places for an instant with those miserable blacks, people wrenched from their own world and introduced into an alien society where they were regarded not as people fully human, but as "chattel."

The word "chattel" originally meant "cattle," though today we understand it to mean something inanimate such as the physical contents of a house. But when the slaves were first called "chattel"—and that is the way they were defined in the Constitution of the United States—the word probably still included the idea of livestock as well as furniture.

It is this idea that still rankles the hearts of American blacks in the twentieth century—the thought that their ancestors, their own flesh and blood, were once bought and sold like cattle. If white Americans take pride in the achievement of their forefathers in casting off the chains of European monarchy, then they must understand how we blacks feel about the degradation of our forefathers during the very same period, the painful knowledge that those who exercised an almost absolute control over their lives regarded them as less than human.

There can be no pride in that past without a corresponding

sense of shame. There can be no pure memory of an American Revolution that published a declaration that liberty was a right accorded to "all men" and then created a Constitution that specifically prohibited blacks from enjoying that right. The only logical conclusion that modern blacks can draw from such circumstances is that their forefathers were not regarded as "men" by the white founders of this country.

Yet, though slavery as an institution was wicked and foreign to the will of our Lord, it was not uniformly cruel and abusive. Some slaves, in the midst of their degradation, were treated with a measure of Christian charity, just as some prisoners of war have always been treated better than others. In the worst of circumstances, the human heart is still a mysterious variable.

Thus the conditions on the plantation of "Master Abernathy," who owned my great-grandparents and grandparents, were—relatively speaking—more tolerable than the conditions endured by other slaves. My great-grandfather, Jake Abernathy, was apparently brought from a plantation in South Carolina, sold to the highest bidder in a slave market near Linden, and lived the rest of his days as the property of this white man whose name he was given. Our family name, then, derives not from ancestral achievement of place or origin, as is the case with many white people, but from a man not of our flesh and blood who held us in bondage by virtue of economic power.

Some black people have come to reject their names because of the arbitrary manner in which they were conferred by white plantation owners. Many of these blacks choose to adopt African names which have an origin more ancient and more "honorable" than their white names. But while I certainly sympathize with such feelings, my grandparents and more particularly my parents made something out of the Abernathy name, investing it with a dignity that was theirs alone. In Marengo County during the first half of the twentieth century, the name "Abernathy" meant integrity, responsibility, generosity, and religious commitment— and it came to mean that largely through the life and testimony of the *black* Abernathys. And in the second half of the twentieth century, the name has national and even international status, as my grandmother predicted at my birth. So I feel no shame in going by a last name to which my father and mother brought such character and dignity. It was *their* name. They didn't just borrow it from a long-dead white man. They paid for it with their exemplary lives and therefore owned it outright when they passed it along to me.

Of the first black Abernathy, I know very little except that his name was Jake; he married and was the father of six children: George; Jake, Jr.; Sharlott; Martha; Lizzy; and Lucy. The oldest, George, was my grandfather; and he was born a slave, as best we can tell, between 1851 and 1854 because he said he was twelve years old at the time of emancipation. The Emancipation Proclamation was issued in 1862 and took effect on January 1, 1863; but most slaves did not learn of its existence until northern troops arrived somewhat later in the Civil War, in some areas as late as 1865. Several family members have speculated that my grandfather, in speaking of his freedom, was referring to the passage of the Thirteenth Amendment. But southern slaves were actually freed earlier than those slaves in Union states where the institution was abolished only by amending the Constitution. (Northerners like to believe that their region of the country was totally free at the time of the Civil War; such was not the case.)

So my grandfather was born into slavery; and since he lived almost a hundred years—until I was a young adult—he did tell me a few anecdotes about life in bondage. From what I can deduce, his master was reasonably kind and just, given the absolute power he wielded over his "property." Two examples will suffice.

My grandfather told us of a time when as a child he pushed his white master's daughter into a shallow pond and was ordered by the little girl's mother to remain in a parlor of the Big House until the master came back from the fields and could punish him. He remembered sitting in the room in misery, waiting for the sound of his master's boots on the front steps, anticipating the worst beating of his life. Finally the dreaded moment arrived, and my grandfather heard the mistress telling her husband that he would have to punish George severely, because he had been disobedient and unruly. A few more mumbled words were followed by footsteps in the hall. The door opened, the master came into the room where my grandfather was waiting and stared at him for a moment, a frown on his face.

"George," he said, "I've had a bad report on you. I've heard that you pushed your little mistress into a pond. Now is that true?"

My grandfather admitted that it was.

"Now, George," he said, "I've told you that it's your responsibility to watch out for her. So why did you push her in the water?"

"Because," said my grandfather, "she pushed me in first." Then he set his jaw and added, "And if she pushes me in again, I'll just have to do the same thing again to her."

He couldn't have been more than ten years old, but he had such a defiant look on his face that the master burst out laughing.

"Well, I guess that's fair enough," he said. "You can run along now, George."

My grandfather told me that story when I was about the same age he had been; and I still remember him when he finished it, his huge head of hair, white and frazzled, his eyes crinkled with laughter as he smiled and shook his head. Despite the conditions under which he'd been born, he harbored no bitterness over the old ways. He recalled only a time when he hadn't received an expected whipping; it was a good memory and he passed it along to the rest of us for our amusement.

I remember one other tale he told about his days as a slave, though I'm not sure how much of it was a personal reminiscence and how much was an anecdote that he heard somewhere in a half-remembered conversation.

He claimed he had been passing an old cemetery (he called it a "graveyard") when he heard two voices speaking from behind some tall tombstones. Terrified, he listened as they spoke. It was, in fact, two adult slaves who had stolen some walnuts from the master's orchard and were dividing them. Unable to read or to count, they had to resort to the simplest division of the spoils—putting the nuts one at a time into two separate piles. This my grandfather found out later. But as he stood there, unable to move, all he heard was a disembodied voice saying, "One for you and one for me. One for you and one for me."

When he could muster up enough courage to move, he fairly flew down the hill, across the yard, and up to the master's house, where he beat on the door. The master was summoned, and when he had calmed the boy he asked him what had happened.

"The devil and God," my grandfather gasped. "I heard them down in the graveyard. They were dividing up all the souls there."

"They were doing what?"

"They were dividing up souls. I heard them saying, 'One for you and one for me.'"

The master tried to reassure him, to tell him no such thing happened; but my grandfather was unconvinced.

"All right, then," said the master. "Let's go up to the graveyard and see about it."

Reluctantly, my grandfather went with him, and when they had mounted the hill and entered the gate, they saw the two men, who in turn saw them, leaped up, and ran as fast as they could down the other side of the hill. Then the master took my grandfather over and showed him what had been going on.

"You see, George," he said. "Things weren't nearly as bad as you thought. And besides, it appears as if they've left you something for all the trouble they caused you."

My grandfather looked down and saw two large mounds of walnuts, which he gathered up and took home to eat.

When I heard this story he was nearly ninety years old, and by no means at the end of his life. He lived almost ten years longer; and during that time he was able to move around, enjoy other people, and fill his life with simple pleasures. One of the greatest of these was eating cheese, which he loved and which, on one occasion or another, he shared with the entire countryside.

In part his cheese feasts were mildly self-indulgent and in part a matter of necessity. My grandmother, Manerva, who was almost one hundred herself, was forever off at someone else's house, so Grandpa George had no one to cook for him and had to scratch in order to survive. The country store was within walking distance and his credit was good (largely because he was my father's father), so he ate fine cheese constantly.

I must say in my grandmother's defense that she was not off gossiping. As a matter of fact, she abandoned my grandfather in the line of Christian duty; for whenever anyone became ill in the vicinity—whether my grandmother knew the family or not—she would cook a chicken, boil some eggs, put them in a basket, and walk to the house where there was illness, no matter how far away it was located. There she would feed the family, clean the house, and nurse the sick person until he (or, more often, she) recovered or died. Then and only then would she return home to take care of Grandpa George.

In the meantime, he would have dined on bologna, sardines, crackers—and pounds and pounds of cheese. If a friend or stranger passed by the house, he would wave his frail arms and call out, "Come on up to the house. I've got a little *cheese!*"

This went on for years and years, the bill at the country store mounting each month. The economics of storekeeping during the Depression was different than today, when most of us go to the supermarket, pick out our groceries, and pay cash for them at the checkout counter. In the thirties and early forties, there was precious little cash to be had, and then it was only likely to appear in the fall, when the crops came in. So the whole country—or at least the part we inhabited—was run on credit. The storekeeper would maintain a complicated set of books for each of his regular customers, and when money came in the customers would settle up with the grocer.

It's that last part that my grandfather never quite understood. He knew that the grocer had cheese. He knew that whenever he wanted some he could go in and get it. He may have been aware that the grocer wrote something in his books each time, but that was as far as his understanding went. From time to time, the grocer tried to explain this last stage of the transaction, but he met with little success. Finally, when the bill had grown from hundreds of dollars to over a thousand, he fell into despair and turned the whole matter over to the law.

One day a deputy sheriff came out to our farm, standing on one foot and then the other, terribly apologetic, knowing very well that my father would accept full responsibility for the debt and that he alone among my grandfather's children would be willing to do so. My father smiled grimly, nodded, and said that he would take care of the matter immediately.

"You might want to talk to the judge first," the deputy told him. "He asked me to tell you to drop by his office. I think he has some advice to offer."

My father thanked him, and the next morning he went to see the judge, a white man he had known most of his life. The judge explained that since the responsibility for my grandfather's debt rested with all the children and since my father was planning to pay the full amount, he should be the one to have my grandfather's forty-acre farm, which Grandpa George had inherited.

"Here's what we can do," he said. "Instead of paying, allow me to render a judgment against your father for the debt. Then I'll order the farm sold to satisfy the obligation. I will see that the farm sells for exactly what is owed. If any of your brothers and sisters will go in with you to bid on the place, then they can share in the ownership. If they are not willing to help your father stay where he's always lived, then you will own the house outright. Then, when your father and mother die, you can do with the place as you choose."

And that's how my father added the last acreage to our family place. But things did not work out the way the judge had predicted. Unfortunately, my father never received compensation for paying the great cheese bill: he died before my grandfather on March 26 at the age of sixty-two. (The date would continue to be significant to my family. My sister Ella Louise ["Doll"] and my brother Kermit Theodore ["K. T."] would both, at the age of sixty-two, die on this date—in Doll's case at exactly the same hour of the day my father died.).

I will never forget the pathos of that moment on March 26 when my grandfather, now almost one hundred years old, was led into the darkened room where my father lay, dead of a stroke, his face still stern and uncompromising even in death. My grandfather's mind now often wandered back through the confused roads of the past, where he spoke with his mother, the white master who had once owned him, the playmates dead and buried the past seventy and eighty years. Occasionally, he would return to the present for a time, recognize his "Babe" (Grandma Nervy), his grandchildren, his great-grandchildren, talk about his current friends and neighbors, and then suddenly be gone again, beyond the reach of those who sat next to him at the dinner table.

Now his most dependable son was dead, and none of us believed he could ever comprehend the loss. Yet the entire family agreed that it was appropriate for him to be brought into the presence of the body, just for the sake of propriety.

As we all stood in the room, curious as well as dutiful, my mother led him through the door, his white hair glowing like a halo from the light behind him, his clothes hanging loosely on his shrunken body, a look of puzzlement and wonder in his eyes. Peering around at all of us, his gaze finally fell on the solemn face upturned to him, its lids closed, its lips drawn.

Then, as we held our breath, we could see the understanding flood into his eyes, and he began to shake his head, his mouth trembling.

"Oh, why has the Lord done this to me?" he whispered. "Oh, why has he taken away my son, my strength and support?"

Then my mother led him out of the room, his cheeks bright with tears. He had lived too long and seen one thing too many. His heart was in pieces. And from that day forward he was a child again and slave to a shrinking world of memories where neither his aged wife nor his smiling great-great-grandchildren could follow. Then, as if Death were correcting an old oversight, he was finally, mercifully, freed.

In addition to these three strong characters—my father, my mother, my grandfather—there were others who were an important part of my upbringing. I will always remember my carefree, irresponsible uncles who taught me to laugh—particularly Uncle Clarence "Buddy" Abernathy, who at times seemed to love me more than my own father. My older brothers and sisters also watched over me, almost as if they were of the same generation as my parents, yet still able to remember living under the same benevolent tyranny to which I was subject. And there were all of the young members of the family with whom I played and who made their mark on my character: my cousins Mary Lester, Reola, M. C., Alfred, Bessie, and Budlam; my sisters Lula Mae and Susie Ellen; my brother James Earl; and my nephews Sonny and Freddy, the children of my sister Doll.

But in those days childhood was not all play, at least not in the country. On a family farm everybody worked; and while young people today look on such a life as tedious and hard, it had its advantages. For one thing, none of the children in our family had to worry about a job, the way black teenagers today do. We all had a job from the time we could walk—and it was not an unimportant job, one that was trivial in the eyes of the world. Children can't plant and plow and hoe and weed and pick as well as experienced adults, but we worked together and did things as well as we could.

At least my brothers and sisters did. As for me, I was given a slightly different role. Perhaps because I was the tenth child and there were already enough field workers in the family, perhaps because my hands were smaller than the hands of the others, for whatever reason, my father assigned me to my mother—to help her in the kitchen, around the house, and wherever else she might need me.

On August days, when everyone else came in sweating from laboring in the heat, I would smile, hold out my hands, and tell my brothers and sisters that the Good Lord had not made my hands to hold a plow or, for that matter, anything heavier than a pencil. Sometimes they would laugh and take it well; but I learned not to push the joke too far, because one of my outside duties was that of "waterboy," and if all of them timed their thirst just right, they could keep me running back and forth for the rest of the afternoon.

Not that my life was soft, as my brothers and sisters like to tell me these days. They forget that my father woke me around 4 every morning, while he and everyone else still lay in bed. He would call my name just once—"David!"—and I was expected to answer "Yes, sir!" and roll out of bed. During all those years it never occurred to me to go back to sleep, because I knew if I ever did, he would come into the room after me, maybe with a belt or a razor strop. One advantage of being the tenth child is the wisdom you gain from noting the mistakes of your older brothers and sisters. I had seen my father deal out punishment to them, and I wanted no part of such treatment. So I was a good boy in the early mornings.

In cold weather I would make the fires before the others got up to dress—and there were fireplaces all over the house, since in those days few people had furnaces. In addition, I had to make the fire in the wood stove, on which my mother cooked breakfast. I also milked the cows before dawn, fed the mules, and the chickens, and gathered the eggs. Then I would wash my hands and churn butter, all before we sat down to breakfast, just as the sun's rays began to cast shadows on the kitchen floor.

Later in the day I would do other tasks, like picking vegetables in the garden, peeling potatoes, snapping beans, slicing onions, and shucking corn. I didn't know who did these chores before I came along and didn't really care. I just knew that I had to get them done before there was any time to slip off and read a book or take a short nap.

There were also errands to run. If my mother needed anything from the store that my father hadn't picked up on his Saturday trip to town, I would be dispatched to get it. And every Saturday I would ride a mile to the mill, hauling heavy bags of corn for the miller to grind so that we could have meal and grits and "chops" (feed) for the chickens.

The chickens were entirely my responsibility. I not only fed them and watered them, but I was also the chief chicken killer in the family. Though at first the job made me queasy, very soon I learned to grab a chicken by the neck, twist it around three or four times the way you used to crank a car, and then pop the head off and watch the body flap around on the ground, quite unaware for a few seconds that it no longer had a head.

Back then, chicken was the best of all meals to serve—better than ham, better than pork chops, better even than roast beef or steak. We did not get to eat chicken every day. In fact, there were only three occasions when we were sure to get chicken. First, of course, we always had it for Sunday dinner, which was served in the early afternoon. Come Sunday, the Lord's Day, we would have a feast. On Monday, Tuesday, Wednesday, Thursday, and Friday, we would have ordinary meals—one meat, three or four vegetables, cornbread, butter, maybe some preserves, plenty of milk. And Saturday—well, that was a day when everyone was busy with special tasks. My father was in town, laying in the week's supplies. My mother was cleaning the house as diligently as most people today do their spring cleaning. Lula Mae and I swept the yard while Susie and James Earl, the babies, looked on and jeered. William was off courting. Louvenia was receiving company. So on Saturdays we were lucky to get leftovers.

But, come Sunday, things were different. Come Sunday, we would have a feast—we would always eat chicken. So we lived for Sunday.

We would also have chicken when the preacher came, because that too was a grand occasion, and one in which I played a special part. Our church—the Hopewell Baptist Church—was small, its congregation consisting of no more than our family and its connections, so we could not afford to have a full-time minister. As a consequence, the preacher came only on the second and fourth weekends of the month. The rest of the time he lived in another town, but when he did come he stayed with us, remaining for several days.

Because my father was the head deacon (what Baptists now call the chairman of the Board of Deacons), it was his responsibility to provide for the preacher when he came to the Hopewell community. The first preacher I remember was the Reverend G. H. Connor, who was associated with my family for over forty years, having married my parents and preached at my father's funeral. I also remember the Reverend J. W. Wilson, the Reverend J. R. Davis (our first educated preacher), the Reverend Columbus Young, and another man named Twilly. These men all stayed at our house, took their meals with us, and were entertained from the time they arrived on Friday afternoon till the time they left on Monday morning. And, like taking care of the children, the current preacher was also my responsibility.

When he was due on Friday, I would walk down the dirt road to the highway and stand there till the Greyhound bus lumbered into sight and squealed to a halt at precisely the same spot every time. The preacher would get off, wearing a black suit, a black tie, and carrying a dark leather suitcase. I would take the grip, which for me was a little heavy, and carry it back to the house, where I would set it in the front room, which was reserved for him because it had fine furniture and lace curtains.

While he was with us I was often excused from my usual chores so that I could wait on him, talk to him, and—if the occasion demanded it—even entertain him. I was always glad to see him come because it meant a lighter work load, despite the long haul from the highway; and it also meant chicken for dinner at least one additional night.

The third occasion on which we had chicken was when my father would hear one of the hens attempting to crow. A devout Christian who knew the Old Testament, chapter and verse, as well as the New Testament, he believed that men should behave like men and women should behave like women. And he extended that law to include chickens. If he heard a hen trying to behave like a rooster on our farm, she would be in a pot before the sun went down. But her wicked pride was our good fortune, and we were always happy when one of the hens got out of line.

As I look back on these times, I realize that even if we didn't have much money, we had the essential things: we had plenty to eat, a place to live, and many things to do—most of them useful and a few of them fun. There were sports to play—in open fields rather than in Little League parks—and several of my brothers were excellent athletes. In fact, one of them, K. T., was a prodigious baseball player who could do it all—pitch, field, and hit the ball a mile. People around our part of the country said he was as good as Babe Ruth, and in a later time I'm certain he would have been a major league star, though of course no such career was open to a black in the 1930s.

My brother William also played baseball as well as basketball; and he too might well have been a famous professional athlete, but I'm afraid I was a different matter. I had little aptitude for sports and therefore little interest. When I found a few free moments to amuse myself, I would usually go to a quiet corner in the house and read a book or a newspaper. More often than not the book was the Bible, which for me was more fascinating than any popular novel.

As was the case in most country homes, the Bible was the central book in our family, the single source of wisdom that bound us all together, and we spent a good deal of time learning about it. As children we had to memorize a verse every week and recite it at the family prayer meeting we held every Sunday morning before breakfast. No matter how busy the week had been, no one was excused from reciting, and my father's memory was too keen to repeat last week's verse, so we never tried.

After recitations, my father would teach from the Good Book and we would listen. Then, at some point, my mother would slip away to prepare breakfast, which was always a very special occasion. We would usually have biscuits, sausage, eggs, and at the end of the meal—the greatest treat of all—the residue from my parents' coffee cups!

Of course, coffee was a stimulant, so the only people who drank it in our family were my father and mother. But the younger children would get a taste of it on occasion, when my parents would pour sugar into the cup, drink the coffee almost to the dregs, and then leave a dark, sweet crystallized mixture at the bottom. After they left the table, we would fight over the remaining treat more that we would have fought over a candy bar.

Such moments come back to me now as more important than the troubles that plagued society, yet somehow never seemed to intrude on our sheltered world. Just as I had no experience of a Great Depression, so was I relatively unaware of racism or segregation, matters that would occupy much of my time and energy in later years. Of course, all the children in our family recognized that racial distinctions existed and that from time to time they could cause trouble. In fact, my father told us never to play with white children. "If you do," he said, "every joke will be at your expense. If you wrestle or box with a white child, you will always have to let him win, otherwise he may become aggravated, and that could lead to trouble."

But such a warning was merely hypothetical to us. We lived on five hundred acres, which gave us plenty of breathing space, and most of the farms around us were owned or run by our uncles and cousins. Our nearest white neighbors—Mr. and Mrs. Robert Jones—had children who were off at college. So we didn't sit around and brood about whether or not to play with whites our age. We'd never met any and had no desire to.

We were also perfectly content to drink out of our own water fountains and to enter and exit by doors marked "COL-ORED." We were so secure in the honor accorded our family that we didn't consider such practices demeaning or even important. If white people wanted their own fountains and doors, that was just fine with us.

Ironically, my first experience of racial animosity came out of my firm resolve to maintain my private vision of Jim Crow. I remember the occasion well—the words spoken, the hostile gestures, the man's name—though not with any bitterness. What happened was at worst annoying, at best highly amusing (at least in retrospect) then—though the society it was symptomatic of was no laughing matter.

One of my responsibilities as a child was to run errands at the country store, which was operated by our neighbor Mr. Jones. This store fronted on U.S. Highway 43, which ran from Mobile to Linden and then to points north (to places as strange and foreign as Tennessee). It was like most country stores of that day—a white, wooden building filled with anything that any reasonable human being could want, from flour and baking powder to hammers and shoes and bolts of cloth. You went about gathering up your own items, except for a few things on the shelves behind the massive counter where Mr. Jones stood and totaled your purchases on a fancy brass cash register. If you charged the goods instead of paying cash, he would pull out a huge, dog-eared ledger and record the items you had bought and their prices. We always paid cash or else brought eggs for barter.

That morning I had brought in a sack of three dozen eggs to trade for things my mother needed in the kitchen, and when I came through the door I knew from the sudden silence that something was different. Then I saw Mr. Fitzhugh, a white man who lived down the road. He was leaning up against the counter, drinking a Nehi soda, and from the expression on his face, I could tell he was drunk.

I moved down to the other end of the counter and told Mr. Jones my business, handing him the sack of eggs. In addition to being our neighbors, the Joneses were our friends. They came to call on us from time to time, visiting in our living room the way other friends did; and despite the fact that they were white, I was even allowed to go over to their house and help Mrs. Jones shake pecans out of the big trees in her backyard. But Mr. Fitzhugh was another kind of neighbor, another kind of white man.

After watching me deal with Mr. Jones, he took a gulp from his Nehi and held out the half-empty bottle.

"Here, boy," he said. "You finish this." It was more a command than an invitation.

Now, my mother had taught us never to drink behind anybody. Not behind members of the family. Particularly not behind a stranger. And *certainly* not behind a white man. So I shook my head and told him, "No, thank you."

His eyes narrowed immediately and he shoved the bottle in my direction.

"Drink this, nigger!"

I shook my head and said firmly, "I'm sorry, but I don't care for it."

He couldn't believe his ears.

"What in hell do you mean? Are you saying you won't drink after *me*?"

I stared at him for a moment, then nodded my head.

With a cry of rage he drew back his hand to hit me. At that moment Mr. Jones, who had been watching to see how far things would go, came halfway across the counter.

"Don't you touch that boy!" he cried. Then he added, "That's the son of W. L. Abernathy."

The change in Mr. Fitzhugh was remarkable. I can't think of a more dramatic testimony to the standing of my father in the community. From a towering bully he was transformed into a bundle of quivering nerves by the sound of a black man's name.

"Oh," he said quietly. "I didn't know that."

Mr. Jones relaxed a little and then turned to me and said, "Now, David, you run along home," and handed me my sack of groceries.

Of course, I did what he said, because he was our friend; but as I left the store, I glanced over my shoulder to see the two white men glaring at one another. To this day I don't know what happened after I left. If Mr. Jones said anything to my father about the confrontation, I never heard about it. I do know that it was the only such incident in my childhood, or at least the only one that stands out vividly in my memory, so strong a figure was my father, and so protective was his shadow.

It is important to understand that the community I grew up in and the privileged status we enjoyed were not to be found everywhere, certainly not in the larger towns and cities of the South, or for that matter in places like New York, Chicago, or Detroit. In a rural area where land was available to people who were willing to work for it, it was possible for a few blacks to enjoy both freedom and a kind of equality—one based on mutual respect and a certain standoffishness. It was not an ideal community by any means, or even a particularly good one, because it lacked the possibility for the kind of fellowship that exists, or should exist, among true Christians. We could only approximate friendship with people like the Joneses. Indeed, that world was a fragile one; and its survival depended on staying in the country and living among people you had known all your life and who had known you.

But we couldn't all do that. Land only goes so far, particularly when there are twelve children in the family and no more than five hundred acres. So it was inevitable that some of us would leave home, settle in other towns and cities, and find there something entirely different from the honor and respect that our parents and grandparents had earned for the rest of us. It was our destiny, our burden—not only as human beings but as black Americans—to live beyond the dignity of our father's house, in a cold and hostile land somewhere east of Eden.

2

Lay Down My Sword and Shield

I HAVE ANSWERED many difficult questions in my life, some of them posed by hostile reporters, some by policemen, some by lawyers and judges, some even by jailors. But the hardest questions I have ever had to answer have come from my own children, who usually wait until I'm off guard and there is plenty of time to pin me down—like on rainy winter days when everyone is trapped in the house.

At such times, I am usually asked to explain in great detail the kind of life I preach about and the ways in which my own conduct falls short of the ideals I say I believe in. My children are still too young to be merciful and too fond of me to let me off the hook—for my own good, they make me face my shortcomings, so that maybe I'll improve in my old age.

One of the questions that has come up on several such occasions is why I fought in World War II, given the fact that I advocate nonviolence as a way of life. And they further remind me that, at the time I served, I lived in a segregated society and was drafted into a segregated army. The answer to this question is complicated and invariably unsatisfactory to anyone under fifty. Today's youth, black and white alike, fall easily into the habit of challenging old ways and rebelling against authority. They think this attitude is natural to youth, that it comes to them by right along with a curiosity about the world and a preoccupation with the opposite sex.

But such is not the case. When I was eighteen years old and suddenly eligible for the draft, it seemed natural for young people to accept and obey authority, to do what we were told without question. Why? Because our parents and preachers said so—and they were older, more experienced, and therefore wiser than we were. Oh, we questioned this rule or that practice, complained about the unreasonableness and immorality of society, and in our better moments swore to change things when we were adults. But though we knew institutions like Jim Crow were wrong, we felt too intimidated by the *pervasiveness* of it and by the fact that it seemed so old and so ingrained, a part of the landscape, like the slant of a hillside or the hang of a massive oak tree.

Besides, in 1944 no one questioned the rightness of the war we were fighting. The Japanese had attacked us. They were guilty of atrocities in Asia. If the war with Japan had any racial overtones (as many people now believe), we were unaware of them. The Japanese, we had been told, were imperialists and meant to rule the world.

As for Hitler, every black in the United States knew that the Nazi regime was racist, the worst in the world. The German talk of a master race was certainly more disturbing to us than it was to whites—with the exception of the Jews. Our attention was focused on the issue by the treatment of Jesse Owens at the 1936 Olympic games and by the two Joe Louis–Max Schmeling fights. We remembered in 1941 that Hitler had referred to Schmeling as "Our Max" and had proclaimed his lucky victory over Louis as proof of Aryan supremacy over the black race. When Louis destroyed Schmeling in their return match, most American blacks were crowded around their radios shouting, cheering, and then laughing at Hitler and the Nazis.

So when Americans went to war against Nazi Germany,

young blacks were quick to respond to the call; in part because we were an obedient generation, in part because we knew the enemy and despised him.

I was no exception. The year was 1944 and the Allies had already invaded Europe, sustaining heavy casualties in the process, so there was no decrease in the demand for more troops. At seventeen you were permitted to enlist, and at eighteen you went whether you wanted to or not, unless severely disabled or a conscientious objector. I was in excellent health; and while I doubted that I could bring myself to kill another human being, it never occurred to me not to go.

When my notice arrived, only three weeks after my eighteenth birthday, I was excited and a little nervous. During the early months of the war, the U.S. armed forces had been outnumbered and outgunned; and while we had recovered our balance by 1943, a number of young men, black as well as white, had died in the process. Practically every sizable community in the nation had lost at least one member, and I had personally known boys who marched off to the music of a military band and never came home. So no one with any sense could have received the notice without sober reflection. My mother tried not to show her concern, but I could see the furrows in her brow as she moved around the house and I could feel her extra measure of attention. I had brothers who were already in uniform; I was her fourth to go.

The first requirement was a physical examination. On the appointed day, I was driven down to the bus station where—to my great surprise—I saw hundreds of men gathered in the parking lot, waiting for the bus to take us to Fort Benning. As I stood on the fringe of the crowd, I saw the head of the local draft board, wearing a porkpie hat, looking around for someone, a sheaf of papers in his hand. Then his eyes fell on me, and he started to move through the crowd, one white face among hundreds of black ones.

He spoke with a sense of urgency and self-importance as he shoved the sheaf of papers in my hand. He had known my father well, and now I was to bear the consequences of their friendship.

"David," he said, "I'm putting you in charge of this entire

group. It will be your responsibility to see that they all get to Fort Benning without jumping the bus. Then, after you take your physicals, you'll be responsible for getting everybody back to Linden. Do you understand that?"

Well, I wasn't sure that I did. I was barely eighteen, and as I looked around me I saw men who were well into their thirties, a few of them outweighing me by one hundred pounds or more. So what would I say if one of them caused a ruckus or tried to jump off the bus? What could I do?

"All aboard," called out the bus driver.

At that moment, the draft board leader shoved the papers in my hand, along with 300 meal tickets.

"Here you are, David. These are orders. You give them to somebody at Fort Benning."

"Who?" I called out as I turned and, obeying the driver's command, moved toward the open door of the bus.

"I don't know," he shouted after me. "Somebody will be there, I'm sure." Then he turned and disappeared into the crowd, leaving me with a handful of papers and a group of men who were staring at the bus and mumbling to one another, wondering if they were supposed to get on it. All of a sudden I was a military commander.

In a voice that sounded faint and childlike to me, I told the men standing near, "OK, let's get on board."

What happened next surprised me: the small bunch standing nearest me began to file mournfully into the bus, and then all the rest followed. It was just like cows. Once you got one or two moving through the gate and into the next pasture, the others would follow without hesitation. All they required was the smallest amount of authority—and that was about all I had to offer, since my only badge of office was the sheaf of papers in my hand.

From the moment we left until we reached Fort Benning, I was terrified that somebody would decide to jump off, everyone else would follow, and by the time the bus reached its destination I would be the only person left, sitting in an empty vehicle holding a list of deserters.

But of course no one escaped. The men laughed and joked

for a while, then a silence settled over the bus, and most stared out the window at the rural landscape, each lost in his own thoughts.

We stopped first at Selma, then at Montgomery, where we changed drivers and were allowed to buy a sandwich from a segregated window at the terminal restaurant. The next stop was Phenix City, and after we left that town I saw we were crossing a muddy river. Then I saw something that filled me with wonder: a sign that read WELCOME TO COLUMBUS, GA. For the first time in my life, I had crossed a state line!

The bus rumbled through Columbus and on to Fort Benning, where we all piled out, a little apprehensive. I held up the papers, waved them back and forth, and in a moment or two a white man in uniform came along and snatched them from my hand, without so much as saying "Thank you." Then he told us to line up while he called the roll. I held my breath, but every man answered, and I was off the hook—at least for the time being. But I remembered that I had also been given the responsibility of taking the men back to Linden, so I still continued to worry just a little bit.

We were taken to a building that looked like a giant warehouse, where we stripped and were put through a series of medical examinations, all of which were either uncomfortable or humiliating. I can't even remember what they were—which is probably just as well. But after we had finished, dressed, and were lined up to return to the bus, I received a shock: I had flunked the physical. I would have to remain and be reexamined.

When I heard that I had to stay behind while all the others returned to Alabama, I was thrown into despair. I wouldn't be able to deliver them back to the Linden bus station as I had been instructed. But then a greater worry began to emerge in my mind: that they had discovered I had some rare and fatal disease. I worried about it until late that afternoon, when I discovered that my blood pressure had been abnormally high for someone my age.

In retrospect, I realize that the nation was running out of men to send overseas. Casualties had been high. The war was about to enter its fourth year and the Selective Service had begun drafting thirty-nine-year-olds. So while in a later time I might have simply been rejected and sent home on the bus with the others, in 1944 they wanted to keep me behind and see if they could get a more favorable reading on the blood pressure machine. Every warm body was precious in their sight—red and yellow, black and white.

Well, when they retested me that afternoon I was so worried that it probably affected the next reading.

"Lie down," I was told. "Stretch out on the examining table and relax completely. Go to sleep if you can. Then we'll wake you up and try again." I lay down for a couple of hours, brooding over my condition; they took my blood pressure again, and again they shook their heads. The reading, though down, was still too high.

"You'll sleep here tonight," they told me, "and we'll take it again in the morning."

After a night of troubled dreams, I awoke shortly before dawn with the sensation that a powerful giant had grabbed me by the arm and was trying to pinch it off. I sat up in bed to find a blood pressure device wrapped around my upper arm like a black snake and an unfamiliar white face staring down at me, smiling.

"Congratulations," the face said cheerfully. "You're in the Army!"

When we were inducted a few weeks later at Fort Benning one gray afternoon in November, no one was smiling. After we raised our hands and repeated the oath, we were assembled and marched haphazardly to the reception center, where we were turned over to the meanest black men I had ever seen in my life. At the time I was something of a Holy Innocent, still living under the protection of my family. No black man treated me with disrespect. Nor did any white man. I was accustomed to speaking politely and pleasantly to strangers, and I expected them to treat me with the same kind of courtesy.

So the obscene abuse that greeted us at the transient company headquarters came as a shock. We were called names I'd never heard before—and for no apparent reason. We were ordered to do irrational things, shouted at while we did them, and then told we had done them poorly. We were awakened at all hours of the night. We were incessantly sweeping and mopping floors, washing windows, scrubbing urinals and commodes, picking up trash in the yard, and marching to and from remote buildings where we stood in line for hours, saw no one, and accomplished absolutely nothing.

During this period, we were taught "military courtesy," which is another name for kowtowing to those in authority. It was a lesson that blacks learned easier than whites, I suspect, because most already knew how it felt to be helpless in the grasp of an arbitrary power. We were told how to salute officers, to call them "sir," and to obey their commands without hesitation or question. All of these lessons were deliberately humiliating; they were intended to crush out of us all that remained of our sense of individual worth and to make us mindlessly responsive to authority. With the war in full swing, we were made to understand that such obedient behavior would contribute significantly to our effectiveness as fighting men and to our own chances for survival.

Daily we grew more apprehensive about the future because everyone kept telling us that basic training would be much worse than our time at the reception center, and after that, things would really get rough.

After several days of contradictory rumors, our orders finally came. We were told we would be moving out at the first glimmer of dawn, that we would have to be "standing tall" in front of our barracks at 5 A.M. So we piled out, duffel bags packed, and stood in the chill darkness. But no trucks came to haul us to the train station. Then it was six, seven, eight, and finally noon. At noon we were told to fall out and go to chow, then return to wait. Sometime after 2 P.M. the trucks rolled into sight to take us to the depot.

When the train pulled out of Fort Benning, none of us had the slightest idea where we were heading. No one told us, certainly not the bulldog of a sergeant in charge. He sat in the rear of one of the cars reading a tattered Western and refused to answer questions.

Someone said we were going to Ozark, Alabama, where

there was an army camp. Someone else said we were on our way to Fort Bragg, North Carolina. Still another was certain we would simply be transported to the other side of Fort Benning and unloaded at one of the training companies there. But as confident as all of these rumormongers were, all we knew for sure was that we were in the hands of very powerful people and that they would set us down wherever they pleased—and whenever they pleased.

After about an hour staring out the window, we knew we had long since passed the outer limits of Fort Benning, and after four hours we had pretty well crossed off the possibility of Ozark. So it had to be Fort Bragg. We were going all the way to North Carolina. The thought of traveling that far disturbed and excited many of us. How would people up there treat us? How would they dress and talk? As the train rumbled into twilight and we saw mountains appear on either side of the train, we began to wonder if this state of North Carolina were not in some sort of foreign country, with its own separate language and customs. And still we rattled and swayed along, never slowing down, the whistle in the darkness wailing like some lost soul.

Late that night as we roared through a rural station, someone shouted out, "Virginia!" Virginia? Above Virginia was Lord knew what—Pennsylvania, New York, Ohio? Early in the morning we backed into Washington, D.C., and we all strained our necks to see the Capitol or the White House, uncertain of just what we *were* seeing, as elegant marble buildings drifted slowly past. Later we chugged through Philadelphia and Newark, and by then we were sure we would never stop.

Finally, the sergeant came through the car and told us that we would be getting off in New York City. By then we were red-eyed and groggy, prepared for anything, seasoned continental travelers! We piled out at Pennsylvania Station and were herded into buses, the fortunate ones sitting, the rest stuffed in the aisles so tightly that if one of us had died he would have stood at attention until we poured off the bus at Grand Central Station. There we were marched through the waiting room, past the famous Oyster Bar, and onto another train headed north.

It was late afternoon the next day when we pulled into Boston. As we stepped off the train, we knew we were in another world with an entirely different climate, where winter was already crowding autumn. The wind was a sheet of ice, and we could see our breath when we exhaled. Then and only then did we learn that our destination was Fort Devens, Massachusetts, which was located just a few miles from Boston and (as best we could tell) within walking distance of the North Pole.

There we would undergo basic training, which would include learning to fire the M-1 rifle, throw hand grenades, crawl through the infiltration course (with machine gun fire overhead), and finally—and worst of all—camp out in the bitter New England weather, where we had to clear away the snow before we could pitch our tents.

As incredible as it may seem to young people today, the army that fought World War II was almost completely segregated; so all the enlisted men in my company were black, but our officers were white—in part, I suppose, because the regular army was commanded by graduates of West Point and a few other military colleges, all of which were segregated. When World War II came along, the army perpetuated this bigotry when it structured the vast civilian army that was required to fight a global war. Some of the general staff even said that blacks would not follow other blacks into battle and that black regiments had not performed well in World War I. While these tales had little basis in fact and were no more than rumors that had been accepted without question, such myths die hard, particularly in a segment of society as hierarchical and inbred as the professional military.

I once heard a story from a white officer that illustrates just how hard it was for the few black officers who served between the two world wars. He said he had known a black officer, a man of great ability and dignity, who served in the Philippines. So contemptuously was he treated that the enlisted men refused to salute him because of his color. Finally one day, when a sergeant had deliberately passed him by without raising his arm, the black officer called him back. "You don't seem to understand," he said, "that you are not saluting me but the uniform and all that it stands for."

Then he took off his coat and hung it on the branch of a

tree. "Now salute that coat or I will see that you are court-martialed."

The sergeant, ashamed of himself, not only saluted the jacket but thereafter, when he passed the black officer, he saluted him as well. And so did the other enlisted men on the post. But it was a victory hard won in a time when it was all but impossible for a black men to be "an officer and a gentleman."

By the time I entered the army things had changed some, but not enough to make much difference. Indeed, the armed forces were not integrated until after World War II had ended—after thousands of blacks had died on foreign soil and thousands more had come back carrying permanent scars. We all knew these things when we accepted the hardships of military service, and we were good soldiers anyway, sent to Fort Devens to receive our infantry training under white officers and to accompany those leaders to the front lines, where so many had died before us.

When we first lined up and faced our commanding officer we must have looked like a sorry band of misfits, bunched in one shivering knot, slumped over, arms wrapped around our chests to keep warm. Our captain was named Patton; and he looked like the kind of soldier who could rightly bear that famous name. Tall, big-boned, and authoritative, he must have weighed 220 pounds, all of it muscle. But he spoke with a quiet, scholarly voice in a strange accent I had never heard before. I soon learned that he was a New Englander and that, while he didn't actively dislike black people, he felt uncomfortable around them. Someone said that in the part of Maine where he lived the only blacks they had ever seen were in the movies or on the pages of *National Geographic*.

But while he was quiet and distant in his relations with his men, Captain Patton was fair; eventually, all but the most hostile enlisted personnel grew to respect him, even if they didn't regard him with affection. Indeed, my own attitude toward him changed during the time we served together.

Our platoon leader, Lieutenant Butcher, was also white; but a man who stood in sharp contrast to the company commander. Butcher was a Southerner, a "cracker," one whose neck was literally red from years of working outdoors. While Captain Patton was educated, Lieutenant Butcher obviously had never gone beyond high school. Rough-featured, rough-talking, he was what some Southerners of an earlier generation might have called a "plain man"; and I must admit that when he first began to bark orders at us, his eyes narrowing to grim slits, we thought we were dealing with an unsheeted Klansman.

But this was a hasty generalization, born of all-too-real experience with such types; as the days became weeks and everyone loosened up, we learned that Lieutenant Butcher was playing the role of a tough guy in order to cover up a heart excessively tender for a combat officer. He was no more the stereotyped "redneck" than we were the blacks of minstrel shows. Instead, we were complicated human beings caught up in a cruel moment of history, desperate to protect our lives and to retain our dignity. In those weeks of basic training and the subsequent time overseas, Lieutenant Butcher and the men who served under him learned a lesson together that the nation at peace was to learn imperfectly only after decades.

As for me; I made up my mind that I was going to do everything right during the training period, that I would emerge from the experience as a leader. I knew that only four of us in the entire company would become platoon sergeants and that the rest would be no more than bodies to be moved from place to place as the situation demanded. I was determined to be one of the sergeants.

So whatever we were asked to do, I did—twice if I thought there was a point to be made. My uniform was the best-pressed. My brass gleamed more brightly. My boots shone in the sun like prisms. The coin the inspecting officer dropped on my tightly made bunk bounced higher than on anyone else's. My footlocker was neater than the one in the photograph on the orderly room wall.

In the field, I made certain that I learned every posture required for the firing of the M-1 rifle. I aimed more carefully, squeezed off the round more steadily, came closer to the center of the target. I slithered under the barbed wire of the infiltration course with studied recklessness, pretending I didn't mind the whining bullets and explosions that surrounded me. And when everyone else was dragging in after a long day's training, I was careful to have an extra spring in my step, just to prove I was capable of any hardship, man enough for any ordeal.

Meanwhile, I was making friends with many of the other men—some of them different from me in almost every respect. This was particularly true of Jack Hatchet, a dark-skinned and rugged giant of about thirty-five, who had led the kind of life the preachers in our church had always warned us against. Hatchet was a professional gambler, and he fascinated me because he was everything that I was not and never would be.

He was the most worldly human being I had ever met in my life. He had been everywhere, done everything, and—as a popular song put it—he had the world on a string. His sole source of income had been cards and dice, and I have no doubt that he had made a good living, because when he was bent over an olive-drab army blanket, looking down at a deck of cards or pair of dice, he was infallible. During those years the marines were occasionally routed and Ella Fitzgerald sometimes missed a beat, but Jack Hatchet never lost at five-card stud or craps. In an uncertain world, on that much you could count.

How the two of us ever became such friends I will never know. Besides the almost twenty-year difference in our ages, I was a country boy who couldn't even shuffle a pack of cards, much less tell the difference between a straight and a flush. As for our attitudes toward the army, I was out to be the best soldier I could be, and Jack's chief ambition was to be totally anonymous, the man whose name is never remembered and consequently never put on a duty roster.

Yet from the beginning, he liked me and I liked him. I guess we first became acquainted because I used to watch the poker games at night, drawn to them, I'm sure, because I had been told that they were wicked and because everyone seemed to be having such a good time.

After a while, Jack began showing me his cards, teaching me the game—though I never understood it well enough to play. Later, after we had gotten to know each other well, he called me aside one night and pulled out his roll of money. "Young soldier," he said, "I want you to keep this for me. And whatever you do don't turn loose of it."

I told him that he could protect his money much better than I could, and he smiled ever so slightly. "You don't understand," he said. "It's *me* I want you to keep it from. You take it. Put it in your footlocker or some other place where I can't get to it. Then don't let me have it, no matter how I beg and plead. Don't you give me more than $25 a day, regardless of what I tell you. OK?"

Wide-eyed, I agreed. Sure enough, a week or two later he came to me, asking for his entire wad, but when I refused to give him more than $25 he accepted my authority like an obedient child. And for as long as we were in basic training, I was his "banker."

Another man I came to know well was Fred Johnson. Like Hatchet, he was older, but there the resemblance ended. Jack was tough and outgoing while Fred was a quiet, gentle-natured man. Jack and some of his followers made a point of being a little careless in their dress, but Fred was neat in everything he did—not merely to avoid trouble with inspecting officers, but because it was part of his nature. He seemed to enjoy polishing shoes, folding fatigue jackets, tying his tie in front of a mirror. He would have done all these things had he lived alone on a remote island, while Jack Hatchet was determined to try the patience of the U.S. Army, just as a matter of principle.

Because of Johnson's mild manner and sunny disposition, I automatically assumed that he was a good, church-going Christian—I suppose because that's all I knew back in rural Alabama. As a matter of fact, Fred had very little religious faith, never having been exposed to the church as a child. However, because he knew it would please me, he would accompany me to the chapel every Sunday morning and Wednesday night, smiling happily and enigmatically at what went on, without ever fully participating. Even at that stage of my life I was already a preacher at heart; and I decided that at some point I would lead this man into the church, where I was convinced he belonged.

I was also worried that Fred had no family and was alone in the world. That was something, I told myself, that I would fix too. Someday I would officiate at his wedding and would see this man settled down with a girl who would appreciate his even temper and docile nature. In the meantime we became good friends, hung around together, and talked a lot in our leisure time.

W. J. was another of my friends, though in a special way. W. J. probably shouldn't have been in the army, because he was clearly retarded. You could see it in his eyes and hear it in the slur and imprecision of his speech. But at a time when every able-bodied man was needed at the front, recruitment officers made exceptions to the rules. We even heard rumors that a blind man and one born without arms had been drafted and put to work filling buckets of water, the blind man turning the faucet on and off, the armless man telling him when the bucket was full. It was a cruel joke, but it contained an element of truth, as the case of poor W. J. illustrated.

Yet I have found that such people often have a special kind of grace, a sweetness of disposition that makes them more lovable than most normal people. Such was the case with W. J.—most of the time. But when he became confused or frustrated or when someone was deliberately cruel to him, he would fly into a rage and strike out at anything and anybody within reach. Stout and strong, he was like a mad elephant on the rampage, and even people like Jack Hatchet would clear out of his way. Or else find me wherever I was.

I could always quiet him with a smile and a few sympathetic words, though I don't know precisely why. Others tried the same technique and ended up flat on their backs; but all I had to do was speak his name and he would stare at me for an instant, glassy-eyed, and then break into a twisted smile. He was a strange person, full of gentle impulses and uncontrollable wildness; and no one knew how he would behave under the kind of extreme circumstances we expected to face overseas.

One soldier who seemed as determined as I was to do well in the army was Rudolph Williams. He was Captain Patton's favorite. Somehow I knew from the beginning that we were in competition with one another, and though I wasn't certain what the prize was, I did know that he seemed to be ahead.

The lightness of his skin wasn't his only advantage over me—he was a Northerner. For reasons that are probably too complicated to understand fully, Southerners (whether black or white) have sometimes been regarded as categorically inferior to people who know little of the region's infinite complexities. But while southern whites, by the institution and practice of legalized segregation, earned a good deal of this contempt, it is ironic that southern blacks have had to bear the burden of regional bigotry as well as racial bigotry. So I could never tell which gave Rudolph Williams the greater edge in the captain's eyes—the fact that he was lighter skinned than I was or the fact that he spoke with a New England accent and had come from an urban area. Certainly both elements were important.

Yet I liked Williams. He was clean-cut and wore the crown of favoritism gracefully. He became company clerk almost immediately, a position that excused him from some of the dirty jobs around the company area and also kept him close to the center of power, the captain. Often when the rest of us were sloshing through frozen mud and counting cadence, he was sitting in the orderly room, dressed in his wool jacket, toasting his delicate skin in front of an electric heater. I can't say that I didn't envy him half the time, but I was grateful that he wasn't more condescending than he was, that he even seemed to be sympathetic to our suffering, though from a comfortable distance.

With these men, and with many more I could name, I shared a special bond that few civilians could understand, certainly few *white* civilians. First of all, we came to an intimate understanding of one another through shared suffering: we were outcasts; we were the lowest of the low; we were infantry recruits. Each of us knew that the other felt the same sense of indignity, the same apprehension of the future, the same icy terror when we thought about what lay ahead. It was not only a fear of death, which all normal people feel—but also a dread of the unknown. If we could have been told in specific detail what lay ahead, we might have prepared ourselves to endure it. But we had only a few "war stories" from the cadre who trained us, and our active imaginations—more than enough to make every man occasionally lapse into quiet meditation and stare through a window pane without really seeing what was happening outside. Only in the years of the Montgomery bus boycott and afterward did I again feel the same sense of commitment to a group of people that I felt among those men, some of whom, we all understood, were doomed to die.

Toward the end of basic training, when the time drew near for the company to be shipped overseas, we were told that each man should take stock of himself and decide what specific assignment he wanted to try for—rifleman, heavy weapons expert, squad leader, platoon sergeant, or company clerk. I don't mean to suggest that all of these jobs were distributed on the basis of our stated preferences. The army was not as "democratic" as it is now. But even in those times the company commander was interested in your own assessment of your talents and limitations.

I chose to apply for platoon sergeant, which meant that if I qualified and was selected, I would be promoted and placed in charge of all the other men in my platoon, serving directly under Lieutenant Butcher, the platoon leader. It was a bold and even presumptuous move on my part, but I was urged to apply for the position by a number of the other men, some of whom were fifteen and twenty years older.

While I knew that I had scored higher than Rudolph Williams had in most of the training exercises thus far, there was still a written examination to pass—and even then, Captain Patton had the prerogative to choose whomever he wanted for the position. I was certain that I was as bright as Rudolph, but I wasn't as sure about the relative worth of our educations. I had gone to the best schools available to blacks in Alabama, but I still felt ignorant about a whole host of things. Nevertheless, after I'd finished the written examination on leadership, I felt I'd done well. Most of it was based on what we had learned in training, and the rest required nothing more than common sense.

For two or three days afterward, I wandered around in a state of suspense, my insides snapping to attention every time the first sergeant or duty officer looked my way. Then, gradually, I came to accept the fact that I had not been chosen. While I didn't show it on the surface, I was hurt and a little angry with the world.

In the play *Othello,* Iago, the villain, does terrible things because he has been passed over for promotion. Some critics have argued that he is not sufficiently motivated to perform such evil acts. But these critics, I am certain, have never served in the army, which is a "closed society" where the smallest honor or privilege is to be treasured more than pearls and rubies. While I was not envious of Rudolph, I was angry at the captain and at the system itself; and I found it difficult not to brood in the darkness like a sullen, eighteen-year-old Iago.

Then, almost a week after the examination, I went into the orderly room for some reason and found the clerk absent. I was turning to leave when I heard conversation behind the half-open door of the company commander. I recognized Captain Patton's deep voice and then Rudolph's quiet tenor.

"I told you to study for that exam," the captain was saying, "but you didn't listen to me, did you?"

There was a muffled response.

"Well," said the captain, "there's nothing we can do about it now. This means I'll have to make that ignorant Alabama boy the sergeant of your platoon."

Again I couldn't hear Rudolph's answer, but by then I was tiptoeing out of the orderly room. Halfway across the street I let out a yell and offered a quick, impromptu prayer. Up to that point in my life, winning the rank of platoon sergeant was my greatest triumph.

However, once I had my sergeant's stripes and the few extra dollars that came with the promotion, I realized that I had also taken on responsibilities that in some way I was ill-prepared to handle. In the first place, I would be heading a combat unit, one that was preparing to go into battle. It would be my job to plunge into a clearing, turn to my men crouching in the woods behind me, and shout out, "Follow me!" That kind of heroic gesture, common enough in John Wayne movies, is not something that comes naturally to eighteen-year-olds, particularly after only a few weeks of basic training. It is one of the minor miracles of American history that civilians have always been willing and able to perform as soldiers in time of crisis, but I can't believe that many of them have done so without grave misgivings—and certainly I was no exception.

Also—and more immediately—I was responsible for the conduct of the men in my platoon during the remainder of the basic training cycle. Before, when I had been a lowly recruit like everyone else, I looked on shirking and small breaches of discipline with amusement, even admiration. Now I realized that any derelictions of duty would reflect directly on my character and my ability to lead. Henceforth, I would be less a comrade to the other enlisted men and more a member of the white captain's party. For a few days I felt very uncomfortable in my new "intermediary" position.

But my earlier friendships with the men now reinforced my assumption of authority. Jack Hatchet in particular came to my rescue. While he had little ambition for advancement or respect for the petty regulations under which an army is routinely operated, he knew that I was committed to doing my job as well as I could, so he became my unofficial "straw boss," keeping all the others in line with a quick flash of his narrowed eyes or a sudden sharp command.

There were others who also helped, and I still remember most of their names and faces after more than forty years: young and clear-eyed; afraid of the future, yet desperately seeking to shape it, to be a part of it; intimidated, yet cheerful, their voices in unison calling cadence across the years. When I recall these difficult times, I am always startled to realize how vivid they still seem, how much more alive we were during that period of severe adversity than in the docile years that preceded the war. By comparison, my childhood seems like a painted landscape in a museum, but my days as a soldier are carved in granite, a few incidents, some of them irrelevant, still standing in bold relief after the erosion of forty years.

I see Jack Hatchet sitting on an army cot dealing a poker hand, his long fingers moving rhythmically as he flips the cards onto the olive-drab blanket. Jack sits at the head of the bed; another man, perhaps Benny Bennett, sits at the foot. Two more squat on the floor, and I stand behind Jack as he picks up his own cards, exposes them one by one with the thick of his thumb, then turns to me and winks. I don't know whether he has a good hand or not, as he well knows; but I smile and look at the others, who are already nervous. They know that somehow he will beat them, regardless of how lucky they are or how well they play. And sure enough, after the bets and the showdown, Hatchet has won again.

I see his huge hands reach out to scoop up the pot. He is as adept at handling money as a bank teller. He counts the bills, keeps a pile of ones, and then wads up several twenties and hands them to me.

"There you go, banker. Put these with the rest."

So I take out my wallet, which is now bulging with Jack's money, and I add these new winnings to the wad. I don't need to count it because I know that with this additional sixty dollars, the amount I am holding totals $885. Two months ago it had never occurred to me that there was so much money to be won from army privates.

The next hand is dealt. Bets are made. Benny and Jack are left in the hand; and while Benny only takes one card, Jack takes three. Benny bets. Jack raises. Benny, gun-shy now, merely calls.

"Aces over," he says nervously.

Jack tosses his cards down on the blanket, one at a time. "Three nines," he says quietly and reaches for the pot.

I have just been appointed platoon sergeant, and we are marching into the Massachusetts woods, packs on our backs, our breath white in the afternoon air. There is snow on the ground, and everywhere the leafless trees are like wet skeletons against a gray sky. Our toes are numb and our gloved hands ache from the cold. The army has told us that with our long-johns and our sleeping bags we will be plenty warm for the ten days we will spend in the field, but already we are beginning to suspect—and it wouldn't be the first time—that we have been told a lie.

Suddenly, we hear shouts from behind. Captain Patton, who is leading the march toward a rendezvous with the rest of the company, calls out, "Plato-o-o-n halt!" and we are standing at attention, uncertain whether we should be grateful for the opportunity to catch our breath or sorry because standing still we will get much colder.

A jeep drives up and out of the corner of my eye I see a sergeant from another company behind the wheel. In the back sit Jack Hatchet and one of his cronies.

"I caught these two trying to make their way back to the barracks," the sergeant says. "They belong to you?"

Since the question seems to be addressed to me, I answer, "Yes, sir. They're ours."

Captain Patton shakes his head and swears silently. His tail is in a crack. A sergeant from another company, maybe a battle veteran, has just caught us on the way to bivouac, minus two men; and we weren't even aware they'd gotten away. I look at Hatchet and he grins and shrugs his shoulders. Patton sees the gesture, and so does the sergeant in the jeep.

"OK, sergeant," Captain Patton tells the smirking driver. "We'll take it from here. You two get out of that jeep and fall in at the rear of the column."

Hatchet and his friend climb out, not quickly, but not slowly either. There is still a casual defiance in Hatchet, an arbitrariness about his character that won't submit itself completely to army discipline. He is going to do what Captain Patton says, but he is going to take his own sweet time about it.

Patton watches him with resentment and discomfort. Then, to the relief of nearly everybody, the sergeant wheels his jeep around and goes bouncing down the hillside. Now Patton must face Hatchet and the distinct possibility that the man will defy him in front of the entire platoon. He glares first at Hatchet and then at me, a known quantity and much more easily managed.

"Sergeant," he says in a voice that is just a little shrill, "it's your responsibility to see that the men are all present and accounted for at roll call. You reported the platoon at full strength. You must have known that these two had taken off. You were covering for them."

I assure Captain Patton that I have done no such thing, but he has gone too far now to withdraw the allegation.

"We'll hold an investigation when we get to the campsite," he says. Then, somewhat gratuitously, he adds, "You may just lose your stripes for this."

For a moment there is silence, except for the chill wind that whips through the naked branches of the trees. Everyone simply stands and stares—Captain Patton at me, I at Captain Patton, everyone else at the two of us, the whole detachment shivering on the hillside.

Then Hatchet's voice cuts through the silence.

"Captain Patton," he says, "what Sergeant Abernathy has told you is true. We were present at roll call. We lined up at the rear. Then, after we'd marched awhile, we dropped out and took off across the woods. The sergeant had no idea we were gone."

Captain Patton looks at him and blinks his eyes. He is wavering. He doesn't quite know what to do. Hatchet, the poker player, sees this indecision and goes a step further.

"Captain, you can't take away Sergeant Abernathy's stripes for something he didn't know about and couldn't help. Sergeant Abernathy always tells the truth. If you take his stripes away, you'll have a sit-down strike on your hands."

Patton turns and looks at the men, shivering there in the gray New England winter. They are too cold to reply, or maybe too scared. What Hatchet is saying comes close to mutiny. It's certainly against the Uniform Code of Military Justice—and this is wartime. Yet a number of them finally nod and mumble their agreement, just below the level of hearing.

Captain Patton stares at them, panic in his eyes. What he does next will not only determine his own immediate fate but that of the entire platoon, maybe the company. If he chooses, he can bring more than one of us up before a general court-martial. All of this has become extremely serious business.

Then he makes his decision involuntarily because, in spite of himself, he breaks into a grin. Then everyone else smiles too, exhaling one great white cloud. It is now nothing more than a big joke.

"OK, you two," he says to Hatchet and his buddy. "Fall in. When we get back to the company area, you'll be on pots-and-pans for a week."

Then he turns to me and says more gently, "Carry on, Sergeant Abernathy."

We are in a large building, sitting on benches in front of wooden tables. Each of us has a pencil in hand and a sheet of paper as well, a government form. An officer is standing in front of the entire battalion. We have never seen him before and he has never seen us; but he has seen hundreds and hundreds like us, perhaps many thousands. He is instructing us on how to fill out our GI insurance forms; and he treats us as if we were five years old. Later we learn that we have not been discriminated against. Everyone passing through this center, black or white, is treated in precisely the same way.

"Hold up your right hand," the officer commands, "and keep it in the air until I tell you to put it down."

Then he looks around the room and tells two or three men they have raised their left hands. They are embarrassed. Everyone laughs. Then the officer tells us we can lower our hands. Next he tells us to arrange the sheet in front of us so that the number is in the upper right-hand corner, the same side as the hand we raised. By now everyone is mumbling with resentment, but the process continues.

We are told take the pencil in our writing hand and then hold it up in the air. After the officer has inspected the entire room from his vantage point on the platform, he tells us that when he says "Now," we are to write our last name in the first space provided us on the form. Two or three men drop their hands and prepare to write, but he patiently tells them to wait until he gives the command. Then he repeats the instructions, pauses for a full five seconds, and then says, "Now!" We all busily write our last names. Then, as instructed, we raise our pencils in the air.

This procedure continues for the better part of an hour, after which we have filled out some ten lines of information, surely no more, and we are thoroughly humiliated. If this insulting procedure is any measure of the army's regard for us, then we wonder just how bad things will be after we get overseas.

We continue to grumble about the indignity as we march to one more generic army mess hall where we eat chow out of tin trays.

"What was all that about?" someone asks.

"Your GI insurance," someone else replies.

"What insurance?"

"The ten thousand dollars your folks will get if you're killed in action."

"They'll get ten thousand dollars?"

Suddenly everyone at the table grows silent and thoughtful. Ten thousand dollars is a lot of money, more than most black families have ever seen. Wouldn't it be nice to have $10,000! Then we follow that line of reasoning to its logical conclusion, realizing the circumstances under which such a large sum would be paid. And we all know that the families of some of the men at this table will probably collect that insurance. We hear nothing for a long moment but the clang and scrape of forks making contact with trays. Then someone cracks a joke and the conversation begins again.

After lunch we march back to the building where we spent the morning filling out that one form, and the officer reads the names of those who have made mistakes. Surprisingly there are quite a few; more than I would have thought. W. J. is among them.

Our ship is named the USS *George Washington*. We hit the gangplank about nine in the morning, dressed in our first-class uniforms and soft caps. Everything else we own is in duffel bags on our shoulders, and henceforth we will live like old-time vaudevillians, except that instead of moving from theater to theater we will be moving from battle to battle somewhere in Europe.

Later, after we have been stored in the hold of the ship like cargo, the NCOs are allowed to climb two stories of ladder rungs to stand on the deck and watch as we slip out of New York Harbor past the Statue of Liberty. I lean on the rail and stare at this Caucasian giantess with a thousand thoughts running through my head.

*   *   *

By the time we get to Le Havre, France, the war is almost over, though people are being killed every day in what the press describes as "mopping up operations." We are trucked from one devastated city to another—Düsseldorf, Bonn, etc.—apparently in an effort to catch up with the battle lines so that we can relieve veterans who have accumulated enough points for rotation. Some of the men are ambivalent about our status: They hope to see just a little combat in this Greatest of All Wars, yet fear ending up like the casualties we see passing us on their way to hospitals at the rear.

Germany is a rubble heap. At least, the part we see is utterly ruined. At the time, I think that, while Hitler brought this terrible destruction on himself and his people, there is little to be said for modern warfare. It is gigantic in its dimensions and terrifyingly impersonal, like some blind monster roaming the land, knocking down ancient trees and toppling buildings, unsure of where it steps or whom it crushes. I see Americans who have lost arms, legs, eyes, faces—and Germans who are in the same desperate condition. At first the sight of maimed and bloodied bodies makes me weak and faint. Later, I find it does not affect me physically; but I still feel a sickness at heart. I'm not certain how the rest of the men feel, but I for one am hoping for an immediate surrender and a merciful peace.

Then one day the war in Europe is over and I thank God that I have been spared—not merely from death but from the necessity of confronting the enemy and either participating in his destruction or else refusing to kill another human being and as a consequence risking death myself. I have by now concluded that I am committed in principle to a life of nonviolence.

Meanwhile, after rejoicing over the victory, we have a morale problem in the company. Still untested in battle, we are alert and restless, a cannon waiting to be fired. Our cruise to Europe seems to have been for naught, but there are rumors that those units recently arrived in Germany will be shipped immediately to the

Far East, where the Japanese are still defending every Pacific island with an unprecedented ferocity and, in some cases, engaging in suicide missions in order to forestall the invasion of their homeland. Fresh American units will be needed. It is only fair that veterans be given a rest from battle. We hear these rumors, wait, and again the pressure mounts.

One day two men, assigned to a meaningless detail, decide to skip out and hide down at the PX. The Colonel—Captain Patton has been promoted by now—finds out and is furious. He knows that too many derelictions of this sort can lead to a dangerous collapse of morale. If he is to lead a strong fighting unit to the Pacific he must maintain order and authority until we ship out. So he calls the two offenders into his office, chews them out, and then tells them to wait outside. He calls me in and closes the door. Outside it is growing dark. Although it is only four in the afternoon, the streetlights are already on, orange blurs in the savage rain that has begun to drench the cobblestones. Periodically, the wind whips sheets of water against the windowpanes as he tells me what I already suspect.

"Sergeant Abernathy," he says, "I am giving these men the severest punishment I can think of without bringing them to a court-martial. They're going to dig a hole in the middle of the company area. It will be six feet long, three feet wide, and six feet deep. The spot I have in mind will be easy to find. It is in the field next to the orderly room, and it is marked by a big puddle. I want them to dig there, in the middle of that puddle, and I want them to do it now—while it is raining. They are not to quit until the hole has been inspected and satisfies my conditions. Then the hole is to be covered up."

I stand there waiting for the rest of the order, the trace of a grin on my face. I understand and even approve of this measure, but I don't like what I know is coming next.

"Sergeant," he says, "in order to be effective, this detail will have to be supervised. And since they're in your platoon, I suppose you can figure out who will have to stand watch over them."

I tell him that it's not too difficult to guess whom he has in mind.

He grins sympathetically. "It's a tough war," he says and returns my salute.

Shortly after midnight the chill sets in. At first I think I have simply been soaked to the bone and that what I experience is nothing more than normal under such circumstances. Then I begin to feel pain in the pit of my stomach and a sudden nausea. The men are working without speaking now, standing up to their waists in a mud pond, shoveling what looks more like water than dirt, watching it seep back into the black hole, which fills up as fast as they try to empty it. I have been holding the flashlight so they can see what they are doing, but now the spot begins to waver like a sick moon. My legs become weak and I try to lock my knees so that I can stand; but I feel the world slip sideways, and then I am lying in the mud as the two men stand over me, calling my name.

The next thing I know I am in a clean bed, propped up on one elbow, vomiting into a bedpan while a nurse holds my head. Her hand feels like it's made of wet snow. Then I sink into darkness again.

Days later my head is clear and the pain has left my joints; but I am so weak it takes every bit of strength I possess to hold a glass of fruit juice. Somewhere along the way I have been told that I have rheumatic fever, but I don't remember when or by whom. The doctors and nurses check me often, their worried faces floating in and out of my view every few minutes.

Then a familiar face appears—Colonel Patton's. He is smiling, but his brow is furrowed. "Sergeant," he says, "we've gotten our orders. I've tried to delay our departure. I've told them that you're going to be my first sergeant, that the company won't be the same without you. But you know how the army is. They do things their own way."

I nod and the motion almost exhausts me.

"So I guess I won't be seeing you for a while," he says. "Not until you get well and catch up with us. Till then. . . ."

He stops. His lip is trembling. He is trying to control himself, but already the tears have filled his eyes. Suddenly he bends down and puts his arms around me. There are tears in my eyes too, and I try to embrace him but my arms fall back on the sheets.

Then, with a final effort I raise my right hand slowly and touch my forehead. He returns my salute, wheels, and is gone. The next day I learn what he already knew—that I will not rejoin the company, that I am being sent back home with the wounded, that for me the war is over.

These incidents and many more return to memory from time to time; and somehow, despite the pain and agony they represent, they seem sweet and clear, refined of their impurities by time and by my growing awareness that suffering is not only a burden but a gift, sometimes meant to be cherished in secret and shared only with God. I feel particularly strong about this when I remember an incident that occurred many years later.

I was walking down the streets of Atlanta when a figure stepped quickly out of a doorway and confronted me on the sidewalk.

"It can't be. Sergeant Abernathy!"

It couldn't be, but it was. "Benny!" I shouted and shook his hand. He was older, heavier, but I had recognized him the moment I saw his face. He was the boy who had played poker on the bed with Jack Hatchet.

I asked him what he was doing in Atlanta, how he had been and finally if he knew about any of the others in the outfit. By then the war was a fading memory, but as soon as I asked the question I dreaded the answer. We were not talking about schoolmates or friends from church camp. We were talking about men who had been sent into combat in the last savage days of the war.

"You haven't heard what happened?" he asked almost in a whisper.

I shook my head, and while I listened with growing horror, he told me the story. They had indeed been shipped to the Far East to participate in the final invasion of Japanese-held islands shortly before the atomic bombs were dropped. They had been forced to learn jungle fighting quickly because they had been dropped into the roughest country in that part of the world, a maze of trees, snarling vines, dense tropical growth—a place populated by insects, wild animals, snakes, and an occasional Japanese detachment.

It seems that one night my company blundered into the wrong part of the island and became caught in deadly crossfire from two machine gun nests. Every single man in the unit— every white officer and black troop—was lost that night. Only Benny survived, badly wounded and left for dead. He and I were the sole survivors. They were all lost.

All lost! For an instant I didn't understand the words Benny had spoken. They were dead then—the whole roster. Had I been there, I would be dead too, lying in one of those foreign cemeteries underneath a numbered marker identical to a thousand others, neatly and anonymously ranked on some green hillside. For a moment I grappled with the thought as if it were no more than a mathematical problem.

Then faces rushed from the darkness of memory into my consciousness, and I was seeing them all again: Captain Patton, the white man who had become my friend; Lieutenant Butcher, the gruff redneck with a soft heart; simple W. J.; and Rudolph Williams, a rival no more. Then one face replaced all others, and suddenly I saw Jack Hatchet, his easy grin and quiet voice speaking to me across the years from the silence of the grave.

Why that one face haunted me above all others I don't know. As I said, we were so different from one another in temperament; he was everything I had been told to reject. Yet when I remembered him and tried to speak his name, I was shaken by an overpowering grief; and there on the street, struggling to speak, I stared at Benny Bennett through eyes blurred by bitter tears.

3

And Study War No More

WHEN I CAME BACK from the army I was thin and weak, but my mother soon took care of that. She fed me the right things: chicken, beef stew, sweet potatoes, black-eyed peas, butter beans, biscuits, and all the pies and cake I could handle. After a few weeks I had put on ten or fifteen pounds and had regained my strength.

The war wound down in Europe and in the Far East, and then my brothers came home—all three of them. The four of us had survived, and out of the group I had come the closest to death, not from an enemy bullet but from rheumatic fever.

The country was generous to those of us who fought. I received some disability because of the damage to my heart, and in addition we were eligible for GI housing loans and—most important of all to me—an allotment to attend college. I had always assumed I would earn some kind of degree, but after my father's death I had resigned myself to years of hard work in order to earn the tuition. With the GI bill I would have tuition paid and a living allowance. Also I had my mustering-out pay. So the future seemed assured—at least for a while.

But though I had enough money to go to college, I had not yet finished high school, so I had to get what is now called a GED, a certificate that I had taken a test and proved that I was capable of performing at the level of a high school graduate. The test was easy enough, and I came out certified to enter college. I was ambitious and confident after my success in the army, but I had to settle for one of the black universities in Alabama, because at the time I couldn't afford to go to a private school, and higher education in the South was still segregated. My dream had been to go to Morehouse in Atlanta, which was known among blacks as the "Little Harvard of the South." In retrospect I realize that I might well have gone to Morehouse had I known just a little more about the world; but for a war veteran who had just returned from Europe I was still relatively unsophisticated, so I enrolled at Alabama State University in Montgomery and told myself I would have to be satisfied with the fine education they had to offer.

The one thing that bothered me about the immediate future was my mother's deteriorating condition. In the time I had been overseas—a little less than a year—she had slowed down considerably, and I knew she was in constant pain from rheumatoid arthritis, a condition that had plagued her for years. She never complained, and I could only see the suffering in her eyes, because she was able to put up a good front when we were around her.

Having lost my father only a few years earlier, I had not allowed myself to think that my mother would not live for many more years. But as the summer of 1945 began to give way to fall, I realized that her condition was not merely painful but might in fact be dangerous; so without asking her I called our old family physician, Dr. Dunning, a white man in his seventies who had long since quit practicing but who readily agreed to examine her.

I remember waiting outside while he made his examination and seeing the look on his face as he came out of the room and shut the door behind him.

"She's in terrible pain," he said, shaking his head. "Why didn't she let somebody know before now?"

"She didn't want to be a bother," I said. "Is there anything you can do for her?"

He nodded. "Oh, yes. I can ease the pain considerably. But I can't cure her."

I suddenly panicked. "What do you mean?"

"I'm afraid she isn't going to last too much longer," he said gently. "But I can see that she won't suffer."

I felt hollow inside. "How much longer?"

"I don't know that," he said. "Maybe a few months. Maybe a year. Maybe even longer."

He patted my shoulder and walked slowly into the living room where he eased into a chair and began to write a prescription in a quivering hand. At the time he had only a few months to live himself. I walked him outside and discovered that he had come in a horse-drawn wagon because he could no longer drive a car. As I watched him sway and bump around the corner it was as if a whole era had disappeared with him.

When I went back in the house my mother was sitting in a chair, rocking and singing. She smiled as I came into the room.

"He's a nice man," she said, "and a good friend, but he's so frail."

I nodded and told her that she was going to be fine, that as soon as I went to town and got her prescription filled she would be without pain; but even as I said it I knew she didn't believe me. That was in late July.

In September I packed my clothes and left for Montgomery to begin my studies at Alabama State University. My sister Doll drove me to the campus, where for the first time I saw the capital city of Alabama and the campus of the university, dominated by Bibb Graves Hall, which stood at the top of the hill, its steeple lifted high above the landscape. I remember being deeply impressed by the sight and by the story of Bibb Graves, the benevolent governor who, though a segregationist, had been committed to black education and had done a great deal for Alabama State University.

Though I was as intimidated as most freshmen by the long academic road ahead of me, I found adjustment to dormitory life easy enough, having spent many months in an army barracks, and I soon fell into a comfortable routine. I went to every lecture. I took good notes. I studied hard and did my homework. And I always had my hand in the air. I was determined to be the best student in the university, just as I had been the best soldier in my company.

But I also wanted to make a mark in other ways. I had never been as athletic as my older brothers, and with my weakened heart I could not have gone out for athletics anyway. So I decided to gain recognition from my fellow students in some other area, and I chose dramatics. I tried out for every play and, even as a freshman, I became known for my performances.

The football players were in the habit of receiving a standing ovation after they had won a big game, and I longed for the same kind of recognition. Finally, during my sophomore year—when I was starring in *Deep Are the Roots*, a popular and well-reviewed play—I got the same standing ovation when I entered the dining room. It was old hat to the football players, I'm sure; but it may have been the height of my college career. Certainly it fed my youthful vanity and probably made me impossible to live with for a day or two, though I tried to be as modest as I could.

Alabama State University was not as sleepy and docile a place as it seemed to be when you looked at it from a country hill. Unbeknownst to the all-white state legislature, which voted us a few crumbs from the educational table every year, we were being taught all sorts of useful and subversive ideas by our faculty members, some of whom were openly urging us to make a difference in our people's struggle for freedom.

The most influential of these was probably Professor J. E. Pierce, who taught political science. He had come from Lowndes County, which was reputed to be the most racist of all sixty-seven counties in Alabama. At that time not a single black there was registered to vote and, as a consequence, Professor Pierce was careful to make us understand how important the ballot was to our future and how courageous we would have to be to ensure black suffrage. He talked about these matters often in class, and I began to realize the degree to which our problems were solvable—if we were willing to do what was necessary.

But he was not the only one talking about such matters. Dr. Emma Payne Howard, who directed many extracurricular activities, was also stressing the need for racial progress; and it was she who first made me understand that a religious vocation could be compatible with a social conscience. Dr. V. E. Daniel was talking about black deprivation in his sociology class, and even Dr. G. Garrett Hardy, who taught drama, used the plays we studied to illustrate social and political ideas important to black people.

Dr. Edward Weaver, head of the Bio-Social Studies Department, became a dear friend during my undergraduate years. An open and informal professor in class, Dr. Weaver often invited me to his home on Saturday nights. He and his wife, Geneva, would allow me to mow their lawn or perform other household chores in exchange for home-cooked meals.

In addition to these, I also remember Dr. Susie Robinson, not because she was any more committed to social justice than the others, but because she was such a stern grader. I remember her telling us: "You're not going to get an A from me, so don't expect it. The only person who deserves an A is the man who wrote the textbook, because he understood everything in it when he wrote it. I only give myself a B. As for the rest of you—you'll be lucky to get a C."

She wasn't quite that strict, but I was certainly proud of the B I earned in her class.

Even as we were being prepared intellectually to lead a more militant generation of black people, a campus controversy arose that gave me my first opportunity to lead a demonstration in protest against discriminatory practices. The controversy was not merely symbolic but was about something very concrete and basic—the food in the dining hall.

Early in my sophomore year we had begun to notice that there were two separate menus for every meal: one for the students and one for the faculty. For breakfast we would sometimes get nothing but toast while the faculty had eggs and bacon as well. Or we would get huge piles of grits with one sausage in it, the sausage grease serving in lieu of butter. For lunch we would usually get heaps of steaming pork and beans—and nothing more, not even a piece of bread to sop it up. And the best dinner we ever got was Spam, again with unbuttered grits, while the faculty would be enjoying huge hunks of real ham.

After several weeks of this fare, we were sick to death of it and were dreaming every night of fried chicken and biscuits. That's all we talked about in the dormitory and between classes. We were obsessed with food, so much so that it was difficult to concentrate in class or to study in the evening.

By then I had been elected president of the student council, so I became the chief recipient of all student complaints. There were approximately three thousand students on campus, and I think every one of them must have come up to me at one time or another and said, "Man, when are you going to do something about that food?"

I had several conferences with the Johnsons, the man and woman who ran the dining hall, but the meals didn't improve; and Mr. Johnson retaliated by patrolling the hall even more carefully, jerking students out of line who were talking too loud or whom he suspected of neglecting to pay their fees. Clearly something more drastic had to be done. But what?

Somewhere I had heard about another college campus with similar problems. The students had organized a hunger strike and had forced the school officials to give them something better. So at the next meeting of the student council I brought in a plan and put it before the group: We would call a strike of the entire student body, boycott the dining hall, and refuse to eat anything until conditions were improved.

Everyone was enthusiastically in support of the idea, and we agreed to begin in two days—as soon as we could spread the word. Two mornings later the faculty trooped in to eat their usual meal of eggs, bacon, and cereal; and the Johnsons fixed hundreds of pieces of toast for the students—but no one showed up to claim them. We had students stationed all over campus, ready to intercept anyone who hadn't gotten the message; and as far as we knew, the boycott was 100 percent effective. The same was true of lunch and dinner

After breakfast the next morning, as I was entering my first class, a student came up to me and handed me a note. It said to report after class to the office of the president. I must admit that I went with a queasiness in my stomach, only partially explained by the fact I hadn't eaten in twenty-four hours. Dr. H. C.

Trenholm, president of Alabama State University, was the kind of man I held in awe. Had he been a policeman or a state senator, I might not have felt the same way. But he was a brilliant scholar whose erudition I both admired and envied. I had heard stories of his withering remarks and cold eye. So I prepared myself for an ordeal.

When I entered his office he was seated behind a huge oak desk that was covered with papers. I had knocked and had heard him tell me to come in, but when I stood in front of him he behaved as if he didn't know I was in the room. He read a letter, made a few notes on a pad, then picked up another letter and slit it savagely with a sterling silver letter opener.

Finally, as if by accident, he glanced up and saw me standing in front of him. He pushed his glasses down to the end of his nose, reared back in his swivel chair, and stared at me with cold and inquiring eyes. I felt my knees begin to tremble.

"Mr. Abernathy?"

I swallowed and nodded my head.

"I understand that you are responsible for this hunger strike. Is that true?"

"Yes, sir," I said in a voice I barely recognized.

He reached down, fumbled among the papers, and came up with a sheet. "This is your academic record," he said, and began to stare at it.

I wasn't too worried, because my grades were excellent, but I was a *little* worried. Finally he put the grade sheet down.

"Well," he said, "I can't ask you to do much better than you've done in class, Mr. Abernathy, but there is something else I want you to do."

"Yes, sir?" I asked.

"I want you to tell the students to stop their hunger strike and lead them back into the dining hall this evening."

I was tempted to give him my promise and rush out of the office, but suddenly I felt my resolve stiffen. I was representing the entire student body, so I had no right to give in.

"The food has to improve," I said firmly. "We won't return until the food improves and we are treated with more courtesy by Mr. Johnson."

He stared at me for a moment, as if trying to back me down by the force of his gaze. "Things will improve," he said.

I hesitated. "When?" I asked in a steady voice.

He blinked his eyes behind the glasses. "Immediately," he said.

"In which case," I said, "we'll certainly call off the boycott, and we'll be there for the evening meal."

He nodded slowly, both to acknowledge my cooperation and to dismiss me from his office. It almost looked as if he were about to smile, though I was sure I knew better than that. As soon as I was out in the hallway I began to breathe normally again. Then I hurried back to the dormitory, where several members of the student council were waiting for me. When I told them the results of my visit they were jubilant—with just the slightest reservation. We would postpone our celebration until after we had eaten the evening meal.

We put the word out all over the campus, and by the time we got to the dining hall around six, there were already long lines outside. Mr. Johnson was walking up and down with a frozen smile on his face, and the smell of something good was in the air. When they threw open the door we saw huge platters of fried chicken waiting at the counter. I was a campus hero.

This experience taught me a lesson that I filed away but never quite forgot: You can deal with the most awesome authority on an equal basis if the people are on your side. It really wasn't too great a distance from the Alabama State campus to downtown Montgomery, where we staged our bus boycott only a few years later, and a number of people would then remember that I had been instrumental in starting the campus boycott.

During my college days I did not forget about my religious commitment nor did I lose my faith as so many college students do. As a matter of fact, I was the superintendent of the student Sunday School, which met at nine o'clock every Sunday morning in Patterson Hall; and everyone believed that it was just a matter of time before I announced a call to the ministry, that is, everyone but me. For some reason I was fighting the idea, though I still knew I would eventually heed the call I had first heard as a child.

One day when I was home visiting my mother, my cousin Louise Walker came by to see us; and in the course of conversation she said, quite casually, "David, why haven't you started preaching yet?"

"What do you mean?" I said.

"Well," she said, "you're going to be a preacher sooner or later, so why haven't you already announced your call?"

"I don't know why you say that," I said, a little too vehemently. "I'm not going to be a preacher."

"You're not?" she said. "Why I thought you made up your mind about that years ago."

"Absolutely not," I said, and as I did so I noticed my mother watching my face very carefully. As soon as Louise had left, my mother turned to me.

"David," she said, "I don't want you to ever lie about preaching. You know that you are going to be a preacher, that God has called you to preach. So don't be afraid to admit it."

I didn't answer her, either to confirm or deny what she had said. I quickly turned away and pretended I hadn't heard. Then I changed the subject. She didn't press me further on the matter. She had spoken her piece and knew that I had heard.

During this period I had a girlfriend, someone I saw on a regular basis during my first four years in college. I'll call her "Jackie," since there is no point in causing her unnecessary distress after all of these years. I met her right after I had started at Alabama State, though not in Montgomery but back in Linden.

I was home for Christmas vacation, and with the holidays almost over and with very little to do, I was hanging around Linden, waiting for the next semester to begin. One day I had stopped in to see a friend at his dry cleaning establishment. Because he was shorthanded, I was asked to fill in for the afternoon, receiving dirty clothes, delivering clean clothes, and taking customers' money.

Toward the end of the day a young man in a shiny 1939 Buick drove up, screeched to a halt, and came barreling into the building to pick up some clothing. I looked through the plate-glass window to see that he had left a beautiful girl lounging in the front seat, staring out of the window. I had not seen her around town before, and she definitely caught my eye.

"I don't have a receipt," he said, "but the clothes belong to my friend in the car. Her name is Jackie Summers."

I went back to the racks of clean clothing and immediately saw her clothes, hanging in plain sight; but I pawed through the rows two or three times, then turned and shrugged my shoulders.

"I can't find the order," I said. "Maybe if she could come in. . . ."

Then he did precisely what I'd hope he would do. He stuck his head out of the door and yelled, "Jackie, would you come in and help him find your clothes."

She came in, waving the piece of paper, which she presented to me.

I took it and smiled. "I believe I must know you from somewhere," I said. "What's your name?"

"It's Jackie Summers," she said, and because everybody knew who everybody else was in a rural Alabama county, I identified her family, and we chatted for a minute, while her boyfriend frowned. Then I took the receipt and found the suit. As they were leaving I heard him commenting on how slow-witted I was, that the suit had been right in front of my nose all along.

I asked around and found out that she was unmarried and that she was a little older than I was. That didn't deter me, however. I had been in the army. I had been to Massachusetts. I had even been to Europe. I was a man of the world at the age of twenty.

She must have thought so, too, because when I asked her out she was quick to accept, and that was the end of the boyfriend and his 1939 Buick. We went everywhere together, and I'm sure that for a long while we were as much in love as most young people get. She was intelligent, had a good sense of humor, and got along beautifully with my family.

Jackie was particularly good to my mother. She would drop by, help with the housework, sit around and talk, and behave very much like a daughter-in-law, particularly when I was back in school. I was grateful for her thoughtfulness, and began to feel comfortable with her as an important part of my life.

One thing stood between us, however; she did not want to be married to a preacher. In fact, she went so far as to say that she would never allow such a fate to befall her. When I would try to tell her that a preacher and his family were among the most loved and honored members of the community, she would shake her head and refuse to listen. Preachers were all right in their place, but she had no intention of marrying one. Finally I stopped trying to talk to her about the question, and we went on as before, but always with this unresolved quarrel in the back of both our minds.

I studied hard and went to church services, church meetings, and church suppers, and didn't pay a great deal of attention to young women—at least not for a while. That part of my life seemed settled. I was certain that when the time finally came and I declared my intentions to become a preacher, she would go along with the decision. (On the other hand, she was just as certain that I would eventually give up such a foolish idea and do something more sensible with my life.)

After a few years of this steady company, I allowed myself a little leeway. At church some social events were held especially for young couples; and too often I was left out of the picture because I never brought a girl along, except on those rare occasions when Jackie was willing to come over from Marengo County. So I decided to expand my social life a little by occasionally asking somebody to accompany me to a picnic or dance. At first I made my situation quite clear. Then, as I continued to date girls other than Jackie, I sometimes neglected this clarification.

During this period I met a girl I found unusually attractive, and for the first time I began to question my long-time commitment to Jackie. This new girl's name was Juanita Odessa Jones, who lived about eighty miles from Montgomery and who came from a fine old family in Perry County, where many of the blacks were prosperous and well educated. As a matter of fact, Coretta Scott King and Andrew Young's wife, Jean, came from the same county.

The more I learned about Juanita, the more I admired her.

She was extremely bright, with a marvelous sense of humor, yet she had a backbone of steel. Unlike some of the other girls I had gone out with, she made no attempt to pretend that she was either fluff-headed or helpless. From the beginning I had the sense that she could take care of herself in the world, with or without help from me. While some men were a little intimidated by her, I found her strength and independence refreshing, and I enjoyed being with her.

She could talk about ideas, and she wasn't afraid to express disagreement. After our second date I found out she too wasn't interested in marrying a minister. I tried to suggest that she might be willing to make just one exception; but she was adamant.

"I'm sorry," she said firmly, "but I just don't see myself as a preacher's wife."

"But I'm going to be a preacher," I protested.

"Then you'll have to marry somebody else besides me," she said with a smile.

I changed the subject quickly, because I didn't want her to stop going out with me. We were having a good time. We enjoyed each other's company and there was no need at this stage to talk about getting married when neither of us was ready for that step. Better to drift along the way we were and take things as they came.

I drove over to Uniontown, Alabama, in Perry County on more than one occasion and did meet Juanita's parents. They had a beautiful house out in the country. Some people might have called it a mansion, but it was really a big farmhouse from another era, with a huge porch or "gallery" and white clapboard walls that always seemed as if they had been newly painted. It was situated firmly among huge oak trees that provided cooling shade in the summer and shelter from the wind in the winter.

I remarked that it must have been a good house to grow up in, but Juanita explained that she had spent most of her life in the dormitories of Selma University in Selma, Alabama. It was at Selma University that she had attended nursery, kindergarten, elementary and was currently a senior in high school. In that respect our parents were very much alike: Both sets had always valued education and done whatever was necessary to see that their children received the best possible schooling.

From talking to her parents, I learned that she had always been strong-willed and independent, and even as a young girl she had not submitted to many of the indignities other blacks were willing to bear. As a teenager she had come to town one day to buy the week's groceries at the white-owned and -operated supermarket. While her purchases were being rung up, she watched as a young white girl about her age followed behind while a bagboy carried her groceries out to the car. When the cashier handed Juanita her ticket she refused to pay it; she just stood there while the people behind her waited.

The cashier looked at her for a second, then shook his head.

"What are you waiting for?" he asked.

"I'm waiting for the boy to carry out my groceries," she replied.

The cashier looked puzzled, then his mouth fell open.

"But we only do that for white customers," he said.

"You charge me the same amount for my groceries, don't you?" she said.

"Sure," he said.

"Then I should get the same service," she said, and dug in her heels.

The cashier stood for a moment, uncertain of what to do. The line was getting longer, but still the cashier wouldn't instruct the boy to carry her groceries.

"Well," she said finally, "if the boy can't take my groceries to the car, then I guess he'll just have to put them back on the shelves." Then she walked out of the store.

The next day, however, someone from the white community stopped her father on the street.

"You better keep that daughter of yours out in the country," the white man said. "If she comes back into town, she's going to get into real trouble."

That was in the late 1940s, and the civil rights movement was not even a plan in the minds of its eventual leaders, much less something committed to paper. Yet she was willing to take on an entire community just to make a point. Her father, afraid for her safety, suggested that she stay out in the country for a while, but she refused to do so, and was back in town the next weekend. Yet nobody bothered her, probably because they knew that she could cause at least as much trouble as they could.

Even though I was not quite ready to get married, I wondered if I would ever find a woman as formidable as this young girl who "didn't want to marry a preacher." Still, I put the matter out of my mind. Next year, perhaps, I would think about it more seriously.

During this period I took Juanita to a dance or two and a few parties, and we agreed to write. When she enrolled in Tennessee State University at Nashville, I turned my attention to other matters, including Jackie—at least, that's what I tried to do. But somehow Juanita stuck in my mind. Then something happened that seemed to eliminate any possibility that we might ever get together.

I had come home for Thanksgiving 1947; and though we were all there and tried to be as happy as we had always been, we were worried about our mother. Even with the medicine she took constantly, she was clearly suffering. When asked about it, she would smile and say that she was doing just fine, that the medicine completely eliminated the fiery pain in her joints. We talked among ourselves about it, but we all knew there was nothing we could do.

During all the years I had known her, my mother had never missed a Sunday in church that I could remember. Attending services in that small country church was not only a duty, but her chief joy. She was always moved by what went on there, and she never failed to come away from a sermon full of joy and dedication, no matter who the preacher was.

So I was surprised when, on the Saturday following Thanksgiving, I was called aside by my sister Lula Mae.

"Mama's not going to church tomorrow," she said, her lips trembling. "She says she doesn't feel well enough."

I shook my head. "Then she must be in pretty bad shape," I said, trying to hide my alarm.

The next morning I went to her bedroom door, and she looked up from her book and smiled. Her eyes were tired and filled with pain.

"Mama," I said, "I know you don't feel up to sitting through church today, but I have an idea. Why don't I take you over in the car. We can drive right up to the side of the church and we can listen to the service. You can hear the music and even the sermon."

She smiled and shook her head.

"That's mighty kind of you, David," she said, "but I don't need to go to church today because I've gone all those other Sundays for all the years. The matter is settled."

She said it very quietly, and I just nodded; but I didn't want to think about what she had just told me. I eased down on the side of the bed and held her hand while the others stopped in and spoke on their way to the church. It was a bright, cool autumn day; but I didn't move from where I sat. For a while she simply lay on the bed, eyes closed, though I knew she wasn't sleeping. Then she opened her eyes.

"David," she said, "will you help me up?"

I took her arm and, leaning heavily against me, she walked with great difficulty from one room to another, stopping in each to let her eyes fall on familiar objects, things she had lived with for most of her life. Finally she asked to go on the porch, where she sat in a rocking chair and stared for a long time out across the land that my father had farmed during their years together.

She could see fenced pastures, cows standing in stubble, harvested fruit trees, fields plowed and planted with winter wheat and greens. It was the last week in November, and already we could feel a chill in the morning wind; but she stayed on the porch as long as she could bear the pain. Then, just before she asked me to take her back to her bed, she turned to me.

"David," she said, "I want you to go on to church. Then, after church, I want you to go back to school. You have to get a good education, because the world you live in will be different from the world I lived in."

I opened my mouth to protest, but she held up her hand.

"Go back to college," she said.

I didn't bother to argue. The look on her face stopped me before I could speak a word. With tears in my eyes I nodded and led her back to the bedroom. Then I went to church, just as she had told me to. Later that Sunday afternoon, when I was ready to leave, I went to her room and held her in my arms for a long moment. Then I left.

The following Tuesday I had spent most of the day in class and in the library and by evening I was exhausted, so I took a shower and put on my shorts. I lay down on my bed, intending to study, but I quickly fell asleep, the book open on my chest.

I awoke when somebody began to shake my shoulders. I finally focused my eyes and saw that it was the vice president of the university. So I sat up in bed, a little embarrassed because of the way I was dressed.

"You have a long-distance phone call," he said in a quiet voice that immediately alarmed me.

"Is my mother dead?" I asked.

"I don't know," he said, glancing quickly away.

I threw on a bathrobe and ran down to the phone, knowing what had happened, hoping I was wrong. I picked up the receiver and heard my brother Garlen on the other end of the line, his voice unnaturally high and strained.

"It's Mama," he told me. "She's gone."

I couldn't speak, so I listened while he told me to drive back by way of Selma University and pick up my sister Lula Mae. I only nodded at first, then finally was able to say I understood, that I would be home as soon as possible. My roommate insisted on making the drive with me; and after picking up my sister, we went on to Linden.

When we got to the house my sister Doll met us at the door—Doll, who would do so much in later years to fill the void in my life that my mother had left. We embraced, but I felt numb and cold, and at that moment there was no help for me.

Immediately I went into my mother's empty room and stared for a long time at the indentation in the pillow. I felt an aching in my arms and legs, but I couldn't cry. I simply stood there alone and listened to the others gathering in the living room, talking quietly, occasionally crying. But I didn't want to join them or share in their conversation. Instead, I tiptoed out of the room, slipped down the hall, and out the back door, into the darkness.

A thick autumn haze hung over the land, and the stars were hidden from sight. As I walked aimlessly out into the pasture toward the woods, it seemed as if I were alone in a gray void, separated from everything and everybody, numb, incapable of either grief or pain. I don't know how long I was out there, probably an hour; and though I had no jacket on, I didn't even feel the chill.

Then I looked up and saw a figure come through the haze, a woman's figure. Then she called my name. It was Doll.

I stood there without moving or replying, so she came over and put her arms around me.

"I know how you feel, David," she said. "But you've got to come back inside with the rest of us. You can't stay out here in the cold."

"I've lost my mother," I said.

"Come back inside with the rest of your family," she said, crying. "I'll be your mother."

My first impulse was to push her away, to shut her and the rest of them out of my grief. But I found I couldn't do it, and suddenly I was crying too. She was old enough to be my mother, and for that moment she was stronger than I was, so I held her until I had gotten control of myself.

"Are you ready to go back inside?" she asked.

"Sure," I said, and smiled.

So she led me back to the house, where I joined the rest of the family, and together we shared our mutual loss. That was the only time I had ever felt separated from my family, and I have never felt that way since.

The next day we had to decide about the funeral. We agreed that the men would deal with the funeral director while the women would stay at home and choose the clothes for the burial. So six of us drove over to the People's Funeral Home in Demopolis to buy the casket. (James Earl, the youngest, was spared this responsibility.)

The funeral director was a man named Ed Weiss, who met us at the door, shook hands with all of us, and then led us into the back room. When Weiss had come to Marengo County many years earlier, he had told everybody that he was black, and, in the strange and complicated world of Jim Crow, he had been accepted as such. But he was, I believe, Jewish—a white man who, for his own reasons, had chosen to live as a black man. No one, black or white, ever questioned his self-identification or pried into his background. He was, as far as we were concerned, just as black as we were—at least when it came time to do business with him.

As we stood among the caskets—some wooden, some metal, some covered with cloth—Mr. Weiss quite logically turned to my brother Jack, who was the oldest.

"Which one would you like?"

Jack looked around at several and then pointed to one. But Mr. Weiss, a man of subtle sensibilities, looked around at the rest of us and knew that we were hesitant. So he turned to the next oldest, K. T.

"What about you?" he asked.

K. T. paused, looked around at the rest of us, and then gave his answer.

"I want David to pick the casket," he said.

Mr. Weiss raised his eyebrows and turned to Clarence, who said immediately, "I know Mother would rest easier if David picked the casket."

Then he turned to Garlen, who said, "David should pick the casket."

William nodded and said the same thing: "David should pick the casket."

Jack agreed. "Let David do it."

So I walked among the caskets for a minute or two, then chose the gray, steel casket in which my mother would lie. Then we went home, where my sisters were supposed to be choosing the clothes she would wear for her burial.

When we walked in the door they were all sitting around in the living room.

"Have you picked the clothes yet?" I asked.

They looked at one another, then shook their heads.

"We can't agree," Doll said. "So we decided to wait and let you decide."

"That's right," said Susie Ellen, "you do it."

Lula Mae and Louvenia and Manerva all chimed in and said the same thing, so I went back into the bedroom and laid out the clothes for my mother to wear, gradually realizing as I did so that an extraordinary thing had happened: Without anyone consciously planning it, I had been "elected" by my brothers and sisters to be head of the family.

I was barely twenty-one years old, not yet holding a responsible position in the world; and my brother Jack was old enough to be my father, but at that moment I took my father's place as head of the Abernathys, and from that day forward I have tried to behave as I think he would have behaved in matters regarding the welfare of us all.

Yet after the preacher had spoken the final prayer and we had lowered my mother's casket into the earth of the McKenney Cemetery churchyard, I knew for the first time the meaning of the words "Sometimes I feel like a motherless child," and I cried along with my brothers and sisters.

When I got back to the house, I suddenly felt utterly exhausted, as if I had been working in the field for days. Without saying more than a few words to the rest of the family, I went into my old room and got into bed. Before my head had sunk into the pillow I was asleep, and I didn't wake up until early afternoon of the next day. I still felt weary and half-sick, the way I had felt after my bout with rheumatic fever, so I simply stayed in bed. Doll brought me a tray at supper time, but I took only a few bites and then turned over and fell asleep again. When I awoke it was daylight, and I felt thoroughly rested. I remembered almost immediately that my mother was dead, but the pain I felt wasn't quite as sharp, and I knew I was ready to get up and be with the rest of the family.

At this point I thought about Juanita Jones, and for some reason I felt compelled to go to town and send her a wire, telling her that my mother had died. We were not yet engaged or even talking about marriage, and I wasn't sure that she would understand why she was getting this telegram. But for some reason I wanted her to share in my loss, to be a part of my life at that point. So I went down to Western Union and wrote out a terse ten-word message.

For the next few days I expected to get a letter, but nothing came. As the days became a week, I was disappointed, then outraged. How could she possibly fail to respond to me in such circumstances? She must be the most callous person in the world! Then, almost three weeks after I had sent the telegram, I got a letter from her, telling me when she would be home for Christmas, saying she hoped to see me. I wasn't sure that I wanted to see her, though I still had the slightest reservation in my heart, hoping she had some reasonable explanation for her conduct.

By contrast, Jackie had won my heart all over again. She had spent all her time with me. In fact, she wouldn't let me out of her sight, knowing that when I was alone I tended to dwell on my loss. Even when I went back out to the cemetery to visit the grave, Jackie insisted on coming, holding my hand, reminding me that life was still sweet and full of promise. I appreciated her sympathy and support, and I made up my mind that henceforth she would have my undivided attention.

However, I did drive over to Uniontown to see Juanita that Christmas vacation, just to let her know that things were not going to work out between us, that we weren't meant for each other. It was then that I learned what had happened to my telegram: its delivery had been delayed for a week by a terrible snow that had brought traffic to a standstill in Nashville and caused a number of problems on the campus, including the problem of mail delivery.

"By the time I got your wire I knew it was too late to write, so I wanted to send a wire. But I didn't have enough money, and I couldn't borrow any at the time. By then I thought it would be better just to tell you in person."

I accepted her explanation, and we parted friends; but my feelings had changed toward her, and I was certain she belonged to the past. After all, I was going to marry Jackie anyway; and she had been perfect during my mother's illness and death. But there was still the matter of my vocation. Jackie was hoping that I would change my mind about going into the ministry, and I was still committed to the idea, though for some reason I had not taken the final step and either made plans to enroll in a seminary or else look around for a small church where I could begin my career. Now my conscience began to bother me as I remembered my mother's words the last time we had talked about the matter; and I told Jackie that sometime in the very near future I would have to announce my call. Again she argued with me, repeating her reluctance to be the wife of a preacher.

But at this point I began to believe that she would accept my vocation once I had made a final, irrevocable commitment.

Late in April of 1948 I made up my mind that on Mother's Day, the 2nd Sunday in May, I would announce my call to preach the Gospel. I chose this particular day in tribute to my mother, who from the beginning had shown me the way to my true vocation. I believed that God would somehow permit her to be standing at the balconies of glory just to hear me announce my call in the Hopewell Baptist Church, where she had gone to church her entire adult life.

I had left the college on Friday and before leaving I told Mrs. A. L. Bratcher—my pastor's wife, who worked at the college—that I would not be at church on Sunday because I was going to Linden to announce my call to the ministry. But on my way I had a stop to make. I dropped by the rooming house where Jackie lived.

"I don't have more than a minute or two," I said, "because I'm driving back to Linden. Tomorrow morning I'm going to the Hopewell Baptist Church and announce my call to the ministry."

She looked at me, and her eyes clouded with tears.

"Why do you have to do it now?"

I explained to her about my mother and what it meant to

her to know that someday I would be making this commitment.

"Please don't," she said. "Wait a while longer. For me."

"I can't do it," I said. "I've waited five months too long as it is."

She dried her eyes and regained control of herself.

"Will you come by and pick me up on your way to the church tomorrow?"

I felt a great sense of relief. She would accept it after all. I smiled and put my arms around her.

"I'll come if I can; but if I can't, somebody else will be here around 10:30 A.M."

As it turned out, I couldn't make it, but my brother K. T. picked up Jackie. I was already seated in the church when they arrived, and she came immediately to the front and sat down beside me. She took my hand and squeezed it, and I knew the message she was sending was not one of support for my decision. It was another kind of message entirely. She moved close to me and leaned her head lightly on my shoulder and whispered in my ear, "Please don't do it."

I merely shook my head and pointed at the preacher, who was opening the Bible, about to read from the scriptures. During the entire service she made her presence known to me, and I knew that she still hoped, even at this late hour, to change my mind.

Then, after the sermon, the preacher stepped forward and asked if there were any announcements. Someone stood up and talked about the men's Bible class, and someone else announced choir practice.

"Any other announcements?" the preacher said, looking pointedly in my direction.

I felt Jackie's hand grip mine with all her strength.

"Brother pastor," I said, rising. "I have an announcement."

I took my hand out of Jackie's.

"I want to announce my call to the ministry of Jesus Christ."

There was loud applause.

"I have been convinced ever since I knew my name that I am called to the Christian ministry. My father, Deacon W. L.

Abernathy, always said that preaching was a man's job, not a boy's. For that reason I have waited to make this announcement. Now I am ready. I am a man. I've been obedient to my father, but now I have to be about the Father's business of preaching the Gospel to the poor. I have to heal the broken-hearted. I have to free the captives. I have to set at liberty them that are bruised and proclaim the acceptable year of the Lord."

There were shouts of joy and more applause. The preacher smiled at me.

"Brother Abernathy," he said, "we are overjoyed to hear this announcement. We have been waiting for it for many, many years. We knew that you were going to preach the Gospel one of these days."

He gave the signal, and the congregation began singing the final hymn, "Leaning on the Everlasting Arm."

Filled with a sudden joy, I had the feeling that the Lord had somehow allowed my mother to see me in this moment. For the first time I glanced down at Jackie and saw tears pouring down her cheeks. I'm sure that everyone else believed they were tears of happiness, but I knew better. I tried to take her hand, but she withdrew it.

I was twenty-two years old, and I believe that at that moment I was perfectly happy.

As for Jackie, she got over it, or so I believed. Certainly it removed any ambiguity from our relationship. No longer was she under the illusion that she would be able to change my mind about my vocation. That struggle between us was over. Now she had to decide whether or not she would continue to see me, knowing that after I had finished my schooling I would be looking around for a church. When I went back to school that night, I found a letter waiting for me at the dormitory. It was from Rev. Bratcher, inviting me to preach at the First Baptist Church in Montgomery on the following Sunday.

I was flattered and a little intimidated. The First Baptist Church seated twelve hundred people, and to me it seemed as big as the Hollywood Bowl. I was a little nervous about preaching to that many pairs of eyes and ears. On the other hand, I hated to think that my appearance would excite so little interest that the church would be no more than half full. I finally decided that the latter would be more difficult to bear than the former, so I went to the church that following Sunday morning nervous that no one would show.

But my fears were in vain. My friends at the university were so interested in watching my performance that they filled the huge sanctuary to overflowing. As a matter of fact, some of the regular members complained because the students had taken all the seats and left the deacons and their wives sitting on folding chairs outside. In part, my activities as boycott leader were responsible for this popularity, but whatever the reasons, I was pleased to find a full house when I stepped into the pulpit. I was nervous, but I had prepared well, and I found that after a moment or two I was completely at ease. Afterward, my friends crowded around to congratulate me.

The next week I went back to Hopewell Baptist Church, where I preached my first sermon before my family and oldest friends. It seemed strange at first to stand in that pulpit, remembering my father and mother, half expecting to see them come through the door, my mother with a smile on her face, my father stern and forbidding, waiting to see if I would measure up to the high standards he had always set. But at the same time, I was comfortable there, as if I had preached a hundred times before. And indeed I had—at least in my imagination.

I received the congratulations of all my brothers and sisters who could be there and from many other friends as well. Then I waved good-bye and drove back to school, where I still had a lot of work to do before I got my degree.

The next year, though I was older than many graduates, I became a junior and was elected president of my class. And that's when we had our second protest. This time the issue was not food but shelter—and again we were the victims of substandard conditions.

The men were living in army barracks that had been moved in from Maxwell Air Force Base. In part, this was a necessity of the times, as we all recognized. In addition to those who would ordinarily be there, colleges were having to accommodate men who had been serving in the armed forces for as long as four years. As a consequence, many institutions had doubled their male enrollments, so barracks were common to campuses all over the country.

Those of us who were veterans did not object to living in barracks. We had grown used to them. But those at Alabama State University were like no barracks we had ever seen, even in basic training. In the first place, few of the showers worked. None gave out hot water. And most of the toilets failed to flush. In addition, there was no heat in the winter, and the icy wind whistled through the cracks in the buildings. Those of us who had been in the service began to wish we were back again. At least the U.S. government knew how to maintain plumbing and heat.

So we organized another uprising, and again I was the leader of the protest. This time we were not only protesting against the university administration but also against the local veteran officer, Dr. Levi Watkins. These people were responsible for making certain that the government and the board of regents of the university provided us with adequate facilities. We figured that if we brought pressure to bear on the campus authorities, they would in turn be more motivated to fight for our welfare.

I hated to go back in to see Dr. Trenholm because of my respect for him and because I knew he wasn't really to blame for the neglect—he habitually worked from before dawn until after midnight trying to solve the many problems of the university, most a product of the unequal educational system in Alabama. He regularly reviewed every student's academic progress during the course of the semester, and he even made out the schedule for all three thousand at the beginning of each term. So he was both academic dean and registrar as well as university president, and his wife often complained that he came home to a late supper each night, only to fall asleep at the table and remain there until breakfast, too exhausted to come to bed. I knew all this about him and hated to contribute to his work load.

Yet, once again, I was the elected representative of the students and I had to speak and act for them. So this time I didn't wait to be called; I made an appointment myself, and took with me a huge mob of students, who waited outside while I led a small delegation into the president's office. The people I took in with me were all top students, so when Dr. Trenholm pulled out our grade sheets (as I knew he would do), he could find no excuses to exclude us from the discussion that followed.

Dr. Levi Watkins was also in the office; while they both listened, we outlined in detail the conditions we were forced to endure. We were respectful, but we didn't soft-pedal our complaints.

Dr. Trenholm turned to Dr. Watkins and asked if he had any contrary evidence.

"No," said Dr. Watkins, "I have no reason to question what they've said."

"In which case," said Dr. Trenholm, "I believe we should try to rectify these matters."

Dr. Watkins nodded his head.

"I'm in total agreement," he said. So conditions in the men's barracks were significantly improved, and again I received much of the credit, in part because I had been willing to go in and confront the august Dr. Trenholm in his office, something no other student had ever done before. The victories I won were relatively small, but their importance to my own self-confidence cannot be overestimated. I believe that my later dealings with mayors, governors, and presidents were significantly facilitated by these two meetings in Dr. Trenholm's office. As a matter of fact, no man ever intimidated me in the same way that Dr. Trenholm did; and when I met Presidents Johnson, Nixon, Ford, Carter, Reagan and Bush they somehow seemed lesser men than this stern black scholar, with his regal bearing and his steady, dispassionate gaze.

I would add only one postscript to these incidents. Neither Dr. Trenholm nor Dr. Watkins held my militancy against me. When I had finished my degree, Dr. Trenholm offered me a position on his staff as dean of men; and after a year of graduate study at Atlanta University I accepted his offer and returned to my alma mater.

Years later, after the civil rights movement had peaked and

I had taken over as president of the Southern Christian Leadership Conference, Dr. Watkins, by then president of Alabama State University, arranged for me to receive an honorary degree along with Governor George Wallace, columnist Carl Rowan, and Dr. Watkins himself. Considering the individual histories of each honoree, and the history of their relations with one another, we were probably four of the most unlikely people ever to share a podium.

Governor Wallace, by then restricted to a wheelchair after having been paralyzed by a would-be assassin's bullet, shook hands with me and welcomed me to the state of Alabama.

I smiled, realizing that he had forgotten all about Montgomery and Birmingham, and particularly Selma.

"This is not my first visit," I said. "I was born in Alabama— in Marengo County."

"Good," said Governor Wallace, "then welcome back."

I really believe he meant it. In his later years he had become one of the greatest friends the blacks had ever had in Montgomery. Where once he had stood in the doorway and barred federal marshals from entering, he now made certain that our people were first in line for jobs, new schools, and other benefits of state government. Carl Rowan (who had attacked Martin and me for opposing the Vietnam War) stood to one side, shaking his head, and Dr. Watkins grinned. He, more than anyone there, knew it was a time for reconciliations.

4

The Summer of 1950

After I graduated from Alabama State, I was still interested in the pursuit of knowledge, although I knew I would eventually become a Baptist preacher, I wanted to do graduate work in sociology, perhaps even get my doctorate before I studied theology and then accepted the call of a church. So I applied to the master's program in sociology at Atlanta University and was accepted for the fall semester. That summer, in order to make enough money to live during the next year, I took a job with the Booker T. Washington Insurance Company, a black-owned business that was well-known in Alabama and surrounding states.

In an earlier era blacks were so poor that they worried all their lives about whether or not there would be enough money for a burial when they died. As a consequence, small "burial leagues" and "burial insurance companies" were set up so that these final expenses would be taken care of. The Booker T. Washington Insurance Company had grown out of such a fund, started by the Smith and Gaston Funeral Home of Birmingham. But by the time I came to work for them in 1950, the organization had expanded to include life insurance and other kinds of standard coverage and was one of the largest and most prosperous black-owned businesses in the South.

I had been highly recommended for a position by Dr. Trenholm, president of Alabama State; when I reported for work I didn't know exactly what I would be doing, though I assumed I would be some kind of clerk. When I arrived, I was ushered into an office, where a black man in a business suit peered at me over his bifocals, glanced at his watch, and said, "Why aren't you over at the radio station?"

"Am I supposed to be over at the radio station?" I asked.

"Yes," he said, "five minutes ago. Now you run on over there, and I'll tell them you'll be a little bit late."

As I rushed out the door I asked the secretary which radio station. I ran most of the way, and when I got there I was out of breath.

When I arrived I was told to go back into the studio, where I found a couple of white engineers waiting for me.

"Are you Ralph Abernathy?" one of them asked.

I nodded, still trying to get my breath.

"OK," he said. "You sit over there by the turntable, and we'll sit behind the glass window and run the controls."

"What am I supposed to do?" I asked.

"Talk," the man said with a grin, "that's what disc jockeys are for, isn't it?"

So I became a disc jockey. As a matter of fact, I was the first black disc jockey ever on a white station in Montgomery—so I integrated radio five years before I would have a hand in integrating public transportation and public accommodations.

It was fun and I had a lot of fans in the black community—particularly among the students at Alabama State, but when summer ended I resisted the temptation to stay on with Booker T. Washington Insurance Company and left Montgomery to register at Atlanta University. I had too many things to learn yet before I settled into any permanent job, and I knew that eventually I would end up in a pulpit somewhere. I didn't think radio work was compatible with preaching, failing to anticipate the tremendous growth of "electronic ministries" in the coming years.

*   *   *

When I enrolled in Atlanta University for graduate study, that fall, I hardly noticed the change from one university to another. Soon I was back in the swing of college life, studying hard, learning a little bit about the city of Atlanta, dating girls.

As for a church to attend while I was there, I made the rounds, listening to different pulpit styles, looking for the first time with critical eyes at the "business" of being a preacher. One day after class another student had said to me, "Ralph, you should come with us over to Ebenezer Baptist Church this Sunday. There's a young guest preacher who's supposed to be pretty good. He's just finishing his first year of studies in theology at Crozier Theological Seminary in Chester, Pennsylvania."

"Well, I might do that," I said. "You say he's pretty good?"

"That's what I've heard," was the reply. "His name is Martin Luther King, Jr."

So that Sunday I went to hear him and he was indeed impressive. He was about my age, but already he had begun to build a reputation in a city the size of Atlanta. So I sat there burning with envy at his learning and confidence. Already he was a scholar; and while he didn't holler as loud as some of the more famous preachers I had heard, he could holler loud enough when he wanted to. Even then I could tell that he was a man with a special gift from God.

After the service was over he was standing at the door, greeting the congregation. I stopped to shake his hand and comment on his sermon. At that meeting we both recognized in one another a kindred spirit, and he asked me to repeat my name. The next time he saw me, not more than a few days later, he remembered who I was, despite the somewhat strained circumstances.

I had found yet another girl I thought might measure up to my hopelessly idealistic standards and had begun to pursue her. In retrospect I realize that she was never really interested in me, but at the time the idea never entered my head. I asked her to go out with me several times, and she finally agreed to let me take her to a Thursday evening choir recital at Sister's Chapel of Spelman College in Atlanta, Georgia.

On Thursday afternoon, however, she called up to tell me in a croaking voice that she had a terrible cold and that she was certain she would still be sick that night, if indeed she survived at all. I was very sympathetic and suggested that we not cancel the date until she saw how she was feeling later. She recovered her voice sufficiently to protest that there was certainly no reason to anticipate that she would recover so quickly and insisted that I make other plans so that my evening wouldn't be spoiled. I assured her that I had no other plans, that since she couldn't make it I would undoubtedly stay in my room and study.

I listened for the telephone, hoping that she would be feeling better and call; but by late that evening it was clear that she wasn't going to get in touch with me, so I started to think of alternative plans for the evening and finally decided that I would go to the choir recital without her. There would be good music, refreshments afterward, and other girls to talk to. Why sit at home and mope?

I dressed and strolled across the campus of Atlanta University into the gate of Spelman College, where I found myself on the green lawn outside Sister's Chapel. As I scanned the crowd for a familiar face, I suddenly saw two—my date for the evening on the arm of Martin Luther King. In an instant it came to me that the croaking voice I had heard was just a little overdone. On an impulse I walked quickly across the lawn and we converged under a huge limp oak tree near the chapel's entrance.

"Well, hello, Mr. Abernathy," Martin said, waving to me with his free hand.

At the mention of my name, her eyes widened and her mouth became an O.

"Good evening, Mr. King," I said and he stopped. I stopped too, and as he turned to face me, she ducked around behind him, still holding his hand.

"I just want to tell you again how much I enjoyed your sermon," I said.

"Thank you," he said. "It's kind of you to say so."

By this time his shoulder was pulled around so that he had some difficulty facing me.

I remarked that it certainly was a nice evening for a musical event, not too warm, just a touch of fall in the air. He agreed. By this time the girl, crouching behind him, was twisting his arm as if she were trying to tear it out of its socket.

"I've heard this is a mighty fine choir," I said.

"One of the best in the South," he said, a look of pain on his face.

I finally had mercy on both of them and went my separate way, curious to know how she would explain her behavior to him. Years later, when I reminded him of the incident, he remembered the girl and the particular evening, but couldn't recall exactly what she had said to him.

If my heart was broken that Thursday night, by Saturday I was probably going out with somebody else. At that age your heart can be broken innumerable times and mended so quickly and so perfectly that you can't see the former cracks with a magnifying glass. Besides, on reflection I realized my interest in this girl had been more a matter of curiosity than grand passion. After all, I already had a girl back in Marengo County. Or did I? I wasn't sure at this stage of our relationship if I still loved Jackie. Perhaps we had been going together too long. And then there was Juanita.

I hadn't forgotten Juanita, despite my resolve to do so. Every so often I would remember how she looked or something she had said, and I would feel a pang of regret over having written her out of my life for no reason at all. It occurred to me that she might not remember my name when we met again, but I have since wondered if Juanita didn't have an active hand in our reunion (not that I would ever presume to ask her).

I was back in Montgomery for homecoming weekend, when a dear friend, Ruth Franklin, came around to the dormitory where I was staying and asked to see me. We went into the lounge of the dormitory and talked, bringing each other up to date on our lives. Then she came to what I have realized in retrospect was the point.

"By the way, Ralph," she said, "did you know that Juanita is in town this weekend? She's staying with me."

"She certainly does look lovely," she continued. "I think she's one of the prettiest girls I have ever seen."

I agreed wholeheartedly with that assessment and promised that I would contact her. I waited only until the door had closed behind my visitor, ran upstairs, shaved, put on my best clothes, and hurried around to the Franklin's house where Juanita was staying, hoping she would have some time for me.

I was lucky. She had come for the Thanksgiving Day homecoming game but none of the other young men she had been seeing had found out she was there, so I immediately asked her to dinner that night. She was more beautiful than I had remembered and more alive than ever. We drove around that evening and after I took her home, I came to a sudden and irrevocable decision. As she was going up the steps to the house she paused, the moonlight caught her hair, and she turned and smiled. In that moment I knew I had to have her, that she was the one for me.

From that day forward I saw her every moment that I could. It was clear that she was beginning to feel the same about me, and at some point she made up her mind that she could be a preacher's wife after all, a decision that filled me with joy. We didn't set a date at that time, but we were both completely and unalterably committed to one another.

And that left me with a problem—indeed two problems. There was Jackie, and there was "Louise." Louise was a lovely girl I had dated while I was at Alabama State, with the most beautiful hair I had ever seen—so long that it fell below her hips. She was a music student in Montgomery, and I had long been aware that she was beginning to regard our relationship as a serious one, despite the fact that I had not so indicated. So I knew I owed her an accounting as well as Jackie, though I soon discovered I had not really fathomed the depths of her attachment.

I took Louise out to get a hamburger and there, sitting at the table, I quietly told her I was engaged to be married to somebody else. Instead of congratulating me, she jumped to her feet, tears welling up in her eyes, and ran out of the grill, her face buried in her hands. I paid the check and tried to find her, but she had disappeared. The next day I found out what had happened.

She had returned to the boarding house where she was living, shut the doors and windows in her room, and then turned on the gas. Fortunately, her landlady had found her before she had inhaled enough of the fumes to kill her, but it was a narrow escape; and it made me feel guilty at the time, not for wanting to marry Juanita, but for failing to be fully sensitive to the deepest feelings of another human being.

When I told Jackie—seated in the parlor of the house where she was staying—she was more composed, though naturally she was hurt. I think in retrospect she must have realized that a relationship like ours, one that had gone on for so many years, had passed beyond the point of mutual excitement. But she was still upset, and I felt a deep sadness when I said goodbye.

Several weeks later I heard that she had been involved in an automobile accident that same day. She had been driving alone and had lost control of the car. Her injuries were not serious, but I couldn't help wondering to what extent I had been to blame. And again I engaged in self-recriminations, learning all over again the degree to which we hurt one another almost as much in our loving as in our hatred.

After I had finished all the course work for my master's degree, I had to make an important decision. Dr. Trenholm, against whom I had led the student demonstrations, wrote me a letter, inviting me to return to Alabama State as dean of men. The salary was low compared to what some of my classmates would be making, but after a year of living on a couple of dollars a day, a full-time job was a great temptation.

However, the Reverend L. M. Tobin, pastor of the Providence Baptist Church in Atlanta, of which I was a member, discouraged me from taking the job. Sitting in his study, he warned me against postponing my theological studies to go back to Alabama State.

"Abernathy, I know what will happen. You'll go back there, and in a year you'll be married. It happens every time. Then you'll have children, and you won't be able to afford to go back to school."

"I won't let that happen," I assured him.

"It will happen," he insisted. "Take my word for it. What you should do right now is apply to Colgate-Rochester and do your seminary work before you make another move."

I nodded and told him he was probably right. But even at the time I was saying it I knew I wanted to go back to Montgomery and hold down a paying job, at least for a year or two. Besides, I had another offer as well, one that I could accept and still hold down my job as dean of men.

The members of the Eastern Star Baptist Church in Demopolis, where I had preached on more than one occasion, had asked me to become their pastor. Like Hopewell Baptist Church, Eastern Star and a number of small Baptist churches in the region could not afford to have a full-time preacher, so they would pay someone to come in and preach a sermon once or twice a month. The other weeks they would have Sunday school. Eastern Star Baptist could afford to bring in a preacher two Sundays a month, and the man who had been supplying that pulpit had died.

I knew that taking the job at Alabama State would not cut me off from my true vocation but would in fact give me the opportunity to preach and to be a pastor of a small congregation while making a decent salary at the university. So I ignored Reverend Tobin's advice and accepted Dr. Trenholm's offer. (Reverend Tobin was right, of course. I got married while in Montgomery, and never returned to school to pursue my theological studies.)

The Good Lord had other plans for me, or so I believe in retrospect. He wanted me to be in Montgomery during those years, and He provided me with the opportunity to stay there and do his work at the same time, not as dean of men at the University but as pastor of the First Baptist Church.

After taking up my duties in Montgomery, I drove to Demopolis on the first and third Sundays of each month to preach and minister to the small congregation at Eastern Star Baptist Church. At least it was small until I came. But since Demopolis was only ten miles from my home town of Linden, that first Sunday the church was half full of my relatives. My second Sunday the church was completely full, and my third Sunday they had to put chairs in the aisle. By the end of the year it was the largest and most active black Baptist church in Demopolis, and they began talking about someday soon having a full-time preacher.

Meanwhile, I was giving my full time during the week to keeping the peace in the men's dormitories at Alabama State and dealing with other disciplinary and personal problems on campus. In a sense I was a preacher on alternate Sundays and a pastoral counselor during the week, since most of the matters that came before me were problems that students might have taken to their clergy had they been at home. So I didn't really feel I had strayed too far from my chosen path.

The First Baptist Church of Montgomery, one of the most historic black churches in Alabama, was having trouble with its pastor, the Reverend Mr. Bratcher. Reverend A. L. Bratcher, whom I started preaching under and who later licensed me to preach the Gospel, was a scholarly man. This church was proud of the fact that they had never dismissed a preacher—something they were empowered to do—but they knew how to wait out a stubborn man and conduct themselves in such a way that he decided to leave of his own free will. Mr. Bratcher got the message after a few months and agreed to accept a call from a larger church in Birmingham.

Shortly after he had made his decision, he was standing outside of the church, talking to several fellow preachers after a meeting, and broke the news to us.

"Gentlemen," he said, "I'm leaving First Baptist, and I thought I'd tip you off. It's a fine old church. One of you might be getting the call."

At the time it never occurred to me that I might be chosen. I was brand new at the game, I hadn't finished my theological training, and the church was fine enough to bring in someone of genuine stature. So why would they consider someone with as little experience as I had? Some of the others responded to Dr. Bratcher's announcement with eager questions, but I held my peace and concentrated on the idea that I could make Eastern Star the best church in Demopolis.

Then Reverend Bratcher came to me and talked about my future and a possible permanent position.

"Ralph," he said, "I don't know who will be picked for the First Baptist Church. It's an historic congregation, you know. The Alabama State Baptist Convention was organized here, as well as the National Baptist Church. In its hundred-year history it has only had six pastors."

As he talked on and on about the importance of the church, I concluded that he was trying to tell me I wasn't experienced enough to handle such an important responsibility. He might have saved us both some embarrassment. I never expected to be considered for First Baptist. Finally he got to the point.

"I have a church picked out for you," he said. "Do you know Greenwood Baptist Church in Tuskegee?"

"I've heard of it," I said. "It's a pretty big congregation."

"It's a fine church," he said, "and I have some influence there. The pulpit's empty right now, and I'm going to get you an invitation to preach there in the next several weeks. I'll also speak to my friends there and see what they can do. The fact that you're a dean and teacher at Alabama State may help you in a college town like Tuskegee."

I was pleased enough with that arrangement; but then, to my surprise, the deacons at First Baptist invited me to be acting pastor while they conducted a search for someone to replace Dr. Bratcher. I considered it a rare opportunity to stand in that pulpit, with the stained glass windows reflecting multicolored lights, and preach to a congregation that looked as big to me as the crowd at a championship football game.

Meanwhile, other people were intervening on my behalf. The Hall Street Baptist Church in Montgomery was also vacant, because my old friend, the Reverend C. K. Steele, had left to go to Florida. When he heard that I was looking for a pulpit, he drove up to Montgomery to act in my behalf.

Having been a powerful pastor when he was there, he

assumed that he could come back and exercise the same authority he had exerted when he was in the pulpit. He met with the
deacons and told them to call me immediately. But the deacons
weren't going to be ordered about by an ex-pastor, particularly
one who had forsaken them for a church in a small city like
Tallahassee, Florida. In particular Mr. George Sly (well named)
rose up to tell him that according to the bylaws of the church, the
deacons had to have two weeks' notice before calling a pastor to
make such a decision, so they would wait. C. K. got in his car and
drove back to Florida. But he had set things in motion. I was
invited to preach at Hall Street one Sunday shortly after I
preached at Greenwood church in Tuskegee.

In the meantime, First Baptist was having visiting preachers, looking them over and finding something wrong with all of
them. Preachers were coming in and out of Montgomery and
Tuskegee from all over the region, and nobody was impressing
anybody. Apparently I didn't impress the people over at Greenwood, because they issued a call to Rev. Francis Harvey. And
Hall Street was unimpressed with the candidates they had
brought in to show C. K. Steele they could pick their own pastor.

Finally, Hall Street broke down and admitted to themselves
that C. K. was probably right after all and decided to hold a
meeting of the deacons on Wednesday night to vote to call me. I
found out about it and was pleased, if for no other reason than
that I could stay in Montgomery, a city I had grown to love. I
would be able to maintain some relationship with Alabama State
and also continue to see the many friends I had made at First
Baptist.

The next Sunday—three days before my call to Hall Street—
I finished preaching at First Baptist and was about to give the
benediction when one of the deacons, and the church clerk,
William Beasley, came forward and held up his hand.

"Brother pastor," he said, "I wonder if you would mind
holding off on the benediction. We need to have a brief meeting.
If you'll just wait for us down in your study, I'll come and get you
in a couple of minutes."

I agreed and went downstairs.

In no more than a minute or two, Beasley came back into

the study and said, "Congratulations, brother, you're no longer just acting pastor. You're the pastor now."

"What do you mean?" I asked, genuinely bewildered.

"We just elected you pastor."

"I don't understand," I said, still a little confused. "I'm going to be called to Hall Street on Wednesday."

"We beat them to it," he said with a grin. "Mama heard you were going to get the call at Hall Street, and told us we had to call you first. You know how Mama is. We did what she said."

I did indeed know how Mama was. "Mama" was Mrs. Susie Beasley. She was one of the most powerful members of the congregation, not only because her children were among the most successful people in the black community, but because of her great faith and strong personality. (Later, on the darkest day of the Montgomery boycott, it would be Mrs. Beasley who would pull me back from the brink of despair and give me one of my greatest lessons in the meaning of faith.)

As for their offer, I was flattered and extremely happy that they wanted me, but not entirely comfortable with the idea. I had concluded that Reverend Bratcher didn't want me to succeed him, that he believed I wasn't prestigious enough to occupy such a distinguished pulpit—and I was inclined to agree. If I accepted, it would seem as if I were overreaching myself. He had been my friend and pastor. He had licensed me to preach out of his church. He was like a father to me, and I didn't want to do anything to displease him.

Then, too, there was C. K. Steele, who had pushed my candidacy at Hall Street and who had driven all the way up from Florida just to speak in my behalf. I had already begun to look forward to Hall Street. Now I didn't know what to do.

So I went back upstairs and bought a little time. I told them I appreciated what they had done and that I was deeply honored. I explained, however, that I still owed it to Hall Street not to make a decision until after I had met with them. But I said if they would all come for the Wednesday service, I would make an announcement at that time.

I thought about it all day long, and the more I weighed my options the more I realized two things: one, First Baptist was the church I really wanted and, two, I was going to accept the offer from Hall Street. It was a bitter choice, but I felt that since I had the two options, I would be betraying Reverend Bratcher to accept at First Baptist when I knew his feelings.

However, I hadn't counted on the machinations of George Sly, who still wanted to give Steele his come-uppance. When he heard that First Baptist had issued a call to me, he immediately went to the Hall Street deacons and persuaded them to cancel the meeting on Wednesday night, I suppose on the grounds that I would surely accept the offer from First Baptist since it was a larger and better endowed church. So on Wednesday night, instead of having two calls to choose from, I had only one; and with no overriding reason not to accept, I stepped into the pulpit and told them I would be honored to be their pastor. As I did so, however, I looked up at the stained glass windows and saw the Reverend Dr. Stokes gazing solemnly into the heavens, and wondered if I really belonged there. I was twenty-six years old.

Of course, I had one matter to clear up. I was still preaching at Eastern Star in Demopolis, and I had to let them know of my decision so they could find somebody else to take the pulpit. I regretted having to leave Eastern Star, particularly in view of the fact that it had grown so rapidly during the eighteen months I had been there. I had some sense of accomplishment, and I was really hoping that at some point the church would be able to support a full-time pastor. In fact, the eighty-six-year-old chairman of the Board of Deacons, Joe "Papa Joe" Hogan, had broached the subject with me on more than one occasion, though he had always spoken in the future tense.

So before I left on the following Sunday, I drafted a letter of resignation to read at the end of the service. Then I got in my car and drove to Demopolis, a little sad that I would be leaving, though optimistic about its future as a congregation. Soon, I knew, they would have a full-time pastor and be meeting every Sunday.

When I finished my sermon I read my letter of resignation to a silent congregation, and when I had finished, Papa Joe immediately rose to his feet.

"And when do you plan to leave, Reverend Abernathy?" he said, a frown on his face.

"The first Sunday in June," I said, aware that I was giving them more than the ninety-day notice customary among Baptist churches.

He nodded and his frown deepened.

"I move we accept the resignation with deep regret," someone said.

"I second the motion," said someone else.

"All in favor signify by saying aye," said Papa Joe.

And that was that. Or so I thought.

Late that afternoon I came back to conduct the evening service, and Papa Joe was waiting for me on the front step. The frown was gone. He greeted me with a broad grin and a warm handshake.

"Reverend Abernathy," he said, "let's go for a walk." He led me into an area adjacent to the church. "How do you like this piece of property?" he asked.

"It's beautiful," I said. "A lovely spot."

He smiled and nodded with satisfaction.

"If you will stay with us and be our full-time pastor," he said, "we'll build you a parsonage on this very spot. You can draw up the design and we will build it to your specifications."

I started to shake my head, but he held up his hand.

"I haven't finished yet," he said. "Hear me out."

So I listened.

"Whatever First Baptist in Montgomery has offered we will match. And we'll have church every Sunday. So what do you say to that?"

I shook my head sadly. "You can't really afford to do that," I said. "First Baptist is a much larger church. There's so much more for me to do there, and they have the money to pay me."

That probably wasn't the right thing to say. I could see that he was unhappy with my reply, but when I also said that I had already accepted their offer and couldn't go back on my word, he would not listen, and we walked back to the church in silence.

The following Thursday I went back to my dormitory to find a letter waiting for me with the name "Deacon Joe Hogan" in the upper left-hand corner of the envelope. I opened it up, and it read:

Dear Rev. Abernathy:

When a man decides to leave a woman, he doesn't give her ninety days notice. He just leaves. And that is what you are going to do.

I called a meeting of the church on Monday evening, and we voted the pulpit vacant, so you are not welcome to come back any more.

Yrs,
Joe Hogan

At the age of twenty-six you do crazy things, and the letter made me so angry that I decided to go down to Demopolis the following Sunday, set up a tent across the street from the church, and conduct a worship service. Nobody would go to Eastern Star Baptist Church except Papa Joe. Everybody else would be across the street, shouting and stomping with me.

But as the week wore on, my anger died down, and I realized the futility of such a gesture. Papa Joe and his deacons had had their feelings hurt. They had offered me everything they had to offer and I had turned them down. I thought a little bit more about the comparison in the letter and began to sympathize with them. They had been spurned.

And despite the bitterness of our parting, I still remember that church and the people in it with great fondness. During the years when we were fighting civil rights battles all over the state of Alabama, I frequently drove through Demopolis; and I never failed to stop in at Eastern Star and speak to the pastor and to the people I knew there so long ago. It was the first of only three churches in my entire ministry.

The people at First Baptist were delighted to hear that I would be with them every Sunday rather than having to share me with Eastern Star. They had been resigned to the idea of a substitute two weeks out of the month, but they preferred to have me there full-time, and I was pleased as well, particularly after Papa Joe's message.

I threw myself into my pastoral duties with all the energy of a young man just beginning his career. As soon as I accepted the call, however, a question kept cropping up in conversations with members of the congregation, particularly older women with daughters.

"Reverend," they would say, "we aren't used to having a single preacher around. Are you planning to get married? Have you picked out anybody yet?"

Any single man or woman is always an object of speculation. But none more so than a Baptist preacher, black or white. His congregation is always looking to make a match for him, because they know that the sooner he's married the less likely he is to get into trouble. And until he's married, every smile he smiles, every prolonged conversation, every compliment is examined with care and suspicion.

Dimly (though by no means fully) aware of my precarious status, I tried to lay some of the gossip to rest by announcing from the pulpit that I was planning to be married soon. As I explained this to the congregation, I could see the approving smiles. The date hadn't been set, but in my own mind the matter was settled forever. In the meantime, I wasn't being too careful about appearances, mainly because it never occurred to me that anyone would suspect my motives or try to take advantage of me.

For example, on a beautiful day during one of the breaks I decided to take a stroll with Joy, a young woman who worked at Alabama State. She lived with her grandmother in a small house just behind the Hall Street Baptist Church, and occasionally we would meet by accident on the campus, which is what happened that day. We were almost to her house when we walked by Hall Street Church. I spotted the pastor, the Revered Alfred Vaughn, who was my fraternity brother, at Kappa Alpha Psi, in his office and waved to him. He got up from his desk and came out to greet us.

After we had chatted for a few minutes, the young woman

and I said goodbye, and he said, "Abernathy, on your way back please stop in and see me."

I said I would enjoy a visit and after I had escorted the young woman to her door a block away, I returned to his office as he had suggested. After I had settled down in a deep leather chair, he began to question me.

"Ralph," he said, "when are you getting married to Joy?"

At first I was amused. "I'm not going to marry Joy," I said. "I'm going to marry somebody else, a girl who lives in another town."

"Then you'd better be very, very careful," he said. "Those people are highly respected members of the First Baptist Church, and if you give the community the wrong impression, you may find yourself in serious trouble. It happened to me once, and it can happen to you."

I shifted uncomfortably in the chair. "What happened?"

"I had to get married," he said. "Oh, I've long since divorced the woman, and I'm happily married now. But with the threat of a scandal, they can have you at the altar before you know it—no matter what your intentions. I would advise you to bring this involvement to a close."

"Involvement?" I said. "There's no involvement. We're just friends. I was just walking her home. But thank you for the advice."

"I just don't want you to end up at the altar before you want to be there," he said. "I know the men in that family, her uncles. They're deacons in your church. And the aunts are active too. All she has to do is say that you have tampered with her in an improper way and you will be a bridegroom in a matter of days or else thrown out of the church."

I nodded, thanked him, and left, wondering if he knew something a little more specific about these people, something I had yet to find out. By the time I had walked back to the parsonage, I had decided to take his advice and avoid further involvement with Joy.

But it wasn't easy. After the Sunday night service I had been in the habit of dropping by the grandmother's house, where she always laid out a delicious supper for the young pastor. Joy had been there too, but mostly I paid attention to the food. As a bachelor, I had come to anticipate those meals much more than the company that went with them.

The grandmother was one of the best cooks in the congregation, and she spent all day Sunday in the kitchen, frying, baking, and frosting to prepare for my visit. Since it never occurred to me that I was being stalked, I decided that I would not break off that part of my relationship with the family. But the next Sunday I found out that I had gone one time too many.

As I was finishing off a plate of spare ribs before getting ready to tackle the pie, Joy went into the kitchen and the grandmother sat down across the table from me to sip a cup of coffee.

"Reverend," she said as casually as she could, "when do you plan to marry my grandbaby?"

I put down the spare rib in my hands, wiped my fingers with a paper napkin, and carefully weighed my words. "Oh, Mrs. Miller, I'm not going to marry Joy. I've already announced my marriage to Juanita Odessa Jones."

She took a sip from her coffee cup. "Where does this Juanita Odessa Jones live?" she asked, not unpleasantly.

"She lives in Uniontown, Alabama."

"And where is that?"

"It's about thirty miles below Selma," I said.

"That's eighty miles from here," she said. "And you live here? And my grandbaby lives here?"

About that time Joy came back in the room and the grandmother turned to her.

"Little sister," she said, "you sure don't have any of my blood in you. If he had been here and this other woman and been eighty miles away I would already have had this man in the marriage bed."

Joy was embarrassed almost to tears.

"Grandmama, I've got my own plans about marriage and not to Reverend Abernathy. I respect my pastor. We're good friends, that's all; so don't try to make anything more of it."

I must say that a great weight fell off my shoulders and I walked home that night with an extra spring in my step. But Joy's declaration had long-range consequences that I found less satisfying. Shortly thereafter the little intimate suppers ended, and on Sunday night I had to go back to my room and open up a can of Campbell's vegetable soup.

The next Sunday, when I delivered my sermon, I worked into the text the fact that I was engaged to marry a young woman named Juanita Odessa Jones of Uniontown. I told them that she was young, beautiful, and innocent—everything that a young man could hope for in a bride. The reiteration of what I had said earlier may have cost me a few social engagements, but it certainly cleared the air and allowed me to speak to young women without exciting hopes or suspicions.

Obviously, however, the time had come to get married; Juanita and I agreed on a date and she sent out the invitations. I asked my brother William to be my best man, Juanita asked my sister Susie to be a bridesmaid, and my brother Clarence supplied limousines from his funeral home, so the Abernathys were well represented. We also asked the entire congregation of First Baptist Church to attend and some of my closer friends there to be in the wedding party. According to the invitations (composed after careful consultation with Emily Post and Amy Vanderbilt) the ceremony was to take place on August 31, 1952, at 6:59 P.M.

An old college classmate of mine, the Reverend James Dixon, officiated, and it was a traditional ceremony with one exception: The bride insisted that the word "obey" be deleted from the text. The wedding was held in the First Baptist Church of Uniontown, and it was the largest wedding that anyone in my family or hers could remember. After the ceremony and the reception at Juanita's family home, we drove to Nashville and spent our honeymoon in the segregated black hotel there.

When we got back to Montgomery we found that the parsonage had been completely redecorated and that we were expected at a second wedding reception, where all my Montgomery friends gathered and presented us with more gifts. After that final celebration, we settled down to the realities of a life that was more rigorous than most young married couples face. For one thing, Juanita still had a year left to teach at the Monroe County Training School in Beatrice, Alabama. That was about eighty miles away, and she would leave on Monday and return on Friday night. Then she would spend most of the weekend cooking food for me to last through the week while she was gone.

However, I was too lazy to warm up what she'd left for me. It was too easy to go down the street and eat at the restaurant run by Mrs. Jeanetta McAlpine, who was the best cook in the Black Belt and who refilled my plate everytime it approached emptiness. In exchange for her kindness, I would pick her up every Wednesday evening along with Mrs. Rachel Maddox and take her to prayer meeting; and if I was tempted to eat too much at her table, those car trips reminded me to restrain my appetite. She had consumed so much of her own fine cooking and was so large that it took several minutes to make the long walk from the front door to the car; and when she slid slowly, laboriously into the back seat, I was always afraid the tires of my car would blow out.

After a year of commuting, however, Juanita was home for good, and that was just as well, because by then we were expecting our first child.

We were both overjoyed, and so were the people at First Baptist Church. In the hundred-year history of the congregation, no child had ever been born to a pastor, probably because all of the previous preachers had been older men of great distinction before they received the call. I was the only "boy" among the seven and everyone was delighted.

The women began sewing and knitting immediately, and those that didn't have these skills went out and bought elaborate presents. By the time the baby was born, every closet and dresser drawer in the parsonage was packed with baby gifts.

As usual, the first baby was a little late, but when our boy came on a Sunday morning our happiness was complete. The people from the church drove across town to St. Jude Hospital just to file past the glass window and stare in at the tiny brown ball in the bassinet, and the hospital nurses shook their heads at the seemingly endless parade of people.

"You have more family than any parents we've ever had," one of them told Juanita, and she nodded in agreement.

I spent as much time as I could at the hospital, peering at my tiny son and occasionally holding him, but unfortunately I had a full schedule of regular pastoral duties. In addition, I had agreed to conduct a revival at a church in Helicon, Alabama— about thirty miles from Montgomery. The pastor there, Reverend G. W. Smiley, was a man well into his nineties, and I had agreed to come to his church many months earlier, so I couldn't let him down. Besides, I enjoyed his company and the people at his church.

Tuesday night after the baby was born, I stopped by the hospital on my way to Helicon to see Juanita, and she told me that he had been a little sick and began to cry. I felt terrible about having to leave her, but the pediatrician had been by to see the baby and I assured her that nothing serious was wrong. Finally, she calmed down and told me to go ahead, that she knew that I had to go to Helicon. So I kissed her and took off in my car, watching a row of dark clouds rising above the trees in the east.

I drove first to pick up Reverend Smiley in Snowden, just a few miles from the Helicon church. The sky was so overcast by then I had to turn on my lights, though it was only around three o'clock in the afternoon. As usual during this revival week, we were invited to dinner at one of the homes of Dr. Smiley's church families—this evening the McClains. Dr. Smiley told me what was in store for us.

"The daughter is a student at Bennett College," he said, "and she has an exotic recipe she's going to try out on us. Her mother tells me it will be a rare treat."

The McClains lived in an old country house at the foot of a steep hill, and as we pulled into the dirt driveway, the lightning flashed, the thunder clattered, and the first rain began to fall— huge scattered drops that left widening spots on our dark suits as we made our way onto the porch, where Mrs. McClain was waiting anxiously. She was particularly concerned for Reverend Smiley, who was spry for his age but as frail as a dried leaf.

Dinner was ready, and it was indeed delicious; but we couldn't hear the conversation, because the rain was coming down in heavy sheets onto the tin roof and the wind was rattling the windows. I have never seen more rain fall in so short a time. As I sat facing the window I could see the driveway turn into a stream and then the yard become a lake while I ate my meal. By the time we had finished dessert we were in the middle of an ocean, fed by all the water that had poured off the hill.

About that time the telephone rang, and it was for Reverend Smiley. When he came back he threw up his hands in despair.

"That was my head deacon. He says the whole area is flooded and that nobody will show up for the revival. So I guess we might as well get on back home."

Mr. McClain, who was looking out the window, turned and laughed. "There's no way you'll make it home tonight, Reverend. When it rains this hard, that hill is as slick as ice. You'd never make it to the top."

"Well, fine," said Mrs. McClain. "We'll have a cup of coffee and when you're ready to go to bed, I'll turn down your covers. We have plenty of room."

Under ordinary circumstances, I would have enjoyed such company; but I wanted to get back to Juanita and the baby.

"Let's just go out," I said, "and see if there's any traffic."

So we went out in the front yard (it had stopped raining) and glanced down the dark, glistening road. Sure enough, after a few minutes a car came along, slowed down, then stopped. The window rolled down and a young white man stuck his head out.

"Uncle," he called out to Mr. McClain, "has anyone gone over that hill after a rain?"

"No sir," said Mr. McClain.

"Well, I'm going to try it," he said, and rolled up the window. He gunned his motor, took off as fast as he could, and hit the hill at about fifty miles an hour. We watched him slip and slide from one side of the road to another, spin to a halt at the top, then in a final burst sail over the rim of the hill and disappear on the other side.

"He made it," I said. "If that white man can make it, I can make it too. We're going over that hill."

"We'll never do it," said Reverend Smiley, sounding his age for the first time that night.

I hated to put him through it, but I felt I needed to get back.

"If the elevator of success is broken, take the stairs," I said. "That's what my grandmother told me and I've always believed it."

So we got in the car and waved goodbye to the McClains. Following in the tracks of the last car I jammed the accelerator to the floor, skidded and fishtailed to the top, and started down the other side. Then I spotted him walking toward me: a man on foot, waving a flashlight for me to stop.

"I know that man," said Reverend Smiley. "He goes to my church."

So I slid to a halt, and the man ran over to my car.

"Reverend Smiley," he said. "You OK?"

Reverend Smiley was grinning. "I'm doing fine. We not only have some preacher, we have some driver."

The man stuck his head in the window and spoke very quietly.

"I walked up here to tell you that we got a call at the church for Reverend Abernathy. The hospital called. They say his baby died."

I was stunned. I couldn't believe it. When I got married I prayed to the Lord for one thing: a wife who would be the loving mother of a fine family. I longed for children, and it never occurred to me that I would be denied that one prayer. I thought of that small brown ball, lying in the bassinet, and my heart ached.

I drove quickly to Reverend Smiley's house and let him off. The old man patted me on the shoulder and said, "Son, don't bother to come tomorrow night."

"I'll be at the church," I told him. "But I won't make it for dinner. Please express my regrets."

I spoke as evenly as I could, trying to control myself, because I knew Juanita would need all the strength I could lend her. Somehow I made it to the hospital, parked the car, and dashed inside. When I got to the room, Juanita was sitting in a chair, staring at the wall, tears pouring down her cheeks.

"The baby," I said.

"Oh, Ralph, he's sick," she said. "He's not going to make it."

I was confused, but at that moment the doctor looked into the room, saw me, and entered.

"I'm glad you're here, Reverend Abernathy," he said. "I wanted to tell you both at the same time."

"It's true, then," I said.

He nodded, hesitated, then said the words. "The baby died about an hour ago. We don't know what was wrong with him. We still don't know. These things happen sometimes and there's nothing we can do about it. I'm terribly sorry."

Juanita was shaking with grief and I held her for a long time while the doctor stood there silently. Then, when she had quieted down, he spoke again.

"It was through the goodness of God that he died," he said, "because he had brain damage. You can be thankful to God he's at rest."

I'm not sure it helped to say that. Juanita stopped crying and stared out the window for a long time as the doctor turned and moved quietly out of the room.

Then she said, "Ralph, would you go and make the arrangements so I can go home?"

I nodded, and though I hated to leave her alone, I went down to the desk, signed the release, and then returned as quickly as I could to the room. She was quiet and tearless now, and I wanted to get her out of the hospital and back home—away from anything that reminded her of the baby.

As we stepped out into the dark night, a streak of lightning crackled across the sky, and I drew her close to me, but she seemed almost in a dream. Driving home neither of us could think of a word to say. When we got into the house and switched on the lights, she went into the nursery, stared for a moment at the piles of tiny clothes on the bassinet, and then began to weep as if she would never stop.

It was the congregation that really brought us both through that terrible period, the love and generosity of people who had taken us to their hearts from the moment we arrived and now treated us as members of their family. Mrs. Susie Beasley was the first to come by the house, and she called me aside for a few minutes so that Juanita wouldn't hear.

"I know you haven't thought about a cemetery lot," she said, "so I've told the Ross-Clayton Funeral Home that the interment will be with my family, if that's all right with you. We've had an extra plot for years and years. It's in the Oakwood Cemetery, right across the street from the church. It will be near the front."

I thanked her as best I could. It was a generous gesture, one that I could not easily have refused had I wanted to—which I didn't. I hadn't really decided what to do, and she had relieved me of a great burden.

Someone contacted the Reverend B. J. Simms of Alabama State, who agreed to officiate at the funeral. On Thursday morning we stood in the midst of all granite tombstones and, surrounded by scores of friends, watched as a car drove up, bringing the tiny wooden casket. The youngest boys in the Cherub Choir served as pallbearers and the little girls carried flowers. After they had set the casket down on the catafalque, they sang "Jesus Loves the Little Children," after which Reverend Simms said a committal prayer and the casket was lowered into the grave. From the grave site we could see the gothic steeple of the First Baptist Church, and Juanita and I always felt that Ralph David Abernathy, Jr. continues to watch over the church.

After more than thirty years have passed, the grief can still come back like a sharp pain.

As everyone had predicted, Juanita soon became pregnant again. This time, with the same doctor in the same hospital, she had a normal delivery of a healthy baby girl. We were both delighted, and after thinking long and hard, we decided to name her Juandalynn—a combination of Juanita, David, and Lynn (an old friend). She brought a renewed joy to our house, as did the other two children born in the next few years: another daughter, Donzaleigh, and then a son, whom we decided to name Ralph David Abernathy III. These were the children born during the Montgomery years, and they grew up surrounded by the love and concern of a huge congregation, all of whom thought the preacher's children were at least partially their own.

But life during those years was by no means idyllic, even for these children. The community we lived in was becoming increasingly dangerous. Following World War II, American society as a whole began to grow and prosper, black society as well as white. The war had given us new economic independence. Many blacks had moved north to work in defense plants, learning skills that earned them higher wages than they had ever dreamed possible. Others, like me, had been overseas and saw the freer, more color-blind nations of Western Europe. When they came back they were not willing to settle for Jim Crow life, not for long, not when they knew there was something better.

Also, the politics of America was changing. Roosevelt's New Deal had been kind to blacks, and they responded by voting for the national Democratic ticket after generations of commitment to the Republicans. People forget that until the late 1940s there was virtually no *white* Republican party in the South—only a few blacks who were occasionally given some morsel of political patronage by the national Republican party. It was only in 1952, when Eisenhower ran against Adlai Stevenson, that the white South began to break away from the Democratic party; and it wasn't until the late 1960s that Republicans began to win local and statewide elections in the South.

And strange as it may seem to younger political science students, it was the Democratic party throughout the Roosevelt years that prohibited blacks from voting in its southern primaries. At that time, with no Republicans running, whoever won the Democratic primary was automatically elected. The word they used was "tantamount": Winning the Democratic primary was tantamount to being elected.

To disenfranchise blacks, the Democratic party declared itself a private club for whites only. Blacks were allowed to organize a segregated Democratic club of their own, which was used to bring out the vote in national elections in support of the Roosevelt ticket. But often we were not allowed to vote for U.S.

senators, congressmen, governors, lieutenant governors, state senators, state representatives, mayors, councilmen, water commissioners, or dog catchers. And heaven knows we weren't allowed to run for any of these offices.

So the Democratic party during those years was either schizophrenic or hypocritical—take your pick. The national party spoke of helping the poor and downtrodden, including the black population, and the local party was the chief mechanism for keeping us in political bondage. President and Mrs. Roosevelt would speak benevolently about us, and Senator Bilbo of Mississippi and Governor Talmadge of Georgia would yell "nigger" in the county squares of Mississippi and Georgia as well as in the halls of Congress. (Ironically Bilbo died of cancer of the mouth.) It was the unspoken political scandal of that day, and for decades it appeared as if nothing would ever change.

In 1948, however, the Democratic party underwent a traumatic change. Its national convention became a battle royal in which all the disparate elements of the party fought with one another. The "Young Turks," led by Sen. Blair Moody, Franklin Roosevelt, Jr., and a young Hubert Humphrey proposed civil rights planks for the platform that threatened the home rule of the southern Democrats. The Southerners, still dominant figures in the party, used all their power to resist the proposed liberal planks, but this time they couldn't prevail, and the liberal forces carried the convention. Without waiting to greet the nominee, President Harry S. Truman, the Southerners—calling themselves "Dixiecrats"—stormed out of the convention to reconvene and nominate their own candidate for president, Governor Strom Thurmond of South Carolina.

Truman, whose defeat the Southerners thought they could ensure, won a miraculous come-from-behind victory, consolidated the party under a more liberal leadership, and the Southerners came creeping back into the Democratic tent, and tried to curl up in a warm place. But things were never the same again. The southern political establishment, which had ruled in part by virtue of its power within the national Democratic party, found itself persona non grata in Washington; and when Eisenhower appointed Earl Warren to the Supreme Court, the doom of Jim

Crow was sealed. The Democratic appointees, vastly in the majority on the court, found in Warren a man whose lead they could follow. With the coming of bipartisan unanimity, the Court declared segregated schools unconstitutional, and for the first time it appeared as if the dark night were about to end.

But we weren't certain of that. In the first place, though few people remember the facts, Brown versus the Board of Education did not end segregation in southern schools but in Kansas, the state that contributed the most Union dead in the Civil War. Those of us who had spent our lives in Mississippi and Alabama did not necessarily believe that the same thing could be accomplished in our part of the country. Though we were told the law would be applied equally throughout the land, we were skeptical. We had heard that before.

When you are born under a system and see it enforced every day of your life, you get to the point where you can no longer conceive of life being any different. So most blacks in the Deep South states looked with curiosity at what was going on in the high courts, shrugged their shoulders, and went back to their day-to-day lives, not necessarily disbelieving the changes that people said were about to occur, but not necessarily believing them either. After all, they had waited a lifetime and seen no change at all.

But among the educated blacks, and particularly among the clergy, there was talk—lots of talk—and with each subtle shift in the political landscape we eyed the new situation and calculated our chances of forcing the issue, of bringing about our freedom more quickly. Some of the older clergy tended to be overly cautious, and many of them were largely unconcerned with social issues. They preached the Gospel of "other worldliness," of a better time in the sweet by and by. Their ultimate solution to Jim Crow was death—when you died you were equal in the eyes of God. For such people, the idea of desegregation was either frivolous or else threatening. Some of these same preachers became chief stumbling blocks in the way of progress when the civil rights movement developed.

Many of the older clergy were in favor of sweeping social

change, but they were willing for it to come about slowly, when white society was ready to accept it. They preached a strict adherence to the law and peace at any price. The last thing they wanted to see destroyed was their precarious credibility among white leaders, who occasionally gave them minor posts of honor in the community in order to use them to keep the rest of us in line. Behind closed doors these "moderates" would join the rest of us in denouncing the oppression of the white establishment, but publicly they would say nothing to incur the wrath of those they privately denounced.

But a new generation of black men and women was coming along. Those of us in our twenties were less patient and less afraid of making trouble. While we too had been born and reared in a Jim Crow world, we had not lived in it quite as long and many of us had traveled beyond its boundaries. We knew that life could be different, and we were half-inclined to believe that the promised changes were really going to come about. As we talked with one another, we began saying that we were willing to help tear down the old walls, even if it meant a genuine uprising.

So instead of preaching about submission and the virtues of patient suffering, we started talking about courage and justice and the necessity to gain equality in this world. We warned our people of struggles to come in the near future. We explained to them that we would be fighting not only for our own dignity as creatures of God, but more importantly for the dignity and well being of our children and grandchildren.

We also began preaching about specific injustices on the local scene. It was one thing to talk in broad generalities about freedom and justice and equality. White people didn't like that kind of talk, but they didn't really fear it. What most upset them was a black who was willing to say in public that this *particular* act or this *particular* white man was vicious and unjust; or that this *particular* practice—in force for generations—should be abolished. That kind of talk was dangerous, and blacks who were guilty of it were "uppity niggers" and had to be dealt with as quickly and as harshly as possible—legally if possible; if not, illegally.

So even though Topeka, Kansas, was a long way from

Montgomery, Alabama—and even though many blacks were still not ready to risk their lives for their freedom—something was in the air, an invigorating feeling, like the first chill of autumn. At the age of twenty-seven, I knew that something tremendous was going to happen in my lifetime—probably very soon, so I watched and waited for a sign.

One of the older preachers who agreed with the younger generation was Vernon Johns, pastor of Montgomery's Dexter Avenue Baptist Church, located on the city square in sight of the Capitol—the only black church so situated. Vernon was in his sixties, an eloquent preacher, and absolutely fearless in the face of local authority. When something happened in Montgomery that he felt was unjust, he spoke out publicly, calling for responsive action from the black community. When I first returned to Montgomery I was attracted to his courageous and colorful style, and when I assumed the pulpit of First Baptist Church, he became my closest friend among the other Montgomery pastors.

Vernon had enjoyed a distinguished career before coming to Montgomery. He had been president of Virginia Seminary, and had also been pastor of the historic First Baptist Church in Charleston, West Virginia. In fact, I think it would be no exaggeration to say that the black community never produced a finer preacher than Vernon Johns. He is remembered today by all who ever heard him as a genius in the pulpit. He preached perfectly structured sermons without ever using a manuscript, and he could quote the Bible verbatim for hours. I have seen him on more than one occasion "read" from a Bible in front of him without ever really looking at the pages. He could also quote poetry for hours without ever making a mistake or repeating himself.

Johns was also interested in economics and read extensively in the field. He would often say that blacks "must become a producing people and not just a consuming people." Like my father, he thought that our temporal deliverance would come through economic progress.

He was not afraid of the white establishment, and was always ready to challenge the authority of those whites who enforced Jim Crow laws inhumanely or brutally. Five years before the Rosa Parks case he had attempted to organize a bus boycott, but the time was not ripe.

He had gotten on a bus in Montgomery and because he was an old man and his hands were trembling, he dropped his dime as he was trying to put it in the fare box. The coin rolled over by the driver's foot, where Vernon could not reach it without getting down on his hands and knees, whereas the driver could have reached down and picked it up with no difficulty.

Instead the driver snarled, "Uncle, get down and pick up that dime and put it in the box."

His tone was clearly threatening, and Vernon responded with defiance rather than fear. "I've surrendered the dime. If you want it, all you have to do is bend down and pick it up."

The driver was furious. "Get down and pick it up right now, or I'll put you off this bus."

Johns turned to the passengers on the bus, all of whom were black. "I prefer to get off the bus rather than to remain where I'm not wanted. Obviously this driver doesn't want us on the bus, so let's all get off."

They stared at him blankly, frozen in their seats, terrified at the idea of defying the bus driver.

"Come on," Vernon told them. "Stand up. Get off."

But he was the only one who had the courage to leave, and later, when he told me about it, he shook his head more in sorrow than in anger.

"Even God," he said, "can't free people who behave like that."

From that time forward he refused to ride the Montgomery buses, and instead he bought a car. The trouble was that he was never quite sure where he'd left it. A genius who was always preoccupied with matters spiritual, he would park his car somewhere and not be able to find it for days.

One day I went by Dexter Avenue Church to see him and

after we had talked for a while, we decided to go my house and eat lunch.

"Let's go in my car," he said, and I said that would be fine.

As we left the church, he suddenly stopped and snapped his fingers.

"Ralph, I just remembered where my car is."

"And where is that?" I asked.

"I parked it," he said, "on Auburn Avenue in Atlanta, Georgia."

You can tell the class of the people who go to a black church by how much noise they make during the sermon. The less noise the higher the class. And the Dexter Avenue congregation—composed mostly of Alabama State professors and their families—was habitually silent during the sermon. No matter how fervently they agreed with what was being said, you seldom heard an "amen" or a "hallelujah."

The story went round, however, that one Sunday a new-comer attended services at Dexter Avenue and, not knowing exactly where he was, became so carried away with Vernon's sermon that he let out a loud "Amen" from the back pew. All eyes turned around and glared at him, but in his enthusiasm he didn't notice.

As the sermon continued he was moved again and shouted out "Hallelujah!" At that point an usher rushed back, bent over, and in an angry whisper, said, "What's the matter with you?"

The newcomer said, "Why, I'm responding to Dr. Johns' sermon. I got the Holy Spirit."

"Well, you didn't get it *here*!" said the usher.

Vernon and I often discussed the differences between Dexter Avenue and First Baptist, and it was his contention that First Baptist, though more religious, was less responsive.

"At First Baptist," he said, "they don't mind the preacher

talking about Jesus, though they would never stoop so low as to talk about Him themselves. At Dexter Avenue, they would prefer that you not mention His name.

"On the other hand," he continued, "when you preach at Dexter Avenue at least people will smile at you sometimes. At First Baptist they just stare at you with cold faces, and that makes the temperature in the church drop about five degrees."

Sometimes when I was out of town Vernon would replace me in the pulpit, and when I was gone on the first Sunday of the month—Communion Sunday—he would come over and administer communion to the congregation, though he really didn't approve of giving communion after the Sunday morning service: "It's the observance of the Lord's supper," he said, "and not the Lord's lunch."

His wife, whose name was Alternate Johns, was a gifted pianist and music teacher. Before coming to Montgomery, where she taught at Alabama State, she had taught at Virginia State University at Petersburg, where she returned after Vernon's retirement.

I shared a great compliment with Mrs. Johns. Vernon said to me once that there were only two people he had ever known who were qualified to enter the Kingdom of God without being born again. "One is my wife and the other is Ralph David Abernathy. Jesus said to repent and believe in Him and thou shalt be saved. But you, Ralph, are better by nature than most men are by practice. You don't have to be born again; you are already qualified to participate in the society of the redeemed."

(You understand that I didn't believe a word of it. At the time he said this, I was praying to be able to just get through every day without committing some grievous sin against God and the people with whom I came in contact. But it was certainly encouraging to have someone who held me in such high esteem. It made me try a little harder to live up to his idealized portrait of me.)

I had first seen Vernon Johns in 1951 when I was a student at Atlanta University. He had been chosen by all-male Morehouse College as their speaker for Religious Emphasis Week.

Because he was a well-known preacher, I felt compelled to attend his first talk on the campus and I remember it well.

His text was from Genesis, the story of how Moses was first chosen to lead his people, and Vernon began by summarizing it as follows: "God saw Moses when he slew the Egyptian and buried him in the sand, and he turned to an angel and said, 'Write that man's name down. Later on I can use him in my program.' "

Then he said to the young men assembled before him: "If I were to summarize in a single phrase my remarks to you today, I would title them—'Constructive Homicide.' "

Vernon was not a believer in nonviolence, as Martin Luther King, Jr. and I were. He believed in taking whatever measures were necessary to achieve our God-given or constitutional rights.

A poor black man was shot down in the street just below Vernon Johns' church one Saturday evening. Everyone in Montgomery knew that he had been killed by a white man, and everyone was reasonably certain who the murderer was. But there was no serious investigation by local authorities, and it was clear that the killing was to be swept under the rug like so many other such killings over the years. The black leadership in the community grumbled behind closed doors; but this was before Martin and I had arrived, so no public protest was voiced—with one exception. The following week Vernon posted on the bulletin board outside his church this sermon topic: IT IS SAFE TO KILL NEGROES IN MONTGOMERY.

The newspapers reported that he was going to preach this sermon on Sunday morning and the white community was up in arms. As it happened the all-white grand jury was then in session; and when word reached them of the sign in front of Vernon's church, they charged that Vernon Johns was inciting people to riot and subpoenaed him to show why he should not be indicted. So the police department sent an officer to pick him up and bring him into the station.

When the policeman arrived at the Dexter Avenue Church, he found an old man in overalls sweeping the steps and, thinking he was the janitor, asked him: "Do you know this preacher, Vernon Johns?"

Vernon nodded his head. "Oh, yes. I know him."

The policeman walked over to make sure the board still had the sermon title on it, then he came back. "Do you think he would actually preach that sermon?"

Vernon scratched his head and thought for a moment. "Knowing him," he said, "I believe he would. He's inclined to do what he says he's going to do."

"You think he's that crazy?"

"Well," Vernon said, "he's pretty crazy."

The policeman shook his head. Things were obviously worse than he had expected. "Is he in the church or in his office?"

"No," said Vernon, "he's not."

"Well then where does he live?"

Vernon gave the policeman very specific directions to get to his house, and the policeman got back in the patrol car and sped off to serve his subpoena while Vernon finished sweeping the steps in front of the church.

Later in the day he called up the sheriff's office and told them he would be happy to come in and testify before the grand jury, and agreed to appear at ten A.M. the next morning. When he came in, dressed in a fine suit, the same policeman was dozing in the back row. But the man woke up about the time Vernon had finished reciting the oath and jumped to his feet.

"Why didn't you tell me you were Vernon Johns, you old scoundrel," he shouted.

"Because you never asked me," Vernon said.

Then he sat down and answered all the questions put to him, carefully pointing out that a black man had indeed been shot and killed in broad daylight, that nothing had thus far been done to bring his murderer to justice, and that until such time as an arrest had been made, the words on the board outside his church were no more than a statement of fact. .

When they realized that he could not be bluffed or intimidated, he was allowed to leave. The following Sunday he preached the sermon, exactly as advertised.

*   *   *

Vernon was forever tendering his resignation to his Board of Deacons as a means of whipping them into line. He was a famous preacher, scholarly enough to please the faculty at Alabama State, and a man of fiercely independent will, so it never occurred to him that the deacons would accept his resignation.

But one day they did. There were people, after all, who were nervous about the spirit of commerce that permeated the church; and there were others who thought that Vernon was too vague and preoccupied to keep up with all his pastoral duties. So after the fifth resignation had been offered, the chairman of the board told Vernon that his resignation was accepted, that they would declare the pulpit vacant and begin looking for a new pastor.

Vernon was stunned. I don't believe he had any intention of leaving and, after thinking it over, he decided that he would stay after all. Mrs. Johns, however, could see that the board meant business. She resigned her position at Alabama State and re-claimed her post at Virginia State, which had always been waiting for her. When fall came, she told Vernon they would have to move; but he was determined to stay at the Dexter Avenue parsonage and fight for reinstatement, confident that the Board of Deacons would change their minds. So Mrs. Johns moved back to Petersburg and Vernon remained in Montgomery.

During that difficult period he spent a great deal of time at our house, particularly after the deacons ordered the electricity and gas turned off at the parsonage. For a while Vernon used the stove to cook his meals, burning back copies of the *New York Times* and the *Washington Post*, to which he subscribed and which for years he had saved. He could get enough of a fire going to heat up a can of spaghetti or Vienna sausages, but he was always grateful for an invitation to dinner at our house, where Juanita, who loved him dearly, tried to cook his favorite dishes.

When the first hard frost came, however, Vernon knew that he was beaten. The house was a deep freeze, and the *New York Times* barely cut the cold that settled into the floors and walls. He wore two and three sweaters to bed and several pairs of socks; but he still shivered all night. Of course, he was welcome to stay at our house—as we told him on more than one occasion—but he knew that he could not spend the rest of his life with us. And he was finally convinced that the deacons at Dexter Avenue were not going to change their minds or make any concessions. So the old prophet packed up his remaining belongings and went back to his farm in Virginia, where he worked in the soil he so dearly loved.

I believe that what made Vernon so stubborn in his last stand against the deacons was the knowledge that he would be without a post or a pulpit from which to preach the Gospel. For a preacher of his genius, such a realization was devastating. He saw himself unable to do the thing he was most qualified to do; and his spirit fought against it until his body forced him to surrender.

Yet he soon discovered that a man of his ability and fame could find a pulpit any time he wanted one. He was constantly being invited to speak at churches and on campuses around the country. He spent more time on the road than at home, and during those last years more people heard him than at any other time during his life.

A few weeks after he left Montgomery, I received a terse note from him:

Dear Friend Abernathy:

Am invited to speak at Religious Emphasis Week at Dillard University in New Orleans. Would like to stay with you and Juanita on Saturday night and preach at the First Church on Sunday of next week.

Vernon Johns

I wrote him and told him that Juanita and I would be delighted to have him as a guest and that the pulpit of First Baptist was always available to him at a moment's notice. Had I known the full story, however, I might have had second thoughts about letting him preach that particular Sunday because I later discovered that the deacons of Dexter Avenue Baptist Church, in the middle of their search for a new pastor, had invited a candidate to preach that Sunday. I know that Vernon's appearance at First Baptist would certainly attract many of his loyal supporters on that particular Sunday. Not only could people construe my scheduling of Vernon as an attempt at proselytizing, but also as a discourtesy to the visiting preacher. When I realized what was going on, I was embarrassed and unhappy.

Vernon, it seems, had known about the Dexter Avenue plans, though I don't believe it occurred to him that he was placing me in such an awkward position. As a matter of fact, so oblivious was he of the problems he was causing that he decided to take advantage of these circumstances. The young preacher who was competing for his former pulpit lived in Atlanta; so Vernon made his travel arrangements with this fact in mind. He hitchhiked from Petersburg to Atlanta, asked to be let off at the bus station, and then called the father of the young preacher and asked if he could ride down to Montgomery with his son. The father agreed readily, so Vernon was chauffeured from the Atlanta bus station to our house by the man whose appearance he would compromise the next day.

Meanwhile, we were waiting in Montgomery, wondering when and how Vernon would arrive. Juanita was in the kitchen, preparing Vernon's favorite meal: chopped sirloin steak, green beans, sweet potatoes, and hot rolls. Knowing Vernon's habit of hitchhiking wherever he went in order to save money, I expected to hear the telephone ring and to learn when and on what highway to pick him up. It was almost four o'clock in the afternoon, and already the gray, drizzling sky had begun to turn black so I was beginning to worry a little. Then I heard a car turn into the driveway. I peered through the blinds and saw Vernon get out of the front seat, carrying a suitcase, and then the driver got out as well.

In the gathering gloom, I could recognize Vernon. The driver—a short, lean young black man—also looked familiar. I tried to figure out why. Then I realized that I had met him before.

It was Martin Luther King, Jr.

I met them both at the door, shook hands, and invited Martin in. He hesitated.

"I'm going to spend the night with one of the Dexter Avenue deacons," he said, "but I could stop in for just a minute."

Juanita came out from the kitchen, and threw her arms around Vernon.

"Juanita," he said, "next to Alternate Johns you are the most beautiful and talented woman in the world."

She had heard it before, but as usual, she smiled. Already the aroma of chopped sirloin was floating in from the kitchen, and she excused herself to return to her cooking.

"That certainly does smell good," said Vernon.

"It certainly does," agreed Martin.

"Please stay, Reverend King," said Juanita from the kitchen door. "We have more than enough."

Martin smiled and said that he would like to, but he had a previous engagement.

For a while we talked about the drive down, the grim weather, and then—ever so lightly—about the situation at Dexter Avenue. Meanwhile, other aromas were floating into the room, and Vernon would occasionally say how much he was anticipating another of Juanita's famous meals and Martin would say that he certainly understood why.

Finally, I said: "Why don't you just stay and eat with us. You could tell Dr. and Mrs. Brooks that you were delayed. It wouldn't be a lie."

"You'd better do it, boy," said Vernon. "I've eaten at both houses, and there's no comparison. At the Brooks' house you will get white people's food: a little cheese and crackers and a salad. Here you'll get the best meal you've ever had in your life."

At that moment Juanita came back in the room. "Dinner's ready," she said, "and, Rev. King, I've already set a place for you."

I could see the surrender in his eyes. He knew he shouldn't stay, but the chopped sirloin was already on the dining room table, in plain sight, and while he was standing there, trying to gather his strength to leave, Juanita went back into the kitchen and brought out the hot rolls. That did it.

He laughed, threw up his hands, and joined us at the dinner table.

Afterward, we sat in the living room, the talk became more

serious. We talked about the oppression of our people and about the growing belief that a sea of change was taking place. We all agreed that Brown versus the Board of Education had altered forever the conditions on which the continuing struggle would be predicated. No longer was the law unambiguously on the side of Jim Crow. It now appeared as if the law was on our side, that the federal government might eventually be pressed into service in our fight for freedom.

Vernon and I knew each other well and had talked about these matters before; but King, though a relative stranger, was forthcoming in his advocacy of an active program to force the issue and to bring about freedom more rapidly. He was, he said, committed to the preaching of a social Gospel that would awaken the Christian churches and mobilize them in the fight against segregation. He indicated that he had been working on plans to do just that and when the time came to do battle, he hoped the churches would be ready.

Vernon and I looked at one another with satisfaction. We had been talking about just such a plan of action, though only in the vaguest of terms.

"How long do you think it will be before we can make a move?" I asked Martin.

"Not for a long time," he said. "At least several years. We must move slowly and carefully, so that when the time does come, we will be sufficiently prepared."

He stayed as long as he could, then reluctantly rose, thanked Juanita for the marvelous meal, and drove off to the Brooks house, where he probably had to eat another meal, though from what Vernon said, not a particularly hearty one.

The next morning I got up early and drove out to the radio station, where I took my turn in a devotional series, preaching a short sermon for the benefit of those people who got up at 7:00 A.M. and didn't want to go to church. At the end of my presentation I was surprised to be told by the station announcer that I had a telephone call. It was Martin Luther King, who told me how much he had enjoyed dinner last night and my sermon this morning. It was a thoughtful gesture on his part, and I was beginning to hope that he would be called to Dexter Avenue, though I knew enough about the politics of the congregation to know how unlikely that would be.

The chairman of the Board of Deacons had already made his choice, and the man he had anointed had preached a highly commendable sermon two weeks earlier. The rest of the board had concurred with the chairman's judgment, and most of the congregation was likewise in agreement. Martin Luther King's visit was no more than a formality in which everyone had to participate because the clerk of the church, Robert Nesbit, had insisted Martin be invited.

As a consequence, many of the members of Dexter Avenue, knowing that the deacons had made up their mind, came over to First Baptist that Sunday to hear Vernon Johns, a man whom they admired and loved. But those who did missed one of the greatest sermons ever heard at Dexter Avenue. Martin—who was not a natural performer like Vernon Johns—was at his best, and at his best no one was more learned and eloquent.

His topic was "The Three Dimensions of a Complete Life," and when he was finished, the congregation was in awe of him. He had all of the erudition of Vernon Johns and twice as much eloquence as his rival. The deacons who had been so certain in their decision before the service began were now just as certain that this new man was sent to them by heaven. The chairman of the board pounded the table and reminded them that they had already made a decision. They replied that it was their prerogative to change their minds. Besides, they pointed out, no final vote had been taken. The chairman insisted that they ratify the earlier decision immediately, and the board said they were not prepared to make such a move—not after hearing about the three dimensions of a complete life.

They argued all afternoon about what to do and finally struck a compromise. The earlier candidate would be invited to preach a second sermon, after which the board would make their final decision. With that they adjourned.

The following Sunday the chairman's candidate returned for a second appearance in the pulpit. He had been briefed about the nature of the situation, as was clear from the topic of his sermon, published on the bulletin board outside the church: THE FOUR DIMENSIONS OF A COMPLETE LIFE.

That fourth dimension did him in. By the time he was finished, the deacons and congregation knew they wanted Martin. When the chairman was confronted with this unanimity of opinion, he gave in and Martin got the call.

I had been following the drama from a safe distance, and I was overjoyed when I heard that he had won out. The Lord had sent me a friend to replace Vernon Johns and I offered up a prayer of gratitude.

Like Vernon, Martin was someone I could not only talk to but learn from. He had more formal education than I did, having finished all but his doctorate at Boston University, and he had the same hopes for the future, the same vision of a transformed society. I eagerly looked forward to his arrival in Montgomery. Once again, I had that same feeling about his move to Montgomery that I had had on that Sunday when I first met him in Atlanta: Somehow we were meant to be friends and partners in some extraordinary enterprise.

Vernon left that afternoon on the Hummingbird, using a ticket that his honorarium at First Baptist had bought. We received a letter from him a few weeks later, telling us how much he enjoyed the visit and how he would be back some day soon.

But he never made it. We kept up with him for the next several years as he traveled around the country speaking at colleges and to large congregations. Then, one Sunday, speaking at Howard University chapel, he preached one of the strangest and most eloquent sermons he had ever preached, entitled "The Romance of Death." People were spellbound when they heard it and haunted by it long after they had left the church.

The next day Vernon entered the hospital, and before the end of the week he had died.

As soon as Martin and Coretta moved to Montgomery we called on them, and from the beginning he and I became inseparable. Though both of us had heavy responsibilities as pastors of important churches, we tried to meet for dinner every day to talk and to make plans. Many people believe that the civil rights movement came together by sheer accident as the result of a confluence of events in the mid-1950s. Certainly chance played a role in the timing of the movement, but the shape it took was in part the result of our conversations during the weeks before we suddenly found ourselves at the center of the Rosa Parks controversy.

Had we been white men during those times, we would probably have met at one of a half dozen restaurants and made notes on paper napkins, but there was literally no black establishment where we could meet and talk quietly. Because of Jim Crow we could only have dinner at home. So the four of us had dinner every night, with Coretta preparing the meal one evening, Juanita the next. And usually conversations among the four of us would last way beyond midnight.

For me it was an exciting time, because we were talking about large and important projects, while at the same time spelling them out in terms of actions we could take right here in Montgomery. Martin had some general ideas about the means of attaining freedom, while I had the specific understanding of Montgomery that he lacked. Together we formulated a plan to turn the city into a model of social justice and racial amity. Both of us recognized the seeming impossibility of the task, but we also understood that change was inevitable and imminent and that we could provide the proper means of achieving these important social ends without completely destroying the community.

Martin provided the philosophic framework for the whole plan and we both insisted that its implementation be completely and militantly nonviolent. Martin and I had thoroughly read and absorbed the teachings of Henry David Thoreau and Mahatma Gandhi on this subject. We had seen the possibilities in applying the same ideas and practices to the elimination of segregation in America. We thoroughly explored all the ramifications and pitfalls, and knew in general what had to be done.

As Martin expounded philosophy, I saw its practical application on the local level. When he talked about how to make a witness to the white Christian community, I understood what he was saying specifically in terms of Montgomery. To use a military analogy, while he was talking about strategy (the broad, overall purpose of a campaign), I was thinking about tactics (how to achieve that strategy though specific actions). Juanita and Coretta also contributed significantly to these plans, which were the product of detailed dialogue. When we spoke of implementing the plans, we were still thinking in terms of years rather than weeks or even months.

For one thing, Martin said that he needed to spend several years in Montgomery, getting to know the city and its leaders, both black and white. He believed that he would have to establish his credibility in the black community before he could hope to lead them into a nonviolent crusade for freedom. He also wanted to gain the respect and trust of those progressive white leaders whose help might prove invaluable in the struggle. All of this would take two or three years at the very least.

As for me, I felt that I needed the same kind of academic credibility that he had; and I made up my mind to take a leave from First Baptist Church, return to school and get my doctorate, then come back and reclaim my pulpit. At that point, we would be ready to attack the central problem of our society and free our people from their long-term bondage.

It all seemed so reasonable and yet so remote on those autumn nights when we sat over a bowl of soup or a plate of stew and outlined the future. Then, as we put the final touches on our plans, God intervened with a plan of his own and a more urgent timetable.

5

The Montgomery Bus Boycott

MOST ACCOUNTS of the Montgomery bus boycott begin with the refusal of Rosa Parks to obey a bus driver's order. As a matter of fact, two black women had already been arrested earlier in the year. One of them, Claudette Colvin, a fifteen-year-old student, had been dragged from the bus and charged with assault and battery as well as failure to comply with Jim Crow laws governing public transportation. In each of these earlier cases, Mrs. Jo Ann Robinson, a professor of English at Alabama State University, had represented the defendants in negotiations with bus officials and city fathers, hoping to put an end to such incidents before they resulted in violence.

Mrs. Robinson, who headed an activist group called the Women's Political Council, had invited black pastors to join her in confronting the white establishment, if only to emphasize the point that our entire community was disturbed by what was happening. At that time, few of the other clergy were concerned with questions of social justice and Martin was too preoccupied with finishing his dissertation, so I was the only one who had accepted her invitation. We were joined by E. D. Nixon, president of the local chapter of the National Association for the Advancement of Colored People (NAACP).

At these meetings, we discussed not only the two women who had been arrested, but also a number of additional bus incidents that never found their way into court, no doubt because the victims were black passengers. Several of the white drivers were determined to harass our people at every opportunity. For example, when the bus was even slightly crowded, they would make blacks pay their fare, then get off, and go to the back door to enter. Sometimes they would even take off with a squeal as a passenger trudged toward the rear after paying. At least once a driver closed the back door on a black woman's arm and then dragged her to the next stop before allowing her to climb aboard. Clearly this kind of gratuitous cruelty was contributing to an increasing tension on Montgomery buses. We tried to reason with local authorities and with bus company officials. They were polite, listened to our complaints with serious expressions on their faces, and did nothing.

On December 1, 1955, Mrs. Parks took her now-famous bus ride and set events in motion that would lead to a social revolution of monumental proportions.

First, it is important to realize the kind of person Mrs. Parks was in order to understand fully why her arrest caused so much reaction in the black community. A seamstress at a large department store, she was a slight woman, soft-spoken and courteous. Though she was the secretary of the local NAACP chapter, she was not the kind of bold and aggressive activist who usually challenges civil authority. She had an air of gentility about her that usually evoked respect among whites as well as blacks, and I doubt that anyone who knew her could have imagined that she would ever end up in jail.

But that Thursday afternoon she had a pain in her shoulder, she was tired and—more importantly—black passengers had been goaded beyond endurance. When she boarded the bus and paid her fare, the day was gray and overcast, the kind of winter gloom that drags the spirit down. With her shoulder aching and a long day behind her, she found a vacant seat on the only row that wasn't filled—the eleventh row from the front. This is significant because of the peculiarity of Montgomery's Jim Crow law pertaining to buses.

Throughout most of the South, the law prescribed that blacks begin seating from the rear forward and whites from the front rearward. Under this arrangement, on a predominantly black route our people might well occupy all the seats on the bus or, if there were a few whites aboard, almost all. On the other hand, on a predominantly white route, blacks might be found only on the back row. The boundary would be established by the proportion of blacks to whites and by who got on first. This method was used in several Alabama cities, including Mobile.

In Montgomery, however, the first ten seats were reserved for whites only—whether or not there were any white riders on the bus. This meant that blacks could not sit in the three-seat benches in the front that faced each other or in the four first-row seats. So Mrs. Parks was acting within the law when she sat down in an outside seat in the eleventh row, with a black man to her right (next to the window) and two black women across the aisle.

Clutching her purse and a shopping bag, she tried to relax while the bus rattled along, taking on more passengers at the next two stops. At the third stop a white man got on, and the driver glanced back and saw that whites occupied rows one through ten of the already crowded bus. Looking at the passengers in row eleven, he called out, "All right, you niggers. I want those seats."

No one replied or moved, perhaps because they weren't sure he meant them, perhaps because they knew he had no right to give such an order. The regulation specifically stated that no black could be moved unless another empty seat was available. What the driver was commanding meant that four blacks (three women and a man) would have to stand so that one white man could sit down. It was neither legal nor logical, and everybody knew it.

"You all better make it light on yourselves and let me have those seats," the driver said, this time with a decided edge to his voice. Everyone knew that refusal meant war, and after a second's hesitation the two women and the man rose, but Mrs.

Parks remained seated. She did move her legs to let the man slip by. Then she slid over next to the window. The move spoke for itself: she was digging in, though she remained expressionless and said nothing.

Anger shone in the driver's face.

"Look, woman. I told you I wanted the seat. Are you going to stand up?"

"No," she said quietly. And nothing more.

He exploded.

"If you don't stand up I'm going to have you arrested."

Again she said she wouldn't move, and with that he shook his head and stomped off the bus. As he headed toward a pay phone on the corner, people began piling out both doors. Some left because they knew there would be a delay. Others wanted to avoid trouble with the law. Mrs. Parks sat quietly in her seat and watched as the driver finished his phone call, walked back to the bus, and stood outside, peering down the street.

Soon a patrol car drove up and two officers got out. After talking to the driver for a moment they followed him onto the bus, where he pointed out Mrs. Parks. The policemen came down the aisle and one asked her, "Why didn't you stand up?" He seemed more puzzled than angry.

"Why do you push us around?" she asked him quietly.

"I don't know," he said, "but the law is the law, and you are under arrest."

Remembering Claudette Colvin, Mrs. Parks rose, indicating her willingness to go quietly. One policeman took her purse and the other took her shopping bag, and the three left the bus, while the driver stood to one side and watched, a look of grim vindication on his face. The policemen drove Mrs. Parks to headquarters, where she was booked, then on to the city jail.

That was Thursday evening, and I didn't hear about any of this until early Friday morning, when I got a call from E. D. Nixon. He told me about the arrest and about the circumstances surrounding the incident. I fought to keep my temper, not only because it was another serious example of racial abuse but also because it had happened to Rosa Parks.

"Is she still down there?" I asked.

Nixon said he had signed for her bond, so she had not spent the night in jail. Clifford Durr, a white lawyer friendly to blacks, had advised them that she clearly couldn't be charged under local law since no other seat had been available to her. But even though Montgomery statutes were on her side, state law gave a bus driver arbitrary powers over passengers, an authority comparable to that of a captain on the high seas. So she was subject to prosecution for disobeying his command, even though he had been wrong in ordering her to move.

Nixon said he was ready to take action. Jo Ann Robinson, who had met with Mrs. Parks after her release the previous night, was already passing around a leaflet calling for specific action in response to the incident. In part it read:

> This woman's case will come up Monday. We are, therefore, asking every Negro to stay off the buses Monday in protest of the arrest and trial. Don't ride the buses to work, to town, to school, or anywhere on Monday.
>
> You can afford to stay out of school for one day if you have no other way to go except by bus.
>
> You can also afford to stay out of town for one day. If you work, take a cab, or share a ride, or walk. But please, children and grown-ups, don't ride the bus at all on Monday. Please stay off all buses Monday.

Nixon himself was a Pullman car porter and was scheduled for a trip that would keep him on the road for the next three days, so he wanted me to take charge: How should we proceed in order to rally public support? Whom should we call?

I thought for a moment.

"I believe we should ask Dr. Hubbard to call a meeting of black leaders under the auspices of the Baptist Ministers Conference. He's probably the most highly respected clergyman in the black community. If anyone can speak with authority to both races, it's Dr. Hubbard."

Nixon was hesitant. He didn't think Dr. Hubbard was dynamic enough, even though he was his own pastor. But I knew that

Hubbard was well loved in the community, so I pressed the matter. Besides, in making the suggestion, I was really taking the burden on my own shoulders, since as secretary of the Baptist Ministers Conference, I would probably end up doing all the work.

The Reverend Dr. H. H. Hubbard, a man in his late sixties, had learned the trick that old mules always know: to let the young mules pull the load most of the time, holding back until a moment when great effort is required. Then the old mules heed the biblical injunction to "Come to the forefront and take thy rightful place." Until that moment arrives, however, they simply lay back and watch the foolish young mules pull all the weight. That's the way Dr. Hubbard ran the Baptist Ministers Conference. I was the foolish young mule and he would let me run around, full of authority, doing all the drudge work. Then, when the moment of genuine importance arrived, he would step into the spotlight. I was counting on that happening this time.

"Anybody else you can think of besides Hubbard?" Nixon asked.

"Why don't you ask Martin Luther King?" I said. Martin was new in town and highly educated, so Nixon was a little intimidated by him.

"I don't know Reverend King, but since I'll be out of town, I'm going to leave the situation in your hands. Do what you think is best.

"And one more thing. We have to get our people to stop riding those buses for at least a day or two. That's the only way we'll ever get what we want."

I agreed and said I would get to work on it. As soon as he hung up I called Martin and told him the story of Mrs. Parks.

"We have to do something this time," I said.

Martin agreed but said he couldn't help—not at this particular moment. He was preparing a plan to present to his church's annual conference, which was scheduled a week from the following Monday. It was a major responsibility of every pastor to present to his congregation a detailed program for the upcoming year—complete with a schedule of events and a budget. This was Martin's first such conference at Dexter Avenue Baptist, and he wanted to call his church to a renewed sense of dedication. It was his moment to take charge, so it was important to him that he prepare a detailed and convincing plan. I understood his predicament.

"We need to hold a meeting of community leaders," I continued, "no later than tonight."

"In which case," he said, "let my contribution be the meeting place. The people will be gone from the capitol by nightfall, and the whole square will be lit up. You can all gather in the basement. There'll be plenty of room and plenty of parking space."

Next I called Dr. Hubbard. Sure enough, he immediately told me to make the arrangements—the old mule up to his tricks—but that was fine with me. I called all the black Baptist preachers and told them there would be a meeting that night at Dexter Avenue Church, a very important meeting. I urged them to attend, though as I recall I made no mention of why we were gathering because I didn't want the white establishment to find out in advance and try to intimidate us, either individually or collectively. Already I was forming some plans, and I knew they could be quickly undone by fear. Besides, since Dr. Hubbard was ostensibly calling the meeting, the preachers probably assumed they were merely attending an extra session of the Baptist Ministers Conference.

Of course, I knew that the Baptists alone could not act in behalf of the entire community so as soon as I contacted the last member of our Conference, I began to call the Methodist clergy, most of them African Methodist Episcopal (AME) Zionist pastors, but I couldn't find any of them at their churches, and when I tried at home I had the same luck. Finally, one pastor's wife told me why: the AME Zionists were gathering that morning at Hilliard Chapel AME Zion Church to meet with their bishop. Since they were by far the largest group of black clergy outside the Baptists, I decided to go speak to them all at once.

When I arrived at Hilliard Chapel, I found Jo Ann Robinson waiting outside, passing out leaflets announcing our meeting. My message had spread all over the black community by word of mouth. I suspect that had I simply turned around and gone home, we would have had a formidable crowd at Dexter Avenue Church that night, so effective was the grapevine.

As soon as I stepped through the door of Hilliard Chapel, the Reverend Dr. L. Roy Bennett recognized me and came down the aisle to meet me and to take me up to his bishop. I explained to the bishop why I was there; he immediately presented me to the assembled group so that I could recite in detail the story of Mrs. Parks's arrest. Then I invited them to the meeting and was assured that they would turn out in force. (Someone would later characterize this as the first speech of the civil rights movement.)

When I came out of the church, Mrs. Robinson was waiting for me. She told me she was planning to give out boycott leaflets to the children leaving Carver and Booker T. Washington high schools, and I offered to go with her and help. For one thing, I was worried that if she passed out the leaflets by herself she might be blamed for everything and lose her position at Alabama State. Though teachers theoretically were free to engage in political activities, in reality, she was extremely vulnerable; so we kept her authorship of the leaflet a secret, despite the efforts of a number of white leaders to find out who was responsible.

After we had given a leaflet to every child in sight, I went home and made a few more telephone calls. Late that afternoon Dr. Hubbard came by my house, settled down in a chair, and asked me what he was supposed to do that night.

"Just have a short prayer and open the meeting for general discussion. At that point we can map out our strategy and be out of the place in an hour. We can't let the meeting run too long."

He nodded in agreement, and waved goodbye.

After dinner I went by to pick up Martin, who said he could break away from his work for an hour or so, and by the time we got to the meeting Dr. Hubbard was fully in charge, with more than seventy people in the room, waiting for the action to begin.

First Dr. Hubbard recited a lengthy prayer and then we sang a hymn. After that he read a passage of scripture. Then to my horror he turned the meeting over to Reverend Bennett of the Mount Zion AME Zion Church because he was head of the Interdenominational Ministerial Alliance, an organization whose sole activity was to sponsor the annual Easter sunrise service. Dr. Bennett cleared his throat and launched into a speech about his own past experiences in organizing boycotts. From the moment he began I had the feeling that we were running the risk of losing our audience, and as the minutes went by, I was more and more certain of it.

He rambled on about past successes without any reference to present difficulties and for a while people listened. Then they began shifting in their seats, checking their watches, and looking longingly at the exits. Each time Bennett paused to breathe we all prayed that he was going to sit down, but always he got his second wind and began to speak again.

One or two people in the back got up and disappeared out the door. Then a few more followed. Soon most of the back rows were empty. Then someone in the front row slipped down the aisle and hurried toward the rear. At that moment it appeared as if Dr. Bennett would inadvertently resolve the matter in favor of the bus company before the rest of us had a chance to speak.

Finally, with only about twenty people left in the hall, I panicked. I jumped up and joined him at the pulpit, a frozen smile on my face.

"Brother Bennett," I said, "we've got to settle down to business. It's getting late."

To my relief he turned, nodded, and without resentment yielded the chair, which I retained for the rest of the evening—just in case. Unfortunately, we had only a handful of people to work with, but in fact there was very little to decide. Everyone agreed we should support the Monday boycott, and we also agreed that we should hold a mass meeting Monday night to decide whether or not to extend the boycott into the week or even longer. We decided that the Monday meeting would be held at Holt Street Baptist Church, located in the heart of the black section of town. After the meeting Martin and I stayed behind to turn out another leaflet, updating our plans.

Saturday morning more than two hundred volunteers showed up to pass out the leaflets, and after they picked up their supply they scattered all over the black part of town, going from house to house and store to store. We also made certain that every clergyman who had left the meeting early had an update on what had happened and also a supply of leaflets for his flock. We were reasonably certain that every congregation in town would get the word on Sunday morning. As Martin and I talked it over, we were satisfied that we had touched every base.

Then something occurred to us: the "saints" would get the message, but what about the "sinners"? A hard core of blacks, most of them men, just didn't go to church or associate with church people. Would they get the word—and, more importantly, would they feel welcome at the meeting? The more we talked about them, the more we worried. They had as much of an investment in this issue as we did, yet we were running the show.

We agreed that we would have to contact them by visiting the clubs and dives that night. Just after dark I picked up Martin and we began to make the rounds. Most of these joints were small, wooden-frame buildings, no more than lop-sided shacks jammed with tables and chairs; and each time we entered it would be the same. The room, lit by a feeble bulb or a neon sign, would be heavy with smoke and the smell of beer or cheap whiskey. Sometimes a jukebox would be playing, but more often we would hear rising voices and laughter. Suddenly someone would see us and the conversation would falter, then die.

Though many were strangers to us, we recognized familiar faces, and usually a voice would call out, "Come in, Reverend Abernathy," or "Good evening, Reverend King." A few revelers even invited us to sit down and have a drink; but we smiled, declined, and then got to the point. We needed a big crowd at the meeting on Monday night. It was very important that we present a united front. We urged them to attend.

They were enthusiastic in their support; sometimes after we had spoken, they broke into applause. By the time we had visited all the night spots we knew, we were reasonably certain the "sinners" would be with us as well. If anything, they were more vocal in their support than were the "saints."

Sunday morning we got some unexpected and unintentional help. A black maid in a white household had given a copy of our leaflet to the woman for whom she worked, and the woman had in turn given it to the *Montgomery Advertiser,* which ran a front page story in the Sunday edition, quoting a good portion of our announcement. Of course, a lot of whites who read the account were stirred to anger against us, and the local police commissioner went on television to denounce the boycott, promising to provide police protection for anyone who wanted to ride the bus.

But in addition to angering whites, the article also touched another readership and stirred them as well. Blacks read the *Advertiser* and those who hadn't known about the boycott and meeting before, learned about them over the breakfast table on Sunday morning.

Thus, by Sunday evening we were reasonably certain we had spread the word throughout the black community. The only question that remained was how well our people would respond. No one knew the answer and several of us slept uneasily that night.

On Monday morning we awoke wondering what the day would bring. The first question was whether or not our people would respond to our pleas and stay off the buses. If they climbed aboard and trudged to the rear as they'd done every weekday for as long as many of them could remember, then the white establishment would be grinning and nodding their heads. Nothing would have changed. We would still be safely, securely under their thumb.

On the other hand, if the boycott worked, then the final outcome of the confrontation would still be in doubt. We might eventually force the authorities to alter local laws or we might find that they could hold the line as long as we could. We might become the plaintiffs in a massive law suit, or we might be attacked or even killed. Yet despite the uncertainties it would bring, we were all praying for success.

About an hour before sunrise, Martin came by my house and we watched out the window as the Jackson Street bus made its first run from Alabama State. Ordinarily the driver would have taken on a few blacks at the university. Then he would have come around the curve and stopped across the street, where a crowd of blacks would be huddled together, mostly women on their way to work as maids in white houses. When we peered over at the stop, however, no one was there. Not a single passenger. We held our breath as we watched the road lighten up and then the headlights nose around the corner. For a moment the driver slowed down, then ground his gears, picked up speed and roared on past. Martin and I leaned forward and squinted our eyes. There were no passengers on the bus. We looked at each other and grinned. The boycott was working—it was working perfectly. For the first time in the history of Montgomery, blacks were acting together to resist racial injustice. Juanita broke the silence with a loud "Thank you, Jesus!" It was indeed a new day.

But only the beginning of that day. Shortly before nine Martin and I arrived at the courthouse and found it swarming with our people. All the leaders were there and many faithful followers as well—around two hundred in all. No one was hiding at home, trying to keep out of harm's way. They had turned out to show their support for Rosa Parks.

Court convened at 9:00 and by 9:05 it was all over. After local officials had huddled with lawyers for the state, Mrs. Parks had been charged with refusing to obey a bus driver, a state offense, rather than with a violation of local seating regulations. The judge had listened to the brief recitation of the facts and had pronounced Mrs. Parks guilty. He'd assessed a fine of ten dollars plus court costs, hoping to move on quickly to another case. However, her black attorney, Fred Gray, had announced that he would appeal the ruling on the grounds that Jim Crow laws were unconstitutional—then the trial ended. Short and perfunctory, it had nonetheless been one of the most significant court cases in American history, given its long-range consequences.

For us, however, Mrs. Parks's conviction was not the end of the issue but the beginning, and we had a long day ahead. Though we really hadn't expected any other outcome, we were nonetheless angry, and the word went out among all the leaders as we left the courthouse: There would be a meeting at 3:00 at Mount Zion Church. We would form some kind of plan to keep the issue alive. With the success of our boycott—the chief topic of conversation all over Montgomery—we were certain we could make a difference this time. All we needed was the right kind of organization. As we left the courthouse I heard more than one person ask, "What are we going to do?"

Martin and I had already come up with some possible answers to that question between bar stops on Saturday night. On Sunday evening, worried about the boycott, Juanita and I had organized our thoughts and put a plan down on paper: officers, meetings, committees, activities. We had everything outlined before we'd finished, and it was a good plan, something to circulate among the leaders before the next meeting.

But the question of who would head the organization was going to prove more troublesome. Neither Martin nor I had the time to take on the job. In fact, in all likelihood, we wouldn't even be asked, since we had both turned down the presidency of the Montgomery chapter of the NAACP, not only because we had more pressing duties, but also because we thought the organization was moribund.

The two most likely candidates to head a new organization were E. D. Nixon and Rufus Lewis, and neither man was ideal. Even Martin and I disagreed on who would be better. I preferred Nixon because he was authoritative and militant. A huge man with almost blue-black skin, he had a powerful voice that he used to great advantage, sweating prodigiously as he waved his arms or pounded the table. I thought he would be intimidating, while I saw Rufus Lewis as too mild and easygoing.

Martin, on the other hand, objected to the fact that Nixon was uneducated and used poor grammar. He felt Lewis, an imposing brown-skinned man who was also polished in speech, could command more respect from the white community. We had debated the matter that morning before coming down to the courthouse, but we hadn't reached any conclusion. As I was leaving after the trial, I was reminded of our discussion when I saw Nixon, who was back in town after his trip to Chicago. I made it a point to go over and speak to him, because I wanted to enlist his support for the plans we had worked out.

Nixon and I ended up talking in the office of Rev. Edgar N. French, which was the national headquarters of the AME Zion Church pension fund. It was located above Dean Drugstore, the only black-owned pharmacy in the city. While Nixon and French listened, I told them in detail about the success of the boycott and the plans for the leadership meeting we would hold that afternoon. When I mentioned the meeting, Nixon suddenly came to attention, the politician in him fully activated. A meeting meant an opportunity.

"They won't have an agenda," he said, "and without any agenda they'll have to accept ours." (By "they" I understood him to mean Rufus Lewis and the Methodists.)

Before I talked about the agenda, I told him that Martin and I believed the first order of business should be the establishment of a brand new organization, one that would not be associated with the issues or the failures of the past. Nixon was silent for a moment. He was naturally reluctant to accept this idea, since he believed that the NAACP should carry the fight. It was our oldest and most respected national organization, but in Montgomery it had recorded few or no accomplishments. In fact, we had made more progress that morning than the Montgomery NAACP had made in its entire history. Nixon and I argued back and forth about the matter with French listening quietly, but I soon saw we were getting nowhere.

So I brought up another matter, one on which we could agree. I said we should demand:

1. A pledge from the city authorities and from bus company officials that blacks would be treated with courtesy when we rode the bus. No more name calling. No more closing the door in our faces.

2. A new ordinance that would allow blacks to seat from the rear forward, and whites from the front rearward. No reserved areas. Nobody standing when there were empty places on the bus.

3. Since many routes (e.g., Jackson Street) were almost exclusively for black passengers, blacks should be allowed to apply for positions as bus drivers.

Nixon has since said that this third demand was a serious negotiating point, a goal we expected to attain. Such a suggestion—which would seem not only reasonable but inevitable in the 1980s—ignores the perversity of the system we lived under at the time and its infinitely subtle inconsistencies, which defied all logic. Though in 1955 it was quite common for blacks to act as chauffeurs for whites, no white political leader of that day would have acceded to the demand that we be hired as bus drivers. While a chauffeur was subject to the directions of his passenger, a bus driver had some small authority over his passengers by virtue of the fact that he was in charge of the vehicle, and the State of Alabama had magnified that authority, primarily to enforce segregation. Black bus drivers would therefore have been given a kind of unprecedented power over white passengers, and the last thing the city government wanted us to have was power. So we never expected either the local authorities or the bus company officials to allow blacks to apply for jobs as drivers.

Knowing how they would react, however, gave us the opportunity to engage in a little strategy. We knew that our first two demands were reasonable, so reasonable that the establishment might well be willing to grant them—except for one problem: They could not appear to be giving in to black pressure. It was a matter of their racial pride, their manhood. So we had to provide them with a way to give us what we wanted while seeming to be tough and unyielding. We did this by adding one unreasonable demand at the end of two very reasonable ones. We figured they just might promise the courtesy and new seating plan and make a big show of rejecting our third demand. That way they would give us what we wanted and still save face by denying us something we never hoped to get in the first place.

After we talked a little longer, Nixon and French warmed up to the whole agenda, and Nixon even stopped arguing over the creation of a new organization and began to speak in favor of it, recognizing that he could be elected leader only if he seemed enthusiastic in his support of the idea. Before I left them, we had put everything down on paper and agreed that I would open the meeting with a few words and then French would read the specific proposals.

I went home to lunch, made a few calls, and then I went by and picked up Martin. On the way to the meeting I told him about my conversation with Nixon, and we both agreed he would probably be elected president of the new organization, though neither of us was absolutely certain. When we got to Mount Zion AME Zion church, we were pleased to see a large crowd. The success of our boycott that morning had given people hope, and Mrs. Parks's trial had rekindled their anger. On the other hand, too many speakers could kill the meeting before anything constructive was accomplished. When we got inside we saw literally hundreds of people jammed into the pews.

Reverend Bennett called the meeting to order, and I was certain that it would be Friday night all over again. Then something happened that eventually proved fortuitous. In the back of the church someone shouted, "Don't say anything! A stool pigeon just came in the door." Instantly the room grew still. One of the known Uncle Toms was seated in the rear. Those of us who were recognized leaders were called to the front; where we huddled, trying to decide what to do next. Although our entire plan would be public in a few days, we wanted a couple of our moves to be a surprise to the white establishment. Some of our people could be cowed by economic threats and a few extra patrol cars cruising the black neighborhoods.

Finally Mrs. Erna Dungee spoke up, suggesting that a group be delegated to meet in private, acting as a steering committee. We put the matter to a vote of everyone present, and eighteen people were chosen to represent the body as a whole. Those of us who were elected decided to meet upstairs in the pastor's office, where we would plan initial strategy and then spread the word to the rest of the black community. As we trooped up the stairs, Bennett was ahead of me, and I stopped him on the first landing.

"We've got all the stuff down on paper," I whispered. "Call on me first."

He nodded and proceeded up the stairs ahead of me.

After we had dragged in enough chairs to accommodate most of the group, Bennett called the meeting to order, and I raised my hand.

"The chair recognizes Brother Abernathy," he said.

I stood up and told the assembled group that several of us had been talking about the need for a new organization to represent the black community during the current crisis. I said we had talked among ourselves for the past several days and had come up with a structure and a plan of action for the immediate future. I reminded them of the success of the boycott and pointed out that because we had been able to act together we were on the verge of an important victory. For that reason, I said, we needed an organization that would unify our own people and let the whites know that this time we really meant business.

Then I turned the meeting over to Reverend French and asked him to read what we had composed that morning in his office. First he read our list of demands and then outlined our strategy for achieving victory, including the extension of the boycott and the establishment of an organization. When he finished and sat down there was silence except for a few words of approval from around the room.

Then Bennett moved that we adopt the plan as presented, including the new organization, precisely as I had outlined it. Someone seconded the motion and it passed without a dissenting vote.

Immediately the question was raised: What should we call the new group? While others were arguing over the matter, I was coming up with a name of my own, one that would not only have the right meaning but also the right connotations. I immediately rejected any word that limited membership to the black community. We knew there were whites who shared our hopes for a freer, more open society and I wanted our organization to be for them as well as for us—at least in principle. I wanted "Montgomery" in the title to imply that it was a group for all the city.

Next came the question of its aims. Would it be formed merely to address the current bus crisis? Would it be a group that dealt with broader racial issues—and nothing else? Or would it be better not to limit the organization's activities by its name? The last line of reasoning seemed best to me, so I thought of the word "improvement," to give it the broadest range of options possible.

Finally, how should the organization be structured? Would

it be a "committee" or a "union" or what? Being a Baptist, I always liked names that suggested a loose and voluntary arrangement, where each congregation (or person) could participate without surrendering any autonomy or freedom. I didn't want a Methodist name. So I thought about calling it an "association."

Just as they were moving to postpone the naming of the organization, I came out with it: the Montgomery Improvement Association. Everyone paused, thought about it for a moment, and agreed that it would serve quite well. So we became the Montgomery Improvement Association (MIA) by unanimous vote.

The next order of business was the election of officers, and under parliamentary law the floor should have been opened for nominations. I fully expected both Lewis and Nixon to be nominated and then the nominations to be closed, but Lewis had apparently made some plans of his own. Opposed to Nixon, he wasn't sure whether or not he himself had the votes, so he proposed a compromise candidate by way of a motion rather than a nomination. His choice took me by surprise.

"I would like to move that we elect Reverend Martin Luther King as our president," he said.

"Would you accept, Dr. King?" someone asked.

Martin hesitated for a moment, then answered quietly.

"Well, if you think I can render some service, I will."

I was stunned.

"Martin," I whispered. "I had no idea that you would accept. I would have nominated you myself."

He smiled and shrugged his shoulders, indicating he had no prior knowledge of Lewis's intentions. I looked over at Nixon. He was frowning. He must have thought we were all in it together. The vote was unanimous, and from that moment until the end of the meeting, Martin presided. We elected Rufus Lewis vice president, Nixon as treasurer, French as corresponding secretary, the Reverend U. J. Fields as recording secretary, and an executive committee of twenty-five members, including those of us present. I was elected program chairman. As it turned out, this structure meant that Martin and I did most of the work—he as the chief officer, I as the chief organizer of activities.

With a good organization in place and with Martin to head it, everyone felt a sudden surge of joy. Something important had happened in that room and we sensed it. We had come upstairs, confused and shaken by the idea that there was a traitor in our midst. We came down with a sense of dedication and unity. We had been together in the Upper Room and we were going into the world to do the Lord's work.

That evening I picked up Martin, and though we had thus far accomplished everything we'd set out to do, there was still one more question to answer: even though our people had stayed off the buses all day (we spotted fewer than ten), would they turn out in force tonight? We were certain most blacks knew about the meeting, and we knew many would come, but Holt Street Baptist Church held one thousand people, and even if five hundred showed, people would still say the meeting was a failure, since we didn't fill up the church.

As we drove through the darkened streets we told each other the people would turn out, but we didn't really believe it. About five blocks away from the church we saw cars parked on both sides of the street; and when we were about three blocks away, the driveways and front yards were also filled up. First we thought it was a party, then Martin and I came to the same conclusion simultaneously—somebody extremely important had died, the head deacon or the preacher himself.

I turned at the next corner and drove away from the church until I finally found a space and parked. When we got out we heard the first sound—a low growl somewhere in the distance. It took a moment before we realized that what we heard was a huge crowd of people, not shouting or cheering the way they do in a football stadium, but talking among themselves. I think at that moment, I realized what it was, and I felt my spine tingle.

When we rounded the last corner we saw them, milling in the dark shadows of the overhanging oaks—hordes of people, a whole army of them, more people than I had ever seen in my life. As my eyes scanned the horizon in both directions all I saw was the crowd. It seemed to spill into the next neighborhood on all sides. The church yard was literally too small to contain them all. Someone who made an effort to count them said there were more than four thousand in the church yard and another thousand inside.

I heard Martin mutter something under his breath, an expression of surprise. As we approached someone saw us and called out, then they all turned toward us and began to make a pathway for us to pass through.

Then the crowd started applauding, politely at first, then louder and louder. Finally they were applauding wildly and cheering. The mayor and his two commissioners must have heard that whoop clear over on the other side of town. When we entered the church the noise was magnified ten times. They were crying out of a sense of newfound freedom, not cheering us so much as cheering themselves for what they had done that day, what we had all done. I don't think I have ever heard a more joyous sound in my life, and as I looked over at Martin I knew he felt the same extraordinary sense of unity among our people. At that moment we both knew that we were on the brink of a great victory, though how great and how costly we could not at that moment have imagined.

The crowd applauded and cheered for fifteen minutes. We stood there, smiling and waving, then Martin signaled for order. But a lifetime of pent-up emotions had been released and the people were enjoying their newfound freedom. So we waited until the crowd had finally shouted and screamed enough. Then, as presiding officer, I motioned for them to be seated. At that moment complete silence settled on the church, and outside the loud mumbling also ceased. You could have heard a dog bark on the other side of town.

Then I called for Gladys Black, the outstanding minister of music at Holt Street Church, to lead us in "What a Fellowship, What a Joy Divine," which became the first hymn to be used in the new movement. Everyone knew it by heart, and since it had no revolutionary overtones, we could always sing it publicly without fear of suspicion or criticism. So the crowd rocked the rafters.

At some point—probably when they saw the size of the crowd—Reverends Powell and Huffman, who had told me they were too ill to read the lesson and lead us in prayer, experienced miraculous cures. The scales fell from Powell's eyes and he was able to open the meeting with a lengthy reading of the scripture. Huffman's laryngitis had disappeared and he was able to recite a long and remarkably resonant prayer. These were the first of many miracles that would occur over the next fifteen years, the proof that God helps those who have the will and courage to help themselves.

Then, because I was better known, I introduced Martin to the crowd, and he stepped forward and began to speak. He recited the now familiar story of Mrs. Parks's arrest. Then he explained what had happened at the afternoon meeting—the formation of the new organization and its slate of officers. Again spontaneous applause and shouting broke out, and we could hear the crowd outside joining in, even though few could under-stand every word over the primitive loudspeaker system that Reverend Wilson had hurriedly put in place. In a few weeks there would be many more audiences like this one outside, all over the country, not physically present in the churches where we held our mass meetings and demonstrations but cheering us on just the same as they heard the words over radios or occasionally saw our black-and-white images on television screens.

What happened after Martin had finished his report about the afternoon meeting was crucial to the success of the Montgomery bus boycott and, on a larger scale, the civil rights movement itself: After talking about the new developments in the Supreme Court, developments that would soon pave the way for racial equality, he began to explain in careful detail the theory of nonviolent protest. I'm sure no white person in Montgomery that night could have dreamed that a thousand blacks—many of them uneducated, some illiterate—were sitting quietly in a church while one of their preachers lectured to them on Henry David

Thoreau and Mahatma Gandhi. Yet that is precisely what Martin did—and at some length.

That lesson was crucial. We were asking these people to go into the streets and to accept whatever punishment the white community had to offer, whether jail or beating or death; and we were asking them to take this risk *without ever raising a hand in their own defense.* So it was only fair that they understand thoroughly why they were being asked to do something so contrary to human nature. The success of this strategy depended on every single person in the black community reacting in precisely the same way. If one small group (or even a single individual) struck back with fist or club or gun then we would lose the moral advantage we were striving to achieve. It was absolutely essential that the decent people in the community, as well as in the nation at large, see Jim Crow for what it really was—an oppressive system maintained by the persistent threat of violence. It was that violence we wanted to expose. For only when it came out from behind the mask of legalism and respectability could people of good will fully understand our predicament and act to free us. This is the lesson Martin taught that night.

To be more precise, that is the lesson he *began* to teach, because nonviolence wasn't just a technique you learned in a single evening. It was a habit of mind, a way of life that had to be learned slowly and thoroughly. It was not just one lesson but an entire curriculum, and this was the first of many lectures that Martin gave to these same people—at least twice a week for the next year, and sometimes three and four times a week. Later we introduced Saturday workshops in nonviolence during which people would undergo simulated attacks, both verbal and physical, learning how to be silent in the face of shouts of abuse and how to fall limp in the arms of arresting policemen. These workshops became a regular part of our training programs in Birmingham, Selma, Chicago, and Mississippi. It was the philosophical groundwork for these workshops that Martin began to lay on that very first night.

Unbeknownst to us, we were also creating the format for later meetings. After Martin had finished with his speech on nonviolence, I stepped forward to read a resolution calling for all blacks to stay off the buses until the white establishment had acceded to our demands. Now the chips were on the table. We were asking them to suffer substantial inconvenience in order to bring about a modest change in procedures and had they chosen to balk, we would have closed down the show and gone home.

But of course that didn't happen. When I asked them if they supported the resolution, they came to their feet, shouting their willingness to go forward with the plan. It was a glorious moment, the single instant in which we knew they had committed themselves wholeheartedly to our leadership. Although from time to time they experienced doubts and faltered briefly, they never really turned from the purpose to which they committed themselves that night. And in the final analysis, it was their commitment that ensured our final victory.

This first meeting was so successful that we repeated the same format in future rallies, both in Montgomery and elsewhere. We would begin with scripture, prayer, and perhaps a hymn. Then Martin would talk about the abuses we were facing, the remedies we proposed, and the way in which nonviolent protest would accomplish our ends. Usually other leaders would follow Martin in saying a few words. Sometimes we would have a guest "pep speaker" from another city. But I would almost always close out the meeting with a plea to "stay off the buses" or "meet at such-and-such a church" or "be sure not to resist when you are arrested"—whatever practical advice was needed to put the current plan into operation. So the meeting would begin with the enunciation of principles and broad strategy and would end with attention to particular tactics. As program chairman, I was in charge of tactics.

We closed the meeting that night with a rousing hymn, and the huge church trembled from the vibrations. Later I wondered what the white sheriff's deputies must have thought, parked a block away, hunched down in their cars, ordered to report everything they saw and heard. The sight of five thousand blacks in attendance must have impressed them, but the sound of our cheers and singing must have unnerved them even more.

The only question left to answer, both for them and for us, was: How long could we keep it up?

*   *   *

The next day Martin met with the press and made our position quite clear. We would end the boycott only when our demands were granted, which were reasonable and should pose no problems for local authorities.

"We are not asking for an end to segregation. That's a matter for the legislature and the courts," he was quoted as saying. "We feel that we have a plan within the law. All we are seeking is justice and fair treatment in riding the buses. We don't like the idea of Negroes having to stand when there are vacant seats. We are demanding justice on that point."

It is important to note the modest nature of our demands and the reasonable tone in which they were spoken. At this stage we were not breaking current law, at least not to our knowledge. (Later an obscure labor statute would be used to intimidate us.) In fact, we were merely calling for "justice" under current law, which prescribed that we could not be driven from our seats unless other places were available. We were not even asking that the buses be desegregated—only that a more acceptable form of segregation be adopted, one used throughout the state and region.

After the first month, the struggle ceased to be a series of attacks and counterattacks and became trench warfare—a prolonged confrontation that required a special kind of character in order to survive and achieve victory. For Martin and me it meant the daily revitalizing of our people's will to stay off the city buses and—despite the inconvenience—to make alternative arrangements to get to work. At the beginning this was an easier task because Mrs. Parks's case was fresh in everybody's mind and because it was something of an adventure. In addition, the national press gave us increasing attention. We saw the story of our struggle move to the front page of the *New York Times,* and after that to the front pages of newspapers throughout the country. As long as we were a major item it was easy to hold our ranks and continue to march to and from work every morning and every night.

But very soon the press lost interest in our daily routine. A story with no new developments is no story at all. And when our struggle was not being carried on the Associated Press wires, the nation forgot about us. The torrent of telegrams and letters slowed to a trickle and then stopped altogether. It became increasingly difficult for us to keep our people's spirits from flagging, even with Sunday sermons and Wednesday prayers. With daily urging by local whites to give up the struggle, some blacks were longing to return to the peace of years gone by, even if it was a peace without dignity or hope. As days became weeks, morale was more and more the central concern of the black leadership.

By the same token, the white leadership was not having an easy time either. The bus line was losing money and one route after another was dropped in order to cut losses to a minimum. The parent company in Chicago was unhappy, and they blamed the local politicians for an unmanageable mess that the Cook County machine would never have permitted.

As for the white politicians, in their frustration they were beginning to go for one another's throats. The more reasonable among them, not a large group, were pushing for an accommodation with us, one that would give us some of what we wanted. The racist-populist element was hoping to ride to power on a new surge of anti-black sentiment, a viewpoint already being exploited by citizens councils throughout the South. Several politicians were leading the Alabama Citizens Council, and while their public statements were politely and peaceably racist, in private most were saying that they were prepared, if necessary, to use violence, just as their fathers and grandfathers had done to keep us in our place.

Knowing that such people historically resorted to terrorism when they couldn't get what they wanted by legitimate means, we took special care to emphasize the fact that our protests would be peaceful and nonviolent. If we were to win we would have to gain the sympathy of the nation by exemplifying the Christian principles we professed, even if it meant being reviled, beaten, and possibly killed. In carrying this message to our people, Martin and I made a good team.

As his speech at the Holt Street Baptist Church revealed, he was a student of history who had made a careful study of civil disobedience, particularly as preached and practiced by Mahatma Gandhi. Martin could explain the theory of civil disobedience to our people in terms they could understand, and these explanations were crucial to our movement, since you can't expect people to undergo pain and humiliation without having very good reasons to justify such suffering. Martin supplied those reasons with clarity and authority, and during the months that followed, no one forgot what he had taught.

On the other hand, at that time I was more experienced and pragmatic in addressing crowds. It wasn't enough for our people merely to know how they should behave and why. Knowing something and having the strength to put it into practice are two entirely different matters. While Martin's task was to teach them, mine was to move them to act—or rather not to act—in accordance with those principles. So at each meeting I would take the pulpit to whip them into a fervor, exhorting them to remain true to our cause—to stay off the buses, to endure whatever abuses the white community had to offer, to outlast the enemy. Martin would speak earlier in the program; I would speak last so the assembled crowd would go out the door singing and shouting, full of resolve to hold firm till we got what we wanted.

But in addition to these speeches, as I mentioned, we also decided to hold workshops in nonviolent protesting, just to make certain that our people were prepared for any indignity the white community might have in store for us, including physical violence. Consequently, we instituted "dress rehearsals" for just such an occasion, knowing that when people are smote on one cheek the natural tendency is not to turn the other cheek but to smite back. We wanted to drill our people so thoroughly in the philosophy and techniques of nonviolence that when they were attacked their instinctive reaction would be to protect themselves as effectively as possible without lashing out at the enemy— which in all probability would be the law.

The workshops were held on Saturdays in one of the churches (frequently in First Baptist). Martin and I were usually the instructors, though from time to time others were invited to

join us (e.g., Glenn E. Smiley from the Fellowship of Reconciliation). We planned this training very carefully, utilizing the chief
virtues of our people, which were a deep, abiding faith and an
almost infinite supply of patience.

Both of these qualities had long been recognized by the
white community, and the leadership had taken advantage of
them in the institution and maintenance of a Jim Crow society.
Our faith in the promise of Heaven had made us less concerned
about our lot in this imperfect world, and because patient
suffering was commended in the Bible, we suffered patiently the
indignities of white supremacy and enforced segregation.

But genuine virtues are strengths rather than weaknesses,
and we realized that these same qualities could be employed to
defeat the very people who had used our Christian submissive-
ness against us. Faith in God's justice and mercy could help us
endure even greater suffering that we had previously experienced. Our patience, strengthened by years of trial, was strong
enough to live through the long night that lay before us. The
white people thought they could wait us out. We were more
practiced in waiting than they were. We could endure their anger
and their violence—if we truly believed we were doing God's will.

We talked to our people a great deal about the power of
redemptive suffering. To suffer, we reminded them, was the
experience most typical of the life of Jesus. He suffered the
indignities of persecution by secular authority and eventually He
suffered the humiliation and final agony of the Cross. We too
could suffer, and in so doing share His martyrdom and rejoice in
His resurrection. Whatever happened to us would happen to
Him. If we were killed, our blood would cry out from the earth for
justice.

But in addition to the theology of suffering, we also had to
teach them the techniques of survival. At some point we would be
arrested and perhaps even physically assaulted. If we endured to
the point where the boycott successfully threatened the survival
of public transportation in Montgomery, we figured that the
white leadership would abandon their pose of calm deliberation
and try to intimidate us physically. We even warned our people
that someone might be killed. We showed them what to do in

specific instances of abuse or violence. For example, we taught them Bible quotations to use when they were accosted and verbally abused. Martin and I would yell and scream at them, then listen as they replied in a quiet and dignified manner, usually with a quotation from Jesus familiar to most church-going whites. Others watched, then took their turn in enduring and replying to verbal taunts.

Assuming that one day we again would be riding the buses, dealing with the same mean-spirited drivers, we rehearsed them in what to say when they dropped their dime on the floor and the driver shouted obscenities, as had often been the case. Our suggested response: "Mr. Driver, I'll pray for you." (Years later in Georgia, one bus driver, after hearing that line, would snarl back: "I don't want any of you niggers praying for me. A few years back y'all prayed for Ole Gene Talmadge and he died.")

Though we knew that our people could follow the path of nonviolence while in control of themselves, we also knew that in moments of sudden anger almost anybody could be tempted to strike back—and one injured policeman prominently displayed could nullify the work of weeks. So we took particular care to teach our people to count to ten before they responded in any way to verbal or physical abuse.

We also showed them how to march along bent over, elbows guarding their stomachs and hands covering their ears and temples. We devised this technique for use in the event that we were bombarded with flying rocks and bottles while demonstrating. We also taught a modified version of the same maneuver for use while being beaten with fists or billy clubs.

Then, too, we told everyone to go limp when anyone laid hands on them during an arrest. In the first place, it signaled to the arresting officer that he would encounter no active resistance; hence there was no need for excessive force. But equally important, a limp body was harder to handle, took more time to haul into a paddywagon, and therefore limited the efficiency of the police. In fact, over the years, this technique probably saved us enormous sums of money since it reduced significantly the number of bail bonds we had to pay.

It is surprising how many of the situations we would later

face were actually anticipated and discussed in these Saturday workshops. By the time we reached the end of our years together, Martin and I had seen people assaulted with fists, clubs, bottles, and rocks and were moved by the manner in which they endured such abuse. Almost without exception they behaved exactly as we had taught them to behave. They protected themselves from the full force of blows, but they didn't strike back, even when their lives were endangered; and for the most part they replied with courtesy and charity.

Of course, we didn't anticipate everything in our workshops. Later, when Eugene "Bull" Connor set the dogs on us in Birmingham, we were unprepared. There was really no way we could have protected ourselves, if they had been turned loose. All we could do was pray and continue to move forward. There was also little we could do about the hoses. But other than these two techniques—so discredited at Birmingham that they were never again used against us—we had prepared ourselves for the entire obstacle course right there in Montgomery.

For a while the white establishment bided its time, assuming that eventually we would weary of the daily chore of walking to work and come trudging by twos and threes back to the bus line. We worried about that possibility as well, and very early in the game we decided to create our own transportation system.

We immediately organized a car pool to help those people in the greatest need—those who lived a great distance from town and who could walk to work and to shop only with great difficulty. Soon we established regular pick-up stops, where people could stand and be certain that when another black drove past, he or she would stop and take on passengers. Later, when we began to receive contributions from around the country, we decided to buy a fleet of station wagons, enough so that each church could have one. Then we would run a free service for all who needed a ride. We would establish regular routes with a regular schedule and then adapt to special needs and circumstances. Our ultimate goal: That no one in the black community should suffer because of the boycott.

It took us a while to collect enough money, but we made our needs known to blacks and sympathetic whites throughout the nation and, in a shorter time than we could have hoped, we had gathered enough to buy the wagons. Each church had a different color. Ours was red, because that was my favorite.

Needless to say, when the whites saw us inaugurate our free service, they were infuriated. It was something they hadn't anticipated, if for no other reason than because of the expense involved. They were used to seeing blacks driving around in ten-year-old Buicks, not in brand-new Ford wagons. For several weeks they fumed.

Their morale was further weakened by the report of the bus company after the first of the year: they were losing twenty-two cents per mile under current conditions, even with routes curtailed or eliminated. At that rate they would soon be out of business. With no relief in sight, they asked for an increase in the fare—from ten to twenty cents. That amount seems paltry by today's standards, but in 1956 it was not an irrelevant sum to people living on marginal incomes, white as well as black. And since by then the boycott was virtually 100 percent effective, that meant the increase in fare was going to be borne by whites.

At this point things turned ugly. We began to get threatening phone calls, many of them obscene. Virtually every one of MIA's known leaders received such calls; and no matter how often you told your wife that anyone making anonymous threats would be too cowardly to carry them out, you never quite convinced her or yourself. You knew that in the past blacks had been gunned down from cover of darkness or else dragged to obscure wooded areas by masked men and then lynched. So violence was always a very real possibility, even when your demands were modest and expressed in the most moderate of terms.

For a long while our meetings were routine. On Mondays and Thursdays we had our pep meetings at which we would have a speaker, usually from Montgomery, sometimes from out of town. Then on Friday nights and Saturday mornings we would hold workshops in which we would train our people in nonviolent techniques. On Sundays and Wednesday nights we would have regular church meetings, and on Tuesdays we would try to spend some time with our families, though often enough Martin and I would have to meet with one of the officers or committees to plan some upcoming event. All of this was tiring, but it soon became routine. When we wanted to know what was scheduled for the evening we simply had to remember what day it was. Then one night, January 30, 1956, the routine was suddenly, frighteningly broken.

We were holding a mass meeting at the First Baptist Church, and Martin was in the pulpit, entreating the assembled crowd to stay off the buses and to maintain peace and order in the face of growing pressure on the black community. He had just begun to hit his stride when I noticed a young man enter the rear of the church, look straight at me, and then signal with his hand. His name was Roscoe Williams and I could tell by his face that something was wrong.

He made his way down the side aisle and I moved quietly to the edge of the platform and bent over in order to hear what he had to say. Martin, who didn't notice the slight disturbance, went on with his speech.

"Somebody bombed Reverend King's house," he whispered.

"Bombed his house? Is anybody hurt?"

"We don't know," he said. "My wife was staying with Mrs. King. I've got to get over there immediately. How do you want to handle it with Dr. King?"

"Take three or four men with you and get on over there. See if everybody is all right. Be as inconspicuous as possible, but hurry. I won't tell him anything until you come back."

The parsonage was only about five minutes away, but I sat there in agony, watching Martin preaching his message of love and defiance, never dreaming that he was about to face a stern test of the faith he was trying to instill in others. I kept glancing at my watch, and after what seemed an hour I saw Roscoe coming back down the aisle. I couldn't tell from his expression whether or not everything was all right.

"They're all right," he said. "Both the women and the little baby. The house is OK too, except for one window. They threw the bomb up on the porch, but just barely. Nobody's even hurt."

He broke into a broad grin.

Suddenly I was aware that a silence had settled over the church. I looked up and Martin had paused. I could see in his eyes that he knew something was wrong. So I joined him at the pulpit and addressed the assembled people.

"The home of Dr. King has just been bombed. I want you to know, Dr. King, that your wife and daughter and Mrs. Williams are safe. And according to Mr. Roscoe Williams the house has sustained very little damage."

Martin kept his composure, and when I had finished he took over again.

"I have to go home now," he said, "but before I go I want to say something to everybody here tonight about nonviolence. The time has come when we will have to test our faith and our dedication to this principle. We cannot win this battle if we respond to violence by retaliating. I want you to go home and decide for yourselves if you really believe that the most powerful force in the universe is on our side. An eye for an eye and a tooth for a tooth will only end up in a blind generation and a toothless people."

Then he left, and many left with him, though the meeting had not yet been concluded. They followed him over to his house and when he arrived home there were hundreds, perhaps thousands of black people there, all having come to protect him and to demonstrate unity in the face of this attack. With such a gathering present he felt he needed to speak to them, so he stood on his damaged front porch and delivered an eloquent speech, quoting passages from the Sermon on the Mount, urging them to remain peaceful and to give thanks to God that no one was hurt. Later that scene would be shown on national television—the first of many such televised speeches during the course of his career in the public eye.

Meanwhile I was back in the First Baptist Church, winding up the meeting, where about three-fourths of our followers had remained. As soon as I had finished, I rushed over to the house to see for myself what I had already heard—that no one had been hurt.

As soon as I saw Coretta, Yoki, and Mary Lucy Williams, I

took off for home, worried about Juanita. When I got there I was relieved to see an undamaged house and a light in the window. Juanita came to the door, and as soon as I saw her I felt a great sense of relief. But we sat up most of the night with the lights off, staring out the window.

The next day we pondered what the reaction of the Montgomery establishment would be. As far as we could tell, there was no official action, except for the policeman at the scene of the bombing, who had told everyone to go home, that this was a police matter. No one was called in for questioning. No one was indicted. No one convicted. Mayor Gales and the commissioners seemed to take it all in stride, as if it were no more than an everyday occurrence.

The black population most affected by the boycott were the women who worked as domestic servants and they were also the ones whose relationship with the white community was most personal and intimate. Entire days were spent in the households of white families, performing a number of highly personal services. They would cook breakfast in the morning and wash the dishes and then clean the house. At noon they would prepare and serve lunch; in the early afternoons they would often hand wash and iron clothes; then in the late afternoon they would prepare the evening meal and serve it, always in a white uniform and white cap; and in the evenings some would even stay with children while the white couple went to a party or movie.

In an earlier time they often lived in the garage apartment and were on call twenty-four hours a day. By the 1950s, however, almost all of them lived in their own homes and worked five or five-and-a-half days a week, with Wednesday afternoon and all day Sunday off. They were the mainstays of the white households, and many white women had to come to regard them as a necessity of life. So when black house servants started coming in later every morning, white women began to feel the earth beneath them tremble just a little.

The miracle of this period was how little the relationship

changed between most whites and blacks, how calm and civil everyone remained. Our quarrel was not with the white race but with the city officials and the bus company, and most white people understood this distinction and did not attempt to retaliate against individual blacks because of our political quarrel with the establishment.

Of course we all knew who elected the mayor and the commissioners and, had we analyzed the situation in any detail, we might well have a felt a resentment against the entire white community; but it was precisely that kind of attitude that we were deploring and we guarded against it throughout the years. I can confidently say that no group of which Martin Luther King and I were members ever let their disapproval of unjust laws and social institutions turn into racial hatred.

So as difficult as it may be for some people to believe, Montgomery was a relatively friendly place during the year of the bus boycott. White firms continued to do business with the same black customers. Black employees continued at their jobs with white employees. Two or three nights a week we held some kind of rally to mobilize the black community against Jim Crow. In retrospect it seems like the oddest society that human beings ever invented.

But while most white people and black people got along fine in their day-to-day relationships, white officials, particularly those at the state level, were harsh and vindictive. For example, Dr. L. D. Reddick, a professor at Alabama State, caught the eye of John Patterson, the newly elected governor. Patterson called Dr. Trenholm, president of the college, and told him to fire Reddick before sundown. Dr. Trenholm whom I so admired, had to obey, though he was outraged at such an order. Then Trenholm was summoned before a committee of the state legislature, where he was treated like a boy, though he was an elderly man of great dignity and character. Those supporters who witnessed his humiliation could hardly bear to remain through the cross-examination.

And Dr. Reddick wasn't the only casualty. Robert Williams, our driver, who was choirmaster at the college was fired at the end of the year, though he was one of the finest musicians

Alabama State ever had. Again, his sin was his association with the leaders of the boycott.

Jo Ann Robinson also left; while I never knew for sure if it was because of her activism, I assumed that it was. More than any other faculty member, she helped to bring about the boycott. She was in it from the beginning; and while the rest of us tried to keep her activities as cloaked as possible, obviously the white establishment found out the importance of her role.

Early in January, a letter appeared in the *Montgomery Advertiser* arguing that our action was a violation of an anti-boycott statute passed many years ago to cover an entirely different kind of activity. The law was clearly drafted to forbid what is now called a "secondary boycott"—that is, an action taken against a company not directly involved in a labor dispute in order to influence a company directly involved. Under this law, if workers are striking against a trucking company, they are not allowed to boycott the independent gasoline company supplying the trucks in order to bring additional pressure to bear on the truckers. Clearly such a law was enacted to cover that specific kind of case, and no one could reasonably construe it to apply to what we were doing, where the object of our boycott was the offending company itself. But those who applied the law in Alabama were not reasonable. So when the letter appeared, written by a Montgomery attorney, we got together and tried to determine whether or not we thought they might prosecute us.

"The law doesn't really apply here," said Fred Gray, "but . . ."

"But they are likely to prosecute us anyway," I said.

"That's right," said Fred. "They could certainly arrest the leadership and anyone else participating in a public demonstration supporting the boycott."

"And that would mean large amounts of bail, fines, and then legal costs while the case was on appeal," said Martin.

We talked about it some more, but we kept coming back to the same brutal truth: With the machinery of the law in their control, the white establishment could make our movement so costly that we might eventually have to give up the struggle or else spend a good portion of our lives in jail. That day as we talked about it in Fred's office, we saw the problem in purely theoretical terms, but as our struggle developed we would see that everything we feared in discussing the possibility of that first arrest would come to pass.

We would indeed be arrested not just once, but many times in the next few years. Often the charges would be patently flimsy or unconstitutional, but local authorities would make them just the same, knowing that we would have to suffer the indignities of jail before we could post bond. And bond money would be the single most pressing need over the years, since in some cases those incarcerated numbered in the thousands and the bail per person ran in the hundreds. Much of our fund raising in the black communities of the North took place while Martin and I were behind bars in some southern jail, waiting for enough hats to be passed to buy us out.

In Montgomery we couldn't have imagined the road ahead, but we did see that the invocation of the anti-boycott statute could have devastating financial repercussions, so we decided to try to avoid arrest if at all possible.

"How about calling it something else besides a boycott?" I suggested.

"It might work," said Fred. "What would you call it?"

We finally agreed that "protest" would be the best term, so at our workshops and pep meetings we passed the word: "We're not staging a 'boycott,' we're staging a 'protest.' "

Everyone tried to change the language, but they had been saying "boycott" too long, and even those of us addressing the crowd would forget and use the old, illegal word. Still, we had a defense if they arrested us, one as specious as the charge itself. And for a while we thought we might get away with it. Then the ax fell.

Martin was out of town that morning when I heard the doorbell ring. Juanita answered the door and I was a little surprised to hear the voice of the Reverend Abraham Huffman greeting her. He was a pleasant, friendly fellow, but he wasn't a usual visitor. He had a page of yesterday evening's newspaper in his hand.

"Haven't you seen this?" he asked, holding up the page as I came into the room.

"No, I haven't," I said. "What does it say?"

"It's a list of people who are going to be arrested today for violating the anti-boycott law. I'm sorry to report that your name is on it."

Juanita looked at me with sudden apprehension and I felt a little weak in the knees. I had never in my life been arrested, nor had any member of my family; and though we had discussed the distinct possibility that this moment might arrive, I wasn't really prepared for it, nor was Juanita.

"Is your name on the list?" I asked him.

"No," he said, "and I'm grateful, but I thought we might pray together before they come for you."

I nodded and motioned for him to come into the back room. Juanita followed. We knelt down and Reverend Huffman began to pray. While he was still praying the doorbell rang again. Juanita got up and went to answer it.

"Ralph," she called. "It's someone from the sheriff's office."

I could tell from the strain in her voice that they had come for me.

"Is Preacher Abernathy here?" a man's voice said.

I went up to the front room, and the deputy was standing there, a huge tow-headed man with a grim look on his face.

"Abernathy, Ralph D.?" he said.

"Yes," I replied.

"You are under arrest," he said.

"Just a minute, please," I said. Then I went back to the back room and prayed one more fervent prayer that I be given strength to endure the terrible humiliation facing me. As I did so I could almost see my parents' sorrowful faces watching me, full of disapproval. I had been taught that the law was next to God in its claim on my conscience and that there was almost nothing worse than a jailbird.

Abraham Huffman shared my distress as I got to my feet and began to gather my things together: toothbrush, toothpaste, shaving gear. When I was ready, Huffman and Juanita followed me to the door, and I turned and kissed her goodbye and Reverend Huffman patted me on the shoulder.

"I'll pray for you," he said.

At that moment the deputy sheriff turned to him.

"And what is your name?" he asked.

"Abraham Huffman."

The deputy pulled out a large piece of paper and ran his finger down it. Then he nodded.

"You're on the list too," he said.

Huffman looked at me wildly. Then he turned to the deputy.

"Man, what are you talking about? I just came by here to see Reverend Abernathy. How come you are arresting me."

"Because your name is right here," said the deputy, pointing to the piece of paper.

"Man, I don't even have my toothbrush," said Huffman.

"Too bad," the deputy sheriff said.

So I had company all the way down to the jailhouse.

It turned out that everybody who was anybody in the black community had been arrested that day. Every pastor in town, every prominent businessman, every doctor and lawyer. Even Rev. M. C. Cleveland, aging pastor of the Day Street Baptist Church, was there, a man so upright and so cautious that he had never attended a single one of our mass meetings, much less advocated a boycott. He was the epitome of prudence and conformity, yet there he was, sitting forlornly in the jailhouse, signing a piece of paper, his fingertips blue with ink. Cleveland's arrest gave the lie to the whole procedure. No one in Montgomery, black or white, could have believed he deserved to be there—a man who paid lip service to Jim Crow and bobbed his head when the white people called him "Uncle."

There were so many of us they didn't even bother to put us in cells. They just took our picture and our fingerprints and then released us on our own recognizance. My prayer was heard—my initiation into the mysteries of arrest had been gentle enough. In later years it would be otherwise. I would be manhandled, attacked by dogs and water hoses, beaten, literally thrown into paddywagons, and kept for weeks and weeks. Eventually I would see the inside of jails all over the country, so many that I could almost have written a guidebook to the jails of the Southeast.

Somehow, after that first arrest, the others came a little easier. I never again worried about what my mother and father might have thought, not with the excellent company I always kept during those years—the best and most highly respected members of the black community.

The next morning Martin returned from his trip and I told him what had happened. "Well, I guess I had better go down and check in," he said, so I drove him down to the jailhouse and he went through the same routine. All in all, there were more than one hundred of us booked, and we were "true billed" by the grand jury. But we never came to trial: These senseless arrests outraged the nation, and for the first time Montgomery began to feel the pressure other cities were to feel later when they found themselves in the civil rights spotlight. At some point they must have concluded that a mass trial would play badly to the national audience, so they simply allowed the whole matter to drag on until everyone forgot about it.

I don't know precisely when we realized that what we were doing in Montgomery was the beginning of a genuine and important movement. In our daily conversations about the plight of our people, Martin, Coretta, Juanita, and I always talked about a time when we could form a nationwide organization to eliminate Jim Crow and usher in a new era of freedom. But we always thought in terms of a more distant future. In fact, at first we regarded the Montgomery bus boycott as an interruption of our plans rather than as the beginning of their fulfillment.

Neither one of us believed he was ready to lead a national crusade. Martin wanted a few more years of experience in the pulpit. I wanted a Ph.D. Both of us believed that because we were still in our twenties, we did not have the maturity necessary to confront the formidable white leadership arrayed against us in every state capitol and county courthouse in the South. We were two young and inexperienced black preachers in an old and cynical society—and we knew it.

But events began to change our perspective. In the first place, after months of confrontation we were still alive, a fact that never ceased to impress us. Literally hundreds of blacks in Alabama had been lynched or executed over the years for far less effrontery than we had committed. Yet we had survived with little more than threats and legal harassment. The more we thought about it, the more we realized why: We had organized our own army of believers and the white establishment was afraid of us in a way they had never been before. It's easy to grab one or two men and string them up on the nearest lamppost—provided there are fifty or seventy-five in on it. But you can't lynch five thousand people, and that's how many we could bring together on a good night.

Then, too, we had supporters throughout the nation—not just black people, but white people as well. Since the end of World War II, the nation as a whole had become increasingly impatient with the South's deviant behavior. The United States was embarrassed in the world community, which had become increasingly important; and the idea of equality, which had been a justification for much of the New Deal, was taken more and more seriously by Americans as a whole.

Most important of all, perhaps, was the role television was playing in the growing unrest over racial discrimination. Words accomplish only so much. Photographs move people more readily, and moving pictures on a screen are even more emotionally provocative. Without television I doubt that we could have escalated the Montgomery boycott into the American civil rights movement. With nightly films of atrocities and occasionally even live reports, our opportunities were significantly enlarged.

At some point we began to realize that if we won in Montgomery—and we believed that eventually we would—then we would perhaps have an obligation to help others do the same thing in other places, though at first we didn't conceive of ourselves as leading every march or demonstration. We weren't particularly anxious to think about such matters until after the boycott was settled and we had won a complete victory. Only when the U.S. Supreme Court made its final decision would our thoughts really turn to the future.

But before that happened, December 5, 1956, loomed on the horizon—a year from the day we had first begun our boycott. As far as we knew, no other organized boycott had ever lasted so long, and still the matter wasn't settled. So should we ignore the day or should we hold some kind of commemoration or celebration? We talked among ourselves and decided to celebrate.

After all, we had remained true to our pledge to one another and as a consequence had almost put the bus line out of business. Of course we had done so with great inconvenience and some risk, but we had stuck together, helped one another, sung together, prayed together, and become a stronger and more loving community as a result. So even though we had not yet won a final victory, we could still celebrate our own unity and courage.

We decided to hold a great gathering and invite the most famous and prestigious preacher we could find to speak at the occasion. We talked about the possibilities and finally settled on the Reverend Joseph H. Jackson, president of the National Baptist Convention, at that time composed of over 7,000,000 people, the largest organization of black people in the world.

Reverend Jackson, a well-known black leader in Chicago, was a powerful preacher. He was that rare performer who could render theological profundities in the popular idiom, and we believed that he would not only inspire our local followers to renew their resolve but would also attract a number of outside visitors to come to Montgomery for the occasion.

We invited Reverend Jackson and were pleased when he accepted our invitation. It was a glorious occasion and we were all moved to rededicate ourselves to the cause as we listened to his sermon, delivered at the First Baptist Church, where the National Baptist Convention, U.S.A., Inc., had been founded almost one hundred years earlier. Yet I have often wondered if the intensity and loyalty of our followers did not excite a certain amount of envy in him because shortly thereafter he turned on us and began to denounce us among black people.

Part of the problem arose from his own status in Chicago. In the first place, he was not only one of the most powerful black Baptist preachers in the city, but also president of his denomination's national convention—and there were those who said he was the most important black clergyman in the world. Yet more and more he saw the name of Martin Luther King in the newspapers and watched Martin's image on the television screen. It must have gnawed at him to realize that Martin had become in a year's time the most important black leader in the country, despite the fact that Martin operated in a small arena compared to Chicago.

But there was another factor involved as well. Jackson was one of the few black people in Chicago who could be called an insider. He was believed to be a part of the Daley machine, though not in the same overt way as black Congressman William Dawson. Jackson was a creator of order, one who, in a time of crisis, would step forward and tell his congregation and the black community at large that they must obey the law and accept the role the Daley machine had allotted them.

Jackson would clothe obedience to Mayor Daley's wishes in terms of religious duty, suggesting that submission to the status quo was what Jesus believed. Jackson wasn't the only black Chicago clergyman who performed this role, but he was certainly the most prestigious. He was worth his weight in gold to the mayor and his machine, but only if his message was unquestioningly accepted by Chicago's black community. Yet more and more Martin was telling the nation's black population that their duty was to challenge the establishment rather than submit to an unchristian and repressive regime.

So when people began to quote Martin back to him, Reverend Jackson would fume with anger and denounce what Martin had said. All too often Jackson would come away with the realization that he had lost the argument to a man a thousand miles away. Needless to say, he must have been increasingly beset as Martin's popularity grew and in so doing eclipsed Jackson, who was seen as a less and less reliable calmer of troubled waters.

Later we saw the depth of Reverend Jackson's animosity. In 1959 Martin and I sent in our registration forms and fees for the annual meeting of the National Baptist Convention. When we arrived, however, we were told that we would not be allowed to register. When we asked on whose authority, we were referred to the chairman of the Enrollment Committee, who told us that Reverend Jackson had ordered the committee to reject us.

"On what grounds?" we asked.

"Reverend Jackson didn't say," replied the chairman, his eyes on the floor as he spoke.

"Can we see Reverend Jackson?" we asked.

"I'm sorry," the chairman said. "That will be impossible."

Of course we stayed anyway, but since we hadn't registered, we couldn't vote. We were told by others, however, that Reverend Jackson was displeased with the civil rights movement and thought we were all troublemakers. Whatever his reasons, he incurred the anger of many younger clergymen who were beginning to encourage their own congregations to become active in the movement.

Over the next two years, he was constantly being quoted as opposed to such actions as nonviolent marches and sit-ins. Having anesthetized his community, he was now speaking to the rest of the country, including his native state of Mississippi. The last thing the movement needed was a man of Jackson's stature building a backfire.

Finally, in 1961 a group of people banded together to capture the convention and oust Jackson from the presidency of the National Baptist Convention. They planned a three-pronged attack. First, they put up a candidate to run against Jackson: the Reverend Gardner Taylor of Brooklyn, New York. Taylor, a younger man who represented the future, was an enthusiastic supporter of the civil rights movement and wanted to see the churches used to promote justice and freedom. Articulate and well educated, he agreed to run against Jackson, and Martin and I supported him, though we were in no way responsible for his candidacy.

In a bitter campaign, in which the entire Convention was polarized, Reverend Jackson defeated Taylor in the election for the presidency, though the vote was a lot closer than anyone had anticipated. Reverend Jackson was bitter over the very idea of

Taylor's candidacy and in part blamed us, believing that we were his enemies.

Yet we were not antagonistic toward him, even after he opposed us years later when we came to Chicago to try to end segregation in housing. At the time we thought he was wrong to support the Daley machine in its perpetuation of segregated neighborhoods and schools, but we didn't believe his opposition was in any way directed against us personally, even though we had heard that he blamed us for the trouble at the 1961 convention.

It was only after Martin died that I realized how small and vindictive he was. In a gesture of respect (and perhaps of penance) the City of Chicago renamed Park Avenue, calling it Martin Luther King, Jr., Drive. It was an appropriate street to choose since it wound down through the South Side and was the principal thoroughfare used by black Chicagoans. Everyone seemed to approve of the move—except for Reverend Joseph Jackson.

His great church fronted on Park Avenue and had done so from the beginning. But when the street was renamed he ordered the entrance moved around to 37th Street, just so he wouldn't have to see Martin's name printed on church stationery and his personal calling cards. So perhaps Reverend Jackson had the last word in an argument that only he regarded as personal.

Yet years earlier—in December of 1956—we invited him to come down to Montgomery and speak to us on the anniversary of our movement, and he came and preached an eloquent and appropriate sermon for the occasion. Others came as well— people of renown and influence—and the event was widely covered by the press, who saw in our confrontation one of the most dramatic and important stories of the year.

As I have already noted, one of the ways in which we sought to minimize the inconvenience to former bus riders was the establishment of a car pool, using the money sent in by supporters around the country to buy station wagons. Needless to say, the white establishment was furious with us, particularly when it became obvious that we were driving regular routes and daily moving literally hundreds of black people to and from their places of work.

The first thing they did to combat this stratagem was to arrest Martin as he was driving one of the scheduled routes. They accused him of speeding, though he couldn't have been exceeding the limit by more than a couple of miles per hour. Instead of simply giving him a ticket, they arrested him, took him down to the police station, fingerprinted him, and released him only after he posted bail. The story made the *New York Times,* though the reporter obviously didn't understand the real reason for the arrest.

Later, however, when it was obvious that further arrests would appear to be legal harassment, they went to the courts and sought help to put an end to our car pooling. A local judge issued a restraining order, forbidding us to continue our pick-ups and drop-offs while the case against us was heard. In effect, we were charged with setting up an illegal transportation system to compete with an already existent and duly franchised system.

This charge was absurd. It could have been leveled at every single arrangement set up among white mothers to transport children to dancing school, Little League teams, and Boy Scouts. The restraining order was, in our estimation, an abuse of judicial power; and Fred Gray immediately went to work to overturn it. In the meantime, however, we had to curtail our car pool, though we never completely shut down the operation.

In the end, the judge handed down a permanent injunction, forbidding us to resume the service. We couldn't believe it. Mercifully, it was in effect only a few days, because shortly thereafter the U.S. Supreme Court handed down a decision that pronounced segregation on public transportation a denial of equal protection under the law. At that point the injunction was moot, since our reasons for a massive car pool had vanished. We would be allowed to sit wherever we wanted to on the city buses, and on a first-come, first-served basis.

At that point, the next act of unofficial aggression occurred. The buses had begun to run again and sullen white bus drivers were allowing blacks to sit where they wanted to, though once the point was made no one in the black community was particularly interested in sitting next to white people or even in the front of the bus. As a matter of fact, many of them still went to the back of the bus as a matter of habit.

But on predominantly black routes, the bus was filled to the front with black riders, all able to sit down. For the first time, white men got on and had to stand while black men and women sat. Once the novelty wore off—in a matter of days—this way of doing things seemed as natural as the old way to all but a handful of people.

But there were a few people in the white community who simply couldn't live with the "defeat" they had suffered. Whether out of injured pride or anger or racial hatred or a combination of all three, someone decided to strike out in protest at what had been accomplished.

As usual they chose to hide behind a cloak of darkness. Early on Sunday morning less than a week after the Supreme Court's decision, the Kings were asleep when suddenly they heard a roar and the sound of splintering wood. Martin and Coretta awoke instantly, certain that their house had been bombed again. Cautiously he made his way to the front of the house and found the door splintered by a shotgun blast.

He started to call the police but thought better of it. If they came it would wake up the rest of the neighborhood and keep them up for another couple of hours. So he went back to bed, but slept fitfully. The next morning he called to tell me about it and then reported the incident to his congregation, saying prophetically: "It may be that some of us will have to die."

Later on that evening he told a meeting of our followers:

> I would like to tell whoever did it that it won't do any good to kill me. . . . We have just started our work. . . . We must have integrated schools . . . that is when our race will gain full equality. We cannot rest in Montgomery until every school is integrated.

But that wasn't the end of the violence. It was only the beginning. The malevolent eyes that had stared at the King house that Sunday morning were also watching the buses as they went up and down the streets with their new mixture of black and white passengers. Then, five days after the first attack, a second occurred, this one more irrational and therefore much more frightening to the community at large.

As a loaded bus was moving along its route, a window suddenly shattered and there was a scream. The bus driver stepped on the brakes and careened to a halt. When he looked around he saw a pile of glass on the floor and discovered that a young black woman had been wounded by a sniper. The sniper, who got off one round, apparently had fled into the night.

On the same evening, another bus was fired on, though this time no one was hurt. The police investigated, but could find no evidence to identify the assailant or assailants. Clearly, the bus company was now in more trouble than it had been in during the boycott. At least then they could count on a small number of steady white customers. Now, with bullets flying, it wasn't safe for anyone to ride. Not at night anyway.

The next day the police commissioner announced that buses would not run after 5:00 P.M., a decision that would have the greatest impact on blacks, who worked in white homes and served dinner before they went home.

That policy, however, did not deter the attackers. A bus was fired on in broad daylight, and it became clear that nothing short of closing down the bus line completely could assure an end to the sniping. Someone was acting out of a deep sense of frustration. They were not trying to accomplish any specific political act. They were seeking raw revenge on whoever came within their sights. Given that attitude, no one could predict the time or the target.

With such uncertainty in the air, Martin and I were extremely reluctant to leave our families, but we had an important meeting in Atlanta just after New Year's. We had called for a conference of all like-minded people to discuss the formation of a region-wide organization to extend the influence of the Montgomery Improvement Association and to join forces with other leaders in southern cities.

In fact, the Montgomery boycott was not the only such activity in the region. Similar boycotts had been pursued in four other cities: Baton Rouge, Birmingham, Tallahassee, and Mobile;

and we were already in contact with those organizations. The Baton Rouge boycott, led by the Reverend T. J. Jemison, had lasted only a short time; but it had given us considerable inspiration. The Birmingham forces were led by the Reverend Fred Shuttlesworth, with whom we would work closely in later years. Tallahassee's boycott was led by the Reverend C. K. Steele, who had made considerable progress in the Florida capital, one of the most "southern" of all cities in that state. In Mobile the black forces were divided, with the Reverend Joseph E. Lowery representing the more militant and effective segment.

With all this activity going on in the region, we had long felt the need for a larger organization that could coordinate all these activities and give them greater focus and power. That was why we were going to Atlanta—to organize just such a group. However, we both felt that the danger in Montgomery had somehow increased since our victory rather than melted away as we had expected.

I toyed with the idea of skipping the meeting, but Juanita would not let me consider the possibility. Martin also urged me to go and offered to find accommodations for Juanita and Juandalynn in Atlanta, where Martin's father was pastor of Ebenezer Baptist Church. Coretta and Yoki he said would be going too.

For some reason that idea didn't work out, perhaps because Juanita was pregnant with Donzaleigh and didn't feel like making the trip. Whatever the rationalization, I decided to leave her behind and attend the meeting. In retrospect, I wonder how I could have been so thoughtless. It is not something I would do today, given the same circumstances; but when young, you take foolish chances and pay the consequences.

Martin, Coretta, and I drove up from Montgomery. I remember that as we drove up to Atlanta we talked about the danger that still lingered behind in Montgomery. Martin and Coretta finally convinced me that there was really no further danger since the Supreme Court had ended our struggle over the Montgomery bus system once and for all. I stayed at Daddy King's, as did Martin and Coretta, and when Bayard Rustin arrived from New

York on the evening of the ninth, we sat up late talking about the meeting the next day and didn't get to bed until after midnight.

Sometime later I was awakened from a deep, untroubled sleep by the sound of Daddy King's telephone ringing. I knew it must be early in the morning, but I told myself it was none of my business and put a pillow over my head to deaden the sound of conversation. Suddenly I heard a loud knock on the bedroom door.

"Ralph," Martin's mother called, "it's for you."

I sat up, wide awake, realizing for the first time that something was terribly wrong. I jumped out of bed and rushed to the telephone.

"It's Juanita," Mrs. King told me. "Something's happened."

I listened with apprehension as Juanita told me the story. She had been asleep in our bedroom with Juandalynn close by, still in a baby bed. Suddenly she had been awakened by a loud explosion that almost deafened her. It had obviously been a bomb. The house was in splinters.

"Are you all right? And the baby?"

"The baby's fine," she said. "She's in the bed."

"Are you alone?" I asked.

"Yes," she said, "but there are hundreds of people outside."

I heard someone speaking in the background, then Juanita responding.

"It's Mrs. Norris," she said. "From down the street."

Mrs. Norris was a supervisor in the local school, and I felt a little better. She and Juanita were friends.

"I'll be on the next plane to Montgomery," I said, "I'll call you back in a few minutes to tell you when."

"Mrs. Norris is going to say here," said Juanita. "I'll wait for your call."

I hung up and told the King household what had happened. Later I called Juanita back about the airline reservations, and as I was giving her the information, someone shouted in the background.

"What!" Juanita cried. After a pause, she said, "Oh, no! Ralph, they've just bombed the First Baptist Church."

Daddy King was standing beside me, and I put my hand over the receiver.

"They bombed my church," I told him. "So I guess you were right after all."

"I'm truly sorry that I was," he said.

We were referring to a conversation that had taken place months earlier. He had come to Montgomery to try to persuade Martin to give up the boycott and move back to Atlanta. The Kings' house had just been bombed, and Daddy King was speaking as the father of a favorite son rather than as a clergyman in the black church. He wanted his son and grandchild to be safe from further harm, whatever the cost to the freedom movement.

Martin and I sympathized with his concern, but neither of us was about to give up, even in the wake of this new act of violence. In the course of our conversation I remember saying to him, "The one thing that worries me is the possibility that they might bomb my church. It's an historic building, and I would hate to think that anything I did would lead to its destruction."

His voice filled with emotion, he had turned to me and said, "Ralph, make no mistake about it. Your church will be bombed. It will be bombed!"

Because I respected his judgment I had been momentarily taken aback, but I'd finally told myself that he was so frightened for our safety that he was taking an unnecessarily pessimistic view of the future. Now, as I held the phone and listened to Juanita give the few bits of information she had, I thought about that early warning and felt the first wave of guilt for not heeding what Daddy King had said.

Juanita said that no one knew yet how much damage the church had suffered but that she would let me know as soon as there were more details.

"You're sure you're all right?" I said.

"I'm fine," she said.

After several phone calls during the rest of the night, I eventually pieced together the whole story. Someone had planted a bomb on our front porch, right next to the bedroom. Obviously whoever it was had known precisely where we slept and had tried to place the explosive at precisely the point where it would do the most damage. The fire marshal told Juanita that, had the bomb been positioned three inches to the right, it would have ignited the main gas line and the entire house would have gone up in one great ball of flame, killing everybody inside.

I found one detail of the story particularly chilling: her account of what had happened while we were talking on the telephone the second time. As she had been huddled in our bedroom, talking to me, suddenly the sky had flashed, and then she had heard a distant blast.

"What's that?" Juanita had asked, trembling with renewed terror.

A nearby policeman had looked down at his watch. Then looked back at her with a frozen face.

"That would be your First Baptist Church," he had said.

She had stared for a moment into the coldest eyes she had ever seen, and suddenly the full horror of the situation had dawned on her. The police had known all along. They were in on the plans. There would be no real investigation and no one would be arrested or indicted. And the same would have been true had she and the baby died.

But that was only the beginning of her baptism into the new and sobering knowledge of what this community was really made of. Already the word was spreading through the crowd: Reverend Graetz's home had also been bombed. Reverend Graetz was the white minister of a black Lutheran church and had been sympathetic to our movement. Again, no one had been killed, but only by the luckiest of circumstances.

All together four churches were bombed that night as well as two residences—ours and Reverend Graetz's. The other churches were the Bell Street Baptist Church, the Hutchison Street Baptist Church, and even the Mt. Olive Baptist Church, which was way out in the suburbs. Apparently they had bombed this last one on the way out of town.

And the question was: Why?

After I was reasonably certain that Juanita was taken care of for the night and that my family was safe from further harm, I went into the living room and joined the King family for a cup of pre-dawn coffee. We tried and tried to understand why, after the battle was lost, they would strike in such a deadly and malicious manner with an intent to injure the innocent.

We finally concluded that whoever had done this deed—and it had to be a group rather than one person—had acted out of a desire for revenge rather than for any strategic reasons. Killing us could only have hurt their cause. Only much later did we see the same pattern repeated itself in Birmingham, not once but twice; and we realized that when evil is defeated, when there is nothing left to win, only then does its true nature finally reveal itself—as gratuitous meanness. That's what lay at the heart of Jim Crow, a desire to inflict pain and humiliation on other people. Sitting there in the Kings' living room, thinking about it, I couldn't help but shiver, even though the coffee was so hot it burned my tongue.

"I'll have to go back as soon as I can get out of here," I said. "I hate to miss the meeting, but I need to get home as soon as possible. I'm sorry."

Martin shook his head.

"Don't apologize," he said. "I don't see how I can stay either, not with all that's gone on. The community is going to need us both."

"But you need to stay," I said. "This meeting is too important for you to miss. Bayard's come all the way down from New York, and there are the others."

"I have to go back," he said. "All of this has come about because of the bus boycott. We have to be there. At least for today. Even if we have to postpone the organization meeting."

Coretta, who had listened quietly, then spoke up.

"Can't I run the meeting for a day until you get back?"

Martin thought about it for a minute. She knew what we had been planning during those months of daily lunchtime conversations. For this reason, Martin and I both agreed that it would be better for her to preside rather than someone else. We could go back to Montgomery, appear to make an appeal for restraint and public order, then Martin could come back to Atlanta for the second day, when the final details would be hammered out. I would stay with Juanita and my child.

We flew to Montgomery that morning, where we were met

by Robert Williams, the professor at Alabama State, who had volunteered to drive us.

"Where do we go first?" he asked.

"I want to go to my house," I said, "then to the First Baptist Church."

We drove immediately to the house. The whole area was roped off, and the grim-faced policemen at first would not let us through. Then Juanita ran out to meet us, Juandalynn in her arms. I held her and Juandalynn for a long time before I let them go to walk around and see what damage had been done. It was extensive. A huge wound gaped where there had been a wall, and I could see the bed, and the rumpled bedclothes, and I felt as if our nakedness had been exposed to the world. We couldn't live there until repairs had been made. There were several church women inside the house, packing items in boxes, preparing to move us out of the house while it was being repaired. But where?

"It's all been arranged," Juanita said. "We're going to stay with Frank and Margaret Brown. They've insisted."

I could only shake my head at the desolation around me and the generosity of these people, who had invited me into their home.

The Browns were members of the First Baptist Church and had been among our best friends in the congregation. They were just a little older than we were and had no children, and when we moved in with them it was like living with family. Juanita and Margaret did the cooking, and Frank played with Juandalynn as if she were his own. We enjoyed each other's company, and they made us feel as if we were doing them a favor in staying there, though we all knew that in addition to the inconvenience, our presence also placed their lives in jeopardy. Yet they never once showed any fear.

Their kindness and courage made me forget for a moment the meanness of the previous night, but not for long. As I stood there staring at the wreckage of our household, I remembered how carefully we had saved to add every single item to the bedroom, which was now littered with broken glass and splintered wood. Then I remembered the church.

"I'm going to leave for a few minutes so we can go over and look at First Baptist Church. When I get back I'll help you pack."

Martin and Robert Williams had toured the house, seen the damage, and gleaned some details from the women who were helping to put the pieces together.

"Are you sure you want to see the church right now?" Martin asked, sensing my distress.

I nodded, staring out of the window.

"It can't be worse than the house," I said.

But it was.

As we drove up in front of the church I saw a sign that made me physically ill. It read CONDEMNED. This fine church, the jewel of the black religious community, was a shattered husk of what it had been the last time I saw it. Several of the great windows had been blown out, and the whole building listed to one side, like a great ship about to sink into the sea.

A white policeman was standing in front of the building, as stiff as an Indian in front of a cigar store. When I got out of the car he narrowed his eyes.

"Good morning," I said.

He did not respond, and it wasn't until I started toward the church that he spoke.

"Nobody can go inside," he said. "The place has been condemned by the building inspector."

"But I'm the Reverend Ralph David Abernathy, pastor of this church," I said.

"Don't you see that condemned sign?" he said. "It don't matter who you are. Nobody goes inside the building."

I felt the anger well up inside me. I couldn't help but wonder if this was the policeman who had known the precise moment when the church was supposed to explode. They were now forbidding me to go into my own church and assess the damage.

Martin and Robert Williams were sitting in the car, waiting for me to return; but a sudden impulse told me to go inside the church anyway.

"Mr. Policeman," I said, "I have to go in this church. You can't stop me. I'm going inside."

He reached down and put his fingers on the handle of his revolver.

"If you go inside," he said, "I'll blow your brains out."

He said it with little conviction, and besides, I had made up my mind.

"I know it's your responsibility to guard the church," I said, "but I'm going inside."

Hesitantly, I started down the stairs toward the basement. With each step I wondered if a bullet would rip into my back or if suddenly the lights would go out, but neither happened. Later Martin would tell me that the policemen drew his pistol halfway out of his holster, then let it slide back and stood there shaking his head. He probably thought I was crazy—and in a way I was. The events of the previous night had been profoundly shocking, and I was in something of a daze as I looked at piles of brick and sagging floorboards.

What had I done? My actions and activities had led to the destruction of this fine old church, which was mine only in trust. I checked in my study to see that nothing was destroyed or missing. Then I walked up the inside staircase and into the sanctuary above, where the damage was most obvious—several shattered windows, splintered beams, caved-in walls. The structure of the building was knocked awry.

But the north and south windows, the great stained-glass wonders, were still intact. Dr. Stokes still stood in solemn splendor on a higher plain than Jesus and John the Baptist. Mrs. Beasley could still gaze up at Dr. Stokes in fond admiration when the sermon bored her. The steel frames had been cast well.

But several of the smaller windows lay in multicolored fragments on the floor, and the rest of the church was a scene of desolation. I had come along as pastor of this historic building and as a result it had been destroyed. Suddenly I felt a wave of nausea. I was physically ill; seized with an attack of diarrhea, I rushed for the bathroom. For the next day or two, I was never far away from one. I know that my illness was the result of my deep feelings of guilt over the apparent loss of this magnificent building.

When I rejoined Martin in the car a few minutes later, I told him that I would not be able to return to Atlanta, that I had to stay in Montgomery and see what could be done to save the church.

"We'll cancel the meeting," he said. "I don't want to continue unless you're there."

I shook my head, still feeling weak and queasy.

"No, you have to go ahead. It's too important."

"Well, I'll go back," he said finally, "but maybe we can postpone the final incorporation until another time," which is precisely what happened. At the end of the second session—the only one he attended—Martin announced that there would be a meeting in New Orleans a month later, during which the organization would be officially formed. That organization became the Southern Christian Leadership Conference.

The next day, still sick, I met with the engineering department of the City of Montgomery in their downtown offices, with the building inspector present.

"We have condemned the building in its present condition," he said, "because it may cave in at any moment. Certainly you can't continue to hold services upstairs."

"Is there any way we can save it?" I asked, afraid to hear the answer. What I had seen the previous day had made me very skeptical.

"Probably," said the building inspector. "But it will be enormously expensive and it will take a long time."

"Let me make a suggestion," said one of the engineers. "If you can bring in some good carpenters and shore up the basement you can probably hold services in the large room downstairs while the other repairs are going on."

"Do you suppose we could do that by Sunday?" I asked, afraid to hear the answer.

He thought for a moment. After all, that was Friday.

"I think maybe you could," he said. "But they'd have to get on it bright and early tomorrow morning."

I began to see a little hope, but I was still sick.

Sunday morning, with workmen hammering and nailing until churchtime, we gathered in the basement for our first service following the bombing. I was still sick, and I wasn't sure whether or not I would make it through the service, but I resolved to try. I stumbled through a sermon, trying to make some sense out of a passage of scripture.

My nervousness and discomfort were apparent, however, and knowing what was in my heart, Mrs. Susie Beasley stood up and spoke before I could announce the hymn.

"Brother pastor," she said, "I would like to make a statement."

I nodded, gripping the pulpit to steady myself while she spoke.

"I really want to make a motion," she said, "but I would like to preface it with a statement. The pastor appears to be burdened this morning, and no pastor can lead if he's burdened.

"So I want to reassure this pastor. When we were building this church, the forces that opposed us used to pass these grounds and say, 'When unborn generations pass this spot, they will look at this hole in the ground where the First Baptist Church was supposed to have stood.' They didn't think we could build such a church in the black community. But we built it!

"And I want you to know, pastor, that we will build it again. And if the Klan bombs it again, we are going to build it again. And again and again. God's church is going to stand.

"So lead on, pastor. Don't you be afraid. We are with you always.

"And now, I want to make a motion, brother chairman of the deacon board, that we give our pastor a rising vote of confidence and ask him to lead as he follows Jesus."

The chairman didn't have a chance to put the motion to a vote. The organist, who was playing the piano in the basement, hit the first strains of the Halleluia chorus and the church burst into singing: "And He shall reign forever and ever. Hallelujah, Hallelujah, Hallelujah."

At that instant I was suddenly, miraculously well. No more problems with my stomach. No more headache. Mrs. Beasley's wisdom and courage had cured me. I don't think I was ever quite so discouraged again.

As for the church, we borrowed money from the Booker T. Washington Insurance Company. With its help we brought in architects, engineers, and contractors and restored the building to its former state. The total cost of the restoration was $250,000, which we paid off on the first Sunday of November, 1961, my final Sunday as pastor. So when I left Montgomery, I left a debt-free church.

In retrospect, what seemed like a tragedy was just one more trial to strengthen God's church for the rigors to come. While at the time it seemed a terrible thing to saddle a group of relatively poor black people with such a debt—more money than it is now—it brought us closer together than we had ever been before and called up in us the spirit of self-sacrifice that is so essential to the accomplishment of great things. Today the continued existence of that church, once condemned and doomed to be torn down, mocks the meanness and hatred of those who placed the bomb there in an attempt to destroy God's house and to demoralize his people.

Mrs. Susie Beasley has long ago been laid to rest in Oakwood Cemetery across the street, near where my own first child lies. But every Sunday her spirit catches the slant of the morning sun in those magnificent windows and casts it in variegated colors across the crowd of people congregated there, reminding them that God is continually resurrected in the hearts of those who love Him and follow His way.

6

Atlanta

IN MANY WAYS Martin and I were alike. We both were black
Baptist preachers who believed in a newer social Gospel that many
of the older clergy saw as radical and worldly. We both had visions
of the future in which our people would win their freedom and for
the first time exercise the full rights and privileges of that freedom.
We both liked to laugh and joke in the midst of the grim business
of leading a movement based on nonviolent civil disobedience.

We also had the same style of leadership. Both of us could
give a good rousing speech when it was required, and both of us
were willing to take chances and risk dangers in achieving our
victories. At the same time, we tended to be a little too lenient in
dealing with staff members, too often saying "maybe" when we
should have said "no."

But we were also different in ways that were more superficial yet more noticeable. I had come from the country, and my
speeches and sermons were usually delivered in simpler language
than his and were full of folk sayings and anecdotes from the
world of rural Alabama. Martin, on the other hand, was more the
city dweller and the academic, who drew his illustrations and

language from books, though he knew the dramatic impact of quoting an old spiritual in the midst of a learned discourse on scripture.

Martin of course had more formal education than I did and had gone to better schools. His education had been structured. Mine had been spontaneous and eclectic.

But these differences turned out to be irrelevant when compared to the similarities, and our friendship grew during the difficulties we faced in Montgomery. Instead of being strained to the breaking point under these severe pressures, it grew stronger. Then, in 1957, after the Montgomery victory had been won, it was put to a new test.

After much anguish and prayer, Martin finally gave in to his father's pleas to return to Ebenezer Baptist Church in Atlanta, where, for some reason, Daddy King thought he would be safe. I think Martin sensed that his mission in Montgomery was completed and that he now could move on to a larger city and a more challenging ministry. I know that he, like me, understood that what had happened in Montgomery was just the beginning for both of us—that the forces we had set in motion would continue to operate in our lives and in the nation. We didn't know what the Southern Christian Leadership Conference (SCLC) could or would accomplish, but we had great hope for the organization and for the future. Martin saw his future in Atlanta, and I saw no reason to leave Montgomery.

So he accepted his father's invitation and handed in his resignation to the deacons at Dexter Avenue Baptist Church. At the time he did so, he was not only the most famous pastor they had ever had, but the most famous black man in America; and his return to Atlanta was an important event, even to that great city.

But for the two of us, it meant an adjustment. We had formed a close friendship that both of us depended on for strength and inspiration. We were in the habit of seeing each other frequently, and on those days when we couldn't get together, we usually talked with each other on the telephone. Our families got along well, so we often went on outings together. We had both gotten used to this closeness, and only when the time drew near for the Kings to leave did I really consider what their departure would mean to me personally.

"We can keep in touch by phone," I told Martin, as we stood in front of his church and talked about the coming move.

"And with the Southern Christian Leadership Conference growing," he said, "you'll be coming to Atlanta more and more frequently."

"Sure," I said, not really believing it.

"Well. I'll miss you," he said, "but after all, it won't be too long before we're living next door to each other."

"What do you mean by that?" I asked.

"I mean you'll be getting a call from one of the big Atlanta churches, once the SCLC begins to make the headlines."

I shook my head.

"I don't want to live in Atlanta," I said. "Montgomery is plenty big enough for me."

"You'll change your mind," he said confidently, but I knew better. I liked my church and the city of Montgomery. Despite all the troubles we had faced, I felt comfortable there. Besides, I believed we were making progress, and I wanted to make certain that we continued to do so. While Martin's vision looked outward to other cities in the region, I saw Montgomery as a potential laboratory for the South as a whole. We could accomplish everything here first. Then others could emulate what we had done. As president of the Montgomery Improvement Association, replacing Martin, I looked forward to desegregating the entire city, using the same nonviolent techniques and the same dedicated people.

But I knew that Montgomery would miss Martin, and so would I. I steeled myself for the loss of such a good friend. He in turn acknowledged the loneliness he would feel, despite the fact that he was returning to a city where he had once lived and where his family was now located. I wondered at the time which of us would suffer more, and I found out soon enough—he did.

He called shortly after he got to Atlanta to tell us they had arrived safely, and we had a long talk about the same matters we had been discussing before he left. Then in another day or two he called to report on how the unpacking had gone and what he had done in the way of making contact with local leaders interested in the movement. Then he called the next day to tell me an anecdote or a joke. And then he was calling every day, unless I called him—which I did more and more frequently.

Next he began to try to sell me on Atlanta. First he used the indirect approach. Then, as I continued to tell him how pleased I was to remain in Montgomery, he was a little more direct.

"Ralph," he would say, "you don't realize what you're missing in a place like Montgomery until you move to a big city like Atlanta. Life is just more pleasant and more convenient here."

"Things are pleasant enough for me here," I said. "I can live without the traffic and the high taxes you have in Atlanta."

"But you make more money in Atlanta," he said.

"It evens out," I said.

We went on like this for months, but it was all theoretical, since no one had made me an offer to move. But Martin was working on that problem. Then the conversation about Atlanta became a little more serious.

I was unpacking my suitcase after a speaking trip when Juanita came into the room with a distressed look on her face. As soon as I saw her I knew something was wrong.

"Ralph," she said, "Dr. Franklin Fisher died."

I was stunned. He was only fifty-one years old and seemed ten years younger because of his boundless energy and good humor. The pastor of West Hunter Baptist Church in Atlanta, he had been a good friend. I would miss him.

I asked about Mrs. Fisher, and Juanita said she was grief-stricken but bearing up well under the circumstances. We both agreed we would have to send flowers and attend the funeral. But something else was on Juanita's mind, and I knew that if I waited she would tell me.

"Ralph," she said finally, "Martin phoned. He wants you to call him."

"Did he say what he wanted?"

"Yes," she said.

She paused for a moment.

"Ralph," she said, "I don't want to move to Atlanta."

Suddenly I saw it all.

"Neither do I," I said emphatically. "And I have no intention of doing it."

"Martin wants you to call him."

"No! no! no!" I said. "I won't even consider it."

I knew immediately what he wanted. He wanted to put me in the running to replace Dr. Fisher, even before Dr. Fisher had been laid to rest. I was amazed at how quickly he would move to get me into an Atlanta pulpit when the opportunity seemed to present itself.

Every time a Baptist preacher went on a trip or caught a bad cold, Martin would monitor the situation closely. When poor Dr. Fisher died, I'm sure Martin was on the telephone five minutes after he heard the news. I knew I would have to deal with him now that an opening had occurred, and I didn't look forward to the prospect.

"Don't worry," I told Juanita. "They'll find somebody else. I probably won't even be considered. Besides, there'll be a mourning period, so we won't have to worry about it for months."

About that time the phone rang. It was Martin.

Sure enough, there was a three-month mourning period for Dr. Fisher, during which no one was considered to replace him. Martin called me several times to talk about strategy, but I was not encouraging. I said we should wait and let the Board of Deacons make the first move. He said that he and Daddy King had every intention of making certain what that first move was; and we argued a little about that.

What he didn't know was that Mrs. Fisher, as advisor to the youth department, had asked me to be the preacher at Youth Day—an opportunity to appear at West Hunter before the official search had begun. Such a visit would have given me the inside track, but I turned it down, hoping that Martin wouldn't find out. As far as I know, he didn't.

Every once in a while Juanita would remind me of how

much she liked Montgomery and how little she cared for Atlanta; and I always assured her I felt the same way. Then something happened that seemed to guarantee that I would not be approached by the West Hunter deacons: the Reverend Otis Moss conducted a revival there, and everybody forgot about me.

Martin called to report: "The cars were parked for five blocks around. Everybody was shouting and singing, and the week he was there he must have saved everybody in the church at least three times. You should have worked it so you could have conducted the revival."

I kept my mouth shut and told him how sorry I was the opportunity had passed me by. He grumbled a while longer and then hung up; and I heaved a sigh of relief.

But the business hadn't quite been settled.

It seems that Rev. Otis Moss had displayed his eloquence in more than one place. When the deacons at West Hunter issued him a call, he wired them back saying he had just been called to a pastorate in Cincinnati and had accepted that offer. So the search began again.

This time Martin and Daddy King got on the phone and worried every deacon in the church until I was invited to preach at West Hunter on the first Sunday in May, six months after the pulpit had been vacated by Dr. Fisher's death. I might say here that Daddy King was a formidable figure in the Atlanta community, and a man who usually got his way. Where Martin's welfare was concerned, his father would spare no effort; and because he knew that Martin was really unhappy without my presence in Atlanta, Daddy King had resolved to remedy the situation.

Suddenly I was faced with a crisis of ego: While I did want to remain in Montgomery, I found myself flattered by the prospect of an offer from West Hunter, a larger and more prestigious church. Indeed, it was one of the finest black churches in Atlanta. Under Dr. Fisher's guidance it had flourished. Originally a white church, West Hunter seated more than four hundred people and had a magnificent interior, though I didn't care for the use of colorless stone, both inside and outside. Dr. Fisher had supervised the installation of a magnificent rose window and a spectacular cross that was always kept burning.

I knew that the church was located across the street from Atlanta University and that Morris Brown College was a few blocks away. Though Morris Brown was an AME college, many Baptist students attended there, so I knew there would be a large youth ministry, and that idea appealed to me.

Still, I really didn't want to go and Juanita was resisting the idea just as strongly as she had when it first came up. But I had come to the conclusion that I wanted to be wanted. So, still telling myself I intended to remain in Montgomery, I accepted the offer to preach in May. Already I had relented just a little, even though I didn't admit it to myself.

For a few days, however, it appeared as if the Lord had intervened to save me from my momentary lapse. The week I was supposed to go to Atlanta, C. P. Adams, the chairman of the First Baptist Church Board of Deacons, died; and the death of such an important member of my congregation necessitated that I preach the funeral. Given the importance of the man and the fact that he had died late Thursday, I was certain the family would want a Sunday funeral. If that turned out to be the case, then I wouldn't be able to go to Atlanta: They would look around for someone else to replace me and, if they got the right man, they would immediately issue a call to him. So I figured I would be off the hook.

I went to see the Adams family and, to my surprise, they told me that their mother wasn't up to a large Sunday funeral; so they would prefer there be nothing more than a graveside ceremony on Saturday morning at 10:00 A.M. That cleared the way for me to go to Atlanta, so God wasn't going to make it easy for me.

For a sophisticated city church, the congregation was surprisingly naive. I was the first pastor they ever heard of who went from place to place in an airplane; and because they understood so little about air travel, no one met me at the Atlanta airport. I had to wait for an hour to catch a cab and it took me another hour to get into the city.

Still, I was there on Sunday morning and preached the best sermon I could. It was titled "Bushes on Fire," and was based on the story of God's call to Moses to lead his people out of Egypt. I told the people that there were still bushes burning in our society, speaking out to us, calling us once more to "Go down in Egypt land and set my people free."

When I had finished, perspiration dripping from my brow, I thought the congregation was pleased. When I went back to gather my things at the house where I was staying, my host and hostess told me how inspiring my sermon was. So I left Atlanta with a certain amount of ambivalence. I was afraid I wouldn't get the call and even more afraid that I would.

When I got back to Montgomery, Juanita was waiting, still racked by misgivings, full of prayers that they wouldn't like me. I told her I still didn't want the call, and she asked me why I had gone over to preach in the first place. I explained that I owed as much to Mrs. Franklin and to the Kings, but I really didn't know the answer to the question. I also said that they would probably call somebody else, so there was really no need to worry.

The following week the head deacon at West Hunter called me at my office. When I heard his voice, I was certain that he was going to invite me to be their pastor, but I was wrong.

"Reverend Abernathy," he said. "We'd like to invite you back for a second sermon as soon as possible, and I thought I'd check with you to decide on a convenient date."

I thought about it as I listened. Obviously they were trying to compare me with someone else in the running; and I remembered Martin Luther King's rival at Dexter Avenue and the disaster that befell him when he returned for an encore. So I decided I wouldn't play that game. I was friendly but I made my position quite clear.

"No," I said, laughing. "I'm not going to engage in a preaching contest. But I appreciate the invitation."

He tried to persuade me to change my mind, but while I kept my good humor, I held firm. He said he understood and that was the end of the conversation. When I told Juanita it was all over with, she was delighted.

The following day the phone rang at my office, and it was again the chairman of the West Hunter Board of Deacons.

"Reverend Abernathy," he said, "the auxiliaries would like

to give a reception for you at the church here in Atlanta. Just a little informal gathering with punch and cookies. Would you object to that?"

I thought for a moment.

"Why do they want to have this reception?"

"The heads of the auxiliary would like to question you about theology."

Again I laughed and told them I really didn't think I could come back over to Atlanta, that I thought one Sunday away from my congregation this month was all I could afford. He was friendly and cordial, said he understood, and said he would be back in touch. Somehow I doubted it. This was surely the end and I was glad to have the matter behind me.

On June 13, I got a call from West Hunter saying I would be invited to be their pastor. I was stunned. I thought I had safely eluded their grasp, and all of a sudden I felt them grabbing at my shirttail. The man who made this offer, a Mr. Clemens, obviously expected me to reply immediately.

"What are you going to do about the call, Reverend Abernathy?" he asked.

"First," I said, "I'm going to wait until I get a letter of invitation from the clerk."

"Can't you just let me know what your feelings are?" he begged. "We're about to have a meeting of the deacons."

"Then let me speak to the head deacon."

The chairman of the Board of Deacons got on the phone, and I asked him if they did indeed intend to issue me a formal call.

"We do," he said.

"Then I presume you will send me a letter to that effect."

He told me that the letter would be sent and that they would await my reply. I hung up the phone and suddenly I could no longer avoid the decision. I had come to the moment I had been certain I would finally avoid. I wasn't even sure I could face Juanita that evening, much less the choice I would have to make in the next few weeks.

Ironically, I learned years later that Wyatt Tee Walker, who was filling in at West Hunter during this period, could have had the call had he let them know he wanted it. But he was playing his cards too close to his chest, and as a consequence he was passed over. On the other hand, I had played my cards pretty close as well, and now I was going to have to sit down and really think the matter through.

Juanita and I talked about the move many a night, weighing the pros and cons, trying to consider all the factors that went into making such an important decision: what was good for my career, what it would mean to Juanita and the children, what it would mean to Martin and the movement. All of these things were placed on the scale and weighed against the obvious advantages of remaining in Montgomery where we were already loved and where we had been happy.

In the final analysis, I decided that we should make the move, Juanita disagreed. Beyond a certain point further talk was useless. Her last word on the subject summarized her deep regrets: "Ralph," she said, "I'll go if you want to, but I hate leaving First Baptist, and I wish you would reconsider."

I told her that I was certain God wanted me to make the most out of my ministry and moving to West Hunter increased my potential for service in several ways. Atlanta, after all, was a greater city than Montgomery would ever be.

"I'm sorry," I said, "but I'm convinced I have to go."

It took me until the third week in August to make this decision, and I immediately informed the deacons at West Hunter Baptist Church that I would accept their call. The following Sunday I announced to the congregation at First Baptist that I would be leaving them.

Since it is customary among Baptists to give a church three months' notice before you move on to another pulpit or retire, I preached my last sermon at First Baptist in November and it was a bittersweet occasion for the whole family. West Hunter surprised us all by sending four busloads of people to fill the church. We weren't prepared for them, and many had to stand outside and listen to the sermon over a loudspeaker we hurriedly set up for the occasion.

After I had finished my own farewell, the chairman of the Board of Deacons got up and made a speech.

"If I had the power," he said, "I would cancel the call, and keep Reverend and Mrs. Abernathy here with us because this congregation loves them, and I don't know if the people at West Hunter can ever love them as much."

Then Mrs. Inez Grant of the gift committee presented us with a sterling silver service, engraved with the dates of my ministry, and the Missionary Union gave us a cut-glass punch bowl that sparkled with rainbows in the slant of the morning sunlight.

We had a beautiful reception afterward, even though we had to stretch the refreshments to include the four busloads of people from Atlanta. During all this I could not look Juanita in the eye, because I knew she was still filled with qualms. By the end of the festivities, I wasn't sure about the decision myself.

The next day the movers came, and after having breakfast with the choir, we said goodbye, tears in our eyes, and drove to Atlanta. When we arrived, we watched the movers unload our furniture into a rented house. Unlike First Baptist, West Hunter did not provide a parsonage. Juanita looked as unhappy as I had ever seen her, but she managed to hold back the tears.

In retrospect, I realize the degree to which this move defined for Martin and me the strength and importance of our friendship. For Martin, my coming to Atlanta was an important ingredient in his life, something he had been determined to accomplish, despite my pleas that I didn't want to be "saved" from Montgomery. He clearly felt a deep sense of loss that only this move could remedy.

On the other hand, I can certainly see how much the friendship meant to me since I felt compelled to make the move despite the knowledge that my wife and children would suffer some displacement and my congregation at First Baptist would have to go through the ordeal of finding a new pastor. These were substantial sacrifices on the part of a number of people, including those most dear to me. While the scope of my ministry and the future of the civil rights movement played an important part in my decision, finally I think I made the move because Martin wanted me to come to Atlanta so badly.

Yet once we had arrived in Atlanta, we lived miles apart and probably talked to each other no more often than we had when I was living in Montgomery.

7

Albany

A<small>S ANYONE FAMILIAR</small> with the civil rights movement knows, our history is not one of uninterrupted victories. Unlike the famous Duke of Marlborough, we lost a few battles along the way. The Albany Movement disaster came after a victory in Montgomery and was our first significant failure. The indecisive action in St. Augustine, Florida, discussed in Chapter 9, happened just at the end of the Birmingham campaign and was, to some degree, complicated by the more important Alabama action, where we won an important victory. At one point I hoped to leave these incidents out of my narrative because I don't enjoy thinking about them. But in both places there were local heroes who deserve to be remembered because they were as courageous and farsighted as anybody at Montgomery or Birmingham or Selma.

We failed to achieve our goals in those two places because we were inexperienced rather than fainthearted, and it is that point I want to emphasize in this chapter. I might also note that once we learned something, we seldom forgot it; so these defeats clearly led to some significant victories in succeeding battles.

*   *   *

It is important for anyone interested in the history of the civil rights movement to understand that in the years immediately following the Montgomery bus boycott, segregation continued on public transportation in most portions of the South. We assumed that once the Supreme Court had ruled on the question, bus lines all over the region would immediately discontinue Jim Crow seating requirements and that everyone would accept such a change; but that simply didn't happen.

The first and foremost reason the situation didn't change was because the southern establishment simply would not cooperate in seeking obedience to constitutional law. Instead of taking every opportunity to prepare their states and communities for the great changes that the courts and public opinion were mandating, they used the occasion to win fleeting popularity by promising a gullible white constituency that the Supreme Court's decision could be circumvented, that the status quo could be maintained even though the Constitution said otherwise.

Some of these people were shortsighted and ignorant. They really believed that nothing was going to change. Having known only one world in their entire lifetime, it was inconceivable that a mere court decree could simply wipe out tradition. They were like the passengers on the Titanic who continued to dance even after the ship had struck the iceberg.

But there were others who knew better. They saw the damage and knew the ship was sinking, but they were still willing to exploit the panic everyone felt, hoping to serve their own political ends. These politicians, playing on the ugliest passions in their respective communities, urged defiance of federal law and rallied the forces of bigotry for one last stand. Such people were chiefly responsible for the bitterness and hatred of the next few years and for the deaths that resulted.

However, there was also a natural lag between the time when that historic decision was made and its final and complete implementation. When a landmark decision is made—which certainly was the case—the full extent of its application must be defined in terms of additional cases. To what extent did the Montgomery decision affect other bus systems in the South? Other modes of transportation? Other public services? The meaning of the court's decision was plain to us and to our lawyers: no more segregation on buses, streetcars, trains, planes, ships, or any other form of transportation that solicited public business. But the southern legal establishment was saying, "Maybe we can find some way in which our local system is different. Maybe we can find a legal loophole so we can keep things the way they've always been."

In that spirit they began to devise stratagems to confound the Supreme Court, and the word went out all over the South: "Don't give in. Just keep doing things the way we always have. This will all blow over in a few years." So in the courthouses and in the state houses politicians grew temporarily powerful by pounding on their desks and shouting this message. Today their names are largely forgotten, except where they played a central role in some violent confrontation and then they are remembered all too well: Orval Faubus, Ross Barnett, Bull Connor, Lester Maddox.

These men were powerful symbols of southern resistance because they used the power and authority at their disposal to defy federal courts and to do so proudly and vocally. Their animosity toward blacks was apparent to the nation at large, and as a consequence they actually *helped* rally the nation to our cause. But other southern politicians were subtler and more devious in their defense of segregation, and sometimes they were even harder to deal with than such obvious demagogues as the likes of Governor Faubus.

What happened in Albany is a case in point.

In May 1961, as the result of a number of confrontations over public transportation, Attorney General Robert Kennedy asked the Interstate Commerce Commission (ICC) to declare that segregation in all public transportation facilities was illegal and to force compliance with this regulation nationwide. On September 22 the ICC did indeed declare that all public transportation facilities must be desegregated, and this ruling provided the executive branch of the government with a practical means of implementing the Supreme Court's intentions in the Montgomery decision.

With this ruling to bolster their courage, black groups around the South began to challenge local practices, sitting in at bus stations and train depots, challenging the validity of the "WHITE" and "COLORED" signs that still remained in place five years after Montgomery. Such a group developed in Albany, Georgia, that eventually began a bus boycott like the one Martin and I had successfully conducted in Montgomery. They also boycotted downtown merchants. The techniques were similar to those we had pioneered in Montgomery, but the movement was made up of several smaller groups and lacked the unity we had depended on so heavily in Montgomery.

One of these groups was the Student Nonviolent Coordinating Committee (SNCC), whose leadership decided to test the white establishment in Albany. On the surface, Albany seemed like an easy target for desegregation. Its mayor and police commissioner seemed "moderate" by the standards of the day and the city seemed ready to usher in a new era with relative ease. But appearances were deceptive. Mayor Asa D. Kelley, Jr., and Police Chief Laurie Pritchett were not the scowling, snarling adversaries Bull Connor and Lester Maddox were; in many respects they were much worse—seemingly friendly and progressive white men who were just as adamant about maintaining the status quo as the worst redneck demagogues. But before we figured this out, both the SNCC and the Southern Christian Leadership Conference (SCLC) had suffered significant defeats and learned an extremely unpleasant lesson.

When the SNCC arrived in Albany to test the ICC ruling, they found the facilities there still segregated; and when they attempted to integrate them, they were arrested. Aided by several local black leaders, including a physician, Dr. William G. Anderson, they tried to rally community support. But the local black community was not ready for a massive campaign of the sort we had put on in Montgomery and would later mount in Birmingham and Selma. What few they could muster to protest—a couple of hundred—were likewise arrested.

With this defeat staring them in the face, my dear friend Dr.

Anderson, the local leader of the Albany Movement who had been my college schoolmate, called SCLC headquarters in Atlanta, where I took the call. I listened while he recounted all that had happened, though I knew most of the story already since the newspapers and television news broadcasts had given it major coverage.

"All of our demonstrators are in jail," he told us, "and we have no money to bail them out."

"What do you want us to do?" I asked.

"If you and Dr. King could come down and join the Albany Movement, it might rally more of our local people and also attract some financial help from around the country. We can't let all of these young people remain in jail."

"Dr. King is not here at the moment, Bill," I said, "but I will talk to him when he gets back. I'm sure we can come down."

Martin returned the next day and I told him about Dr. Anderson's call.

"What do you think we should do?" he asked.

"I think we should go," I said, "but maybe we should send somebody down to look over the place first, just to see what to expect."

So a couple of our people drove down to Albany to question the black community and determine how much support we could expect from them. They were immediately arrested, so we never got a full scouting report. Finally, after Martin had talked to Dr. Anderson, we decided to go down ourselves, though even at that early stage we were beginning to suspect that we would not have an easy time turning the tide, because the more the black demonstrators gathered, the more adamant the mayor and the commissioners became. Instead of weakening, the white leaders seemed to be gaining strength and resolve, as well as the support of their constituency.

Part of the reason for this growing support was the militancy of the local newspaper, the *Albany Herald*, which was edited by James Gray, a fierce defender of segregation. Gray denounced the members of the SNCC, and later Martin and me, as "professional agitators," suggesting that we were an army of mercenaries come to tear up the city. That charge was to be repeated over the years, often with the out-and-out accusation that we were paid by the Communist party.

When we got to Albany we discovered the black community—and more particularly, the black demonstrators—hopelessly divided. All of the organizations participating in the campaign had agreed to merge their identity into one group, to be called the "Albany Movement," and to be governed by a steering committee. But by the time we arrived, any unity they may have achieved had already collapsed. Everyone had a different strategy. Everyone wanted to be in charge. Everyone was mad at everyone else. And as soon as we arrived in town, everyone was mad at us.

We went by Dr. Anderson's house and heard the sad story from him. He was president of the Albany Movement, so he was catching all the flak. The Andersons were old friends. Before Dr. Anderson had come to Montgomery to finish his college work, I had known his wife, Norma, when she was a student at Fort Valley State College; as a matter of fact, I was the godfather of their oldest child. Now I had come to Albany to try to help the Andersons out of a mess.

"Which of the pastors are cooperating?" Martin asked.

"Reverend Grant of the Mt. Zion Baptist Church, my pastor, and Reverend Boyd of Shiloh Baptist are the two most active," said Dr. Anderson, "but there are others who will help. There'll be meetings at both churches tonight."

"Will we be given the opportunity to address the crowd?" I asked. Since the churches were directly across the street from each other, we could address the crowd in both places.

Anderson told us that we would, so we went down that cold night in late November and tried to warm up the crowds with nothing more than rhetoric. Since Anderson was the leader of the Movement in Albany, we changed the format slightly. I spoke first, then Martin, and finally Dr. Anderson. Martin and I were able to bring their temperatures to a boil with calls to sacrifice and action. By the time Martin had finished, the building was trembling with the cheers. The Andersons were delighted, and in his final words, Dr. Anderson called for the marchers to assemble the next day for a protest march into downtown Albany.

After the meetings were over, a number of leaders came over to the Anderson house to discuss strategy, and it was there that we first saw the internal tensions that existed within the Albany Movement. Dr. Anderson, a man of remarkable patience, was beset from all sides by ego and dissent. The Movement had already made demands of the city that had been in part rejected, though at one point they seemed to have been near agreement. The U.S. Department of Justice was leaning on Mayor Kelley in an effort to bring the whole matter to a satisfactory and nonviolent conclusion. Some people thought we should do nothing for a while in order to give negotiators time to reconcile current disagreements. Others were ready to call for an economic boycott and another mass demonstration.

Martin and the rest of the SCLC people present did little more than ask questions in order to understand what was really happening. We were still bewildered by the end of the evening when most of those present agreed that a telegram should be sent to the mayor asking for some response by ten the next morning. At that point, if there were no agreement, then we would march on the downtown area. So Dr. Anderson, as president of the Albany Movement, called in the telegram that night, and the others agreed to round up as many potential marchers as possible, just in case we could accomplish nothing through negotiation.

That next morning we drove down to Shiloh Baptist Church and found a moderate crowd waiting there, perhaps three or four hundred, certainly not the group we had begun with in Montgomery. There were no signs of policemen, and for the first time it appeared as if the Albany Movement would demonstrate its ability to mount a genuine march without internal dissent or massive arrests. But first, of course, we had to see what Mayor Kelley's response would be.

Ten o'clock came and went without reply from city hall. Finally at around noon a hand-carried letter arrived from Mayor Kelley, rejecting the demand for some sort of immediate reply to the Movement's demands, and accusing Dr. Anderson of betraying an agreement to work through already established negotiators.

"We feel you are not acting in good faith," he wrote, "and until you can do so we can give no response to your demand."

Anderson and one of his local leaders immediately went down to City Hall to confront the mayor and try to persuade him that the telegram was neither a breach of good faith nor an unreasonable action. Martin and I waited in the pastor's study with several other people, and they were gone well over two hours. When they returned we could see defeat in their eyes. They reported their confrontation in detail and we listened in growing frustration. The more we heard, the more we were certain that with a little more pressure at the right moment the whole conflict could have been resolved.

"So what do we do now?" Anderson asked.

"What will happen if we march?" I asked.

"We may get away without being arrested," said Anderson, "but I doubt it."

"Do you think he might listen to reason if you called him and talked some more?" Martin asked. "Tell him you want to avoid further confrontations. Tell him there are people here who are pushing you to take action."

Anderson agreed to try, and we sat down and mapped out a new set of arguments to present to him; but after another lengthy conversation, this time by telephone, Anderson finally gave up.

"It's no use," he said. "He's more adamant with every passing minute."

I looked over at Martin and when our eyes met we both saw the same despair. We had not wanted to be arrested quite yet, not this weekend, at any rate. I was particularly unhappy because I had scheduled the Reverend Fred Shuttlesworth as a guest preacher the next day at my church. He, Martin, and I had been known as the Movement's "Three Musketeers," and I had promised to be there to present him to the congregation. However, both of us were resolved to do what had to be done.

We gathered the marchers in Shiloh Church, and after a few words from the leaders, we moved out into the chilly fall afternoon and down the street. For a while it appeared as if we would march unchecked. However, the moment we left the black section of town we looked ahead to see a small army of policemen, standing there with billy clubs in their hands, just waiting for us to march into their trap. Police Chief Laurie Pritchett was there as well, and I began to think of ways to get a message to Juanita, so she could warn Fred Shuttlesworth that I wouldn't be there to greet him.

Chief Pritchett stepped forward as we approached, and in a quiet, matter-of-fact delivery told us that if we did not disperse immediately, we would be arrested for parading without a license. We stood there, silent and unmoving, for what must have been a full minute. Then Chief Pritchett announced that we were under arrest and his officers moved forward to take us in custody— Martin and me and a large portion of those with us.

In fact, there were so many of us arrested that the Albany jail could not contain everybody. Consequently, a good many of the demonstrators were transferred to jails in nearby Camilla and Americus. (The latter is a city located very near Plains, later famous as the hometown of Jimmy Carter.)

Martin and I were surprised and pleased to find that the Americus jail where we had been sent was a brand-new facility, as clean as a motel, though by no means as comfortable. We shared a cell, which made the stay almost pleasant for both of us, since it gave us time to talk in a more leisurely way than we could in the rush of our daily lives.

As we sat there, I reminded Martin that I had a problem with my church.

"Remember that tomorrow is men's day at West Hunter," I told him, "and that Fred Shuttlesworth is coming over from Birmingham to preach the sermon. I'll have to be there, and that means I can't stay with you in this fine new jail."

"I understand," Martin said. "When are you going to pay your fine and leave?"

"I'll wait until late afternoon and then go," I said. "There's a flight back to Atlanta at 8:30 in the evening."

We talked for a while, and then I climbed up on the bed and

took a short nap. When I awoke and tried to get to my feet, the cell started spinning, and I grabbed the bed frame to keep from falling.

"What's wrong?" Martin asked.

"It's that dizziness you get sometimes when you stand up too fast," I said, but I knew it was something a little more serious. I had never lost my balance to that degree. I wasn't sure I would be able to walk. After sitting down for a minute or two I tried again, and it was just as bad; I still had to fight to keep my balance.

"Ralph," said Martin with a worried look, "we better get you a doctor right now."

I tried to shake it off for a few minutes more, but I didn't feel any better.

"I'll let William Anderson look me over before I go back to Atlanta."

I stood up again and the whole world wobbled.

"Maybe we better ask them to take you right to the hospital," he said.

I assured him it was just a problem of balance rather than a loss of consciousness, and he felt a little better.

"You better tell the jailor right now that you want to be released," he said. "He looks like the type who would make things as difficult as possible."

"You're probably right," I said, and the next time he came through, a scowl on his face, I asked him if I could make arrangements to be released.

He was probably the meanest man we encountered in our long career of arrests, and I can still see his face in my mind's eye. He spoke to us between clenched teeth and his eyes sparkled with hatred.

"If it was up to me you'd never get out of here, boy," he said. "But I don't have the authority to keep you or let you loose. You got to be released from the Albany jail."

"But how do I do that?" I asked.

"For right now, shut your nigger mouth," he said and disappeared.

When he came back through forty-five minutes later, Martin spoke to him again.

"This man is sick and needs to be back in Atlanta to see his doctor. If anything happens to him, we'll hold you responsible. Can't you get somebody to take him back to Albany, so he can catch a flight to Atlanta tonight?"

The jailor grinned and disappeared again. He seemed delighted with the idea that I might die in his jail.

Outside the shadows lengthened and the sun went down. I felt no better, but I didn't seem to be getting any worse. Still, I wanted to get back to Atlanta to greet Fred Shuttlesworth, but I gradually began to resign myself to the fact that I wasn't going to make it tonight.

Around 8:00 P.M. the jailor came in, stopped in front of our cell, and took out his key ring. He didn't say a word. He just pointed at me and then jerked his thumb in the direction of the door. I made my way down the hall, hanging on to the walls and furniture for support, while he watched me with barely concealed pleasure.

The two deputies assigned to drive me back over to Albany seemed intelligent and reasonably civil, so I wasn't too uneasy when, on the way, they stopped in a roadside joint near Camilla to get a beer. The driver went inside while the deputy in the passenger seat waited in the car. I sat in back in silence, listening to the jukebox music from the honky tonk, and watching the neon beer sign blinking. There was a crowd of about twenty white men hanging around outside, drinking beer, and occasionally shouting and laughing raucously.

After a minute or two one of them noticed the patrol car and sauntered over, a bottle in his hand. He leaned against the car and spoke to the deputy in front, failing to see me sitting in the back seat.

"How you doing, bo?" he said.

"OK," said the deputy. "How you?"

"I hear y'all made some arrests today."

"Yeah," said the deputy, "we made a few."

"Them damn niggers really tore up Albany, didn't they?"

The deputy nodded, and maybe he gestured toward the back seat. I couldn't be sure. The newcomer shaded his eyes and peered into the car.

"Who you got back there?" he asked.

The deputy was silent for an instant as he stared over at the crowd outside.

"That's our yard man," he said. "We're taking him home."

The man laughed and said, "I thought it might have been King. Where is he?"

"I think they took him to Americus," the deputy said.

"What about Abernathy?" he said.

The deputy shrugged his shoulders.

"I don't know where they took him."

"What about William Anderson?"

"I don't know," the deputy said.

The man finished his beer and tossed the bottle onto the ground. "Well," he said, "if we could get our hands on any of them niggers we'd hang them up by their balls."

By that time the driver had returned with a six pack of beer and had been listening to the conversation. As soon as he heard the threat he interrupted.

"We've got to be going now," he said. "We've got to get this old nigger home."

He jumped in, slammed the door, cranked up the car, and shot out onto the road, gravel spraying behind him. It was a long drive the rest of the way, more than forty miles, but neither said a word to the other and they left the beer unopened. Their silence spoke eloquently, I thought, for the shame they must have felt yet would never dare put into words, even to their closest friends.

I was resigned to the fact that it was too late to catch a flight back to Atlanta, so I spent the night with the Andersons, where Dr. Anderson examined me and could find nothing wrong that would warrant putting me in the hospital. I flew back early the next morning, just in time to change my clothes, shave, meet Fred

Shuttlesworth, and escort him into the church, where I could barely make my way to the pulpit.

Though by then I was feeling much better, I saw a doctor on Monday. After running a number of tests, he told me he thought I must have lost too much salt from my system. In the meantime, Martin had vowed to stay in jail, through Christmas if necessary, in order to call attention to the intransigency of the supposedly moderate regime in Albany.

In fact, more than seven hundred people were behind bars, an embarrassment and an expense for the local governments in three Georgia cities. Faced with increasing attention from the national media, and polarization on the home front, the Albany mayor and commissioners seemed to relent and grant the Movement some of what they wanted. Weary and distrustful of one another, the black negotiators decided to accept what seemed to them a victory of sorts: the promise that desegregation would be studied and implemented sometime in the near future and that, though charges against them would not be dropped, the jailed demonstrators would never be brought to trial. On the basis of what the negotiators told him, Martin allowed himself to be bailed out, only to discover that none of these promises had been put into writing. It appeared to the public as if the Albany Movement had simply backed down on its demands. And that is what the press reported.

Since Martin had vowed to stay in jail until justice was done, many said he had reneged on his promise, and the more militant young people began to accuse him of being unwilling to practice what he preached. The SNCC in particular suggested that the SCLC had barged in, taken over, and then scuttled the Albany Movement. We were very unhappy with the settlement that had been reached, once we fully understood its nature, and were particularly indignant that we should have been tagged with the blame.

Two months later we returned to Albany to stand trial on the charge of leading a parade without a permit. After the evidence had been presented, the judge announced that he would hand down a ruling within sixty days. But he didn't call us back until July, when the temperature had risen into the nineties.

Then he told us that he had found us guilty and ordered us to pay a $178 fine or serve forty-five days in jail. He seemed surprised when we told him we would choose jail.

Two policemen stepped forward to lead us out of the courtroom to a waiting squad car, which hauled us off to jail, only a few blocks away. We finally met Chief Pritchett, a tall stocky man of about thirty-five, who was smiling and affable. His manner suggested that he was really sympathetic with us and our cause, that he loved black people, and that this arrest was some embarrassing duty he was obliged to perform. When he took us in the back to lock us up, he acted as if he were escorting us to his guest room.

But that illusion was short lived. The cell we stepped into was the filthiest place I had ever seen. Martin and I looked at one another in disbelief. There were two bunks, a commode, and a water fountain. Nothing more. The floor was concrete, as best we could tell, but it was covered by a coat of scum and dirt.

We both in turn peered into the toilet and winced. It was also caked with scum, and the bottom was encrusted with rust. (At least we hoped it was rust.) The fountain was a little better than the toilet, but not much.

We examined the bunk, a double-decker with squalid, stained mattresses no more than a few inches thick.

"Do you want the top or the bottom?" I said finally. Martin shook his head. "I don't want either," he said. "Take your pick." "I'll take the top," I said. "It's farther away from the commode."

Martin sat down on his bunk and a huge cloud of dust ballooned out of the mattress.

"We can't live in a place like this," he said. "I wonder if they'll let us bring in some wash cloths and soap, so we can clean up this mess."

We later learned that we were enjoying special privileges because we were celebrities. The rest of the demonstrators were crammed eight and ten in a cell. We also discovered that Chief Pritchett was as friendly and cooperative about visitors as his manner had suggested.

"Sure," he said. "You can have whatever you want, just as long as it's not a gun or a hacksaw."

"Can we have some cleaning supplies so we can shape up this place?" Martin asked.

"We don't have any of that stuff here at the jailhouse," he said, "but you can send out for it if you want to."

"What about food?" I asked.

"You can bring in all the food you want, though we'll feed you if you don't have anything else to eat."

We made up our minds that we would be sending out for lunch in a couple of hours. Having seen the room, we had a pretty good idea of what the chef would be serving.

We soon discovered that we could look down the hall and see our friends at the desk as they inquired about us. When the Andersons showed up, we called out to them: "How about bringing us what we need to scrub down this place?"

An hour later someone brought us everything we needed: a mop, a brush, rags, ammonia, and a new, shiny galvanized bucket. They also brought clean sheets, pillows, and blankets. Never had we been so glad to see anything. We asked the jailer to fill the bucket for us and went to work. First we tackled the floors. For a while we didn't think we were going to be able to penetrate the scum. But eventually we got down to the concrete and in about two hours the floor was smooth and glistening, probably for the first time since the builder hosed it down after the concrete hardened.

When we had finished with the floor, we washed down the walls, the bed frame, and the fountain, which was gleaming white and silver when we finished. Then we looked at the toilet and back at one another. But it was no use. We couldn't stop until the job was done. So with aching backs and shoulders we went to work.

When we had finished, the sun's rays turned the commode into a shining pearl of white porcelain. We both agreed that it was perhaps the finest looking toilet in Albany, Georgia. Only then did we feel we could sit down on the bed and relax.

In the middle of the afternoon, the jailor came to us with a plate of fried chicken, potato salad, biscuits, and a huge apple pie. We both rolled out of bed, starving, surprised that the city of Albany had done so well by us. Then we looked down the hall and saw a little old black lady smiling and waving.

"Thank you, ma'am," we called out, and waved back.

"You're welcome," she said, "and that's just the beginning."

She was right. From that moment on we were never without food in our cell. Not only did the women bring hot dishes that evening, but they also baked pies, cakes, and cookies; and somebody even churned a couple of quarts of homemade ice cream for us. Just when we had finished off one delivery, a woman would come in with a new basket and we would start eating all over again.

By the next day word had reached Daddy King that we were in jail, and he immediately resolved to get us out. To command as much respect as he possibly could, he persuaded Dr. Benjamin E. Mays, president of Morehouse, and The Right Reverend William Wilkes, bishop of the AME Church, to drive with him to Albany.

When the three of them came back to our cell late that afternoon, we pointed out to them what fine, clean facilities we had and offered them a piece of cake.

"Son," said Daddy King, "please let me pay for both of you, so you can get back to Atlanta."

Martin stuck a piece of cake in his mouth and shook his head.

"We can't do that, Daddy," he said when he'd finally swallowed. "We have to stay here and see this through."

"Couldn't you do more on the outside?"

When I heard this I thought about what it would mean to be "on the outside" as opposed to staying here in the cell. On the outside there was bitter quarreling among the various factions of the Albany Movement. In jail we had one another's company. On the outside we were interlopers and rival leaders. In jail we were martyrs for the cause. On the outside we would be rushing from confrontation to confrontation, with barely time to grab a hamburger or hotdog. In jail we were eating the best cooking that the women of Albany could provide. So I was happy when I heard Martin's reply.

"Please don't post bond," he told his father. "We are making a point by staying in jail, and we can stand it for forty-four more days, if necessary."

Daddy King and the other two gentlemen shook their heads gravely, said their goodbyes, and walked out the door. As they were doing so, they passed two women carrying baskets of food, and by the time Daddy's car left the Albany city limits, Martin and I had finished half a cherry pie.

The following day, however, our fines were paid—or so we were told.

"Who paid them?" we asked Chief Pritchett.

"Some friend of y'all's," he said vaguely. "A well-dressed Negro man. I figured you knew about it."

"What was his name?" we asked.

He pretended not to hear and finished filling out the papers.

"You're free to walk out the door," he said with a friendly smile. "Good luck."

We thanked him for his hospitality and left, still wondering who had paid the fines. Whoever had done it was no friend. He had spoiled our chance to call attention to the injustices of the Albany regime. Perhaps it had been somebody from SNCC or one of the other groups, trying to get us out of Albany before we were able to bring about some genuine concessions from the white establishment. We asked the Andersons and the other leaders of the Albany Movement, but no one knew the answer, so we finally concluded that no one paid the fines, that Mayor Kelley and Chief Pritchett finally came to the same conclusion we had—that our presence in jail was accomplishing more to unify the Albany Movement than anything we could have done on the outside.

Martin made his feelings known when the press asked him about the circumstances surrounding our release: "I do not appreciate the subtle and conniving tactics used to get us out of jail," he said.

After talking the matter over with Dr. Anderson and our Albany attorney, C. B. King, we decided that we had been dealing with the wrong person all along. If Mayor Kelley and the city commissioners would not come to terms with us, then perhaps we could talk to Chief Pritchett, who seemed friendly and reasonable. So we went back down to his office and conferred with him on the whole matter of segregation in Albany.

As always, he was reasonable and even conciliatory. The more we talked with him the more convinced we were that he was the key to solving our problems in Albany. He could listen to us and then talk to the mayor, and eventually we could find terms on which we could build a consensus that would lead to integration of public facilities. When we left we were convinced that all previous disagreements had been the result of faulty communications. Our problems could now be resolved, perhaps in the immediate future.

But dealing with Pritchett proved to be as illusory and as treacherous as quicksand. When he talked to us he was a moderate, ready to do anything that would lessen tensions and usher in an era of racial justice. When he talked to the city fathers, however, he said something else, because they spoke highly of his opinion in these matters and still held to their segregationist policies: There would be no dropping of charges for demonstrators and no appointment of a biracial committee. The buses, the terminals, the library, and the public parks remained segregated.

We knew that if we were going to get anywhere against such shrewd and formidable opposition, we would have to turn up the heat and try to force the city fathers to make concessions or to take some action that would provoke intervention from the federal government. But the role of the Justice Department in the Albany situation was ambiguous. Burke Marshall, with whom we were to confer often during the next few years, was Attorney General Robert Kennedy's assistant attorney general for civil rights. He tried during this period to persuade the local government to make concessions. But we came to realize that the Kennedys' chief concern was not for justice but for peace and order—and I still believe that this priority was what finally caused them to enter the fray on our side in Birmingham. We had turned up the heat to the point where it was obvious that peace could only be achieved through justice. Only then did the president and the attorney general commit themselves to racial justice. But that commitment came long after Albany was an unpleasant memory.

As a matter of fact, we suffered our greatest setback at the hands of Federal District Judge J. Robert Elliott, who was appointed by John F. Kennedy. Fearing further activities in the wake of our growing dissatisfaction, Mayor Kelley went to Elliott in an effort to secure a temporary restraining order, forbidding the leaders of the Albany Movement to conduct any mass demonstrations in the city. Judge Elliott listened to the arguments and agreed to issue the injunction, naming a number of specific leaders, including Martin, Dr. Anderson, and me.

We received official written notification in Chief Pritchett's office, where we had been summoned for that purpose. At this point we were confused as to what we should do. On the one hand, public demonstrations were our best means of calling attention to racial injustice. Since we didn't have the vote or the money to pursue our ends through more conventional avenues, we were dependent on our freedom to assemble peaceably and to speak our minds. Could we forego that right and leave ourselves without further recourse just because one judge had so misinterpreted the law?

On the other hand, who were we to turn on the federal judiciary just because one decision had gone against us? After all, we had made obedience to federal courts a central argument in our efforts to desegregate the South. Our chief complaint against Mayor Kelley and the Albany commissioners was their unwillingness to comply with the Supreme Court's ruling banning segregation on public transportation. Could we now disobey a federal judge and continue to argue that southern whites should submit to the Supreme Court's decrees on schools and busing?

Martin and I discussed the matter at some length and finally concluded that we had no choice but to obey Judge Elliott's ruling, however wrong-headed we thought it might be. To do anything else would have meant forfeiting further appeal to the principle of law—and at that point we would be finished.

However, there was a loophole in the wording of the restraining order. It enjoined only certain people by name. Our lawyers told us that while we could not lead such demonstrations, anyone whose name did not appear on the judge's order could call for a march without being held in contempt of court.

So that very night others took over the Movement, and in Shiloh Church they called for an immediate march downtown. In a rousing affirmation of the principle of nonviolent protest, more than one hundred volunteered. We sat in the church and watched as they marched out the door on their way downtown to certain arrest. So Judge Elliott's injunction had failed to stop our movement. We were still in the game. Now we had to make a move of our own.

We met with our lawyers, including William Kunstler, who had flown in to consult with us; and they outlined a stratagem for us to follow. We would go to Judge Elliott with our own argument and see if we could persuade him that our constitutional rights were being denied by the Albany city government and ask him to void the restraining order. After all, our side had not been presented to him. Perhaps he was unaware of all the circumstances.

We soon discovered that Judge Elliott was out of state, so we were able to go to Chief Federal Appellate Court Judge Elbert P. Tuttle and persuade him to hear our case. He listened to a preliminary presentation and agreed to set up a hearing the next day, one at which both sides would be given an opportunity to plead their case. He then called Mayor Kelley and invited him to send an attorney.

After hearing presentations by attorneys from the Albany Movement and the City of Albany, Judge Tuttle handed down a decision: Judge Elliott had acted improperly in issuing a restraining order. Tuttle then dissolved the order, effective immediately, and we were once again in a position to stage nonviolent demonstrations in Albany. We were overjoyed at the ruling.

But after the initial exultation had passed, Martin and I agreed that we were simply back to the point we had reached two days ago—stalemate. We still had not won a single concession from the mayor and his commissioners. We had failed to bring them to the bargaining table. They wouldn't even let us appear before an official meeting to argue our case. If we had won the right to demonstrate, we weren't certain that demonstrations would do us any good.

Part of our problem lay in the mayor's unwillingness even to talk to representatives of the Albany Movement. We always had the feeling that if we could confront white authorities with the unreasonableness of their position and do so in a public arena, we could force them into revealing themselves. Mayor Kelley and Chief Pritchett were able to define themselves as moderates to the press as long as we were not there to contradict them. The reports going out to national newspapers and on television news programs were highly complimentary to the local establishment, despite the fact that they were not only in violation of the Supreme Court ruling but also an executive order issued by the ICC. We believed that an appearance before the city commissioners would clarify and expose the true nature of the city's position, and apparently Kelley and Pritchett thought so too because they never allowed us that opportunity.

Finally, we decided to force the issue. We asked for a meeting with city officials, were again refused, and as a consequence went down to City Hall in a group, knowing that the door would be barred and that we would in all likelihood be arrested. We tipped off reporters, hoping they would see the degree to which we were being denied equal access to elected representatives of the people but, though they showed up, they still didn't take our part in the struggle.

Chief Pritchett showed up too, all smiles and friendly words.

"Folks," he said, "the next meeting of the commissioners will be August 7. You can come back then."

"But they won't let us into the meetings," Martin said, principally for the benefit of the press. Pritchett knew all too well that we wouldn't be allowed through the door.

"Nevertheless," said Pritchett, "that's the time of the next meeting. Now you can't stay around here in such a large group. So I'm going to have to ask you to disperse and come back on August 7."

We stood in silence and stared at him.

He smiled sadly and shook his head.

"If you don't leave in three minutes, I'm afraid I'll have to place you under arrest. Please don't force me to do that."

At that moment we all knelt in prayer, thereby signaling to him and to the press that we had no intention of obeying his order, that we were choosing to go to jail.

When three minutes had elapsed by his watch, he sighed and signaled to nearby officers to arrest us. Martin and I were driven in a squad car to the jail; where we found ourselves assigned to the same cell we had occupied seven months earlier.

"Look at this place," Martin said. "The floor's covered with grime again."

I nodded. "And our commode has more rust in the bottom. Still, it's not as filthy as it was the last time we moved in."

"No," said Martin, "but it sure is hotter."

And it was. The temperature was in the nineties outside, but in the cell it was easily one hundred degrees. By the time we had been in there ten minutes, our clothes were soaked and sweat was pouring down our foreheads and stinging our eyes. We took off coats, ties, and unbuttoned our shirts; but nothing seemed to help.

"Never mind about the home cooking," I said, "we need an electric fan as soon as possible."

"Let's make that two electric fans," Martin said.

We were in there more than a week, and I was worried about a recurrence of my dizziness. I made certain that I took salt tablets and drank lots of water and lemonade. This time there was some food, but not as much. After the second Albany arrest, we were no longer guests. We were home folks, and home folks don't get pies and cakes baked for them, at least not every day.

While we were in jail we got good national coverage, including an appearance on Meet the Press by William Anderson, who replaced Martin. As a consequence of this sympathetic attention, President Kennedy got a number of letters, wires, and telephone calls from irate citizens demanding that the Justice Department intervene in the Albany situation. Finally, to win some relief from these pleas, he responded to a question at a press conference by condemning the Kelley regime.

> I find it wholly inexplicable why the city council of Albany will not sit down with the citizens of Albany, who may be Negroes, and attempt to secure them, in a peaceful way, their rights. The U.S. government is involved in sitting down in Geneva with the Soviet Union. I can't understand why the government of Albany . . . cannot do the same for American citizens.

It was a good statement, and it gave us some rhetorical ammunition, since President Kennedy had carried Georgia in 1960 and was still popular in the state. Martin wired him, thanking him for his support and encouraging him to speak out more often in support of our cause. On the other hand, we got no legal action from the Justice Department, which refused to intervene despite the fact that the City of Albany was at least technically in violation of the ICC order to desegregate public transportation, since the stations were still segregated.

Finally, we were brought to trial after more than a week in jail and were convicted and fined two hundred dollars and sentenced to sixty days in jail. The judge suspended our sentences and we returned to Atlanta to take care of our pastoral duties. While we were gone, the city closed the library and the public parks to avoid integration; so it was clear that we were getting nowhere.

Since the mayor and commissioners had continually blamed "outside agitators" for their failure to talk with the black community, Marion Page, one of the city's black leaders, took the occasion of our absence to appear before the city commission and ask for desegregation of the bus and train stations and the local buses, as well as for a dismissal of charges against demonstrators. This time Mayor Kelley listened till Page had finished and then refused to comment on any of the questions he had raised, saying that such issues would be decided by the federal courts.

By this time fewer and fewer members of the black community were willing to risk arrest—and for very good reason: They saw no concrete results from the previous demonstrations and trips to jail. The Albany Movement was no closer to victory in August 1962 than it had been in December 1961, when

Martin and I first went to jail. In fact, the city government seemed stronger and more adamant about their position in late summer than they had been the previous fall. They were clearly winning the war, despite our occasional victories along the way.

After Marion Page had failed to accomplish anything of consequence in his confrontation with the white city fathers, William Anderson threw up his hands and said he was through. From the beginning he had been called an outsider, even before we arrived on the scene, and when it became clear that the rest of the black community would no longer do what was necessary to keep up the pressure, Anderson decided to leave Albany and set up his practice in Detroit. He had tried to rally the community and had failed; so rather than beat his head against a stone wall, he simply withdrew from battle, announcing that henceforth the Albany Movement would devote itself to the registration of black voters. It was a bitter defeat for him, but he took it philosophically, waiting until the issue had died down before he made his move. In the meantime we all worked to register as many voters as possible.

The national press understood the meaning of this new direction and wrote their somber post mortems on the Albany Movement, chiefly blaming dissention among the various organizations for our defeat. Certainly had the people in Albany been as unified as the people in Montgomery, we would have forced the city government into some productive negotiations.

Yet we had not been entirely impotent, even with the deep divisions that plagued us. For example, our bus boycott in Albany was quite effective, more so than the one in Montgomery. In Albany we forced the bus company to go out of business. The local merchants had also suffered from the withdrawal of black business. Indeed, we probably learned a great deal about the potential of the economic boycott in Albany, as the campaign in Birmingham would later reveal.

For a time we were able to persuade large numbers to demonstrate and even to be arrested. Lack of unity among the leaders did not deter a number of blacks, many of them young people, from going to jail—as long as they thought something might be accomplished. For a long while we had the will, despite the initial squabbling between the SNCC and the National Association for the Advancement of Colored People (NAACP) and later between SNCC and the SCLC.

It is also true, as Martin would later point out, that we tried to accomplish too many things at once: desegregation of public transportation, desegregation of public accommodations, and voter registration. Martin believed this "scatter-gun approach" was our most serious strategic error:

> I think the main tactical error was that the leadership did not center this marvelous revolt on some particular phase of segregation so that you could win a victory there and give the people the kind of psychological lift, a morale lift they needed.

Perhaps. The principle certainly worked well for us in the future. But I really don't believe that had we concentrated on lunch counters or local buses we would have gotten any further in Albany. The communities in the South weren't willing to grant us anything at that point. We only succeeded in wringing concessions out of them in those places where local authorities were so flagrantly oppressive that the press could present the conflict to the nation in highly simplistic terms. Then public indignation would be aroused; letters and phone calls would pour into the White House, the Justice Department, and other relevant agencies; and either the executive branch or Congress would be forced to act.

I am convinced that had we focused our attention on one single issue instead of several, the press would still have presented the conflict in the same terms: Mayor Kelley and Chief Pritchett were as nonviolent and as civil as we were. In Montgomery our houses and churches were bombed. Later we would have dogs and fire hoses turned on us; our marchers would be clubbed and gassed; people would be murdered in cold blood. But nothing of that sort happened to us in Albany.

As a matter of fact, had Laurie Pritchett been commissioner of public safety in Birmingham, or sheriff of Dallas County, or governor of Alabama during the 1960s, who knows when we would have gotten a Public Accommodations Act or a Voting Rights Act. He was soft-spoken. He was friendly. He was careful in his language. And he too preached the gospel of nonviolence. He made certain that his officers never used clubs or other weapons, and they never abused the demonstrators they were arresting. They were always polite when they hauled us off to jail, and no news photographer or TV cameraman ever got a picture of the Albany police kicking or striking a black civil rights worker. To the contrary, Pritchett conducted arrests the way crossing guards helped school children.

All of this "tender loving care" beguiled many reporters and blinded them to the true nature of segregation in Albany. They saw the Albany establishment as it wanted to be seen, indeed as it saw itself: benevolent, paternalistic, and genteel. Consequently, only at certain times during the prolonged conflict did the true oppressiveness of this regime show itself to the American people, and then it quickly disappeared behind the ingratiating smile of Chief Pritchett.

So no sustained pressure forced President Kennedy to enter the fight in our behalf. He was able to do precisely what he had wanted to do all along: toss us a few rhetorical bones and concentrate on items more important to the New Frontier—like a tax cut to spur the economy.

Martin made more sense when he argued that we wasted our time trying to confront the political leaders of the community, that we should have concentrated our attack elsewhere:

> All our marches in Albany were marches to the city hall trying to make them negotiate, where if we had centered our protests at the stores, the businesses in the city, [we could have] made the merchants negotiate. . . . If you can pull them around, you pull the power structure because really the political power structure listens to the economic power structure.

This truth, which Martin discovered in reflecting back on the Albany failure, was probably worth the humiliation we suffered, since it was the key to our success in Birmingham and elsewhere. The white establishment was under the delusion that it believed in tradition more than anything else; but it was soon to discover that it believed in something else even more—money.

Thus, political leaders like Mayor Kelley and Chief Pritchett could respond to the voices of the segregationists in the community as long as the only alternative voices were those of black people. Given the choice between voters and nonvoters, the decision was an easy one. But when the voices of their most powerful fellow townsmen began to be heard in support of black demands, then suddenly the situation became considerably more complicated.

For the most part, white businessmen paid the city's bills, and they also financed campaigns for reelection. More importantly, they usually belonged to the informal club of "movers and shakers " who ran every southern community. While most were probably segregationists, few were willing to sacrifice their financial security to slow down or even block desegregation. A significant loss of income meant loss of status, power, and influence. So when the time came, they were the first to sue for peace—provided we brought enough economic pressure to bear.

Had we concentrated more on the business community, through picketing and boycotting, I am certain we could have brought about some changes in Albany. (The bus company even went so far as to hire a black driver in order to appease us, though they wouldn't go so far as to integrate the buses.) But we didn't cost the downtown merchants enough money to frighten them into putting pressure on the mayor and the commissioners. In retrospect Martin saw that, and his insight helped us to do better in Birmingham.

Finally, while I don't think the fights among the various factions were as important a factor in our defeat as the behavior of our opponents, we learned a bitter lesson about at least two of the other organizations, the NAACP and SNCC. Neither one of the groups was willing to put the cause of black freedom above its own welfare.

The NAACP had for several generations been the only black civil rights organization and its leaders were proud and jealous of their place in history. Instead of welcoming new allies in fighting their foes, they were more concerned with protecting their own preeminence, so much so that one of their Albany members regularly informed Chief Pritchett of our activities, giving him advance warning of moves and telling him what we had said in executive sessions of the steering committee. Indeed, it is entirely possible that Chief Pritchett was able to maintain his equilibrium throughout the Albany campaign because he so often knew exactly what we were going to do and why.

We had dealt with stool pigeons in Montgomery, but it had never really occurred to us that we might have to worry about informers in the NAACP. Albany put us on guard where they were concerned. The next time we dealt with them we would be more careful. Indeed, when we got to Selma we would find them attacking us again, and doing it when we were the most vulnerable.

As for the SNCC, it was the beginning of a rivalry with them that would become more heated with the passing years. If the NAACP was composed of middle-aged and middle-class blacks, the SNCC was an organization of the very young, originally founded with our support as a nonviolent group, but increasingly violence-prone as the civil rights controversy became heated up.

In Albany they were still holding to a nonviolent course, but they were already a little reckless and imprudent—long on enthusiasm and short on experience and planning. Because they had arrived in Albany first, they regarded us as interlopers, an older crowd horning in on their action. From the beginning they undermined our position within the Albany Movement and tried to turn the other groups against us. They knew that Martin, who was already the recognized national leader of the freedom movement, had commanded the respect and loyalty of the local people before he ever came to town, and they resented him for it. They also saw the SCLC as too moderate and cautious, not as old-fashioned as the NAACP, but too much like the older crowd to be effective.

In later years the SNCC would abandon its commitment to nonviolence and dedicate itself to the destruction of society. Stokely Carmichael would call for younger blacks to reject Martin and the SCLC and mount a radical attack against the existing social order. At every turn we would find them in our way, trying to subvert our followers and replace our constructive approach with planned disaster.

So we really were an organization that occupied the middle ground between the old and the young, the conservative and the radical. We were willing to use techniques and tactics that the NAACP would never try, but we were not irresponsible in our behavior, nor were we ever destructive, as the SNCC later was.

As a matter of fact, in Albany we were the only group that tried to work with William Anderson and the local leaders, and in the end Anderson trusted us in a way that he didn't trust the others. When final decisions were made, they were often made with only us and a couple of local leaders, which made NAACP and SNCC leaders all the more jealous of our presence in Albany.

From all this we learned a great deal. In the years to come we remembered the problems we'd had with these organizations and plotted future actions accordingly. In Selma, for example, we hesitated to intervene, despite a fervent request from local leader Amelia Boynton, because the SNCC was already in the area. Eventually, against our better judgment, we entered into a cooperative agreement with them, only to be sorry at a later date. When we were planning Resurrection City, we had an agreement with the SNCC calling for them to stay out of our way before we finally put our plans into operation, and Martin's last weeks were troubled by the thought that Carmichael, H. Rap Brown, Willie Ricks, and others like them might capture the leadership of the black youth and lead as many as would follow to their destruction.

Albany, then, was not really a total and unredeemable failure but a laboratory where we learned a great deal and lost little but time. Soon enough the buses and depots and public accommodations were integrated, and people like Mayor Kelley and Chief Pritchett, who won their battle against us, lost the war. We went on to Birmingham and got a Public Accommodations Act, and then to Selma and got a Voting Rights Act. In the end, the white establishment in Albany gave us everything we wanted—a few years late, perhaps, but better late than never—and "never" was a word the white segregationists were using in 1962.

8

Birmingham

As I WRITE THIS CHAPTER, Birmingham, Alabama, is regarded as one of the most progressive and racially harmonious cities in the nation. Its black mayor, Richard Arrington, Jr., wrote in *American Vision* a few years ago:

> Today, some 114 years after its birth, Birmingham is "the" place to be in the South. To us [i.e., blacks], no other city in the South offers more potential for growth. Since my re-election in 1983, even more dramatic steps have been taken to ensure an equitable sharing of power. . . .
> Birmingham is on the move. The Birmingham of 1963 and the Birmingham of 1985 are two different cities. Blacks are now active in every sphere of life in this city. They are represented on the city council. They also serve on numerous boards and agencies. Blacks are moving into the economic mainstream in the "Magic City," though much remains to be done in this vital regard. As southern cities begin to "top out" in growth potential, Birmingham will continue to grow, bi-racially, with style.

In 1963, blacks would have told you that Birmingham, Alabama, was the worst city this side of Johannesburg, South

Africa. I knew of black people driving from Tuscaloosa to Atlanta who would go thirty miles out of their way just so they could avoid this bastion of southern racism.

There were several reasons why Birmingham was so hard-hearted, but when you added them together, it didn't quite explain the intensity and scope of the hatred. For one thing, at that time Birmingham was the closest thing the South had to a northern industrial city like Detroit or Chicago, and such areas often provoke all sorts of animosities—economic, ethnic, and racial. There were a number of lower middle class whites working in the steel mills beside blacks who for the first time in history were beginning to make equal, or nearly equal, salaries. Given the history of the South, such a semblance of equality stuck in the craw of poor whites, who dignified themselves by saying they were at least social and economic superiors to the segregated blacks. Now they could rely less and less on this proposition to salve their pride.

Then, too, blacks were living in neighborhoods next to their own, and with the city growing in the post-war industrial expansion, some of these neighborhoods had begun to overlap—a fact that put many lower class whites and blacks into close proximity in the worst possible housing conditions. Such social arrangements led to numerous incidents, some of which were violent and even fatal.

Added to these changes, however, was the nature of the white leadership in the community. Birmingham had a "city commission system" of government that had been in place for fifty years and was clearly antiquated by the 1960s. This system, designed for small communities in an era where government did little, placed control of all the city's affairs in the hands of three men—a mayor and two commissioners, one in charge of law and order, the other in charge of parks and public works. In the best of all possible worlds—with three wise and benevolent men who got along with one another—the system would still have proved inadequate to govern a city of more than 300,000 people.

But the three men who held office at the beginning of 1963 were by no means the ideal public servants. The three were Mayor Arthur J. Hanes, and Commissioners J. T. Waggoner and

Theophilus Eugene "Bull" Connor. Blacks regarded all three as hard-core racists who had fought every effort on the part of the city's few moderates to make accommodations to the changing times. Connor, in particular, was adamant on such matters, and as public safety commissioner he held the reins of police power.

In the summer of 1962, The Reverend Fred Lee Shuttles- worth, a Birmingham activist and member of the SCLC, had led a series of demonstrations in an attempt to persuade downtown Birmingham stores to integrate their facilities and staffs. The merchants expressed some willingness to cooperate, but they told Shuttlesworth and his Alabama Christian Movement for Human Rights that they could not integrate their stores as long as the city government objected—and when they said this, everybody knew they were really talking about the man they called "Bull" Connor.

Yet when their final meeting took place in September 1962, the merchants made a promise (or so Shuttlesworth believed). There was to be a vote in November to decide whether or not to replace the three-man city commission with a mayor–council system, which would expand the number of elected officials to ten—a mayor and nine council members. If changes were made—i.e., if Connor were to be replaced with someone more "progressive"—then the downtown merchants would be in a position to inaugurate new policies.

At that point, Fred Shuttlesworth, who had joined with us during the Montgomery Bus Boycott, came to an SCLC retreat and formally asked us to intervene in Birmingham. We had been considering the possibility for a long time, along with a number of options; but at this meeting we all knew we were going to make a final decision which would irrevocably commit us to the venture. So we considered the negatives as well as the positives, and the negatives were formidable.

First, the history of the city was ugly and suggested a potential for community violence found in few if any southern cities. We knew that the unprecedented bombings we had experienced at the end of the Montgomery boycott were relatively common occurrences in Birmingham and required no extraordi- nary tensions to set them off. As a matter of fact, middle-class blacks, such as attorney Arthur Shores and business executive

John Drew, lived in a part of town nicknamed "Dynamite Hill" because it had a long history of such attacks. Ku Klux Klan members particularly disliked Shores because he was the first black lawyer in the history of the state and also because he played golf regularly in Jamaica with John Drew, a thought that used to drive whites wild with envy.

Second, we knew about the white leaders in Birmingham. Bull Connor was legendary in the state of Alabama. He was also a shrewd and bold adversary in a fight. We could expect a maximum effort on his part, even if he remained in his present post. And if he were elected mayor—a distinct possibility—it would mean a city united in defense of Jim Crow. (There was also a white judge named Abernathy—possibly a distant cousin of mine—who was famous for his hard-hearted attitude toward blacks and for his speed and harshness in dispensing sentences.)

Third, the black leadership was not really well organized. Shuttlesworth was not supported by most of the other black clergy, who believed he was too abrasive and reckless. They were timid and willing to wait—typical of the older crowd who had gained some credibility in the white community and were reluctant to forfeit it. Fred had thus far operated without widespread support, except among college students, many of whom seemed ready to help usher in the new era.

These were the drawbacks to a Birmingham campaign, and they were serious. Some of our staff members were hesitant, even skeptical. But for some reason I didn't feel that way, even though I understood fully the risks involved.

For one thing, though Shuttlesworth may have been a loner without the ability to work with others (as some had charged), he was courageous. He knew what had to be done, and he was willing to do it—regardless of the risks. What he was requesting from us was precisely what everyone knew he lacked himself and needed: the ability to gather together, organize, and train large numbers of nonviolent demonstrators. He was asking us to take over and operate the movement in his own backyard. Such a willingness suggested that his ego problem might not be as big as some had told us.

As for Bull Connor and the City of Birmingham, it was true

that they constituted the hardest and most mean-spirited establishment in the South. Yet if we beat them on their own home grounds, we might be able to prove to the entire region that it was useless to resist desegregation, that its time had finally come. To win in Birmingham might well be to win in the rest of the nation. So in the long run the gamble might actually save time and lives in our struggle for equality.

Besides, the people of Birmingham needed us more than anyone else did at that time. They were ready to assert themselves, and I believed we were strong enough to help them. In addition, I had a personal interest in seeing Birmingham become a safer and freer city: My brother Jack and a host of other Abernathys were living there. So when my time came to speak, I said as much; and in the end the others had to agree.

After we had decided to commit ourselves to a Birmingham campaign, we considered the matter of timing. Under ordinary circumstances we might have gone in a little earlier—and with great fanfare. But the upcoming election affected our strategy and made us quite willing to hold off our announcements for a few extra weeks. We understood that Birmingham was undergoing profound political changes, and we didn't want to interfere with them, since our people could only improve their position under new conditions.

With that end in mind, Shuttlesworth and other black leaders went to their community of 100,000 to 150,000 people and stirred up support for a change in government. Sure enough, in November Birmingham modernized its city government by voting in a mayor–council system.

But the old order had not yet passed. At that point Mayor Hanes and one commissioner decided to retire, but in a move that chilled the hearts of Birmingham blacks, Bull Connor announced that he would run for mayor under the new charter.

He had two opponents in the race, both of them infinitely preferable to the black community. One—the most progressive—was Tom King, probably the man most black people preferred. The second was Albert Boutwell, a former lieutenant governor of Alabama and a popular local figure. Boutwell was also regarded as "progressive," though he was by no means an integrationist. It appeared that if the race were thrown into a runoff, then either Boutwell or King—whoever came out ahead—would have a good chance of defeating Connor. But it was by no means a certainty that there would be a runoff, given Connor's popularity with the hard-core segregationists in the city.

Again, black voters turned out to support King and Boutwell, knowing that any vote against Connor would make him less likely to win a majority; sure enough—Boutwell and Connor ended up in the runoff with Tom King the odd man out.

At this point, we were poised on the border, waiting to invade; but we knew that if we entered Birmingham before the runoff election, we would give Connor's candidacy a big boost and perhaps even elect him. As a matter of fact, we couldn't even run the risk of sending in our advance team to scout the area and recruit protestors. Even the rumor of the coming demonstrations would panic the white voters and perhaps cause them to vote for the man with police experience rather than the more businesslike Boutwell.

Our careful restraint was not something we did out of consideration for Birmingham alone. We were also concerned about our own hides. We knew that in the confrontation to come we would be much safer facing a government headed by Albert Boutwell than one headed by Bull Connor, and we would certainly be happier with a new police chief. Connor's defeat would mean the end of him in every way—or so we thought.

It's important to remember the national political context in which the Birmingham SCLC campaign took place. The Supreme Court had cleared only so much ground for us—mostly ruling on cases that in some way or another involved governmental discrimination or interstate activities. But civil rights law was still in its developmental stages, and it was generally assumed that discrimination in public accommodations would have to be taken care of by the legislative branch, probably at the initiation of the president.

But John F. Kennedy was preoccupied with getting a tax cut in order to stimulate the economy, and major legislation desegregating public accommodations just didn't fit into his agenda. He told us so quite frankly, though he occasionally paid public lip service to the idea.

As a matter of fact, when Martin first approached him about the problems in Birmingham, he rejected the idea that any kind of public accommodations act could be pushed through Congress. "Leave me alone to get through my tax cut," he seemed to be saying, "and someday I might get around to your problems."

In the second year of his term, however, Kennedy became more and more interested in civil rights legislation, not because he wanted to, but because he had to. So there was a difference—and that difference was Birmingham.

Money was always a problem, of course, because the SCLC was run on the generosity of thousands of people, black and white, who believed in our cause and from time to time would heed our call for help and send in contributions. Also, Martin spent a good deal of his time making appearances throughout the country, speaking before groups, soliciting contributions.

We used the money for many things—transportation, literature, legal fees, fines, and for the posting of bonds in case of arrests. But most of it went for staff. At this point Martin and I were still receiving no salary, and the Reverend James Lawson, who was a local leader in Memphis, was unsalaried like the two of us. But our regular staff—Andy Young, Jim Bevel, Wyatt Walker, Hosea Williams, Bernard Lee, Randolph Blackwell, Dorothy Cotton, Septima Clark, and others—were on the payroll; and whenever we would enter a new city, we would also hire a few additional staff members.

In Birmingham we hired several outstanding people, one or two of whom remained with us. For example, we hired James Orange there. And we also hired an extraordinary man we called "Sunshine." He was a retired steel mill worker, an old man who had devoted his entire life to hard labor and who should have been content to spend the rest of his days relaxing. But he came to us, burning to get into the fight, and we put him on the payroll.

When we were ready to pull out some months later, Martin

asked me to write to the temporary staff in Birmingham, tell them that their services were no longer needed, and thank them for a job well done. But when I came to Sunshine's name I could hardly bring myself to write the letter. He had been so loyal and so eager to help that I knew he would be heartbroken. Nevertheless, I sent him his termination notice along with the rest.

A week or so later he showed up in Atlanta at SCLC headquarters and asked to see us. We agreed to meet with him in Martin's office. His back as straight as his years would permit, he marched in and stood in front of us like a soldier reporting for duty.

"Mr. President," he said, "Mr. Pastor, I just want to say something about your letter terminating my service. I had worked in the steel mills for all of my adult life, but when you all came to town I quit the steel mills and joined up with the Movement. It was the greatest thing that ever happened in my life, and I want you to know that you didn't hire me, and you sure can't fire me. I will be with the Movement till they say 'Ashes to ashes, dust to dust' over me. I'm a Freedom Fighter and I'll die a Freedom Fighter. That's all I have to say."

We sat in silence for a moment, and then I said, trying to explain to the old man, "But . . . the money. You see, we just can't. . . ."

He nodded his head.

"If you have the money then I know you'll pay me, and if you don't have any money, that's OK too. But I'm still a Freedom Fighter. You understand?"

"Yes," we both agreed, "you're still on the staff."

Five years later Sunshine was one of the honor guard chosen to accompany Martin's casket down Albany Avenue in Atlanta as he was brought to his grave on a mule-drawn wagon. During that grim march his foot was injured by one of the mules; and because of complications due to diabetes, the foot had to be amputated. But instead of quitting, he got an artificial limb and kept on showing up at every trouble spot we went to, always there to march, or demonstrate, or go to jail—whatever was required at the particular time and place.

Then, a few years after Martin died, I was summoned to

Birmingham to preach Sunshine's funeral and to say the very words over him that he had pronounced in our study that day. In the eulogy that followed, I spoke of him as an old soldier who had enlisted in Birmingham and remained in the service of his people for life. I knew that nothing would have pleased him more than to be remembered in that way.

On April 2, 1963, the election for mayor of Birmingham was held, and Albert Boutwell defeated Bull Connor by a substantial margin, enough to announce to the city's militant racists that they were decidedly in the minority. On April 3—having held off as long as was necessary—Martin and I flew to Birmingham to begin our most ambitious campaign. Fred Shuttlesworth told us that he would meet us at the airport with a delegation representing the various black churches and groups who would supply us with our "troops." I remember we were in a cheerful mood, in part because of Boutwell's victory—which made our venture a good deal less dangerous (or so we thought), in part because after waiting patiently through a long winter, we were at last flying to Birmingham over green southern hills speckled with the white of dogwood.

Our springtime optimism faded when we got to the airport. There we found Fred Shuttlesworth and three other people, two of whom, as I recall, were members of his own Alabama Christian Movement for Human Rights. As we walked toward the group Martin and I looked at each other and shook our heads. We were back in the middle of winter again.

Shuttlesworth introduced us to the others, as Martin looked around the airport, making a point with his eyes.

"Where's Ware?" he asked, referring to the Reverend J. L. Ware, president of the Baptist Ministers Conference. Ware was the most prestigious and influential black man in the city, and his support was important, if not essential, to the success of the campaign. The fact that he was not there shook our faith at the outset.

"He's holding a meeting of the Ministers Conference," said Fred. "The others are probably there too."

That sounded better—but only for a moment. Because we realized that had Ware already decided to throw his weight behind us, we would have received an invitation to speak before his group. No such invitation had been forthcoming. In fact, no one representing Ware had bothered to come to the airport.

We picked up our luggage, stashed it in the trunk, and climbed into the front seat of Shuttlesworth's car, while the others piled in the back. One bad traffic accident on the way into town would have wiped out the entire Birmingham movement. I could tell that Martin was edgy.

"Let's go to Ware's meeting," he said. "If I can speak to the whole group today maybe we can get them to pledge their support."

Fred drove us to the church where the meeting was being held, and as we came in at the back, Ware looked up and saw us. He stopped in the middle of a sentence, and all heads turned around. But there was no burst of applause and no ripple of friendly smiles. Most of the faces were grave and enigmatic.

Martin knew Ware, of course, as did I. We had seen him on numerous occasions at various Baptist meetings and conventions. So it was easy for Martin to walk to the front of the room, shake hands with the older man, and ask him quietly if he could say a few words. Ware asked permission of the group and turned the floor over to Martin, who quietly explained to them why we had come to Birmingham and why we had not made our plans public until now. Then he talked about the necessity to redeem the city and create a new sense of amity between the races, one based on equality, justice, and true freedom.

His presentation was more logical than emotional, in part because he was talking to fellow clergymen, in part because of the cool reception he sensed. There were few scattered "Amens" from the pews, an occasional nodding head, but no bursts of applause. The group was polite but cautious. It appeared as if we would leave with the same number of supporters we had come with; Reverend Ware thanked us, but did not ask that we be given a vote of confidence or a pledge of support.

We drove in silence to the Gaston Motel, which was to be our headquarters for the next weeks. The Gaston Motel was owned by A. G. Gaston, one of Alabama's few black millionaires. Gaston owned an insurance company as well as a considerable amount of property. The Gaston Motel was Birmingham's only acceptable black inn, the place where black business and professional people stayed when they visited the city. It was not luxurious, but it was as well furnished and well decorated as most of the white motels and hotels.

We were given the best suite in the motel—two rooms located right above the lobby—one bedroom with two double beds and a sitting room with chairs, a table, and a desk. It was in that sitting room that most of the strategy was hatched during the campaign, and it was probably under that room that the bomb was planted that reduced the place to splinters and piles of plaster a few weeks later.

Gaston was one of several important community leaders we wanted to enlist in addition to the clergy. He did not donate the motel room to the SCLC during this period; we paid for it ourselves. But he was very sympathetic to our cause and very generous with his financial support. We knew that more than any other man in black business circles, he could help us establish our credibility in Birmingham. So we immediately invited him, Dr. L. H. Pitts (president of Miles College), and several others to form a board of advisors who would help provide liaison with the black business and professional people, as well as with those white business leaders of more moderate disposition. We spent the rest of the day trying to put this board together and talking to other contacts who might prove helpful in organizing the black community.

Already the news was spreading by word of mouth throughout the city, and toward late afternoon we began getting calls from those anxious to help. But only a few calls. Both Martin and I were beginning to wonder out loud just how much support Fred and the others could really deliver. We would get our first count that night, when there was to be a meeting at 16th Street Baptist Church.

By the time we got to church that night, it was already full and overflowing. There were hundreds of people there—an impressive turnout for a first rally, though not as large as we had drawn that first night in Montgomery. Still, we made our speeches, asking for support in the days to come, and more particularly for volunteers to participate in a mass demonstration scheduled for noon the next day in the park at Third Avenue and 19th Street, in the heart of downtown Birmingham. We said that we intended to demonstrate against segregated businesses by "sitting in" at several of the lunch counters.

As we spoke, we noticed several white men sitting near the back, watching us with expressionless faces. We knew at a glance that they were policemen, and possibly FBI. Like hardened criminals we had learned to spot the cops almost instinctively, not so much by their dress as by the way they moved and the expressions on their faces. Not that they were anxious to hide their identities. Several people came up to us afterward and mentioned them by name. They were there to find out everything they could about our activities, and when the meeting broke up, they didn't leave. They stood around, watching informal conversations from a short distance, glaring at us with cold, analytical eyes.

And this surveillance went on for the entire Birmingham campaign. I don't think we held a single church meeting where, in a sea of black faces, you could not spot the same white men, staring straight ahead, expressionless but alert. Later we would discover that they were also bugging every pulpit we stepped into and every room in which we met. Though we never met them or exchanged a word, they were our constant companions for months.

At the end of that first meeting, the response to our request for volunteers was not encouraging. Some people came forward, but not in the numbers we had learned to expect. However, we "work-shopped" them and hoped that others would show up the next day.

The next day, however, relatively few people assembled at noon—a disappointing kickoff to our assault on Birmingham, the nation's meanest city. We knew that it would take thousands to overwhelm these merchants, who had made promises in the fall that they were very reluctant to keep in the spring.

In addition, we couldn't integrate the lunch counters we

had targeted, because in anticipation of our move, four out of five had remained closed. The fifth had hired several burly bouncers, who stood at the entrance wearing signs that said: WE RESERVE THE RIGHT TO REFUSE SERVICE TO ANYONE. Since most of our volunteers were young college students, they decided to heed the old folk saying, "A coward don't tote no broke bones."

Late in the afternoon, however, four of our students were arrested at a lunch counter adjacent to the Hotel Detwiler. Bull Connor, still smarting from his defeat in the mayoral election, was on hand to tell the press that, though he didn't know how long he would remain in charge of the Birmingham police, "you can rest assured that I will fill the jail if they violate the laws as long as I am at City Hall."

Curiously, while we were blaming the merchants for their failure to keep the promises they had made in September, Bull Connor was blaming them for our presence in town. They had encouraged us, he said. In addition, he criticized three store owners who had refused to press charges against earlier demonstrators.

"If the merchants don't cooperate with the police, we can't move those Negroes out of their buildings."

The total number of demonstrators arrested up to that point was twenty-one, and the sentences handed down against them by Recorder Court Judge Charles Brown came as something of a shock to us: They were fined one hundred dollars and sentenced to 180 days in jail. Six months for sitting down at a lunch counter and ordering a cup of coffee!

We immediately announced that we would appeal the sentences and seek bail. The next day we issued a list of conditions for calling off the demonstrations. They were as follows:

1. The desegregation of lunch counters and other downtown facilities.
2. The immediate introduction of a fair-hiring policy in downtown stores—white collar as well as blue collar jobs.

3. The dismissal of all charges against those arrested for demonstrating and "sitting in."

4. The institution of fair employment practices in all city departments.

5. The reopening of city parks and playgrounds, all of which had been closed to avoid desegregation.

6. Establishment of a biracial committee to work out an equitable plan for the desegregation of all Birmingham schools.

As in Montgomery, we did not expect to win all six points immediately. However, we did hope to win a good many before we left Birmingham; at this point, all were reasonable in the context of the rapidly changing times. Today, more than twenty-five years later, they seem to be no more than what decent people would have done as a matter of course. But, back then, Bull Connor had other ideas about decency.

The next day we had a few more volunteers—still mostly young people—and they were led by Fred Shuttlesworth in a protest march to the Federal Building. This time forty-two were arrested. Again they were fined one hundred dollars and sentenced to 180 days in jail. Connor boasted to the press that everyone arrested would be put to work. The women worked in the jail laundry and the men worked on a farm just outside the city limits.

After the arrest we held a press conference at which I warned the white leadership that the momentum would build as the arrests continued. "The demonstrations so far," I told them, "have only been minor." But of course I knew they wouldn't believe me—not yet. Old Pharaoh didn't believe Moses and Aaron—not until they had unleashed ten plagues on Egypt, and even then he changed his mind about granting them their freedom. We figured there would have to be more plagues for Birmingham, particularly as long as Bull Connor was in power.

As I recall, it was the next day that Connor made his first bad mistake, one that eventually turned the nation against him: He used dogs against the demonstrators. The Reverend A. D.

King, Martin's brother, pastor of the First Baptist Church in Ensley, was leading a prayer march into the heart of the city when he was blocked by Connor's guard dogs. Our demonstrators had been trained not to attack, and in turn the dogs were trained not to tear into anyone except when commanded or unless attacked, so our people were not in any real immediate danger.

However, an onlooker—a black man—frightened by one of the snarling dogs, pulled out a knife and slashed at the animal, which in turn attacked him. Blacks rushed to his aid, and several policemen immediately waded into the crowd, swinging their billy clubs. Before it was over, cameramen had gotten a number of action shots, and 26 demonstrators had been arrested. That brought the count to 102 in just five days.

In one sense that's just what we wanted—large numbers of arrests that would dramatize to the nation the lack of constitutional guarantees in Alabama. Clearly, we did not have freedom of speech or freedom of assembly. Bull Connor would not give us a permit to march or to picket in the downtown area of Birmingham, and when we tried to use those traditional means of protest without official permission, we were fined and jailed for a period of six months. No one of intelligence and sensibility could fail to recognize the injustice in such a community.

Yet at one hundred dollars apiece, the fines of our demonstrators totaled more than ten thousand dollars—an enormous amount of money to us. In addition, to post bond for all of these people and keep them from having to serve their full sentences, we would have had to raise many times that amount. And the fight was still in its early stages. Clearly money was going to be a major problem during this campaign and, for some reason, the contributions were not coming in as spontaneously as they had in the past. Perhaps people were becoming accustomed to street confrontations, massive arrests, and even the injudicious use of billy clubs. Whatever the reasons, one thing was certain: We weren't taking in enough to keep our promises to our demonstrators. We had told them they would not have to serve their sentences. Now we would have to raise the money to pay their fines and bail them out. Once we were able to accomplish that, we were certain that we would eventually force the city to drop the charges or else win acquittals in the federal courts.

So while Martin and I were coordinating the local efforts, we were also making frantic phone calls to Harry Belafonte and others, asking them to exert additional efforts to raise the necessary funds for the Birmingham campaign. They had always come through in the past, and now, in the face of greater need than ever, they agreed to try harder. But they told us that Martin's presence at small fund-raising gatherings around the country was essential if we were to raise the kind of money we were talking about. So he agreed to make as many of these events as possible, while still keeping a firm hand on the escalating local confrontation.

But this necessity to be on call for fund-raising activities made it essential that he not be among those arrested and jailed himself. Or so we supposed at the outset. Yet as the days went by, and Birmingham blacks were a little slow in rallying to our battle cry, we began to change our minds. Our lack of presence in the ranks of demonstrators was causing comment, particularly among those local leaders who were opposed to our presence in the first place.

Likewise, the press was beginning to note the lack of commitment and momentum in this campaign, and some began to wonder out loud whether or not we had the full support of the 100,000 to 150,000 blacks in the city.

So we began to rethink our strategy as the first week drew to an end without any significant breakthroughs, either locally or nationally. At that point we allowed our problems to dictate our decisions for us—as they did frequently during these years of struggle. At the time we saw difficulties and complications as the work of the Devil, but in retrospect we usually agreed that it was God instead, creating adversities in order to move us in the right direction.

As we mounted a demonstration each day, only to see our people arrested and jailed under the same harsh terms, we came up to Holy Week, the days preceding Easter, the most important holiday in the Christian calendar. This period, when we traditionally thought about suffering and sacrifice, seemed an appropriate time for the two of us to come out of our command headquarters and make our own witness.

That's why on Wednesday night, at a large and emotion-charged rally, Martin told the assembled crowd: "Ralph Abernathy and I will make our move. I can't think of a better day than Good Friday for a move for freedom."

The situation was further enhanced on Thursday morning when we learned that Judge William A. Jenkins had issued an injunction, forbidding us to march or to participate in any other public demonstration. We had expected such an action at some point during the campaign, and it had come at just the right climactic moment. If we defied a court order, we would further escalate the fight. Not only would we be defying local law enforcement authorities, but also a state court. The nation would know that both the City of Birmingham and the State of Alabama were in it together.

On Thursday we called a press conference at which we announced that we would defy Judge Jenkins's court order and proceed with the march as originally scheduled. It was the first time we had ever defied a court order, but we knew that if we allowed a state judge to deter us, we would never be able to break the power of the white establishment. Martin made our position clear to the local and national press.

He also made it clear that he knew what was in store for us the next day when he said, "I am prepared to go to jail and stay as long as necessary." That was no idle boast. At that point we weren't sure that our directors would be able to raise the money to bail us out, and six months on the work farm would wreak havoc with our lives and, more importantly, with the movement, which might well wither away without Martin's constant public presence. With this need in mind, Martin spent Thursday night talking on the telephone with people who could help us raise bail money.

While Martin was strategizing, I spoke at the Thursday night rally, telling the cheering crowd: "Almost 2,000 years ago Christ died on the cross for us. Tomorrow we will take it up for our people and die if necessary."

Again, I was not indulging in empty rhetoric. The unresolved conflict between our forces and those of Bull Connor was like a boiler whose pressure was built to the point of an explosion. The frustration of our people, who had not been allowed to march or picket, was matched by the rage of Bull Connor and his troops, who watched us slowly grow in numbers and determination rather than disperse and give up, as others had done in the past. Something dramatic and conclusive had to occur and both sides knew it.

As I gripped the pulpit, building up to an emotional exhortation for new demonstrators to join us, I felt something on the underside of the wooden frame. As soon as I touched it I knew exactly what it was—a bug! We had learned to live with them ever since Montgomery, where we even found one under the furniture in our living room. So Bull Connor was listening to everything we were saying. Well, I decided to give him something to enliven his evening.

> It seems they've put one of those electronic doohickeys under this pulpit, so they can find out what we're going to do tomorrow. Well, I want you to know, Mr. Doohickey, that we'll be marching tomorrow by the hundreds. We're going to fill the jailhouses, Mr. Doohickey. We won't let anybody turn us around. We won't let the Ku Klux Klan turn us around. We won't let J. B. Stoner turn us around. What's more, Mr. Doohickey, we won't let *Bull Connor* turn us around!"

The crowd laughed and roared its approval, while somewhere, out in a parked car, old Bull or one of his men was probably cursing as he listened. That night scores of people volunteered to march with us the next day, in part, I suspect, because of Mr. Doohickey.

However, on Friday morning, the day of the planned march, two developments disturbed us.

The first was the appearance in the *Birmingham News* of a statement by eleven leading Birmingham clergymen, including the Right Reverend C. J. Carpenter, Episcopal bishop of Alabama; Rev. Joseph A. Durrick, auxiliary Roman Catholic bishop; and Rabbi Hilton Grafman of Temple Emanuel. In their proclamation they declared our proposed march "unwise and untimely," called us "outsiders," and urged "our own Negro community to with-draw support from these demonstrators, and to unite locally and work peacefully for a better Birmingham."

Martin was particularly disturbed when he read it, shaking his head and wondering how religious leaders could encourage the kind of attitude that had created a city where bombing of black houses and churches had become almost a common occurrence. He brooded about the statement long after he should have dismissed it from his mind.

The second development was similar to the first, though far more damaging to our morale: Our own advisory committee came to us and asked us not to continue the march in defiance of the injunction. They cited the need to obey the law and their own belief that things might get out of hand, that perhaps we needed a cooling off period, that it would be improper to violate the sanctity of the Easter season by acts of civil disobedience that might provoke violence.

We met in our suite at the Gaston Motel and listened while they presented their arguments in solemn language, which they had obviously rehearsed. We recognized the line they were taking. It came from the white Birmingham merchants, who did a brisk business during Holy Week and were terrified that they would lose money if we turned the downtown area into a trouble spot. "A cooling off period" could be translated as "sometime after the Easter sales."

Not that Mr. Gaston and Dr. Pitts were themselves con-cerned with retail revenues. They were too dedicated to the cause to let a few dollars stand in the way of our progress. But they had been influenced by those white men they regarded as their friends, who were merely using them to prevent us from doing what was necessary to bring the city to its knees. For it was precisely the greed of the white merchants on which we were counting. In the end, we were betting they would care more about dollars than they would about Jim Crow, but we could never bring them to make that choice until we could first take away their downtown trade.

So we sat there in the motel suite and for a while allowed them to lecture us on the virtues of prudence and compromise.

Meanwhile, across the park from where we sat, a huge crowd had gathered in the 16th Street Baptist Church, where our staff members were "work-shopping them"—taking away their guns, knives, and razors and telling them that they must learn to cover their heads and never strike out, even when attacked. Many of the new demonstrators were college students out of school for their Easter break, and some were of high school age and even younger. They were cheering and singing so loudly that every so often we could hear them through the open window of the motel. The noise made Martin impatient.

Finally, when he could bear it no longer, he walked over to the window, where I was standing.

"Ralph," he said. "I'm going to march regardless of what they say. But Sunday is Easter, and you're the only preacher at West Hunter Church. If anything happens to me, Daddy will be there to lead the congregation on the highest day in christendom. But your people won't have anybody. So you go on back to Atlanta."

Then he reached out and embraced me. I knew what he was thinking: He might either be arrested and jailed for months or else be killed, given the pent-up emotions about to be loosed. He was giving me a way out. But on this Good Friday, I wasn't about to be Peter.

"Martin," I said, "what are you trying to say to me?"

"I'm just saying you should be at your church on Sunday."

I smiled and shook my head.

"Martin," I told him, "if you're going to march, then I'm going to march too. Don't worry. West Hunter will be all right."

He looked me straight in the eye until he understood that I meant what I said. Then he nodded swiftly.

"OK then let's go. We're keeping a whole bunch of people waiting."

He turned to the assembled advisors, who were talking among themselves, convincing one another all over again that the right thing to do was to hold off until a more convenient time for everybody.

"Gentlemen," he said. "Thank you for your words of advice, but we're going to have to march. Now."

I followed him out, and we left behind a room full of consternation and silence. Outside we were joined by the Reverend Nathaniel Lindsey of Thurgood CME Church, who was determined to be arrested with us. A man of unshakable courage, he never failed to answer our call for volunteers.

We walked diagonally across Kelly Ingram Park, and as we went we could hear the singing from the 16th Street Baptist Church. The crowd was already in full spirit, long since primed to make the march. As we came to the corner, Martin nodded in the direction of a patrol car parked on 6th Avenue. Bull Connor's advance scouts. Undoubtedly we would see more in the church. They knew we were preparing for a major move, and the two policemen hunched in the front seat frowned as they listened to music on their radio. As we walked past we could hear the same music booming from the windows of the church. They were so busy listening to the transmission from the doohickey that they had failed to see Martin Luther King, Jr., and Ralph Abernathy walk right past them. Martin and I smiled and mounted the steps of the church.

When we entered at the back we were immediately greeted by a swelling cheer that must have blasted the eardrums of the two policemen in the squad car. We walked down the aisle and joined the other leaders on the platform. Then Martin stepped up to the pulpit and addressed the crowd, telling them we were ready to march and if necessary go to jail.

Up until then we had too few demonstrators to make our point. This time, however, there were enough: Hundreds and hundreds of people followed us out of the church and down the steep steps.

Bull Connor knew he was facing a full contingent this time, a genuine army of nonviolent soldiers rather than a thin line of rag tag volunteers. He must also have known that any chance he had of regaining political power in the city of Birmingham depended on his ability to repel our demonstration in such a way that he seemed resolute yet responsible, because, on the one hand, he had to please his local constituency, the racists and hardliners who wanted Jim Crow defended at all costs, while on the other hand, he had to reassure a national television audience that Birmingham was not held together by brute force, as many of us had claimed from the beginning. A man of genuine character might have been able to walk that narrow line. Connor—standing a few blocks away from our departure point, glaring into the dusty afternoon—was about to show the world of what he was made.

It was after 2:30 when we finally exited from the 16th Street Baptist Church and walked down the long steps. As we turned east up 6th Avenue, we walked past the same patrol car, and we could hear the hymn from the church blaring over their radio. This time they glanced up, saw us, and frantically grabbed for a microphone to call Bull Connor, wherever he was.

Dressed in jeans and blue shirts, Martin and I led the long column up to 17th Street, where the block was already cordoned off. Again they had the dogs there to intimidate us. They would hold them on a short leash as they snarled and barked, then suddenly release the leash so the dogs could charge forward before they were jerked up just short of us. We were able to maintain a certain amount of self-confidence by snapping our fingers at the dogs as if we were unconcerned with their apparent readiness to tear our throats out. It was obvious, however, that we were walking into a fortress of policemen and dogs, so we abruptly turned south and moved over to 5th Avenue, then headed east again. And again we were met by the police, who were arrayed against us halfway up the block. In the rear we could see Bull Connor's huge frame, his square head crowned by a Stetson.

"Stop them there!" he shouted.

Suddenly two motorcycle policemen roared up and two men in suits appeared at the same time. One pair grabbed me and the other grabbed Martin.

"Don't hurt them! Don't hurt them!" somebody yelled.

Holding each of us by the seat of his pants, they propelled us toward a waiting paddywagon, lifted us in the air, and tossed us inside like a couple of sacks of meal. Then they slammed the door behind us and we were momentarily in darkness, since there was only a small sliver of light slanting in through the roof of the wagon.

Outside we could hear shouts and screams, mingled with the roar of motorcycles and the screech of tires. Obviously massive arrests were taking place, though we couldn't tell how many or under what circumstances. We speculated about the events outside, then lapsed into silence, expecting at any minute to hear the motor crank up and find ourselves on the way to the jailhouse.

Then minutes passed, and the shouts would die down for a moment or two then begin again. Once we thought we heard someone crying, a woman, perhaps, or a young child. It was impossible to tell.

Then we heard voices drawing closer—three men, who must have come over and stood by the paddywagon. One we recognized as the voice of a man we had yet to meet—Bull Connor.

"Where's Martin Luther King and Ralph Abernathy?" he said in a hoarse growl, less than two feet away just outside the wagon.

"Right there inside," said a second voice. "We got them both."

"Well, let's arrest them all and take everybody off to the jailhouse," said Connor.

"What jailhouse?" said a third voice. "The Birmingham jail is full. The Bessemer jail is full. The Jefferson County jail is full. The fairground is full."

There was a long pause.

"OK," Connor shouted, "don't arrest another goddamn nigger."

"What about King and Abernathy?" the first voice asked.

"Take them to the Jefferson County jail. And wait a minute. Make sure they double up a couple of the other prisoners so there are two empty cells. These two have never been separated. They're the Gold Dust Twins. Let's see if they can get along without one another for a change. Put them in solitary."

I heard Martin say something under his breath.

"What did you say?" I whispered.

"I said he's a smart old cracker."

*   *   *

Sure enough, Bull Connor had realized that together we could still make plans and draw strength from one another. We had always done so in the past. Alone our ingenuity and will might be severely restrained. Little did he know that he had unwittingly made a terrible mistake, one that would result in one of the most important actions of the entire civil rights movement.

After we were fingerprinted, we were hauled to separate cells. I was put on the fifth floor and Martin was put on the sixth. There we were kept incommunicado for a long enough period to violate the Constitution of the United States and establish an excellent case for dismissal in a federal court. At the time, of course, no one was as familiar with the rights of suspects as they are today, so we sat in our respective cells and wondered when Andy Young would find a lawyer who could get us out. It never occurred to us that we might be entitled to call a lawyer ourselves.

After they had kept us locked up for an entire day and a night, a jailor came by, keys jangling, and unlocked the door to my cell.

"It's time for you to get some exercise," he said, crushing my hopes. When I saw him unlocking the heavy iron door I had expected to be told that bail had been posted.

We went down gray flights of stairs and outside into a yard bound on all sides by a high chain-link fence topped with barbed wire. As I stood there and examined the grim treeless landscape, I heard the door open behind me and saw Martin step through, followed by a guard who looked exactly like my guard.

Martin grinned and said, "Hello, Ralph."

"Knock it off!" shouted the guard behind him.

"Yeah," said my guard. "You two can walk around, but no talking."

We both nodded and began to walk side by side around the yard.

"You in a cell alone?" Martin said.

"Yeah," I replied in a whisper.

"Shut up!" one of the guards cried.

We walked on a little farther.

"You talked to anyone from the staff?" I asked, moving my lips as little as possible.

"Not yet," Martin said.

"No talking!" shouted one of the guards.

We walked around the edge of the fence, like animals, exploring the farthest reaches of our cage. Martin said, "I'm writing a reply to the letter from those clergymen in the newspaper."

"Did they give you anything to write on?" I asked.

"No," he said, "I'm using toilet paper."

After about an hour of this, they took us back to our respective cells. Martin continued to write his letter of reply, pondering every word in the silence of his solitary cell, framing a document that will be read for as long as the nation exists and is free: "Letter from a Birmingham Jail."

Bull Connor's plan had backfired. Had we been together we would have planned strategy, reminisced, told jokes, laughed, and prayed together. But without each other's companionship I prayed, read the Bible, and when night came, slept—while Martin wrote his famous letter.

When Wyatt Walker, the SCLC executive director, was finally allowed to visit, Martin slipped him the sheets of paper and Wyatt smuggled them out—a few at a time. In the letter Martin answered in specific terms the assertions of his critics that he was pushing too fast, that the demonstrations were ill-timed, and that he was creating "tensions" in the community. He wrote:

> Frankly, I have yet to engage in a direct action campaign that was "well-timed" in view of those who have not suffered unduly from the disease of segregation. For years now I have heard the word "Wait!" It rings in the ear of every Negro with a piercing familiarity. This "Wait" has always meant "Never. . . ."
>
> Nonviolent direct action seeks to create such a crisis and foster such a tension that a community that has constantly refused to negotiate is forced to confront the issue. It seeks so to dramatize the issue that it can no longer be ignored. My citing the creation of tension as part of the work of the nonviolent register may sound rather shocking.

But I must confess that I am not afraid of the word "tension." I have earnestly opposed violent tension but there is a type of constructive nonviolent tension that is necessary for growth.

He then went on to give perhaps the best explanation yet written of why we violated the Jim Crow laws while still believing in the principle of law. It was an important distinction that he made, one that too few people fully understood. He wrote that there are *just* laws and *unjust* laws:

> I would agree with St. Augustine that "an unjust law is no law at all. . . ."
>
> I hope you are able to see the distinction I am trying to point out. In no sense do I advocate evading or defying the law, as would the rabid segregationist. That would lead to anarchy. One who breaks an unjust law must do it openly, lovingly . . . I submit that an individual who breaks a law that conscience tells him is unjust, and who willingly accepts the penalty of imprisonment in order to rouse the conscience of the community over its injustices, is in reality expressing the very highest respect for the law.

He also reminded them of something that by 1963 was a growing reality in American society: We were not the radical element in the black community but the moderates. The Black Power movement was in the ascendency, and more and more the young leaders were talking privately about the necessity for violence. Martin noted this trend and drew some conclusions from it. His analysis of the situation is as valid today as it was in 1963.

> I began thinking about the fact that I stand in the middle of two opposing forces in the Negro community. One is a force of complacency made up in part of Negroes who, as a result of long years of oppression, are so drained of self-respect and a sense of "somebodiness" that they have adjusted to segregation, and in part of a few middle-class Negroes who, because of a degree of academic and economic security and because in some ways they profit by segregation, have become insensitive to the problems of the masses. The other force is one of bitterness and hatred, and

it comes perilously close to advocating violence. . . . I have tried to stand between these two forces, saying that we need emulate neither the "do-nothingism" of the complacent or the hatred and despair of the black nationalist. For there is the more excellent way of love and nonviolent protest.

Finally, he took up the charge of "extremism," which was in the air at the time and used against us frequently by our enemies.

The question is not whether we will be extremists, but what kind of extremist we will be. Will we be extremists for hate or for love? Will we be extremists for the preservation of injustice or for the extension of justice. . . . Jesus Christ was an extremist for love, truth, and goodness, and thereby rose above his environment. Perhaps the South, the nation, and the world are in dire need of creative extremists.

I have often wondered what those eleven clergymen thought and felt after reading this eloquent and persuasive reply to their statement. Were they convinced by it, or did they simply dismiss it as more radical nonsense? Did they eventually feel ashamed of themselves, or did they continue to feel proud that they had defended their city against the outsiders, the troublemakers? I have never read any subsequent statements by these gentlemen—and perhaps that says something about their ultimate thoughts on the subject.

In the meantime, our staff members and followers were expressing outrage at our treatment. They sent telegrams to both President John Kennedy and his brother, Attorney General Robert Kennedy, protesting our treatment. To the president they said:

Both were arrested, along with fifty other citizens, in violation of the constitutional guarantees of the First and Fourteenth amendments. Both are now in solitary confinement, allegedly "for their own safety."

We submit that these two distinguished Americans are political prisoners, and not criminals. We ask that you use the influence of your high office in persuading the city officials of Birmingham to afford at least a modicum of humane treatment. Neither of these men have mattresses or bed linen.

To Robert Kennedy they said: "We remind you that these men are not criminals. They are political prisoners. Their present solitary confinement constitutes police brutality."

On Easter Sunday, while we sat in our cells and contemplated the Resurrection, many of the same clergymen who had criticized us were preaching about the joys of Christ risen to their congregations. To test the sincerity of their faith, several of our leaders showed up at white worship services. In two congregations they were seated, and in one they were refused admission. Two out of three wasn't bad for that period in history, though in one of the two the black visitors were seated in Jim Crow pews.

Later in the day, two of our national board members—the Reverend A. D. King and the Reverend N. H. Smith, pastor of New Pilgrim Baptist Church—led a demonstration in protest against our arrest and continued confinement. Again Bull Connor and his policemen were waiting, but this time they were facing almost two thousand marchers—the greatest number yet. Connor set up a roadblock just beyond 5th Avenue and there the two groups met. The clash was violent. Some of the demonstrators were beaten with nightsticks and during the confrontation bystanders threw rocks at the police. A rock smashed a motorcycle windshield and the young black apparently responsible was surrounded and clubbed to the ground by several policemen. Around thirty protesters were arrested.

During this confrontation, Connor had again deployed his team of firemen, armed with hoses. At the height of the frenzy, with the two thousand lined up against him, Connor screamed to the firemen, "Turn the hoses on them!" Hearing that cry, all of the demonstrators knelt and began to pray. The firemen stared at them, astonished by what they saw.

"Turn on those goddamned hoses!" Connor shouted.

But again the firemen refused to obey the order. The sight of people kneeling in prayer spoke more eloquently than did Connor's authority. Suddenly, in the face of genuine Christian witness, he was powerless to make his own men obey him. It was a moment of revelation that might have epitomized the entire meaning of the civil rights movement.

*   *   *

On Monday while we remained in jail, Albert Boutwell was sworn in as the new mayor of Birmingham, promising a "new era of economic and cultural growth." Standing on the steps of City Hall, he said to the assembled crowd:

> I am determined that we shall present the true and positive picture of both our city and people to the rest of the world. Whatever our shortcomings may be, they are our own local problems and we shall resolve them by local effort and local unity.
> We shall not submit to the intimidation of pressure or to the dictates of interference.

The crowd applauded and cheered when he made that statement, but they were all deluding themselves. Already the events of Good Friday were having their effect all over the country. A number of prominent public figures reacted angrily to our imprisonment, and on the same day Boutwell was sworn in, President Kennedy called Coretta King to express his concern over our arrest and to offer his assistance. Of course, Coretta was grateful for his interest and told him so; though I'm sure she wanted to point out that if his administration had been able to pass a public accommodations act, we would never have had to come to Birmingham in the first place.

The president told Coretta that he hoped the advent of the new Boutwell administration would mean the resolution of racial conflicts in the city and assured her that Martin was doing well. As a matter of fact, he said, he had personally arranged to have Martin call her in just a few minutes. She expressed her gratitude for this news, and the president said, "Feel free to call me or the attorney general or Pierre Salinger."

Although he neglected to call Juanita, I thought it was a gracious gesture on his part, but also the gesture of a man under severe pressure. Calls and telegrams were coming into his office from all over the country and he was beginning to realize that the issue of civil rights was not going to go away while he took care of "more important" fiscal matters. This was one of those times—more numerous, I think, than most politicians will admit—when people were less interested in their pocketbooks than in matters of principle. The conscience of the nation had been touched, and President Kennedy was beginning now to realize just how deeply.

After he had hung up, Coretta waited by the telephone; sure enough, in about half an hour the phone rang and it was Martin, who learned for the first time that it was Kennedy who had forced local authorities to let him make the call (though to save face locally the Birmingham police would deny any presidential intervention). Martin told Coretta to let Wyatt Walker know immediately that the president had called, so we could get word to the national media. We hoped that news of Kennedy's concern would encourage our supporters to press the White House and Congress for further action.

Yet at the same time the president was expressing his public sympathy, Burke Marshall of the Department of Justice was trying to get us to postpone any further demonstrations until Boutwell was firmly in control of the local government. It was an old story to us, one we had already heard from the Kennedy administration: The time isn't quite right, so just wait a little longer until the right people are in office, it's the right month and year, and everybody is ready for change. In effect the Kennedy administration was saying what the eleven clergymen had said in their manifesto.

Ostensibly there was some wisdom to their advice. Connor was now preparing to go to court in an effort to block the new administration from taking power until late 1964 or early 1965. In effect he was arguing that he, Waggoner, and Hanes legally had the right to serve out the balance of their terms, that the change in the form of government did not nullify the previous election. But there was every likelihood that the State Supreme Court would settle the matter quickly in behalf of Boutwell and the new council and that Connor would finally be eliminated from the Birmingham scene, thereby making our task considerably easier. Or so Burke Marshall was arguing.

But we knew better. In the first place, Bull Connor had not retarded our progress in Birmingham; he had accelerated it. His dogs and hoses had proven invaluable to us in mustering national support for our demands. Had someone more prudent and more credible been in charge, it would probably have taken us twice as long to whip up public indignation.

But more importantly, we knew that while Boutwell's style was more moderate and more conciliatory than Connor's, he was no genuine supporter of civil rights. In fact, he represented the status quo and was pledged to defend it with all his considerable experience and skill. Paradoxically, with Boutwell able to convince the Justice Department that his administration would be sympathetic and benign, he might well delay our success indefinitely. He was precisely the kind of local ally Kennedy wanted—someone to control events in Birmingham and make certain that the whole ugly mess didn't become a national scandal and generate a widespread demand for federal action. The last thing President Kennedy wanted was federal action.

On the other hand, Burke Marshall, the representative of the Department of Justice, was an honest and even-tempered man with whom we would be working over the years, even after President Kennedy was gone. He was a good negotiator; and on more than one occasion, both in Birmingham and later in Selma, he presented our position to the white authorities in such a way that they were willing to make concessions and give us part of what we wanted. It was probably Marshall who urged the president to make his unprecedented call to Coretta. While Martin and I were in jail, Burke Marshall arranged negotiations with our staff and the white leadership to see what could be accomplished.

After we had been in jail almost a week, I was told that Juanita was coming to Birmingham and would be allowed to visit me on Thursday. She told me that the children were fine, that they missed me, and that the congregation was getting along without me but that they hoped I would be there on Sunday.

"I think we've stayed in here long enough to make our point," I told her. "We'll probably be out Saturday."

After talking the matter over during our daily walk around the prison compound, Martin and I both agreed that we would post bond and go back to Atlanta on Saturday.

"Is there enough bond money?" I asked in a whisper, still under the occasional scrutiny of our usual guards.

"Wyatt says he talked to Belafonte and that they have raised enough to cover everybody's bail."

"That's a lot of money," I said.

"The hoses and dogs helped," he said. "And Bull Connor. Our arrests on Good Friday put us over the top."

We knew, however, that we could not expect our supporters to pay such fines and bonds indefinitely. If the arrests kept up, sooner or later they would become routine and the press would lose interest. At that point it would be impossible to raise enough money to keep up with the rate of arrests thus far. We would have to take steps to reduce or eliminate massive incarceration. So on Friday, just as we were about to pay our bond and leave jail, our attorneys filed an injunction in federal court to prevent Connor from hauling us off every time we attempted to demonstrate.

In the injunction we charged Birmingham law enforcement authorities with "denying to Negro citizens the right to peacefully protest state-enforced segregation in the City of Birmingham" and also "continuing to deny Negro citizens a permit [or] other appropriate approval to peacefully demonstrate against state-enforced racial segregation in the City of Birmingham by peace-fully parading through the streets in accordance with proper peace regulations."

By the time we were released from jail, the number of arrests from our efforts up to that point totalled almost 350. Two hundred dollars each for bail had totaled some $70,000; and if we ended up paying everybody's fine, that would be another $35,000. The bond money was refundable; the fines were not. So we were extremely grateful to Harry Belafonte and the others who raised the necessary amount.

A week in solitary confinement is a terrible experience. Living with yourself for such a long period is humbling. You realize how dull your own company is and how much you depend on the existence of others to give meaning and color to your lives. I was glad to get back to my wife and children, and to see the members of my congregation, all of whom were extremely supportive. I remember thinking what an odd thing it was for a

Baptist preacher to come back to his people after a week in jail and receive such a warm greeting.

The next week we went back into battle, and it was at this point that we began to enlist children into the struggle, a practice that got us into significant difficulty with the press and with some of our own supporters, who felt that school children should not have been encouraged to skip classes in order to engage in demonstrations.

At the time Martin and I felt that our decision to use children was proper; and from the vantage point of twenty-five years, I still think so. In the first place, we did not believe there was any genuine danger involved in bringing them along. We had been demonstrating for more than eight years by the time we got to Birmingham; and while people had indeed been brutalized by policemen, we were reasonably certain that even the most mean-spirited cop would refrain from clubbing a very small child.

Second, we believed that children had a stake in what we were trying to do, that in fact they had more to gain or lose than we did since they had longer lives ahead of them. We forced no child or teenager to come with us. But if children genuinely understood what we were doing and expressed a desire to participate, then we welcomed them. We felt they had a right to be among those who ushered in a new and brighter future.

Third, the presence of children among the marchers was a poignant reminder to the public that innocence suffered when Jim Crow laws were enforced. The contrast between the small children who walked with us and Bull Connor and his men was sharp and eloquent. Sometimes people can dismiss injustice toward adults of another nationality or race, telling themselves that such people have somehow earned the oppression they are suffering; but it is very difficult to say that children have earned the harsh measures imposed on them by foreign invaders or oppressive local authorities. The whole problem takes on a slightly different dimension when viewed from the perspective of a child. I can't help but believe that many Americans began to take a second look at Jim Crow when they saw young blacks in the ranks of protestors during the latter weeks of the Birmingham campaign.

However, what we soon found out made us just a little less certain of everybody's safety. Now that the jails were full, Bull Connor could no longer arrest our people in order to dispel a march or sit-in. So if he wanted to stop us now he would have to break up the demonstration and scatter the demonstrators. The only way to accomplish this was to do so with force, because we certainly had no intention of peacefully dispersing every time Bull Connor asked us to. The dogs had caused too much controversy, so he decided to hold them in reserve, but he made greater and more creative use of the water hoses from that time forward, sometimes with great effectiveness. And when the hoses failed, he would bring out the dogs.

Day after day we would send out demonstrators and day after day we would be met by water hoses and occasionally dogs. During one water attack, the firemen met the demonstrators in front of 16th Street Baptist Church and black onlookers began to respond by tossing bottles and rocks. Enraged, the firemen moved forward and turned on the hoses at close range. Fred Shuttlesworth, who was standing on the steps of the church, was slammed against the side of the building with such force that three of his ribs were broken and he had to be taken to the hospital in an ambulance.

Though this daily confrontation between our demonstrators and Connor's troops seemed to be nothing more than a prolonged game, in reality we were accomplishing a great deal. For one thing, we were continuing to get national coverage, both on television and in such important publications as *Time, Newsweek,* and the *New York Times;* as a consequence, pressure was beginning to build in support of a Public Accommodations Act. Even President Kennedy, who would just as soon have swept the entire matter under the rug, was getting the message and would eventually introduce such a measure as a means of responding to the calls, telegrams, and letters that were pouring into the White House.

On the local level we were also scoring points with our persistence. Whereas white Birmingham was at first united in its opposition to the integration of public facilities, after a while an increasing number of merchants and business leaders longed for peace, because the longer we kept the downtown area in turmoil, the more money everybody lost.

We had long since organized a boycott of all downtown stores, and demonstrators had began to carry signs that read: DON'T BUY SEGREGATION and DON'T SHOP WHERE YOU CAN'T EAT. While merchants had always assumed that black business was considerably less important than white business, they began to realize that it took all their white customers to break even and so their black customers provided them with their margin of profit.

But of course they were losing a good deal of white business as well, not so much because of the handful of whites who joined in our boycott, but because of the thousands more who stayed away from the downtown area to avoid trouble. With blacks, dogs, and water hoses to frighten them away, white women increasingly did their shopping in other stores; and while there were not as many suburban malls as there are today, there were enough neighborhood shops to satisfy a significant portion of the white population.

Faced with excruciating plunges in sales revenues, downtown merchants began to see the wisdom and justice of some of our demands. "Perhaps we have been a little too harsh and intransigent," they said. "Perhaps a little integration might not hurt. Indeed, perhaps a little bit might be only fair. After all, these people do contribute to the economy, and anyone who has money deserves some respect from the business community. Of course, we will give them as little as possible, otherwise we might anger our white customers, the folks with the *real* money."

With this kind of attitude, the merchants entered into negotiations with us—assuming that we would settle for token concessions and leave their city, claiming a great victory. What they never fully understood was the degree to which the Birmingham campaign was national in scope rather than merely local. We had no real incentive to accept less than full integration of downtown facilities and staffs because what we were really after was a federal law—and we knew we would never get one if we compromised in Birmingham. While the merchants had a vested interest in ending the demonstrations, we had an interest in keeping them going. So we were clearly negotiating from strength the opposition didn't fully understand.

One of the first things the downtown crowd demanded was that the black community repudiate the SCLC, drop Fred Shuttlesworth, and find more acceptable black spokesmen—like Rev. J. L. Ware. Ware, they argued, would be more reasonable and more representative of the majority of Birmingham blacks.

Such an argument might have made sense a few weeks earlier, when Ware was well known and we had just come to town. At that point, Fred Shuttlesworth probably represented the thinking of only a minority of blacks in the city. But things had changed—in large measure because of the behavior of Bull Connor; and now the black community was united in its demand for a greater degree of change than an establishment figure like Ware would have ever dared to request. In longing for the time when Ware spoke for black Birmingham, the whites revealed a misunderstanding of the times, a nostalgia for the good old days of five weeks ago. Their world had been irrevocably altered in that time, and yet many of them hadn't an inkling that the end of Jim Crow was near.

The merchants, however, had seen the handwriting on the wall, the "Mene, Mene" spoken by their cash registers; and they were now trying to salvage what they could of their credibility with the white community. But Burke Marshall, after conferring with the movement's leadership—including such local figures as Gaston and Pitts—went back and told the merchants that Martin and Fred and I spoke for the majority of blacks now and that any deal would have to be cut with us.

At this point we were demanding four concessions; and though these were revolutionary at the time, today they seem like little more than token gestures in the direction of justice and decency:

1. Immediate desegregation of all store facilities including lunch counters, rest rooms, and fitting rooms.
2. Immediate upgrading of black store employees and a program of nondiscriminatory hiring.

3. Merchant pressure on city government to drop all charges against arrested demonstrators.

4. Merchant pressure on city government to establish biracial committee to deal with future problems and to develop specific programs for the hiring of Negro police-men, removal of voter registration obstacles, school desegregation, reopening of all municipal facilities, and the desegregation of movies and hotels.

The business leaders were taken aback by the sheer scope of what we were demanding.

"We could probably put a black clerk or two at some inconspicuous counter in the name of tolerance," they said. "And we could even allow black customers to use the same fitting rooms and rest rooms as whites. As for integrating our lunch counters, naturally that's out of the question. As for points three and four, that's a matter for the city government to decide, and we aren't even sure who is going to be running Birmingham at this point. When the Boutwell regime has finally been legitimized by the Alabama Supreme Court, then maybe we can make some progress. In the meantime, we'll remove a few segregation signs and add a few employees—provided, of course, the marches and demonstrations cease."

With this kind of short-sighted and arrogant response, we were determined to intensify the pressure on the downtown area. By this time, the jails were full; and the authorities could no longer arrest our people. In a sense that was good news, because we never knew whether or not we would have the money to bail them out; and we couldn't continue to ask blacks to risk arrest if we couldn't guarantee that they wouldn't spend six months in jail.

On the other hand, as more and more young people became involved in the movement and as the crowds swelled into the thousands, a certain amount of friction developed between by-standers and police; and from time to time blacks and whites enraged by the conduct of Bull Connor's troops would throw bottles, bricks, and whatever else they could get their hands on. We had no control over people we had not drilled in the techniques of nonviolence, but more and more the nation began to see this kind of behavior and to blame us. So as the crowds increased and the violence escalated, we knew we would be running additional risks of an incident that would reflect badly on our leadership as well as on Bull Connor's.

Consequently, we began to feel some pressure to settle the matter, though we still did not experience the same urgency that the merchants felt. Thus, when a committee representing the broad spectrum of Birmingham interests came up with a proposal, we listened. First, they wanted a one-day truce in order to cool down tempers, which, everyone agreed, had risen to the boiling point. At a meeting in our suite, black businessmen like A. G. Gaston suggested that we agree to the moratorium and try during the one day of peace to come to a settlement. What they suggested was a cessation of demonstrations in exchange for a discussion of very specific demands, such as immediate integration of all facilities, including lunch counters, as soon as Albert Boutwell's regime was certified as the legal city government.

"But that might not be for more than a year," somebody pointed out.

Others replied that the court would undoubtedly hand down an immediate decision and that it would in all likelihood signal the end of Bull Connor and his cohorts. It was a gamble, but not much of one.

Martin listened thoughtfully and while the others were debating the matter, he turned to me.

"What do you think, Ralph?" he asked quietly.

I knew that he relied on me to tell him precisely what I believed, even when he didn't want to hear it. Often I had advocated strong action when others had urged caution. This time I saw no reason why a day's truce could hurt the cause. I didn't necessarily believe we were going to wring out all the concessions we needed in that one 24-hour period, but I did think it would make us look better in the eyes of the press and the nation. If we held back and the merchants offered us little more in the way of concessions, then we would go back into the struggle with an added degree of credibility.

"Let's let them have their day's truce," I whispered.

Martin thought about it a while longer, then voiced his own agreement with the idea of the moratorium. Virtually everybody else agreed, and we made the announcement, as the negotiators went back to work.

And it was then that we learned why so many black leaders had not been willing to support Fred Shuttlesworth. Though he had been in the hospital at the time we came to this decision, he checked himself out and came down to the motel to protest the truce. Bothered by the pain he was still experiencing, and furious that any action could be taken without consulting him, he lit into Martin, calling him a coward and a double-crosser. For a while we tried to reason with him, pointing out that everyone else in the leadership group had participated in the decision; but he was totally irrational on the subject, vowing to go out and resume the demonstrations on his own.

At some point he changed his mind; and when the time ran out while negotiations were still in progress, we extended the truce in order to give our team, led by Andrew Young, the opportunity to get the agreement they felt was near. Shuttlesworth was bitterly angry during these tense hours, because he felt that outsiders had come in and taken the movement away from him though, in reality, without us there would have been no movement in Birmingham at all.

Despite Shuttlesworth and Bull Connor, who raised our bail bonds in an effort to cause trouble during these sensitive hours, we finally reached an historic agreement, one that no one could ever have predicted when we first entered the city in early April. This agreement, approved by both black and white negotiators, read as follows:

1. Within three days after the close of demonstrations, fitting rooms will be desegregated.
2. Within thirty days after the city government is established by court order, signs on wash rooms, rest rooms and drinking fountains will be removed.
3. Within sixty days after the city government is established by court order, a program of lunchroom counter desegregation will be commenced.

4. When the city government is established by court order,
   a program of upgrading Negro employment will be
   continued and there will be meetings with responsible
   local leadership to consider further steps.

   Within sixty days from the court order determining Birmingham's city government, the employment
   programs will include at least one salesperson or
   cashier.

   Within fifteen days from the cessation of demonstrations, a Committee on Racial Problems and Employment composed of members of the Senior Citizens
   Committee will be established, with a membership made
   public and the publicly announced purpose of establishing liaison with members of the Negro community to
   carry out a program of upgrading and improving employment opportunities with the Negro citizens of the Birmingham community.

This agreement, which we announced on Friday, May 10,
was a great victory for the civil rights movement—one that
nobody could have predicted just a month earlier. After having
marched and demonstrated for over a year in Montgomery and
failed to achieve significant results in Albany, we had expected
Birmingham to be the most challenging project yet, one that
would involve us in a long and bitter struggle with powerful
vested interests and a fanatic leadership. A collapse of the
opposition after five weeks was an exhilarating experience, if only
because it suggested that freedom and equality throughout the
South might come quicker than we had dared to hope.

We held a victory celebration on Friday night. We told the
people of Birmingham that while we would be going back to
Atlanta to preach on Sunday, Martin and I and the rest of the staff
would return next week in order to make certain that the
agreement was carried out in good faith and to start a voter
registration drive that would give blacks a greater role in the
affairs of their city.

The next day we chatted with the press for a while and then
left for the airport, happy that such a complicated matter should
be resolved so simply, and full of good feelings about the white

people of Birmingham. Then I gave the key to our suite to Rev. Joseph Lowery, who planned to spend the weekend there; but he didn't go directly to the room—a decision for which he was later to be grateful. Minutes after we rounded the corner and left the Gaston Motel behind, a bomb exploded and blew the suite into a pile of powdered sheet rock and splintered wood.

The office below was likewise destroyed and the damage to adjoining units was extensive. Had we lingered for any length of time we would most certainly have been killed in the blast, and no one had the slightest doubt that the explosion was intended to kill us. Angry blacks gathered to protest the deed, and the police eventually waded in with billy clubs in order to break up the broiling mob. The result: a major riot, with injuries on both sides—a far cry from the peaceful and nonviolent denouement we had expected.

The house of A. D. King, Martin's brother, was also bombed that same evening, though he and his family were not at home and consequently no one was injured. But the bombings did alarm President Kennedy. For the first time he appeared on television to address the nation about civil rights. He announced that he had called up the Alabama National Guard to stand by in case of trouble and had also dispatched the army to an area near Birmingham, just in case the violence spread in the city.

We returned to Birmingham as soon as we heard about the bombing, mainly to make certain that our gains of the past weeks would not be irrevocably lost in a brief period of racial violence. We moved around Birmingham's black neighborhoods, stopping in bars and pool halls as we had done in Montgomery, assuring everyone we talked to that victory was within our grasp, that if they would just restrain themselves we would have everything we had asked for. People listened to what we told them and nodded their heads, though you could see the anger still burning in their eyes. We knew that if we could only keep the lid on for a little while longer, the Alabama Supreme Court would rule in favor of the newly elected government and our problems would be over. One major race riot and the city would again belong to Bull Connor.

My father,
Deacon W. L. Abernathy.

My dear mother,
Mrs. Louivery Valentine Abernathy.

The church of my birth, Hopewell Baptist
Church, Linden, AL.

My wife, Mrs. Juanita Odessa Jones
Abernathy, as a little girl.

Her loving parents,
Ella Gilmore and
Alex Henderson Jones.

And their home.

Gone to be a soldier.

Here I am in my early disc-
jockey days.

My new bride.

My first church, Demopolis, AL.

Rev. Ralph D. Abernathy
Pastor

Our home was bombed in January 1957 during the integration of the buses in Montgomery, AL.

The historic First Baptist Church was bombed the same night, during the Montgomery Bus Boycott.

Dr. William Anderson (the local leader), Martin Luther King, and I announcing the end of the Albany movement in Dr. Anderson's backyard. (© *by Elaine Tomlin, courtesy of SCLC*)

President Lyndon B. Johnson pausing with Dr. Martin Luther King, Jr., Congressman Walter Fauntroy, and me, after he signed the voting rights bills in 1965. (*Courtesy of The White House*)

Marching up Dexter Avenue, Montgomery, AL, in 1965, led by our children Juandalynn, Ralph III, and Donzaleigh. (© *by Elaine Tomlin, courtesy of SCLC*)

The Selma-to-Montgomery March being led by Mrs. Rosa Parks; me; my wife, Juanita; Ambassador Ralph Bunche; Martin Luther King; Mrs. Jean Young (wife of Andrew Young); Coretta Scott King; and Rev. L. V. Reese, the local leader at Selma, AL. Ralph III is on the shoulders of an SCLC volunteer to the left behind Martin. (© by Elaine Tomlin, courtesy of SCLC)

Andrew Maursette, an SCLC staff member informing me and Martin we were about to be arrested, Selma, AL, 1965. (© by Elaine Tomlin, courtesy of SCLC)

Marching in Memphis. *From left,* my assistant, J. T. Johnson, unknown, me, William Kunstler, Rev. J. W. Wells, unknown, Rev. John Thurston, Rev. Edwin Blair. (© by Elaine Tomlin, courtesy of SCLC)

The three musketeers—me, Martin, and Freddie Lee Shuttlesworth. (© by *Elaine Tomlin, courtesy of SCLC*)

At the tomb of my dearest friend, Martin Luther King. (© *by Elaine Tomlin, courtesy of SCLC*)

On the bus to the Poor
People's Campaign.
(© by Elaine Tomlin,
courtesy of SCLC)

J. T. Johnson, me, and Rev. Bernard Scott Lee bringing out the vote in Eutaw,
AL. (© by Elaine Tomlin, courtesy of SCLC)

Picketing in Charleston with Walter Reuther, Mary Moultrie (head of 1199B), me, and Juanita. (© *by Elaine Tomlin, courtesy of* SCLC)

Celebrating the victory in Charleston, SC, and my release from jail, with Jesse Jackson (in daishiki). (© *by Elaine Tomlin, courtesy of* SCLC)

Jesse Jackson preaching with me during
entrance services for the new house of
worship of the West Hunter Street Baptist
Church.

West Hunter Street Baptist
Church.

Sitting with a group of proud children in Greene County, AL, just following the election (by an 80 percent black population) of the probate judge, high sheriff, superintendent of schools, all seven county commissioners, and all nine members of the school board. (© *by Elaine Tomlin, courtesy of SCLC*)

My first family reunion, 1969, in front of the house where I was born: the Louivery and W. L. Abernathy children with their spouses. *Seated left to right*: the late Ella Louise Gibbs, the late Joseph H. Gibbs, Louvenia Coats, V. O. Lawson, Manerva Lawson, Lula Mae Yarbrough, Susie E. Abernathy Hildretch. *Standing*: Tulfa (Jack) Abernathy, the late Isyphine Abernathy, the late Kermit Theodore (K. T.) Abernathy, Susie Dell Abernathy, William A. Abernathy, Norma Easley Abernathy, Garlen Abernathy, Elizabeth Eaton Abernathy, James Earl Abernathy, Joyce McKay Abernathy, Clarence H. Abernathy, Juanita Odessa Jones Abernathy, and me.

My family today. *Seated*: Juanita and me. *Standing*: the Honorable Ralph David Abernathy III (a Georgia state representative), Kwame Luthuli (a student at Williams College), Juandalynn Ralpheda Abernathy (an opera singer in West Germany). *Kneeling*: Donzaleigh Avis Abernathy (a Hollywood actress). *(Courtesy of Joseph Clayton)*

The next weeks were uneasy and filled with rumors of a breakdown in communications and a renunciation of the agreement. Some of the white leaders, in an effort to save face in the wake of mounting criticism, tried to suggest that they had not really agreed to the addition of more than a single black clerk in the downtown area; but we patiently reminded them that those present had understood the wording to mean that each store would employ at least one black salesperson and that this action was only a symbolic gesture of more such hirings in the near future.

As we had hoped and prayed, the Alabama Supreme Court did indeed rule that Albert Boutwell and his nine fellow councilmen were the legal governing body of Birmingham and that Mayor Hanes and Commissioners Connor and Waggoner had been deposed at the time Boutwell and his councilmen were sworn in. Though Boutwell was no integrationist, he was a fair man who respected the word given to our representatives by Birmingham's white negotiators. On July 16, three months after we had entered Birmingham, the biracial committee held its first meeting, and a week later the city council repealed every single segregation ordinance, paving the way for the local merchants to keep their part of the bargain.

The eventual result of this action was the Birmingham described by Mayor Richard Arrington in the quotation at the beginning of this chapter. We had won a great victory, not merely because we had defeated Bull Connor on his home field, but more importantly because we had persuaded the basically decent white leaders of Birmingham to come forward for the first time and take charge of race relations in their own city.

To be sure, they had not wanted to do so. Left to their own devices, they would still be selling merchandise in stores where restrooms and fitting rooms were still marked "white" and "colored" and where black people could not sit down beside white people at a lunch counter and order a ham sandwich. These were not bad people, but they were not good people either. They lacked the character or the moral insight or the religious zeal to do what was right. Perhaps they didn't even know what was right when they did it. That's where we came in. We made it impossible for them not to do the right thing without taking an even greater risk in defense of what was evil.

Near the end of the Birmingham campaign we staged the March on Washington. Everyone involved in the civil rights movement during those years now remembers having dreamed up the March on Washington, and in a way everyone is right. We all talked about the possibility a year or so before a coalition of organizations finally made concrete plans and actually put them into action. It was an idea that recommended itself.

Though we were focusing our attacks on the South—and during 1963–64 primarily on the state of Alabama—we knew that our real target was Congress, and Congress met in the nation's capital. What we wanted was federal legislation, the only sure end to our regional problems; but we had learned that with the media focusing on our struggles night after night, we could catch the attention of the nation's legislators only by exposing ourselves to the billy clubs and paddywagons of the local police. That approach, however, was neither the safest nor the most direct.

So from time to time we toyed with the idea of converging on Washington and confronting Congress itself rather than fighting local battles and hoping the senators and representatives would feel the heat in their faraway offices. Whenever we felt discouraged at the lack of progress in a local campaign, someone was bound to say, "Why don't we just go up to Washington with as many people as we can muster, and tell Congress what we want face to face?"

Everyone would nod and say, "Maybe we ought to do that," but we were always in the middle of some march or demonstration and had too many problems already without taking on another project. Still, we all knew that eventually we would organize such a massive demonstration.

Toward the end of the Birmingham campaign we began to consider the Washington march more seriously because we became increasingly frustrated over the failure of the Kennedy administration to take up our cause with sufficient zeal. Both the president and the attorney general were eloquent in their com-mendation of civil rights. From time to time both endorsed our goals, and when we got into trouble—when we were jailed or our lives were in danger—they would respond. Unfortunately, it always took some significant initiative on our part for them to take positive steps, and we were certain that Congress would never move unless pushed to do so by President Kennedy. He was, after all, not only the leader of the country but also the leader of the Democratic Party, which at the time controlled both houses of Congress.

Before we could make definite plans, however, Bull Connor brought out the dogs, Martin and I were jailed, and the nation saw it all happen on television. Letters and telegrams poured into the White House. The Kennedys saw that at last they had the popular support they needed to take action, and the president proposed the civil rights legislation we had been asking for. On June 19, 1963, he introduced a bill that, though less sweeping that we had wanted, was a major step in the right direction.

In the meantime, A. Philip Randolph had been developing the most concrete plans yet for a major rally in the nation's capital. He was working on a two-day demonstration; the first day devoted to a march on Capitol Hill, the second day to a mass meeting on the Mall where a number of people would speak—civil rights leaders, sympathetic legislators, perhaps the president himself.

Randolph—the dean of civil rights leaders—had for many years used the threat of a Washington march to exact concessions and promises from politicians. He had intimidated Franklin D. Roosevelt with the specter of black people gathering in the capital, and though in the forties he was probably bluffing, by the sixties he knew we had the capacity to deliver tens of thousands of demonstrators, so he began to make plans in earnest.

We all respected him because, in a time when few blacks would speak out, he had organized the Pullman car porters and wielded them into an important arm of the national labor move-ment. An elegant and dignified man, he spoke with an Oxford accent of his own invention, though at times he would forget and say "cain't" instead "cawn't"—a slip that those of us who loved and admired him overlooked.

Initially Randolph's planned march was not directed specifically at civil rights legislation but focused instead on the overall economic plight of black people in America. At the time the leaders of the SCLC were dedicated to removing legal barriers to the freedom of our people and were not as actively concerned with bread and butter issues as we later became, though such matters were always in the back of our mind. However, when Randolph and others began talking about the rally early in 1963, we realized the potential impact that such an event could have on the president's commitment to a civil rights bill.

By June, with the civil rights bill before Congress, it was obvious that a Washington march would be feasible. The financial and logistical support was obtainable, and we saw evidence that we could attract at least one hundred thousand people to the event—more than enough to make an impression on the White House and Congress.

Though Philip Randolph was the most important single figure involved in the planning, the leaders of ten organizations were principally responsible for the final shape of the event. In addition to Randolph, who at the time headed the Negro American Labor Council, the others included: James Farmer of CORE; John Lewis of SNCC; Mathew Ahmann, executive director of the Catholic Conference for Interracial Justice; Eugene Carson Blake of the National Council of Churches; Rabbi Joachim Prinz, representing the American Jewish Council; Roy Wilkins of the NAACP; Whitney Young of the National Urban League; Walter Reuther of the United Auto Workers; and Martin Luther King, leader of the SCLC.

The plan that eventually evolved, which a number of us hammered out in the basement of the Metropolitan Baptist Church, was a slightly modified version of what Randolph had originally proposed. Instead of a two-day event, the group eventually settled on a one-day march, beginning with entertainment and culminating in a rally in front of the Lincoln Memorial. A small, representative delegation would make a courtesy call on the leaders of Congress, and all members of the House and Senate would be specially invited to the rally; but we would not swarm up Capitol Hill by the tens of thousands and surround the legislators. Such an action, we were persuaded, might support the charges of our enemies that we were a group of fanatics.

If the March on Washington seemed like a gamble at the time, in retrospect I realize that we had a great deal more to lose than to gain. Martin and I were both worried about violence. On this subject, Martin had said, "The Negro is shedding himself of his fear, and my real worry is how we will keep this fearlessness from rising to violent proportions." He had also expressed to me his concern that with SNCC involved the march could easily provoke an incident that could lead to trouble.

"If that happens, Ralph," he said, "everything we have done in Birmingham will be wiped out in a single day."

Representative Charles C. Diggs, Jr., of Detroit—one of the few black congressmen—also raised questions about the propriety of the march, and even asked that the leadership reconsider the idea. So it was not only our enemies who suggested that we were going to bring a dangerous mob to the nation's capital. Our best friends were also concerned.

The event was finally scheduled for Wednesday, August 28, and we began making arrangements to transport as many people to Washington as we could possibly muster. As always, buses had to be hired and other needs anticipated. As treasurer of the SCLC and southern coordinator for the march, I had to make certain the money was available and paid out to the right people at the right time. While most people remember only the triumphant moments in front of the Lincoln Memorial, what I also remember are the hard work and enormous expenditures that got us there.

We didn't do everything by ourselves. Not only did the ten sponsoring organizations make significant contributions but outside groups did as well. For example, the National Council of Churches prepared eighty thousand lunches, which they brought to the Mall in refrigerator trucks and sold to the marchers at less than cost. Several labor organizations, such as the International Ladies Garment Workers Union, also paid for busloads of demonstrators to make the trip.

Three days before the march, in response to the expressed fears of politicians and Washington police officials, the leaders of the march issued an eloquent appeal to the marchers, reminding them of precisely why they were there and precisely whom they represented. In part this appeal said:

> [T]he Washington March is a living petition—in the flesh—of the scores of thousands of citizens of both races who will be present from all parts of our country.
>
> It will be orderly but not subservient. It will be proud but not arrogant. It will be nonviolent, but not timid. It will be unified in purposes and behavior, not splintered into groups and individual competitors. It will be outspoken, but not raucous.
>
> It will have the dignity befitting a demonstration on behalf of the human rights of 20 millions of people, with the eye and the judgment of the world focused upon Washington, D.C., on Aug. 28, 1963. In a neighborhood dispute, there may be stunts, rough words and even hot insults, but when a whole people speaks to its Government, the dialogue and the action must be on a level reflecting the worth of that people and the responsibility of that Government.

The appeal called on everyone involved in the march "to resist provocations to disorder and violence" and "to remember that evil persons are determined to smear this march. . . ." It also called for "self-discipline so that no one in our own ranks, however enthusiastic, shall be the spark for disorder," and for "resistance to the efforts of those who, while not enemies of the march as such, might seek to use it to advance causes not dedicated primarily to civil rights or to the welfare of our country."

This appeal, published in newspapers and distributed among participating groups, set the tone for the occasion. Nobody was reassured, however. The Washington police announced that they would be pressing into service almost 2,000 of the 2,930-member force, and Deputy Police Chief Howard Covell told the press nervously, "We expect one hundred fifty thousand persons. We are prepared to handle this number—peacefully. But I tell you this—we could not handle this number if it were not peaceful."

Less than forty-eight hours before the march was scheduled to begin, two things happened that helped to put the event into focus. First, word came from Africa that W. E. B. Dubois had died at the age of ninety-five. Founder of the NAACP and father of the civil rights movement, he had lived till the eve of this great occasion, when the entire world would see his people gather together in a peaceful and eloquent demonstration of their newly found strength. Thus the March on Washington became a kind of memorial to the spirit he had exemplified during his long and fruitful career.

On the other hand, the day after Dubois died, Paul Johnson won a runoff election in Mississippi to become the Democratic nominee for governor, and thus a sure winner in the general election. It was Johnson who had joined with Gov. Ross Barnett to block James Meredith's entrance to the University of Mississippi; and though Meredith had eventually registered, Johnson had run in the primary using his segregationist stance as his sole issue. So as we prepared to go to Washington we were reminded that Jim Crow was far from dead in the Deep South. Its advocates were still holding the highest state offices and exercising the most powerful local authority.

On the eve of our march, we set up headquarters in a green and white tent near the Washington Monument and began to prepare for the proceedings the next day. People were already pouring in from around the country, and the tent became a focal point for the frenzy of activity that always comes at the last minute, when everyone remembers a hundred things that need to be done—sign making, march organizing, speech polishing. All night long people worked over tables in the light from naked bulbs strung from the poles.

By seven the next morning huge crowds had already begun to gather, and by midmorning police were estimating the number assembled at ninety thousand. Already the crowd had exceeded the expectations of many. And still the buses rolled in, unloading scores more, many carrying signs, some black, some white, all in a holiday mood. I can say that of all the demonstrations we ever organized, the crowd at the March on Washington was the happiest and the least likely to cause trouble. I knew from the beginning of the day that we would have no ugly incidents, that all the fears had been ill-founded.

The official proceedings began with our courtesy visits to Capitol Hill. About seventy-five of us went to the offices of House and Senate leaders in both parties to ask for their support during the upcoming fight for passage of the president's civil rights bill. We met with Majority Leader Mike Mansfield and Minority Leader Everett Dirksen in the Senate and with Speaker of the House John McCormack. They listened courteously to what we said and promised to give our words every consideration. I remember coming away with the idea that everyone was walking on eggs until after the march was over. Only then would they know for sure whether or not it was safe to say something positive about our visit.

While we were winding up our business on Capitol Hill, the crowds were assembling at the foot of the Washington Monument to see and hear a number of prominent entertainers who had come to support our efforts. Among those who made appearances were Harry Belafonte; Mehalia Jackson; Joan Baez; Peter, Paul, and Mary; Odetta; Charlton Heston; James Baldwin; and Jackie Robinson.

When we got back from our meetings with the chief congressional leaders, we discovered that a major crisis was in the making. John Lewis's speech, which had been distributed to the press the night before, was causing serious problems; and Cardinal Patrick O'Boyle, who was scheduled to give the invocation at the main ceremony, had announced that he would withdraw unless Lewis made significant changes in his text.

In particular, Boyle and others objected to the attacks on the Kennedy administration and to unnecessarily provocative statements that might be used by our enemies to defeat the civil rights bill. Among other things, Lewis intended to accuse President Kennedy of appointing racist judges and of taking sides against the civil rights movement in Albany. He also planned to say: "We will not wait for the President, the Justice Department, nor the Congress, but we will take matters into our own hands and create a source of power, outside of any national structure, that could and would assure us a victory. . . . The revolution is at hand."

Such statements were not in keeping with the spirit of the march as defined in "the appeal" published three days earlier. Undoubtedly our enemies in Congress would focus on John Lewis's statements, offering them as proof that the civil rights movement was in the hands of radical revolutionaries. The Kennedys were distressed when they read the advanced copy of the Lewis address, and Burke Marshall of the Justice Department acted as a go-between in an attempt to get John to moderate his tone. In fact, it was undoubtedly the president who asked Cardinal O'Boyle to use his influence in the matter.

Predictably, John Lewis refused. He had worked hard on the speech. He represented one of the more militant groups in the coalition, and he wanted his voice to echo that militancy. So he said he would deliver the speech as written.

For a while it looked as if the spirit of the occasion would be marred. First one, then another of the older leaders tried to reason with him. Randolph, whose age and quiet dignity impressed us all, finally prevailed; and with great reluctance John agreed to make the changes. I remember that even as the proceedings were in progress at that Lincoln Memorial, John and two coauthors were huddled behind Lincoln's statue, angrily pounding on a portable typewriter. The result was a speech of great power, but one that could not be used as a weapon against the movement.

A number of people addressed the crowd that afternoon, from Josephine Baker to Roy Wilkins; and all were eloquent and moving. Most of them spoke of the struggles we had undergone and of the even harder challenges that lay just ahead. Most were militant in tone and accusatory in their language, and certainly it was a time for militant accusations: *Brown v. Board of Education* had been handed down nine years earlier, yet most of the schools in the South were still segregated. Though segregated public transportation had been ruled unconstitutional in 1956, there was still segregation on the buses throughout the region. And still black workers were underemployed and underpaid.

John Lewis summed up that side of the ledger when he cried:

> They're talking about slow-down and stop. We will not stop.
>
> If we do not get meaningful legislation out of this Congress, the time will come when we will not confine our marching to Washington. We will march through the South, through the streets of Jackson, through the streets of Danville, through the streets of Cambridge, through the streets of Birmingham.

Roy Wilkins, Walter Reuther, and Philip Randolph took similar lines, as did all of the other leaders, including James Farmer, who had been jailed in Louisiana and whose speech was read by stand-in Floyd McKissick. Thus did they set the stage for Martin, who was the last major speaker of the day.

How he knew just what note to strike I can't say. It was part of his genius to be able to rise to such occasions and somehow transcend them. He did it the last night of his life, and he did it on that hot August day in 1963, standing before a crowd that by then numbered 250,000 people.

Instead of dwelling on the bitterness of the past or the severe problems of the present he gave the cheering crowd, as well as the millions who watched on television, the vision of a future no one else had defined and few black people could imagine. It wasn't that Martin disagreed with the grim messages the others had brought to the crowd and to the American people. The dream he envisioned acknowledged the truth of everything that had already been said. He simply looked beyond the injustice and hatred and division to see what America could become, if and when it realized its fullest potential as a nation. It was a prophecy of pure hope at a time when black people and the nation as a whole needed hope more than anything else.

When he had finished, those present and the nation as a whole knew that they had heard one of the great speeches in American history. Its phrases were already burned into the memory of all who heard it, and people were quoting them verbatim when the newspapers came out the next day, some carrying the full text, most quoting large segments. It was one of those few public utterances that instantly becomes a part of the oral tradition of a people, never to be forgotten. More than twenty-five years later, most Americans, white as well as black, can quote phrases and even sentences from that speech. It was the crowning moment in the greatest ceremony of the civil rights movement.

I say "ceremony," because I doubt that the March on Washington actually led to passage of the civil rights bill or, for the matter, to any other specific improvement in the condition of black Americans. When asked whether or not Congress had been moved, both Senator Mike Mansfield and Senator Everett Dirksen said they doubted the occasion would have any effect. Even Hubert Humphrey, whose support for us was always whole-hearted and unwavering, said: "All this probably hasn't changed any votes on the civil rights bill, but it's a good thing for Washington and the nation and the world."

Certainly he was right. Ceremonies of this sort have an important effect on the consciousness of a community or a people, even if they don't result in concrete actions. After the March on Washington, everyone felt better about themselves and about the country. We had gone to our nation's capital. We had not been unruly or even discourteous. Instead we had been joyously affirmative. We had staged a gigantic political rally—the largest of its kind in the history of the nation—and we had presented a gift to America, a great new affirmation of the principle of equality to put in its National Archives. The administering of a pledge to the entire audience, the benediction by Dr. Benjamin E. Mays, even the conversation we had with the president later in the day were really anticlimactic after listening to Martin's eloquent rekindling of the American dream. The drama had ended when he spoke those last words, and the applause would continue to echo through the years.

9

St. Augustine

WE WERE ALWAYS on the lookout for localities that had particularly harsh regimes, cities that were oppressive beyond the ordinary limits of southern society. Segregation by definition was evil, but evil in this world exists in degrees; and there were some towns and cities that were more dictatorial and abusive than others. We tried to seek out these places, because the black people who lived there were in more immediate need. (In warfare you always take care of your seriously wounded first.)

So we sought out St. Augustine—or to be more precise, St. Augustine sought out us. The oldest European settlement in the nation, St. Augustine was located in the "porkchop" section of Florida, the central part of the state that was more southern than the two coasts, and also more segregationist. It was St. Augustine and Tallahassee rather than Miami and St. Petersburg that produced the racial headlines during the 1950s and 1960s.

St. Augustine in particular had been a center of racist activity for a decade, and the Ku Klux Klan had openly conducted its bizarre seances there, continually reminding blacks as well as whites that violence was always a possibility in the community "if things went too far." As a matter of fact, Klan leader Holsted "Hoss" Manucy was something of a public figure in St. Augustine and was occasionally seen with St. Johns County Sheriff L. O. Davis, one of those southern lawmen who helped to create the familiar TV stereotype—mean-spirited, ignorant, and gratuitously cruel.

Standing up for racial justice in the community were three black leaders of extraordinary character. One, Dr. Robert B. Hayling, was a local dentist and a key member of the St. Augustine chapter of the NAACP. Another was Rev. Floyd McKissick, a local Baptist pastor. A third was Goldie Eubanks, one of the most outspoken black activists and also a member of the NAACP. They had been protesting the white regime for a number of years and were particularly frustrated that ten years after *Brown v. Board of Education* little had changed in St. Augustine, Florida.

The occasion for a major confrontation presented itself in 1964 when the city fathers decided to seek federal funds to defray the cost of celebrating the 400th anniversary of the founding of St. Augustine. Dr. Hayling, speaking for the black community, protested to federal authorities, including President Lyndon Johnson, that no federal assistance should be given to a city that practiced the most rigid form of segregation. When this attempt at intervention became public knowledge, the white businessmen of St. Augustine were furious. The establishment had been wounded in the most vital part of its anatomy—its pocketbook.

The *St. Augustine Record*, yet one more segregationist newspaper, attacked Hayling and the battle was on. Blacks began picketing. Confrontations and fights increased. Arrests were made. And then—as was often the case in such an atmosphere— dangerous violence followed. Someone hurled bricks and fired shots at Dr. Hayling's home. He and others were beaten. Finally, during one of several occasions when armed whites drove through the black section of town, shots were exchanged and someone was killed.

But things were slightly different this time—it was a white man who was killed instead of a black. He had been armed, and the bullets had been fired from such cars in the past. But police determined that the shot had come from the home of Goldie Eubanks, and he had been arrested for murder, along with three other men whom investigators had placed at the scene of the death.

Dr. Hayling, sensing that a legal lynching was about to take place, called for intervention by the federal courts, but nothing happened. In the meantime, the violence escalated, and in a way that was familiar to those of us who had lived through the Montgomery campaign. The house of a black family was set on fire, presumably because they had sent their children to a previously all-white school in the fall. The car of another family was burned. Someone fired four shotgun blasts at Dr. Hayling's front door.

At this point, the NAACP removed Dr. Hayling from his position with the local chapter, perhaps because local white leaders blamed him for the violence, and because the organization had in turn been judged guilty by association. Needless to say, we were shocked at this action. When Dr. Hayling and Goldie Eubanks resigned from the NAACP and asked to be affiliated with the SCLC, we accepted them into our ranks, with the understanding that we would permit only nonviolent activities and nonviolent rhetoric.

The first thing we did was send Willie Bolden, Robert Johnson, J. T. Johnson, Richard Gay, R. B. Cottonreader, Rev. C. T. Vivian, Rev. Fred Taylor, Rev. T. Y. Rogers, and other staff members to St. Augustine to "work-shop" all of the activists there so that they would know and understand both the theory and practice of nonviolent protest. Dr. Hayling had been quoted as saying: "I and others of the NAACP have armed ourselves and we will shoot and ask questions later." Shortly thereafter the white "nightrider" had been killed. We could have no more statements of that sort. Henceforth, everyone involved in SCLC-sponsored activities would go unarmed and would submit to whatever indignity and physical abuse the St. Augustine community could devise.

The next thing we did was support a nationwide call for volunteers to come to St. Augustine and demonstrate against the continuing racial injustice there. The call was answered by a number of young people, as well as by several older women of note, including Mrs. Malcolm Peabody, mother of Gov. Endicott Peabody of Massachusetts, and Mrs. John Burgess, wife of a black Episcopal bishop. Both were arrested for attempting to integrate the dining room of a local motel. In addition, almost a hundred black students were arrested at the same site. This incident brought widespread attention to the problems of St. Augustine, and we saw the possibility of making real progress in the wake of this national publicity.

Because of this almost accidental focus on public accommodations, our efforts in St. Augustine began to center more and more on the integration of the local hotels and motels. Having already accomplished so much along these lines in Birmingham, we hoped to widen the acceptance of integrated public accommodations in this hard-core community, where the Klan still moved about with easy acceptance.

The Reverend C. T. Vivian had come aboard by then, and he was our chief initial contact with Dr. Hayling and his group. The Reverend Hosea Williams had also joined the staff, as had Rev. Andrew Young and Rev. James Bevel; so we were almost at full strength and ready to do battle on a number of fronts around the region.

These new members brought in new ideas, among them Hosea Williams's suggestion that to avoid the terrible heat of midday we hold our marches at night. So after Mrs. Peabody, Mrs. Burgess, and the students had been arrested in late March, we began a series of nighttime demonstrations that began in late May and lasted through most of the summer.

We had a perfect symbol of our demonstrations in the old slave market, an historic section of the city where blacks had been sold to the highest bidder. This center of tourist interest was our destination on many of our marches; once there, we would remind those watching and listening that St. Augustine still condoned practices that were akin to the institution of slavery.

These demonstrations severely disrupted the tourist traffic that was so vital to the city's economic well being, particularly in this quadricentennial year. The businessmen were furious, as were the Ku Kluxers; so from the beginning we had an audience of hostile and at times obscene local onlookers. As tensions built in late spring and early summer, this hostility erupted into violence and bloodshed.

Indeed, we received from the citizens and authorities in St. Augustine what we had never been able to elicit from their counterparts in Albany—brutal unprovoked attacks that were immediately broadcast over the television sets of the nation and published in newspapers across the country. This in turn prompted letters and phone calls of protest to Congress, where, at this very time, the 1964 Civil Rights Act was being held up on the floor of the Senate by a southern filibuster. Reports from St. Augustine and the subsequent reaction by citizens nationwide clearly spurred senators who were straddling the fence to vote for cloture, and debate was shut off by a vote of 71-29, clearing the way for passage. This happened in early June.

In addition, the violence helped us raise money for our growing budget. We were perpetually in financial difficulties, as are most nonprofit organizations dedicated to social change. We were financed for the most part by donations from black churches all over the country, northern synagogues, direct-mail appeals, labor unions, and rallies where Martin and I and other staff members spoke. Many people were generous, and some were thoughtful enough to send money on a regular basis, even when we were not making headlines by being beaten or thrown in jail.

But when the nation's television screens were filled with pictures of policemen swinging billy clubs and nonviolent pro-testers being stoned or gassed or kicked, then the conscience of the nation was awakened, and two or three days later hundreds of checks would begin to pour into our Atlanta office from the farthest corners of the globe. Mayor Kelley and Sheriff Laurie Pritchett of Albany may have instinctively understood that principle. Mayor Shelley and Sheriff Davis of St. Augustine and St. Johns County clearly did not, and their "careless" maintenance of law and order, particularly in the spring of 1964, contributed immeasurably to our bank account at a time when we were genuinely worried about being able to continue.

However, despite the fact that this kind of violence brought in contributions, we looked at it with great apprehension. In late

May, white crowds attacked us during a march to the slave quarters and with a half-hearted defense by the police we found ourselves in danger of serious injury. Then, after we had withdrawn and the attacks had apparently ceased, they fired shots into a house and automobile in the black section.

After that the police told us we could not march at night, because such activity would promote violence. This prohibition was like telling people they had no right to leave their houses at night because they might be attacked by robbers. We had attacked no one. We were the victims of mob violence. The police should have been restraining our attackers, not us. But, as we knew, it was difficult to distinguish between our attackers and our supposed protectors.

David Garrow, in *Bearing the Cross,* reports that a concurrent FBI report revealed that Sheriff Davis "has currently indicated he would rely on Klan members for assistance in controlling any demonstrations. Davis is quite close to Holsted Manucy, exalted cyclops of the Klan at St. Augustine. Davis was also instrumental in helping the Klan hide out . . . a Klansmen responsible for the bombing of the residence [of a civil rights activist in Jacksonville]."

I was not surprised to read this account years later. It merely confirmed what we already knew: that "Hoss" Manucy had a license to do anything to us that the federal authorities could not prove. That is why Martin appealed to President Johnson and our lawyers appealed to the federal courts to intervene and protect us from the Klan and from the deliberate neglect of the St. Johns County Sheriff's Department. President Johnson gave us nothing in the way of help, but Federal Judge Bryan Simpson listened to our case, saw the evidence of the close connection between Davis and "Hoss" Manucy, and he ruled that we had a right to march at night and that local law enforcement agencies had a responsibility to protect us and ordered them to do so. Again we had appealed to the federal courts and had won our point, a process that made us even greater believers in the majesty of the U.S. government, despite the fact that the court order did us very little good a few nights later when rock-throwing whites bombarded us, despite the presence of local police who used tear gas on the mob in an effort to repel them.

Around this time we discovered that some of the local black leaders were urging their friends to stock up on firearms in order to resist the attacks of Klansmen and other groups who might invade the black community armed with weapons. Indeed, whites had set fire to one of the houses where we were staying, and fear reached new heights in the wake of the inability of local authorities to restrain white violence.

As soon as we found out that some of our leaders were misleading our demonstrators, we called them in and chewed them out. They had been through our workshops, we told them, so they should have known better. Only with the use of nonviolence would the indignation of the entire country be stirred up in our behalf. Now was the time when we most needed to practice restraint—when violence had already made the national news and the eyes of the nation were on St. Augustine. We asked them to surrender their weapons and to tell the others to do so, and they agreed. But only a few weapons were turned in, and we suspected that some were still holding out on us. So we resolved to change our strategy in order to avoid further danger to the larger community, as well as the collapse of the nonviolent movement.

Martin and I decided to take on the burden of the campaign ourselves by seeking arrest. It was easy enough in St. Augustine. All we had to do was go over to the Monson Motor Lodge, stroll into the dining room, and ask to be served. The proprietor told us blacks could not be served in his establishment and asked us to leave. We refused and he called the police. The whole process took less than an hour and our arrest made the evening news. That night, when we marched back to the slave market, we did so with less violence than before, perhaps because our arrests had to some degree satisfied the bloodlust of the mob.

Several days later, while trying to come up with a new way to make the same point, Hosea Williams hit on the perfect plan, one that would help us beat the heat and challenge segregation at the same time: We would integrate the motel swimming pools.

"But how will we do that?" I asked. "As soon as we walk down the street with our bathing suits on, the police will surround us and keep us from getting near a pool."

"It's easy," said Hosea. "I've already got it worked out. A couple of our white friends will register at the Monson Motor Lodge. Then, we'll go by their rooms, one or two at a time. We'll change into bathing suits there and then step out the door and walk over to the pool. It's just a few steps. Before they know we're there, we'll be paddling around the pool."

It sounded like a good plan, so we agreed to try it. We slipped unnoticed into the motel and changed into our suits. Then we walked toward the pool, where about ten white people were already swimming. One of them saw us, then several more. They stared at us with uncomprehending eyes, telling themselves we weren't going to do what it appeared we would do. Then, all at once, we plunged into the pool with them. Instantly they clambered out and walked away as quickly as they could. We weren't sure whether they got out because they didn't want to share the pool with us or because they knew that the fireworks were about to begin.

Sure enough, in less than a minute the manager came rushing out of the lobby and over to the poolside, waving his hand frantically.

"You can't do that," he screamed. "Get out! Get out or I'll call the police."

We laughed and waved at him, and he wheeled around and charged back inside. He came charging back out a minute later with a five gallon can and held it poised over the water.

"OK," he said. "This is acid. *Acid!* If you don't get out I'll pour it in the water."

I turned to Hosea at that point and asked him if he thought the man really had acid in the can.

"Probably," he said.

After warning us one more time, the manager turned up the can and some sort of red liquid spilled into the water and made a dark stain that began to spread. For a minute or so we were uneasy, but the stain disappeared before it spread to where we were standing in deep water.

The manager knew at the same time we did that our skins weren't going to burn off our bodies, so he cursed and ran back into the building. Five minutes later we heard the distant wail of a siren that grew louder and louder. At least two squad cars arrived and several policemen came rushing into the courtyard, as if they had been called to quell a riot.

"OK," one of them yelled. "You niggers are under arrest."

"Fine," we said, "come in and put the cuffs on us."

"Come out of the water right now," the ranking officer barked and came to the edge, trying to reach out to grab an arm. Instinctively we all swam to the middle and began waving. The water was lukewarm in the burning Florida sun, but it was still soothing; so we saw no reason to hurry out of the pool and be hauled off to a hot jail. Besides, we were enjoying the frustration of the police, who were trying to arrest us without losing their dignity or getting wet.

They stood on the side, glaring at us and occasionally whispering to one another, while we floated on our backs or paddled around in small circles. One account has a policeman finally wading into the pool to make the collar, but I don't remember it that way. As I recall, we finally got tired of the game; and worrying about excessive exposure to the sun, we swam to the side, climbed out, and submitted to arrest.

During this period, the grand jury was meeting to hear our charges concerning lax law enforcement and to make some sense out of the local chaos. When word came that we had actually invaded an all-white swimming pool, they quickly used the occasion to denounce us as outside agitators and to ask that we leave the community—as if the problem were the demonstrations themselves and not the injustices that had provoked the demonstrations.

We had heard this before in Albany and Birmingham, where the white establishment had tried to convince the world and itself that local black citizens had been perfectly happy until we had come along. But this time they had a bribe to offer us—if we would leave St. Augustine, the grand jury would set up a biracial committee to resolve the questions we had been raising.

It is difficult even now to think that they could have so misread our strategy or our resolve. They had agreed to consider the idea of a biracial committee precisely because we were there, marching down their main streets, affronting their tourists, embarrassing them nightly on the evening news. Hadn't they watched us hang tough in Birmingham? We had no intention of leaving, and we told them so. But we did make a counterproposal: We would stop the demonstrations for one week if they would appoint a biracial committee immediately. The grand jury rejected the offer.

A few days later we had a near riot down at the slave market. Our demonstrators were attacked by a white mob that had been stirred up by the Klan and by J. B. Stoner, self-appointed spokesman for the white race, who would be with us for several decades, turning up in various parts of the region, sometimes running for office, sometimes simply appearing wherever racial trouble broke out, always intent on making things worse than they had been before he arrived. This time he succeeded in so inflaming the swelling crowd that they not only sent a number of our demonstrators to the hospital, but also shot a policeman in the arm.

At this point the direction of the confrontations was clear: Sooner or later someone would be killed, and perhaps a good many people. Though we had wanted to dramatize for the American people the hatred and violence inherent in this ancient city, we did not want to be the cause of anyone's death—and we were certain that at any moment one of our leaders or supporters would be gunned down at night or else bludgeoned to death by someone in the mob that was increasing in size and ferocity with every night.

Fortunately, authorities in both Washington, D.C., and Tallahassee were also alarmed. For the first time, all parties tried to persuade the local leaders to establish a biracial committee so that instead of confronting one another on the streets, blacks and whites could sit down in quiet deliberation and work out a desegregation plan that would eventually lead to an integrated and united community. Governor Farris Bryant met with St. Augustine banker Herbert Wolfe, who seemed to speak for the local business community in his desire to extricate the city from its current difficulties. Bryant, who had not been particularly friendly toward black people in the past, was nonetheless genuinely interested in preventing violence and bloodshed; and we in turn met with Dan Warren, an attorney who could speak for Bryant and the state of Florida.

Our goal at this stage was the establishment of a biracial committee that seemed to have a genuine chance to succeed. We could not afford to carry on another protracted campaign just at this time. After all, we were not certain that we had really finished our work in Birmingham. We had received assurance that the new city government would see that all promises were kept, but already there was some talk that the merchants would not honor some of their commitments, and we were planning to establish a permanent office there, with the possibility that we might have to go back in if the agreement fell to pieces.

If we stayed in St. Augustine, we would need all of our forces. As a matter of fact, Hosea Williams was playing an important role in our night marches, and he was the one we had hoped would be monitoring the situation in Birmingham. Martin was like a general who has a small army and must therefore pick and choose where he will fight his battles. St. Augustine was not a place to fight a major battle. We were vastly outnumbered and were consequently in danger of sustaining heavy losses. Better to wring some significant concession and then leave the field.

According to Garrow, Martin summarized our position to Dan Warren as follows: "I want out of St. Augustine. . . . But I must come out of St. Augustine with honor. . . . I must come out of here with a victory."

What we were worried about, of course, was another Albany. Birmingham was still too fragile a victory to risk another obvious retreat. For the sake of the movement and our people, we had to make some progress in the battle, otherwise blacks would lose heart nationwide, and all our legal victories would be hollow and empty as the South retrenched and reestablished de facto segregation. So the victory Martin called for was not for himself but for justice and equality.

However, even though we suspended our downtown marches to facilitate the progress of talks, the local leaders were still unwilling to grant us the biracial committee. In fact, during the middle of the negotiations they put out warrants for the arrest of Martin and several others because, following the successful example of Birmingham, they had recruited minors to join the demonstrations. The charge against the leaders was contributing to the delinquency of a minor.

Then, when all seemed lost, the governor of Florida suddenly saved the day. Or so we all believed.

He called a press conference and announced that he had appointed a biracial committee to resolve the racial tensions in St. Augustine and that all four men had agreed to serve. The press asked him who these people were, but he declined to name them.

We were delighted. A great burden had been lifted from our shoulders, though we were quite surprised that Bryant, who had been elected as a segregationist, would give us what we wanted— and over the objection of Mayor Shelley and others, who protested the governor's interference in a matter they regarded as purely local. In response to this clear-cut submission to our chief demand, we immediately suspended further demonstrations for two weeks and packed our bags and headed back to Atlanta, stopping just long enough to tell reporters that we were now going to turn our attention to more pressing problems in Alabama.

It was only much later that we learned the truth; There was no biracial committee. Governor Bryant had simply lied to the press and to the public.

I don't think we suspected that the governor would make up a story and tell it to the entire state, just to buy a little peace and quiet. We were prepared for him to make promises that he had no intention of keeping, and we were certainly used to having Old Pharaoh change his mind after making promises that he did intend to keep. But I don't think it occurred to us at the time that Farris Bryant would say he had chosen four people to serve on a committee when he had not done any such thing. Bryant's own account is therefore painful and disturbing, even after twenty-five years.

He reports having told Mayor Shelley that the biracial committee would serve as a necessary deterrent to violence, even if it never met. Bryant wrote that when Shelley asked for clarification of what Bryant meant, he said that I said: "I'll tell you something, Dr. Shelley, if you'll give me your word you won't reveal it."

"What's that?"

"Well, there's no committee. . . . I've told everybody including the Negroes that I've appointed a committee but I have not."

The lack of integrity in public officials is a fact we have learned to live with over the last twenty-five years; yet even in the days of Watergate I'm not sure that high officials lied in quite the same way Farris Bryant lied at this crucial moment in our negotiations. In boasting about it afterward, he was like a con man, bragging about pulling off a million dollar swindle.

And indeed we were conned. Weeks went by before we began to realize that no biracial committee would be meeting, no conflicts would be resolved, and no integration of public facilities would take place in St. Augustine. Eventually, Mayor Shelley told the public why, thereby breaking his word to Governor Bryant, though he probably told himself the statute of limitations had run out.

To be sure, it extricated St. Augustine and the State of Florida from a tight spot. We left town. No one was killed. Racial tensions cooled down for a while. So perhaps in the eyes of many people the end justified the means.

But Governor Bryant's strategic lying cost the white community considerable credibility—if only in future years. We never completely believed an elected official again, no matter how high his office or how sincere his protestations. If Mayor Richard Daley was angered and hurt when we questioned his word in negotiations during our Chicago campaign, he needn't have blamed us. It was Gov. Farris Bryant of Florida who made us doubters.

St. Augustine also put us on notice that the violence we had experienced during our marches in Birmingham was by no means the worst we could expect. With cooperation from local authorities, hate groups like the Ku Klux Klan might go to any lengths to keep us from bringing about the inevitable a day sooner than was necessary. Indeed, as we examined the situation we faced in that oldest of American cities, we realized that we could not always count on the federal government to step in and save us from local forces hostile to our agenda. In this case, President Johnson had shown interest and had tried to influence

Mayor Shelley to reach some agreement with us, but as we left we had the idea that it would have taken no less than a few black bodies to spur the federal government to action if local and state authorities stood by and allowed the violence.

Of course, there were constitutional reasons why Johnson hesitated as well as political considerations. Most of the laws violated by Hoss Manucy and his fellow Klansmen were local or state, and it was the responsibility of local and state authorities to handle their enforcement. But there was plenty of precedent to send in federal troops where law and order had broken down in a community, and we were convinced that such a time had arrived in St. Augustine several weeks before we pulled out. When you are surrounded on all sides by attackers, wild-eyed and screaming, you do not think in terms of subtle constitutional distinctions. You run for cover as fast as you can and wonder where the federal troops are.

But it was the political rather than the constitutional considerations that we found suspect when we analyzed the president's reluctance to help us. Senator Barry Goldwater was to be the Republican nominee for president in the upcoming general election. Goldwater, a conservative ideologue, had voted against the 1964 Civil Rights Act and was using the rhetoric of states rights to court southern voters. While experts gave Goldwater no chance to win, Lyndon Johnson knew that it was entirely possible that the senator from Arizona might pick up electoral votes from the South (which, in fact, he did); so Johnson was tiptoeing around civil rights issues until after November.

In retrospect, I can understand his strategy, if not agree with it. At the time, however, with the screams and jeers of the crowds echoing in our ears, we found it difficult not to condemn him for outright political cowardice, particularly given the insurmountable lead he held in the preliminary polls.

We discussed the matter at some length, wondering if we should pay more attention to the political climate in timing our campaigns, but we finally decided that to do so would be to grant our opponents what they had always argued—that we should wait until all the signs were right before we made a move. Had we assented to that principle, we could have shut the doors on the

SCLC and any chance for racial progress. *No* time was right for a civil rights campaign. There were *always* excellent political reasons for waiting until the next month, the next year, the next century.

So we concluded that we would address problems as they came up rather than in the light of the national political scene. It is important, therefore, to note that in 1968 we not only involved ourselves with the Memphis sanitation workers, but also planned and executed our Poor People's March on Washington—and did so during a time when the Democrats had the most to lose by our activities. We concluded that in doing so we were sending a message to both parties: "Our agenda and yours are two different things. Be forewarned that if you don't want trouble during election years, then you had better pay attention to our agenda the rest of the time."

Sometime later—and no one can pinpoint exactly when— the last motel pool was integrated in St. Augustine, Florida. I don't know the name of the black man or woman or child who plunged into the blue, chlorinated water while the manager stood by, arms folded, perhaps clenching his teeth, perhaps smiling with genuine satisfaction. But I am certain that it happened many years after our 1964 campaign in that city, and I can't even say that our several months in St. Augustine helped to prepare the way for that moment.

I can say with certainty that we learned to be more cautious and less trusting during our confrontation with Mayor Shelley and Sheriff Davis and "Hoss" Manucy, and that these lessons, applied in Selma and elsewhere, were valuable in preparing us for a more difficult and violent future. To be sure, after Albany and St. Augustine, we could hardly have been surprised at the hostility and death that were waiting for us. The first example of it occurred just a few weeks later when word came one Sunday morning that the 16th Street Baptist Church in Birmingham had been bombed and those four little girls had been killed. By then we were talking about going to Selma.

10

Selma

BEFORE OUR MARCH AT SELMA, most white people outside Alabama had never heard of the city. It was just a place they went through on their way from Montgomery to Meridian, Mississippi. But blacks in the South knew it as an intellectual and cultural center. It was a mecca for our students, who could go to Selma University or Lutheran University. It was also a church center, which had produced a number of national leaders, including Dr. D. V. Jemison of the Tabernacle Baptist Church, president of the National Baptist Convention, USA, Inc., the largest black organization in the world; and his son, Rev. Dr. T. J. Jemison, presently the president of this illustrious body. It was to many of us the "Capital of the Black Belt," a place where intelligent young people and learned elders gathered.

But none of them were allowed to vote.

The year was 1965 and we had been circling around Selma, trying to decide whether or not we could stir up enough trouble to force the federal government to act on the persistent denial of voting rights to blacks in the South. What we wanted was a voting rights bill passed by Congress, and we knew that we would

297

never get one unless the American people saw what was going on in places like Selma and registered enough indignation to force their elected representatives into action.

In many ways the right to vote was the one right that ensured all other rights. Obviously, the federal government could not patrol every bus line and every restaurant throughout the South. If public transportation and public accommodations were to remain equally accessible to blacks—and that was now the law—then local authorities would have to share the responsibility for seeing that their states and communities created a climate in which the law was obeyed.

I don't mean to suggest that they could enforce federal law. I simply mean that local governments would have to stop conspiring with the more extreme elements in southern society to circumvent federal law, that local elected officials could no longer speak out in favor of segregation or run reelection campaigns promising to keep blacks in their place—by force if necessary. I mean that U.S. senators and representatives could be voted out of office if they went to Washington and talked about using "interposition" to frustrate the will of the Congress and the U.S. Supreme Court.

In many ways Selma served as an ideal illustration of what we had to face throughout the South. After Congress had passed the 1964 Civil Rights Act, blacks in Selma had begun to pressure local authorities and businessmen to comply with the federal statute; but when black organizations such as the Dallas County Voters League began to meet to discuss ways and means of bringing about compliance, a state judge, James Hare, issued an injunction forbidding all public gatherings to accomplish such ends.

Today such a judicial action seems incredible, a clear violation of the freedom of assembly guaranteed in the Bill of Rights. If any judge at any level were to make such a ruling today, he would be overruled in twenty-four hours by a higher court, exposed to ridicule by the national press, and probably face immediate removal efforts. But in the state of Alabama, *circa* 1964, such high-handed judicial tyranny was not only commonplace but largely successful. Judge Hare's injunction stood for months and its very presence in Alabama was reason enough for us to go to Selma.

In May 1964, we met at the Gaston Motel in Birmingham to talk about strategy in general and Selma in particular. Mrs. Amelia Boynton of the Dallas County Voters League was present and told us of the difficulties they had encountered and of the devastating effect Judge Hare's injunction had had on those activists in and around Selma who wanted to press for voter registration. She pointed out that if this injunction were allowed to stand, then not only would we be unable to push for new civil rights legislation, but we would be unable to seek enforcement of those laws already passed. We would have won a great battle only to lose the war. She pleaded for us to come to Selma next, where our efforts were most needed.

I, for one, was convinced. I said that we needed to look no further for a site to fight our next battle, that we should choose Selma and challenge Judge Hare's illegal injunction. Some others were a little more cautious. After careful deliberation, we came to the conclusion that nothing would change the climate of southern states as much as the emergence of a strong black electorate, one that could mean the difference in a close race between a racial extremist and a racial moderate. We knew that in most places we could not actually elect blacks to office—not yet. But we believed that we could use our voting strength throughout the region to elect people sympathetic to blacks and protective of their rights.

Of course, there were municipalities, counties, and even congressional districts in Deep South states, many of which were now represented by the people who most despised and persecuted blacks, where we believed we could eventually elect mayors, sheriffs, and even congressmen. But initially we merely wanted to get the vote in order to make a difference—to exercise our right as citizens to choose who would govern us—whether black or white.

(May I say parenthetically that time has proven our premise. Whereas, in most of the Deep South, elected politicians routinely made campaign promises to keep us in our place, today no one uses such rhetoric—that is, no one who expects to be elected.

The Gene Talmadges and Theodore Bilbos and John Rankins are gone from the southern political scene. And men who once played a more subdued variation of that game—George Wallace and Strom Thurmond to name but two—in later years have gone out of their way to help the black people and to appeal to them for their votes. Nothing better illustrates the power and importance of the vote than the current racial atmosphere in southern politics, and this was something we knew over twenty years ago when we contemplated going into Selma.)

Of course there were arguments pro and con. For several reasons it seemed like a good cause and a good place to make our stand. First, the local authorities were unreasonable and intransigent. Like Bull Connor, they were unwilling to make any compromises and seemed likely to respond with oppressive measures if challenged. So we would get our confrontation on television, the kind of visual conflict that would best define for the viewing public what we were up against.

Second, the local black churches were powerful, and there were several leaders on whom we could rely for support: the Reverend L. L. Anderson of Tabernacle Baptist Church, the Reverend C. A. Lett of the Green Street Baptist Church, the Reverend M. C. Cleveland of the First Baptist Church, and lay people like Dr. and Mrs. Sullivan Jackson (in whose house Martin and I stayed while we were in Selma). There was also a dynamic young black pastor—Reverend F. D. Reese.

Third, the voting issue itself required emphasis at this particular stage of the movement and no community so clearly reflected the need for intervention in this matter. It was also close enough to Atlanta to enable us to travel back and forth when necessary. We could all spend some time with our families, preach in our pulpits on Sunday, and still be on site most of the time to manage the campaign.

There were, of course, some negative aspects as well, and we considered these carefully before we made a final commitment. For one thing, the SNCC had already moved into Dallas County and was working the communities surrounding Selma. We were not happy to see them there. In the first place, they were not genuinely committed to nonviolence, though on the surface they appeared to be. Stokely Carmichael in particular was more and more inclined to suggest that at some point, perhaps in the very near future, blacks would have to abandon nonviolence and fight back against white oppression with all available weaponry.

In addition, both Stokely and James Forman were personally difficult to deal with. They did not always agree on tactics and they were never willing to listen to others. Then, too, they would sometimes make commitments to perform certain roles in the overall strategy, only to fail to show up or else follow some entirely different course of action. So any field action with them in the area might prove counterproductive and even disastrous.

Also, the hostility of the local authorities meant a heightened sense of danger, one that particularly affected Martin. For some reason or other he was convinced that he would be assassinated in Selma; and while he was prepared to run the risk if assured of success, he felt he needed an extra measure of certitude, given his premonition that he would not survive the campaign.

Taking everything into consideration, we finally agreed to move into Selma and try to make that city the grounds on which the battle for voting rights would be fought. What we wanted to do was force local authorities to permit blacks to register without making them answer written and oral questions to prove they were literate and of sound mind. Whites were not subjected to the same examinations, no matter how little education they had completed. They were often allowed to register when they could only sign the application with an X. And certainly none of them was ever asked to recite the Thirteenth or Fourteenth Amendment to the Constitution verbatim, as were blacks on a routine basis.

We were going to try to register local blacks and do so in good faith, knowing that in all likelihood we would fail in our attempt. Then we intended to demand intervention by the state authorities. We would go directly to Gov. George Wallace, who was then in his segregationist phase and would also refuse our requests.

At that point we intended to go ahead with our own registration and election, what we would call "freedom registration" and "freedom election."

*   *   *

I was chosen to make the opening gambit—an appearance on January 1 (Emancipation Proclamation Day) in 1965. When I got there, I learned that SNCC troops had already moved into Lowndes County adjacent to Dallas County and that they were living in Selma itself, a fact we feared would complicate our activities. Just before I left for Selma, I had talked to Martin at SCLC headquarters and he had given me some words of advice.

"Go down there, speak, get in your car, and drive right on back. We've got a lot more planning to do before we go in there full force."

I detected an ominous note in his voice.

"Do you have reason to believe there might be danger?" I asked him.

"There's been some evidence to that effect."

"What evidence?" I asked.

He hesitated.

"There was an incident involving a snake," he said.

"A snake?"

"Somebody put a rattlesnake in the mailbox of one of our supporters. Fortunately he heard something moving inside the box when he came to pick up his mail. But it was a live snake and it could have killed him."

I shook my head in disbelief. It seemed incredible that people would go that far merely to keep someone from trying to vote, though, as I flew to Montgomery, the closest airport to Selma, I realized that more was at stake than merely one man's vote. A whole way of life was at stake, so maybe it wasn't so incredible after all. We were marching around the walls of Jericho and the white establishment knew it. I couldn't help but feel uneasy.

I rented a car in Montgomery and drove the thirty miles to Selma, still trying to gauge the trouble we would be facing. Chief among them was the local sheriff, Jim Clark, who was, in his own way, as formidable as Bull Connor, though somewhat subtler. Connor would always snarl at his adversaries and use racial epithets. Sheriff Clark would smile and speak softly—as long as things went his way. But he had a temper that could get him into trouble, a temper we were counting on, because when he was angry, he could use his power with the same ruthless abandon as Bull Connor. In some ways he was a greater danger, because he was more credible in his dealings with the press. I had heard about him. I wondered if I would meet him that night.

But there were other, moderate whites in Selma and we were hoping that at some point they would take charge of the scene, realize the reasonableness and inevitability of what we were asking, and allow people to register to vote before the city was torn to pieces and people died.

The newly elected mayor, Joseph T. Smitherman, was a "moderate" by 1960s standards. A young man interested in developing the economic potential of Selma, he was a member of the rising generation that saw accommodation as the best policy in dealing with racial change. He was willing to meet with black leaders and to consider all possibilities, but he was to some degree restricted in how much he could concede to us by the strong presence of hard-line racists in the community, older people of wealth and influence who wanted to fight every change as if it were the battle of Armageddon (and I'm sure they thought it was).

Supporting Smitherman was Wilson Baker, Selma's commissioner of public safety, whose role it was to supervise law enforcement in the city itself. Since Clark's jurisdiction was the entire county, the two men often found themselves claiming the same turf. They had different styles of dealing with racial matters. Baker would talk with the black leadership and try to work out solutions acceptable to everyone involved in the confrontation, while Clark had grown up believing that in dealing with blacks you could only use billy clubs and guns, since that is all we understood.

Clark's constituency was the mass of people scattered throughout the county, many of whom were poor white farmers who particularly feared black advancement, since they believed it would eventually rob them of whatever modicum of dignity they possessed. It was a foolish and fragile illusion, but they clung to it generation after generation, and it helped them to bear their own second-class citizenship.

Baker's true constituency, on the other hand, was the same as Smitherman's: the Chamber of Commerce, the small band of businessmen who wanted to see Selma grow, prosper, and attract new industry. They saw the future in terms of building starts and an expanding tax base. What they feared most of all was what had happened in Birmingham, where the streets were full of protestors and emptied of customers. They didn't want their city to become another symbol of southern reaction—as Montgomery and Birmingham had become; because if that happened they would lose out in the competition with other southern sites for plants and factories.

If Smitherman and Baker could persuade the businessmen that Selma could avoid the fate of its sisters and also survive the wrath of the racists, then we might well have an easier time of it. But if Clark's crowd was turned loose on us, then we would face the same potentially explosive campaign that we faced when we began in Montgomery and in Birmingham. The fact that Selma chose the hard way rather than the easy way is in some measure the result of Clark's inability to control his own temper or those people who looked up to him. Thus, before our campaign was over, the cause would have three more martyrs and we would again hold the undivided attention of the nation as it watched our struggles every night on the evening news. Indeed, for many Americans, Selma would be more synonymous with hard-core resistance to the civil rights movement than any other city in America—all this despite the efforts of Smitherman and Baker, who did their best to avoid the conflict and bloodshed that followed.

When I got to Selma I found Rev. J. V. Reese's church. It had a capacity of only a couple of hundred people, and it was jammed. The crowd was extremely enthusiastic. I talked to some of the leaders afterward, and they assured me that they would support the SCLC. I was inclined to believe them.

Following Martin's advice, I didn't linger too long, but got back into the car and headed toward Montgomery, scanning the rear view mirror. But no one followed me. So far, so good.

The following day the whole crew moved in to take possession of the territory. Beforehand we had made it clear to all concerned that we wanted our behavior to be peaceful and orderly. If the SNCC was in Lowndes County nearby, there could be additional trouble, even violence; and we didn't want anyone to blame us for it. So everyone was warned to be on his best behavior.

The whole staff flew to Montgomery on January 2, where we were met by supporters and driven to Selma. We were planning a meeting that night at Brown Chapel AME Church, where we would rally our forces and bring as many local people as possible into the movement.

James Bevel and others had already done some advance work in Selma and they assured us that the people would be with us.

Martin was to speak that night and as we drove the familiar route from Montgomery to Selma, I couldn't help recalling my own attempts to register, back when I was a student at Alabama State University. Fired up by one of our teachers, who had explained to the class for the first time what it meant to have our suffrage denied, I went to my Kappa Alpha Psi fraternity house and called a bunch of the older brothers together.

"Tomorrow," I said, "we are going down to the courthouse and register to vote."

"Man, are you crazy?" someone said, and the others shook their heads at the absurdity of my suggestion.

"I've never been more serious," I said. "If enough of us go down together, maybe they will be too intimidated to refuse us. We have every right to vote—those of us who are over twenty-one."

"I can just see us right now," somebody else said, "intimidating a deputy sheriff with a double-barrel shotgun in his hands."

But I shamed them into coming with me—about eight of

them—and when we got there we were faced not with a deputy sheriff but with a frail-looking white woman with snow-white hair. As soon as I saw her, I knew we would have to use entirely different tactics. Certainly we couldn't try to crowd her or to confront her with loud demands. The situation called for manners and finesse.

She issued all of us a four-page literacy test, which the others looked at, scribbled hasty answers to, and gave back to her without a word. One by one she told them that they had failed, if for no other reason than they had failed to fill in some of the blanks. I looked at the examination and saw that several of the questions did not apply to us. Could these be the blanks they were failing to fill out? Just to cover every base, I answered those questions as well, writing "This does not apply to me."

After the others had cleared out, mumbling to themselves, I walked up to her, gave her a big smile, and said, "Excuse me, ma'am, but I've finished this test. Would you please be so kind as to grade it for me?"

She glanced up at me, her eyes widening.

"Did you come in with those other boys?"

"Yes ma'am," I said, still smiling.

"Well," she said, "you seem different from them." She took my examination and thumbed through it, expecting to be able to say, "You didn't fill in all the blanks," but as she flipped from page to page she found all the questions answered. Her eyes glazed over. And it was in that moment that I understood what was going on: She didn't know the answers to the questions herself!

She hesitated for a moment.

"Well," she said. "You got them all right."

"Thank you very much," I said.

"But that doesn't mean you get to vote," she snapped back. "I get to ask you an oral question."

"What kind of oral question?" I asked, still smiling. If they didn't get you on one technicality, they got you on another.

"A question on the Constitution of the United States," she said. "Are you ready?"

I nodded.

"All right," she said, "So recite the Thirteenth Amendment."

I knew, of course, that the Thirteenth Amendment freed the slaves, but of course I didn't know it verbatim. I was stumped. It looked as if I wouldn't get to vote after all. But it occurred to me that if she didn't know the answers to the written questions then she wouldn't know this one either.

"It goes like this," I said. "I pledge allegiance to the flag of the United States of America, and to the Republic for which it stands. One nation, indivisible, with liberty and justice for all."

She stared at me for ten seconds without blinking her eyes. Then she reached over, picked up a voter registration certificate, and began to fill it out. Then she glanced up at me.

"You better had known it," she said between clenched teeth.

When I got back to the fraternity house everyone was sitting around, angry at the woman for flunking them, and angrier at me for persuading them to go down there in the first place. I let them chew me out for a couple of minutes, and then I pulled out my voter registration and waved it in their faces. At that point I'd had to run for my life.

A number of years had passed since that incident, and the Supreme Court had ruled that Jim Crow laws were unconstitutional; but if anything, it was more difficult to register in Alabama in 1965 than it had been ten years earlier. I had been one minnow that had slipped through the net. Today we were a good portion of the fish in the ocean, and our enemies now suspected that their net was no longer wide enough to contain us.

On the evening of January 2, 1965, there were more than seven hundred people at Brown Chapel AME Church. Not only were our supporters there, but our enemies as well. The press, usually friendly during those early years, also showed up, just to see what would happen when we violated Judge Hare's injunction.

We prepared for the worst, anticipating that we might well be confronted by a massive force of state troopers and hauled off to jail. Governor Wallace had suggested as much in discussing possible violations of the injunction, and we half expected him to make an example of us. Indeed, we were eager to see him do so.

An *en masse* arrest of Martin Luther King and the staff members of the SCLC would have been the best possible beginning for our campaign.

Martin told the packed church that Selma had become "a symbol of bitter-end resistance to the civil rights movement in the Deep South." He urged all blacks to register to vote and he outlined the plan we had adopted in case the registrars tried to prevent our people from exercising their constitutional rights: We would appeal first to the governor, George Wallace; then we would go to the legislature; and if those appeals were rejected, we would go back to Washington and demand that the Congress of the United States take action.

We knew, of course, that both George Wallace and the all-white Alabama legislature would turn a deaf ear on our demands. Both were irrevocably committed to maintaining the status quo; and the political survival of the hard-line segregationists depended on their holding the line on this one issue. But we wanted to exhaust all existing procedures before we returned to Congress, and we wanted the nation to see precisely what the Alabama establishment was really like—not that they didn't have a pretty good idea already. We figured we would be in jail within a week or two—provided Sheriff Clark didn't let us down—and such treatment would bring opprobrium on our opposition. With any luck we would be visibly abused without being maimed or killed. The line we walked was increasingly thin in these matters, and I understood Martin's jumpiness.

But he was unusually apprehensive about the forthcoming campaign and I worried that he would allow his morbid imagination to get the better of him and be incapacitated at just the time he was most needed. Selma was indeed a challenge, and Sheriff Clark represented a formidable segment of the white community, the most radical and dangerous element of a society with its back to the wall. We were approaching that terrible moment in the course of the region's history when even the diehards would have to admit defeat.

No one knew what the realization of ultimate defeat would bring. When the Confederacy lay in shambles the proud secessionist Edmund Ruffin, unwilling to face the future, blew his brains out. On the other hand, John Wilkes Booth chose to blow out the brains of the man he most blamed for the defeat of his cause. Martin knew enough of the hatred he had generated to expect the latter before the former.

On January 5, I was at West Hunter Church when I got a call from Martin. As soon as I heard his voice, I knew he was deeply disturbed.

"Ralph," he said, "I want you to meet me at the SCLC office right now, if you can. Something just came in the mail that you need to listen to."

I didn't ask him what it was. I immediately drove across town to our national headquarters. First, he sat me down and handed me a letter, then watched as I read it—once, twice, then a third time. It was a puzzling document, a rambling outburst of hatred, supposedly written by another black, but with curious vocabulary that sounded by turns literary and childlike. Martin was described as "a collosal fraud, and an evil, vicious one at that." The writer declaimed that "Satan could not do more. What incredible evilness." And he ended with a command: "King, there is only one thing left for you to do. You know what this is. You have just 34 days to [sic] (this exact number has been selected for a specific reason, it has definite practical significant) [sic]. You are done. There is but one way out for you. You better take it before your filthy, abnormal fraudulent self is bared to the nation."

My first impulse was to laugh out loud. Surely this was written by some harmless old lady. But when I looked at Martin's face I could tell he was taking the whole thing more seriously.

"Before you say anything," he said, "I want you to listen to the tape recording that came with the letter."

The tape recorder was sitting on the coffee table, and he reached over and turned it on. There were muffled voices that seemed to come from a faraway room, and for a moment I couldn't make out who they were. Then I recognized Martin and then myself. But where were we? What were we talking about? I listened, trying to remember, while Martin watched my face to see my reaction.

"Where did that take place?" I asked.

"It was at the Willard Hotel in Washington, D.C.," he said.

He ran the tape forward while the squeaky voices chattered in high speed. Then there were other sounds, and he slowed the tape down. Clearly what we were hearing were whispers and sighs from a bedroom. After about a minute of this, Martin suddenly reached over and punched the stop button.

"That's enough. It just goes on and on like that," he said quietly. We sat in silence for a moment, staring at each other.

"J. Edgar Hoover," I said.

"It can't be anyone else," he said.

"So they bugged our hotel room."

"Make that 'rooms'," he said. "I've listened to it three times, and I believe the tape covers several different nights and several different places."

I shook my head. It was outrageous. I wanted to ask him if Coretta had heard it, but decided not to. I also resisted the temptation to remind him that I had warned against just such tactics when we were in jail in Birmingham. It was no time to say "I told you so."

"How dare they interfere with my private life," he blurted out. "They have no right. It's nobody's business but my own."

"I agree," I said, wondering how seriously to take this threat of exposure. Of course, I didn't bother to say anything about the suggestion that he commit suicide. Whoever wrote the letter had no understanding whatsoever of Martin or his faith. The idea would never have entered his head. Whatever his weaknesses, he had no intention of throwing away the life that God had given him.

Later Andy Young arrived and Martin showed him the letter and replayed the tape. He was equally indignant, and agreed the FBI was clearly the source of the package. We left that night without any clear plan to combat this Second Front. For the FBI had become our enemy just as surely as the Ku Klux Klan and the other racist organizations that were waiting for us at Selma. It was ironic that the Klan was on their list of "subversive organizations" and we were not. Yet they seemed to be spending more time plotting against us than all the rest of the subversive organizations put together.

Since Hoover had the backing of the U.S. government, it was useless at this point to declare war on him. We could barely confront Sheriff Clark and his deputies in Selma. We certainly could not do so without at least the neutrality of the Justice Department's chief enforcement arm. We talked about the problem for the next couple of days, and then came to a conclusion: We would go to Washington and try to reason with Hoover.

I'm afraid it was probably my idea. I can only say in its defense that at the time no one fully understood the degree to which Mr. Hoover had taken leave of his senses. We assumed that, though filled with malice toward us, he was a rational man who was merely misinformed about our ultimate aims. If we could disabuse him of his belief that we were Communists or else willing pawns of the international Communist conspiracy, perhaps he would call off his dogs.

Little did we realize that at some point before this time Hoover had crossed over the line between arrogance and megalomania. Nor did we understand the degree to which he recoiled from the very idea of sexuality. Though the letter seems to have been written by his longtime associate William C. Sullivan, the words echo Hoover's expressed sentiments when he calls Martin "a dissolute, abnormal moral imbecile."

The idea that we could reason with such people was naive. Nevertheless, at the time it seemed the best course of action to follow. So, while Martin kept an appointment in Baltimore, Andy Young and I flew to Washington to meet with Hoover's representative, Deke DeLoach, to see if we couldn't explain our aims and achieve some sort of truce.

It was a waste of time and money. DeLoach was not a man who could really speak for Hoover, and we spent most of our time trying to answer charges he was unwilling to admit the FBI had made. We assured him that Martin was not a Communist, that Communists did not control the SCLC and that we had no desire to tear down American society. We pointed out that even in the SCLC's constitution it states very clearly that, "No member of this organization shall be a communist nor a communist sympathizer." All we wanted, we said, was equal protection under the law—the right to enjoy the full privileges of American citizenship.

He listened soberly, occasionally nodding his head, and seemed to be receptive to what we were saying. We brought up the rumor that they were looking into our finances, and he denied that the FBI was conducting such an investigation. He seemed to bear us no ill will whatsoever; and not only did he deny any FBI interest in Martin's private life, he seemed quite sympathetic with our obvious distress.

Toward the end of the interview we realized that he was playing an elaborate and patronizing game with us, treating us with a strict courtesy that barely hid his contempt. I had the sense that he was really performing for another audience and my eyes wandered around the room, looking for the doohickey, but I never saw it. I had the distinct impression that Mr. Hoover was—or would soon be—listening to every word we said.

We left more frustrated than when we had arrived. Not only would the FBI not cease and desist, they would not even talk to us about the matter. At that time the Freedom of Information Act had not been passed and we were helpless in the face of Mr. Hoover's power, which was almost totalitarian in practice, if not in theory. We had nowhere to turn in our helpless anger, so we flew back to Atlanta and reported our failure to Martin, who shrugged his shoulders. He had not really expected us to succeed, but I could tell that he was disappointed.

During the next week we followed our usual pattern of evening rallies, during which we urged our followers to be courageous in the face of white intimidation, and at the same time educated them in the theory and techniques of nonviolent protest. We wanted to build up as large a group of marchers as we possibly could while at the same time making certain that they followed our methods rather than those of the SNCC crowd, which was now a part of our campaign, working with us to ensure a nonviolent march.

What we were building toward was a march on the courthouse, where we planned either to register everyone to vote or else force them to arrest us in large numbers. We planned that march for January 18, and we let the crowds and the Selma establishment know that come Monday they could expect to see us at the square. So the lines were drawn, and the national media began to gather for the confrontation.

On Monday morning, one of the few days during the month that the county would register voters, we gathered a huge and enthusiastic crowd at Brown Chapel Church. After Martin spoke and there were prayers, we marched down the road to the courthouse, where Sheriff Clark's deputies were waiting for us, while the TV cameras rolled.

Clark himself stood in the entrance of the courthouse, consciously imitating Governor Wallace, his eyes narrowed, his lips taut, trying to look like the meanest man in Alabama. It was his moment in the national spotlight and he knew it. Like Bull Connor, he had misjudged his audience and failed to understand the precarious nature of the support for his stance among Selma businessmen, who were working frantically to preserve the peace. What national TV audiences saw was an all-too-familiar sight: southern law enforcement officers blocking the way of blacks who wanted to claim their rights as citizens and human beings.

To justify his refusal to let us enter, Clark stepped forward and announced that there were too many of us to enter the courthouse. We would have to go stand in an alley, he said, and be called in by the registrars, one at a time. We knew that he was stalling, and we seriously doubted that he would register the first black; but we had waited for almost two hundred years and we could wait a little bit longer. We allowed ourselves to be herded into the alley and milled around for several hours.

In the meantime, as if to underline the kind of mentality Jim Clark represented, the American Nazi leader George Lincoln Rockwell joined the crowd on the square. Rockwell, a rawboned man with black hair and five o'clock shadow, was more of an irritant than a genuine threat to what we were doing. He loved to appear before cameras and strut, but his handful of followers were more like a ragtail remnant of a motorcycle gang than an army of storm troopers. They said vile things and did a lot of posturing, but it never occurred to us that they would either grow or prosper.

We were much more concerned about the secret and sullen

groups of rednecks that met at night in lonely places and talked about planting bombs and bushwhacking us in the cover of darkness. From experience, we knew that the kind of people who committed racial violence never did so in the light of day. Rockwell was too big a talker and too big a con man to risk any overt act of aggression. Years later, when one of his half dozen followers shot and killed him, I actually felt sorry, as much for the squalid little life he had led as for the manner of his death.

Martin actually talked to Rockwell and his followers. After the speech, Martin invited Rockwell to speak at our rally that night, and Rockwell accepted. Martin realized that he was giving the man more publicity than he really deserved, but he also knew that Rockwell would be carried on national television and that what he said would work to our benefit, since Rockwell would put into words what Jim Clark and his deputies were really defending.

After we milled around in the alley for several hours, feeling more and more like a pack of caged rats, Martin finally called several of us together.

"Nothing is going to happen here," he said. "He's going to wait us out. So while Clark is here, let's go over and integrate the Albert Hotel."

Since the 1964 Civil Rights Act was now federal law, we didn't anticipate any trouble; and though Clark's people didn't like it, we had been testing public accommodations for a week or more—restaurants as well as hotels and motels—and so far everything had gone well. As we slipped away from the milling crowd and moved down the street, we were followed by Wilson Baker's people, who—unlike Clark's deputies—were actually trying to keep the peace.

Several of us followed Martin into the hotel lobby, where we were greeted with quiet courtesy by the desk clerk, who had been told we would be coming. Dorothy Cotton, one of our staff members, was on one side of Martin and I was on the other as he stood at the desk. Suddenly I saw a quick movement out of the corner of my eye, then someone rushed past me, pushing me off balance. Next I heard two loud blows and saw Martin falling to the floor and a brawny young white man drawing back his arm to hit him again.

Before I could do anything several people dashed over, grabbed the man, and hauled him out of the place. Dorothy and I helped Martin to his feet, and he assured us that he was all right. There was no blood and the skin was not broken, but he seemed a little dazed. It was a sudden reminder of the hatred that our very presence excited in a number of white people, and I'm sure Martin saw it as an ill omen—a sign that Selma might yet produce the assassin he had thus far avoided.

"Who was he?" we asked.

"One of Rockwell's followers," Baker replied. "He's not from Selma. We've placed him under arrest. He won't bother you again."

Baker told us he would protect us as well as he could, but he said he would prefer that Rockwell not speak at our rally that night, and we agreed to let him handle the matter his way, though we still didn't think we had anything to fear from Rockwell personally.

We held a rally that night, telling everyone to keep the faith and that on Tuesday we would return and things would be different. But as a matter of fact, we weren't too certain that things wouldn't be exactly the same. Monday had been a wash—a day of indecisive milling around. Because he had herded us into that alley like grazing cows and at the same time kept his own cool, Sheriff Clark had been the winner, not only among the home crowd but also among television audiences, who had not yet seen the kind of explosive brutality that lay beneath the surface of racist communities.

While Sheriff Clark deserved some of the credit for controlling himself and his platoon of deputies, we were partly to blame for our lack of progress. We had too easily allowed ourselves to be deterred. After all, our main purpose had been to register voters and not a single black voter had been put on the rolls. At a meeting after the rally we decided on a slight change of tactics: On Tuesday, when Sheriff Clark ordered us into the alley, we would refuse to leave the sidewalk in front of the courthouse. Then we would see how calm he remained.

The next morning we came in about the same numbers and were confronted by the same stony-faced deputies. After the crowd had assembled, Clark strode forward like the cock of the walk and shouted out: "All right. Y'all move on into the alley now, and we'll call your name when it's time to register."

We knew the roll would be called up yonder before the first name was called on the Selma courthouse steps, so we refused to budge. Clark glared at us and we could see the muscles in his jaw ripple.

"I said, y'all move and move now!"

We shuffled around, but there was no real movement toward the alley. Clark's pride was at stake and we could see his temperature rise as he stood there, brow furrowed, his eyes tiny pinpoints of hatred.

Mrs. Amelia Boynton, one of the local leaders, was standing in front of the line, refusing to move, staring at him with undisguised contempt. All he had to do was look into her face to know that he would never intimidate her into moving. The face of this local enemy, backed by hundreds of supporters, must have been too much for him to bear.

Suddenly he rushed over to her, grabbed her by the back of her collar and walked her to a waiting patrol car, manhandling her in plain sight of reporters and TV cameramen. He had gone for the person who most antagonized him, without thinking that that person was a woman and that in pushing and jerking her around he conformed to almost everyone's stereotype of the southern sheriff and fulfilled our highest hopes for him. After a slow and disappointing first day, the Selma campaign was at last on its way.

Mrs. Boynton was only the first. The deputies were ordered to begin arresting all demonstrators who refused to move, and that meant virtually all of us. Of course, our people would immediately go limp as they had been taught, and that meant two and sometimes three deputies were required to haul one person to the paddywagon or patrol car. Consequently they ended up arresting between fifty and seventy-five people before the day finally came to a chaotic end, with reporters interviewing the leadership and then phoning their stories back to newspapers like the *New York Times* and the *Washington Post*. Also, TV footage was on its way to the major networks, who were alerted to the fact that another southern lawman was manhandling and arresting peaceful black demonstrators.

That night we held our most enthusiastic rally to date. Martin spoke eloquently, teaching once more the lesson of nonviolence, explaining patiently the need to remain passive in the face of the taunts and attacks of the forces arrayed against them. He commended those who had gone to jail and warned those who had not been arrested that their time might well come on Wednesday.

When I got up, I said:

"I want to propose a new name for membership in the Southern Christian Leadership Conference. I want to propose for honorary membership the name of Sheriff Jim Clark, who did more for our organization this day than anyone else in the city of Selma."

The crowd roared its approval.

The next day we marched again, wondering what Clark would try this time. He still hadn't allowed the first black to register, but he had exposed the essential racism of the city to the entire nation, and Mayor Smitherman and Wilson Baker saw their chance to avoid the glare of publicity vanish with Clark's arrogance. Would he again insist that we move into the alley? We came to the courthouse curious to find out.

This time he tried to speak with a quiet authority, but the moment he saw us you could see his intentions begin to bubble and seethe. The very sight of us seemed to inflame him.

"All right, y'all," he said in a barely controlled voice. "If you want to register you'll have to go around to the side door. Then we'll let you in to register, but you got to move out of the way, so people can use the front door here."

So it wasn't the alley this time, but the side door. We realized that this was the last day of the week we would be able to register, that if he kept us waiting until the end of the afternoon, he could have turned us back until next Monday. So we refused to move.

"All right," Clark called back over his shoulder. "Arrest them!"

It was Tuesday all over again, with one exception: This time we didn't commit all of our troops at once. To avoid marching in numbers that could be construed as "holding a parade without a permit," we broke our mass of demonstrators into three smaller groups. So just as Clark thought he was beginning to thin us out, he looked up and saw a second group marching down the road, as large and as uncooperative as the first. For a moment he appeared to be unnerved. Then he confronted them with the same order.

"Go around to the side door, and you'll be registered."

The next group was just as recalcitrant as the first, and again Clark's response was the same: "Arrest them all."

When the third group bore down on the scene, Clark was not on site; Wilson Baker stepped in, hoping to offer a reasonable compromise and recover some of the city's lost dignity.

"You people can stay here at the front, provided you keep a path open so people can go in and out."

"No they can't!" Clark shouted, as he came galloping over, and for a minute no one was sure who would arrest whom. The face-off between Clark and Baker showed us that they clearly hated one another more than they hated us, which was as it should be, since in the long run it was the Clarks of the region who made life hardest for those white moderates with some sense of decency. People like Baker and Smitherman would one day govern relatively integrated cities and even gain the political support of blacks. But in 1965 the Clarks were in power and the Bakers and Smithermans had neither the wisdom nor the courage to resist Jim Crow rule. So both types ended up as the enemies of racial amity and justice.

Predictably, Jim Clark prevailed, and the third group was arrested and hauled off to jail. By the end of the day, those arrested totaled more than two hundred. Things were going well. The story was capturing the attention of the nation. People throughout the country were beginning to think about the injustice involved in depriving us of our right to vote. If Jim Clark wasn't Bull Connor yet, he was well on his way.

On Friday a group of more than one hundred black teachers marched in protest against the arrests, and when Martin and I flew back to Atlanta, we were pleased with the progress. Saturday things were looking even brighter. We learned that a federal judge, Daniel Thomas, in response to our lawyers' petition, had issued a temporary restraining order barring Selma and Dallas County officials from hindering voter registration.

The importance of this judicial action cannot be underestimated. For the first time in the Selma campaign, we had been able to set local authorities against the federal courts and the Constitution, thus clearly defining the true dimensions of the conflict: We were not the law breakers, Jim Clark and his deputies were. With that point established—at least for the moment—we could press our advantage on Monday and see if Jim Clark would accept the yoke of the law.

Monday morning we were out on the streets early, marching back down to the courthouse. Clark was agitated from the beginning. I could see it in his eyes. He looked like a man in great physical pain as he strode back and forth in front of us, trying to size us up. He was now under federal mandate to allow us to register, but he knew he still had a certain amount of leeway in controlling such a large crowd. Overruled by the superior authority of a federal judge, he was nonetheless out to prove that he was a force to be reckoned with on his own home turf.

Again he made the mistake of venting his wrath on a woman. Her name was Annie Lee Cooper, and when Clark jabbed her with the heel of his hand in an effort to make her step back behind an imaginary line of his own invention, she threw a roundhouse right and hit him on his temple.

Immediately she disappeared into a swarm of deputies, who managed to subdue her, despite the fact that she was a powerful woman whose muscles had been built by hard work, probably over a wash pot. In that one swing she had managed to pack a lifetime of resentment.

But she didn't stop there. As the deputies restrained her, Sheriff Clark brandished a stick in front of her face.

"I wish you would hit me, you scum," she cried out, and his eyes went wild. He brought the club swiftly down on the top of her head, as she tried to tear loose from the grasp of the deputies. Once again the photographers had a picture to send back to their newspapers and to the television networks. The sheriff had come through for us again, just when it appeared as if the federal courts would save him from himself.

At this point the registrars had begun to process the applications of blacks, forced to do so by Judge Thomas's decree. But they took their own sweet time about it. They continued to open up only on the first three days of the week, and while they did allow those in line to register, they made them use a lengthy and complicated form designed to be as confusing as possible and to take the maximum amount of time. Then, they would go over each application with all the care of a freshman English teacher; and every time they found the slightest misspelling or omission, they would simply reject the applicant and tell him or her to begin all over again. For people who had borne the burden of an unequal educational system their entire lives, this kind of indignity was heartbreaking, particularly to those of us who had been luckier in our educational opportunities. The fact that they didn't apply the same standards to less educated whites didn't make our treatment any easier to bear.

It was clear to us that there would be only token registration, despite the fact that their stalling tactics were clear violations of the spirit if not the letter of Judge Thomas's order. Something obviously had to be done.

So instead of breaking down into smaller groups we decided to march into town in one huge mass and force the sheriff to arrest us all. That action would again remind Judge Thomas that we had come here to register voters and that, despite his specific orders, the white establishment of Selma was still trying to deny us our constitutional rights.

Martin and I marched at the head of the line to make certain we were among the literally hundreds that Clark would send to jail. Martin's arrest in particular would stir up interest in our plight and might provoke Judge Thomas into having another look at our case. Clark was happy enough to oblige us, and we found ourselves once again in a cell together, along with others who were there for the first time. As I recall we stayed until the end of the week, while the press gave us increased coverage. At the same time, our lawyers went back to Judge Thomas with a list of complaints about the manner in which we had been treated. The judge took the complaints under advisement, and on Thursday he acted. He ordered the registrars to stop using the deliberately complicated form they had been using, and he ordered them to cease and desist all disqualifications for minor mistakes or omissions.

He made one more provision that began to penetrate to the heart of the problem: He ordered them to register at least one hundred applicants every day. This particular instruction was the first concrete sign to the black residents of Dallas County that they were actually going to be able to participate in the electoral process, and they were elated. They had actually forced Clark and his cohorts to give us what we wanted.

But while many of our marchers thought the victory had been won, we had by no means achieved all of our goals. In the first place, we knew that Judge Thomas could not set up residence in the courthouse and monitor every day's procedures. Nor would he be around when the Democratic primary was run. There were hundreds of tricks to keep blacks from voting, and this courthouse crowd knew them all.

Also, the local enforcer of election laws would be the chief peace officer of the county, Sheriff James Clark. No, we wanted something more permanent in the way of legal protections. We wanted a federal law that would be enforced if necessary by federal marshals, and we were now beginning to believe that we might get it, provided we could keep up the pressure.

We received a little help in that direction from President Lyndon Johnson, who issued a statement about our situation:

> All Americans should be indignant when one American is denied the right to vote. The loss of that right to a single citizen undermines the freedom of every citizen. This is why all of us should be concerned with the efforts of our fellow Americans to register to vote in Alabama. The basic problem in Selma is the slow pace of voter registration for Negroes who are qualified to vote. . . . I hope that all Americans will join with me in expressing their concern over the loss of any American's right to vote. . . . I intend to see that that right is secured for all our citizens.

This was strong support from the president at a time when his popularity had not yet taken a downward turn as the result of the war in Vietnam. He had just defeated Senator Barry Goldwater by a landslide, and his influence still carried weight even in the South. Indeed, this was the first signal he had sent us that he might consider the voting rights act we were so anxious to see enacted.

As I have said before, I do not share the feelings of contempt that many Americans harbor toward President Johnson. When we needed him, he stepped forward and helped us—and on more than one occasion. He was responsible for the 1964 Civil Rights Act (which Senator Goldwater voted against) and eventually he helped us pass the 1965 Voting Rights Act. It may be unpopular to say so, but I don't believe under President Kennedy we would have gotten either.

But we needed an incident to trigger national indignation, something that would dramatize for the entire nation the hopelessness of our situation. We weren't certain what that would be, but we talked about the possibilities as we sat in jail, hearing about the world's reaction to our arrest on the radio and from the daily reports of Andy Young.

After we were released from jail, Martin and I and a delegation of SCLC staff members flew to Washington, hoping to talk to the president about the necessity for voting rights legislation. We thought that after his strong statement of sympathy he could hardly refuse us what we asked for, but at the last minute we were unable to get through to see him. Or so we thought.

However, we did meet with Attorney General Nicholas Katzenbach and an even more sympathetic supporter, Vice President Hubert Humphrey. The two of them were encouraging and we were led to believe that some kind of bill might indeed be introduced in the current session of Congress, though no one could be certain.

Then, in the middle of our conversation the telephone rang. It was the president, who asked that the vice president and Martin join him at the White House. Through a misunderstanding, we all got up and followed them to the Oval Office, where we spoke to President Johnson. He was cordial to everyone, and we talked with him for a few minutes before he and Martin and Vice President Humphrey spent some time together behind closed doors in the president's office. When Martin emerged he was in excellent spirits. But we didn't ask him what had happened while we were still in the White House.

"What did he say?" we asked, as we went through the gate and started down Pennsylvania Avenue.

"He said the administration would send a voting rights bill to Congress," Martin told us, clearly pleased.

"When?" we asked.

"Very soon," he said.

That was the best we could have hoped for, but I believe we were all a little disappointed that we weren't given some immediate relief. The Selma campaign was beginning to wear us down. Even with the registration of one hundred voters a day, that meant only three hundred a week; and there were thousands of blacks eligible to vote in Dallas County.

At the moment we were locked in a grinding struggle with Sheriff Clark that was clearly building to a crescendo. Both sides were now frustrated and edgy. The confrontations were more personal and the words and actions more provocative. We had been through it before, and we could sense the tension building. Something was going to happen—a major clash, an explosion into violence. We didn't want to precipitate such a dangerous situation, but events had moved us inexorably in that direction.

Martin sensed the coming climax, and when the euphoria of his visit with the president had worn off, he suddenly collapsed under the pressure and had to be hospitalized with the same mysterious ailment that always plagued him during these rugged campaigns. After a day or two of rest, he got up out of bed to resume the battle, but he was not feeling well, and on the march to the courthouse that Monday morning C. T. Vivian took over.

It was a grim wintry day, alternately drizzling and raining, and the marchers shivered as they marched to the courthouse, where once again they met the sheriff and his deputies, standing just inside, out of the rain, blocking the entrance. At that moment Clark was sitting in the catbird seat. He was inside. Our demonstrators were outside. The rain was pouring down, and a cold wind whipped through the crowd. Clark smiled grimly and told them they couldn't come in out of the weather.

Vivian is a man of great personal courage, and he went eyeball to eyeball with Sheriff Clark there on the courthouse steps, sparing no words in denouncing him and demanding to be allowed to enter. Clark had himself been in the hospital, probably with the same kind of nervous exhaustion that Martin had suffered from; and his fuse was even shorter than in the previous weeks. With Vivian denouncing him like Aaron denouncing the Pharaoh, Clark could restrain himself no longer. With a roar he lunged at Vivian and was barely contained by deputies, who knew the whole drama was being played out under the watchful eye of Judge Thomas.

"Go on and hit me," Vivian yelled at him, while the deputies hung on even tighter. Then somebody, one of the deputies in all likelihood, struck Vivian in the face and knocked him back into the crowd. The cameras were grinding away, and it appeared as if Clark himself had landed the blow.

Vivian was immediately placed under arrest, but the nation saw one more example of police brutality on the air, and we figured we were just that much closer to our voting rights act. While Clark lacked the dogs and the water hoses that had made Bull Connor such a perfect foil, he was making up for his lack of style in frequency of attacks. He could be counted on to produce for us on a daily basis, and in the wake of this attack he even boasted on-camera, though according to people close to the action he had not thrown the punch himself.

A couple of evenings later an incident occurred in Marion, Alabama, thirty miles away from Selma, that both saddened and outraged all of us. After a church rally, Vivian had led a group of marchers to the courthouse; but before they had reached their destination, they were met by state troopers, who ordered them to turn around. At that point someone turned out all of the street lights, and in the ensuing darkness the troopers attacked the marchers with billy clubs, while network cameramen stood by, unable to film what was happening.

During this melee, one of the troopers began clubbing an older woman. Her grandson, Jimmie Lee Jackson, intervened in an attempt to shield her from harm. In the ensuing brawl, a state trooper shot and critically wounded the seventeen-year-old youth, who was immediately taken to the hospital. Martin and I visited him in his room the next day, but the doctors were worried. They were not sure about the extent of his internal injuries, and in the next hours his conditioned deteriorated rapidly.

Our response to this misuse of police power was to write Attorney General Katzenbach, asking for help in meeting the official acts of violence directed against us. George Wallace's response was to issue an executive order banning all nighttime marches. He called us "professional agitators with pro-Communist affiliations" and depicted the shooting as the inevitable result of our interference.

Jimmie Jackson lingered for a couple of days and then died—the first person to be killed in an SCLC campaign. It was an unnerving experience for us, but we believed in continuing the fight, if only because it had already proven so costly.

"We'll think about some response for Sunday," Martin said.

The next Sunday would be crucial. We sent the word throughout the State of Alabama that we were planning a massive march from Selma to Montgomery and wanted to bring in as many volunteers as we could to swell our ranks. We would be marching in protest against the careless and vicious murder of Jimmie Lee Jackson. We would begin in Marion, the city where the slaying had taken place, and we would walk the eighty miles to the state capitol building in Montgomery and demand that state authorities put an end to the kind of behavior that was going on in Dallas County and indeed throughout the state and region.

This would be our big push—the event we needed to focus the attention of the nation and Congress on the State of Alabama and the plight of disenfranchised blacks. Our staff was on the telephone for a couple of days, talking to people in a number of towns and cities; and they were reporting an excellent response. It looked as if we would be able to count on a substantial crowd to join us in our march down Highway 80.

That is, if there *was* a march. Governor Wallace had

nothing to gain by letting us leave Jim Clark behind and take up residence on his front porch in Montgomery. He had been watching the proceedings in Selma with growing concern, and he was shrewd enough to understand the impact that the violence and brutality were making on the consciousness of the nation. Although it was a state trooper who had shot the Jackson boy, most Americans were inclined to blame Clark and the local authorities.

While Smitherman, Clark, and Baker were thinking only in terms of their constituency in Selma, Wallace was thinking of his reputation even beyond the State of Alabama. A year earlier he had declared his intention of running for president and had withdrawn only because Senator Barry Goldwater, an arch-conservative, had won the Republican nomination. Now his eye was already on 1968, when he would organize a third party and make a genuine run for the presidency. A limited amount of resistance to the civil rights movement would further his cause with a certain segment of the population, but a bloody confrontation with us and with the federal government would severely jeopardize any chance he would have to win more responsible conservatives to his cause.

So his best bet would be to use his power as governor to make certain that we never left Selma. That way, any violence would be attributed to Sheriff Clark and his hometown boys rather than to Wallace's Montgomery-based state troopers. State troopers could kill a young man in Marion and still Wallace would not be blamed. Better to keep all the action in Selma.

We probably figured all of this out before he did and, for that reason, we weren't counting on getting to Montgomery on that first Sunday. But if we were stopped, that too would make our point on national television: Not only were blacks not free to vote in Alabama, they weren't even free to assemble and walk the streets and highways of the state.

We argued back and forth about what to do. Some people wanted to postpone the march until we could get a court order that would provide legal authority for the activity. Others wanted to march anyway and either peacefully turn back when stopped or else provoke another massive arrest.

As if reading our minds at this crucial moment, Governor Wallace announced in Montgomery that he would use "whatever measures are necessary to prevent a march." Several people told Martin that the march would be dangerous, that it would lead to massive arrests, and that he personally should stay out of the confrontation in the interest of safety.

Martin had been receiving an excessive number of death threats as the result of the Selma campaign, perhaps more than at any other time in his career; and with negotiations in progress between our leader and the president of the United States, no one wanted to risk losing him. Finally, he agreed to go back to Atlanta on Friday, rest on Saturday, take up his pastoral responsibilities on Sunday, and then come back to Selma Monday morning. In his absence it was agreed that one of the others would lead the march, assuming it seemed wise to hold the march come Sunday.

The staff continued to argue about the wisdom of moving against Wallace's well-staffed and highly trained state troopers. Safety, timing, and the propriety of the march were all questions we left unresolved as Martin and I drove to Montgomery and then flew back to Atlanta.

"You see what things look like Sunday," Martin had told Hosea Williams. "Then you let us know what you think."

But both of us knew what Hosea would think on Sunday. Regardless of the situation, he would want to go ahead with the march. In addition to his fiercely militant spirit, he would be in command; and the challenge and glory would be his. So it didn't surprise me when I got a call Sunday morning at West Hunter Church, just as I was about to step into the pulpit.

"Brother pastor," an usher told me, as he handed me the phone, "it's Hosea Williams. He says it's urgent." So I took the phone.

"We got to march," he said. "Everything's right."

"How many people do you have?"

"I don't know exactly," he said. "I haven't counted them. But they're swarming all over the place."

"About how many? Hundreds?"

"Thousands," he said. "You've got to get to the president. You're the only one who can get him to give the go-ahead."

"He's in church now," I said.

"Then call Ebenezer and get him to consent. We need to move now."

I paused for a moment, trying to gauge the intensity of his excitement and to guess at the reality that lay behind it. Did he really have a couple of thousand people crowding around Brown Chapel Church, wildly impatient to make a eighty-mile march, or were there a few hundred of the faithful sitting around, waiting to find out if they were going to make the gesture or go home and have Sunday dinner? In the final analysis I just couldn't be sure, so I agreed to call Martin.

"If I don't catch him before he starts preaching, it may be a while."

"We can't wait much longer," Hosea said. "Call him out of the pulpit."

An usher came up to me, a worried look on his face, and pointed to his watch. I nodded and put my hand over the receiver.

"This is important," I said. "I have to make a quick call. Then I'll be there. Tell them to hold off for five more minutes."

"I'll call Martin right now," I said. "You call me back in five minutes."

I dialed Ebenezer Baptist Church and the phone rang about eight times, which always meant that the service was underway and there was nobody manning the office. Eventually a man answered the phone, and I asked to speak to Martin Luther King, Jr.

"Is this Reverend Abernathy?" the man said.

"Yes."

"Reverend King said you might be calling. He's already started his service, but he said to interrupt him if it was you."

Martin came to the phone, and I repeated what Hosea had told me, including the part about thousands of people.

"Ralph, what do you think?" he asked.

"As for the thousands, I think he's exaggerating," I said.

"So do I," said Martin. "But putting that aside, do you think we ought to let him go ahead?"

I still didn't know the answer, but I offered what advice I could.

"If he wants to get his butt beaten then let's let him do it. Because if we don't, he'll blame us the rest of his life, saying he could have done this or that."

Martin paused for almost thirty seconds and I could hear him breathing deeply. Finally he spoke.

"Tell him he can go."

I got off the phone immediately, knowing that Hosea would be calling back in five minutes. Upstairs in the church I knew that people were beginning to shift around in their pews and glance nervously at their watches. If I didn't get up there in a hurry, a few would begin to leave.

Finally, after what seemed like an eternity, the phone rang and I grabbed it.

"Hosea," I said. "Go to it!"

"We're gone," he said and slammed down the phone.

I went upstairs and preached as usual. But it was not one of my better sermons. I was preoccupied with what was going on in Selma. And I kept asking myself whether or not I had given Martin the wrong advice. Already one youngster was dead at the hands of Alabama state troopers, and I didn't want to see anyone else killed—not in a fruitless attempt to make a march that might well have been postponed.

After church I was standing out in front, shaking hands with the members of my congregation, when someone ran up to me from the parking lot.

"Reverend Abernathy, they crossed the Pettus bridge. They've beat people—Hosea Williams, John Lewis. You've got to come listen!"

I quickly went to my own car and turned on the radio. It was all over the dial. People had been chased, run down, and brutalized. There were scores of injured people. Some of them appeared to be in serious condition. Vaughn Memorial Hospital was running over with people. So was Good Samaritan Hospital. And the black infirmary was jammed. I went back into the church and called Martin.

"Anybody killed?" he asked.

"No known dead," I said. "But it just happened less than an hour ago. The reports are still sketchy."

"Well, thank God no one's dead so far. Can you fly back with me on the first plane?"

"I'll be ready when you are," I said.

We tried to make some sense out of the reports we were getting over the radio and later on TV. At first we thought the marchers had simply been set on by a bunch of state troopers. However, after talking by telephone to Hosea, John Lewis, and several of the other staff members we gradually pieced together what had happened. And with Monday morning's newspaper account in the *New York Times*, we had a fairly complete picture.

There had been about 525 people involved in the march, not the "thousands" Hosea had described; but apparently they had been enthusiastic and ready to take risks. A New York doctor, a member of the Medical Committee for Human Rights, had volunteered his services for such dangerous occasions and had told the marchers while they were still in Brown Chapel: "There'll be tear gas, but don't panic. Don't rub your eyes. Wash them with water, if you can. And we'll be on hand to help."

The whole body had moved out of the church right after I had given the word to Hosea, walked down Broad Street, and crossed over the Edmund Pettus Bridge, just on the other side, still within the Selma city limits. With cold wind slicing into their ranks, the marchers had come face to face with the forces of the law: more than fifty state troopers, a large number of men deputized for the occasion by Sheriff Clark, and at least fifteen mounted policemen. Wearing white crash helmets, the lawmen were standing shoulder to shoulder in a line that stretched across both sides of the four-lane highway to Montgomery, and all were armed—with night sticks, tear gas canisters, and/or whips.

As Hosea and John Lewis, now a U.S. congressman, were leading the thin column toward them, the law enforcement officers donned gas masks and brandished their billy clubs. Then the marchers saw a man raise a bullhorn and a voice came booming through the cold morning air.

"I'm Major John Cloud. This is an unlawful assembly. Your

march is not conducive to the public safety. You are ordered to disperse and to go back to your church or to your homes."

Hosea, trying to find out just who these people were, called out, "May we have a word with the major?"

"There is no word to be had," Major Cloud shouted back.

Hosea tried in vain to arrange a truce so they could talk, but Cloud refused to let him advance. Then Cloud said, "You have two minutes to turn around and go back to your church."

The two groups stood glaring at one another while someone in the ranks of the lawmen, probably Major Cloud, watched the second hand of a watch sweep around twice. The wind blew in cruel, icy gusts as both groups eyed one another.

"Troopers, advance," Major Cloud barked.

Suddenly Hosea, John, and the other people in the front of the line saw a flying wedge of blue uniforms and white helmets rush toward them like charging infantry. They were so unprepared for the speed and force of the rush that they were overrun before they had time to turn and retreat, or even to raise their hands to protect their faces. John Lewis was clubbed to the ground and suffered a fractured skull. Hosea and the rest were knocked to the ground and trampled on by heavy boots.

The marchers reeled backward, their backpacks and extra clothes scattered on the ground. They ran toward the bridge as troopers pursued and clubbed them on the back and head. Screaming in fear and pain, they stopped and crowded together for protection.

At that point, someone fired tear gas into the crowd and suddenly they were engulfed in a white corrosive cloud that blinded many and burned their throats and lungs. Soon the cloud engulfed the entire scene. Wheeling and staggering, they were repeatedly beaten by club-wielding law officers wearing gas masks. Many of those present were old women and very young children but, regardless, they were attacked with equal ferocity. As the main body of marchers retreated, three women were left behind, prostrate on the side of the road, gasping for breath. One of them was Amelia Boynton. But the troopers came over, rousted them up, and told them to get back with the others. Mrs. Boynton and the other two staggered forward, fighting for breath. Later she would be one of seventeen people hospitalized, most of them as the result of tear gas.

Another round of tear gas was fired and then, according to one marcher, a louder blast from a shotgun blew a hole in a nearby brick wall. As the marchers staggered backward and turned to run, the horsemen galloped forward and pursued them, up the high slope of the Edmund Pettus Bridge. Onlookers saw troopers using whips to drive the marchers faster, flailing their backs. Running, stumbling down the other side, they made their way along Broad Street and into the black community. As they did so, four carloads of lawmen came careening off the bridge, turned the corner with a squeal, then screeched to a halt. Armed men poured from the vehicles and began clubbing the blacks who dashed by in an attempt to make it back to the church or to the houses of friends and neighbors.

Standing at some distance, a crowd of about one hundred white onlookers cheered. A cameraman was filming the action from a distance, and three white men attacked him and took away his camera. Later they were sorry they had done so. The cameraman was an FBI agent, and all three were arrested on federal charges. One of the men arrested was a member of the National States Rights Party. It turned out to be Jimmie George Robinson, the same man who had hit Martin in the hotel lobby.

At that point it was not Major Cloud but Sheriff Clark who was leading the attackers. Blacks fell back in the wake of a new, concentrated assault of swinging billy clubs and wildly charging horsemen. But the people in the neighborhood, surprised at first by the sudden swirl of battle in their midst, became angry and began to hurl bricks and bottles at the deputies. One was cut under the eye. Sheriff Clark himself was struck by a piece of brick, but was not really injured. (Later we would explain that it was not the marchers who had launched a counterattack but the residents of that neighborhood, people who had not attended our nonviolent workshops.)

But these people were certainly provoked, particularly those living in the immediate vicinity of First Baptist Church who saw riders ride up the steps and into the building itself in order to pursue and club fleeing blacks. Not only were their friends being brutalized, but their church had been trespassed on and desecrated—and for no good reason, since by then the march had been broken up and the marchers scattered.

Back in the Brown Chapel area, the leaders were quickly converting the ground floor of the two-story parsonage into a makeshift infirmary in order to care for the injured. The members of the Medical Committee for Human Rights were busy trying to treat those who were most injured. Some were bruised and cut. Others had broken ribs. Most were suffering from the effects of the tear gas. Amelia Boynton was stretched out on a table in a semiconscious state while a doctor worked frantically over her.

Even as he was doing so, more people were being clubbed outside by Sheriff Clark's men. Suddenly there was a shout. Wilson Baker, Selma commissioner of public safety, had arrived with some of his own law officers and demanded that Clark and his men fall back. For a moment the two men glared at each other. Then Baker began urging the blacks still under siege to move back into Brown Chapel Church. Recognizing the voice of reason, they immediately did so; and since Clark had no one left to pummel, he ordered his own men back to their cars. Then there was nothing but silence in the neighborhood, except for the loud groans and cries coming from the parsonage.

After dark, in groups of three and four, the marchers and their friends stole from their houses and began to congregate in the church, where Hosea Williams spoke to them of what they had been through, saying, among other things: "I fought in World War II, and I once was captured by the German army, and I want to tell you that the Germans never were as inhuman as the state troopers of Alabama."

The ragged army of veterans huddled in church that night was in no mood to argue with him. Then John Lewis told them: "I don't see how President Johnson can send troops to Vietnam— I don't see how he can send troops to the Congo—I don't see how he can send troops to Africa and can't send troops to Selma, Alabama."

The battered group, roused to anger, cheered.

"Next time we march," he said, "we may have to keep going

when we get to Montgomery. We may have to go on to Washington."

(Perhaps in response to this speech, printed in the *New York Times,* the U.S. Department of Justice announced that FBI agents had been dispatched to Selma to investigate and determine whether or not "unnecessary force was used by law officers and others. . . ." One would have thought they could simply have watched the news films to answer that question.)

In response to numerous requests from the press, Martin issued a statement on Sunday night, denouncing the Alabama authorities and reaffirming our intention to make the march from Selma to Montgomery. In part, it said:

> I am shocked at the terrible reign of terror that took place in Alabama today. Negro citizens engaged in a peaceful and orderly march to protest racial injustice were beaten, brutalized and harassed by state troopers, and Alabama revealed its law enforcement agents have no respect for democracy nor the rights of its Negro citizens. . . .
> When I made a last-minute agreement not to lead the march and appointed my able and courageous associate, Hosea Williams, for this responsibility I must confess that I had no idea that the kind of brutality and tragic expression of man's inhumanity to man as existed today would take place. Alabama's state troopers, under the sanction and authorization of Governor Wallace, allowed themselves to degenerate to the lowest state of barbarity. . . .
> We will go into federal court immediately to seek to restrain Governor Wallace and his state troopers from the unconstitutional and unjust attempt to block Negro citizens in their quest for the right to vote. . . .

In the statement he also announced that he and I would lead a march on Tuesday "in an attempt to arouse a deeper concern of this nation over the ills that are perpetrated against Negro citizens in Alabama."

The next afternoon our lawyers went to Montgomery to

appeal to Judge Frank M. Johnson, Jr., for an injunction forbidding local and state authorities to interfere with our march on Tuesday. The hearing was conducted in the judge's chambers with only our lawyers and Assistant Attorney General John Doar present. At the end of the hearing, Judge Johnson seemed to indicate that he would be willing to enjoin Sheriff Clark and Governor Wallace from interfering with a later march, but he also indicated a predisposition to enjoin us from marching as well, at least until he had heard the inevitable appeals from the other side.

As for Governor Wallace, he was busy putting his own construction on the events of the previous day. When asked by reporters if he didn't think the troopers had reacted with excessive violence, he said they behaved the way they did for our own good. "[W]e would have had all those folks camping out there in the woods. . . . There's no telling what would have happened. . . . We saved their lives by stopping that march. There's a good possibility that death would have resulted to some of those people if we had not stopped them."

On the other hand, there were blacks who were saying things that were almost as absurd. Even the NAACP, an organization known for its timidity, was using rhetoric that hardly contributed to the nonviolent atmosphere we were trying to maintain among our people. Their board issued a declaration that said: "Negroes must either submit to the heels of their oppressors or they must organize underground, to protect themselves from the oppression of Governor Wallace and his storm troopers."

In a further clarification of the NAACP's position, Roy Wilkins, the executive director, said Negroes would be "shooting back" not engaging in an "armed insurrection."

The statement issued by the organization, he said, was "not an ultimatum," but a way to discourage further attacks on blacks. "They start shooting back and you start thinking twice about shooting," he said to his white listeners.

On Monday we conferred with our lawyers and other supporters in the capital. When we finally got back to Selma it was late at night, and we thought perhaps we were too late to make the rally. But when we were a block away we could hear the shouting and cheering in Brown Chapel Church; and when we walked into the church and the congregation saw Martin, they whooped and applauded for five minutes.

He took the opportunity to deliver a scathing attack on the authorities and to praise those who had been courageous enough to take the clubbing and the tear gas without fighting back. He also welcomed the many leaders and supporters who had come to Selma to join us in our Montgomery march. He ended up with a call for unity and a repetition of his announcement that we would indeed begin our journey at 1:00 P.M. the next day.

"We've gone too far to turn back now," he said. "We must let them know that nothing can stop us—not even death itself. We must be ready for a season of suffering."

Even as he spoke these words, however, I knew that Martin was having second thoughts about the march the next day. Judge Johnson, who was much friendlier toward us than Judge Thomas, had told our lawyers that he would indeed allow us to march to Montgomery under his protection. But probably not on Tuesday. To handle the matters according to judicial procedure, he had to hear the arguments of the local and state authorities. Then he would be free to act. But until he had listened to both sides, he felt inclined to forbid our march.

So there was every likelihood that when we began tomorrow we would be met by a federal marshal who would tell us that we had been enjoined from proceeding farther; and that thought was bothering Martin, even as he was talking about tomorrow's march.

After the rally the staff and a number of our friends from other organizations gathered at the Jackson house and discussed our alternatives. We came to no final conclusions, but the discussion was heated and at times enervating. Our main concern at this point was our treatment of the thousands of people who had come from all parts of the country to march side by side with us. How could we disappoint them? We talked about the matter the rest of the night and finally went to bed shortly before daylight.

The next thing I knew I heard Jean Jackson knock on the door and call to Martin.

"Reverend King, I hate to wake you, but there's a man from the president here to see you. It's Leroy Collins."

Martin and I staggered out into the kitchen in our pajamas to meet Collins, who was accompanied by John Doar. Both smiled sympathetically and didn't seem to be bothered by what we were wearing. Over a cup of coffee at the breakfast table we talked about what we would do that day. But first Collins, head of the federal government's new Community Relations Service, listened while Martin outlined the problems we faced.

"We sent out the call nationwide for all our friends of good will, those who believed in justice and equality, to come to Selma and march with us on Tuesday. And there's every indication that they're coming by the thousands. Can we now tell them to go back home?"

Collins nodded sympathetically. He understood that we had a problem, and he wanted to do something that would help us justify the efforts of those who had come to march and at the same time obey the federal injunction.

"What about this?" he said finally. "Suppose we could get Lingo [Colonel Al Lingo of the Alabama State Patrol] and Clark to allow you to make a march of some sort without going on to Montgomery. Would that be enough to satisfy your supporters?"

Martin shook his head.

"I don't know," he said. "We've made marches in Selma before. It would hardly be worth a trip of several hundred miles just to repeat the same stroll downtown."

Collins thought for a moment.

"Suppose you could cross the Edmund Pettus Bridge and go to the spot where the blood was shed on Sunday? You could make it a symbolic journey, a reenactment of Sunday's march. Only this time there would be no billy clubs and no horses. The troops would have to let you come and they would keep their distance. Then you could voluntarily turn around and walk back to the churches, obeying a federal injunction, telling your people that you had made your point."

I could tell that Martin liked the idea. He sat for a long moment, staring at the floor as if searching for an answer. Then he looked over at me.

"What do you think, Ralph?"

"I think it sounds OK," I said, with just the slightest hesitation. There was no easy path. Either route incurred risks and criticism. But this way we could salvage something for tomorrow and still obey Judge Johnson, who, we were certain, would clear the highway for us by next weekend.

Martin asked the others who were there and got a mixed response. Hosea wanted to make the march whatever the consequences. So did some of the others. Several agreed with us. But SNCC would be furious, that much we knew. They would take advantage of the situation to attack our leadership and impugn our courage. On the other hand, leaders like James Farmer of the Congress of Racial Equality (CORE) supported a more prudent policy. In discussions the previous night, he had urged us to postpone the march. His attitude was perhaps the most encouraging of all, since he was the one who had come down in answer to our nationwide appeal.

After reviewing all the opinions, Martin was still skeptical of at least one part of Collins's plan.

"How can we be sure that Lingo and Clark can control themselves, much less their men. They'll come charging into us just the way they did last Sunday, no matter what we agree to."

"Suppose I can get their assurances? Suppose they will support the whole idea?"

Martin was silent. He still hadn't made up his mind, entirely. I knew that he was thinking of all the people, black and white, who were even now gathering at the churches all over Selma, ready to move out when he gave the signal. I was glad I didn't have to make the decision.

"I can't promise anything," he said finally, "but I will try. If you get Lingo and Clark to agree, then I'll try to stop the march. But only after we reach the spot where the blood was shed on Sunday."

Collins jumped to his feet, shook hands, and said that he was off to talk to the lawmen.

"I'll be back as soon as I have an answer," he said.

As soon as Collins had left, Martin was again torn.

"I'm going to call Jack Greenberg and the New York boys," he said.

He wanted reassurance from them that he was making a wise move in postponing the march, but Greenberg, Harry Wachtel, Clarence Jones, and Bayard Rustin, from the vantage point of a thousand miles, were full of clarity and courage. All but Greenberg, who was president of the Legal Defense Fund of the NAACP, urged us to defy Judge Johnson's order and march into the teeth of Al Lingo's state troopers. They would be cheering us on from in front of their television sets, not only when we were being attacked by the state troopers but also while we were serving our terms in federal prison.

In some cases these people had given us strong support and good advice. This time they confused Martin and made his decision that much more difficult and painful. When he hung up you could see the anguish in his face.

Later that morning, as we made our way toward Brown Chapel, we had even graver misgivings about calling off the march. The people were here—they had come literally by the thousands. How they had all made it so quickly we didn't know. Some had come by plane, more by train and bus, still more by automobile. They were swarming like a huge invading army, covering the land, the sidewalks, and the streets. Under different circumstances my heart would have leapt at the sight of them, but this morning I saw their numbers as a mixed blessing. In an hour's time they might all be shaking their fists at us for having sold them out.

Martin mustered them with a bullhorn, speaking to them of the great indignities suffered by marchers on the previous Sunday and calling for them to follow him toward the Edmund Pettus Bridge. He and I were on the front row with a Greek Orthodox patriarch between us, decked out in all his ecclesiastical regalia, his beard flowing down to his waist. On my right were a group of nuns in their black and white habits, and immediately behind me were two rabbis. We were as ecumenical a group as ever gathered together in this country.

We walked down Broad Street, past the intersection where Highway 22 led off toward Linden—the route I used to drive when I was in college—and I stared down that long road toward home as if I had never seen it before. Somewhere along Broad, maybe at Tepper's department store, we saw Leroy Collins push his way through the small crowd of white onlookers and wave frantically. Martin slowed down to a shuffle but continued to move. Collins was holding a piece of paper in his hand.

"Colonel Lingo and Sheriff Clark have agreed to the plan," he said. "They want you to follow this route. It leads right down Broad and onto the Edmund Pettus Bridge. Just the way the march went last Sunday. All you have to do is turn around at that spot, and they'll keep their men under control."

"I'll do my best to turn the column around," Martin said, "but I can't guarantee it. Some of them have come a long way, and they're mighty determined. Just keep those troopers from attacking us."

"I'll stand right next to Lingo and Clark," Collins promised.

"I'll try too," said Martin, and Collins took off ahead of us, walking as rapidly as he could in order to get over to the other side as quickly as possible. By the time we came in sight of the humpbacked bridge, he was already crossing it, a lone figure trying to bring two sides together, a bridge himself.

As we turned left and approached the bridge, a man suddenly stepped from the curb and faced us, holding up his hand. He told us that he was Federal Marshal Stanley Fountain and was there to read an injunction issued by Judge Johnson, an injunction forbidding us to march on Highway 80 to Montgomery.

As Fountain read the legal language I looked over at Martin. He had a strange look on his face, as if he were hypnotized by the language. I wondered if he were praying or if he were in some kind of self-induced trance. I had never seen him look quite the same way before, and I never saw him look that way again. I started to speak to him, but decided to hold my peace until the marshal had finished and Martin had had an opportunity to respond. Behind we could hear the steady drone of thousands of voices, in control of themselves but impatient.

When the marshal had finished, Martin suddenly woke from his trance.

"Let's go, Ralph," he said and stepped past Stanley Fountain, who moved out of the way of the great surging crowd. We walked up that high arc, unable to see what was waiting for us on the other side; but as we crested at the center of the bridge, we could look down and see the army of state troopers and deputies lined up across the road. For an instant I felt my stomach flip, and I knew how soldiers must have felt a hundred years ago when they faced each other on a battlefield. Just before we started down, I turned to look behind us and saw thousands of people winding back down the bridge and along Broad Street. And I knew that some of them were still back at Brown Chapel Church, just starting out. For that glorious instant we had the high ground, and there in the morning sun I thought we were invincible.

But as we came down the slope of the bridge, we saw that the men in front of us were well-armed and standing tall. There were several hundred and their ranks stretched across the road. They were clearly prepared to block our way with clubs, whips, tear gas, and rifles. Would they actually shoot into the crowd? I didn't think so, but I didn't know for certain.

As we approached them, I looked over and saw Collins standing near the troopers, a worried look on his face. In some respects he had as much to lose as we did.

When we were about twenty-five yards from the line of troopers, Martin turned and said, "We'll stop here." And we did.

At that point someone—perhaps another federal marshal—stepped forward and said in a hoarse voice, "Dr. King, you can't proceed any farther. If you do, it will be considered a violation of the injunction."

Martin looked at me.

"You say a prayer," he said, "and then we'll try to turn this column around."

He took his bullhorn and turned around to the crowd, which was still crossing the bridge and fanning out into the fields on both sides of the road.

"Dr. Ralph David Abernathy will now say a prayer," he shouted.

I took the bullhorn from him and turned my back on the troopers.

"Would everybody please kneel," I shouted and literally thousands of people immediately dropped to their knees. I stared for a moment, overcome by the sight. Then I knelt myself.

Closing my eyes, I silently asked the Lord to give me the right words and began. I don't remember exactly what I said. I know it was a long prayer that covered everything that had happened and everything that might happen, including a compromise with what we had originally intended. My words echoed, and between them there was an oddly disturbing silence. When I finally finished and lifted my head, I turned around.

The troopers were gone. They had retreated to one side and left before us an empty highway, a straight shot to Montgomery, the asphalt glistening as brightly as the Yellow Brick Road. It was as if I had prayed them out of our way.

I looked at Martin and he looked at me. For an instant I'm sure he must have been tempted to plunge forward into that gap, with troopers on both sides of the road. Maybe that's what George Wallace and Jim Clark wanted us to do. Had we broken our word and violated the injunction, we would have been fair game. They could have arrested all of us—or as many as they could haul away—and we would have been discredited by everyone in authority. Even Lyndon Johnson could not have defended our actions, if indeed he had wanted to. And we could never again have looked Collins in the eye.

So without another word, we turned the column around and, marching by our own bewildered people, we looped back down the highway and up the slope of the Edmund Pettus Bridge. When we were halfway to the crest, I looked around for the first time and saw that the crowd was following us. All of them. There would be no injuries or arrests this day.

On the other hand, when we got back to Brown Chapel

Church, we had to face another kind of hostility. John Lewis and the leaders of the SNCC were in a rage.

"You made a deal!" they shouted. "You sold out!"

"No, we didn't sell out," we explained. "We made no deal with anyone. We simply obeyed the injunction in order to march later with the full protection of the court."

But they felt betrayed. So did some others, including the press. They too were bewildered by what we had done, particularly after we had been given a clear marching path by the troopers. This point was made time and time again, and we began to realize just how shrewd Governor Wallace had been in creating the illusion that we had been free to continue. Now both our friends and casual observers were beginning to suspect that we had been less than courageous. It was the first time that such accusations would be made, though not the last. Soon, very soon, the advocates of violence would be saying that Martin was too timid to lead the movement, and then that he was too cowardly.

In retrospect, however, I believe that we made the right choice, however difficult it may have been. Because not only was the nation as a whole watching us, but also the Congress of the United States. Had we violated a federal injunction and been arrested by the waiting lawmen, our enemies on the floor of the House and Senate would have been able to call us nothing more than troublemakers and rabble rousers, a mob with no respect for order or for human life. But because we made a prudent judgment and waited till we had the support of the federal court, we were able to make the march to Montgomery under the protection of the very people who had blocked our way when we halted just over the bridge.

It is also worth noting here that, once again, the very philosophy of nonviolence was on trial in Selma. Lewis and the other members of the SNCC, though theoretically committed to nonviolence, were moving ever closer to fighting back. We had reason to believe that they were a kettle waiting to boil over, and too often a kettle that boils over puts out the fire.

No single incident during those years better illustrates the wisdom of our approach than Bloody Sunday and our response to it. The sight of unarmed and unprotected blacks being beaten and whipped and gassed by riot squads was what it took to pass a comprehensive voting rights act. Nothing less than this kind of gratuitous brutality would have attracted such national attention and caused such widespread indignation.

Had anyone been armed or struck back in anger the police would have been able to use such actions to justify what they had done. But because everyone behaved according to the plan outlined in our workshops, what America saw was an unprovoked attack on innocence. That was the message we wanted to send to Congress and the American people.

Had we armed ourselves and spent the next weeks shooting back at policemen, as Roy Wilkins was suggesting, we might still be having difficulties registering to vote in Dallas County and in other polling places throughout the country. Everyone now takes this idea for granted, but in 1965 we were having a harder and harder time defending our approach from the attacks of the more militant members of the black community. Had our approach failed to elicit positive action from the Congress of the United States, I am convinced that Martin would have lost control of the movement and we might have seen even more desperate times than we did experience. Though we were hated and condemned by many whites who should have known better, we clearly stood for ideas and methods that were most likely to bring a peaceful resolution to racial tensions in the South.

But more important to us at the time was that we were the only ones who could win concessions from the nation's white establishment because we understood what would most likely touch their consciences and make them see the error of Jim Crow and second-class citizenship.

So when some of our friends as well as our enemies called us "cowards" and "traitors," we gritted our teeth and bore the charges, explaining our reasons for behaving as we did, refusing to accept any counsel that argued against following federal court orders and continuing to teach our people the techniques of nonviolence. But we didn't like such criticism, particularly in view of our past record; and we were particularly disturbed by the idea that it might affect our marchers in a crucial moment of confrontation.

We were prepared for criticism from the SNCC, but we were surprised to hear that James Forman had called our actions "a classic example of trickery against the people." White reporters were running back and forth from one black leader to another, bringing new accusations and insults. Martin, who had had little sleep since Sunday, finally withdrew from Selma and drove back to Montgomery, staying with the Smileys where he could find a little peace and hear a few kind words from old friends.

The rest of us took the abuse and tried to explain our reasoning to an increasingly hostile opposition. Then, on Tuesday night, something happened that was to make our squabbles over strategy seem petty and irrelevant. The Reverend James A. Reeb of Massachusetts, one of the white people who had answered our call for supporters only a day earlier, was set upon by a group of white troublemakers and beaten severely, along with two of his companions. (They had been beaten simply because they had the courage to eat in a black restaurant.) From the outset it was apparent that he had been critically injured, and on Thursday he died—the second fatality of the Selma campaign.

As the week moved on, we work-shopped the people, teaching them over and over again the language and gestures of nonviolence. In the wake of Bloody Sunday, however, these sessions were much more sober and much more diligent. In the past we had talked in theoretical terms, but now we were lecturing to people who had already sustained a brutal attack, many of them staring at us through bandages or limping.

On Thursday morning Judge Johnson heard our petition for the right to march to Montgomery with police protection. He questioned Martin at some length about the things he had been quoted as saying about the first injunction, trying to determine if, as the state's attorneys were trying to argue, we had in fact violated the first injunction issued against the Tuesday march.

Martin maintained that we had marched over the bridge not to violate his injunction but to make it possible for us to control the marchers.

Finally, we got the word from Judge Johnson. As promised he had issued an injunction that spelled out our right to march and the responsibility of state authorities to protect us. In his ruling he said of the Dallas County law enforcement team: "the evidence in this case reflects that . . . an almost continuous pattern of conduct has existed on the part of defendant Sheriff Clark and his deputies and his executive deputies known as 'possemen' of harassment, intimidation, coercion, threatening conduct, and, sometimes, brutal mistreatment toward these plaintiffs." He accused them of intervening to prevent us "from exercising their rights of citizenship, particularly the right to vote and the right to demonstrate peaceably for the purpose of protesting discriminatory practices."

He concluded by saying that there should be some relationship between the kind of demonstration permitted and the enormity of the wrongs involved. "In this case," he said, "the wrongs are enormous." Thus he concluded that we should be given the right to demonstrate as we had planned to: by marching en masse down Highway 80 from Selma to Montgomery, despite the fact that it meant blocking off one half of the highway and the commitment of a number of state troopers and other state personnel. Johnson specified that on the longest segment of the journey, where Highway 80 was only two lanes, a maximum of three hundred marchers would be permitted. On the four-lane segments, however, we could have as many marchers as we wanted.

This decision was significant in several respects. In the first place, a federal court had specifically ruled that Clark and others in his force had committed intimidating and even brutal acts against our people. In other words, the federal government had once again come down on our side in our struggle with local law enforcement agencies, which meant that *they* rather than *we* were the lawbreakers—a point we had continued to make since the earliest days of the Montgomery bus boycott. That point alone was worth the trouble.

In the second place, Judge Johnson had enunciated a new and subtle principle in determining what was permitted of demonstrators: the magnitude of the demonstration permissible depended on the size of the injustice suffered. So as long as we were protesting genuine and widespread abuse of our civil rights, we had a right to plan events that might inconvenience or even severely inhibit the carrying on of everyday communication and commerce. The blocking off of Highway 80 involved considerable inconvenience and inhibition. Yet these arguments were invalid in determining whether or not we could make our march—not if we had suffered sufficiently. Henceforth, we might even be able to block traffic at the New York World's Fair, something we had been forbidden to do in the North.

But there was one more element to this decision that made it a particularly sweet victory: Governor Wallace, who had sent in Major Cloud and the combat-ready unit of state troopers, would be forced to provide genuine protection this time, on penalty of a contempt of court citation from a federal judge.

Governor Wallace was furious when he received the word, and he went on statewide television to denounce Judge Johnson's decision as coming from a "mock court." He told his audience that the State of Alabama simply did not have the troops to spare, and telegraphed President Lyndon Johnson to send federal marshals to accomplish the task Judge Johnson had assigned.

This speech, a typical Wallace performance, was more rhetoric than substance. Of course he had enough men to protect our marchers. More than fifty state troopers met Hosea and his marchers as they came off the Edmund Pettus Bridge and carried out a well-executed attack against a much larger (although unarmed) force. Fifty dedicated troopers could easily have protected us against the handful of Ku Kluxers who might have had the nerve to attack us, knowing we would have an armed escort.

President Johnson, an old veteran of southern political wars, saw that Wallace had left himself wide open, and Johnson took the opportunity to strike a devastating blow, using a state's rights argument against the governor:

> Responsibility for maintaining law and order in our federal system properly rests with the state and local government. On the basis of your public statements and your discussions with me I thought that you felt strongly about this and had indicated you would take all neces-

sary actions in this regard. I was surprised, therefore, when in your telegram on Thursday you requested federal assistance in the performance of such fundamental duties.

Even more surprising was your telegram of yesterday, stating that both you and the Alabama legislature, because of monetary considerations, believed that the state is unable to protect American citizens and to maintain peace and order in a responsible manner without federal forces.

Having shamed Wallace in this fashion, President Johnson went on to call up 1,863 members of the Alabama National Guard, thereby removing them from state command, and assigning them to protect our marchers. Johnson also pressed into service more than a thousand military policemen from Maxwell Air Force Base in Montgomery and Craig Field near Selma; and he alerted a thousand troops in Ft. Benning, Georgia. We later discovered that two helicopters had been assigned to follow us the whole way, just so they could spot any trouble that could not be detected from the ground. So we were as well protected as a shipment of gold from Ft. Knox—thanks to President Johnson.

Despite the fact that such actions were invited by Governor Wallace, however, O. L. Perdue, president of the Reserve Officers Association of Alabama, appealed to the president not to force the Alabama National Guard "to protect those who have fabricated lies, flouted local law and order, and brought tensions to our state and to all America."

With national guardsmen and military police beginning to pour into Montgomery, Alabamians began to see that their governor had lost control of the situation. Of course, Wallace could later say that he had saved the state of Alabama one million dollars by forcing the federal government to provide protection. On the other hand, Lyndon Johnson had the last laugh, because he sent in Ramsey Clark, one of the most despised men in the South, to oversee the operation, and his presence as coordinator of the Alabama National Guard must have galled both Wallace and his most ardent white supporters.

Needless to say, we were overjoyed at Judge Johnson's

decision and the sympathy that lay behind it. We immediately announced that the march would begin at 10:00 A.M. on Sunday, March 21—exactly two weeks after Bloody Sunday. Though geographically we hadn't budged an inch during this period, we had come a long way in a fortnight. Now we had to make certain that our march was well planned and well executed.

Food and shelter were the most important considerations. While the core group of marchers would number only three hundred, we expected many times that number to start and finish the journey on those stretches that were four lanes. Since we planned to go no farther than about twelve miles on the most strenuous day—a very reasonable expectation—we decided to provide food for at least four nights, with the assumption that we would arrive in Montgomery sometime Thursday. That meant a lot of meals to be cooked and transported to wherever the marchers stopped for the night.

Before we had finished enlisting help, most of the black kitchens in Selma and Montgomery were pressed into service—kitchens in homes, restaurants, colleges. People sent whatever they could, from loaves of bread to more substantial dishes like fried chicken, fish, ham, collard and turnip greens, peas, sweet potatoes, and macaroni and cheese. And there was lots of soup—cooked in pots and brought in the back seats of cars—still hot when it was put on the folding tables we used.

Everyone was welcome to eat, and of course no one was charged a penny. Miraculously the volunteer cooks of both cities were able to feed at least three hundred each day and more than three thousand people on the first and last days—only slightly fewer than were fed on the biblical five loaves and two fishes. No one went hungry in the field, though some of those who sent food had less on their own tables as a consequence.

As for campsites, we would send an advance crew ahead each day to plan for a place to have lunch and a place to pitch our big circus tents. Needless to say, there were a good many people along the way who didn't want us to use their property. Most of the time we were able to find blacks who owned property on or near the highway, and they were usually willing to give us permission to stay. In one instance, however, when we could not locate the owner, we stopped anyway—out of absolute necessity.

We rounded up several huge tents (eventually we were using four), but they weren't big enough to take care of all three hundred full-time marchers; so some people had to use sleeping bags or blankets and sleep in automobiles or on the back of flatbed trucks. It wasn't the most comfortable outing for these people, particularly that Tuesday night, after it had rained all day; but they endured the chill and were as cheerful as those who slept in the relative comfort of the tents. As a matter of fact, the tone of the entire march was that of a celebration. As we walked along the highway we sang songs, told jokes, and generally enjoyed each other's company.

Our stated purpose for the event, which we were now calling the Alabama Freedom March, was to present a petition to Governor Wallace, demanding that our civil rights, long denied, be granted to us. But of course we were still trying to make an impression on the people of the nation in general and the U.S. Congress in particular. More than anything in the world, we wanted that Voting Rights Act passed in this session.

After working out the logistics, we again put out a call, and even more people poured into Montgomery and Selma, so many this time that all the hotels and motels were filled for miles around, and we had to sleep out-of-town marchers in black homes and in our churches. Among those who came to Selma to be with us were such famous figures as Ralph Bunche, Under Secretary of the United Nations; Gary Merrill, the actor; Dick Gregory, the comedian; Mario Savio, then a well-known activist; as well as a number of nationally prominent civil rights leaders. But there were also a number of people who were unknown to the general public but who were equally dedicated to the cause. For example, there was Cager Lee, the grandfather of Jimmie Lee Jackson, the boy who had been killed by an Alabama state trooper. There was Mrs. Viola Gregg Liuzzo, mother of five, a white woman who had taken an incomplete in her classes at Wayne State University in Detroit just so she could participate in this demonstration. And there was Jim Letherer, a one-legged man who was determined to make the entire march on crutches.

As a matter of fact, when we assembled at Brown Chapel Church there were more than three thousand people present, a considerable improvement over Bloody Sunday. Martin had prepared a rousing speech before we left, and I was chosen to introduce him. Standing there, looking at the multitudes of bright and smiling faces, I couldn't help but see the whole undertaking as a joyous adventure.

"When we get to Montgomery," I told them, "we are going to go up to Governor Wallace's door and say, 'George, it's all over now. We've got the ballot!'"

The crowd laughed and roared its approval, but when Martin spoke it was with more eloquent sobriety:

> You will be the people that will light a new chapter in the history of our nation. Those of us who are Negroes don't have much. We have known the long night of poverty. Because of the system we don't have much education, and some of us don't know how to make our nouns and verbs agree. But thank God we have our bodies, our feet and our souls.
>
> Walk together, children, and don't you get weary, and it will lead us to the promised land. And Alabama will be a new Alabama and America will be a new America.

With those words we began our march—the third and final one—down Broad Street and across the Edmund Pettus Bridge. But this time there was a difference. Instead of troops waiting for us on the other side of the Alabama River, we had a military escort all the way. Jeeps and motorcycles ran ahead at each crossing, and guards would jump out and position themselves at the intersecting roads to halt all traffic, while two helicopters wheeled in the sky above us, ready to swoop down on anyone who stood in our way.

There was another difference: Sheriff Clark was no longer in charge of the operation. As a matter of fact, as we filed out of town, singing our songs, he was standing on the steps of City Hall, only a block away, wearing a button with a one-word message on it: NEVER. He told about fifty people who had come to hear him speak, "The federal government has given them everything they wanted." In saying this he probably never realized the degree to which he had contributed to the outcome of the conflict.

Since we didn't leave until almost one o'clock, we only walked a little more than seven miles on the first day, the whole journey on two lanes of a four-lane highway. This meant that the many celebrities who had come to lend their support at the beginning of the march would not have too strenuous a walk and could be transported back to Montgomery in order to leave in late afternoon or early evening.

The day was chilly, with the temperature in the high forties; but we were not uncomfortable, certainly not as much as we were in succeeding days. Some of the onlookers were hostile and abusive. One man held up a sign that read "Too bad Reeb," referring to the Unitarian minister who had been beaten to death. And another brandished the slogan "I hate niggers." But many of the onlookers were supportive, and we were in too good a mood to be soured by the presence of a handful of self-identified bigots. After all, we knew that no one dared attack us.

We didn't know how vulnerable our friends were elsewhere at that very moment. For in Birmingham a number of bombs, six in all, were discovered in the black community, set to explode as we were embarking on our march. One was found in a Roman Catholic church and another in a Catholic parsonage, probably because a number of Catholic nuns and priests were prominently involved in the march. Two more turned up in black mortuaries, and a fifth in an all-black high school. The sixth was planted near the former home of the Reverend A. D. King, Martin's brother. Obviously the bombers had not been told that A. D. had long since moved to Kentucky.

Clearly these acts of pure malice were perpetrated by people seeking revenge for the manner in which we had triumphed over local and state white leadership. While the school was empty on Sunday morning, the other buildings were in use, and the Catholic church was holding service with 120 people present. The fact that the bombs were discovered and that they were poorly wired does not alter the grim implications of such a plot. The people involved were political murderers, and their hatred toward us was measureless. When we heard about it along the road, I felt a chill that had nothing to do with the weather.

On the other hand, if we had our enemies in another part of the state, we also had friends around the country. There were demonstrations and supporting marches in New York City; Washington, D.C.; Linden, New Jersey; Portsmouth, Virginia; New Rochelle, New York; Montreal, Canada; and even Guam. Some of these events involved hundreds of people. So if Birmingham wasn't with us, the rest of the world was.

At the end of the first day we stopped in a field owned by David and Rosa Belle Hall, a black couple who lived in a three-room house and had never voted in their lives. But they owned eighty acres of land, had a few animals, and farmed in much the same way my parents had done thirty years earlier. They were good and simple people who, though not politically active or socially sensitive, were willing to run the risk of allowing us to use their property, aware that everyone in the state would know what they had done by the next day.

That night we put up two of the circus tents, hoping that they would be enough to take care of everyone who had remained. It was icy cold after sundown, and someone started a wood fire in an old oil drum. A lot of people sat around the fire, singing and telling stories until early in the morning; but most of us were too tired to do anything but fall into bed. Martin and I slept in a van in sleeping bags on the floor.

Martin had been in pain during the last couple of miles because of a large blister on his foot. He got some first aid before he went to sleep, but he told me he didn't know whether or not he'd be able to last four more days. Fortunately, he would get a break from the marching because he was due to make a speech on Tuesday.

"When do you plan to leave?" I asked.

"As early as I can," he said, wincing.

The next morning the trucks brought coffee and oatmeal for breakfast, and we started out on the second leg of our journey.

After several stops we reached the Lowndes County line where the highway narrowed to two lanes. In obedience to Judge Johnson's restrictions, we stopped to determine which marchers would be allowed to continue and which would have to leave for the slightly less than fourteen miles of two-lane traffic.

In addition to the leaders of the march, we decided that all those who had been arrested or beaten during the Selma campaign would have the privilege of making the entire journey, which everyone wanted to do. Then we looked at the rest and tried to make a determination based on contributions thus far. One of the people we allowed to continue was Jim Letherer, the man with one leg. He had said at the outset that he wanted to make the entire journey, and some of the white onlookers back at Selma had laughed at him and shouted out insults. So he was chosen. Also chosen was a red-headed Irishman named Murphy, who spoke with a brogue of his belief in freedom and equality for all men. These, and the others who made up the three hundred, started out on the single lane of Highway 80 while the others climbed into vehicles and went back to Selma or forward to Montgomery. During that 13.8 miles, however, some people dropped out and others took their place, so that a good many more than three hundred could actually say they had marched for the entire five days.

While we marched down the single lane, U.S. Army personnel patroled the other lane, making certain that all cars drove slowly and that there was no harassment. There were a few exchanges between our marchers and the Alabama troopers, and one of our drivers was arrested for speeding, but by and large we got along well. That night, when we again stopped in a field, our camp was guarded by sentries, as if we were combat troops in enemy territory—which in a way we were.

So wary were we of intruders and troublemakers, that we set up our own security patrol within the camp, making certain that everyone who came among us—and there were many reporters, well-wishers, and sightseers each night—was first checked out for weapons. But the second night there were fewer of these, and no one was sitting around the fire singing songs. For one thing, we were all too tired; and for another, the rain had begun.

Tuesday we had to walk through a steady and chilling downpour. A few people carried umbrellas, and a few more made ponchos out of plastic sheets. Some even tried to make rain hats out of cereal boxes, but most of us were soaked to the bone before we had been on the road an hour. We felt sorry for the drenched cattle standing in the glistening pastures, but we felt even sorrier for ourselves, particularly since by Tuesday many people were beginning to feel the ravages of having walked so far without the right type of shoes.

For those who could no longer bear the blisters or who felt near collapse from exhaustion, we had a large mobile hospital that was lent to us by the International Ladies Garment Workers. They treated anyone who suffered from minor complaints, but we all knew that their real purpose for being there was to handle more serious life-threatening injuries, such as severe beatings and gunshot wounds.

One thing about the rain, however; it certainly would have discouraged anyone who might have wanted to attack us from the nearby fields and woods since the low land on both sides of the highway was filling up with water. As a matter of fact, when we pitched our tents that evening, we did so over ground so wet that we could not even make the floor dry by scattering straw. So those who slept in the tents did so on a cold bed, and those of us who slept in cramped vehicles had the better bargain for the first time.

When we started out Wednesday, we were in much better spirits, despite the night of rain, if only because we would move into the city limits of Montgomery before the end of the day and that night would be entertained by the greatest assembly of talent ever to perform before a predominantly black audience.

Those listed on the bill included: Harry Belafonte; Mahalia Jackson; Tony Bennett; Billy Eckstein; Pete Seeger; Odetta; Sammy Davis, Jr. (who closed his Broadway show to come); Dick Gregory; Alan King; Nipsy Russell; Bobby Darin; the Chad Mitchell trio; George Kirby; Joan Baez; Peter, Paul, and Mary; Ossie Davis; Elaine May and Mike Nichols; Ina Balin; Arthur Davis; Ruby Dee; James Baldwin; Shelley Winters; Leon Bibb; John Killins; Godfrey Cambridge; Ella Fitzgerald; Nina Simone; Leonard Bernstein; and Floyd Patterson.

One or two of these weren't able to make it, but almost all of them were waiting for us when we crossed the city limits, as were literally thousands and thousands of other people who had flown in from all over the country to join in the last few miles of the triumphant march. Of course, it might have been even more joyous an occasion had not the skies opened up and dumped tons of water on us the very moment we entered the city. But we sang out with "We Shall Overcome" and survived the fifteen-minute downpour, just as we had survived the others, and marched all the way to St. Jude's Church behind a band, with people cheering on both sides of the road.

That night, we camped on the still-soaked grounds inside the St. Jude's complex, and watched all of these famous and talented people perform on a makeshift stage. Few audiences in the world had ever watched such an array of stars on a single stage; yet we watched them for the price of a four-day march along Highway 80.

Many of them stayed on for the last leg of our journey—a 3.5-mile procession from St. Jude's to the steps of the state capitol itself, where we would celebrate the end of our march and present our petition to Governor George Wallace—or so we intended, though we had reason to believe he wouldn't receive us or the petition. Indeed, he showed his contempt for us and for our cause by declaring Thursday a holiday for all female state employees, as if somehow our presence in Montgomery constituted a danger to white womanhood. It was a shrewd and mean-spirited insult, calculated to appeal to racial stereotypes so familiar to white southerners that they could hardly have failed to make the connection. With defeat imminent, he was putting us on notice that he was not going to surrender easily. We would have to drive a stake in the heart of Jim Crow.

But on Thursday we were prepared to overcome any obstacle. Of course the four-day hike had been physically exhausting, but the anticipation of our triumphant appearance at George Wallace's doorstep with our own army started our adrenaline flowing. As we marched out of the St. Jude's complex and into downtown Montgomery, we were met by literally thousands of people, waving, shouting, and falling into step with us as we marched onward. Up Dexter Avenue we came, past Dexter Avenue Baptist Church, where Martin had begun his ministry, around the square—crowded by now with more than twenty thousand cheering people—and right up to the steps of the Alabama State Capitol, where a platform had been built out of new lumber so that we could speak to our followers and, through television, to the nation as a whole.

It was a glorious homecoming for Martin and me. Juanita and Coretta joined us in our moment of triumph, and we stood before our old friends and a host of new ones we didn't know as they cheered our triumph over the Alabama white establishment. I made sure that our children, Juandalynn, Donzaleigh, and Ralph III, all of whom were born in Montgomery at the St. Jude Hospital, were among the marchers. In fact at one point they led us up Dexter Avenue. Although they were only ages seven, six, and five, they were freedom fighters. Not only had we come from Selma to Montgomery—a distance of more than fifty miles—but we had come from the outer regions of second-class citizenship to the threshold of full participation in American democracy. Even as we stood there in the shadow of the capitol, once the seat of the Confederate States of America, things were happening in Washington, D.C. A number of people in both the executive and legislative branches of government were preparing a bill to guarantee voting rights to all Americans, but particularly to blacks in the South. As we stood on that platform, in the knowledge that such a bill was in the works, I couldn't help but think that sometimes the mills of the gods grind pretty fast—that is, if you put your shoulder to them and help push them along.

The speeches given that day were full of hope and the promise of a new day for Alabama blacks. Everybody understood that our march had been more than a symbolic journey. Our ability to make that fifty-mile trek was a concrete demonstration that a group of determined blacks could successfully defy local and state authorities when their cause was just, even to the point of using public property to their own ends. Highway 80 belonged to the motorists of Alabama and the rest of the nation, but we had claimed it for our own in our moment of need—over the objections of the Jim Clarks and George Wallaces—and we had done so with the superior power of the federal government behind us.

I don't know what Governor Wallace and Sheriff Clark thought as they watched the spectacle of our celebration on television that night, but they should have recognized that their cause, whether states rights or white supremacy, was doomed as we stood there on the capitol steps, usurping what had always been exclusively white territory for our own political rally. For that hour we owned the capitol of the State of Alabama, just as for four days we had owned Highway 80. At that moment we were confident of eventual victory. Martin spoke:

> They told us we wouldn't get here, and there were those who said we would get here only over their dead bodies, but all the world today knows that we are here and that we are standing before the forces of power in the State of Alabama saying, "We ain' goin' to let nobody turn us around."
>
> The Civil Rights Act of 1964 gave Negroes some part of their rights, but without the vote it was dignity without strength.
>
> Once more the method of nonviolent resistance was unsheathed from the scabbard and once more an entire community was mobilized to confront the adversary. And again the brutality of a dying order shrieks across the land. Yet Selma, Alabama, became a shining moment in the conscience of man.

The crowd roared its approval, and seventy-five yards away, in a window of his office, George Wallace parted the venetian blinds slightly and peered out at twenty-five thousand people gathered on the square to protest his actions and his ideals. Certainly Martin didn't spare the governor's feelings: "So I stand before you this afternoon with the conviction that segregation is on its deathbed in Alabama and the only thing uncertain about it is how costly the segregationists and Wallace will make the funeral."

Then, in one of his finest climaxes, he brought the crowd to its feet in one great, prolonged cheer:

I know you are asking today, "How long will it take?"
I come to say to you this afternoon however difficult the
moment, however frustrating the hour, it will not be long,
because truth pressed to earth will rise again.

How long? Not long, because no lie can live forever.

How long? Not long, because you still reap what you
sow.

How long? Not long, because the arm of the moral
universe is long but it bends toward justice.

How long? Not long, cause mine eyes have seen the
glory of the coming of the Lord, trampling out the vintage
where the grapes of wrath are stored. He hath loosed the
fateful lightning of his terrible swift sword. His truth is
marching on.

He has sounded forth the trumpets that shall never
call retreat. He is lifting up the hearts of man before His
judgment seat. Oh, be swift, my soul, to answer Him. Be
jubilant my feet. Our God is marching on.

Later a delegation led by Joseph Lowery tried to deliver our
petition for redress of grievances to Governor Wallace. At first
they were not allowed to enter the capitol. Then, when the guards
finally permitted them inside this public building, they were met
by one of Wallace's assistants who announced that the governor
had left for the day.

In effect, we had driven him from his own citadel, forcing
him to vacate the seat of government. Had he come out, received
our petition, and behaved in a gracious manner, he might have
salvaged some dignity for himself and for his cause. As it stood,
our triumph over him was complete, and we left the square in a
state of joyous vindication, certain that we had won a great
victory.

But such moments of triumph and absolute certitude are
always illusory. The world is not a fairy tale or a Hollywood movie,
and its innumerable stories never end "happily ever after" or with
a perfect kiss at the fade-out. There is always trouble around the
next bend in the road, and in this case the road was Highway 80.

That day, after the cheers and the confident speeches were
over, all of the marchers had to return to their homes. Since many
of them had come from Selma, we set up car pools to take them
fifty miles to the place where it had all started. One of the cars

used in this operation was driven by Mrs. Viola Liuzzo. Accompanied by nineteen-year-old Leroy Moton, one of our Selma supporters, Mrs. Liuzzo had taken several loads of passengers back to Selma, and had been subjected to considerable harassment along the way. People had yelled insults because she was in the car with a black male, one car had deliberately rear-ended her, and another had tried to force her off the road.

That night, when she and Moton were en route to Montgomery after dropping off a load of weary marchers, a car sped up behind them, began passing, and suddenly someone fired at least three shots through the window on the driver's side. Mrs. Liuzzo slumped over the wheel and the car veered onto the shoulder and traveled several hundred yards before Moton was able to put his foot on the brake and steer it out into a pasture, where it finally jerked to a stop against a rusty barbed-wire fence.

Fearing there would be more shots, Moton tried to pull Mrs. Liuzzo to the floor to avoid being hit. As he was trying to revive Mrs. Liuzzo, he saw a car coming from the other direction slow down, and he ducked. Since he was covered with Mrs. Liuzzo's blood, he lay perfectly still, as if dead, as the other car pulled up and stopped. He heard footsteps and then someone aimed the beam of a flashlight into the front seat. Whoever it was remained for an instant, then Moton heard rapidly retreating steps, a door slam, and tires screeching as the car leapt forward. Again he tried to elicit some response from Mrs. Liuzzo, but she lay still. She was dead.

So we were robbed of the happy ending to our Selma march, and the nation was reminded that what we had achieved was not without a heavy cost. Three people had died—Jimmie Lee Jackson, James J. Reeb, and now Viola Liuzzo. One was black; two were white. This third tragedy was especially poignant because of the small children Mrs. Liuzzo left behind, but all three deaths were heartrending, since in each case the victims were not instigators of the march but people who had instinctively reached out to help others in distress.

The Liuzzo death reminded us that while we had come a long way on that march from Selma to Montgomery, we still had a long way to go. This became increasingly evident as we watched the arrest and subsequent trials of the klansmen who had killed Mrs. Liuzzo. The FBI, through the use of an informant, had the assailants under arrest by the next day and it appeared that justice would be done. We even publicly praised Hoover for the swift actions of his agents.

But we had forgotten the way justice operated in south Alabama during those years. Despite the fact that an eyewitness testified for the prosecution, a jury refused to convict the first klansman tried, and for a while it appeared as if the murderers would go completely free. Our outrage was to some degree tempered by the fact that the same men were later indicted and convicted of violating Mrs. Liuzzo's civil rights, a federal crime, and were all given the maximum sentence of ten years. But everyone knew that these men were guilty and should have been prosecuted and convicted for murder—and the fact that they weren't properly punished embittered many of our followers and pushed them in the direction of a more violent leadership.

11

Chicago

WE SHOULD HAVE KNOWN BETTER than to believe we could come to Chicago and right its wrongs with the same tactics we had used in Montgomery, Birmingham, and Selma. We entered a different world when we came to this northern city in 1966, a world we didn't fully understand. While in some respects it was much better than the segregated South, in some ways it was much worse; and before we had fully understood the differences between the two societies, we had suffered our first significant defeat since Albany. It was an embittering experience, and I'm not sure that Martin ever got over it.

Perhaps the most important difference we encountered in Chicago was the sheer size of the city. I remember arriving for our first "scouting expedition" and being driven around the city by Jesse Jackson, who was living there at the time, in charge of the SCLC's Operation Breadbasket. As we drove through the South Side, where a large segment of the city's black population lived, we kept waiting for the slum tenements to give way to warehouses, vacant lots, and then country stores and open fields where cows were grazing. Instead we saw more slum blocks. And more. And more. And more. We had the feeling that if we drove much farther south we were going to see the Gulf of Mexico.

"That's nothing," said Jesse. "Wait till you see the West Side."

Sure enough, when we drove over there, it was even vaster and more devastated—a rubble heap of infinite proportions, owned and operated by absentee landlords.

I recall looking over at Martin and both of us shaking our heads. The number of people living in this squalid devastation was beyond our comprehension. We were used to dealing with constituencies that numbered in the thousands. Here we would be dealing in behalf of hundreds of thousands. The prospect cast a pall over our spirits as we wondered if we could ever bring order and enlightenment to a wilderness so vast and monotonous. We were acutely aware after that tour that the problems we would face were infinitely more complicated than they had been in Selma or even Birmingham.

Also, we had not yet reckoned with the equally formidable presence of Mayor Richard J. Daley, perhaps the last of the great city bosses of the North. In the South we knew and understood the infinite subtleties of a Jim Crow world, and for that reason we could play the political game with the likes of Montgomery's Gayle and Birmingham's Boutwell, both southern mayors of a recognizable stripe. But while we had Chicago advisors to help us with our moves, we were unprepared for Daley's devious strategy and we were naive in our belief that, in a portion of the country where segregation had not been the law, it could still be so firmly institutionalized and so vigorously defended by the establishment. To us it seemed like a new form of cheating.

I later learned that much of this attitude was the result of the state's history. Contrary to what I had always assumed, Illinois, the Land of Lincoln, had been a racist society since before the Civil War. As a number of historians have pointed out, the Black Codes instituted in the Middle West in the early nineteenth century were designed to keep blacks from entering the state and settling there. Indeed some people argue that the so-called "Free Soil Movement," which opposed the expansion of slavery into the western states, was based not so much on a love of liberty as on a hatred of blacks and a desire to keep them out of their part of the country.

Indeed Lincoln's own attitude was by no means pure or enlightened by modern standards. While opposing slavery, he spoke out against social and political equality, denied that he wanted to give blacks the vote, said that the two races could not live on the North American continent in harmony, and suggested that the best solution to the race problem was to ship blacks back to Africa. His Emancipation Proclamation did not free the slaves in the five Union states where the "peculiar institution" was still legal in 1863; it didn't even free them in those parts of the South then occupied by federal troops.

That historical legacy had left Illinois with what many northerners would regard as the best of two possible worlds: a segregated society without the stigma of Jim Crow laws. How well such a society has functioned over the years can be measured by the number of major race riots in the City of Chicago since the turn of the century. No area, North or South, has produced so many. With the exception of the New York City draft riots of 1864, the Chicago uprisings may have produced the highest number of fatalities for such brief and violent confrontations. In Alabama and Mississippi the lynchings and murders were perennial, an ever-present possibility in even the smallest communities. Over the years they added up to more racial murders than occurred in the state of Illinois, but they were spread out and were therefore less spectacular. In Chicago all the hatred and frustration would build up over a long period and then explode from time to time in an orgy of mass violence and bloodletting that made headlines all over the country.

The last such explosion had occurred in the forties. In 1965 it appeared as if the time were ripe for another. It was into that world that we stepped when we got off the plane at O'Hare Airport, ready to take on the City of Chicago.

As usual, the whole episode began with the failure of local blacks to achieve any progress in their struggles against the white establishment. The occasion in Chicago was the attempt on the part of black activists to integrate a public school system that the mayor and his superintendent blandly asserted had never been segregated in the first place.

As a matter of fact, blacks were not only going to separate schools, but in some instances they were receiving instruction in trailers and cast-off military barracks. The inferiority of these facilities and the instruction that went on there constituted an injustice apparent to even the most casual observer. The superintendent of schools, Benjamin C. Willis, was the chief architect of this system, though he received wholehearted backing from the Daley machine, and indeed was one of its insiders. Willis claimed the Chicago schools were integrated and uniformly high in quality.

Frustrated by the long-term maintenance of what amounted to a dual school system and unable to make any real headway themselves, a group calling themselves the Coordinating Council of Community Organizations (CCCO) appealed to Martin for intervention. Since we had long been talking about a major campaign in the North, Martin told Al Raby, head of the group, that we would consider the possibility of coming to Chicago with the same kind of commitment we had made in Birmingham and Selma.

Jesse Jackson, who had studied in Chicago and had headed our Operation Breadbasket there, was eager for us to come. He knew well the need for progress in integrating the schools, and he also felt that his own operation would be given additional impetus with the added presence of Martin and the entire SCLC staff. He assured us that we could make a difference in Chicago, that our presence would help to unite the black community in its opposition to the Daley regime. What he didn't fully explain was how that was going to work, given the enormous inroads Daley had made into the black power structure of Chicago.

Indeed, it might be more accurate to say that Daley had *created* the current black power structure in order to serve the ends of his own political organization. The Daley machine was as powerful and as delicate as a nuclear reactor. It had innumerable parts, all of which worked with fine precision toward the creation of incredible energy, which in turn performed all sorts of useful tasks, and some not-so-useful ones.

Some of the parts of the machine were blacks, and within certain well-prescribed limits these people exercised power in partnership with the mayor. Among those were leaders like Rep. William Dawson, who had been in the U.S. Congress for some years and handled the patronage both locally and nationally for his black constituents. Dawson knew he was in Congress for life, and he might well have broken with Daley had he chosen to do so, but he also knew that if he played ball he could live a relatively comfortable life and still maintain some illusion of autonomy.

Of course, he could do nothing about Chicago's local segregated school system, but he could make certain that his constituents received some slices of the municipal pie. Those who supported that arrangement argued that it was the best possible deal in a fallen world and that blacks got a lot more in Chicago than they did in other major cities, largely because Dawson believed in "going along to get along."

But Dawson had to deliver his constituency when they were needed, and that meant when anyone attacked the Daley machine or the world it had created. So when we came to Chicago, the congressman was one of the chief defenders of the status quo. He suggested that the city had no racial problems and that we were nothing more than dangerous outsiders who were causing trouble for our own selfish reasons. In making this point he was echoing Mayor Daley, who also said Chicago was a racially harmonious community without segregation. We had expected to hear something like this from Daley; we were somewhat taken aback when Congressman Dawson chimed in. Other black leaders also backed up their declarations of racial amity, including our old friend Rev. Joseph H. Jackson, who praised both Daley and Superintendent Willis, saying that they were chief among the friends of Chicago blacks.

What was going on here was no different in kind from what had gone on in Montgomery and Birmingham. The white establishment in both those communities had also won the obsequious loyalty of a few black leaders, who could always be counted on to speak to the black community in behalf of the status quo and to the press in behalf of the black community. But while the character and function of these black leaders were essentially the same in the North as in the South, there were certainly differences of degree and effectiveness.

For one thing, since southern whites had given their black pawns no share of the power, they had no real credibility; and blacks soon abandoned them when genuine leaders appeared. In Chicago, however, Dawson and the black aldermen and block captains had a real though minor role in the organization that ran the city, and that meant they could deliver genuine benefits to the people in the South Side. So when Dawson and his lieutenants spoke, many blacks listened, more than had listened to the powerless establishment preachers in Alabama, who had no genuine authority and no patronage to dispense.

Another difference was the fact that, while in the South the press tended to view apologies for the status quo with a healthy skepticism, in the North the same people would accept the explanations of a Daley and a Dawson without seriously questioning the validity of what they said. As a consequence, the national coverage we got seemed spotty and less sharply focused. There were even those commentators who suggested that we had made a mistake in coming to a northern city, that we should have remained in the South.

By the time we had finished our work there, we wondered if they weren't right.

As usual we sent a team of staff members into Chicago for a preliminary evaluation of the problems we would face and the resources on which we could draw. Their conclusions were mixed, but their final recommendation was to go ahead. Chicago, after all, was the "Birmingham of the North," the most segregated of all the major northern cities and the one with the most powerful establishment. If we could do as much with Chicago as we had with Birmingham, then we would win a great victory and take a giant step toward the solution of those problems that were peculiarly northern.

As Martin put it in a preliminary statement, "If we can

break the system in Chicago, it can be broken anywhere in the country."

We began with the idea that we would go into Chicago, unify the various black groups that were fighting separate battles, wield them into a coalition of several hundred thousand, and via marches and demonstrations dramatize the plight of urban blacks to the decent people of Chicago and to the nation.

By this time we realized that although we had won the legal right to check into any hotel in the country, we still had problems checking out, because we didn't have the money to pay. In large measure that was the problem with the blacks living in Chicago. They didn't have the money to buy their way out of the squalor and degradation that surrounded them. They needed good jobs; and if they didn't have good jobs, then they needed some source of regular income to survive. Martin had begun to talk about a minimum income guaranteed to every American—an idea that in recent years has been supported by conservative economists.

So, at first, our point of attack was the slums themselves and the economic inequities that had caused the slums. For the first time since Albany, our purpose was again broad and ill defined, since the existence of slums meant problems in a number of areas: schools, jobs, and housing to name but three. We started with schools, since that was the issue that Al Raby had originally brought to our attention.

But before we could really begin to focus on Benjamin C. Willis, the man we had pegged as the Bull Connor of Chicago, he announced his retirement. In addition, Alderman Ralph Metcalfe, a black member of the Daley machine, announced that he was forming his own committee to investigate the questions we were raising. At this point it appeared as if the school issue would not be as productive as we first believed. Then Mayor Daley announced that the schools were indeed in need of desegregation and he would take care of the matter shortly. As we eventually learned, what Mayor Daley promised and what he did bore little resemblance to one another, but for the moment he had blocked our move against the school problem.

So by the time we got to Chicago, we were talking about slums again, and most specifically about housing. Housing was the key to much of what was wrong in Chicago, and we resolved to show by example precisely how bad things really were: Martin and I were going to live in low-rent apartments and use our own presence to dramatize the primitive squalor in which black Chicagoans had to live.

Martin probably didn't know what he was getting into, but I did. When he said we were going to live in the slums my mind went back to 1951, the last time I had been in Chicago; and I gave an involuntary shudder. I had spent several nights in Chicago under just such circumstances. I didn't want to do it again.

The occasion was the National Baptist Convention. I went to Chicago on the train with the Reverend H. H. Johnson, traveling from Montgomery to Birmingham to Atlanta to Nashville to Chicago. I was the newly elected pastor of the First Baptist Church, and Rev. Johnson, as pastor of the Hutchison Street Baptist Church, was probably attending his thirtieth meeting, so he took me under his wing after we got to Chicago.

"Now, Ralph," he said, "there's no use going to the housing committee to find a room. The only thing left will be boarding houses, and believe me you want to avoid boarding houses. I'm an old pro at finding good rooms at a good price, so we'll just stroll around a little and see what's available."

As we walked along the dirtiest and most dismal streets I had ever seen, he continued to give me the benefit of his wisdom.

"Remember that when you get in the room, hide your shoes, socks, and any clothes you don't have on your back. And pin your money in your underwear."

We finally spotted a housing project on East Cottage Grove, and Reverend Johnson seemed interested. The place looked unpromising to me, but Reverend Johnson said it might do just fine. We walked up the steps, knocked on the door, and were met by an old lady, who looked at us suspiciously and said she didn't want to rent us a room.

"Because of him," she said, and pointed to an old man in the parlor who stared straight ahead with a glazed look in his eye. She explained that he had had a stroke.

However, Reverend Johnson sweet-talked her into renting us her guest room on the first floor.

"How much would it be?" Reverend Johnson asked, all business.

"With or without meals?"

"Without."

"Two dollars a night apiece," she said belligerently, almost as if she expected us to quibble. We agreed and paid her the money for five nights. We didn't bother to look at the room, probably because Reverend Johnson figured it would look much better after dark. As we left to go back to the convention hall, I noticed that she had four locks on the door.

Since we were attending evening sessions at the convention, we never got back before about 11:00 P.M., and each time we came to the front door, we would knock loudly, she would peer between the lace curtains, a worried look on her face, and then open each of the locks, crack the door just wide enough to admit us, then close it quickly and lock each of the four locks.

"Well," she would say with obvious relief, "you didn't get killed tonight."

So when Martin suggested we live in the slums ourselves, I remembered what it was like fifteen years earlier and was apprehensive.

"On the South Side?" I asked.

"On the West Side," he said, and I said, "Oh, well that's more like it."

But as I mentioned, it turned out the West Side in 1966 was worse than the South Side in 1951. And Chicago was worse than either Selma or Birmingham. Martin and I went down looking for the worst possible housing in order to dramatize our plight and we certainly found it. The apartment houses reminded me of the buildings I had seen in Europe right at the end of World War II—windows broken out and mounds of rubble instead of yards.

And the odor was unbearable. It was a little like a city dump, except that along with the garbage you constantly smelled human waste. There was no escaping it. The hallways were filled with rotting food and piles of feces, and always you could see the rats patrolling—so large and bold that you wondered if they weren't going to attack you. Indeed, I was told that sometimes they did.

Since our wives were going to spend part of the time with us, we got separate apartments, each the epitome of filth and disrepair. As soon as we moved in, however, the word got back to Mayor Daley. By the time Martin had flown back to Atlanta, taken care of pressing business, packed a minimal wardrobe, and returned, the entire place had been painted, repapered, and redecorated. It didn't look like an apartment in *House Beautiful,* but it was clean and bright—probably the best looking quarters within fifty blocks of that location. Not a place you would show the press to let them know how bad life in the slums could be. Again Mayor Daley had blunted our attack.

On the other hand, since I was not the chief focus of media attention, no one even swept my floor. When I got back to Chicago at the same time, there was yet another layer of filth over everything and a new generation of rats roaming the hallways. I knew that I could never bring Juanita into such a place. I will now confess, years later, that after a night or two to make a point, I checked into a hotel in the black community and spent the rest of my Chicago visit there. Juanita stayed with her sister, Mrs. Eloise Percival, far out on the South Side. As I lay on a comfortable mattress and listened to the hum of the air conditioner, I thought about the place I had left behind, and I was doubly resolved that we would free those blacks in Chicago who genuinely wanted to get out of the slums.

But that proved to be a much more difficult task than we had anticipated. Things began well. We held rallies at some of the larger Chicago churches like Liberty Baptist Church and Mount Pisgah Baptist Church. Their pastors, the Reverend A. J. Jackson and the Reverend Joseph Wells, were among the many Chicago clergymen who supported our presence in the city and spoke out in our behalf. Among the others were the fearless and eloquent Reverend Daniel and Reverend Owen Pelt of Shiloh Baptist Church, Reverend John Thurston of New Covenant, and the Right Reverend Archibald Carey of the AME Church, later elected a judge in Chicago. We used rallies at these churches to raise money and to educate the black people of Chicago concerning the issues we would be focusing on, explaining the techniques of nonviolent resistance, and building toward the time when we could put a hundred thousand marchers into the streets and dramatize for the white people of Chicago the strength of black resistance in their city.

Al Raby was our Chicago chief advisor, and we found him intelligent, articulate, and easy to get along with—a rare combination. He was perhaps the best local leader we worked with during those years. A tall lean young man, he was a school teacher of the newer breed who had the courage and imagination to make things happen in a city that with the help of black leaders like Dawson had held its black population in political and economic bondage for generations. Raby was ready to lead a fight, and he gave us the best advice we got in Chicago.

But we needed more than advice. We needed unity among the city's blacks and it became increasingly evident that we weren't going to get it. First, there was our old nemesis Rev. Joseph Jackson, who spoke out against us among the city's black Baptist clergy and began to chip away at our support. For example, knowing we had to stage a dramatic event in order to galvanize our supporters, we scheduled a rally in Soldier's Field, which holds nearly one hundred thousand people. It was our belief that we could pack in that many if everyone in the religious community turned out his congregation; but Jackson vocally opposed the rally and urged blacks to boycott the occasion.

Then there were the Muslims, led by the aging Elijah Muhammed, a frail little man who wore a fez and told his followers that white people were devils and would some day have to be destroyed. While we were speaking out for integrated schools and integrated housing, the Muslims were preaching the gospel of separatism. They kept in their own part of town, went to their own church, dressed in their own special way, and whenever possible shopped only in Muslim-owned stores and ate only in Muslim restaurants.

They were a proud and well-disciplined people whose standard of living was considerably above that of most other blacks in Chicago. In addition, the last thing they were willing to support was a move to put black students and white students in the same schools or blacks and whites in the same neighborhood. If anything they were more zealous in support of segregation than Mayor Daley, since the mayor paid lip-service to racial tolerance and the Muslims were black supremacists. They would probably have joined us if we had proposed killing all the white people, but they certainty didn't want to listen to anyone preach the gospel of brotherly love. So they too boycotted our rally.

So did all the black city employees and ward heelers in the Daley machine, all of whom were afraid to disobey the explicit orders handed down by Congressman Dawson, Alderman Metcalfe, and Daley's other straw bosses. While these three groups— Joseph Jackson's Baptists, the Muslims, and the municipal employees—did not constitute a major part of black Chicago, they did make up a significant portion of those blacks who were politically aware.

As a consequence of this opposition and the general apathy of the majority of blacks in that vast, anonymous city, we had a miserable showing at our midsummer rally. The stadium, one of the largest in the world, was less than half full, and the press and our enemies took note of our failure to meet our much-publicized quota.

This "short-fall" not only hurt our credibility but also cut into our operating capital, since it had been an expensive operation. As treasurer of the SCLC, I had to bear the burden of our money troubles. Although Martin made several fund-raising trips, including one to Europe, we were looking at a tight squeeze; and we clearly could not afford to indulge ourselves with mass arrests, since we would not have the bail money.

And nobody, least of all the Reverend Ralph David Abernathy, wanted to spend five minutes in a Chicago jail.

I had seen one.

During some confrontation with a slum landlord, an SCLC staff member had been arrested, and I went down to bail him out. Or so I thought. When I got there, I discovered that he had already been jailed.

"But I'm here with bail," I said to the warden, a black man who looked at me with cold eyes.

"You can't bail him out now," he said, and turned his back on me.

"I'm Dr. Ralph David Abernathy," I said, with as much dignity as I could muster, "and I'm with Dr. Martin Luther King."

"Get out of here," he said. "It's past visiting hours."

"But I. . . ."

"Get out!" he yelled as he wheeled around to face me.

But I held my ground.

"I'd like to see the jailor," I said.

For the first time his face changed expression as he smiled a razor-thin smile and left the room. In a moment he returned through the door followed by a huge black man with an angry frown on his face. I knew the moment I saw him why the warden had smiled.

"What the hell you want?" he asked.

I explained to him that I wanted to put up bail for one of our people and that I had come at this hour because I didn't know anything about their rules.

"You can come back at three o'clock," he said. "Now get out of here right now, or you'll end up back there with him, and the two of you may never get out."

I believed him and came back at three, utterly amazed that the jail system would be completely segregated, right down to its jailor, warden, and guards. Later it occurred to me that someone had probably told them to be as rough on us as they possibly could, an order they obeyed with a vengeance. The whole experience caused me great grief, partly because it never occurred to me that blacks would hold such jobs and treat other blacks in such a manner.

What our staff member had been doing was attempting to get landlords to make basic repairs on slum housing so that the apartments were at least structurally safe and no longer a health hazard. We wanted to see roofs waterproofed, windows replaced, and plumbing fixed. When the landlords refused to do the first thing in the way of minimal improvements, we began counseling the tenants to withhold rent payments.

Then we came up with a better idea. We would collect the rent, hire people to repair the building, and then, when it was habitable, let the tenant begin paying the landlord again. We introduced this plan by actually occupying a building with the announced intention of assuming financial control until all of the major health and safety problems had been fixed.

At this point the establishment reacted with great cries of outrage. Judge James Pearson, a black who sat on the federal bench, said we were thieves and revolutionaries, and several members of the Daley machine echoed these sentiments. But our bluff worked to some degree: the building inspectors did inspect the building we had chosen and cited the owner for numerous violations. On the other hand, it was clear that the city would withhold rent subsidies from those apartment dwellers cooperating with us, so we had to back away from that approach and try something else.

Then something happened that seemed to give us an opportunity to unite public opinion behind us. It was mid-July and the temperatures were running in the nineties. With no air conditioning in the slums and no public swimming pools to use, a group of youngsters somehow managed to turn on a fire hydrant and then begin playing in the water that poured out onto the streets. Technically, it was a violation of the law, but a wise and friendly police force might have stood by for a little while and let them cool off before stepping in and shutting off the valve.

But instead of allowing a little leeway in view of the weather and the nature of the slums, the police immediately moved in, shut off the hydrant, and arrested half a dozen of the youngsters. Martin happened to drive by just after they had been hauled off to jail, when a hot and angry crowd was gathering. Sensing he was looking at the start of a major riot, he stopped, found out what had happened, and went immediately to the police station, where he was able to secure the release of the six "desperate criminals."

Then he went back to try to cool down the crowd. At first they listened to him with respect. He was, after all, a famous

man. Besides, he had been able to get the young people out of jail.
But having lived in this desperate climate for so long, they were
finally beyond reaching.

When he started to explain to them the importance of
nonviolence, they refused to listen. Finally, they grew sullen and
rebellious and either walked away in disgust or else began
shouting obscenities and other insults at him. Then, like a
hurricane forming, they became a mob, then a riot.

The streets overflowed with them. People were running in
all directions, knocking each other down, breaking windows,
shattering streetlamps, shouting, cursing, and attacking automobiles. It was all Martin could do to get out of the neighborhood
and back to the safety of his hotel room.

He had encountered for the first time a crowd of blacks that
he could neither reason with nor overpower with his rhetoric. He
had seen the myriad faces of the black power movement and
taken some stock of their fierce anger.

As if that experience itself were not discouraging enough,
he turned on the radio the next morning and heard that Mayor
Daley was accusing him of starting the riot. For the next few days
we tried to dispel that notion and to talk with the various factions
that crowded the streets of Chicago every day, making trouble for
the city and for each other.

We were particularly disturbed by the youth gangs, young
black boys wearing identical costumes, swaggering along the
sidewalk, carrying sticks and pipes on the outside of their
clothing and knives and guns in their pockets and inside jackets.
They stole whatever they wanted from helpless merchants,
roughed up passersby, and at night patrolled the streets in search
of trouble. Sometimes they got into wars with other gangs, in the
course of which members of both sides would be wounded,
tortured, maimed, and occasionally killed.

At night they would run up streets and down alleys, looting,
robbing, raping, and terrorizing whole neighborhoods. We had no
idea that such gangs existed in Chicago and we were really at a
loss when it came to dealing with them. They had nothing but
contempt for the church and for religion, which meant that we
could not appeal to them on the same grounds that we appealed

to our followers in the South. While we had to teach black Alabamians to defy the authorities in the service of a good cause, these young hard-eyed black boys had no respect for anything or anybody. To them a preacher was the next worse thing to a policeman, and religion was for old folks and suckers, both of whom they regarded with a fine contempt.

These young men, already with police records and facing short and violent lives, were enough to send us packing off to Atlanta, flying the white flag. And yet we somehow had to reach them if we were to reform this society in the way we had reformed Montgomery, Birmingham, and Selma.

So we began by having a meeting with the leaders of these gangs—the Roman Saints, the Cobras, and a group that with considerable pride called itself the Vice Lords. We met with them in Martin's apartment and tried to explain nonviolence as a positive strategy rather than a failure to fight at all. They listened, argued, listened some more, and finally said they understood what we were trying to do and would cooperate.

Martin, who always believed in the power of reason more than I did, was delighted. It appeared as if we were finally making headway in solving one of the major problems in the city. But I wasn't so optimistic. I didn't believe in instant conversions. I figured hundreds of thousands of people walked along the road to Damascus without seeing anything unusual.

I told Martin I was convinced that these young thugs would be back at each other's throats by nightfall the next day, and he shook his head.

"I don't think so. I really don't. I believe they understand now."

But my pessimism was deepening over the whole enterprise. I was beginning to believe that we weren't going to make a dent in Chicago, that when we left, things would be exactly as we had found them, with blacks on the South Side and West Side terrorizing one another while Mayor Daley continued to run the city like his own private kingdom.

Yet the mayor also met with us, in the same atmosphere of open exchange. He listened carefully. He raised questions. He usually agreed with at least part of what we were saying. But always he would say that he was already in the process of confronting the problem or that we didn't understand the full complexity of the situation in Chicago—an argument that had a certain amount of validity.

Meanwhile, his black henchmen were denouncing us at every turn. Ralph Metcalfe, Ernest Rather, and others were saying that we should leave Chicago to Chicagoans—a cry similar to the ones we had heard from whites in Birmingham and Selma. The strategy was simple and it worked: Let the white mayor play the benevolent and rational servant of all the people, while the black detractors undercut the credibility of any black activist who might want to challenge the establishment in order to correct its many ills.

We understood that we had to do something besides hold mass rallies and try to put out the fires at would-be riots. The mayor was effectively dodging every charge we threw at him; and the news reporters, interested in us at the outset, were now finding better copy in the attacks of our enemies. So we decided to step up the pressure and narrow our focus.

By then we saw the situation more clearly—or thought we did. The most fundamental problem of black people was their confinement to the slums of the South Side and the West Side. The school problem would be solved for many blacks if they could move into the white sections and the suburbs, where the facilities and teachers were infinitely superior to those in the black schools. We had to begin with the children, since they still had a chance to escape from the slum world in which they were now living.

And what was keeping blacks from making that type of move? In the South it had been state law, which decreed that the schools be segregated. But housing patterns had not been quite so rigid, particularly in the rural South; but in Chicago, everybody lived in neighborhoods inhabited by people of the same ethnic background. The Poles, Lithuanians, Irish, and Hispanics lived in their own discrete sections as surely as the blacks did. There were no state or city laws mandating this rigid housing pattern, but there was something else that worked just as well—a tacit conspiracy on the part of the real estate agents to keep the same mix in the neighborhoods—and particularly the same racial mix.

This conspiracy had some legal manifestations, particularly in the covenant that every owner signed before he could buy a house in places like Gage Park, Belmont-Cragin, and Chicago Lawn. But in addition, the real estate agencies simply would not show houses in those areas to black buyers. At that time, there was no Illinois open housing law, as there is today, nor was there a Chicago statute with teeth in it. So these covenants and discriminatory practices were perfectly legal.

A comprehensive open housing ordinance was needed in Chicago as well as enforcement of those provisions already on the books. These became our specific goal, just what we had been lacking up until that point. So we decided to picket the realtors who were most flagrant in their discriminatory practices and lead protest marches into the white suburbs where covenants were traditional. For the first time we had a clear strategy apparent to all. After trying to be resident problem solvers, we were going after something we had a chance to get.

During this period I was flying in and out of Chicago as frequently as was Martin, involving myself in some of the activities, then flying back to Atlanta to take care of other SCLC matters, mostly financial, and to fulfill my obligations as pastor of West Hunter Church. In retrospect I remember arriving in time to be a part of the frequent mass meetings and, toward the end, the mass marches, which were unlike anything we had encountered, even in Selma.

In the South when we conducted a major march, we always outnumbered the spectators who lined the sides of the roads, except at times in Birmingham, when large crowds of black onlookers gathered, either sympathetic or else just curious—but never hostile. When there were actively hostile white onlookers, as during our two marches out of Selma after Bloody Sunday, they were usually no more than small bunches of hecklers who held up abusive signs or shouted out racial epithets. Even in Mississippi, when we were surrounded by a coldly hostile mob, they were only potentially violent.

In Chicago we sometimes had the feeling that this huge sea of snarling white faces was going to sweep over us and kill every single black marcher. They shouted. They screamed. They cursed. They threw rocks and bottles. They howled with delight when someone was knocked down or cut or carried off to a waiting ambulance. They made their wishes perfectly clear: They wanted to maim or kill us. Nothing else would really have satisfied them.

Even now I can lie in bed at night and feel something of that old terror, just recalling the sound of the mob, surrounding us on all sides (or so it seemed), ready in an instant to surge forward and get their hands on us. Even crowded together in a phalanx of four or five hundred, we somehow knew there were several pairs of hands for each of us, enough to tear us limb from limb.

In the South, particularly in Birmingham and Selma, it was the police that we most feared, with their dogs, hoses, tear gas, and billy clubs. They, rather than any white spectators, constituted the enemy. But in the North we had expected to find the police standing up for law and order. In Montgomery they had apparently known about the bombings even before they happened, but we had told ourselves that in Chicago they would at least be neutral in carrying out their duties.

But they were just as much in cahoots with the white racists in the northern cities as they were in the southern. I remember seeing an officer stare at a white woman as she hurled a rock into the crowd. His eyes followed the route of the missile as it arched downward and struck a black man on the side of his face. The policeman broke into a grin and made some remark to her—then they both laughed. And that was not an isolated incident. That attitude prevailed during the tense days we marched into the suburbs to dramatize the injustice of the real estate brokers and the all-white constituencies they served.

Our first target was Gage Park, an area that had been particularly discriminatory. We decided we would move in on Friday night and hold an all-night protest "vigil" in front of one of the most well known and racist of all the brokers. It was a modest beginning, one that should not have alarmed the local residents. After all, we had turned out thousands in Alabama and in Mississippi.

But again there was a difference. White people in the South were used to seeing blacks in their neighborhoods, if only as domestic servants. Many of the people in Gage Park had seen blacks only at a distance and rarely, if ever, on the streets of their own neighborhood. So the fear of the unknown played a large part in their reaction.

In addition, they were terrified that a massive influx of black settlers would turn their quiet, suburban neighborhoods into instant slums and they would have to sell their houses at a tremendous loss, wiping out a lifetime of savings. Or else they would have to remain where they were and risk robbery, murder, and rape every time the sun went down. Such were the stories that were circulating throughout Chicago at this time.

As I reflect on it, I can see the continuity in their attitude from the first half of the nineteenth century to the second half of the twentieth. They were still living in the Land of Lincoln, the state that had hated slavery because it had feared blacks.

So the screaming mob that met our fifty demonstrators and drove them out of Gage Park that night were in a state of frenzy born of terror. They thought of themselves as an invaded people, standing at the last barrier of civilization. It is the kind of unreasoning fear that has always lain just beneath the surface of racism, a fear nurtured by generations of segregation and all the myths that surround the unknown.

Of course, we had to go back the next day. We couldn't allow even this kind of unexpected violence to deter us. If we had backed off, we would have lost the respect of Chicago blacks and would have sent a signal to the white establishment (i.e., Mayor Daley) that we didn't really mean it when we said we were willing to risk death in our fight to win our freedom.

So Saturday and Sunday our people went back into the suburbs, determined that they would complete a protest march, no matter what the risk. I remember getting a report on the march by telephone and thanking the Lord I had come back to Atlanta to tend my flock. On Saturday they had gone into Gage Park in the afternoon, led by Al Raby and Jesse Jackson. Before they had moved a block into white territory, they were attacked again. The air was filled with bottles and rocks, and both Al and

Jesse were struck, as were many of the others. During all this the police were mostly behaving as if they were disinterested bystanders, though they made a few arrests.

Because they failed to take preventive action on Saturday, the police had to deal with a much more dangerous situation on Sunday. This time the mob not only attacked the marchers with rocks and bottles (the weapons of choice in Chicago) but also turned over and burned several black-owned automobiles. As many as fifteen cars were destroyed during this binge of destruction.

During the first three days of the following week, Martin and I were attending the SCLC convention in Jackson, Mississippi, which was keynoted by Sen. Edward Kennedy, then among the youngest men in the United States Senate. As I recall, we had tried to get his brother, Robert Kennedy, who had been President John F. Kennedy's attorney general; but he was unavailable. The younger brother made a rousing speech, however, and reminded many of us of the late president.

During this period Martin contracted his virus, the one he always got during the tensest moments in a campaign, when it became clear that lives were to be endangered. He went to bed, took reports from the convention in his sickroom, and kept in touch with Chicago by telephone. I was certain that the events in Gage Park had triggered this new outbreak, but as usual neither one of us said anything about it; and there was never any question that he would return to Chicago and join the marchers as soon as he got there.

By the following Thursday I was back in Chicago, as was Martin. It was very clear that everyone in the movement was unnerved by the hatred and violence they had encountered and by the failure of the police to do more than go through the motions of defending them. We also discovered that Jesse Jackson had stirred up a hornet's nest by announcing to the press that we intended to march into other suburbs, including Cicero. Both black and white leaders were disturbed at the thought that we would consider moving into such a dangerous area. I remember somebody talking about how foolish such a move would be, and I recall asking why.

It was then I found out that Cicero was famous for its race riots, one of which had occurred only a few years earlier, within the memory of almost every adult in Chicago. Though Cicero wasn't a part of Chicago and therefore not under the benevolent protection of Mayor Daley, he knew that he might be held accountable if all hell broke loose in this neighboring suburb, so he too took note of Jesse's statement.

Some people have suggested that Jesse made such a statement off the top of his head; but as I recall, we had talked about such a move in our strategy sessions and therefore he was correct in suggesting that we might take on Cicero at some time in the near future. Martin was a little angry, however, because he had not wanted to tip off our future plans and because our demoralized army did not want to hear about even more difficult battlegrounds at a time when they were encountering enough trouble in Gage Park and Marquette Park.

But we did not back away from the idea of going into any segregated white community in order to dramatize the injustice of housing in the Chicago area. In fact, as in our choices of Birmingham and Chicago, there was some strategic value in storming the most heavily defended position. If you could handle the highest and most well fortified ramparts, then you would send out the strongest possible message to the rest of the enemy: If we can beat these people then you might as well surrender.

Whether, as some people have argued, the threat to march in Cicero brought the establishment to the negotiating table, or whether the activities in Gage Park were sufficient, no one can say for sure, though I am inclined to believe that what happened over the weekend in the suburbs was sufficiently provocative to alarm Mayor Daley. The city was attracting the attention of the national press and Daley was nervous about this kind of scrutiny. He knew what it had done to Birmingham, Selma, and other southern cities. He did not like the prospect of being compared to Bull Connor and Jim Clark.

But more important, I believe, with his concern for the City of Chicago. To be sure, *his* Chicago was not *black* Chicago, though he probably believed that he was equally concerned for all its citizens. Whatever the relative measure of his concern, he loved the city of his birth and genuinely wanted what was best for it. Besides, he was not the kind of political leader who was willing to sacrifice domestic tranquility in order to maintain a status quo that was no longer tenable.

He did not like the idea of Chicagoans killing Chicagoans, nor did he approve of the destruction of private property. In addition, he knew that the burning of fifteen black-owned automobiles today could easily lead to the destruction of a hundred white-owned cars and houses in the near future. Whites owned a lot more property than blacks did and were therefore substantially more vulnerable—black gang members learned how to make Molotov cocktails before they learned to do long division.

So at the start of the new week, after the consequences of our marches had been fully assessed, the mayor's Commission on Human Relations was ready to negotiate. They asked the Chicago Conference on Religion and Race (CCRR) to conduct discussions that would include all parties involved in the conflict— representatives of the SCLC, the CCCO, the CCRR, the Chicago Real Estate Board, and the city's business community. Since I was spending much of my time traveling back and forth from Atlanta, I did not participate in these negotiations, which were carried on over a number of days. Martin was the chief negotiator on our side, and Andy Young was part of the group representing the Chicago Freedom Movement, as were Al Raby, Jesse Jackson, and Jim Bevel.

I think we all sensed from the beginning that we might be betrayed, that in the end we might get nothing but empty words and deferred actions. Daley was known as a shrewd manipulator of boards and commissions, and already the local press was against us, with the *Chicago Tribune* leading the way in calling our activities dangerous and demanding that we stop all marches and remain quiescent, calling us anarchists and outside agitators. Of course, they had been very supportive when we were marching in Alabama and Mississippi; but now we had clearly overstepped the boundaries of propriety, which were apparently synonymous with the Mason-Dixon Line.

So with the media on his side and with the power in his hip

pocket, Mayor Daley brought a lot of strength to the bargaining table; and we expected him to be tough. But we also knew from Al Raby and Jesse Jackson that he could be devious. His typical ploy was to give assent to high-sounding principles and to make vague promises about an unspecified future, while refusing to be pinned down to any specific goals and timetable.

In the past groups had come away with what they thought were significant concessions, only to discover in six months or a year that they had been given a beautifully wrapped box with nothing inside. We were familiar with that kind of victory as well. We were still trying to make headway in our attempt to integrate schools in the South, despite the fact that *Brown v. Board of Education* had been handed down more than a decade ago; and we were beginning to realize that Lyndon Johnson was not going to implement the civil rights legislation passed in 1964 and 1965, or at least not as thoroughly or as quickly as we had been led to believe.

For some reason I was particularly skeptical about making any real progress. Perhaps it was because I was not fully involved and could therefore see the whole picture with more objectivity. But I had the feeling that no one was going to win in Chicago, that we were going to come away empty-handed, leaving that vast slum as hopeless as it was the day we arrived. I conveyed my pessimism to Martin and the others and discovered that they shared my skepticism.

"You're probably right," Martin had said with a sigh. "Still, we have to try. But that doesn't mean we have to trust the people we are dealing with. We will not be satisfied with empty promises."

So Mayor Daley and the Chicago Real Estate Board were not dealing with a bunch of spring lambs when everyone sat down to negotiate. Martin and our people were prepared to be betrayed, and they were leading from a position of strength for one good reason: The marches were still going on. As long as the city was teetering on the brink of chaos, the Mayor had some reason to make genuine concessions, and the white people had reason to accept them. By now it was an old game to us, and we could play it as well as the mayor—or so we hoped.

Sure enough, the first thing they asked for was a discontinuation of the demonstrations while the negotiations went on; so we were faced with our first opportunity to show our strength. When asked what we wanted to achieve, we outlined nine demands:

1. The enforcement of the open housing ordinance already on the book.

2. The amendment of the ordinance to include a provision that outlawed discrimination by owners as well as brokers.

3. An agreement by the Chicago Real Estate Board to drop their legal challenge to the existing ordinance.

4. An agreement to end opposition to a state-wide open housing provision.

5. A demand that the Chicago Housing Authority stop building all public housing projects in slums.

6. A demand that the Public Aid Department stop discriminatory practices.

7. A demand that banks and other lending institutions stop discriminating in their lending practices.

8. A demand that local labor unions end all discriminatory practices.

9. A demand that those responsible for urban renewal in Chicago stop discriminating against black neighborhoods.

Each of these demands addressed complicated issues that had a long history in Chicago and there was no way they could be easily resolved since a number of groups and organizations, both public and private, were involved. But Mayor Daley took no note of this fact. Instead, he asked if we would halt our demonstrations once our demands were met. Warily Martin suggested that we might, whereupon Daley went down the list of demands and quickly agreed to every one of them. Presto! The race problems in Chicago had been solved, and after only a few minutes of discussion.

In effect, Mayor Daley was saying, "Well, if that's all you want then we can adjourn and go home—just as soon as you agree to halt the demonstrations."

It was not a shrewd move on his part. In that instant he revealed to us the strategy he intended to follow: Promise them anything so long as they stop the marches; later we can figure out ways to circumvent the granting of their demands. Had he balked at some of the points or at least argued for a while, his final acceptance might have been credible. But having collapsed so eagerly he only angered our negotiators and put them on their guard. Even the representatives of the white establishment were a little embarrassed by what was clearly a patronizing attitude on his part.

So the discussions focused on specific details; how and when these demands would be met, how the good faith of the establishment could be guaranteed. On the other side the question remained the same: When will you stop the marches? How quickly can we tell our people that they can go back to business as usual?

But as the conversations continued—and they took place during several lengthy meetings—the unwillingness of the real estate brokers to change basic policy became more and more apparent. They blamed their reluctance on the white customers they served, making the same argument we had heard from restaurant owners and hotel managers in the South—though not bigots themselves, they were nonetheless forced to pursue discriminatory policies in order to stay in business.

As Martin put it, "[White southerners] said that they were just the agents, that they were just responding to the people's unwillingness to eat with Negroes in the same restaurant or stay with Negroes in the same hotel. But we got a comprehensive civil rights bill and the so-called agents then provided service to everybody and nothing happened and the same thing can happen here." We had also demonstrated in the South that we could cost them more business than they could retain by resisting our demands.

Likewise an unspoken threat hung over the heads of the whites sitting around the negotiating table: "If you don't agree

with our demands then we will bring chaos to your neighborhoods, and what will property there be worth after a year of daily
marches?" When Mayor Daley heard allusions to this argument—
and it was never voiced in such explicit terms—he became
agitated and began to push the realtors for some kind of commitment that would rescue the city from impending disaster.
Indeed, all of the white representatives turned on Real Estate Board representative Ross Beatty and demanded that he
take a more positive attitude. He in turn began to reframe his
argument and to make room for some concessions down the
road.

But what Beatty was trying to save was a tradition of
informal segregation that spanned generations, and it was not
easy for him to sweep all this aside with a wave of his hand as
Mayor Daley had done. He was not, like the mayor, an absolute
monarch of the constituency he represented. Nor did he believe
he could escape accountability so easily. We came to believe that
anything Daley told us was seriously suspect, even when it was
repeated before the television cameras. But Beatty was unable to
make promises for which he alone would be held responsible, so
he was still hedging everything he said, making certain that he
didn't commit the entire real estate industry of Chicago to the
principle of justice—an uncharacteristic stance for that particular
segment of Chicago business.

On the other hand, with the rest of the Chicago business
community staring daggers at him, Beatty gave a lot of ground
each time the group met. In the end, he begrudgingly conceded
everything we had asked for, though we had to wring every
concession and every specification out of him with hard arguments and threats, always alluding to the marchers and their
potential to make worse trouble than before.

Nevertheless, things seemed to be going well, with each
side expressing a guarded optimism, when suddenly Mayor
Daley revealed his essential duplicity—he attempted to take the
only weapon we had away from us. He sought and got an
injunction from a Cook County circuit court judge that severely
restricted the kinds of marches we could launch and where we
could go.

Most restrictive of all was the limitation of demonstrations to no more than five hundred people. Such a restriction was unfair for several reasons. In the first place, it meant that we could never dramatize the true strength of our movement in Chicago. No matter how great our support grew, and it had been gaining momentum all along, we could still only put forth five hundred representatives. Thus, the very idea of a "demonstration" was being undermined, since we couldn't "demonstrate" our sizable strength. No one knew better the importance of crowd sizes than an old politician like Mayor Daley, and we suspected that he might have passed along this information to Judge Cornelius J. Harrington, the judge who had approved the injunction. Now our marches on television could never appear to be as large or as broadly based in support as the earlier marches at Birmingham and Selma.

But a second and perhaps more important consequence of the five hundred figure was its guarantee that when we marched into the ethnic neighborhoods, we would always be outnumbered by the same people who had bombarded us with rocks and bottles and had burned our automobiles. Literally a thousand people or more had converged on our fifty at Gage Park. Had there been more of us, the onlookers might have been less demonstrative and violent. Now Judge Harrington was making sure that the odds remained heavily in favor of his own people, despite the fact that we had not engaged in a single act of violence.

Also, we were forbidden to demonstrate at more than one place at a time, we could not do so after dark nor during rush hours; and we had to give the police advance notice of at least twenty-four hours (i.e., tip off our plans and risk further retaliatory action by neighborhood mobs that would have ample time to organize their assaults). The time limits imposed dictated that we would have to demonstrate during midmorning or midafternoon hours, thereby eliminating any of our people who held down jobs.

Of course, all of these restrictions were justified on the grounds of public safety, and there was just enough logic in each provision to make the injunction credible to the press and to a large majority of the white people. But for those blacks negotiating with the Mayor and his friends, the injunction was a betrayal of the spirit of frankness and growing trust that they thought the group was striving to achieve.

We said so, and several of the white members of the CCRR agreed with us. The matter of stopping the demonstrations had been freely and openly discussed. We had explained why we had to retain that option, but Martin had indicated we would stop invading the surburbs when we had an agreement that included specific implementation plans. To ask us to cease our marches was to ask for one side to disarm unilaterally in the middle of a war.

Not only were we disinclined to do that, but we could not have taken such a step even if we had wanted to. In the first place, too many leaders in our coalition would have simply continued the marches on their own, with overwhelming support from Chicago's black people. In the second place, had we agreed to forfeit our right to march, it would have been the end of SCLC credibility as the middle-of-the-roaders in the black community. We represented a more militant spirit than William Dawson but by no means the lawlessness and violence that Stokely Carmichael was advocating. The Dawsons were relics of the past. Their day was almost over. The future belonged either to Christian nonviolence or to Black Power, and Black Power in 1966 meant something akin to civil war. We couldn't quit the field and leave the nation to face such a fate. That is why we continued to hold to the strategy of nonviolent demonstrations, and that is why we resented Mayor Daley's end run.

However, while we were angry at the injunction, we weren't really surprised. What we had to decide was whether we would defy the court order or accept it, and we finally agreed to do the latter, concluding that it still left us enough room to maneuver. The judge had not said, after all, that we couldn't march. He had simply made certain that we would be unable to demonstrate our growing strength and unity to the rest of the nation by bringing ever increasing numbers into the streets.

Within our own ranks, opinion was divided. Some said we could live with the injunction, but only as long as negotiations were progressing. Our lawyers advised us to obey the injunction, since, unlike earlier such legal restrictions, it was reasonable and would be so perceived by the public. Others said we should defy the court order and force them to arrest us en masse, just as we had done in Birmingham. Martin sat back and let the two sides argue the question. Then he made his own decision and persuaded the others to go along with it: We would accept the limitations of the injunction—for a while.

We also used the clear betrayal of our negotiations to win points with the more fair-minded whites during subsequent discussions. Mayor Daley had his injunction, but he paid a price for it in credibility at the negotiating table. No longer did anyone say, "You have no right to question the mayor's word." When we continued to voice our demand for something concrete and detailed in the way of an implementation plan, more and more whites saw our point—we just *might* be betrayed again.

In the meantime we found ways to circumvent the judge's orders and still remain technically within the law. Since the injunction applied only to Chicago, the following Sunday we launched three demonstrations simultaneously—one in Chicago and two in suburbs beyond the city limits. Again we were pelted with rocks and bottles, and these acts were recorded by the television cameras.

When Martin held a press conference the next day in Atlanta, he told the assembled reporters that our obedience was conditional on progress in the CCRR negotiations. If our demands were not met at the next full meeting of negotiators, we would defy the court order, and that could mean a massive march into downtown Chicago. Martin also indicated that we might also march into Cicero.

With this announcement the fat was in the fire. We had set our own timetable for the resolution of this problem; furthermore, we had shown our willingness to take on Cicero. Already the white racists were organizing for a last-ditch stand, as if the march into Cicero were the equivalent of the Normandy invasion. The American Nazis were in town, a handful of troublemakers trying to increase their numbers in the face of this threat to their mean and ugly world. There were also local residents who were making wild and irresponsible promises. Cook County Sheriff Richard Ogilvie begged us to cancel the Cicero march, which he called "suicidal," but at this point we could not back down. And Martin told Ogilvie as much.

"We fully intend to have the march," he said to reporters. "We have talked with Ogilvie about this and announced our plans last Saturday. We gave more than the seven days' notice."

Ogilvie and Cicero responded by asking Governor Otto Kerner to call out the Illinois National Guard. Kerner, after pondering the potential consequences of the Cicero march, agreed to grant Ogilvie's request. So the battle lines were drawn—as they had been drawn in Montgomery and Birmingham and Selma.

Meanwhile, a subcommittee had been meeting every few days to draft an agreement that would meet all our demands and at the same time be acceptable to both the Chicago Real Estate Board and the mayor. I am certain that their deliberations were greatly facilitated by the threat of the Cicero march. Over the years we found that white elected officials were seldom willing to negotiate in good faith unless an army was poised at their gates or already loose in the streets. Then they would make concessions they would never have considered if we had stood in their offices, hats in hand, and pleaded in the name of justice.

During those days of working out a final draft, there were people on both sides who were dissatisfied with the results. David Garrow in *Bearing the Cross* has given an excellent blow-by-blow account of the final negotiations and the accord that was reached when Mayor Richard Daley saw that his back was to the wall.

Fortunately, Al Raby, Jim Bevel, and Jesse Jackson were sufficiently negative to frighten the other side into believing the whole negotiations might break down, even at the end, and leave them facing Armageddon in less than forty-eight hours. Had we all seemed docile and happy we might have gotten considerably less than we had hoped for. As it stood, we got everything; and there was even some possibility that the city might come through on all its promises.

When, after lengthy and at times heated debate, the agreement was approved unanimously, Martin made the following speech to the assembled group, an eloquent impromptu statement of his faith and optimism over what had been accomplished:

We read in the scripture, "Come, let us sit down and reason together," and everyone here has met that spiritual mandate. There comes a time when we move from protest to reconciliation and we have been misinterpreted by the press and by the political leaders of this town as to our motives and our goals, but let me say once again that it is our purpose, our single purpose to create the beloved community. We seek only to make possible a city where men can live together as brothers.

Yet even at the threshold of what appeared to be our greatest triumph, he was not so filled with hope that he did not see the fragile nature of an agreement that was thus far no more than words:

I know this has been said many times today, but I want to reiterate again that we must make this agreement work. Our people's hopes have been shattered too many times, and an additional disillusionment will only spell catastrophe. Our summers of riots have been caused by our winters of delay. I want to stress the need for implementation and I want to recognize that we have a big job. Because I marched through Gage Park, I saw hatred in the faces of so many, a hatred born of fear, and that fear came because people didn't know each other, and they don't know each other because they are separate from one another. So, we must attack the separation and those myths. There is a tremendous educational job ahead of us.

Finally, he left them with a warning and a word of clear, if guarded, optimism.

Now, we don't want to threaten any additional marches, but if this agreement does not work, marches would be a reality. . . . I speak to everyone on my side of the table now, and I say that this must be interpreted, this agreement, as a victory for justice and not a victory over the Chicago Realty Board or the City of Chicago. I am as grateful to Mayor Daley as anyone else here for his work. I think now we can go on to make Chicago a beautiful city, a city of brotherhood.

As the world knows, that didn't happen.

*   *   *

Martin appeared before the press with Mayor Daley to celebrate the agreement, which he said would lead to "the total eradication of housing discrimination." At the moment I know he hoped and perhaps half-believed that it was true. Certainly the words were there—with all the clarity and fire of diamonds. And who could question the Mayor, as he stood under the glare of lights, smiled, and told the nation, "This is a great day for Chicago."

What was in his mind and heart at that moment? None of us will ever really know. He was, like all human beings, ultimately inscrutable in his deepest thoughts and feelings. Did he know at that very moment that he had no intention of making good on any of the promises contained in the agreement? Did he stand before the public fully intending to renege on all the promises, to maintain the status quo after signing his name to a document designed to usher in an entirely new way of doing business?

Or did he genuinely believe at the time that all of these fine things would be done precisely as everyone had pledged they would? Did he sincerely expect his own machine to turn on itself and undo all of the injustices it had perpetrated—and was still perpetrating at that very moment? Only the Good Lord knows the answer.

But I didn't believe him at the time, and neither did many of the black leaders in Chicago, the ones who dealt with the poor on a day-to-day basis. Some of them thought we had sold them out for a superficial media triumph that would be repudiated by future events. Others even suggested that the march into Cicero should be undertaken as planned—that the black community should demand even greater concessions before they forfeited their momentum. On the other hand, most blacks were optimistic and believed that something would be accomplished, that we had won a significant victory if only because the mayor and other members of the white establishment had signed their names to a document that admitted the status quo was discriminatory, unjust, and had to be changed. Tragically, a few even believed that very soon they would be looking at houses in Gage Park and the other exclusively white neighborhoods.

The weeks turned into months, and gradually reporters stopped asking the mayor when his administration would enact open housing initiatives and begin to keep its promises to the black community. When someone did remember to raise that question, Mayor Daley would make some vague excuse and move on to other, more important matters.

But our enemies in the black community did not forget. The broken pledge of Chicago became a key arguing point in the rhetoric of Black Power advocates. "That's all you get from nonviolent approaches: a lot of talk and no action. Force is the only thing the white man understands. So burn, baby, burn!"

In a sense Chicago was the high-water mark of the civil rights movement. We came North hoping to expand our influence to the nation as a whole—and with a great opportunity to do so. We were attempting to establish a pattern of desegregation in the nation's second-largest city that would serve as a model for the rest of America's urban communities. We had encountered a hatred there that both surprised and challenged—a hatred that many of us regarded as greater than anything we had seen in the South—and yet we had survived and exacted from the white leadership a promise to follow our blueprint for integration. That could have been the culmination of the dream Martin had spoken of at the Lincoln Memorial three years earlier.

But like Herod, Richard Daley was a fox, too smart for us, too smart for the press, too smart for the white leaders who sat in the room and signed the agreement in good faith, too smart to give any credence to dreams, too smart for his own good and for the good of Chicago. He was the essential politician of our time, wise enough to survive and dominate an arena in which only money and power make any real difference.

So did we make a mistake in taking his word and leaving Chicago with our signed agreement and our high hopes? Martin had less than two years to ponder this question before he was taken from us, but I have had twenty years.

I believe we did the right thing, even though the outcome was bitterly disappointing.

Unless you are in a position to destroy your enemy completely, you have to stop the battle at some point and try to achieve peace, however unlikely the prospect. Whatever Mayor Daley's behavior had been in the past, we owed him one chance to respond to reason and do what was right. Everybody deserves to be trusted one time in his life, just to be given the opportunity to be better than he is. Besides, that negotiated agreement was a necessary step in the road to real progress, because if we had not tried it, the establishment would have forever blamed us, saying our suspicion had cost the city its chances for real peace. Our failure to negotiate in good faith would have been the reason given for every harsh and repressive measure in the future, so we really would have had to try what we did, even if we had known for certain that it would fail.

Had we continued to march into Gage Park and Cicero, someone would surely have been killed—and maybe more than a few. What could have come out of such bloody encounters but another agreement, another document filled with words that the mayor and his learned legal staff could twist and squeeze to suit their own purposes. Eventually the success of any movement in Chicago depended on the genuine willingness of white people to commit themselves to justice and equality—and that, I now realize, was nothing we could ever have wrung out of the Daley machine or any of its followers. Our only hope was to invoke a greater power than the mayor himself wielded, or else to take that power away from him. And eventually we did both.

First, when the City of Chicago refused to pass an open housing ordinance with teeth in it, the advocates of justice in the State of Illinois went to the legislature and eventually forced the passage of such legislation, which of course applied to Chicago. The story of how they achieved that victory both amused and touched me. It was told to me by a friend who knew the man involved, and I believe that it must be true.

His name was Bill Barr, and he went to the Illinois House of Representatives as a Republican from Joliet, though he was anything but typical of his party at that time. During his first session, when he was too naive to know that legislators don't vote on principle but on self-interest, he listened to a debate on the legalization of bingo, a question that came up in every session. After hearing the arguments, he decided that sponsors of the bill had made a good case, so he voted for it, despite the fact that he was in the minority.

Later that day he was summoned to the office of the old Chicago politician who had sponsored the bill. When he stepped in the office, the man looked up at him and narrowed his eyes.

"OK," he said, "what do you want?"

"What do you mean?" Barr said.

"You voted for our bingo bill. So what do you want out of it?"

"I don't want anything," Barr said. "I thought it was a good bill, so I voted for it."

The veteran looked at him for a minute, blinking his eyes.

"Are you kidding me?"

"It's true," Barr said.

"We owe you," said the veteran, speaking for himself and the half dozen politicians in his little group, who were Cook County irregulars, Republicans who did business with the mayor of Chicago while maintaining membership in the opposing party.

"You don't owe me," Barr said. "Besides, the bill lost."

"We owe you," the veteran said.

A couple of years later, Barr became interested in the open housing bill that was introduced each year in the legislature but never came to a vote. Barr had always assumed that the idea of forcing realtors and homeowners to sell to minorities was a bad one, but the more he heard about the housing conditions black people had to endure, the more he became convinced that the passage of a strong state law was the only solution to this terrible problem.

When he asked why the bill was never brought to a vote, he was told that they knew they were three votes short, so they avoided a defeat, which would hurt the chances of passage at some time in the future. Knowing that the bill would never come up, Barr nonetheless astonished his Republican friends in the

House by becoming a cosponsor along with the black caucus.

At that point the old Chicago veteran called him into his office again.

"What are you trying to get from the niggers?" he asked.

"Nothing," said Barr. "I listened to their arguments, and I think they deserve a break. Like I did on your bingo bill."

The veteran stared at him for a moment.

"And that's it?"

"That's it," said Barr.

The veteran shook his head in disbelief.

"How many votes you need?" he asked.

"We're three short," said Barr.

"Call it up for a vote," said the veteran.

"What do you mean?" Barr asked.

"I said call it up for a vote."

So Barr went back and huddled with the black cosponsors of the open housing bill. They didn't quite understand what was going on. Finally one of the black leaders said, "Why not? We've been afraid to put it on the floor for years. Maybe something will happen."

So they asked for a roll-call vote, which, in the Illinois legislature, was done with buttons at the desks, green for yes and red for no. As they went down the list alphabetically, the legislators would call out their vote and punch the button, lighting up one of the two lights on the tote board.

Barr and the others were watching as the clerk called out the name of the veteran, the leader of that half dozen irregulars from Chicago.

"Six votes for Barr and his niggers!" he called out, and punched not only his own button but those in front of his five team members. The bill passed and became law in the State of Illinois—or so I have been told—in part because a good man went to the legislature and voted his conscience, not only on the question of open housing, but also on the game of bingo.

But something else happened in Chicago that turned the tables on the Daley machine—the people elected a black mayor. In

1983, a good friend of mine, Congressman Harold Washington, running against a divided Daley machine, captured the Democratic mayoral nomination and went on to win in the general election. Though he did not live to see the end of all discrimination in the City of Chicago, the very fact that a coalition of blacks and liberal whites were able to put him in office will probably mean that never again will a Chicago mayor and his administration so cynically treat the black leaders of the city when they ask for equality and justice.

Perhaps we had nothing to do with the climatic change in that great city that elected Harold Washington in 1983, seventeen years after our frustrating experience, but I like to believe that we did, if only because it would have pleased Martin so much and would have removed some of the sorrow he felt until the day he died.

As a postscript let me add that as we were winding up our Chicago campaign, an invitation came from Carl Stokes in Cleveland: He wanted us to help him in his campaign to become the first black mayor of a major city. As soon as I heard the news, I rushed into Martin's office and urged him to accept.

"What can we hope to achieve?" he asked.

"The most important goal I can think of," I replied. "We can get the hell out of Chicago."

12

Jesse Jackson

WHEN WE LEFT CHICAGO to return to Atlanta, Jesse Jackson remained behind as our representative in that part of the country. His job was to operate Operation Breadbasket, a program we had developed in consultation with the Reverend Leon Sullivan, whose success in procuring jobs for blacks in Philadelphia, Pennsylvania, had caught our attention. We hoped to replicate his program on a national level, and it was that task that we assigned to Jesse, who was eager, articulate, and had made a name for himself in Chicago.

Many people thought from its name that Operation Breadbasket was a handout program in which poor families were given free food. In some ways it was the furthest thing from such a program, although there is nothing wrong with feeding the hungry. The purpose of Operation Breadbasket was to force companies doing business in the black community to hire blacks as employees; not just at the lowest levels but throughout the corporate hierarchy. So we were not so much interested in giving blacks handouts as we were in providing them with the means to be self-sufficient and to feed themselves.

The program worked like this: We would first target businesses that were located within the black community and did business exclusively, or almost exclusively, with black customers. We would check to see how many black employees they had and at what levels. As surprising as it may seem to many Americans today, many of these businesses had no black employees at all, or only one or two at the janitorial level. White owned and white operated, they set up in the middle of black neighborhoods, took money from black customers, and then spent it in white establishments in white neighborhoods.

Obviously, such a system conspired to keep blacks poor and jobless while at the same time taking what money they did have and recycling it in the white community. It didn't take a Harvard economist to realize that if some of the employees in those companies were black then they would spend their paychecks in black establishments located in black neighborhoods, and such a practice would help enrich blacks at every level.

Essentially we were saying that businesses should give back a little of their wealth to the people who helped to create it, that if you want black people to spend money on your goods or services, then you should be willing to hire black people in your company. It was simply a matter of being fair.

We began by going to the owner or general manager of a targeted business and asking them to tell us how many black employees were currently working in their operation and in what positions. It was a simple request for information, but it is surprising how many of them refused to give us the information, invariably because they had either no blacks on their payroll or only one or two who were working in menial tasks at minimum wage.

Usually we knew the answer to this question before we asked it, but when the targeted company refused to give us the information we asked for, we called on the chief executive, explained our purpose, and asked that blacks be employed at whatever population ratio was current in that particular city or county: If the proportion of blacks to the total population was 12 percent, then we would ask that 12 percent of the employees be black. We also asked that blacks be hired at levels of responsibility for which they were qualified. For example, we often found that many of these corporations didn't even employ black truck drivers, much less black accountants, black supervisors, black assistant managers, black store managers. Was it too much to ask that a corporation that depended heavily or exclusively on black patronage be asked to integrate blacks into its lower and middle echelon job structure? We weren't asking that they be made chairman of the board or president or even vice president (though Leon Sullivan ended up on the Board of Directors of the U.S. Steel Corporation). We just wanted an opportunity to recover in a small percentage of paychecks what we were paying out in day-to-day patronage. That's what we told them.

Sometimes they lied and said they had a large number of blacks working for them, expecting us to trundle off like so many Step'nfetchits, mumbling our gratitude. But we didn't take anybody's word. We asked to meet and talk to the black employees, and at that point the management usually asked us to leave, knowing we had them; and we would leave.

At other times they would lecture us, saying we had no right to tell them how to run their businesses, that no one could order them to make decisions that were contrary to their better judgment. We would agree with them, admitting that they certainly had the right to refuse if they wanted to, and then we would leave.

At still other times they would simply refuse to see us under any circumstances. When we wrote, they wouldn't answer. When we phoned, they would refuse to talk to us. When we came to their offices, they would remain behind locked doors. Again we would leave.

Leaving was always the first stage of the game. The second was a boycott; and to call for a boycott was *our* right.

The boycotts were generally promoted from the pulpits of the city's churches. The preachers would get up on Sunday morning, explain the whole rationale of Operation Breadbasket, tell their congregations which business was being targeted, why they had been chosen, how they had refused to cooperate, and what we intended to do in return. Then the preacher would close with an exhortation to his entire flock to be faithful to the boycott and to pass the word.

By Sunday noon everybody would get the word, and the convenience store or drugstore or restaurant would suddenly be devoid of customers. Nobody would cross the threshold. The manager would wonder for a while what was wrong, and then gradually he would figure it out. If he was his own boss—and hence the man responsible for his plight—he would grit his teeth, dig in his heels, and swear he'd wait us out. The days would become a week and the weeks would move toward a month, and during that time there wouldn't be a single sale unless some outsider came into the neighborhood and didn't know what was happening.

If the manager of the store were not the boss of the company but the owner or operator of a franchise, then he would get on the phone to the main office and beg the management to give us what we wanted. Under such circumstances, we had an ally in the poor man who had to bear the financial burden of corporate bigotry.

But we didn't just boycott places of business. We also boycotted products. For example, we would research a certain product that blacks bought in abundance—a food item, a beauty aid, a health item—and we would determine just how many blacks were employed in the company at every level. Then, when they refused to hire blacks in proportion to the number in the local population, we would tell blacks to boycott that particular product.

Salesmen or delivery men would leave their usual order, drive off, return in a few days or a week, and find every item still on the shelf. In the case of perishable foods, this would mean disaster. Everything would be spoiled or sour or dried up—a total loss. And when you were delivering that particular product to twenty or thirty stores in the black section of town, you were talking about dangerous losses of revenue, the kinds of losses that could result in almost immediate insolvency. Few people realize how precarious the food industry really is, how vulnerable to such an attack.

But no manufacturer or distributor can bear the loss of a major market for very long. If you are turning out five thousand items a week and anticipating the sale of five hundred to black people, then you will lose 10 percent of your business and in many competitive markets that's your margin of profit. As a matter of fact, we finally came to the conclusion that in many, if not most, of the businesses in the United States the whites get a company to the break even point and the blacks get it the margin of profit. Once we understood that economic fact of life, Operation Breadbasket picked up steam.

In the end, of course, most, if not all, of the businesses capitulated to our demands—at least they did so in places where we were well organized. We would get a frantic phone call a day, a week, or a month into our boycott. Would we reconsider our actions? Could we talk about it? How fast could we reach an agreement? The transformation was miraculous.

In less than a week, the most scowling bigot could be turned into a pillar of tolerance and brotherly love. When we entered his office he would come rushing out to greet us, offering his hand this time, ushering us into his office, offering coffee or cigars or both. We would not be ungracious. We too would be smiling, happy that he had looked deep inside himself and found this wellspring of virtue.

Then we would get down to negotiations, and he would begin by telling us how many black loaders and truck drivers he was going to bring aboard—just as soon as the next vacancy occurred. We would then tell him that we were not willing to wait for these vacancies, that we wanted to see blacks in jobs right now.

"Are you asking me to fire white drivers already on the job?" he would ask incredulously.

"How you manage it is your business," we said. "Perhaps you can find work for some blacks without laying off anyone on the job now. Perhaps, on the other hand, you will have to make adjustments for the neglect you have practiced in the past. Again, you have the right to do whatever you want to, including refusing to hire *any* blacks—provided you are willing to pay the consequences."

In some cases, whites did lose their jobs, but they were much better able to get other work than were the blacks who replaced them. We were sympathetic with anyone who might have been displaced, but we saw no other way to accomplish this goal. We were breaking eggs to make omelettes, and we insisted that businesses not postpone their responsibility to correct an historic imbalance. As surprising as it may seem, almost none of them tried to defy us once they had felt the sting of our boycott. They were convinced that we could deliver on any threat we made—and we could.

This, then, was the strategy of Operation Breadbasket. First perfected by Leon Sullivan, it had worked in Philadelphia; and Martin and I both thought it could be used as a tool to gain social justice for blacks throughout the country. So we invited Sullivan to come to Atlanta and talk to us about his success. Once we heard his story, we were convinced we could expand the movement to include this strategy, and with such an end in mind we started Operation Breadbasket and put Jesse in charge.

Originally, it was our intention to move him to Atlanta and allow him to coordinate his national operation at SCLC headquarters. Jesse, on the other hand, didn't want to make the move. He knew his way around in Chicago, he had made a lot of friends, and he was reluctant to leave it all behind. Then, too, Jesse was never the kind of mule to submit too easily to the bit. He had a tender mouth and would be pained by the slightest pull of the rein. Staying in Chicago was a way of remaining almost independent while at the same time enjoying the benefits of SCLC connections. Martin was forever threatening to go up there and move him back South, lock, stock, and barrel, but he kept postponing the decision because he knew it would be so unpleasant.

Besides, we had to weigh the benefits of forcing the issue against the losses we might incur. At best we would have a slightly more authoritative control over Operation Breadbasket— but at what cost? A major squabble in the press? The resignation of Jesse Jackson? With the momentum of the movement already diminishing, we decided we couldn't afford to run the risk.

We were not entirely pleased, however, with the progress of

Breadbasket. At its inception we believed it would become a primary instrument to liberate our people from economic bondage. It was the Montgomery boycott applied nationwide to the entire economy. A means by which blacks in every American city could claim the jobs that had been systematically denied them for generations. All that would be required would be a willingness to work together and to refrain from buying certain products for a short time.

In our initial enthusiasm, we could see chapters of Operation Breadbasket springing up all over the country and immediately becoming significant local forces, as significant and active as the Red Cross or the United Fund. All that was required was one highly successful model and the right man to market the idea nationwide. Such a man, I was convinced, was Jesse Jackson.

In retrospect, I realize that we expected too much too soon. The civil rights movement was beginning to heat up in those later years, and instead of boycotts, more and more people were turning to violence. Then, too, taking the concept nationwide was probably too big a job for one man. Perhaps Martin could have done it successfully, but not without sacrificing all the other activities to which he was committed—and that would have meant a whole new direction for the SCLC.

So we turned Operation Breadbasket over to Jesse, counting on his irrepressible personality to carry the day, forgetting that he was still a very young man with human limitations just like the rest of us. When he failed we were unfairly critical.

The main problem with Breadbasket was that it never existed outside of Chicago, except on paper; and even the paper organization was sketchy and full of holes. We had a few scattered chapters elsewhere, most no more than meaningless pins on a map. The flagship chapter in Chicago was our only genuine success, and it never measured up to what Sullivan had done in Philadelphia.

Indeed, there were problems with the Chicago operation. For one thing, it was poorly organized, and the members were forever squabbling with one another. For example, Jesse had brought in his half-brother Noah Robinson to work with him, and Noah was a chronic troublemaker—if anything, more stubborn than Jesse. Unfortunately, Jesse couldn't control Noah, so some of the disciplinary problems were passed along to headquarters back in Atlanta.

In fact, I remember on one occasion Noah was so out of control that we were afraid he might do something to land us on the front pages of the *Chicago Tribune*. When the matter came to our attention I called Jesse and asked him to keep his brother in line.

"I can't do anything with him," Jesse said. "He won't listen to me."

"Then who will he listen to?" I asked, more to make a point than to elicit an answer.

"He'll listen to his Daddy," said Jesse.

Noah's father was Jesse's natural father as well, a big man with a booming voice who was sometimes a preacher and sometimes something else. He lived in Greenville, South Carolina, a long way from Chicago; but it wasn't so very far from Atlanta, and we were ready to try anything. So we brought Noah to Atlanta, and Mr. Robinson drove down from Greenville to confront the young man and straighten him out.

When Noah saw his father walk in the door, he wilted like a morning glory; and then we retreated and shut the door behind us. Suddenly we heard shouts and threats the likes of which we had never heard before. We stood outside in the hallway, looking at one another and shaking our heads at the ferocity of old Mr. Robinson's rage. Later we would agree that we didn't hear Noah's voice interrupt one time, a fact we found incredible.

Finally it was over, and when the door opened, Noah walked out looking like the angel in the Christmas play, while Mr. Robinson mopped his brow with his handkerchief, a frown still evident; and that was the end of Noah's tantrum, at least for that time. In retrospect, I wonder why we didn't send Mr. Robinson up to Chicago to run Operation Breadbasket. (The last time I heard anything about Noah, he was on trial in Greenville for murder.

But it wasn't just personnel problems that plagued Operation Breadbasket. There were also problems with the book-keeping. Jesse was apparently incapable of keeping financial records, nor was he able to find anyone else who could do it for him. Since the Chicago project was part of our overall operation, we were responsible for submitting financial reports at the end of each year to retain our tax-exempt status. What we got from Chicago was little more than a paper bag full of cancelled checks and receipts—and more of the former than the latter. Eventually we were able to make some sense of what records Jesse's staff sent us, but our accountants were always red-eyed and short-tempered by the time they finished.

On the positive side, Jesse showed tremendous skill in dealing with the press to gain their attention in order to advertise the projects of Operation Breadbasket. The quicker the word was spread throughout the community, the quicker Breadbasket could gain widespread support in the black community. Jesse had a flair for publicity and could promote a press conference on the smallest pretext and end up the lead story on the evening news. It was this talent that eventually gained him his national following and catapulted him into the political spotlight in 1984 and 1988.

He was also a genius at motivating people. Nobody could do more with a crowd of potential supporters waiting to be told what to do. He instinctively knew their hearts, and he was a master of the right phrase to bring out their passion. When he spoke to such crowds he always quickened their blood. Though not a preacher with a permanent pulpit, he could take the language of the sermon and translate it into the language of practical politics and that made him an extraordinary leader of black people—something I recognized in him the first time I heard him speak at Selma.

But he also had a talent for hatching entrepreneurial schemes that occasionally got him into trouble. He was always coming up with ideas for new projects and new money-making operations. When Martin was still alive, he could keep a lid on Jesse by virtue of his recognized preeminence in the movement, but that didn't stop Jesse from hounding him constantly about some new project that was "sure to make us a fortune" or "get us on the cover of *Time*."

After Martin was killed, I inherited the problem of Jesse's entrepreneurial zeal along with the other assets and liabilities of the SCLC. The difference between me and Martin, however, was that I was less inclined to say "no" and more inclined to say "maybe"; and for Jesse "maybe" invariably translated into "yes."

One of the projects he proposed, eventually called Black Expo, seemed to have particular promise because it grew directly out of the concern of Operation Breadbasket to promote the entrance of blacks into business and the market place. As a matter of fact, Black Expo was based on one of the cornerstones of Breadbasket: the idea that white businesses needed black customers, a fact on which black economic progress would be built.

Essentially Black Expo was a trade fair for companies who did business with the black community—a means of displaying their wares and showing their gratitude for black patronage. Many of the businesses were white-owned. A few of them were black-owned. Both types of businesses were welcome to set up booths.

But in addition to being a trade fair, Black Expo was an entertainment extravaganza to which a number of actors, singers, dancers, and sports celebrities donated their services. People came by the hundreds of thousands, and in 1969 SCLC's share of the proceeds was $66,000. The next year our share dropped to $11,000. And the following year, the finances were so confused that the whole matter became a controversy in the Chicago newspapers. I didn't know what to think, but I had other matters to worry about, so I put Jesse and Black Expo out of my mind. Then something happened that made it impossible for me and the board members of the SCLC to ignore the charges and countercharges appearing in the Chicago newspapers.

As I was returning to Atlanta after a long and tiring trip, I was met at the airport by a young black reporter named Angela Parker, who introduced herself and then began asking me questions about SCLC's ownership of Black Expo. When I assured her that the trade fair was indeed sponsored by our organization, she produced documents that indicated otherwise. It seemed that a group of Chicago businessmen incorporated the project under a separate charter, first as a foundation, then as a nonprofit corporation.

I was tired and confused, and when Angela Parker asked me for a statement, I said, "This is most unusual. I find it difficult to believe. Although there may not have been any mishandling of funds by this move, still, if it is true, it was wrong. Black Expo should not have been incorporated without approval and knowledge of the board of directors and the SCLC president. If this is true, the Reverend Mr. Jackson had no right to direct the founding of either a foundation or a corporation. No department had that right according to the policies of the national organization. It cannot make any legal moves without the approval of the president and the board of directors of the national office. We cannot, at this time, allow a department to get out of line. It can hurt the entire organization."

The truth is, I really didn't want a confrontation with Jesse over this or any other matter. We needed to maintain a united front against our common adversary, and internal bickering merely weakened the cause. I put it this way at the time.

"I have considered the liberation of the black and the poor people much more important than dissipating energies and resources seeking to deal with ... Reverend Jackson. ... We have been bogged down with matters of getting America to feed its hungry, house its poor, and redirect its national priorities. This has had to take precedence over everything else."

At this point, however, we were forced to confront the issue. Angela Parker published the story in the *Chicago Tribune,* including my quote, and everyone demanded some sort of action from me and the other SCLC officials. We discussed the alternatives open to us and finally decided to fly the board to Chicago and hold an inquiry at the Marriott next to O'Hare Airport.

Jesse came, we heard evidence, discussed the matter at some length, and finally decided that we needed more details and legal advice. We did conclude that at the very least Jesse had allowed irregularities to occur, and we suspended him for sixty days with pay while we continued our investigation. His pride hurt, Jesse immediately resigned from the SCLC. It was then that he organized Operation PUSH and began his climb to national prominence.

*   *   *

Jesse's best talent is his ability to inspire people to be better than they are, particularly young people. Jesse's PUSH for Excellence program, in which he attempted to keep young blacks in school, may have been one of the few successful programs that actually made a difference to our young people. It was put together with rhetoric and a few simple procedures, yet in many predominantly black schools parents for the first time were actually beginning to work together to prevent dropouts—and mostly they did so because Jesse came into town, got everybody together, and then he talked.

What he said was important: that black children now had the opportunity to be anything they wanted to, that school provided them with the means to break out of the poverty cycle and make a name for themselves.

"I am some*body*," Jesse would shout, echoing Dr. William Holmes Borders of Atlanta's Wheat Street Baptist Church, and then make the youngsters repeat the statement after him. Soon the rafters of the school gymnasium would be shaking with that cry, and afterward the youngsters, many of them members of street gangs, would rush to sign one of Jesse's "contracts" to do homework on a regular basis, study so many hours a week, and stay in school until graduation. Parents would sign pledges to check homework, and teachers promised to keep parents informed about academic progress as well as problems.

When Jesse was promoting PUSH Excel in the late 70s he was performing a great service for our people, and I always regretted the fact that he became involved in presidential politics and dropped the PUSH educational program. Not since then have we shown any significant improvement in motivating black youngsters to get the most out of their education.

Yet I have supported him twice in his bid for the presidency, and I suspect that I will support him again if he chooses to run. Over the years I have come to love and admire Jesse, in part because he has matured into a great leader, in part because he has been so supportive of me.

13

Memphis

THE ROAD TO MEMPHIS really began in Quitman County, Mississippi, in 1968, when we were marching in behalf of James Meredith, after he was wounded by a shotgun blast. We were in a small schoolhouse in the dusty little town of Marks, talking to a teacher who was trying to help rural black children learn enough in their earliest years to carry them through high school graduation and a decent job. We had asked her how well she was doing, and she had confessed that the task was difficult. Most of the children came from poverty-stricken homes where illiterate parents could give them no help. They tried, but they simply couldn't keep up the pace, even with preschool preparation to enter the first grade.

We looked around the primitive schoolroom and saw them watching us, wide-eyed and silent, having been told who we were. We smiled and waved, and several of them broke into broad grins. They seemed bright and alert, but something bothered me about them. Then I realized what it was: Virtually all of them were underweight, a condition that lent a special poignancy to their enormous eyes.

As if reading my mind the teacher glanced at the clock.

"Can you excuse me," she said. "It's lunchtime. I need to feed them. It won't take but a minute. Please don't leave."

We watched as she brought out a box of crackers and a brown paper bag filled with apples. The children sat quietly as she took out a paring knife and cut each apple into four parts. Then she went around to each desk and gave each child a stack of four or five crackers and a quarter of an apple.

I watched with a growing awareness of what we were seeing. This was not just a snack. This was all these children would be eating for lunch. I nudged Martin.

"That's all they get," I whispered.

Turning to me, he nodded his head; and I saw that his eyes were full of tears, which he wiped away with the back of his hand.

As we drove around that day, meeting various people, he was strangely silent. That evening, lying on his bed in the motel, he stared at the ceiling for a long time, then spoke to me.

"Ralph," he said. "I can't get those children out of my mind."

"I thought that was bothering you," I said. "They bother me too."

"We've got to do something for them," he said. "We can't let that kind of poverty exist in this country. I don't think people really know that little school children are slowly starving in the United States of America. I didn't know it."

It was true. He had grown up in a middle-class household, as had I. Neither one of us had ever gone hungry, nor had any of our family. Oh, we had seen some poor homes in our ministries, but we had never lived in a poverty pocket like northern Mississippi. So that day we were confronted with something we knew existed but had never seen firsthand.

"I've been thinking about it," Martin continued. "We have to take all these people to Washington and show them to the government. The president and Congress have to be shown that there are Americans who have nothing to eat and who live in shacks."

"How can that possibly be done?" I asked.

"I'm going to propose to the SCLC executive committee that we organize a Poor People's Campaign to expose poverty, so that everyone can see it."

I must confess that I didn't fully understand what he had in mind at that moment. I couldn't grasp the scheme he had been thinking about all day. But as he told me more, it all began to make sense.

"We'll go to Washington and camp out, if necessary," he said. "We'll take these people into the congressional hearings and to the various departments of government. We'll let these elected officials hear firsthand what kind of conditions these people have to endure. I would like every official of the U.S. government to see what I saw today. Then something would be done."

"But what can be done?" I said. "What will we ask for?"

"I've thought of that, too," he said. "First, we need a guaranteed minimum wage in this country, so that no family will be without the means to buy the necessities of life. Second, we need vouchers or stamps for free food; so that the parents of those children can go to any grocery store and buy the right kind of food. And third, we need to do away with the commodity program, where people are given whatever surplus food the government has—when they have it. All poor people get is starches and fats. No wonder so many of them have such short lives."

"When do you want to do this?" I asked him.

"As soon as possible," he said. "Right after Chicago if we can. We'll go for broke. We'll move the whole operation to Washington and stay there till we get a hearing."

He looked over at me.

"Well, what do you think?"

"It's an entirely new direction for us," I said. "But it's certainly needed. I'm ready to try it if you are."

At the time I made my own commitment I was under the spell of that classroom, filled with bright-eyed black children who had probably never eaten a nourishing meal; but I hadn't really thought about the details. Martin had them worked out in his mind, and he was generally an excellent strategist; so I assumed he would have a fully developed plan by the time he talked to our staff and executive board and that, as usual, they would support him. But this time he ran into real opposition.

Back at Ebenezer Baptist Church, sitting in his study, we tried to sell the staff on the plan and ran into formidable opposition. The most vocal adversaries of the idea were James Bevel and Jesse Jackson, who were surprisingly vehement in their objections.

"How do we bail out?" they asked.

"What do you mean?" Martin replied.

"If we don't succeed, if we don't get any concrete results, then how do we bail out of the situation?"

Martin's eyes flashed. "I don't care about bailing out," he said. "I just want these people to be *seen* by the American public. They're invisible now. If the public could just see them, then something would be done."

"We don't like it," they said. "If we don't make any progress then we'll lose face."

Martin listened with barely constrained anger. He had seen a vision in Marks, Mississippi, that would haunt him for the rest of his short life and these two were talking about "bailing out" and "saving face." He argued with them at great length, trying to make them see the logic of his plan, trying to convince them that we had to take chances if we were going to accomplish great things; but they were unremitting in their opposition—two young pragmatists who were lecturing the older and more experienced idealist. Finally, Martin broke off the debate and left the meeting.

Over the months he would come back to the Poor People's Campaign time and time again, hoping to make Jim and Jesse see the basic necessity of this new direction for our movement, trying to convince them with logic and example when in reality his own commitment to those pathetic children was of the heart rather than of the head, a commitment they clearly did not share. Theirs was the carefully reasoned argument, based on practical considerations rather than on passionate zeal. So nobody changed anybody's mind.

But on the strength of Martin's vision of what the Poor People's Campaign could accomplish, we went ahead with plans. We talked to our advisers in New York, including Bayard Rustin and Stanley Levison. We traveled around the South recruiting people to make the journey. We explored various strategies for dramatizing the plight of the poor, including the idea of bringing some of the actual shacks to Washington on flatbed trucks, just so people could see the kind of housing in which the poor of Mississippi lived.

Then, in March 1968, the garbage worker's strike in Memphis began to occupy some of our attention. This strike came at a time when Martin was already concerned with the economic plight of poor people, so it was natural that he would be sympathetic to what was going on in Memphis. After a discriminatory action that deprived black sewer workers of the opportunity to remain at work and draw pay, Local 1733 of the AFSCME, a union of primarily black membership, called a strike, demanding fair treatment; but Mayor Henry Loeb of Memphis refused to recognize the union's right to bargain with the city, a decision regarded as racist by the black community.

Martin made one speech there late in March and was impressed by the size of the crowd and the fervor of their response, so he agreed to come back and lead a nonviolent march in support of the embattled sanitation workers. But when the time arrived we were in Newark, meeting with a number of potential supporters of the Poor People's Campaign, and Martin asked me, as he had done many times before, to stand in for him.

"You go to Memphis and make the speech. I'll come just one day later, in time to lead the march."

"What do you want me to say to them?" I asked.

"Just give your usual inspiring and rousing talk," he said.

So I went and gave a talk at the Mason Temple, headquarters church of the Church of God in Christ. The speech turned out to be one of my best efforts, an emotional plea for unity and courage that people were kind enough to say was inspiring and arousing. Afterward they took me to the Peabody Hotel, which was a little more expensive than others, if only because of the famous trained ducks that marched through the lobby in military precision. Because the Peabody had a contract with the union I got to stay there. (I believe it was the first Deep South white hotel I ever stayed in. They had just integrated under union pressure, and I was one of the first blacks to register there.)

The next day I went with the Reverend Solomon Jones to pick up Martin and Bernard Lee. Solomon always acted as our driver when we were in Memphis, and we always rode in a Cadillac lent by the funeral home that would eventually prepare Martin's body for burial. Martin and Bernard landed around 11:00 A.M., although the march had been scheduled to begin at 10:00, so we drove as fast as prudence would permit to the Clayborn Temple AME Church, where huge crowds were waiting. We had planned to go inside and "work-shop" the people in the theory and techniques of nonviolence; but as soon as our car pulled up, a bunch of young men crowded around, peering in, pressing their noses against the glass, speaking courteously to us but refusing to step back so we could get out.

"It's my fault," I told Martin. "My speech last night was too inspiring and arousing."

He laughed, and for a few minutes it seemed like a big joke; but after an hour the joke had worn a little thin.

Finally Bernard grew impatient.

"I know who those fellows are. They're the Invaders. They're a bunch of troublemakers who are trying to horn in on the march."

At that moment the Reverend James Lawson, one of our national board members who lived in Memphis, pushed his way through the crowd and stuck his head through the window.

"The only way we'll get away from them is to get out and start the march."

So we left the automobile and began to walk. There were thousands of people pressing all around, and we could hear the young men yelling greetings designed to distract us from what they were doing.

"Dr. King!"

"Reverend Abernathy!"

"We're glad you came to Memphis!"

"You're the hope of America!"

Then, after a few blocks, we heard what sounded like gunshots, though we later learned it was the smashing of glass windows. The Invaders had used the cover of our march to commit acts of violence. Suddenly what had started out as a peaceful demonstration was turning into a riot. Once again the younger members of the movement had betrayed our principles and used us as a stalking horse behind which to lash out at the white community.

The sound of breaking glass grew louder. There were shouts and screams. We heard whistles blow and then, in the distance, the whine of sirens. Looking behind, we could see people scattering in all directions.

Martin turned to Jim Lawson, the official leader of the march, who was just ahead of us.

"Jim," he yelled. "There's violence breaking out, and I can't lead a violent march. Call it off!"

Lawson hesitated for a moment, then obeyed.

"The march is off!" he shouted. "The march is off! Everybody go home! The march is off!"

"Let's get out of here!" Martin shouted, but that was easier said than done.

We looked ahead and saw a chain of state troopers beginning to form. For an instant it looked like we would all be crowded in together, like fish in a closing net. Then at the corner we saw a car, a Pontiac driven by a black woman, and suddenly a policeman stepped in behind her, indicating that her car would be the last allowed across the intersection.

"Let's get in that car ahead," Bernard said. "They're letting her drive on."

The three of us pushed our way up to the car and begged to be allowed inside. The woman took one look, recognized us, and motioned for us to get in. Bernard opened the front door on the driver's side, and she immediately slid over and let him behind the wheel. Just then the state troopers ahead began to lower their gas masks. They stepped aside to let us zoom across the intersection, and as we looked out the rear window we saw the canisters flying through the air.

In complete silence we drove till we reached the Mississippi River, where we saw two motorcycle policemen. Bernard rolled down the window, signaled for them to stop, and shouted.

"Will you please help us get Dr. King out of here."

"Where are you trying to go?" one of the policemen asked.

"The Peabody."

"Forget it," said the policeman. "There's pandemonium at the Peabody."

"What about the Lorraine Motel?" I called out.

"Pandemonium there," said the policeman. "As a matter of fact, we've declared a curfew. We're going to clear the streets."

He thought for a moment.

"I have an idea," he said. "Follow us."

The two of them escorted us down Riverside Drive, sirens wailing; finally we pulled into the Riverfront Holiday Inn. They motioned for us to wait in the car, went inside, and then emerged with a key. So we didn't even have to check in. They took us straight to our room and let us in. We thanked the woman for the use of her car, waved goodbye to the officers and settled down in our accommodations—a two-bedroom suite with a living area in between. Bernard and I took the room with two beds, and Martin took the one with the single bed.

He sat down immediately and turned on the television, and it was only then that I realized how upset he was. The picture widened from a pinpoint of light to an image of street violence. We were getting live coverage of the riot. Martin shook his head in disbelief and wrung his hands.

"This is terrible," he said. "Now we'll never get anybody to believe in nonviolence."

"It's not our fault, Martin," I told him. "Those young men. . . ."

"It doesn't matter who did it," he shouted. "We'll get the blame."

And that was just the beginning of what proved to be a long afternoon and night. The television reported that it was indeed the Invaders who had been responsible for the riot. One of their group had been killed that morning. They were a militant organization and had been marching with the group led by Dr. King. The commentators made that point more than once. "Never have I led a march where the demonstrators committed acts of violence," Martin said to nobody in particular.

"It wasn't our fault," I repeated.

"We should have work-shopped the people," he said.

"But they wouldn't let us out of the car," I said. "Maybe they did that on purpose."

But he still wanted to be reassured that we would not be blamed nationwide, so he got on the telephone and began to call everyone he knew around the country. He wanted consolation and reassurance. He was particularly anxious about what the incident would mean to the success of the Poor People's Campaign. He wondered if the press would turn against the project.

Most of the people he called were supportive, but apparently some were less convincing in their reassurances than others; so he brooded for hours after the last call.

"Maybe we'll just have to let violence have its chance," he said over and over again. "Maybe we'll have to let violence run its course. Maybe the people will listen to the voice of violence. They certainly won't listen to us."

But I disagreed.

"You know better than that. Violence will never get us anywhere. We can't let these people take over. They'll ruin everything we've built up."

I pleaded with him to stop worrying and get some rest, but he said he wasn't ready to go to bed yet, and kept on making calls. Finally about 4:00 A.M. he fell asleep, and I tiptoed out, exhausted.

It seemed as if I had just fallen asleep when I heard a bell ringing. When I realized that our suite probably had a doorbell, I staggered out of bed and stumbled into the living room as the bell rang again. When I opened the door I saw three young men standing there.

"We'd like to speak to Dr. King," one of them said.

"What time is it?" I asked groggily, thinking it couldn't be more than six or seven.

One of them looked at his watch.

"It's a little after ten," he said.

"Why do you want to see Dr. King?" I asked.

"We want to apologize for yesterday," he said.

"Who are you?"

"We're the Invaders."

"He didn't get to sleep until early this morning," I said. "You wait here. I'll see if he's up."

I went back and woke Martin. When I told him who was here he blinked his eyes.

"I can't see anybody," he said. "I've got to shave. I'm due at a news conference right now."

"These young men want to make a confession to you," I said. "I think you ought to listen to them. It won't take too long."

He hesitated for a moment, then sighed.

"If there's any apology," he said, "they can apologize to you."

I couldn't tell whether or not he was in any better spirits, but I thought an apology might have helped—assuming they were really there to apologize. When I confronted them at the door again I told them, "He can't come out. If you have anything to say, tell me and I'll pass it along. But be sure and make it brief. We're supposed to meet with the press this morning, and we're already late."

They assured me they wanted just a minute and then they'd be gone. As a final precaution, I looked them over carefully. They were well dressed, well groomed; and I didn't see any signs of weapons, so I ushered them in. They told me they had been wrong in instituting the violence, that one of their friends had been killed during the skirmishes, that they were deeply sorry.

I listened, nodded, and then tried to explain to them the reasons why nonviolence was the only way to freedom for black people. They said they understood and assured me that they were with us 100 percent. At the time I believed them.

After they left, we dressed and dashed downstairs. We had had very little time to talk, and I wasn't sure whether or not Martin would be able to maintain his composure in the face of a strong interrogation by hostile newsmen.

Bernard Lee had planned to introduce him to the room full of reporters, but Martin stepped forward and took over immediately.

I held my breath.

"Ladies and gentlemen," he said, "what I'm going to tell you is on the record, off the record, any way you want it."

He went on to tell them precisely what had happened the previous day. He was precise. He was detailed. He was witty.

After he had finished, he answered all the questions that were thrown at him in a firm, upbeat manner. It was perhaps his finest performance with the press.

After he had thanked them, he turned to me and I threw my arms around him.

"Martin," I said, "you were just great."

He smiled.

"Were you really pleased, Ralph?" he said.

"Completely pleased."

"If you were pleased," he said, "then you can do something to please me."

"What's that?" I asked.

"Get me out of Memphis!"

"You got it," I said and went to a pay phone immediately to make the reservations.

We arrived in Atlanta around five o'clock that afternoon. My old '55 Ford was waiting at the airport, and on the way back, as we talked, I realized he had still not shaken the depression he was feeling the previous night.

"Martin," I said, "let's do something different tonight, something to take our minds off all this turmoil."

"Like what?" he said.

"How about going to a movie?"

He thought for a moment then shook his head.

"I believe I'd release more tension if I worked out. Why don't we go down to the YMCA Health Club right now."

"I've got to go home," I said. "You know, we've been on the road so long I haven't seen my family in days and days. I want to go home so Juanita can see that I'm really alive."

"You're right," he said. "Drop me off at home, and I'll get Cody to drive me to the Y."

We were standing in the parking lot of Ebenezer Baptist Church and already the sun had set behind the hills west of Atlanta. The sky was a deep rose color and, though it wasn't yet six o'clock, already darkness was settling over the city. Winter wasn't far away. It had been a bad day and we were both ready to relax.

"See you in an hour," I heard him call out as he led me out of the parking lot. I followed him for a block, then turned in one direction while he turned in the other.

About an hour later he called from the YMCA.

"Ralph," said Martin, "tonight Corrie and I are going by to pick up some fish. Why don't we get enough for you and Juanita. We'll bring it on by your house and the women can cook it up in your kitchen."

"That sounds fine to me," I said. "Give us an hour to feed the children and settle them down."

When I got home Juanita was already feeding the children, and she seemed genuinely pleased to hear that the Kings would be coming over.

"But I've already cooked up something special—my annual casserole. Why don't you call and tell them to skip the fish?"

This casserole, which she still makes once a year, contained all the leftovers of the pig—pig's feet, pig's ears, pig's tails. I don't know of anyone else who makes it and, though it may not sound like the most appetizing dish in the world, it is uniquely delicious, one of the finest delicacies I've ever eaten.

"We'll have the casserole and the fish," I said, knowing that Martin would love the casserole and that we could both eat a lot of fish.

Sure enough, the Kings brought enough fish to feed three families, but as soon as Martin saw what Juanita had fixed, he grabbed the bowl and took it into the living room.

"We'll eat some of this while the two of you fry fish," he called, and we both dug in.

He didn't talk about the movement that night. Instead he talked about the times before the Montgomery bus boycott when we were all younger and hadn't taken on the burdens of the black people. He remembered people long forgotten, did some of his imitations, and told a few stories. Juanita and Corrie brought in a platter of fish that scraped the ceiling, and we shared what was left of the casserole. By the time we finished, we were absolutely stuffed—all of us. We were also thoroughly exhausted—Martin and I because we had had a trying day, Coretta because she was just recuperating from an operation, Juanita because she had been out all day and had come home to cook and serve two meals.

Martin and I made our way into the family room and collapsed into two matching love seats, our heads propped on one arm, our legs hanging over the other.

I remember him saying, "Ralph, I wish you'd had enough money to buy a whole sofa instead of just a half sofa."

Juanita overheard him and brought in a pillow, which she installed under his head.

I laughed and then settled more deeply into the cushion. We talked for a few minutes, but the silences grew longer, and finally we both fell asleep. I figured we would be awakened when Juanita and Coretta finished in the kitchen, but things didn't quite go that way. Coretta, out of the hospital only a week or two, had gone back into our bedroom to lie down, and Juanita had put her head on the kitchen counter, just for a moment. We all were awakened around eight the next morning when Ralph III came into the kitchen, ready for breakfast.

It was the last evening our two families spent together.

I hurried into the bathroom to shave.

"Martin," I called to him. "I'm going to make the staff meeting [at Ebenezer Baptist Church that morning]. Why don't you take your time and come in late?"

"I think I'll do that," he said. "I need to stop by the house first."

Both of us were slow starters in the morning. Together we could tie up a mirror for the better part of an hour. So even though I got a head start on Martin, I was still late for the meeting. As executive vice president, Andy Young had begun without us, but when I arrived he yielded the chair.

The chief item on the agenda again was the Poor People's Campaign. While Jesse Jackson, James Bevel, and Andy were offering a whole list of objections to the project, I saw Martin slip in and sit down in an old wooden school desk with an arm on it. After whoever was talking had finished, we changed places so that he could preside. He listened for a while, then began to get restless. Occasionally, he would try to interject some comment, but mostly he just sat back and listened to the bickering and sniping.

Jesse had taken the floor and was enumerating all the reasons why Martin's Poor People's Campaign would never work, why we should try something entirely different. Once again that morning he went on at great length and I could tell that Martin was getting more and more restless. Finally, without saying anything in response to Jesse, he got up, walked over to the chair where I was sitting, and said, "Ralph, give me my car keys."

I was puzzled.

"I don't have your car keys, Martin."

He smiled. "Look in your pocket."

I felt in my pockets and fished out an extra set of keys. I frowned, still bewildered, and handed them over to him. I suppose he had left them on the desk, and I had sat down there, played with them while listening to the debate, and then stuck them in my pocket. Obviously he had seen me.

"I'm getting out of here," he said, then turned and left the room.

Forgetting the meeting, I followed him into the hallway and down the stairs.

"What's wrong, Martin?" I asked.

He stopped on the landing. He shrugged his shoulders.

"Nothing, really," he said. "I'll be all right. Wasn't I all right Friday?"

"You were fine," I said, still worried. "But where are you going now?"

"I have to take Yoki to ballet."

I couldn't shake off a deep sense of foreboding. He seemed preoccupied and depressed.

"Will you let me know where you'll be?"

Before he could answer I looked up and saw that Jesse Jackson had come to the staircase and was staring down at us.

"Doc," he called out.

Martin whirled and glared at him.

"Jesse," he barked, "it may be necessary for you to carve your own individual niche in society. But don't you bother me."

Such an outburst was uncharacteristic of Martin and Jesse was stunned. His mouth fell open and for one of the few times in his life he was speechless. Martin stared at him for a moment, then turned and continued. When we reached the parking lot, Martin climbed into his car. I suppressed an impulse to say something more to him; instead I returned to chair the meeting. I thought it was time to let them know that Martin needed support at this particular time, that he was undergoing a period of severe strain.

"There are times when the staff ought to come together," I began. "Especially when the leader is confused. Now we have to go back to Memphis, and then we *are* going to Washington to make this Poor People's Campaign a successful operation. The only questions we have to settle are matters of logistics—who will go where and do what. Now that's what we're going to talk about for the rest of this meeting."

Martin had been invited to preach at Washington Cathedral on Sunday, so we had to alter some earlier plans. We decided that Hosea Williams, James Bevel, and Andy Young would go to Memphis on Sunday. They would work-shop the people in preparation for a march. Jesse and the others would come in Monday. On Tuesday, Martin, Bernard Lee, and I would arrive in Memphis.

Once the plans were finally established everyone was eager to tell Martin that we had finally come to an agreement.

"The Holy Spirit has come," they announced. "We want him to know it."

Hosea Williams told me to go find him, but by the time I did, the Holy Spirit had come and gone and everybody had fallen asleep. When I finally got him on the phone, he was still in a strange mood.

"Ralph," he told me, "I'm going away."

"You're not going off alone?" I asked.

"Well," he said, "I hope Coretta will come along."

"Where are you going?"

"I have a church member who has a farm in South Georgia."

It sounded like an evasion, but I let it pass. (Later I would ask numerous members of Ebenezer Baptist Church, but no one owned such a farm or knew anyone in the congregation who did. The story is still one of the mysteries surrounding his death.)

I told him the staff had asked me to call.

"They want you to come back so they can tell you how they feel and ask you some questions."

He was silent for a long time, then sighed and said he would come. But it took him several hours to get there. We sat and waited on the third floor of Ebenezer Baptist Church, periodically looking at our watches and wondering out loud about the delay. After two hours we became somewhat alarmed, though we knew that Martin was chronically late, even to important press conferences. Finally, as the afternoon wore on, some of us stretched out and went to sleep.

Later we found out where he'd been. "My son never had time to talk to me very much," Daddy King said, "but on that last Saturday he came by my study and we talked for about three hours."

So he was right downstairs all the time, in his father's study. Finally, when their talk was ended, Martin came upstairs and the meeting reconvened. Martin and I sat in silence while Jesse and Hosea did most of the talking. They told him they wanted to go to Washington by way of Memphis.

"We want to prove to the people there that we can have a nonviolent march," they said. "You go on to Washington and preach at the cathedral."

They even told him what sermon they wanted him to preach, but he told them he would preach on an entirely different topic, and they seemed reasonably content. After the meeting had broken up I noticed Jesse with a hangdog look on his face, waiting near the door. I remembered that he needed a ride to the airport, and I knew that he was still burning from the rebuke Martin had given him.

"Please take care of Jesse," Martin told me. "Drive him to the airport."

Clearly he wasn't ready to talk to Jesse. He was still in a strange mood, so I agreed.

All day Monday I waited in Atlanta for Martin to call, from Washington, but I didn't hear from him until Tuesday in the middle of the afternoon.

"Hello, David," he said casually. "How are you doing?"

"Where are you?" I asked. "Where have you been?"

"Around," he said. "Don't worry about it. We can go tomorrow."

"But we're due today," I reminded him.

"Please, let's not go till tomorrow."

I heard the plaintive quality in his voice and, though I knew the others would be disappointed and even angry, I avoided acting as the voice of his conscience.

"OK," I said, "we'll go tomorrow."

So we waited till Wednesday. I drove over to his house on Sunset Avenue a little early, knowing he wouldn't be ready, hoping I could hurry him along so we wouldn't have to run for the plane. When I got there he was still back in his bedroom, just beginning to pack. Mostly what he was stuffing in his briefcase was books. On trips he would always end the day with his nose buried in some old theological tract. Coretta came in and offered to make me breakfast; but I told her we didn't have time so we both helped Martin pack. Even so, we still had to break the speed limit to make the plane, pushing my 1955 Ford to its capacity, and when we got there we saw that Bernard Lee and Dorothy Cotton were about to panic, but all four of us were in our seats when they closed the door and taxied onto the runway. It was an Eastern Airlines flight, scheduled for a short flight to Memphis, but we sat there on the runway for more than an hour. Everyone was looking at his watch and craning his head to look down the aisle, but there was no word from the cabin.

Finally, the pilot broke the silence. "Ladies and gentlemen," he said, "we have a celebrity on the plane and we had a bomb threat. Though we guarded the aircraft all night, we were still required to check every piece of luggage. That's why we've been delayed. Now we're cleared for takeoff."

Martin gave a dry laugh. "Well, it looks like they won't kill me this flight, not after telling all that."

There it was again, this sense of foreboding. I tried to shrug it off. "Nobody's going to kill you, Martin."

He smiled thinly and stared out the window as we started to roll down the runway.

Solomon Jones was there to pick us up and on the way to the Lorraine Motel, Martin loosened up a little bit. After checking in and unpacking, we were driven over to James Lawson's church for a meeting with some of our supporters. When we got there, however, there was bad news. A judge had issued an injunction and we would not be allowed to march on Thursday. Martin fell silent again. Nothing was going right in this town.

Nonetheless, we held a meeting with the clergymen present, and when we got back to the motel, federal marshals were waiting with an official copy of the injunction, which they presented to Martin. Later in the motel room Martin expressed his dissatisfaction with the way things had been handled down at the courthouse.

"Didn't Andy explain what we had in mind?" Martin asked as he stretched out on the bed.

Solomon Jones stood in the doorway and stared down at his feet.

"Andy didn't go to the hearing," he said.

Martin was furious. Some things couldn't be helped, but this omission was inexcusable. Andy was made executive vice president of the SCLC just so he could speak for the organization on such occasions. He was second in command. He had failed to come through again. Martin was highly vocal in his expression of dissatisfaction.

Our flight had landed just ahead of bad weather, and outside the motel we could hear the wind whipping against the glass window and see flashes of lightning. By 4:30 it was dark outside and rain was beating down on the roof. In the distance we heard a siren.

Later, after eating, we held a meeting in our motel suite, but nothing much was decided. Then someone reminded Martin that he was scheduled to speak that night.

I could see his face cloud up. It was storming again, as bad a wind and rain as we'd seen in months, and it was clear that few people would show up at the speech. Martin never liked to address small crowds, and already the phone calls had begun to come in from friends and advisers, offering help in circumventing the injunction.

Martin looked at me.

"Ralph, I want you to go and speak for me tonight."

I hesitated, as I knew that the people who showed up, however few, would be deeply disappointed to hear a substitute.

"Why don't you let Jesse go?" I suggested. "He loves to speak."

Martin brushed the suggestion aside.

"Nobody else can speak for me. I want you to go."

"Can I take Jesse?"

"Yes," he said, "but you do the speaking."

That night the elements conspired to keep the crowd small. The rain poured steadily most of the evening, and every so often the drizzle would turn to sudden sheets of water that washed across the windshield of the car and rendered the frantic wipers useless. Lightning streaked, followed almost immediately by loud explosions of thunder. At some point during the night a tornado tore across town and ripped the roof off a house. Later people would say nature was trying to tell us something.

With Solomon driving, we made our way slowly across town to the headquarters church of the Church of God in Christ, where I was certain we would find a couple of dozen people huddled in the doorway like half-drowned chickens. To my surprise, when I entered the sanctuary I saw about five hundred people—a small crowd compared to what Martin had drawn the previous week, but more than I had expected to find.

As I stepped in the door, a crowd of TV cameramen converged on me, while flashbulbs exploded. I counted seven or eight television cameras already set in place. The networks were there, as well as the Memphis channels. That meant the audience would be national, so the event was much more important than a poorly attended local rally.

Besides, the people who had driven through rainy, wind-swept streets to get here had done so because they expected to see Martin Luther King, Jr., not Ralph D. Abernathy. I knew that better than anybody, and I was overwhelmed by the fact as I walked down the aisle and onto the stage. Nobody shouted or applauded. Clearly they were all waiting for the evening's attraction.

I stood there for a second, then made up my mind.

Turning to a technician I asked if there was a telephone in the building.

"What do you want with a telephone?" Jesse asked.

"I'm going to call Martin," I told him.

"Don't call him," Jesse said. "If you don't want to speak then I'll speak."

Instead of explaining, I looked questioningly at the technician, who had his mouth open, ready to answer.

"There's a telephone in the vestibule of the church," he said. "You can either go out the door and up the outside stairway to the bishop's office or you can go back up the aisle and take the front stairs. That way you'll keep out of the rain."

I decided to stay dry, so I walked back between the puzzled rows of spectators and found my way to the vestibule, and after overcoming the shock of discovering the tomb of Bishop Mason, for whom the church was named, I called the Lorraine Motel and asked to speak to Martin.

He seemed to be in a slightly better mood when he took the receiver.

"Martin," I said, "all the television networks are lined up, waiting for you. This speech will be broadcast nationwide. You need to deliver it. Besides, the people who are here want you, not me."

He responded so readily that I was surprised.

"OK, I'll come."

I tried to assess the tone of his voice. I thought he might be kidding me.

"Martin," I said. "Don't you fool me now. You are coming, aren't you?"

"David," he said, "did I ever tell you I'd do something and then not come through?"

I thought he was probably serious.

"When will you be here?" I asked. He hadn't been too punctual in the past few days.

"As soon as the limousine can get me there," he said.

Still a little uneasy, I went back and joined Jesse onstage.

"Is Doc coming?" he asked.

I nodded and I could tell he was a little disappointed. The man who was going to preside over the meeting came up to us and we chatted for a while. Then I heard a sudden cheer followed by applause and turned to see Martin coming down the aisle. They were standing now and, though there were only five hundred of them, they sounded like several thousand. I glanced over and saw the red lights glowing on the television cameras. Thanks to me, they would get their footage after all.

Martin came up on the stage, acknowledged the crowd, and then came over to sit down beside me. The presiding officer stood, then turned to us.

"Which one of you wants to go first?"

Martin had always spoken first before, providing the inspiration. Then I had followed with a more practical discussion of tactics and logistics. But tonight I was inexplicably moved to alter that sequence. "Let me go first," I said.

Martin raised an eyebrow, but nodded. He figured I must have had a reason. But in fact, I had no reason, just an impulse. I wanted to talk about him, and for the first time at such an occasion I did.

"Brothers and sisters," I said, "ladies and gentlemen. Too often we take our leaders for granted. We think we know them, but they are really strangers to us. So tonight I would like to take a little time to introduce you to our leader, Dr. Martin Luther King, Jr."

With that lead-in I began at the beginning—with his birth, his early schooling and then moved on to college, the beginnings of the civil rights movement, and finally to the current confrontation in Memphis. In doing so I was trying to sum up the greatness of the man in a way I had never done before. I don't think he quite understood my motives, and I'm not sure even now I understand fully myself. But when I finally gave him to the audience they went wild.

He turned with a grin on his face and said, "You took a terribly long time to introduce me." He turned quickly to the crowd and said, "I want everybody to know that my dearest friend in the world is Ralph Abernathy." Then he addressed the audience for more than an hour and a half. He was at the height of his powers. I never saw him better.

Finally, after he had moved from specific actions to general principles and back again, he went into that strangely prophetic finale that still haunts the memory of America:

> Well, I don't know what will happen now. We've got some difficult days ahead. But it really doesn't matter with me now, because I've been to the mountaintop. And I don't mind. Like anybody, I would like to live a long life. Longevity has its place. But I'm not concerned about that now. I just want to do God's will. And he's allowed me to go up to the mountain, and I've looked over, and I've seen the promised land. I may not get there with you. But I want you to know tonight that we as a people will get to the promised land. And so I'm happy tonight. I'm not worried about anything. I'm not fearing any man. Mine eyes have seen the glory of the coming of the Lord.

I had heard him hit high notes before, but never any higher. The crowd was on its feet, shouting and applauding— even some of the television crew. It was a rare moment in the history of American oratory, something to file along with Washington's Farewell Address and the Gettysburg Address. But it was somehow different than those speeches because it was an eloquence that grew out of the black experience, with its similarities to the biblical story of captivity and hard-won freedom. Everyone was emotionally drained by what he had said, including Martin himself, whose eyes were filled with tears.

It took us a long time to tear ourselves away, but we had other plans. One version of what happened later that night has it that we went to a late dinner with Ben Hooks at his house. That is not what happened at all. The real story is a little more complicated and a little less satisfying.

A "friend" of Martin's invited us to have steaks at her house, three of us—Martin, Bernard Lee, and me. When we got there, we found three ladies waiting. Martin's friend had provided dinner partners for Bernard and me, and we had a very heavy meal along with some light conversation.

I was exhausted at that stage of the evening; and since I was a happily married man, I was not particularly interested in developing a closer relationship with my companion. Nor was Bernard Lee, as best I recall. I remember trying to keep up my part of the conversation during the meal and then, when the women went back into the kitchen, beating Bernard to an easy chair with an ottoman and falling fast asleep. When I awoke, I saw an empty living room, except for Bernard stretched out on the sofa. Shortly thereafter, Martin and his friend came out of the bedroom. The other women had long since left. It was after 1:00 A.M.

We drove back through the rain, which hadn't slackened all evening, Solomon Jones leaning forward, occasionally wiping off the windshield, which was clouding up on the inside. We didn't talk and by the time we drove back into the motel parking lot, I had long since fallen asleep again, a gift I have always had that has enabled me to keep going for days at a time, without losing much needed energy. Martin, on the other hand, never took catnaps and never ran out of gas.

When we arrived at the motel, the level of his energy would again be tested. A light was on in two adjacent downstairs rooms; and as we drove up Martin recognized the car parked in front with a Kentucky license plate. His brother A. D. had arrived from Louisville.

"Let's go and see if A. D. is up," Martin said.

I said I would go with him, so Bernard went off to bed. When we got to A. D.'s motel room, we found that he was not up. A. D. had had a couple of drinks, and there was a white woman with him.

But there was a black woman in the room as well, a member

of the Kentucky legislature; and she had clearly come to see Martin. They had known each other before. Their relationship was a close one. Knowing that someone would be with Martin to watch out for him, I spoke to the women, then excused myself, and went off to bed.

When I got back to the motel room, I left the door unlocked so that Martin could get in if he needed to, though I didn't necessarily expect him. By then it was almost 3:00 A.M. and I was asleep before my head had sunk into the pillow.

Sometime between 3:00 A.M. and dawn, I believe another young woman Martin knew well must have slipped into the room, looking for him but had not found him.

Between 7:00 and 8:00 A.M. Martin came upstairs. Maybe because he knew this young woman had been expecting to see him the previous evening, he stopped by her room. I don't know what he told her—maybe that he had gone to bed early (which was technically true). Whatever he said, she knew better and told him so. Obviously, she had a few other things to say as well, because when he came back into our room he was visibly upset. He lay down on his bed, curled up like a small child, and looked over at me.

"She's mad at me," he said. "She came in this morning and found my bed empty."

I opened one eye and quickly closed it.

"Ralph, do something. I need you to help me. Call her and see if you can straighten things out."

I tried to go back to sleep but he begged me, so I sat up, cleared my head, and called her. She answered on the first ring and she sounded wide awake. I tried to ask her how she was, but she let loose a storm of abuse.

"Don't you call me, trying to fix things. It's partly your fault anyway. Why don't you tell him not to behave the way he does instead of trying to cover for him."

Then she called me a couple of names and hung up.

"What did she say?" Martin asked.

I told him and he shook his head.

"She's really mad this time."

I agreed that she was and got dressed.

While we were still talking about her, she walked past our window, carrying her suitcases. She glanced in and her eyes met Martin's, then she turned away and moved on.

Martin called her name. Then, turning to me he said, "Go stop her, Ralph. Don't let her leave."

I moved toward the door, but she walked back into view, slowly, hesitantly, her face half hostile, half forgiving. She really loved him, and I had an idea that if he said the right words, she would take her bags back to the room and that would be the end of the quarrel.

But Martin didn't say the right words. Instead, he tried to disarm her by being indignant himself.

"Why did you hang up on Ralph like that."

"Because Ralph is a poor counselor. Instead of telling you what you really are, he tells you what you want to hear. Then, when you get caught, he takes up for you."

"What are you talking about?" he said.

"I'm talking about Ralph!" she snapped.

Suddenly Martin lost his temper. "Don't you say a goddamn thing about Ralph," he shouted and knocked her across the bed. It was more of a shove than a real blow, but for a short man, Martin had a prodigious strength that always surprised me.

She leapt up to fight back, and for a moment they were engaged in a full-blown fight, with Martin clearly winning. Then it was all over. They glared at one another, eyes flashing, breathing heavily. Then she rushed past him and out the door.

He watched dumbly for a second, then shouted, "Don't go! Don't go!"

But she was gone, on her way to the airport, headed home. The next thing she knew for certain about Martin Luther King was that he had been shot and killed. It must have been doubly bitter for her, remembering those last few hours, knowing that they had parted in anger.

Martin and I ate lunch together in the Lorraine Motel, and I remember that the waitress never got the order right. The specialty of the day was catfish, and for both of us it was a treat.

"We'll have two orders," Martin said, "and two glasses of iced tea."

In a minute she came back. "You want one order of catfish or two?" she asked.

"Two orders," Martin said, and held up two fingers.

We discussed the injunction for a while, agreeing that we couldn't let it stop us now, that we had to reaffirm the integrity of the nonviolent move in the face of what had happened the previous week. The staff would be in agreement. We would have the march, injunction or no injunction. However, we would try to persuade the judge to change his mind, something Andy had not taken care of on Wednesday.

Both of us were hungry, and we kept cutting our eyes over to the kitchen door, expecting the waitress with our catfish at any moment. Finally, she came through the door with a tray of food. On it she had one platter piled high with fish, and two glasses of iced tea. She had brought a double order instead of two orders.

As she approached, I opened my mouth to say something, but Martin raised his hand.

"Oh, Ralph. Don't bother her anymore. She probably doesn't get paid minimum wage, and you know what the tips must be like here. We'll just eat from the same plate."

And that's exactly what we did. It was the last meal we ate together.

After lunch we held a staff meeting and talked over the upcoming events. We still had some concern over whether or not the Invaders would attempt to disrupt the march and turn it into a violent upheaval. Some of the younger staff members were nervous about this new consideration. Martin was impatient with them. There was no more reason to be frightened now than in the past, he said.

"I'd rather be dead than afraid," he said contemptuously, as much to himself as to the rest of us.

It was a choice of words we would all remember just hours later.

After the meeting we worried about whether or not Andy had made any headway with the judge. We had expected to hear from him by early afternoon, and somehow we believed that the longer the delay, the less likely the decision would be favorable. Finally, Martin decided to go down to the first floor and spend some time with A. D.

When he came back he told me they had called their mother in Atlanta and talked to her for about an hour.

"She was happy that we were here together," he said.

That night we were supposed to have dinner over at the Reverend Billy Kyle's, and Martin lay back on the bed and started speculating about what Mrs. Kyle might be serving. After running through a couple of possible menus, he turned to me and said, "Ralph, call her up and ask her what she's having."

"You're not kidding, are you?"

"No," he said. "Call her."

I shrugged my shoulders and made the call.

"Let's see now," she said. "Roast beef, asparagus, cauliflower."

I repeated the menu to Martin.

"And candied yams, pig's feet, and chitlins."

Martin said that he could hardly wait and got up to shave.

His skin was so tender that he couldn't use a razor; instead he used a depilatory called "Magic Shave." Where he first came up with it, I don't know. Few people used it and I well understood why. In the first place, it was a paste he had to make from a fine, white powder. Then, too, it was the worst smelling stuff anyone ever rubbed on his face. After he plastered it on, he had to wait until it ate through the hair, after which he would scrape it off with a knife. Under similar circumstances most men would have grown a beard, but Martin was meticulous about this particular procedure, and it was one reason he was always late.

As he prepared his face I brought up something that had been on my mind.

"Martin," I said, "I won't be able to go to Washington on the days we agreed."

"You're going to have to," he said.

"I can't," I told him.

The minute I said it, I remembered another meeting many years ago in Montgomery.

We'd held a meeting of the Montgomery Improvement Association that afternoon and I was sitting at home after supper when the phone rang. It was Coretta.

"What happened at the meeting?" she asked. "Martin came home, took a tranquilizer, and went to bed."

I thought for a moment.

"There's only one thing I can think of. We had a disagreement. He wanted one thing. I wanted another. The board voted with me."

"Well, I guess that's it," she said.

I rushed over that evening to straighten things out. "What's wrong, Martin?" I asked.

"You can have anything you want," he replied, "but please don't disagree with me in public."

"I won't do it again," I said, and I didn't.

That afternoon in Memphis was different, of course, but something about the way he spoke reminded me of that day long ago when I had hurt his feelings. I explained again why I couldn't go to Washington, though he'd already heard my reasons.

"It's Revival Week. I have to get an evangelist to conduct the revival because Reverend Otis Moss can't come."

He knew it. Earlier in the week he'd tried himself to find someone for me. Now, in the motel, I began to realize how much my presence in Washington meant to him.

"Ralph, I would never think of going to Washington without you," he said. "West Hunter is the best church in the world. They'll do anything for you. You go tell them you're going to have a different kind of revival, one in which we are going to revive the soul of this nation. Will you do it?"

I sighed and nodded.

"Yes, I'll do it."

Satisfied, he began slapping his face with cologne. When he had finished, he said, "You ready to go?"

"Let me put my cologne on," I told him.

He started toward the door. "OK," he said. "I'll wait on the balcony."

As I was putting cologne on my face, I heard him talking to Jesse, who was down below in the courtyard. I was pleased to hear the conversation and the warmth in Martin's voice. Relations between them had been cool for the past few days, ever since the exchange after the Saturday meeting. Now Martin was clearly going out of his way to assure Jesse that everything was all right.

"Jesse," he called out, "I want you to go to dinner with us tonight."

Then I heard Billy Kyle's voice, coming from the opposite end of the balcony.

"Jesse took care of that even before we had a chance to invite you," he yelled. "But tell Jesse not to invite too many other people."

I heard Jesse say something and then another voice, that of Ben Branch, who played the trumpet.

"Will Ben be there?" Martin asked Jesse.

"Yeah," Jesse called up.

"I want him to play my favorite song, 'Precious Lord, Take My Hand.'"

Then I heard another familiar voice from the parking lot below, that of Solomon Jones.

"Dr. King, it's going to be cool tonight. Be sure to carry your coat."

I'll never forget it. I had sprinkled Aramis on my hands and was lifting them to my face when I heard a loud crack, and my hands jerked reflexively. It sounded like a backfire from a car, but there was just enough difference to chill my heart. I wheeled, looked out the door, and saw only Martin's feet. He was down on the concrete balcony.

I bolted out the door and found him there, face up, sprawled and unmoving. Stepping over his frame I knelt down, gathered him in my arms, and began patting him on his left cheek. Even at the first glance I could see that a bullet had entered his right cheek, leaving a small hole.

"Hit the ground!" someone shouted from the parking lot below.

"Oh, God!" someone else yelled, and I heard scuffling feet.

I looked down at Martin's face. His eyes wobbled, then for an instant focused on me.

"Martin. It's all right. Don't worry. This is Ralph. This is Ralph."

His eyes grew calm and he moved his lips. I was certain he understood and was trying to say something. Then, in the next instant, I saw the understanding drain from his eyes and leave them absolutely empty. I looked more carefully at the wound and noticed the glistening blood and a flash of white bone.

Then Kyle was standing over me, terror in his face.

"Billy, quick! Go call an ambulance!"

He disappeared inside, and I glanced at the courtyard below, consciously aware for the first time that somebody somewhere had fired a gun. It had been only a matter of seconds, but no one was visible in the parking lot. Jesse, Ben Branch, and the others had apparently taken cover—where, I didn't know.

I scanned the street, the rooftop, but I saw no one with a gun. The seconds ticked off. A couple of cars drove leisurely by. I cradled Martin and tried not to think what might happen next.

Then somewhere I heard a loud wail. I peered into the motel room and saw Billy Kyle, face down on the bed, screaming.

"This is no time to lose our heads," I said, as calmly as I could. "Get an ambulance."

"I can't get a line," he yelled. "Something's wrong with the phone."

Later I would learn that the black woman operating the motel switchboard at the time of the shot had suffered a heart attack and died, thereby making outgoing calls impossible. However, somebody somewhere called an ambulance.

I felt as if I were on that balcony cradling Martin for hours, but it was actually less than ten minutes from the time the shot rang out until the time the rescue squad arrived. After a couple of minutes I heard shouts from the courtyard below, then tentative conversation. At some point police arrived from the far end of the parking lot.

Meanwhile, a man from Community Service Relations had come up the stairs, frightened enough to be crawling on his hands and knees, but brave enough to bring a blanket to spread over Martin for the treatment of shock. Then Andy Young followed and knelt beside me.

He looked down at Martin, then cried out, "Oh, God! Ralph. It's over!"

More in anguish than anger I said, "Andy, don't you say that. He'll be all right. He'll be all right."

Then Bernard Lee was there, and I was aware of an insistent sound that grew louder and louder, but it wasn't until Bernard spoke that I realized what it was.

"Here comes the ambulance. OK, there won't be room for all of us. Just Dr. Abernathy."

The siren screamed into the courtyard, and the ambulance backed right up to the foot of the concrete staircase. They came scuffling up the steps, and I helped them lift Martin onto the stretcher. Then I followed him into the ambulance, hardly aware that by now a small crowd had gathered, some of them familiar faces, some of them strangers. Several people I had never seen were crying.

They strapped him in and I sat down beside him. Before the engine had cranked up, one of the attendants was taking his pulse while the other was wrapping a black band around his arm to take his blood pressure. The engine roared and we jerked forward. As we careened onto the street, the siren began screaming. I wondered if he heard it and if he was afraid.

"Is he alive?" I asked one of the attendants.

The man gave a quick nod.

"But just barely."

The ambulance turned sharply, stopped, swung around, then began backing toward the hospital entrance. I jumped out, then stood until they had brought Martin down onto the pavement. Then I followed them into the emergency room.

A doctor and two or three nurses were waiting, all three white. They motioned for me to leave the room, but I shook my head.

"I'm staying," I said.

The doctor looked at me for a second, then nodded his head and turned to Martin. I saw them cut the shirt away and noticed for the first time that it was bloody. Then I saw a hole in his chest large enough for me to put both of my fists in.

Two more doctors entered the room and moved into the circle surrounding Martin. One doctor bent forward, then turned to me.

"You'd probably do better to wait outside."

Again I refused. Bernard Lee and I remained there, and I walked around in a daze, trying to pull my thoughts together. At some point the others must have arrived in the hallway outside. I wasn't even sure who was there.

One of the doctors turned, saw me, and came over.

"I assume you're the Reverend Ralph Abernathy."

I nodded dumbly.

"I'm sorry, but I have to tell you that it would be an act of mercy if God took him. If he lives he'll be a vegetable—paralyzed from his neck down."

Another doctor left the room, looked over at us, and shook his head.

"That's the brain surgeon," the doctor said. "Did you see him shake his head?"

"Yes," I said.

"He won't make it."

"Then why are they still in here?" I asked.

"There are things they have to try," he said. "With somebody as well known and important as Dr. King, you try everything. But nothing's going to work now."

He turned.

"I'll keep you posted."

Later I saw one or two leaving, and the same doctor came back over to me.

"He's going," he said gently. "If you'd like to spend a few last moments with him, you can have them now."

I walked over with Bernard to where he was lying, his breathing nothing more than prolonged shudders. Somehow I knew that they would be taking his body as soon as he was gone, so the first thing I did was remove the things from his pockets and put them in my own. Then, as the remaining doctors and nurses stood and watched, I took him in my arms and held him. The breaths came farther and farther apart. Then, a pause came that lengthened until I knew it would never end.

I turned to one of the nurses.

"What will they do with him now?"

"First, they'll take him to the morgue."

I nodded, laid his head back down on the blood-soaked pillow, and walked out the door and down the hallway to the waiting room. The others were there—Andy, Jesse, Hosea, Jones, Bevel. I told them that he was dead. We were all in deep shock, but somehow someone—maybe Jesse—told me that Coretta and Juanita were on their way from Atlanta; it occurred to me that they would not know he had died. If they had to learn the truth at the airport, I wanted to be there to tell them rather than have them hear it from some reporter.

I turned to Solomon Jones.

"How about taking me to the airport."

Driving along the dark streets, covered with glistening puddles, I was aware for the first time of a terrible ache in my arms and legs, and my head was throbbing. I felt like someone running a high fever, though I dimly understood that I had just gone through a terrible trauma and was feeling the physical consequences of what had happened. On the surface I was composed, but I knew in my heart that I was closer to being unconscious than being calm.

When we got to the airport and entered, I heard my name being paged. At the desk a young woman said she had a message for me.

"It's from Mrs. King," she said with a crisp smile. "She said she had already gotten the word and would not come to Memphis until tomorrow."

I nodded and thanked her, and she made some cheerful

remark, never realizing the significance of the message she had just delivered.

"Now take me where my friend is," I told Solomon Jones.

"That would be at the morgue."

We finally found it, and when I walked in the door I was met by a young white man with an anxious look on his face.

"I'm glad you have come," he said. "We need someone to officially identify the body."

I nodded and sighed. The horrors of the day weren't over yet.

I followed him down a long hallway and into a room and saw, on a metal table, a body covered with a piece of brown paper that reminded me of the wrapping paper butchers used in country stores. Protruding from underneath were two feet, and on one of the toes a tag was tied.

The young man lifted the piece of paper, and I saw him again, somehow more dead than he had seemed when I left him in the hospital room.

I nodded.

"This is the body of Martin Luther King, Jr.," I said.

The young man let the paper settle with a crackling sound.

"There's one other thing," said the young man. "The coroner would like to do an autopsy, but he'll need permission. Would you be willing to sign?"

"Not really," I said. "That's something Mrs. King ought to decide."

"I'd like you to call her," he said. "It's important."

"How is it important?" I asked. It seemed incredible to me that such a procedure could make any difference now.

"It might tell us something we didn't know before, something that could save another person's life."

I hesitated.

"All right," I said finally. "I'll call Mrs. King."

I didn't really want to bother Coretta. I was certain she was in shock, as I still was. And she had the children to comfort. Why burden her with this decision? But I dialed the number anyway, partly in response to what the man had said, partly because to do so was the course of least resistance.

Coretta sounded terribly tired, and we talked for a minute about what would happen tomorrow. Then I asked her.

"I don't know," she said, "I'll leave it up to you. I guess Martin would have agreed to it. But you make the decision."

I hung up and turned to the young man.

"All right," I said. "You can do the autopsy."

"Who'll sign?" he asked.

"I'll sign," I told him, and I did.

In retrospect, I wonder if it was strictly legal. I suspect not. Yet if you check back through the records you will find somewhere a permission to do a postmortem with only my signature on it, not that of close kin.

"What will you do with him after you finish?" I asked.

"He'll be turned over to a local funeral home, whichever one you specify."

"How long will it take?" I asked.

"Not long. A couple of hours at the most. We'll try to get started immediately, just as soon as the coroner can get down here."

I don't remember who made the decision concerning the funeral home. Probably Solomon Jones, since the car we were using had been loaned to us by the funeral home. Somehow the arrangements were made and we went back to the motel. The first thing I did was call a staff meeting, not absolutely certain of what I would do or say—only sure that we still had unfinished business. As horrible as it was, we couldn't let one single bullet kill the entire movement.

With everyone gathered in the meeting room of the Lorraine Motel, I found words to express my feelings. I said that we had to go on, that Martin's life had been given for his people, that we would be betraying him if we let his death either frighten us into retreat or destroy our hope in ultimate victory.

Then James Bevel stood up and said, "Our leader is dead. In many respects I loved Dr. King more than Jesus. But now he is gone, and we have a new leader. And that leader is you, Ralph David Abernathy. So you lead and from this day forward we will follow."

Hosea Williams and others seemed to join in a chorus of approval, and I was pleased to see that no one was giving up the fight.

After the meeting broke up, Jesse called me aside.

"Listen, Ralph," he said. "I want to go back to Chicago and get my troops organized. I want to bring a huge delegation down to Atlanta. We need to bring in thousands and thousands of people from around the country. The funeral has to be the occasion where we demonstrate our strength and our numbers."

"That seems like a good idea," I told him. "Go ahead. We'll see you in Atlanta. Call tomorrow and we'll tell you what's been decided about the funeral."

So Jesse turned and left.

The next hours were filled with the conversation of people who came by to express their shock and sympathy. Mostly they were local friends, people involved in the struggle for higher wages, or those who had followed our campaigns from the very beginning. There were a few white people, news personnel, some in tears along with the rest of us. But mostly blacks came, those for whom Martin had given his life.

At about 3:00 A.M., I suddenly felt the need to get out of the motel—and to be with my friend, who was by now lying all alone in the funeral home. So I found Solomon Jones and pulled him aside.

"Take me to the funeral home," I said.

Ben Hooks overheard and said he would go with me, a gesture I greatly appreciated. Then others said they would go—and so we eventually had several carloads. We wound through the dark streets of Memphis like a dress rehearsal of a funeral procession.

The funeral director met us at the door and offered his hand. He told us it was a very sad occasion and asked how he could help us.

"I'd like to view the body," I said.

He shook his head slowly.

"You don't want to go in right now, Reverend Abernathy," he said.

I assured him that I did.

"I promise you that you don't," he said. "Take my word for it. Please."

But I insisted, so he shook his head sadly and said, "Follow me, but I want to warn you that we have just received the remains from the hospital and haven't had a chance to do our own work."

I nodded, pretending I understood, but I really didn't. Ben Hooks said he would go in with me, and later I was glad he'd done so, though I wonder if he was glad, given the nature of what we saw.

I had never before viewed a corpse that had undergone an autopsy, and I never want to see another. The sight haunts me yet, though for some reason I had to see it, would never have felt I'd satisfied my obligation to Martin if I hadn't seen his body at that moment.

They had cut open his forehead at the hairline and rolled the scalp downward until it covered half his face. Then they had sawed his head open to expose the inside of his skull. What we saw was not a face but the curved dome of a still-glistening brain. I stared for an instant, a mute witness to the final dehumanization of Martin Luther King, Jr., his transformation from person to thing. I knew in that moment that I could leave this body now, leave it forever, because it no longer belonged to my friend. I was ready for the burial.

So I picked a temporary casket and a suit to clothe the body for the trip back to Atlanta.

I went back to the motel, aware that they had only a short time to prepare the body. Already reporters were flying in from all over the world, heading for Memphis, gathering like bees around a honeycomb. I didn't know whether or not the funeral home would attempt to repair the indignity of the autopsy. Worried, I went back to the funeral home the next day and again viewed the body. It appeared to be unblemished. The morticians had done their job well.

At some point during the long night, I was asked if I could be on *The Today Show,* and I agreed, not certain that I could make it, but willing to try. It was only when I was already on the air that I learned Jesse would be on at the same time, live from Chicago. I didn't pay too much attention to what he said. I was exhausted and barely listening, though I do remember being a little confused by his account. It was only when I got back to the room that I learned what he had said, not only that morning, but the previous evening, after I had gone to the hospital. Most of it came from Hosea Williams, who had seen it all.

It seems that shortly after the ambulance had left, the press had converged on the place, camera crews and reporters, local staff and network, all eager to put someone on camera to tell the story. Jesse and Hosea had both agreed that until they knew what had happened, they would avoid the press and stay out of sight. At least that's what Hosea had thought was the understanding.

So he was more than a little surprised to look out the window and see Jesse, standing in front of several cameras, speaking into a microphone that a reporter was holding in his face. Curious, Hosea slipped outside and eased up behind Jesse, though on the other side of a chain-link fence.

"Yes," Jesse was saying, "I was the last person he spoke to as I was cradling him in my arms."

With a roar of anger, Hosea started cursing and was halfway up the chain fence before one of the others pulled him down and held him until his anger had cooled. But Jackson had told the same story, or very nearly the same, that morning on *The Today Show.*

We have never talked about this matter, though it was very much in the spotlight during the 1988 presidential campaign, when Mayor Koch and others brought it up. I never thought a great deal about it, though others in the group were vocal in their anger. If I had any theory about why Jesse had said what he did, I would have to say he was somehow in shock, reliving the whole scene in his mind, and acting out what he might have wished to do during those last seconds. Certainly, at such a moment, none of us was quite normal or even rational—and the state of confusion lasted for several days. (Indeed, that afternoon Jesse appeared before the Chicago City Council wearing a blood-stained shirt and saying that it was the same shirt he had been wearing the previous evening when he had held Martin.)

Calls and telegrams were pouring into the Lorraine Motel and into SCLC headquarters in Atlanta, and one contained an offer from Nelson Rockefeller: He would be happy to make his plane available to us for the return of the body to Atlanta. It was not only a gracious gesture, but it solved a practical problem for us and made it possible for the family and close friends to accompany the body.

When it was time to go to the airport, we drove in a procession to the funeral home, where we found hundreds of reporters and photographers taking pictures of the open casket. As soon as we arrived, the funeral director closed the casket and some of the staff carried it to the waiting hearse as the rest of us climbed into waiting limousines and drove in a slow processional to the airport.

Governor Rockefeller's plane had not yet arrived, and as we walked forward, ahead of the casket, I saw Coretta, standing, waiting. When she saw me she moved forward.

As I recall, there were about thirty-five of us on the plane, with the casket in the rear. It was a solemn trip, and most of us stared out the window and thought our own thoughts. As for me, I thought about Juanita and the children—and how they might have felt had it been my body en route to Atlanta in a metal box. I also thought about the future, already crowding in on me with measuring tape, ready to fit me for the next casket.

But as the plane banked and then nosed downward toward Atlanta, I thought again of Martin and what he had said as we took off only three days earlier—the brittle smile on his face when the captain announced the bomb threat and reassured us that everything was safe. There had been normal and very human fear behind that smile. Now, he was unworried, at peace. For just an instant, staring at the greening woods below and thinking of what was to come, I almost envied him.

*   *   *

The news of Martin's death was on every television network and every radio. It was one of those moments in history that Americans can use to punctuate their lives: Pearl Harbor Day, the assassination of John F. Kennedy, the killing of Martin Luther King—everyone remembers where he or she was when the news about these tragic events first broke. I have heard hundreds of black people tell stories about that April night, detailed recollections of where they were, how they first heard, what they thought and felt, and what they did. Many of them wept. Many prayed. A few went to church. And a number rushed into the streets and wreaked havoc on the communities in which they lived.

The violence began in Memphis and spread like an ugly stain until it touched every part of the country and most major cities. In Nashville four thousand members of the National Guard were called up to respond to the growing disorder. In Greensboro, North Carolina, blacks, mostly teenagers, threw bottles and smashed windows. In Jackson, Mississippi, crowds gathered and people began smashing car windows. In Washington, D.C., Stokely Carmichael led a mob into the streets and eventually some of his followers began to break into windows and loot stores. In New York City, despite Mayor John Lindsay's attempt to pacify the city's black inhabitants by a personal visit, people began looting and smashing windows and burning buildings.

Some of the nation's black leaders were quick to call for restraint, reminding the nation in general and black people in particular that Martin had always preached the gospel of nonviolence. James Farmer, while expressing his sense of outrage, said: "Every racist in the country has killed Dr. King. Evil societies always destroy their consciences. The only fitting memorial to this martyred leader is a monumental commitment—now, not a day later—to eliminate racism. Dr. King hated bloodshed. His own blood must not now trigger more bloodshed."

Hosea Williams, speaking for the SCLC in Atlanta (where there was no rioting), said: "Let's not burn America down. . . .

We must—we must—maintain and advocate and promote the philosophy of nonviolence."

Fred Shuttlesworth reminded the black community of Martin's belief that "not one hair on the head of one white man shall be harmed by us."

But these voices—the voices of Martin's friends and followers—were drowned out by the cries of his enemies in the black community, who took the occasion of his death to attack the whole premise of his life.

Julius Hobson of ACT, said: "The next black man who comes into the black community preaching nonviolence should be violently dealt with by the black people who hear him. The Martin Luther King concept of nonviolence died with him. It was a foreign ideology anyway—as foreign to this violent country as speaking Russian."

Lincoln O. Lynch, chairman of the United Black Front, said: "The assassination of Martin Luther King, in my opinion, will wake up black people to the fact that it is imperative to abandon the unconditional nonviolent concept expounded by Dr. King and adopt a position that for every Martin Luther King who falls, ten white racists will go down with him. There is no other way. White America understands no other language."

And Floyd McKissick, then national director of CORE, said: "Dr. Martin Luther King was the last prince of nonviolence. . . . He was a symbol of nonviolence, the epitome of nonviolence.

"Nonviolence is a dead philosophy and it was not the black people who killed it. It was the white people that killed nonviolence and white racists at that."

These statements, made on the night Martin was murdered, indicate the severe antagonisms that polarized the black community, its divisions at that particular moment. Nothing would have pained Martin more than to know that his death had been used by his enemies to undermine the movement he had begun. His last months had been haunted by the thought that at some point in the near future the apostles of violence were determined to have their day. As a matter of fact, some members of our group even raised the idea that a black man had shot Martin, just to bring about that day of armed revolution.

I never entertained such a thought. When I got over the shock of the incident and began to speculate about the person who might have committed such a crime, I immediately narrowed my suspects down to two types—both white. The first was a typical klansman—uneducated, mean-spirited, and essentially stupid—whose self-esteem was so low that he could only raise it by an act of violence against a black man of character and stature. The second was someone trained or hired by the FBI and acting under orders from J. Edgar Hoover himself.

But while I didn't believe that black radicals had played any part in Martin's death, I began to realize that in the short run they and they alone were the ones who would profit from it. For the next few days, the crowds and the headlines and the attention of the nation belonged to them. They had their chance to try the doctrine of violence, and they took full advantage of the moment. In cities throughout the nation the gang leaders who bragged about how much better they could run the movement than we could began to lead their wild, grief-stricken bands into battle— smashing, burning, looting, and toppling buildings, neighbor- hoods, blocks, sections of cities. For days they were at it— fighting policemen, state troopers, and national guardsmen throughout the nation. They beat people and were beaten. They shot people and were shot. They killed people and were killed.

Here are just a few examples of the chaotic violence that occurred in the three days following Martin's assassination:

1. In the nation's capital a black mob, responding to the leadership of opportunists like Stokely Carmichael, went on an orgy of rioting, burglary, and wanton destruction that left whole sections of the city devastated—black sections. They looted stores, many of them black owned, and burned down or tore down entire buildings, often where blacks were living.

    Some white people were grabbed on the streets or pulled from cars and beaten. In fact, one white man died from such an attack. But seven black men died: Two were shot while looting; one was crushed to death when a wall collapsed and fell on him; three were found burned to death in stores they were robbing; and one cut his throat while trying to crawl through a smashed window.

Along with the 8 dead, there were 987 injured, 4,613 arrested, and hundreds of people left homeless and without jobs. Virtually all of these were black people rather than white. As a matter of fact, the *New York Times* had the following to report about the victims of the Washington rioting: "No reports of damage to government buildings or white residential areas of the city. [The disorders] were primarily confined to a pie-shaped wedge of the Negro area of the city."

2. In Baltimore, the black section of town was patrolled by six thousand national guardsmen and two thousand troops after rioters tore down their own neighborhoods, torching buildings, looting stores, and throwing bricks, bottles, and firebombs at firefighters who tried to extinguish the blazes.

   During the three days, 258 people were injured, 12 listed in critical condition. Four people were killed: two were shot by the police—they were black; two died in a building that had been firebombed—one was black and one was white.

3. In Chicago sixty-seven hundred national guardsmen were called up to quell the rioting, looting, and burning that took place over the three worst days. But they could not do the job; and at Mayor Richard Daley's request, President Lyndon Johnson sent in five thousand troops.

   When the smoke cleared after the third night, the South Side and the West Side were patched with smoking piles of rubble. Two hundred ten buildings had been burned down. Thousands were homeless. The police had arrested approximately 1,800 people, 90% of them black. Their bonds were set at five hundred to five thousand dollars, and most could not bail themselves out.

   More than five hundred people were injured, virtually all of them black; and eleven people died—*all* of them black. Seven young men—ages eighteen to thirty-two—were killed during the rioting. Six were shot and one was stabbed. Two other blacks were burned to death. Another was shot. Yet another was found with a crushed skull.

Of the Chicago riots, the *Times* wrote: "All the riot damage was in the Negro neighborhoods. The rioters had torn down and burned down the stores and apartments they themselves needed for shelter and sustenance. No white neighborhood was touched by the destruction, and most Chicagoans have not seen any of it. They would not know a riot had occurred without radio, television, and newspaper reports."

4. By the time the rioting had begun to diminish, Stokely Carmichael had left Washington, after telling the rioters to "get guns." People who listened to Cuban radio heard him say in an interview: "[N]ow there won't be any other leader who will tell his brothers not to burn the cities. . . . This means that it will be necessary to fully enter into a revolution."

He went on to predict that "guerilla warfare will rapidly develop in the cities."

Not only does that statement seem strident and childish in retrospect, but it seemed so at the time. It was perfectly obvious to me and to the other members of our movement that rather than these events tolling the death knell of nonviolence, they signaled its rebirth. After three or four days of an abortive attempt at "revolution," radical leaders had clearly failed. Nationwide, twenty-eight people had died, all but two of them black. The army and national guard had moved in and put down the rebellion rather handily. White neighborhoods had remained untouched. Tens of thousands of black people were homeless, jobless, without money or food, and injured or languishing in jail, unable to pay the bail. The white people were not particularly jubilant in their victory, but they had no doubts about their ability to handle this kind of civil disorder.

More importantly, the white enemies of black progress were openly rejoicing; those who had warned of "revolutionary tendencies" and "foreign influence" could point to a Stokely Carmichael and say, not without justification, that he was plotting the violent overthrow of the government.

But the advocates of violence, black as well as white, had not correctly read the signs of the times—and they had underestimated the strength of the organization that Martin had left behind. They had also failed to take into account my own firm resolve that what Martin stood for would be carried forward, no matter what.

In the early morning hours after Martin had been shot, I called a news conference in Memphis and made our plans for the future quite clear. First, I reaffirmed our continuing commitment to nonviolence and our willingness to risk our lives for that principle.

"We're all willing to die for what we believe in," I said to the press and to the nation. Then I told them that we would return to Memphis on Monday and complete the nonviolent march we had planned to make in support of the striking sanitation workers. We would make a silent march, I told them, not only for our original purpose, but also as a memorial to Martin.

The days immediately following Martin's death were filled with anguish and hard work. We all knew that despite our private grief we would be the central figures in a tremendously important public occasion, the nearest thing in our history to a state funeral for a black. Coretta set a strong example for the rest of us. She was controlled and efficient during the planning and execution of the details, with help from everybody, including Daddy King, who was surprisingly calm in the midst of a tragedy he had been dreading for so many years.

Together we decided that the body, after being prepared at Bell Street Funeral Home, would lie in state at Sisters Chapel at Spelman College. Then on Tuesday there would be two separate ceremonies, one service in the church, the other a public memorial service to be held outdoors at Morehouse College, almost five miles away from Ebenezer Baptist Church. All plans were conditioned by the fact that literally tens of thousands of people would be coming from all over the country and that most of the black people in Atlanta would probably want to take part in some way. Clearly the Morehouse ceremony would accommodate the many simple people, white as well as black, who wanted to pay tribute to Martin, while the church funeral would be for family, friends, and a few dignitaries of national prominence. Coretta asked me to officiate at both services, and of course I agreed. She also asked me to conduct the committal service at the graveside.

Meanwhile, I had a congregation to face on Sunday and a march to lead on Monday back in Memphis. In many ways the West Hunter service on Sunday would be more difficult than officiating at the three events on Tuesday. "Officiating" meant acting as a kind of master of ceremonies, but at West Hunter I would have to stand before my congregation and talk about Martin's death—its meaning to me, its implications for the nation, and its religious significance. I wasn't sure I could sort out all these meanings so soon after the event, but on Friday evening and Saturday I had to try.

On Sunday morning, I mounted the pulpit and delivered my sermon in the form of a letter to Martin, which I shared with my congregation. I called it "A Short Letter to My Dearest Friend in the City Called Heaven."[*]

As plans for the funeral began to crystallize, we found that their implementation was sometimes more difficult than the planners had anticipated. For example, to emphasize Martin's commitment to the poor people of the nation, we decided to have the casket transported from Ebenezer Church to Morehouse on a cart drawn by two mules. Many people still remember the stark and grim image of the cortege rolling down the streets of Atlanta; as a symbol, the mules and cart had served their purpose. But they had not been easy to come by.

We had to search the countryside before we found two mules who could work in tandem. I put Hosea Williams in charge, and he must have driven up a hundred red clay roads

---

[*] The text of this sermon can be found in the Appendix.

searching for a pair. Finally he found what he was looking for and was able to persuade the owner to lend them to us for a day. But the cart turned out to be even more elusive.

Finally, on Sunday afternoon, Hosea came by the church to give me the news.

"Well," he said with a sigh of relief, "we've got a wagon."

"Where did you get it?" I asked.

"At a farm about thirty miles down the road. Remote place."

"Did you have any trouble talking the owner into letting you have it?"

"No," he said evenly. "I stole it."

I couldn't believe my ears.

"You *stole* the cart!"

He nodded grimly.

"Nothing else to do. Nobody was around, and I couldn't take the chance they'd say no."

I tried not to think about it. I could imagine the owner as he watched the funeral on television suddenly recognizing the wagon and leaping to his feet in rage. Before the casket reached Morehouse he might be there with an officer and a warrant.

"We'll have to find the owner as quickly as possible and pay him for the wagon," I said.

"Yes," said Hosea gravely. "We'll have to do that."

The funeral was on Tuesday, but first we went back to Memphis to make our nonviolent march along the same route we had hoped to follow when the Invaders had begun their disruptive tactics. Instead of singing hymns, we would be marching silently in tribute to Martin. While we hoped that what had happened already would discourage any further violence, we had no idea what the atmosphere in Memphis might be. There were people who might well find that the spilling of one man's blood had only whetted their appetite for more violence and death.

My fears were unfounded. It was a memorable occasion, proving that black people could conduct a nonviolent march in Memphis, Tennessee.

All the members of the SCLC were, of course, in the march.

So were Coretta and the children. So were Juanita and our children. So were the surviving Kennedy brothers, Robert and Edward, though very soon Robert would also be killed by an assassin's bullet. So were a number of other nationally known figures including Walter Reuther, Dr. Benjamin Spock, Harry Belafonte, Ossie Davis.

I remember walking down Main Street, seeing the somber and grieving faces of the black people lined on either curb, and then the white faces, some pained and others enigmatic, all of them clearly anxious in the wake of the terrible event of the previous week. For the first time, I had to wonder if the next person I passed wouldn't pull out a gun and start blasting away or if a bullet fired from some distant window wouldn't suddenly tear into my head, even before I heard the sound of the shot.

It was during that march that I first came to the realization that I had become the number one target of racist assassins now that Martin was gone. I had never really worried about it before, except during a few minutes in Mississippi when I thought we might be grabbed by the mob and strung up to the nearest lamppost. Now I realized the specter that had haunted Martin from time to time, particularly in his final years. I knew that if someone wanted to kill me badly enough, there was nothing I could do to stop him. The thought was sobering, but I didn't let it bother me too much, and during the next few years I would be plagued by much more mundane considerations, such as how to revitalize our sagging spirits and where our next dollar was coming from.

We ended up at Memphis City Hall, where both Coretta and I spoke to a huge crowd of at least twenty thousand.

Coretta pled with the people of America to eliminate poverty, saying: "If this can be done, then I know that his death will be the redemptive force that he so often talked about in terms of one giving his life to a great cause and the things that he believed in."

And I said: "I have been to the top of the mountain. I have talked with God about it, and God told me that Martin did not get there but you have been so close to Martin I am going to help you get there. If God will lead me I am going to lead my people into the promised land."

The national television networks carried the march and for a moment we received their undivided attention and sympathy. But it was the last time. When we got to Washington we were the object of exasperation and contempt, and I began to learn the loneliness of being at the top. I knew just how Martin had felt, and at the same time, I had no loyal friend to give me comfort and counsel. He had Ralph Abernathy. I had no one.

One good thing came out of Memphis, however, In the wake of what had happened, the strike was settled there in favor of the sanitation workers. A small victory bought with a great man's life.

On Tuesday we buried Martin, and it was a day of great ceremony and strain. It began with the arrival in Atlanta of a number of dignitaries from around the nation—governors, senators, and several announced candidates for president. Because of the presence of these important figures, the basement of West Hunter Church was converted into a communications center, set up by Earl Gray, then a staff member for Robert Kennedy. He installed fifty telephones and made certain that during the entire day everyone was in touch with his own particular headquarters.

Among those the *New York Times* listed as attending were the following: Vice President Hubert Humphrey, Attorney General Ramsey Clark, Secretary of Labor Willard Wirtz, Under Secretary of State Nicholas Katzenbach, Associate Justice Thurgood Marshall, Secretary of HUD Robert C. Weaver, Sen. Edward Brooke, Gov. Nelson Rockefeller, Gov. George Romney, Sen. Jacob Javits, Sen. Edward Kennedy, Sen. Robert Kennedy, Sen. Eugene McCarthy, Sen. Wayne Morse, Sen. Harrison Williams, San Francisco Mayor Joseph Alioto, Atlanta Mayor Ivan Allen, New York Mayor John Lindsay, U.N. Ambassador Arthur Goldberg, U.N. Under Secretary Ralph Bunche, Mrs. John F. Kennedy, and a number of well-known entertainers.

The church was so crowded, in fact, that for a while it was impossible for members of the family to enter. People were jamming all doors, some attempting to get inside, others simply hoping for a glimpse of the casket. When the family could not enter, A. D. went to plead with the crowd.

"At this hour our hearts are very heavy," he said. "Please let the family through. You would want Dr. King's wife, children, mother, and father to have an opportunity of seeing this service. Please don't make Mrs. King have to fight her way in."

But even this plea accomplished nothing, so determined were the people outside to keep their places near the door. Finally, A. D. told them, "If we can't receive your cooperation, we have but one choice—to remove the body and bury it privately."

Eventually, the family members were able to push their way inside and take the seats waiting for them, but the service began more than an hour late and made the whole ordeal more difficult for everyone involved.

I remember looking out at the crowd sitting solemnly at attention, and thinking that something was wrong with the scene, though for a moment I couldn't figure out what it was. Then I realized: This was Ebenezer Church, yet most of the people jamming the pews were white. So many politicians and celebrities had come for the funeral that there wasn't room for all of Martin's friends and relatives, the people who came to this very church to hear him preach on Sundays. Fortunately, they would have their opportunity to see and hear a memorial service at Morehouse later in the afternoon.

But I began the service by pointing out that we were here to bury a man rather than make a political statement, though I acknowledged the larger importance of Martin's death. I didn't want to offend those present, but I wanted to point out the essentially religious nature of what was about to happen and to remind them that a funeral is a very private and very personal occasion.

Perhaps the most moving moment came near the beginning of the service when they played a tape recording of Martin's instructions concerning his own funeral. Excerpted from a sermon he had delivered at this same church, the words were almost too painful to bear.

"If any of you are around when I have to meet my day, I don't want a long funeral. And if you get somebody to deliver the eulogy, tell him not to talk too long. . . .

"I'd like somebody to mention that day that Martin Luther King, Jr., tried to give his life serving others.

"I'd like for somebody to say that day that Martin Luther King, Jr., tried to love somebody. . . .

"I want you to be able to say that day that I did try to feed the hungry. I want you to be able to say that day that I did try in my life to clothe the naked. I want you to say on that day that I did try in my life to visit those who were in prison. And I want you to say that I tried to love and serve humanity."

Mary Gurley, a singer from Ebenezer Church with an extraordinary and beautiful voice, sang the hymn "Where He Leads Me," while we all wept. The choir sang "When I Survey the Wondrous Cross," "Softly and Tenderly," and "Then My Living Will Not Be in Vain."

(I might say parenthetically that we violated every instruction he had left behind, and probably the violations would have been to his liking.)

The sermon was preached by Dr. Harold DeWolf, who had been Martin's Major professor at Boston University. A white man, Dr. DeWolf spoke of Martin's dedication to the cause of the poor and oppressed and then talked of the responsibilities the living have to the dead.

> It is now for us, all the millions of the living who care, to take up his torch of love. It is for us to finish his work, to end the awful destruction in Vietnam, to root out every trace of race prejudice from our lives, to bring the massive powers of this nation to aid the oppressed and to heal the hate-scarred world.

At the end of the service I led the congregation outside reading the words of the Twenty-third Psalm, and we watched as the pallbearers—members of the SCLC executive staff who had helped him build the organization—lifted the highly polished African mahogany casket onto the wagon and saw the mules lean forward and begin to pull their load down the street. Fifty thousand people followed behind while another one hundred thousand watched along the way.

The walk from Ebenezer to Morehouse was almost five miles and the heat was merciless. With the funeral lasting an hour longer than scheduled and with the strenuous march and blazing sun, it was small wonder that by the time we got to the Morehouse campus, people were beginning to pass out.

I had hoped to be able to start as soon as we arrived, but the crowd was milling around and talking as if they were at a lawn party rather than at a formal ceremony. When the family arrived, however, they surged around them; and we had chaotic shouting and screaming for about ten minutes.

At that point I wasn't certain we would be able to hold the memorial service. I thought of the mob at Memphis on the first day when Martin had suddenly shouted "Call off the march!" I had that same sense of panic.

Obviously, others felt the same way, because people in the crowd began to faint and medics were kept busy carrying them off in stretchers. As I began to speak, I heard the cry of someone else keeling over, and when I tried to carry on, Daddy King jumped to his feet and called out, "Ralph, you've got to get this over! People are dying!"

The first time he said it I nodded and went right ahead; but he stood up again after about three minutes.

"We wanted him to live," he shouted to the audience, "but they killed him!"

Then he turned to me.

"You've got to cut it short, Ralph! You've got to cut it short!"

I thought things would calm down once we began the program, and several eminent clergymen were waiting to speak; but before I got three words out Daddy King was on his feet again.

"Get Mays up there, Ralph, so we can end it!"

At that point I gave up and called on Dr. Benjamin E. Mays, president emeritus of Morehouse, who was scheduled to give the principal address. (Some of those eliminated included Joe Lowery, who may never have quite forgiven me.)

Dr. Mays, who knew Martin well, was one of the most

famous public speakers in the black community; and he did not disappoint his many admirers. In his famous high style, he moved all who could hear him, which unfortunately was only a small portion of the increasingly unruly crowd:

> He drew no distinctions between the high and the low; none between rich and poor. He believed especially that he was sent to champion the cause of the man farthest down. He would probably say that, if death had to come, I'm sure there was no greater cause to die for than fighting to get a just wage for garbage collectors.
> He was supra-race, supra-nation, supra-denomination, supra-class, and supra-culture. He belonged to the world and to mankind. He now belongs to posterity.

Mercifully, the four-mile journey to South View Cemetery was made by motorcade, with the hearse and family limousines leading the way. Most of the political celebrities had quietly slipped off, either after the church service or after the memorial service, but crowds of simple and anonymous black people were lined on both sides of the road to salute Martin one last time.

The old cemetery, its sternly erect tombstones scattered over a green hillside, was also crowded with people, most of them black, a good many of them close friends and associates. We were like Gideon's army now. All the faint-hearted had fallen by the wayside.

By this time I was exhausted, as was everyone else, so I made it brief and from the heart, the way those of us in the black Baptist church do it best. Consequently, I don't have a text of my remarks. But one newspaper account contained the following excerpt.

> This cemetery is too small for his spirit but we submit his body to the ground. The grave is too narrow for his soul, but we commit his body to the ground. No coffin, no crypt, no stone can hold his greatness. But we submit his body to the ground.

At that moment I bade him a silent goodbye and turned my back on the grave, determined to make his spirit live in the army and marching orders he had left behind.

But it turned out that I had not really committed his body to the ground, at least not permanently. For I was to see him one more time—not figuratively, but literally.

After the funeral and readjustment to life without him, Coretta decided to build a center in memory of Martin, an institution to carry on his work. I had encouraged her to become active in the SCLC and had even prepared an office for her in our headquarters. But she wanted to pursue the future independently, and certainly there were many donors who were eager to contribute to a fitting memorial for Martin.

So with seventy-five thousand dollars from the Ebenezer Baptist Church and seventy-five thousand dollars that the SCLC contributed, she bought a piece of property next door to the Ebenezer Church, and went forward with plans to build the Martin Luther King, Jr., Center for Nonviolent Social Change. One of the things she intended to do during construction was to relocate Martin's body in a tomb on the grounds of the center, on an island in the middle of a small man-made lake.

So I was not really surprised when she called me one day and asked me to accompany her and other members of the immediate family to exhume the body and move it.

"I'll be happy to be there," I said. "When will it be?"

"Tonight," she said. "We'll meet at 2:00 A.M. at South View Cemetery, so there won't be any curiosity seekers."

It was a dark night when we gathered on that hillside and stood there, watching as the cemetery and funeral home workers, illuminated by flashlights, unsealed the mausoleum and slid the casket out. Coretta, A. D., Christine, Daddy King, Isaac Farris and a few other close family members were there, and we stood in silence as the men swiftly and efficiently carried the still glossy casket and installed it in the hearse. Then we followed behind—a three-car entourage winding along the dark road into the sleeping city.

When we got to the funeral home, the family went into a waiting room, but A. D. and I accompanied the casket into the back.

The man in charge then explained to me what they had to do.

"When we removed the casket from the chapel at Spelman, we didn't have time to seal it properly. So that's what we're going to do now. We'll take off the top, put glue on it, and then press the top back on. It will take about ten minutes."

I started to leave, then something made me stay—a vague sense of responsibility to Martin. As his best friend, I couldn't allow his body to suffer this last indignity at the hands of strangers. So I stood and watched with A. D. as they took the hinges off the lid and lifted it from the casket.

Then I saw him, lying there underneath a thin sheet of glass.

His face, his features were still intact—solemn, though perhaps a little pinched, as if he had suffered a long, long illness. But his shoes and pant legs were covered with green moss. As I looked, my eyes riveted on the figure lying there, I realized that the sight of his corpse disturbed me less now than the first time I saw it lying under the brown paper in the Memphis morgue, a tag tied on its toe.

They worked quickly, efficiently to clean off the moss, paint the lid with glue, then fit it back on the casket, several of them pressing down with their full weight to make sure the bonding was perfect. Then, when they had finished, the man in charge nodded to me and A. D.

"That should do it," he said. "He should last two hundred years now."

As we left the room I thought that if history was just, he would last a good deal longer than that in the minds and hearts of his people.

14

Martin Luther King, Jr.

SOME PUBLIC FIGURES reveal themselves completely in their media appearances while others, for whatever reason, withhold a significant portion of themselves. President Reagan, for example, is what he seems to be, whereas Richard Nixon is still an enigma. The public knew and loved the lighter side of John F. Kennedy. They knew considerably less about Lyndon Johnson's earthy sense of humor.

Martin Luther King, Jr., was not a man the public knew fully, and for this reason their appreciation of him was to a significant degree diminished. What they saw was a stern and righteous prophet—a man single-mindedly dedicated to social justice and nonviolent protest. In him they found much to admire—courage, devotion to God, uncompromising commitment, eloquence, moral vision. What they missed was his humanity, warmth, and, above all, his unflagging capacity to have fun and to make everybody else join in.

I suppose the "public man" he became was not entirely of his own making. The press helped to create that Martin Luther King. But so did the circumstances under which he first caught

467

the attention of the American people. We were in Montgomery in the middle of a dangerous struggle, the outcome of which was still very much in doubt. Martin's house had been bombed. Telephone threats were a daily occurrence. No one knew when the next stick of dynamite would go off. Everyone in the black community felt he or she could be a future victim.

To confront such a situation with frivolity would have been to trivialize the dangers we faced and to suggest to the general public that we were the happy-go-lucky "characters" of story and song. We were in serious trouble. So was the entire country. Martin felt that his public appearances had to reflect the grim realities of the situation. America needed a Jeremiah not another black comedian. So he became Jeremiah, and continued in that role until the end.

I'm not suggesting that he was play-acting when he spoke to the American people as the stern Baptist preacher. He *was* a Baptist preacher and one side of him saw the world in moral terms. For Martin, the racial conflict was a struggle between the forces of Good and Evil, one that required a stern and uncompromising stance. When he spoke at the Lincoln Memorial or at Memphis on the last night of his life, he was speaking from the heart, with words that came to him naturally.

But he did have another side, and those of us who knew him well enjoyed his company in a way that outsiders could never understand. Martin was fun-loving, and when he was offstage you could usually find him telling a joke or teasing somebody. He had a perfect sense of timing and he instinctively knew what was funny. Some people have that gift and some people don't. He had it. I'm convinced that if he had wanted to be a stand-up comic he could have been almost as famous in that role.

He was also a mimic, with an ear for peculiarities of speech and an eye for facial mannerisms and gestures. When he imitated somebody the resemblance was always uncanny and usually extremely funny. I have seen a room of staff members helpless with laughter as he launched into one of his routines.

One of the people he "did" was an Atlanta preacher named Hilly Thomas who had a stutter that became increasingly pronounced as he became more and more excited. Martin had a repertoire of Hilly stories that could keep people laughing for hours.

As a service to the black religious community, Martin used to teach a course in grammar to seminarians. Some of the older preachers would also sit in, just to give them a little extra polish; and Hilly Thomas was among them.

One day Martin was dealing with pronoun case endings, and more particularly with the question of when to use "I" and when to use "me." Having finished his explanation he put a hypothetical question to the class:

"Let's say you've been out too late at night, you come home at 2:00 A.M., and you find your wife has locked the door. You knock and in a minute you hear her voice saying, 'Who is it?' Which do you say? 'It is I,' or 'It is me'?"

Hilly waved his arms and begged to be allowed to answer.

"If I stayed out till t-t-two in the m-m-morning and knocked on the d-door and m-m-my wife asked m-me, 'Who is it?' I'd answer," he said in his most seductive voice, "*B-b-baby*, this is m-m-me."

Martin used to recreate an entire sermon he once heard Hilly Thomas preach at Chapel Hill Baptist Church on Northside Drive.

"Hilly began," Martin said, "by announcing, 'I'm going to preach this m-morning on the t-text "God is Love." And m-my subject is: "is." Now "is" is not a noun; "is" is not a verb. "Is" is just "is." Like "is you got your ticket?" "Is you going?" "Is" is just "is." ' "

At that point Martin would be screaming, whooping, and waving his arms and the rest of us would be on the floor, holding our sides. He could continue the sermon until we gasped for breath and begged him to stop. When I finally met Hilly Thomas one day at Operation Breadbasket headquarters, I broke into a big grin the moment he opened his mouth. Martin had him down so perfectly I almost had to leave the room.

*   *   *

Martin could also find fun in the stuffiest occasions. I remember one day we were sitting on the stage at one of the great Ivy League schools, listening while the president was introducing me so I could introduce Martin to an auditorium jammed with students. As the president droned on, Martin leaned over and whispered to me, "Look at that man's shoes."

I looked and saw that when the man rose up on his toes to make a point, he revealed that both of his soles had holes in them.

Martin whispered again, quoting from "Amazing Grace": "It looks as if those shoes are saying 'Through many dangers, toils and snares I have already come.' "

At that moment the man ended his very serious introduction, and I had to walk to the podium, bent double with laughter, while Martin nodded soberly.

Martin loved food and was particularly appreciative of good cooks. He was fond of Juanita because she was bright and quick-witted; but it was also her cooking that made her among his favorites. I remember one night in Montgomery when she had served homemade ice cream and he was about to start on his second bowl. Suddenly he stopped with his spoon in midair.

"Juanita," he said, "I believe we can solve this whole boycott problem if we carry a bowl of this ice cream over to George Wallace. I think I'll take it over right now."

He started to rise, then sank back in his chair.

"No," he said. "He doesn't deserve it. I'm just going to sit here and eat it myself."

Much has been written in recent years about my friend's weakness for women. Had others not dealt with the matter in such detail, I might have avoided any commentary. We all fall short of the mark, and an excessive preoccupation with one another's shortcomings is a form of pride that we should avoid. Sexual sins are by no means the worst. Hatred and a cold disregard for others are the besetting sins of our time, but they don't sell books or tabloid newspapers—and that's the reason why people have talked about Martin's failings and left the flaws of some others alone.

Unfortunately, some of these commentators have told only the bare facts without suggesting the reasons why Martin might have indulged in such behavior. They have also left a false impression about the range of his activities. While I can't completely set the record straight without violating my own sense of what is proper and decent, I think I can make some attempt to render justice to the dead without causing too much unnecessary pain to the living.

In the first place, Martin and I were away more often than we were at home; and while this was no excuse for extramarital relations, it was a reason. Some men are better able to bear such deprivations than others, though all of us in SCLC headquarters had our weak moments. I don't think it had anything to do with our respective views of what was right or wrong. We all understood and believed in the biblical prohibition against sex outside of marriage. It was just that he had a particularly difficult time with that temptation. His own principal explanation of that difficulty is one I choose not to repeat here.

But in addition to his personal vulnerability, he was also a man who attracted women, even when he didn't intend to, and attracted them in droves. Part of his appeal was his predominant role in the black community and part of it was personal. During the last ten years of his life, Martin Luther King was the most important black man in America. Indeed, he was the most important leader our people had seen in many generations, probably the most important ever. That fact alone endowed him with an aura of power and greatness that women found very appealing. He was a hero—the greatest hero of his age—and women are always attracted to a hero.

But he also had a personal charm that ingratiated him with members of the opposite sex. He was always gracious and courteous to women, whether they were attractive to him or not. He had perfect manners. He was well educated. He was warm and friendly. He could make them laugh. He was good company, something that cannot always be said of heroes. These qualities made him even more attractive in close proximity than he was at a distance.

Then, too, Martin's own love of women was apparent in ways that could not be easily pinpointed—but which women clearly sensed, even from afar. I remember on more than one occasion sitting on a stage and having Martin turn to me to say, "Do you see that woman giving me the eye, the one in the red dress?" I wouldn't be able to pick her out at such a distance, but already she had somehow conveyed to him her attraction and he in turn had responded to it. Later I would see them talking together, as if they had known one another forever. I was always a little bewildered at how strongly and unerringly this mutual attraction operated.

A recent biography has suggested without quite saying so that Martin had affairs with white women as well as black. Such a suggestion is without foundation. I can say with the greatest confidence that he was never attracted to white women and had nothing to do with them, despite the opportunities that may have presented themselves.

Of course, J. Edgar Hoover became preoccupied with Martin's private life early in the civil rights movement, and this preoccupation was a significant factor in Hoover's pathological hatred of him and the movement he headed. Early in the game the FBI began to bug our various hotel rooms, hoping to discover our strategy but also to gather evidence that could be used against Martin personally.

I remember in particular a stay at the Willard Hotel in Washington, where they not only put in audio receivers, but video equipment as well. Then, after collecting enough of this "evidence" to be useful, they began to distribute it to reporters, law officers, and other people in a position to hurt us. Finally, when no one would do Hoover's dirty work for him, someone in the FBI put together a tape of highly intimate moments and sent them to Martin. Unfortunately—and perhaps this was deliberate —Coretta received the tape and played it first. But such accusations never seemed to touch her. She rose above all the petty attempts to damage their marriage by refusing to even entertain such thoughts.

As soon as Martin heard it, he called me over to his house and played the tape for me and for one or two others. The message accompanying the tape was grim and explicit—Martin had thirty-four days to kill himself, otherwise he would be exposed for the monster he clearly was. While there was a certain irrational, even desperate tone to that message, it was not something we could dismiss. We had to do something.

So I decided to talk to the FBI myself in an effort to dissuade them from further harassment in the midst of what we considered to be a movement of vital importance to the strengthening of America. We knew as well as Mr. Hoover that foreign governments took a strong interest in the unrest among the nation's blacks. They had long cited racial injustice as one of the great weaknesses in American society, and from time to time their agents had recruited and used black dissidents to stir up trouble.

Hoover had heard enough of our conversations to know that we were not agents of any foreign ideological plot, but were loyal Americans attempting to reform the system from within. At least I assumed the FBI had that much sense; so I went in to reason with them, to say:

> Look here! We are engaged in a crusade to bring racial justice to America. Our chief enemies are precisely those people you have identified as among the most dangerous groups in the country—the Ku Klux Klan, the American Nazi party. If such people are opposed to what we are doing, doesn't that prove that we're a threat to the hatred and divisiveness that they represent?
>
> What you're doing is not only something the Nazis and the Klan will approve, but you are also treating Martin Luther King in a manner that is unfair and perhaps even illegal. His private life should be his own business. No government agency has the right to bug the bedroom of an American citizen in order to monitor his sex life. There is something especially outrageous about such behavior. How about stopping it and leave us alone to pursue our political and social goals with the full protection of the United States Constitution.

In retrospect, I realize how naive I was to have believed that such a plea would have had any effect on Mr. Hoover. He was clearly a man whose mind was made up on a number of issues and who had gone beyond the point where he listened to opinions that contradicted his own, even when they were supported by facts. But I made the trip anyway, a waste of my own time and the resources of the SCLC, which paid for my ticket to Washington.

Contrary to the testimony of others, I saw no evidence that Martin was greatly disturbed by Hoover's tapes or the knowledge that FBI agents were spreading tales about his sexual exploits. In fact, he seemed less concerned about public exposure than I was.

I had only one real conversation with Martin on this subject. He was involved with a young woman and her closeness to Martin had been spotted by some of the reporters covering our story. I was worried that with the materials being circulated by the FBI as an incentive, some of the more hostile members of the press might be tempted to make something of Martin's relationship with this woman and use it to discredit him and the movement.

As fate would have it, soon after the question had begun to trouble me, Martin and I were thrown in jail again and once more shared a cell, where we were left alone for most of the day. Realizing that I would never have a better opportunity, I brought up the matter.

"Martin," I said, "you can't really disguise the nature of certain friendships. If a man and woman are particularly close to one another, it shows in the way they behave—the way they look at one another and the way they talk. Don't sell these reporters short. They're much more alert and perceptive than you give them credit for.

"Besides, a single female among a group of men is bound to excite their imaginations. It's natural for them to want to 'assign' that woman to one of the men, and it's just as natural for them to assign her to the biggest man around.

"So whatever your relationship with her, you need to cool it down. With Hoover's men hiding under every bed, you just can't afford to continue the way you have."

Sitting there on the edge of the cot, he stared at the wall for a long time, weighing what I had said. When he answered, it was with a friendly but firm tone.

"Ralph, what you say may be right, but I don't care. Nor do I care what Mr. Hoover thinks or says. The FBI can do whatever they please, but I have no intention of cutting off this relationship."

I nodded my head and changed the subject. I was disappointed in his reaction, but I think I understood it. At that particular time, he was bearing a lion's share of the burden, and he felt he couldn't do so without this source of strength.

We never talked about the matter again.

To clarify my friendship with Martin, I feel compelled to discuss at least one incident in some detail—my designation in the SCLC bylaws as Martin's successor in the event of his death or incapacitation. The matter first came up when we were driving through Alabama, after Lyndon Johnson had become president following Kennedy's assassination. Because Johnson had no vice president, the question was raised concerning what would happen in the event he was incapacitated in some way. Who would take over the reins of government? The Constitution prescribed who would succeed him as president in the event he were to die, but the other question was not easily answered. In response to some national uneasiness, Johnson wrote down specific instructions and made them known to his administration and to the public at large.

As we were driving from Montgomery to Selma, with me behind the wheel, and Martin leaning back in the seat, eyes closed, he suddenly said to me,

"You know, Ralph, if Lyndon Johnson felt the need to provide for his successor, maybe I ought to do the same thing. What do you think?"

I immediately told him I thought such a move would be completely unnecessary, that nothing was going to happen to him. "Johnson is a middle-aged man who's already had one heart attack. You're barely in your thirties."

He sat up and stared at the straight road ahead, silent for a moment. I thought he had let the matter drop, and with a sense of relief I refocused my attention on my driving.

"You know," he continued, "I had the feeling I was going to be killed in Mississippi. I was certain of it. I'd already written off the rest of my life. Fortunately, it didn't happen. But I'm sure it will in Selma. This is the time and the place. I know it."

I tried to laugh him out of it. Sometimes that technique worked. This time it didn't; he was determined to talk about his apprehensions.

"I know you don't want to talk about it," he said, "but we have to plan for all possibilities. I'd like to know that if I'm no longer here, then you'll be carrying on for me."

My reaction was again negative. In the first place, I didn't want to consider the idea that he might be removed from the scene, even temporarily. No one could replace him. He had all the qualities needed to lead the movement. He was educated, eloquent, and had a presence that moved men and women to follow him in perfect faith. Then, too, he was already a symbol of the conscience of the nation in racial matters, not only for black people but for whites as well.

Certainly, I had significant reservations about my own ability to fill his shoes. I had stood in his shadow for most of the years, choosing to act as his counselor and sounding board rather than as a public presence or press spokesman. Andrew Young had stood in the spotlight more than I had; and with his youthful charm and his extremely light skin, I thought he might be more acceptable to our white friends and supporters than I would. Jesse Jackson also had a willingness to seek the spotlight that was almost at times a compulsion. I suggested these two people as possible successors, emphasizing again that such a move was unnecessary and perhaps even foolish, since it might give some sharpshooter ideas.

But Martin was adamant. He knew me better than any man alive, and he was confident that I would do what he would do, that with me at the helm the right decisions would be made, the right path chosen. It was flattering, to be sure, but the whole idea made me extremely uncomfortable and I argued with him for the entire distance between Montgomery and Selma.

But he had clearly made up his mind.

"The second week in April," he said, "we'll be having a board meeting in Baltimore. I'm going to propose to the board that you become the vice-president-at-large. You'll still be financial secretary-treasurer, but it will be understood that in case something happens to me, you will automatically become president."

The whole idea made me a little queasy, not only because we were talking about his death in such a casual way, but also because I didn't like to think of myself in the role of SCLC leader, with all the responsibility that the job entailed.

"We can't do that," I said. "The constitution won't permit it."

He nodded, still staring straight ahead.

"That's right," he said. "We'll have to change the constitution. But I'm sure the board will go along with whatever I recommend."

"Please don't ask me to do this, Martin," I said.

"Ralph," he said, "I've thought about it and prayed about it, and you are the only person who can keep the team together. And if the team stays together, then the program will come out of the team."

"I can't possibly map out strategy the way you do," I said, "I. . . ."

"You don't have to do all the planning," he said impatiently. "The others can do that for you. But you will have the same instincts I do in these matters.

"You know, Roy Wilkins told me not too long ago, 'Martin, if you ever need my opinion on a matter and can't reach me, then call my assistant, John Morsell. Whatever he says is what I would say, because he thinks the way I do.'

"Well, you think the way I do. You can be in California and I can be in New York, and if newsmen ask both of us the same question three thousand miles apart, we're going to come up with the same answer. That's why I want you to be my successor. Is that so difficult for you to accept?"

"No," I said quietly. "I suppose not."

I realized that in anticipating his own death, he wanted to

do whatever he could to assure that his work would continue, that things would be done his way. Somehow the idea of my being in charge reassured him at a time when he was extremely anxious about the future. By the time we arrived in Selma, I had assented to the idea of my being named without really expecting anything to be done.

Martin often fell into these moods of apprehension, but they never lasted long; and I figured that when this one passed he would drop the idea of a constitutional amendment. I was wrong, however. Once convinced that this move was prudent and businesslike, at the spring meeting of the board, he presented the proposition and insisted that they make a provision for his successor, and that I be designated as the man.

The board, feeling as I did that Martin would probably outlive us all, went ahead with the action, if only to humor him. I was designated as his automatic successor in the event he were to die or be incapacitated; and when he was shot down in Memphis I took over the direction of the organization as soon as I left the hospital. (Later, as if to affirm their belief in the wisdom of that constitutional change, the board convened in Atlanta on the evening of Martin's funeral and "confirmed" the fact that I was now head of the organization.)

But I had no part in devising or promoting this scheme, and it was only later that it occurred to me how resentful the others might have been, particularly Andy and Jesse, both of whom were ambitious. I'm sure it seemed to them that I was no more than an appendage to Martin, someone who served as a part companion, part bodyguard, but who never played an important role in the decisions that affected the direction of the movement.

In a sense that evaluation was right. What they didn't realize was the degree to which Martin depended on me for counsel when we were alone and how many of his ideas originated with me. As long as he was our leader, I gave him my complete and unqualified support in meetings and with others. If I had any reservations about what he was planning to do, I expressed them when only the two of us were together. We were a team, and each of us was severely crippled without the other. That is why I stuck so close to him during those years.

*   *   *

Martin Luther King, Jr., was probably the most famous preacher of his day, black or white; but contrary to what most people believe, it was not a skill that came to him naturally or even easily. He worked hard to achieve the eloquence for which he became so famous. (On the other hand, his brother A. D. was a natural, like their father, Martin Luther King, Sr. It was said of A. D. that he preached better drunk than did his more famous brother sober, which may have been why he was drunk a good deal of the time.)

But Martin was brighter and better educated than A. D., and he learned something from his "Boston exposure" that enabled him to "invent" the marvelous figures of speech and biblical elaborations that were so often quoted by newspapers and magazines. It was almost a trick, yet it was no more than what poets and storytellers have done throughout the ages: He stole his ideas and illustrations from older works.

I use the word "stole" here in the same way T. S. Eliot used it when he said that the mark of a mature poet is when he stops borrowing from other poets and starts stealing outright. Martin would study the homilies of earlier clergymen, take what he could use out of them, and then turn them into new and contemporary sermons, speaking them in his own idiom with his own voice.

When I say "earlier" clergymen, I mean eighteenth century and early nineteenth century figures, men who wrote and spoke in a language long outmoded, in fact virtually unreadable to the average country preacher. As incredible as it may seem to twentieth century readers, eighteenth century preachers were among the best-sellers of their time. A good volume of sermons would sell proportionately as many copies as a good mystery novel would today. Martin learned this at some point in his graduate studies and saw an opportunity to supplement an ordinary talent and turn it into an extraordinary one.

I think this practice might provide some doctoral candidate with a good topic for a dissertation, because much of what Martin said publicly had its origins in the works of clergymen long dead and in English as well as American graves. He never traveled

anywhere without a suitcase full of these musty volumes—
leather-bound, with beautifully decorated end sheets and gold-
tipped pages. Whenever we left a motel room, you could always
find bits of dried leather and paper on the floor beside the bed
where he had slept, because he was forever poring over his books
to find new figures of speech and flights of rhetoric.

Martin was not the only person who learned this trick. The
Reverend Dr. Benjamin Elijah Mays, another famous black
preacher, did the same. Dr. Mays had also experienced the
"Boston exposure," having attended Bates College before getting
his doctorate at the University of Chicago. He served first as dean
of the School of Religion at Howard University and then came to
Atlanta as president of Morehouse. There Martin and I knew
him, and there the controversy developed over who stole ideas
and sermons from whom.

Mrs. Mays was forever reading passages from Martin's
speeches in the *New York Times* and finding them hauntingly
familiar. Then she remembered where she had heard them: in
the sermons that Dr. Mays preached at every Morehouse chapel
service. She was perfectly happy to see Martin win national fame
and admiration using her husband's material. Imitation, after all,
was the sincerest form of flattery. But it annoyed her that Martin
didn't give Dr. Mays credit for the original ideas. It wasn't exactly
plagiarism, she said, but it wasn't quite honest either. "That was
Benny's idea," she would say. "Why won't Martin just say so?"

What annoyed her even more was the fact that many people
thought Dr. Mays was stealing from Martin and not vice versa.
Dr. Mays would preach to five or six hundred students at chapel.
Martin would preach to several thousand at Washington Cathedral. The *Washington Post* would quote liberally from Martin,
and everyone in Atlanta would assume that Dr. Mays had
plagiarized.

It is important for people to realize that while Martin was an
extremely important and even powerful man, he was by no
means a rich one, and in that respect he may have been unique.
Most men who gain fame and political power, whether in elective

office or in private political organizations, find ways of enhancing their income. Few U.S. senators, for example, leave office in modest circumstances. They have earned large legal fees along the way. They have been a part of lucrative investment groups. They have acquired and then sold important properties.

Martin, on the other hand, had almost no income other than what he earned as co-pastor of the Ebenezer Baptist Church, probably no more than ten thousand dollars. He was paid no salary as president of the SCLC. In fact, his only perquisite in that office was a chauffeur, who drove him around Atlanta, and also to nearby cities. But Martin supplied the car.

Of course, our expenses were paid as we traveled around the country; but more often than not, when we went into a city for a campaign or demonstration, we raised more money for the SCLC than we spent. So the organization wasn't really supporting Martin and the rest of us; we were supporting it.

Martin was expected and encouraged to supplement his co-pastor's salary by taking the proceeds from two speeches a month that he made as a representative of SCLC. The honoraria for the rest of the speeches—and sometimes he gave eight or ten a month—were put into the SCLC account and used for ongoing expenses.

As a consequence of this strict set of rules and Martin's adherence to them, the Kings did not live any better than the rest of us. Indeed, Martin and Coretta never owned a house until the last years of their marriage. They lived in a parsonage or in rented places, and to my knowledge they never had the kind of savings account that allowed them to make profitable investments or draw large amounts of interest.

Through sacrifices in other areas, the Kings and the Abernathys were able to give their children some of the advantages they had lacked: music lessons, ballet lessons, and later college educations. But the children went to public schools and they were no more privileged than any other children there. In fact, there were many families in Ebenezer and West Hunter Baptist churches who were far better off than the clergy, so fame and influence did nothing to further our fortunes—in part because we made a conscious choice to avoid any appearance of profiteering, lest our many critics take advantage of the situation to impugn our motives.

Of course, it would have been easy to appropriate money for our own use. Much of what we collected while we were on the road was in cash and no one knew how much there was. At the beginning of the Montgomery bus boycott, when we were traveling around the country raising huge sums of money, we would often take what we had collected at a rally and give it to the local preacher to deposit in his church account. Then he would send us a check through the mail.

Very early in the game, however, we began to notice that some of these checks were disappointingly small. We would pack a major metropolitan church to the rafters, make eloquent pleas for sacrificial giving, watch as the ushers went around, and see virtually every person in the place piling bills onto a heaping plate. Then, three or four days later, a check would come in that would average less than a dollar per person for that large audience. Then, in several months, we would hear that Reverend So-and-So had taken his entire family on a trip to the Bahamas. It took little imagination for us to know who had paid for that trip.

So sadder and wiser as the result of several such incidents, we made certain we were right there when the plate—spilling over with ones, five, tens, and twenties—would arrive in the pastor's study. We would count the collection, bundle up the bills, and put them immediately into a satchel, which I would then take into custody. We were gracious and friendly when we did all this—but we did not deviate from the procedure, regardless of whose church we were visiting. Better to be slightly distrustful than to tempt our brother pastors.

On these trips I was always the "bagman," and that meant I had to be especially careful to keep my hands on the satchel at all times and to look out for strangers. It also led to many nights sleeping in the Atlanta airport with the satchel between my knees.

Often we would get into Atlanta late at night and have to wait till the next morning for a flight to Montgomery. At that time Atlanta was still a segregated city, regardless of the succession of court rulings that gradually eliminated Jim Crow. The continued segregation of public facilities meant that white taxis would not serve blacks, and when you came out of the Atlanta airport and looked around, all you saw were white taxis. In fact, there was only one black cab company; and because there were only a few black airline passengers in those days, and because the Atlanta airport was twenty miles out of town, the Lincoln Cab Company did not station one of their few vehicles to meet incoming flights. If you had just flown in and wanted a cab to pick you up, you had to call into Atlanta. Then, because the interstate highway had not yet been built, you had to wait until the cab wound through a network of back roads—usually for about an hour—and you had to pray that it didn't have a flat tire or blow a gasket on the way. Even if you were picked up in an hour, it would take you at least another hour to get home.

Many times Martin and I would fly into Atlanta and be scheduled to fly out the next day. If we wanted to spend the night in Atlanta, we were faced with a two-hour ordeal before we got to bed, as well as another hour of travel time in the morning, usually to catch an early flight out. That meant a minimum of three hours of sleep lost.

Early in the movement, Martin decided that he would prefer to make the cab trips and enjoy what little sleep he could steal and still get up in time to leave the next morning an hour and a half before flight time. He needed a certain amount of comfort in order to sleep well—a bed, a pillow, the luxury of being horizontal, and he could always go to the home of his parents. So when we would arrive late in the evening, Martin would call the taxi, wait for the inevitable hour, and then wind home to his own bed.

On the other hand, I have always been able to go to sleep anywhere and in any position. I believe I learned this trick in the army, where you used every ten-minute break to catch up on the sleep you'd lost the night before. I can sleep stretched out on a wooden floor, or seated in a rocking chair, or even on a hard wooden bench. So it was no problem for me to sit down in the Atlanta airport, close my eyes, and in a couple of minutes fall sound asleep for the rest of the night, awakening only occasionally at some sudden noise.

But our splitting up at the end of the flight posed one question: What would we do with the satchel of money? The most obvious answer was for Martin to take it home with him. But the more we thought about that solution the more problems we discovered. After all, Martin, driving along those dark and winding back roads, would be much more vulnerable than I was, seated in the well-lit lobby of Atlanta International Airport, where there was always a policeman stationed.

So we finally decided that I would keep the money at the airport, squatting on it in such a way that it was imprisoned between my calves and my buttocks. That way, if anybody tried to move the satchel, I would wake up and scream "Bloody murder!" knowing full well there was a policeman nearby. In a way I looked like a chicken perched in a hen house, and Martin would laugh at me getting comfortable on my nest egg as he started for the cab. But I had the last laugh. Before he had exited from the airport, I would be fast asleep; and sometimes he would have to wake me when he came in the next morning.

In all those years, we never lost a dollar from the satchel.

When we first came to Atlanta in 1961, our children were just starting in school. Juandalynn had completed kindergarten and was ready to enter the first grade, Donzaleigh was just starting nursery school, and Ralph III was almost two years old. Juanita, who was determined to find the best schools available, enrolled Juandalynne in Frank L. Stanton, a neighborhood school, and put Donzaleigh and Ralph in the nursery school at Spelman College. The King children were also enrolled in these schools, and Cody Perry, Martin's driver, picked up all the children, took them to school, brought them home, and then took them to various lessons and athletic practices in the afternoon.

As a consequence, our children were good friends with the King children and saw a great deal of them. Then Juanita and Coretta decided that the oldest children—Yoki, Martin, Juandalynn, and Donzaleigh—would receive the best possible education at Spring Street School, located near the downtown area of Atlanta. This was the school the children of governors and congressmen had traditionally attended, and Juanita wanted only the best for our children. At that time the city had instituted a system allowing all children to choose the school they wanted to attend. We thought there would be little trouble enrolling our children at Spring Street, and filled out the forms.

Juanita drove the four of them to school the first day and was shocked at what she saw. A mob of white parents surrounded the school, and in order to get the children inside the building, she had to lead them past a line of screaming cursing adults, who called them every vile name imaginable. When the five of them were inside, they were met by the principal, a Mrs. Douglas, who treated them with a cool courtesy.

Since two of the children, Juandalynn and Yoki, were both in the third grade and two, Marty and Donzaleigh, were in the second grade, we assumed that two would be in one class and two in another, but Mrs. Douglas divided them up, placing each child in an all-white room. It was then that they discovered for the first time that they were the only black children in school.

Each morning for a week Juanita—a strong and courageous woman—would take the children past the line of abusive adults, and each day the group would get smaller and less vocal. Then, the second Monday, she drove up and saw the schoolyard empty. The white parents had given up. From that time forward black students were admitted to Spring Street School and other all-white schools in increasing numbers.

So our children and the King children had their own campaign and final victory in the civil rights movement, a local version of what we were able to accomplish on a national scale. That common experience bound them close together, even though, in later years, they went to separate high schools and colleges.

Martin was mild mannered in his relationships with others and slow to anger. But occasionally he would become so angry that he would completely break off relationships with people with whom he had worked. One person who angered him was Carl Stokes, mayor of Cleveland, and it happened like this.

We had just finished up our negotiations in Chicago, and the air around us was heavy with hatred. We were unnerved by what we had seen of that city, yet we could not easily withdraw, because there were still details to iron out and we had no other project in sight. Then we were given an opportunity to exit gracefully from the Chicago scene. Carl Stokes was running for mayor of Cleveland, and for the first time in history it appeared as if a black might be elected mayor in a major American city. We were invited to come to Ohio and play an important role in the campaign. The most attractive aspect of this invitation was the excuse it gave us to leave Chicago, and when I read the letter I immediately took it to Martin and urged him to accept. He read it once through, then looked up at me.

"I'm already packed," he said.

When we got to Cleveland, we were still skeptical that Carl could win, but after we looked at the numbers we agreed with the Stokes backers: It was just possible he could make it. However, it was clear that he had to make some inroads into the white community in order to pull off a victory and that posed a dilemma: If he tried to court the white vote then he couldn't spend the time necessary to get out the black vote; on the other hand, if he waged the kind of campaign necessary to turn out the black vote, then he would alienate too many of the whites he needed to win. So he turned to us for help.

"If you could come in and organize the black community," he said, "then I could devote all my attention to the whites and say the kinds of things that would appeal to them. Your organization is the only black group in the country with sufficient reputation and experience to manage this operation. How about it?"

Given the importance of electing blacks to office in an era when there were almost none, we concluded the Cleveland race could be a breakthrough, so we agreed to help. We moved in, set up a headquarters, and put together a full-scale campaign organization, although we had never done such a thing before. We registered voters. We prepared and distributed literature. We organized blocks and precincts. We recruited workers. We established a phone bank and made thousands and thousands of calls. And on election day we provided transportation for everyone who needed it.

The campaign was exhausting. We worked day and night, came home to a motel room to fall into bed, and then rolled out at the crack of dawn the next day and went back to work again. Finally election day came, and we worked in our headquarters until the very last minute before the polls closed. Then Martin hung up the phone after reminding the last voter to go to the polls, and said, "Well, we've done all we can. Now let's go and enjoy the party."

We caught a cab from the black section and arrived at the downtown hotel a little after the rest of the workers, since we had stayed at our post until the last minute. We took the elevator up to the suite Carl had rented for the occasion, and when we arrived we were greeted by Carl, his wife, and the Reverend Eddie Osburn, our old and good friend. Eddie had kept the SCLC alive in Cleveland over the years and, though it was not our most active chapter, Eddie alone had accomplished many fine things. We talked to him for a minute, and then Carl came over and called us aside.

"I want you to come with me down the hall."

"OK," we said, assuming that he wanted to introduce us to somebody. He led us to another room, took out a key, and let us in. We found ourselves in a tiny single room.

"This will give you some privacy. I'll be back to get you when the time is ripe for you to make your appearance."

We thanked him, sat down on the narrow bed, and turned on the television set, which was black-and-white and about the size of a cereal box. The election returns were just beginning to come in and things looked bad for Carl. But the newscaster kept stressing that these were figures from white boxes. The black boxes had yet to come in, so we felt a little better.

Then, after a while, the black boxes started coming in, and we had done our job better than anyone expected: The turnout was heavier than usual, with Carl getting virtually all of it. His white opponent was beginning to lose ground. Soon they were neck and neck. Then, as the black boxes continued to pour in, Carl pulled ahead. Finally, he was so clearly the winner that even the newscaster began to concede his victory.

During this dramatic contest, Martin and I had sat on the edge of the small bed, bent over, staring at the tiny television set, rejoicing over the fact that our work had given Carl his margin of victory. The white boxes had come in as expected. The black boxes had exceeded all predictions.

Then suddenly we found ourselves watching Carl Stokes himself, standing on the platform, claiming victory, surrounded by his wife, Eddie Osburn, and a crowd of other supporters. They were all screaming, cheering, and waving drinks around, joining in the celebration. Then we realized we'd been had. Carl had stashed us in this room to keep us away from his victory party. He didn't want us on the platform with him. He didn't want to acknowledge the importance of our help. In the middle of Carl's victory speech, Martin turned to me.

"Come on," he said. "Let's get out of here."

We left the hotel unnoticed and caught a cab back to our motel in the black section of town, riding in silence, both of us contemplating what had happened. When we got to the room where we had stayed for so long, Martin finally spoke.

"You make the reservations while I pack. I want the first plane out to anywhere."

Fortunately, there was an Atlanta plane early the next morning, and we were on it. Later that day, Eddie Osburn called. After hearing what happened, he apologized profusely. He had not been in on Carl's little trick.

But Carl Stokes never apologized, nor has he thanked us to this day for the role we played in getting him elected that first time.

Much has been made in recent narratives of Martin's fears that he would be killed during the course of the movement, and some people have even suggested that he was cowardly. These charges are not new. They were made during his lifetime, particularly by advocates of violence who wanted to attribute the worst possible motives to his insistence that we not strike back at our attackers. The charge was made when we turned back that Tuesday in Selma. It was made again in Birmingham when we agreed to a truce while negotiations for a peaceful settlement were in progress. And it was made after we had left Chicago, only to be betrayed by Mayor Daley, who reneged on his promise to promote an open housing policy.

In more recent accounts, derived from interviews with former staff members, historians have begun to probe the day-to-day relationships Martin had with his associates and to discover chinks in his armor hitherto unrevealed. With this kind of information in circulation, I feel a certain obligation to discuss this question of Martin's courage (or lack of it) in some detail. I knew him better than any of the staff members and I was with him from the beginning. He also talked to me at some length about his reservations and fears, so I believe I can make a contribution to this dialogue.

First, however, let me point out what Plato had to say on the subject. In discussing the courage in battle he said there were three kinds of men. First, there were those who knew the risks involved in warfare, understood what it meant to die, and were desperately afraid. When faced with the enemy, they turned and fled, unable to control their fears in the face of mortal danger. These men, said Plato, were cowards.

Second, there were those who went to war with absolutely no understanding of what might happen to them. They had no sense of their own vulnerability, and they had never considered what it meant to die. When faced with the enemy, they charged forward without the slightest thought of the consequences. Plato called these men fools.

Third, there were those who entered the fray fully aware of the dangers they faced and fearful that they might lose their lives. They had contemplated death and knew that it was an ever-present possibility on the field of battle. Yet, afraid of the enemy's ability to wound or kill them, they nonetheless controlled their fears, marched into battle, and fought for their people. Only these men, according to Plato, were truly brave, because only they were willing to risk their lives in full knowledge of the dangers involved.

Martin Luther King, Jr., was a truly brave man.

It is certainly a matter of fact that at times he was preoccupied with the imminent possibility of his own assassination. Some have described this preoccupation as "morbid" and have suggested that others did not feel the same gloomy apprehension. But events have certainly vindicated any sense of doom he felt. Those other staff members who now suggest that he was overreacting miss the obvious point that they are alive and he is not.

They never learned what it was to be the "point man" for the entire movement and to know that all eyes, all conspiracies, all gun sights are focused on you. Martin felt that for almost fourteen years, during which he was the target of two bombing attacks, one knife attack, and literally thousands of threats, sent through the mails and breathed over telephones by people who were pathological in their hatred of him.

His house was bugged, his phone lines were tapped, and everywhere he went he could be certain that he was being monitored by the latest electronic devices. He wasn't always certain that these belonged to the U.S. government. After all, his enemies consisted of some of the most desperate and dangerous hate groups in America—the Ku Klux Klan and the American Nazi party to name but two. Also, he never ruled out the possibility that his own government might want him dead as fervently as did those ragged bands of zealots.

It wasn't as if these people were just big talkers who never took action in support of their warped beliefs. Four little girls in Birmingham, three victims in Selma, Medgar Evers and three Freedom Riders in Mississippi—these were just the most famous of those who died during this era in the service of the civil rights movement. Small wonder that Martin, a man of great intelligence and sensibility, considered his own death from time to time and was appalled at its high level of probability. Indeed, there were times when he was terrified.

Sometimes his fear manifested itself in a melancholy moodiness. He would be lost in thought for long periods of time, and when he talked about the future he would be pessimistic and even apocalyptic. More than once he talked about retiring, turning the movement over to somebody else, or just letting it drift for a while in order to let those in favor of violence have their day.

Occasionally, he would talk about leaving the public scene and retiring to some remote hideaway, far from the limelight that he had inadvertently stumbled into. We took a vacation to Acapulco when he was in such a mood, and during that final week he spoke of retreating to a remote farm in Georgia, where he could live a simpler life without the conflict that surrounded him during his every waking hour. This periodic longing for Bali Hai was just one more way he had of coping with fears that from time to time gripped him. But he never made the final break with the movement that would have ensured his ultimate survival.

He would often dwell on the possibility that he might be killed and would begin to make plans in anticipation of that time, for instance, by choosing an SCLC successor should something happen to him.

Another manifestation of his fear was the illness that would sometimes overtake him when he was about to face danger. Again the best example was Selma, where for a number of days he was so sick with "a stomach virus" that he was unable to function as leader of the movement and had to delegate responsibilities to me and to others.

This was no mere attack of nervous stomach. He ran fever and was racked by chills, alternating with heavy sweats. No one could have doubted that what he suffered from was a genuine illness. This happened not once but a number of times during the years between 1954 and 1968. Sometimes he was even hospitalized.

Yet when his presence was absolutely essential to accomplish some important goal, or when a genuine confrontation was at hand, he always showed up and marched at the head of the line, his calm and assured manner a model for others to emulate. In Birmingham, when the entire black business community was telling us to obey the court injunction and call off our march rather than risk Bull Connor's dogs, it was Martin who decided to lead the demonstration himself and then tried to persuade me to go on back to Atlanta and let him bear all the risk.

In Selma, after waiting to get a favorable ruling from the federal court, Martin led the march out of Selma, believing that he would die in this campaign and knowing that along that lonely highway a sniper would have his best shot at those who walked at the head of the line. With two people already dead it was a brave move on his part, not *in spite* of but *because* of the illness he was suffering as the result of his fear.

In Chicago, where we encountered the largest and most hostile crowd in our long experience, it was Martin who overrode the fears of the other staff members and moved to the head of the line to lead the march into the suburb of Gage Park. For his gesture he was struck in the head by a rock, a blow that might well have been fatal. Yet he picked himself up off the ground and proceeded forward.

These are only three examples of many when he overcame his well-founded fears to face his enemies in the field. Memphis would be a fourth, for I am certain that his reluctance to go there that week and his desire to get out of the city as quickly as possible were the result of yet one more premonition. Certainly, his speech at the church that last night suggests that he was once again contemplating the possibility that he would be killed soon—as indeed he was.

If Plato was right about the nature of true courage, then Martin Luther King certainly fit the definition. Fearful that he would be killed, and well aware that he was vulnerable every time he sought public confrontation, he nonetheless continued to place himself in jeopardy on literally hundreds of occasions over more than a decade. And while he may have privately complained about the dangers he had to face, publicly he was always the embodiment of the kind of courage that was required if the civil rights movement were to succeed. Had he been a coward rather than a truly brave man, then none of the rest of us would have followed him and we might still be riding in the back of buses and eating in segregated restaurants.

*   *   *

It has been more than twenty years now since Martin died, the man who knew my mind and heart better than any other man. The pain of that loss has diminished in years, but I have never quite gotten over it. Every so often I will see or hear something and reach for the telephone, saying, "I need to tell Martin about that." Then I remember that he is not sitting in his study at Ebenezer Church, but lying in a crypt on a small island— separated from the rest of us by the deep water surrounding him and by the widening years.

15

Resurrection City

WHEN I TOOK OVER FROM MARTIN, I did so after the civil rights movement had peaked and the SCLC had already begun to decline in influence. In Montgomery we had begun in hope and had won a great victory. We had grown in strength and purpose at Birmingham and Selma. But we had been tricked in Chicago and went away empty-handed. We still had a number of tasks to accomplish, but we had lost our fighting edge and the single-minded allegiance of our people, who were beginning to look in other directions for leadership. As I have already suggested, Martin's last months were troubled by this loss of momentum and by the opposition that had sprung up against us, both in the white press and in a small but vocal segment of the black community. When I took over after his death, I inherited his deep concern along with the other responsibilities and burdens of office.

As I think back on those times, I realize that we had begun to falter for several reasons, some of them unavoidable, some of them a product of our own miscalculations. In no particular order, I would list them as follows:

494

1. The first reason we declined in influence was our remarkable success—we had eliminated virtually all of the statutory barriers to our own advancement and equality. Through our efforts and those of others, legal segregation in most areas of public life had been eliminated, either by a decision of the U.S. Supreme Court or by the passage of legislation in the U.S. Congress. All schools and other federal, state, and local institutions; all public facilities; and all public accommodations had been desegregated or were in the process of desegregation. We were now guaranteed the right to vote, so in those places where we made up a significant segment of the population we had the opportunity to exercise some control over our own political destiny.

   These things had been the major goals of our movement from the beginning, and they had been achieved in a decade of great upheaval, something no one could have predicted when we first began our boycott to protest the arrest of Mrs. Parks. But when we had accomplished these things, there were many who said this was enough, that we should be satisfied with theoretical equality, despite the fact that we were still manifestly unequal in a number of ways that really counted.

   In fact, our situation was very much like that of the slaves following emancipation. In *Up from Slavery*, Booker T. Washington describes how a Union officer rode into the plantation where young Washington had been born a slave, read the Emancipation Proclamation, and rode out again, leaving the free blacks to figure out how they were going to make a living for the rest of their lives. Their solution: go back up the Big House, hat in hand, and tell their former owners that they would remain and do what they were told.

   If you are not economically independent then you are not free in any meaningful sense of the word—and that was just as true in the 1960s as it was in the 1860s. Once again, the legal barriers had been removed and yet life had not changed for most blacks—not yet. We recognized that fact, but some of our critics did not.

When we tried to change our focus and attack economic injustice, we lost many of our former supporters, including some members of the press.

2. As noted in the discussion of Chicago, our shift of the battleground from South to North also cost us support. Since the Civil War, many non-southerners had regarded racial discrimination as a regional problem. The South had patently unjust laws mandating segregation. The whole society was openly and unapologetically racist. And southern politicians like Theodore Bilbo, Gene Talmadge, and John Rankin continually reminded the nation that they represented an all-white electorate, that blacks could not vote in southern states and were therefore less than citizens. So the rest of the nation seemed to many people enlightened and tolerant, an ideal society compared with what was going on in Mississippi, Alabama, and the rest of the region.

Thus, when we went northward many non-southerners were outraged, because they had never thought of themselves as anything but exemplary in their race relations. When blacks demonstrated at the opening of the New York World's Fair, Walter Cronkite announced on CBS News that we had gone too far, and when we went to Chicago black congressman William Dawson said they had no racial problems in that city. The national news gave us little coverage; when Mayor Daley denied that Chicago was segregated, they took him at face value.

Had Chicago been a southern city I'm certain that the press would have exposed the mayor's duplicity, conducted in-depth interviews with local blacks, and uncovered the racism that permeated the Daley machine. But the story simply didn't please as many people, nor did it appeal to anyone's sense of moral superiority, as stories about Birmingham and Selma did. When you attacked Mississippi, New Yorkers and San Franciscans felt good about themselves. When you attacked Chicago, everybody felt uncomfortable. So the press backed off, and when we went back down South, they never quite rejoined us, not with their previous enthusiasm.

3. The doctrine of nonviolent protest had increasingly come under attack by newer and younger black leaders who neither understood what we were doing nor cared about the progress we had made. Many of them did not want to make further progress within the system. They wanted to capture the movement in order to tear down society rather than reform it. They were filled with hatred and anger and they wanted to stir up the same emotions in their followers.

We saw them on the rise, and tried to persuade the best of them to join us; but they were beyond listening to reasons. Martin said to me shortly before he died: "Why don't we just step back and let the violent forces run their course? They don't know what they're doing, and it won't last long. But we need to prove to the nation that violence is wrong. The Stokely Carmichaels and Rap Browns are famous for coming into a community and leaving it in turmoil."

He said this, I think, just to hear me reassure him that what we were doing was right, and I immediately did just that. We couldn't abandon the Poor People's Campaign, I told him. We had to go on to Washington. He nodded his head and agreed with me, saying it would be a terrible sin if we didn't stand up for nonviolence; but he still worried about the increasing influence of Carmichael, Brown, and the newer breed of black leader.

And his worries were justified. They had begun to undermine our credibility with blacks and also with some of the white press, who found their style more confrontational and therefore better news. Thus the black community was divided and so was the attention of the nation as a whole. Not only did we fail to recruit the supporters that we once did, but our contributions began to dwindle, because some of what we used to get went to more militant groups.

It broke Martin's heart to be attacked by his own people, and it was also extremely difficult for me to bear, particularly since I had never experienced the outpouring of affection and loyalty that he had enjoyed during the early years of the movement. I had to accept increasing criticism from the advocates of violence, while at the same time answering the charges of whites who were saying we had gone far enough, that the things we were asking for could never be achieved.

4. The focus of the later years was no longer on race alone but on the disparity between the rich and the poor; and there were many people who opposed racism as a matter of principle, but who didn't want to see the economic apple cart upset. They were perfectly willing to help us do whatever was necessary to gain racial equality, but they believed that economic equality was an impossible goal and perhaps even an immoral one, since it meant redistributing the wealth through taxation and federal legislation.

Of course, blacks suffered greater economic deprivation than did whites, but many people did not think that this discrepancy should be eliminated by such governmental initiatives as affirmative action programs. Thus, when we started talking about economic issues, we began to alienate old friends and make new enemies.

5. Finally, after a decade of fighting for racial justice, many people, black and white, were weary of the struggle and were ready to give up, to lay down their swords and shields. Just as we were getting to the point where we could address the most basic needs of our people for the first time, our soldiers wanted to go back home and live in peace and poverty. It was as if the Israelites had seen how high the walls of Jericho were and had decided they would recross the desert and make a deal with old Pharaoh after all.

Our financial supporters were weary too. They had written checks over the years whenever we asked them, and now we were starting out again on a project the end of which they could not foresee. We had expanded our constituency to include Hispanics, American Indians, and poor whites. No longer did the cause seem as clear-cut or the motives as pure. We were now talking about money rather than desegregation, and to many that was not as compelling a cause. So we lost substantial financial support.

*   *   *

Martin had been facing all of these problems in the months before he died, and they weighed him down. Now they were my problems, but I had to bear some additional burdens as well. I was not, after all, Martin Luther King, Jr.; and as far as the white press was concerned, that made quite a difference.

For one thing, I didn't have as many degrees as he did and I didn't have his polish. In addition, my skin was darker, a more important factor in dealing with the white press than anyone would dare admit. As Andrew Young put it, in advising me during those first days as president: "Now the national press isn't going to be as kind to you as they were to Martin. You're not the fair-skinned boy. Your ancestors weren't 'house niggers.' So they'll treat you differently."

In an attempt to try to "sell" me to the press and to the American people, Andy contacted *Ebony* and *Jet* and arranged for them to do cover stories to give me a boost. In retrospect, I realize this approach did more for me in the black community than in the white press, which wanted to see me as another Martin Luther King, something I was not and could never be, any more than he could have been a Ralph Abernathy.

Since Martin had already been receiving criticism from various sources for the faltering pace of the movement, I was also attacked by people from the same quarters. I had no honeymoon. I went immediately to the kitchen, which was already plenty hot.

So in order to confront the issue I told the press: "I want to make it crystal clear that no man living, dead, or unborn could fill the shoes of Martin Luther King, Jr."

But I went on to point out that each man has something to offer, and that I would make my own unique contribution to the movement now that he was dead.

After the Memphis march I called a staff meeting to plan the Poor People's Campaign, and we tried to take up where we had left off. We had already decided to build a model city in Washington, a place where the poor people of the nation could come, live in "homes" of their own, and remind the nation at large of the poverty that still existed within its boundaries.

We had decided to build this city on the Mall, the long strip of green grass that runs from the Lincoln Memorial almost to the Capitol, flanked on either side by the several Smithsonian museums, and the gathering place for Americans who come to visit the capital city. So in a sense the Mall belongs to everybody in the country in a way that no other piece of land does. A number of groups during the year are allowed to lease a portion of the Mall and set up whatever structure or display suits their purposes, using the property for a while as if it were their own. Depending on when you are there, you might see a folk music festival, a tenthouse evangelist, a political exhibition by an eccentric political party, or a food vendor.

On the Fourth of July the ground is completely covered with people lounging on blankets, listening to radios, and eating every conceivable kind of food: fried chicken, hot dogs, tacos, gyro sandwiches, egg rolls, spaghetti, potato salad, sardines, spare ribs, knockwurst, sushi, barbecued beef, bagels, nachos, chitlins, hamburgers, corn dogs, baklava, cotton candy, ice cream, and peanut butter sandwiches. If you've never really understood what America is all about, then go to the Mall on the Fourth and walk among those tens of thousands of people. Then you'll have a better idea.

They are all jammed up together, lying within inches of one another, and yet they get along fairly well, particularly when the fireworks begin. Then they are all like a mass of small children, staring wide-eyed at the explosions of red and blue and green and purple that fill the sky and light up the Washington Monument, the Lincoln Memorial, and the White House—all of them visible if you are located in just the right place. It's quite a sight, and it was a little of that spirit that we were trying to capture in our plans for the Poor People's Campaign.

Before Martin was killed, we had dreamed up the idea of the city, and we had even named it. Sitting there in SCLC headquarters in Atlanta, we had tried to come up with something that would capture the essence of what we were trying to accomplish.

"We need to make it something positive, something hopeful," Martin had said.

"What about City of Hope?" somebody suggested.

"That sounds good to me," I said.

"There's already a City of Hope in California," somebody else pointed out.

Somebody then suggested "Dream City," but that didn't seem to fit either, since it sounded much too ethereal and unreal.

Finally, somebody came up with "Resurrection City," and we settled on it, though with some people expressing misgivings.

Later, however, when we came back to discuss the project after Martin's death, the name seemed even more appropriate. The more we thought about it, the more it seemed to fit what we were doing. We wanted to make the project a living memorial to Martin and what he had dreamed of, so that through the success of our campaign he would be resurrected in the fulfilled aspirations of the poor people of America, who would live better, fuller lives for him, now that he had died for them. The idea of resurrection would counter the new wave of cynicism and anger that was sweeping across the nation in the wake of the assassination, a hatred that Stokely Carmichael and his followers were growing powerful on. It had just the right touch, and I was pleased.

It was easy enough to lease a large portion of the Mall for this event, and we immediately did so. But the name and the place were among the easier aspects of our planning. Where would we find the poor people to live in our city, and how would we get them to Washington?

"We should be able to get enough poor people within thirty miles of Atlanta," someone said. "We've got all the poor people we need in our own backyard."

"No. We'll get them from everywhere," I said. "From the four corners of the nation. That way the entire country will bear the burden of the problem and not just one part of it."

Everyone agreed.

"Now what about transportation?" I asked.

At first we were thinking about transporting them directly to Washington in buses, the cheapest of all public transportation.

We had used buses before with great success. But buses had little symbolic value. They would simply be fast, inexpensive, and practical. We would use the buses for most of the trip, but we needed something else.

Then, even before Martin's death and funeral, somebody had come up with the idea of mule-drawn wagons and, again, the idea struck us as appropriate. To most of us who grew up in the rural South where poverty and farming were almost synonymous, the wagon was the perfect image of deprivation. We had all seen people as late as the 1960s come to town in a wagon because they couldn't afford to own and operate an automobile. A number of rural blacks and whites still lived this way. We imagined things were much the same for Mexican-Americans in Texas and California.

But, then as now, the worst poverty in the country could be found in the inner cities, where generations of blacks had grown up jammed into squalid, crumbling tenements, starving to death, without any hope of moving three blocks beyond where they lived for an entire lifetime. These people had never ridden in a wagon and they never knew what a mule was.

Yet the nation as a whole understood what we were driving at when we announced our plans. We would start out from the four corners of the nation in caravans—from the South, Southwest, Midwest, and New England, all leaving at different times, all converging at about the same time, all homeless people, come to Resurrection City to start a new life.

We would set up a model for the rest of the nation to emulate. Everyone would live together in peace and mutual respect, the way they did for a brief while on the Fourth of July. We would have people of all races, ethnic backgrounds, and religious beliefs. Since everyone would be poor, there would be no greed or envy. We would have a common dining room where everybody would eat together, and our business would be to go from government agency to government agency, representing the poor, speaking out for their interests, asking for several concrete things from our government, the richest in the world.

First, we wanted free food stamps for those who were out of work and had no money to buy food. Up until then, the government had supplied not stamps but commodities—usually butter, cheese, milk, and other dairy products that black people often could not eat because of our metabolisms. Food stamps would allow the poor to choose a healthier and more varied diet, thereby prolonging their lives and giving them the additional health and vigor to work at good jobs.

As for jobs, we wanted those too. But since what was needed, then as now, were skilled laborers, we would ask the Department of Labor to set up a job-training program to give those able to work the skills to find decent jobs. We would call for the creation of a million jobs a year until we had full employment.

Finally, we wanted housing for low-income families. This demand more than anything was symbolized by the city itself, which dramatized the great need for adequate shelter nationwide. All of these things were basic to survival—food, shelter, and minimal jobs; so we believed our demands in behalf of the hungry, the penniless, and the dispossessed were just and would be recognized as such by the people and their elected representatives.

As for me, I realized more every day the loss I had personally suffered and the terrible burden I had inherited. At the same time, I was beginning to feel a certain enthusiasm for the project we were planning and a hope that it might be successful. It occurred to me that if we could achieve the goals we set out to achieve, American society would indeed be miraculously transformed by Martin's death into the good and just society it should have been from the beginning; and I found this a very exciting prospect.

As for Resurrection City, I thought of it as a new founding, the creation of a model for the just society. We would teach Americans how to live with each other in their own cities, and we would accomplish this by simplifying existence to the point where everyone could understand what was truly important and what was merely irrelevant and inconsequential.

All our citizens would start out equal because they would arrive at Resurrection City in equal need: No one would have a larger house or a fuller stomach merely because of what he or she had inherited. No one would have an advantage over another because everyone would have nothing. No one would need an extra push because no one would have a head start. No one would be greedy and no one would be envious. We would all be back on the frontier, where liberty and equality were not two mutually exclusive ideas, but achievable goals. It was an invigorating prospect, and I found myself looking forward to the establishment of this City on the Hill, where we would live the Good Life as a witness to the entire nation.

"But wait a minute," someone said at one of our many planning meetings. "We have no real excuse to march on Washington—not yet. You only demonstrate when your demands haven't been met. We haven't even asked for these things."

Others argued that poor people had been asking for them since the founding of the nation, that these were the basic necessities every human being should be guaranteed in order to ensure "life, liberty, and the pursuit of happiness." Still others argued that specific demands (i.e., food stamps, job training, etc.) should precede any call for a massive convergence on Washington, and I tended to agree.

"We need a 'test run,' " I said. "Maybe a group of us should go to Washington as an advance delegation. We could call on the Department of Labor and the Department of Agriculture, present our list of what we want to achieve, and see what the response is. Then, when they say 'no,' we can immediately call for all the poor people in the country to come to Washington and stay till the government changes its mind."

So a small group flew into Washington, called a press conference, announced our intentions to see officials in those departments, and then went through the motions of calling on the bureaucracy.

We saw under secretaries, assistant secretaries, and deputy assistants—all of them high enough to recognize our importance as newsworthy black leaders but not high enough to make final decisions.

At the prodding of Walter Fauntroy—now congressman, then head of our Washington SCLC bureau—the Department of the Interior granted us a permit to build our city in the area between the Washington Monument and the Lincoln Memorial.

This plot of ground included the famous reflecting pool and about fifteen acres of the most beautifully kept grass in the world, and we concluded that we had acquired one of the best pieces of real estate available at the time.

Our permit specified that we could use this property for slightly over a month. We planned to take occupancy around the middle of May and vacate no later than June 16—our deadline. At least that was our original plan. Very little went according to schedule, and at the end of our lease, we were forced to ask for an extension.

So we called a press conference in Washington and announced that we had come in search of help for the poor people of the nation, and that their government had refused to listen. Therefore, we were going to bring a larger delegation to Washington and see if our combined voices would not then be heard. As symbolic of this moment, we went back to the Mall and drove the first stake in the ground for the raising of "City Hall," the tent that would be the headquarters of Resurrection City. Then we issued a call for the poor people to come to their nation's capital and help us out.

A number of newspapers and television commentators were supportive of these efforts, but some were not. The old consensus we had counted on in the past was no longer there for the asking. Neither was the money, not in the same quantities it had been before, and that posed a problem.

We estimated the Poor People's March would cost around one million dollars, a huge fortune in 1968. We had collected about three hundred thousand dollars, which we figured would be enough to put us on the road and get us to Washington. After that, we would have to rely on the grace of God and the generosity of Americans, black and white. Thus far our contributions had ranged from an anonymous gift of twenty-five thousand dollars to thirty-seven cents, given by a poor black who had come to our headquarters, eager to help but a little strapped for cash.

In addition, we had received gifts of food and clothing, including one thousand denim jackets sewn by a group of black women in Crawfordville, Georgia. During our stay in Washington we were constantly receiving additional gifts of this sort, mostly from black churches in nearby places like northern Virginia and Philadelphia. AT&T also donated some free telephones. For the most part, however, we paid for such things. Not only did we have to install telephone lines into our city, but we also had to put in temporary sewer lines, showers, electrical wiring, and medical supplies. The cost for these preliminary "hook-ups" ran around thirty-nine thousand dollars—a fairly expensive camping trip.

The most important expense we incurred, of course, was the feeding of all these poor people, almost none of whom could afford to buy their own meals. To give some idea of how close we were cutting corners, we had only $1.30 per person per day budgeted for meals. Yet considering the fact that we had approximately three thousand people to feed almost every day, our five-week food bill was staggering.

Our major expenditure was transportation, and we weren't sure that we would be able to take everyone home after the march ended, but we had enough support to go on with our plans, and we immediately arranged for the organization of the caravans. There were too many tasks to be performed by the current staff, so we had to hire additional personnel.

As a reminder of the origins of this Poor People's March, we began the southeastern caravan at Marks, Mississippi, where Martin had first seen those small children subsisting on such minimal food. We managed to assemble a number of people in a short amount of time, since the homeless and jobless are always numerous and have little to keep them rooted in one place. We promised daily meals and hope, two commodities they had long since found in short supply, so they flocked to our support. Hosea Williams was the leader of the southeastern caravan, and for a while my entire family joined the group and traveled down the highways: Juanita, Juandalynn, Donzaleigh, and Ralph III (Kwame had not been born then).

At the very outset we encountered difficulties with the weather. In Mississippi, for example, it rained on the day we had planned to leave, so we had to postpone our departure. But that wasn't the biggest problem we ran into. Our greatest headache was the mules.

We planned to leave from our various destinations with mule wagons leading the way, but the most important departure would be from Marks, Mississippi; and for that site alone we calculated we needed at least fifteen mule-drawn wagons, or a minimum of thirty mules.

First, it was hard to find that many mules "at liberty." The region had changed radically since the days of my childhood, and very few farmers were using mules any more—only a few of the older and poorer sharecroppers. Consequently, the animals were relatively scarce, even in Mississippi. Most of the extant mules were owned by blacks, so after inquiring for miles around, we finally located thirty fairly sturdy specimens and put them in a fenced pasture in Marks.

Our next problem was getting them shod, a necessary step if we were going to use them on the paved highways. In the old days this would have been no problem, but in 1968 there were few blacksmiths left, even in rural America—and there were even fewer who had shod mules.

We finally located an old man who said he could do the job, and we brought him to Marks, only to find that a local deputy sheriff had cut the fence and let out all thirty mules. Being of an independent mind, each mule had struck out in a different direction, and it took us the better part of a day to round them all up again and get the blacksmith to work.

However, many of these mules didn't like the idea of wearing shoes, and a mule that has made up its mind is the best example I know of an "immovable object." The blacksmith hammered and cursed for a couple of days, trying to do a job that with thirty horses would have taken no more than several hours—and I don't think he shod more than half of them.

By then it was past time to get on the road. It was at that point we discovered that we didn't have enough drivers to handle what mule teams we had put together. Again, times had changed. Younger blacks, many of whom had never worked on a farm, were terrified of the animals, viewing them with the same suspicion they would have felt toward a team of tigers. By the same token, the mules sensed this fear and reacted to it by snorting and kicking up their heels. Faced with this menacing behavior, some of our drivers withdrew, and as a consequence our wagon train was considerably reduced in size by the time we actually hit the road.

I flew around the country trying to spend some time with each of the eight groups; when I got to Mississippi I was given the honor of driving the mule train that was leading the caravan. Mules did not frighten me. I had spent some hot summer days plowing behind my father's mule, Annie, and I knew how much could be expected from one of them. So the mules and I got along just fine.

There was a crowd of curious onlookers, white as well as black; and I tried to make a speech wherever I went—not a long stem-winder, but a few words to commemorate the occasion in whatever town we found ourselves along the way.

The two mules pulling my wagon were named Eastland and Stennis, after Mississippi's two senators, both of whom we knew would be opposing the legislation we were going to Washington to promote. So when I was asked by someone why we had picked these names, I said:

> That mule there is named Eastland. I didn't know why. Then I found out he's old and forgetful, and he doesn't even want to carry his part of the load. The other's Stennis. They gave me the task to lead him. Now, Stennis is still full of life. But he's so stubborn. He wanted to get off the road and eat grass. I said, "All these years, you been leading us around, but today, thanks be to God, we're leading you."

A *New York Times* reporter there was surprised that I would say such a thing in front of a crowd of whites, and puzzled that many of them thought it was just as funny as the blacks did.

Unlike the marches in Montgomery, Birmingham, and Selma, this was a joyous occasion. Everybody was in high spirits, and there was much laughing and singing along the way. For one thing, we knew—or thought we knew—that the time for massive violence was over. An individual, like James Earl Ray, might gun one of us down; but we no longer expected to be met by official violence, like the dogs and water hoses the City of Birmingham had used. Besides, our movement was no longer racial but multiracial. So poor whites had little reason to view us as a threat to their tenuous respectability, as they had once done.

It was a slow trip, mostly along the backroads and highways of the rural South and no one bothered us until the group crossed over into Georgia. By then I was traveling with another caravan, but I received word from a reporter covering my movements that my entire family had been arrested in Georgia.

"On what charge?" I asked the reporter.

"For trespassing on Georgia's highways."

"For what?" I asked.

He grinned. "That's what it says on the AP wires."

Sure enough. They had been stopped and arrested by the Georgia State Patrol under orders from Governor Lester Maddox. Maddox, who had resisted the integration of his Atlanta restaurant by brandishing an axe handle, was the last of the racist-populist governors in Georgia, a state that had produced more than its share in the twentieth century. Maddox was playing to his constituency when he issued such a ridiculous order, and the federal courts soon intervened to rule that we had every right to use the highways. But for a while my wife and children were under arrest.

As usual, such outrageous behavior on the part of the white establishment just gave us additional publicity and enlisted sympathy from people who might otherwise have yawned at the whole venture. Maddox, despite his militant racism and his ostensible political success, was never any real hindrance, as earlier racist demagogues had been. On the whole, because of his absurd posturing and irresponsible rhetoric, he was a help; in later years, when we were opposed by more subtle opponents, we had a much more difficult time achieving our ends.

After the federal injunction was issued and my family and the caravan were back on the road, I worried for a few days, because I thought the incident might provoke some isolated act of violence. But none occurred. They passed out of Georgia and into South Carolina, where they were met with no such outrageous tactics and the trip was relatively uneventful.

Of course, the wagons and mules didn't make the entire trip. They traveled a portion of the way in each state and were then loaded into vehicles and transported into the next state. We tried to stagger the caravans so that those who were traveling from a farther distance would arrive at the same time as those who began at locations closer to Washington, but our timing was slightly off, and the eastern caravan was ahead of the others.

On May 11, I flew to New York and met them for a huge rally in Central Park. It was a noisy crowd, and I told them that we would stay in Washington "until the walls of poverty are torn down." At that point the crowd, warming to the occasion, shouted back.

"They will do everything they can to stop us," I said.

"That's right, brother," they cried.

"They will do everything they can to turn us around.

"They will do everything they can to provoke us to violence.

"But we are not going to inflict violence on property or person.

"Under the leadership of Martin Luther King, we tried to rock this nation until things fell into place, but under the leadership of Ralph Abernathy, we're going to show them something—we're going to turn it upside down and right-side-up."

The crowds cheered and began singing as we marched out of Harlem and East Harlem, down Fifth Avenue, where the famous Easter parade had taken place and where the great heroes were greeted with ticker tape parades after returning home from foreign wars and Olympic triumphs. We hadn't won a great victory—not yet—but we took that walk down Fifth Avenue as a symbol of our revived spirits after Martin's death. Though it had only been a few months, I thought it was important to stress that we were looking toward the future rather than the past, and that we had won our battle against despair and the attempt to wreak our vengeance on the white community.

As we walked past black onlookers, we yelled out, "Give us

some help. We're doing this for you. Just one block. Just half a block."

And many responded by leaving the sidewalk and joining our columns to march a block or two before they fell away and waved at us. One woman expressed the feelings of many after she had walked a ways and then returned to watch.

"I should go to Washington," she told a reporter. "I'm deeply considering it."

Officially we opened the Poor People's Campaign on May 12, with a rally in Cardozo High School Stadium, located in the heart of Washington's worst black slum. The surrounding area had been devastated by riots following Martin's death, and the stadium rose out of great piles of bricks and rubble that served as a reminder both of Martin's death and of the inevitable consequences of violence, even in the face of such cruel injustice.

Thousands came to hear Coretta King give a stirring speech, calling for "black women, white women, brown women and red women—all the women of this nation—[to join] in a campaign of conscience." She called for welfare reform, and a restoration of benefits for women with children, saying: "Our Congress passes laws which subsidize corporation farms, oil companies, airlines and houses for suburbia, but when it turns its attention to the poor, it suddenly becomes concerned about balancing the budget."

She was joined on the platform by my wife, Juanita, and Mrs. Robert Kennedy, as well as Mrs. Harry Belafonte, Mrs. Phillip Hart, and several other prominent women, who supported our efforts by sharing in that moment. It was an impressive kickoff for the campaign; and after the rally a number of us returned to the Mall to begin setting up our model city.

There were Mexican-Americans from the Southwest, American Indians from the Dakotas, Puerto Ricans from New York City, poor blacks and poor whites from all over. They believed deeply and firmly that they had come to find a better life, and they took the idea of their own City on the Hill quite seriously. For the first time in their lives, they were to have their own homes and own street addresses. You could see the excitement shining in their eyes when we told them what we had in mind.

We had spots staked out along streets named for the heroes of the movement: King Boulevard, Abernathy Street, Fanny Lou Hamer Drive. As they scrambled out of wagons and buses—carrying all their belongings in bundles, cardboard boxes, or cardboard suitcases—we met them, took them to City Hall to register, and then tried to assign them "property" on a first-come, first-served basis.

On May 13, we had a brief dedication ceremony, at which I drove the nails into the first plywood building and then said a few words. I announced that we had come "to plague the Pharaohs of this nation with plague after plague until they agree to give us meaningful jobs and a guaranteed annual income."

I also vowed that our marches and demonstrations in the city would be nonviolent, but I warned the government that we were there for the long haul.

"Unlike the previous marches which have been held in Washington," I said, "this march will not last a day, or two days, or even a week. We will be here until the Congress of the United States decide that they are going to do something about the plight of the poor people by doing away with poverty, unemployment, and underemployment in this country."

I pledged that we would stay until Congress adjourned. "And then," I said, "we're going to go where Congress goes, because we have decided that there will be no new business until we first take care of the old business."

Then we sang "We Shall Overcome." Since the Indians had originally owned the land and had suffered greatly at the hands of our government over the years, I symbolically alluded to this injustice by asking an Indian girl for permission to use the land, and she granted it. Then I said, "I declare this to be the site of our new city of hope, Resurrection City, USA."

After this brief ceremony, we began to build the first home on our property for Minnie Lee Hill, who had come from Marks, Mississippi. Mrs. Hill was there with eight of her children and she symbolized the need and deprivation that Martin had recognized and responded to in that community.

The "homes" we were building were not, strictly speaking, tents although they were often called that in the news stories and although there were some real tents on the site. They were actually, A-frame huts made of plywood. In size they were about eight by twenty feet, not the Taj Mahal by any means, but with the square footage of a fairly spacious bedroom. Since these had been prefabricated, they were fairly easy to put together, and by nightfall we had constructed about a hundred. We continued, however, by spotlight; and as hammers pounded nails and saws bit into wood, the city took shape between the marble formality of the Lincoln Memorial and the Washington Monument, its progress evident in the still waters of the reflecting pool. By the next day, Washingtonians were surprised (and probably shocked) to see about six city blocks of raw plywood structures covering the green lawn of the Mall.

We had moved in.

At first the "shacks" had the same unpainted look about them, as if they were made out of huge wooden playing cards leaning against one another. Later, however, the graffiti that decorated them gave each its distinctive character. One was named "Big House of John Hickman." Another contained "Soul Sisters Shirley, Mary, Ruby, Joyce." Still another was called "Cleveland's Rat Patrol." There were also some bearing Spanish names, and a few with pictures drawn on them. We allowed them to write what they wanted to, as long as it wasn't offensive or obscene.

In addition to the individual shacks, we also had a large mess tent where everyone ate, as well as tents that housed doctors, dentists, and a nursery. During the first days, which were sunny, barbers gave free haircuts on a first-come, first-served basis.

We even had our own zip code, 20013.

I was too busy to ponder at length the meaning of all this; but when I stopped to watch these people, I was touched by the eager and grateful way they responded to these services, usually unavailable to them in the towns and cities where they lived. For the first time, many of them felt genuinely part of a real community, something most people take for granted since it is part of our nature as human beings to be social animals rather than loners. We had taken a few of the nation's loners and brought them together with one another—and for a brief while it appeared as if they were going to meld into a genuine family.

At the beginning we also had some distinguished guests as visitors. Early on, for example, Sidney Poitier came by and led a cleanup brigade to police the area. Later we had a visit from politicians from both parties, including a young congressman from Texas named George Bush. The press also came, though even at the beginning their stories were skeptical and ironic, an attitude that had not been in evidence when they covered Birmingham and Selma. In part, I believe their cynicism came from the fact that we were in the nation's capital, where belief and optimism were always in short supply. In addition, the Black Power leadership had captured their imaginations with their wildly revolutionary programs and their Robin Hood rhetoric. Nonviolence was middle-class and establishmentarian by late 1968, and I was a middle-aged preacher full of ten-year-old platitudes. It was more interesting to do profiles on Stokely Carmichael and Rap Brown.

But we did have one young man with us who was a new face with a flair for quotable aphorisms—Jesse Jackson. Over the years I had watched Jesse grow in his ability to accept responsibility and deal with problems, and after Resurrection City was built I named him its manager. It was the first time he had ever played a central role in a major civil rights campaign, and he received some attention from the media. The *New York Times* ran a profile with a picture and he was interviewed from time to time by other newspaper and television reporters. In general, he acquitted himself quite well.

One of the first crises occurred when a group of young blacks from Chicago and Detroit attempted to behave in the same way they behaved on the streets of these troubled cities. They organized into an angry gang, swaggered around the city, drinking, cursing, and set up a "protection" business.

To cope with them, we tried to use psychology and made a

few of the leaders "marshals," though the only people who really needed disciplining were their own ranks. But the stratagem didn't work. They continued to cause trouble, particularly at night when others were settling down and attempting to go to sleep. So we had to ship them back home. Unfortunately, we did not locate them all and they made trouble until the day we left.

Then more trouble developed when we tried to assign a family of Mexican-Americans to a lot next door to a black family and across the street from a white couple. Speaking in Spanish they protested, pointing back down the gravel path, greatly agitated. Someone came to get me at City Hall; and when I got there, a small crowd had already gathered, staring suspiciously at this confrontation between the poor family and the Resurrection City authorities. I could tell by looking into their eyes what they were thinking: "It's started here as well. Nothing is really going to be different. They'll push us around just the way the authorities have done everywhere else we've been." I knew this could be more than a mere misunderstanding. Indeed, it might turn into a nationally televised incident. So I was very anxious to reassure these people that we were going to help them, not tyrannize them.

A young black woman who could speak Spanish was talking with the man of the family; and when I walked up, she explained the problem.

"They say they want to live next door to the Mexican-Americans they saw over on the next row."

I nodded, thinking they simply didn't understand what was going on. "Tell them that we're all living together as one people, that we don't assign anyone to separate neighborhoods according to race or national origin."

She turned and spoke to the husband, a short middle-aged man with shining white teeth. His wife listened too, and as the interpreter spoke, I saw her face dissolve into anguish.

"No, no, no," she shouted and began to speak in Spanish at an astonishing rate. It was difficult for me to believe anyone could understand what she was saying, but the young black woman nodded, smiled, and said something in return. Then she turned back to me.

"She says they have three small children who speak nothing but Spanish. She wants them to have other children nearby with whom they can play. She says they're not used to living next to people who speak only English."

We had agreed from the very beginning that we were going to have a completely integrated society, that property assignments would be made according to time of arrival, and that no exceptions would be made. However, this was a problem I had not anticipated. I didn't want to cause anyone undue hardship, nor did I want to complicate the process of registration, which was threatening to be a major headache, now that everyone had suddenly piled in on top of us.

"All right," I said, "tell them they can go where they want to."

My translator rattled off some Spanish, the Mexicans broke into bright smiles, and suddenly the problem evaporated. The crowd around smiled and nodded their heads. I was a hero. For about sixty seconds I thought I was Solomon. Then I started to think about what I had done and I was less self-satisfied. I had made a significant concession, a compromise with the very idea of Resurrection City. Above all we wanted to have a society that was completely amalgamated—a genuine melting pot to prove to the nation and the world that it could be done. I had just permitted the first exception to that principle, and for an hour or so, as I walked around watching people help each other pound stakes and put up tents, I worried about it. Then I shook off my misgivings. What difference could this one exception really make?

But that wasn't the end of the exceptions. This one family's complaint was only the first of many—the Mexican-Americans were not the only ones worried about language barriers. Every group wanted to stay with its own kind, and when we tried to encourage complete integration, we met with resistance—first mild protests, then heated entreaties, and finally cold, stubborn intransigence. They not only preferred to live in separate ethnic groups, they *insisted* on it.

So Resurrection City was flawed from the beginning. It rapidly became a camp full of ghettos, with no one having a great deal to do with anyone else. All the Indians wanted to live together, all the blacks, all the Mexican-Americans, Puerto Ricans, whites—every single group you found in its own little neighborhood in major American cities. I was bitterly disappointed at the beginning, but I finally resigned myself to the fact; and after that I tried not to think about it, as I walked from group to group, seeing different kinds of faces, hearing different kinds of talk and different kinds of music. It was like New York City, only we got along better with one another than New Yorkers. At least most of the time we did.

Next, the heavens opened up and it began to rain. It was one of the wettest springs in the history of the nation's capital. Day after day, the gray skies poured water, huge sheets that swept across the Mall like the monsoons of India. The first day or two it was an adventure, sitting in the City Hall tent, listening to the persistent rapping of raindrops on the canvas. But after a week the green grass that had provided us with a natural carpeting sank under our feet into soft mud. You could emerge from your tent, take a couple of steps, and suddenly find yourself ankle deep in cold, brown slush. The gravel pathways, built for the steady foot traffic of tourists, held up better, at least for a while, but once you left the path to walk down one of our own "streets" you did so at your own peril.

I remember that, at some point shortly after the rains came, Juanita and Coretta came to Washington to see Resurrection City and arrived on the scene to find the sea of mud already deepening, the rain still falling, and people sloshing around in obvious misery.

"How can we possibly go in there?" they asked.

"We'll find a way," I said, peering up at the sky, wondering when it would ever stop.

"There's only one way I can think of," Juanita said, "and that's on somebody's back."

She was right. No vehicle could move ten feet down one of those roads without getting stuck. So I found two strong-backed young men who were willing to be human horses, and they carried the two ladies around so they could see the city. It was a sight to behold: the two of them on the backs of young men, umbrellas over their heads, squealing in alarm every time one of their bearers stumbled. The whole business looked like something that might have happened in ancient China and, after about a ten-minute tour, Juanita and Coretta went back to the hotel and shortly thereafter returned to Atlanta.

One of the things that made our city different from other cities was the absence of any business or industry. Nobody was working and therefore there was no commerce among the residents. But that was one of the reasons why we were in Washington—to demand that training be supplied for the jobless.

So we made our primary vocation the very process of searching for jobs, as well as demanding that the hungry be fed with food stamps. Each day a huge group of us would walk over to the Department of Labor and Department of Agriculture, camp on their doorsteps, and send representatives in to talk to the same people we had talked to before—when we got to talk to anybody. Our demonstrations, which were peaceful and friendly, drew some press coverage in the first days; but soon they became routine, and the television crews stopped coming, as did the newspaper reporters.

When they decided that nothing was going to come of our efforts, they began to follow the more militant black leaders, who were providing them with inflammatory rhetoric and an occasional bombing or killing to liven up the evening news. Mired in the mud and therefore unable to provide them with colorful glimpses into Resurrection City home life, we were yesterday's news and last week's headlines.

Occasionally, however, something happened that was a little out of the ordinary and, if they got the word in time, the news teams would come rushing back. One such episode began when a group of American Indians came to me and said they would like to go over to the Supreme Court the next day and ask the justices to force the legislative and executive branches to live up to the treaties that the American government had signed with their ancestors and then broken. I knew their claims deserved serious consideration. They were a part of our community. I told them I would go with them and see if we could prick the conscience of the Supreme Court.

On the morning we were scheduled to go, the Indians, about twenty-five men, came to my tent dressed in their various tribal costumes, their faces covered with colorful paint, carrying tom-toms, ritual tomahawks, and peace pipes. From there, looking like a war party on patrol, we walked over to the Supreme Court, climbed the steps and announced our presence to a woman at a large polished desk. As usual, the bureaucrat who was sent out to greet us was courteous, expressed sympathy with our concerns, and asked us to wait.

As we sat down, I had the feeling that this was as far as we were going to get, but I think the Indians—this was their first trip to Washington—believed that shortly we would be brought into the court chambers, where nine justices in black robes would listen while they told their historic story of betrayal. They sat quietly, tom-toms and tomahawks at their feet, smiles on their painted faces; and every time a door opened anywhere within hearing they would sit and stare straight ahead at attention.

When lunchtime passed and we had moved into the middle of the afternoon, the frowns on their faces deepened, and they began to mutter among themselves. I tried to reassure them that nothing was unusual here, that they weren't being singled out for special abuse, that the court was probably in session and that someone would get around to us eventually. (That much I believed, though I was certain we wouldn't get so much as a glimpse of a justice.)

Finally, one of them—perhaps a chief—said something in Indian and made a signal to the others, whereupon one of them picked up a pipe and brought it to the chief. He slowly, carefully stuffed the bowl of the pipe with some kind of tobacco, and lit it with a long wooden match that he struck with his fingernail. He took three or four puffs on it, sent a great cloud of blue smoke into the air, and then passed it along to the next person, who took a few puffs and then passed it to the next man on the bench.

Smoking was not as universally banned in Washington as it is today, but at the time it occurred to me that you probably weren't supposed to smoke in the Supreme Court; and I fully expected some clerk to come rushing up to us and tell us the pipe had to go. However, I overestimated their awareness of our presence, because the pipe smoking ritual continued for the better part of an hour without interruption, except to refill the empty bowl. At the time I wondered if this was, as we had always heard, a peace ritual, or if they did it when they were mad at other tribes.

Later I became more concerned when two of the braves, on orders from their chief, took up their tom-toms and began to beat them slowly and softly. Again I expected a clerk, but again no one came. Apparently infuriated by this period of waiting, the drummers picked up the tempo of their beat and also the volume. The tom-toms became louder and more frenzied. Finally the noise was so loud that I was convinced the justices would be able to hear it, no matter where they were in the building.

Then all twenty-five of the Indians began to chant to the rhythm of the drums, while I sat there, a smile frozen on my face, trying to appear interested in what they were doing, as if this were a demonstration staged for my benefit. But they weren't looking at me. Every so often their fierce glances would shift from one another to the huge wooden door that seemed to separate them from the people they wanted to confront.

The door didn't open. It was as if nothing they did could possibly impinge on this court, with its ancient traditions and its great authority. My embarrassment finally subsided, because I understood that no matter what they did, nobody would take note of it; and I began to understand some of their special frustration.

Finally, I looked at the chief, he looked at me, and we both shook our heads. He turned to the chanters.

"OK," he said, "you can knock it off. We're going."

The Indians weren't the only ones who had their own private agenda. So did some of the other groups and this too helped to blur the focus of what we had come to Washington to accomplish. For example, the Puerto Ricans were intent on gaining independence from the United States, though, from what I had heard, the majority of the people on the island didn't hold to that view. Nevertheless, in the Puerto Rican section of Resurrection City, that's all they talked about. Every so often one of their leaders would stand up on a wooden box and make an impassioned speech on the subject, always in Spanish and therefore incomprehensible to most of the other people in the community.

Of course the Mexican-Americans could understand these speeches, but they didn't care anything about Puerto Rican independence. They cared about bilingual education, and their leaders wanted us to drop the call for job training and instead expend our energies trying to persuade Congress to pass national legislation mandating classes in Spanish for members of their community who did not learn English as a first language.

"Why talk about jobs," they said, "when Mexican-American children could not understand what was going on in their classrooms."

Sitting in City Hall, I tried to explain to them that while their argument had a great deal of merit, we had to use our combined forces to address issues of common interest to all the poor. But this reasoning failed to impress them, and they were clearly unhappy that we wouldn't abandon our agenda and concentrate on theirs. That night they drank heavily, played ranchero music on their guitars until three in the morning, and had to be visited several times by the national park rangers, who served as our official police force.

We also had a Town Council that, after much thought, was appointed rather than elected, since no one knew anyone else well enough to vote with any degree of authority. I tried to appoint representatives from all the various "neighborhoods," and in general the council worked effectively together. They made decisions to keep peace and order in the city, and established rules to govern the conduct of such communal activities as the mess tent.

We all ate together under one canvas roof, and everyone seemed pleased with the food, which was better and more plentiful than anything they had been used to. Most of this food was donated, and the rest we bought out of gifts from our supporters. With the land free and the food continuing to come in, we figured we could spend a week, a month, or a year in

Washington—as long as we needed to make the government understand the needs of the poor people.

Of course, we had little money left over for other than necessities, and occasionally that lack led to trouble. For example, one day Jesse Jackson took a large group over to the Department of Agriculture to talk about the necessity for food stamps rather than dairy products. After spending all morning talking to a little white man with rimless glasses, the man took them all down to the cafeteria and waved goodbye as they started through the line. Jesse assumed that the Department of Agriculture would be picking up the bill, so everyone piled his plate high with food. When they got to the end of the line, the cashier held out a hand for payment, and as our people came through, they all pointed behind them. Jesse who was at the end of the line, had about ninety-five cents in his pocket, and it took him a while to realize that he was supposed to pay for some ten meals in addition to his own.

"Charge it to Resurrection City," he said, and sailed on by.

About fifteen minutes later I got a telephone call from the manager of the Department of Agriculture cafeteria, and after hearing the story I told him we would foot the bill if we could raise the money from the poor folks who were living in Resurrection City. We passed the hat and managed to come up with enough to cover the bill. But we really didn't have the money to cover eating out, and after that Jesse ate in the tent with the rest of us, as did the others who had accompanied him.

After we had chosen June 19 as the day for our giant rally—which we were now calling Solidarity Day—we had to face the fact that the on-site leaders could not operate Resurrection City and lead the demonstrations on Capitol Hill if we were preoccupied with staging this gala event, so we agreed that Bayard Rustin would be in charge of the whole operation. We tried to work with Bayard, but with less than two weeks to go, he was causing more problems than he was solving, and finally he resigned when he could not have his way on all important matters, so we replaced him with Sterling Tucker, director of the

Washington Urban League. Sterling did an excellent job and as the days passed and the event approached we had enlisted the support of around forty national organizations and had put together a stellar panel of speakers. These included Roy Wilkins of the NAACP, Walter Reuther of the United Auto Workers, Whitney Young of the Urban League, Senator Edward Brooke of Massachusetts, Dorothy Height of the Council of Negro Women, and Coretta King.

We also invited all of the current presidential candidates. There were some famous names among them: Hubert Humphrey, Richard Nixon, Nelson Rockefeller, and Ronald Reagan, but only two out of the considerable field agreed to appear— Senator Eugene McCarthy of Minnesota, whose candidacy had discouraged President Johnson from seeking a second elective term; and Harold Stassen.

In addition to the afternoon speeches, we planned entertainment in the morning, and Ossie Davis was in charge of that portion of the program. After the entertainment—which was planned for 10:00 on the morning of the nineteenth—there would be a march from the Washington Monument to the Lincoln Memorial, where the main event was to take place between 2:30 and 4:00 in the afternoon.

I was scheduled to give the major address of the day, and I thought and prayed about the challenge of that appearance. Everyone was prepared to measure the success of this event against the march on Washington of five years earlier, when two hundred thousand people crowded onto the Mall and heard Martin give his "I Have a Dream" speech. Such a comparison was intimidating, and there was no way we could match the stunning success of 1963.

The civil rights movement had been at its height at that time, and Martin was still a leader who could do no wrong. We had money in the bank and hope in our hearts. That was before Chicago and before Memphis. In 1968, the nation had just experienced a spring of widespread student riots on scores of campuses, and by the time June 19 rolled around, there had been major civil rights disturbances in cities throughout the country. If you were black or poor and wanted to make a statement, the chances were you could find a march or demonstration within a hundred miles of wherever you were.

As for me, I did not think for a moment that I could match Martin's performance that day in 1963, which many believe was the rhetorical highpoint of his career. Part of what made Martin's speech so inspiring was the joyous note of hope in it; it appealed to the best aspirations of the American people, their belief in themselves and in the future. Five years later, things were different. As I thought about what to say, I was sure Martin would have come up with the right words but I couldn't imagine what they would be.

As the plans developed we saw evidence that we would indeed draw a large crowd, so we started to take more seriously the possibility that we would be evicted from Resurrection City on the sixteenth and find ourselves in a state of confusion when Solidarity Day arrived. So we went back to the Department of the Interior and formally applied for an extension of our permit, which was granted—for a week.

This action infuriated some members of Congress, who had hoped to see our encampment dispersed before the nineteenth and our rally ruined as a consequence. As soon as the extension was granted, someone introduced a bill that would make it illegal for demonstrators to camp on federal land anywhere in the country—a measure that suggested the degree to which we had disturbed the leadership on Capitol Hill. They were holding the bill like a sword over the head of the Interior Department, just so they wouldn't renew our permit again. Later, after we were gone, they dropped it.

For the moment, however, we were safe, so we turned our attention to the logistics of handling an estimated forty thousand people coming to the Mall from highways, bus depots, airports, and train stations. Our figure was based on the assumption that each of the groups to which we appealed for help could account for at least one thousand people, though we had no real way of judging their effectiveness. We hoped for more, but did not want to predict a larger turnout than we could produce. We figured that forty thousand would be sufficient to impress the Congress and the nation with the seriousness of those interested in the welfare of the poor; anything smaller would be considered a failure. As it turns out, we exceeded our predictions and surprised a lot of people.

On the fifteenth, four days before Solidarity Day, I issued a call for a massive turnout to demonstrate that America still believed in the spirit of the march in 1963 and had the will "to redeem the national dream." I called on people "from all regions, urban and rural, of all creeds, races and minorities, and from all economic levels and professions" to come to Washington to show their support of the poor.

I reminded them of Martin's speech five years earlier:

> It is sad for us to say today that the dream has not been fulfilled. On that day we felt that America had great promise for her poor people. Today we can see that that promise was empty.
>
> This is a last call to save America. If the call is not heard, the national crisis of poverty and hunger will only deepen. I must caution America, and especially the Congress, once more that this time we must listen to the voices of Solidarity Day.
>
> They are the voices of reason and the voices of judgment. They are nonviolent voices. But there is anger in the voices of the people.

On Tuesday people began to pour into town, and the doubters began to revise their low predictions. Clearly, there were huge crowds of new arrivals walking the streets and coming by Resurrection City to see for themselves what they had read about and seen on television. By the morning of the nineteenth the hordes began to gather on the Mall. There was no doubt about it: we had outdone our own predictions.

Crowd predicting in Washington is an old political game, dominated by the people in power. You can see a huge swarm of marchers glutting Pennsylvania Avenue for a mile and then be told by the police the next day that what you saw was only twelve hundred people. On the other hand, when a preferred group comes along, they miraculously swell to ten times the apparent number.

We figured we had somewhere between one hundred to two

hundred thousand people on the Mall that day, but the Washington police estimate was fifty thousand—which was ten thousand more than we had predicted and many times what our enemies had suggested. We were pleased and confident that we had made a point with Congress.

As a matter of fact, we had reserved one hundred places for members of Congress, though fewer than that actually showed up. Vice President Hubert Humphrey came, however, as did David Rockefeller, representing his brother Nelson. Senator Robert Kennedy had been assassinated only weeks earlier, and we were particularly touched by a wire from his widow, who had stood on the platform at Coretta's speech. Coretta prefaced the reading of the telegram by saying that it had come "from another lady who was just recently victimized by the same tragedy which my family and I were victimized by."

Mrs. Kennedy said in her wire: "Today, on this most important day for all Americans, my heart and prayers are with you. The finest memorial to Dr. Martin Luther King would be the tangible action our country takes now to implement the programs he and my husband cared about so deeply."

Mrs. Kennedy's gracious message was only a reminder to those present of the times we were living through in the late 1960s. And it is important in evaluating our words on Solidarity Day to remember just how troubled the nation had been by violence and conflict. Indeed, it is difficult to remember darker days.

The Vietnam War was at its bloody height; young men were being killed daily and their deaths screened nightly on the evening news. Americans were sickened by what they saw and frustrated that our reasons for being in that southeast Asian country were so tenuous and yet our leaders so determined to keep us there.

As a consequence of the war, America's young people were up in arms and we had just experienced a year of riots on college campuses. Unlike the panty raids of an earlier time, these were bitter confrontation in which students clashed with police and stormed into administration buildings. They also burned draft cards and fled to Canada.

Coretta set the tone when she said that our Campaign was "maybe the last opportunity to save the nation and the world from destruction."

Whitney Young spoke in the same spirit and said that "America lies to us, and we know it." As for the establishment's attitude toward such occasions as the Poor People's Campaign, he said that protest demonstrations "have become a kind of entertainment for millions of morally impoverished people who view the demonstrations of the oppressed on television sets in comfortable homes and then turn to other diversions, unmoved, uncaring. . . . Their hearts are ragged, their decency tattered, their morals shabby. . . . These people too, these morally impoverished Americans, have to be rehabilitated."

Strong words and with a certain irony the *New York Times* called us all "apocalyptic." Perhaps we were. But we earnestly believed that if the nation didn't come to its senses and turn from violence and self-indulgence, it might easily fall prey to the anarchy preached by these young arrogant leaders, black and white, who wanted to tear society down, just to see if they could do it.

I spoke last, and I took pains to reassure those present that we did not intend to pack up our tents and roll out of town as we had been told to do. We intended to stay and fight, at least until we were arrested and thrown in jail, something I thought we would probably have to face. I said:

> We will stay in Washington and fight nonviolently until the nation rises up and demands real assurance that our needs will be met. . . . I don't care if the Department of the Interior gives us another permit to stay in Resurrection City. . . . I intend to stay here until justice rolls out of the halls of Congress and righteousness falls from the administration, and the rough places of government agencies are made plain and the crooked deals of the military-industrial complex become straightforward.

As for the militant tone I was taking, I explained that "Some people call this kind of defiance of government 'civil disobedience,' but if that is so, it stands at the heart of the Judeo-Christian tradition. . . . We may be placed in jail but I know my God is able to deliver us." Then I alluded to the violence and death of the past three months in making my own determination quite clear.

> We will not bow down to a racist Congress. We will not bow down to an administration that refuses to administrate the blessings of this nation to the poor. We will not bow down to the militarism and violence of this nation. I don't care what they do to me. If I must join Robert Kennedy and Martin King, I still will not bow."

I concluded by making the demands of the Poor People's Campaign clear. They were as follows:

> That no child go hungry . . . that no family lack good housing . . . that no man be without a job . . . that no citizen be denied an adequate income . . . that no human being be deprived of health care . . . that every American be educated to the limit of his hope and talent . . . that no more of our people be murdered by the violence which torments America.

When I finished, the crowd cheered, and though I did not make the same kind of impact Martin made in 1963, I knew at the end of that speech that I had established my authority as head of the SCLC. For the first time, I felt comfortable in the role that had been thrust on me.

I also felt that the entire Poor People's Campaign had been justified by that one great rally in which the voice of the poor had at last been heard throughout the land. Standing there, listening to the cheers and watching the ragged masses wave their signs, I was prepared to say that we had been successful, even if we were thrown off our land come Sunday night.

After the meeting, a number of out-of-town demonstrators came up and introduced themselves, some of them black, some white. Many were representatives of local civil rights organizations, labor unions, and other grass-roots organizations who told me how important they thought the campaign had been for the morale of the people. Since we were doing something, they would sit back and see what happened.

After I had shaken everyone's hand, I went back to Resurrection City to see how things were going. In the back of my mind I had been worried about the deterioration of the community, but I hadn't allowed myself to think about it until Solidarity Day was behind us. Now I had to face some formidable problems.

First, we were now down to fewer than one thousand people. For a variety of reasons, a majority had already left. Some were discouraged over the apparent lack of success on Capitol Hill, though we had actually won several important victories in Congress: The elimination of commodities as sole sustenance, the introduction of food stamps, the promise of a jobs program (never fulfilled), the alteration of rules on welfare. Others had personal reasons for leaving—responsibilities back home, families to attend to. Still others had found it difficult to live in close quarters with people of different racial and ethnic backgrounds.

But we were faced with other, more serious problems in the encampment. We had never really eliminated the small gangs that had roamed the city from the day we arrived. Mostly young blacks, they had continued in Washington the life they had led in the streets of Chicago and Detroit—stealing, robbing, and intimidating their neighbors. In such a small community, their presence was felt more acutely, and the older people in particular resented them, in part because they had been victimized by such hoods before. Here in Resurrection City they were simply reliving the nightmare of the ghettos.

The day after our mass meeting we went back to the Department of Agriculture and held another demonstration. Some people in the crowd of bystanders threw rocks at the police; and later that evening, as officers patrolled the area around Resurrection City some of these same young blacks bombarded them with rocks and bottles, then disappeared back into the maze of plywood shacks. In response, the police fired tear gas into the middle of the camp and several older people experienced severe discomfort as a result.

I understood the frustration of the police officers at being attacked. We were also frustrated by the activities of these gang members. But the tear gas had not been directed at the troublemakers but had been fired indiscriminately into our midst.

Clearly, we were not settling down for the long haul. If

anything, the situation was deteriorating day by day, and we began to be concerned with the possibility of violence by law enforcement officials as our army declined in numbers. We even considered the possibility that things might get as bad as they did in Birmingham and Selma. We knew that the upcoming weekend would be crucial in determining whether or not we might be able to hang on.

One of the problems was getting the younger people to demonstrate. They apparently looked on the marches and demonstrations as work, and in Detroit and Chicago gang members didn't work. They "hung around," occasionally robbing older people or shaking them down for money—too much of that was going on in and around the camp. When the young punks weren't doing that, they were hanging around the camp. We tried to roust them out to board the buses so we could go relieve the protesters already over at the Department of Agriculture, but they wouldn't budge from their shacks, except to go into the food tent at meal times and eat twice as much as anyone else.

The older people were complaining about this behavior, and it was beginning to demoralize them, particularly the ones who had answered the bus call every day, despite sore feet and aching backs. The *New York Times* sent a reporter to the camp and reported the bickering among our people, which didn't add to our credibility among those we were asking to support us. It was at that point we began to suspect that these younger gang members might have been sent there to make as much trouble as they could so that the press would see us in the most unfavorable light possible.

Certainly, they were our most pressing problem, and perhaps we might have taken care of other difficulties had they not been constantly stirring in the pot. For example, we were continuing to improve the facilities, though it was taking us longer than we had anticipated, and it appeared as if we might have all the lights and showers installed just about the time the police moved in and closed us down. So we were making progress at the same time we were falling to pieces.

Because of the bad publicity we had gotten, on Friday I attempted to direct the attention of the nation once again to the problems we had come to Washington to solve. I held a press conference and called on President Johnson to answer a simple question: "Why is there still poverty in a nation as rich and as productive as the United States of America?"

Addressing Lyndon Johnson directly, I said, "We keep running into a wall of silence or a pack of excuses or a counterattack against the people of Resurrection City, USA, when we repeatedly ask these questions. . . . We do not want a speech about the Great Society, we want a direct answer."

President Johnson had said at one point in the earlier days of his presidency that he intended to eliminate poverty. He even had the audacity to suggest that the person who had said the poor would be with us always didn't know what he was talking about. So with this background, I thought the question I was posing was a fair one and deserved an answer.

"If the president, speaking for this society, has the courage to answer directly," I said, "then maybe America can find the courage to deal with all the problems suggested by this question. And if not, then God help this sick nation."

Then I posed a more specific question that suggested what some of these problems were.

"Why does the United States government pay the Mississippi plantation of a United States senator [James Eastland, Dem., Mississippi] more than thirteen thousand dollars a month not to grow food or fiber, and at the same time why does the government pay a starving child in Mississippi only nine dollars a month, and what are you going to do about it?"

(Twenty years later, after thinking about this question, I am still bewildered by the long-term inequities in government policy, particularly in the area of agriculture. As best I can tell, since 1968, small farmers have gone out of business in ever-increasing numbers while "agribusinesses" owned by such companies as Prudential Life have gobbled up most of the federal dollars allotted for farming. However, I can certainly answer my own general question at this point: There is still poverty in our society because there is still greed.)

Some of the newspapers carried my question, but President Johnson chose to ignore it not only for the rest of the day, but for the rest of the time we were in Washington. Later that afternoon Jesse Jackson led another group to the Agriculture Department, where they were met by a substantial body of policemen. Jesse announced that the demonstrators would stay there until Monday morning when the employees returned; and though it was illegal to obstruct the entrances to federal buildings, the police allowed us to stay there, saying we would pose no problems over the weekend.

"They'll have to walk over us or remove us on Monday," Jesse said, "because no business inside that building is more important than the fact that people are starving."

He also said that "thousands of people will be coming in over the weekend to be with us on Monday morning. We're going to make a home at the Agriculture Department until they let us go home with enough food for hungry people."

Jesse was bluffing, and perhaps hoping to generate some enthusiasm in the neighboring communities. We had sent out a call for reinforcements, but we had no evidence that they would arrive. Some of the staff believed they might come, most of them believed they wouldn't, that we had peaked on Solidarity Day. Andy Young was particularly pessimistic at this point and was looking for "a way to bail out." However, I still believed we could bring pressure to bear on Congress and accomplish something even more significant that we had accomplished thus far.

Meanwhile, the weekend loomed ahead; and while we hoped for a new influx of eager supporters, we realistically had to face the prospect that the troublemakers and agitators would be even more active now that the time was drawing near for the expiration of our permit.

As it turned out, the weekend went badly. Violence increased, and several ugly incidents occurred that further compromised us in the eyes of the press and the nation. Four white youths were robbed and beaten by blacks. A white man was attacked by four black youths inside the camp and was robbed of his wallet and his wrist watch, then shot, though he was not seriously injured. Later, on Sunday night, the same young troublemakers again threw rocks and bottles at passing automobiles; and the police again responded by firing tear gas into the camp.

By then we already knew that we were going to be evicted from the site at some time in the not-too-distant future. We called all the people together and told them that in all likelihood they would be forced to leave Monday or sometime later in the week.

"They said we had a reasonable time to get out," I told them, "so we don't think anything will happen Sunday night."

"Will we go to jail?" someone asked.

"That depends on what you do," I replied. "If you leave voluntarily, then no one is likely to bother you. But if you refuse to leave or resist, then you'll probably go to jail."

"If we go to jail, will you bail us out?"

Everyone laughed, but it was a serious question. In the past we had been able to guarantee bail for anyone arrested, even in Birmingham when the bail and fines assessed had been unconscionably high. This time, however, we were just about dead broke; so we couldn't afford to come up with that kind of money this time.

"This is strictly jail-without-bail," I told them. "If you don't have the money and don't want to spend time behind bars, then leave quietly when they ask you to."

"What are you going to do?" somebody asked.

"I'm going to jail," I said.

Sunday a man came to tell us that our appeal for an extension had been denied.

"The permit expires at eight P.M. tonight," he said. "You'll have to vacate by then."

"What will happen if we remain?" I asked.

"Then you'll be arrested," he said simply.

We had not really expected to be granted an indefinite stay, but somehow until we heard these words we thought we might be allowed to remain, at least through the congressional session, which we figured would last only a few weeks more. Now we would have to make other arrangements for everyone remaining to quit Washington or else go to jail—something most of the staff had done before.

But it all seemed anticlimactic, particularly when we remembered the bright optimism we had shared at the beginning. We had won concessions from the Congress, but we had failed to gain everything we had asked for. We were soldiers fighting for a cause, and we wanted to be taken in battle, not waiting in camp.

"Who's left?" I asked Bevel.

"Maybe five hundred," he said. "Some of them are old folks and children."

"Well, let's wait and see what happens," I said. "Could be this is a bluff."

The others shook their heads. They didn't think so.

"If it's not a bluff," I continued, "then they won't actually come to arrest us till tomorrow or the next day. Probably they'll come in the morning. I think we should make one last march to Capitol Hill tomorrow, try to get on the Capitol grounds and force them to remove us. Then we can at least make our arrest count for something."

Everyone agreed, though we eventually modified the plan somewhat so that a few staff members, including Jim Bevel and Andy Young, would remain at Resurrection City to make certain that the people we left behind would not have to face the police alone.

The next morning we awoke to rain again, and I remember thinking how much the weather had influenced the Poor People's Campaign, how different it might have been had we not lived in a giant mud puddle during most of the five weeks we had been here. Today we would be marching again in the rain, and perhaps arrested. At least it would be dry in jail.

Sure enough, as we were preparing for our morning assault on Capitol Hill, the first enemy scouts appeared.

A small group of park rangers drove up, got out, looked around, and then walked over to where we were standing. One of them approached me, and I knew what he was going to say.

"Reverend Abernathy," he said, "I'm sorry, but we've got our orders. We've been told that your permit expired Saturday night and that you'll have to move along."

I looked around at the stricken faces staring at me, several hundred people who were about to be deprived of their homes. They had the same look on their faces you see in news broadcasts telling of great natural disasters, like hurricanes and forest fires, where families have lost all their possessions and don't know where to turn. Now these people were in Washington, D.C., some of them a thousand miles from where they'd begun, and once again the police were telling them to move along.

"I understand what you're saying," I said, "but I'm not sure exactly what we're going to do now. Give me a chance to confer with my staff."

He nodded and walked off so we could confer in private. We no longer had a City Hall in which to make our plans, but we walked over to one side and tried to assess the situation. Essentially, we agreed that simply to pack our bags and skulk out of town would be unthinkable, particularly since, at that point, we had only promises and no concrete legislation. We still needed to fight to make certain that Congress and the administration did not renege on their verbal commitments.

In addition, we didn't want those people to feel that we had turned tail at the first sign of real trouble. They knew that, unlike them, we had homes to return to, even though the mortgage might not yet be paid. We also had jobs, medical insurance, and all the perquisites that went along with regular employment. When we left Resurrection City behind, it would be to return to a more comfortable life. So it was all too easy for us to submit to the law and stroll off into the sunset.

But they were trapped in Washington without food, without shelter, and without money to buy those things. If they couldn't remain on the Mall, then where would they go? To another park? To jail? To the streets of downtown Washington, where a block from the White House people were living in the streets and begging for food?

After tossing the question back and forth, we finally realized we had no real choice. We would have to resist this action, if only to let them know that somebody cared about them, that we had not just used them to achieve specific political goals and then tossed them aside when we no longer had any need for them.

Besides, if we all went to jail, everyone would have some-place to sleep tonight and something to eat tomorrow morning. Of course, we could probably put together enough money to get them back home where they came from, but even that activity would be significantly facilitated if we went to jail and in so doing stirred up public indignation.

We walked back to where we were standing before, and the park ranger came over. "You figured out where you'll be going?" he asked.

"We won't be going anywhere," I said. "We've decided we're going to stay here."

"But you can't do that," he said. "I've been told to arrest you if you don't leave."

I smiled. "Then I guess you'll just have to arrest us," I said.

He must have read Birmingham and Selma and Chicago, but I could tell by the look on his face that he never expected to be faced with such a situation himself.

"Look," he said, bewildered, "I'm not kidding. I've got no choice. I'm under orders."

"I understand perfectly," I said. "Go ahead and arrest us."

He turned in a panic to the four or five rangers he had along with him.

"You'll probably need to call for extra transportation," I said helpfully. "Usually the city can get some help from the suburban departments."

"Yeah," he said in a fog, "that's a good idea."

He returned to his men, conferred with them for about two minutes, then sent somebody running across the field.

"We'll have somebody here shortly," he called over to me.

"Take your time," I yelled back, keeping a note of good humor in my voice so he wouldn't feel too intimidated.

"All right," I said, "let's get the marchers together and go up that hill one more time. See if we can get everybody who's able-bodied. Tell them it will be the last time."

We mustered somewhere between two hundred and three hundred marchers, a far cry from what we had done in the past, and tens of thousands fewer than had gathered here only five days earlier. As we started down the Mall, already wet with rain, I stared at the Capitol looming in front of us, and wondered what kind of country America had been when that dome was first constructed. Certainly, a country that condoned legalized slavery, but was it one less compassionate toward the poor and homeless? In 1968 things may have been better, but not so much better that we could just pull up our stakes and go back home.

We came to the end of the grass strip, crossed the street, and mounted Capitol Hill for the last time, determined to get inside the Capitol or at least on the Capitol grounds—something any American could do on almost any day of the year. But as we moved toward the crest we were met by a large contingent of policemen, who formed a living wall between us and the huge dome towering over us. John Layton, chief of the D.C. police, was standing at the head of the line, and I halted the march and walked forward to meet him. He was courteous but firm.

"You can't march onto the Capitol grounds," he said.

"We expect to be arrested," I said. "But we don't want to cause any trouble. We want to be nonviolent above all else. If we could just be allowed to walk into the Capitol itself, then we would immediately give ourselves up for arrest and move into your patrol wagons without any resistance."

He shook his head. "I'm sorry, but we won't be able to allow that."

I walked away, then came back. "In which case, how about our walking onto the Capitol grounds and then submitting to arrest?"

Across the street a crowd had already gathered, many of them black; and I'm sure that both our marchers and the police were viewing them with apprehension. The police were afraid of being bombarded with rocks and bottles, and we were afraid of being blamed in the press for whatever they did, since reporters weren't always careful to make a distinction between bystanders and our nonviolent protesters.

After hearing my second request, Chief Layton again shook his head.

"No," he said. "It's against the law for demonstrators to congregate on the Capitol grounds, and we intend to prevent that from happening."

"You mean that as taxpayers we can't walk on public property?" I asked.

"Not if you've come to demonstrate."

I went back to the others and told them what was happening.

"Let's just move on anyway," someone suggested.

"I'd like to avoid the risk of injury," I said. "I'm hoping we can reach some kind of agreement that will take the risk out of the situation."

We tried several more times, but to no avail. The chief was adamant: He would make no deal in which we were permitted to cross the line he was guarding. It appeared as if we would be denied a chance to make a final symbolic gesture toward Congress.

"What about just sitting down," somebody suggested. "If we blocked the sidewalk and the street they'd have to arrest us."

We talked about it and finally agreed that this was the best compromise we could contrive. So we all sat down.

The chief stared at us for a few moments then walked over.

"If you continue to sit down," he said, "we'll have to arrest you."

"In which case," I said, "you might as well get on with your arresting."

We waited until the paddywagons came, and while we were waiting we prayed, not only for ourselves and for the nation, but more particularly for the peaceful acceptance by our people of this final end to Resurrection City. The increasingly ugly mood of the last few days had filled me with foreboding. When the wagon arrived, I was among the first to get in, and I remember thinking that this time there would be no close friend to share my moment of solitude. As I was locked inside a couple of reporters came to the barred window and asked for a statement.

"I just hope that people will continue to demonstrate in a nonviolent way," I said.

They took almost everybody across the river to Lorton, Virginia, in part because there was more room there, in part, I suspect, because they believed our presence there would be less likely to cause riots. As for Lorton, I don't remember too much about it, so it must not have been the worst jail in the country.

Meanwhile, back at Resurrection City, the dismantling of our camp was in progress. Shortly after we had left several busloads of police had arrived, dressed in crash helmets and carrying gas guns and pistols as though they expected some violent outbreak. What they found there were some docile SCLC staff members and mostly old people and small children. They announced over a public address system that all who wished to return to their homes could do so; that their bus fares would be paid by the Travelers Aid Society. Then they moved in and began breaking into every hut and tent, rousting out the few people they found remaining there. Then, when everyone was rounded up and moved away from the city, they began to tear down the fence. Our first and only confrontation with the federal government was over, and the victory we had won was too ambiguous for people at that time to appreciate fully.

That night, when they heard that Resurrection City had been invaded and dismantled, the black people in Washington's poor neighborhoods rioted, and Mayor Walter Washington had to declare a curfew and call in the National Guard.

16

Charleston

CHARLESTON WAS, AND IS, A UNIQUE CITY, full of old memories and historic pride. In 1969, the year we conducted our campaign there, South Carolina was celebrating its tricentennial and Charleston was at the center of that celebration. The site of revolutionary war activities, it was of course the place where the first shot of the Civil War was fired. If you go down to the Battery along the seashore, you can see the cannons that fired on Ft. Sumter. Their muzzles are filled with concrete after all these years, but they are still pointed seaward, as if ready to be put into service at the slightest provocation.

Some of the houses that look out on the Battery "south of Broad" were as old as the city itself—three and four stories high, filled with chandeliers as big as magnolia trees. The white people who lived in those houses had names as old as any in America, and these same names were on the quaint signs along Broad Street where the law firms were located. These were the people who ran Charleston in 1969 and would do so for a few more years, before the real estate crowd moved in to take over so they could "redevelop" the city and get rich.

540

If you turn off Broad onto Meeting Street and drive a few blocks, you come to a square where, on a high pedestal, stands the statue of John C. Calhoun, the South's most renowned antebellum statesman and advocate of the doctrine of nullification, which held that if the states didn't like what the federal government was doing, they didn't have to obey the law.

While Broad Street was the dividing line between fashionable whites and not-so-fashionable whites, Calhoun Street was the dividing line between whites and blacks, or at least one dividing line. King Street north of Calhoun became first a black business area and then a black residential section. West of King Street were lots of three-story houses in which blacks lived, sometimes two and three families in one ramshackle building. These houses, not so old and elegant as the houses on the Battery, were once owned by middle-class white families that could better afford to keep them painted and in good repair. Now they were fire traps, rat infested with peeling paint and leaking roofs.

The blacks who lived there were holding menial jobs or none at all, and though they lived only a few blocks from what was left of the elegance of the Old South, they might have been ten thousand miles away. While Charleston seemed like a friendly city to outsiders, it was in reality the most closed society in the entire region, and maybe in the nation. Even whites who were "outsiders" could not gain admission to such inner circles as the Carolina Yacht Club, and blacks entered only as waiters and busboys.

But that wasn't the only problem, nor even the most aggravating one. South Carolina was, and is, one of the strongest anti-union states in the nation—and in more than one way. Not only did it have a so-called "Right to Work Law," but it had resisted persistent attempts on the part of the AFL-CIO and other national unions to organize workers in such important industries as textile manufacturing and agriculture. Union organizers were regarded as troublemakers, not only because they drove up wages and spoiled the climate for new industry, but also because they brought with them "Negro problems" from the North. The chamber-of-commerce mentality of "progressive Charleston" was a chief factor in this anti-union sentiment, so when Dave

Livingston, a white man, went down into the slums of the city to organize black hospital workers for Local 1199, he struck a raw nerve.

The city fathers met, brooded about the threat to the established order, and vowed to fight any attempt to organize the hospital workers, though it would have meant very little in the way of a budgetary increase. But there was a more important consideration: South Carolina law prohibited any government agency—state, county, or local—from negotiating with a union. That gave local authorities a good reason to ignore union activities. However, when twelve people became too active in organizing workers at the South Carolina Medical College Hospital, they were fired. All of the other union workers struck in protest, and they were followed by the union workers at Charleston County Hospital.

As soon as this happened, Dave Livingston called and asked for help. "It's not as big as Washington," he said, "but it's a tough town and we can't do it alone. If you led a campaign down here, they would be more likely to listen to reason, particularly if they had to deal with a couple of thousand demonstrators and the television crews grinding away."

I was a little skeptical.

"I've heard that Charleston has a mind of its own. I've got a lot of questions to ask before we commit ourselves. Such as what support do you have from the churches?"

"We've got plenty of support," he said, and named the local preachers who would back us. "You can have a meeting at a different church every night."

"What about the local newspaper?"

There was silence for a moment.

"The *Charleston News and Courier*," he said finally. "They're against us. I would say they are probably the most conservative newspaper in the state. I have to admit that we'll get no help there. Let's not talk about the local press. Let's talk about the *New York Times* and CBS News."

I was beginning to have second thoughts. A local newspaper, particularly in 1969, could make a big difference in the white community's perception of what was going on, and we needed as much white support as we could get. As we had seen before, without some local pressure on the city leaders, we would have a difficult time bringing them to the bargaining table.

It was obvious that we would have a hard time getting support from the business community of Charleston. In Birmingham, for example, the merchants finally turned on Bull Connor because nobody would come downtown to shop as long as we were demonstrating and being savaged by dogs and fire hoses. In Charleston, however, it was the merchants who most feared unionization, because they were certain it would stop the trickle of industry from the North that moved into the state seeking cheap, manageable labor. It appeared as if the merchants would be the last people in Charleston who would intervene in behalf of our cause. And if they wouldn't help, then who would? The answer seemed obvious: Nobody from the white community.

I knew that meant a hard and bitter struggle with major disruption of the city, and that knowledge led to my next question.

"How are the jails in Charleston?"

Dave said we were in luck, that they'd just built a new jail.

After talking the matter over, the SCLC decided to go there, though we could not mount a campaign for another two weeks. I suppose part of the reason we settled so quickly on Charleston was because of the challenge. Few cities represented so clearly the old way of looking at southern society. Ironically, the upper classes of the Carolina Low Country opposed Jim Crow laws when they were first proposed in the 1890s, and the *Charleston News and Courier* denounced such measures on their editorial pages. But in 1969 the Charleston establishment had refused to accept the idea that Jim Crow was dead and buried. The thought of attacking this citadel of reaction was therefore appealing.

But the economic issues there were so clear-cut that there was a real possibility of an unambiguous victory, something we had not won in Washington. We needed to win something big in order to reestablish the credibility of nonviolence as a means of social change, and the unionization of Charleston, South Carolina, would be something big, not only to blacks but also to labor unions around the country.

In fact, we figured we could count on some help from national labor, and in that respect we were not disappointed. That alliance would help to build our credibility among those people who might have been leaning toward the violent approach to black·liberation. We also hoped it would bring us some new financial support.

We were finding it harder and harder to fund our activities. We needed time to raise some more money since the Poor People's Campaign had ended up costing us considerably more than we had planned. Nevertheless, we agreed to go to Charleston and stay as long as was necessary in order to achieve a settlement.

The Charleston hospital workers' strike was in many ways a replica of the sanitation workers' strike in Memphis. The parallels between the two were obvious to leaders on both sides of the conflict, and the actions of the City of Charleston and the State of South Carolina were dictated to some degree by their fear that the same kind of atmosphere would prevail and that in the end they would somehow be forced to capitulate to our demands.

In the first place, both strikes came about because a municipality refused to recognize the bargaining rights of a union. In Charleston the union was Local 1199B of the Retail, Wholesale, and Department Store Workers, who wanted to represent those hospital workers who performed the most menial tasks and received the most meager wages. In the end Mayor Loeb of Memphis refused to recognize a particular union, but the city of Charleston refused to recognize *any* union, because they said it was against South Carolina law for an agent of a state or local government to negotiate with a union.

The second similarity between the Charleston and Memphis confrontations lay in the identity of the workers involved: Both groups, performing unpleasant drudge work, were almost 100 percent black. So the issue was not just economic; it was also racial. We were convinced that the low wages these workers received could be explained in part by race. Since white workers had greater job opportunities than blacks, they could demand higher wages. Black workers, their options limited by the color of their skin, had to accept whatever jobs were available. For most of these hospital workers then, it was sweep floors and empty bedpans or else go hungry. For that reason, we were interested in pursuing their quarrel with the city of Charleston.

Third, in both cases, the city authorities had said unequivocally that they would not bargain with the local black union—period. As Richard Black, Charleston County manager put it, "The facts are simple. The county will not recognize the union." The local hospital administrators took the same position and it seemed to local black workers that their situation was hopeless. But still they persisted, encouraged by a biracial Concerned Clergy Committee (CCC), a first for Charleston.

A final resemblance between the Charleston and Memphis strikes was the time of year both broke out. SCLC involvement in the hospital workers' strike came in March, almost one year to the day after our intervention in the Memphis strike. As a matter of fact, I made a speech in Memphis on April 4, the anniversary of Martin's assassination, and then flew to Charleston to make an appearance in behalf of the hospital workers. The parallels made Juanita and others uncomfortable, and I must admit that I half expected some attempt to be made on my life during the struggle in Charleston. As a matter of fact, at one point I told a large crowd at one of our many rallies, "I personally am willing to die for this cause if need be."

The strike began in the middle of March when twelve hospital workers, members of the union, were dismissed from their jobs for what seemed to them irrelevant reasons. Hospital officials denied that the dismissed workers were fired because of their union activities, but those twelve were clearly the most active union organizers.

At that point the union issue had to be resolved; so rather

than submit to the purging of any member who happened to be active on behalf of the union, the entire membership of Local 1199B walked out—over four hundred laundry workers, kitchen helpers, nurse's aides, licensed practical nurses, orderlies, and maids. They struck two hospitals—Medical College Hospital and Charleston County Hospital, the former run by the state, the latter by the county.

The hospitals responded by hiring replacements as quickly as they could, so the union threw a picket line around the hospitals. The hospital authorities, complaining that the pickets made entrance to the hospitals difficult and therefore endangered lives, sought and received from Circuit Court Judge Clarence Singletary an injunction, restricting the number of pickets to ten. When the union still mounted a full picket line, police were sent in to enforce the injunction and violence ensued. Pickets were beaten and manhandled, and over one hundred had been arrested before I arrived on the scene.

We had been monitoring several union controversies throughout the South, in part because we recognized in them a means of bringing a better standard of living to our people, in part because Martin had given his life during such a confrontation, and we wanted to make certain that we honored that sacrifice by doing what we could to help the kind of people he had helped. In addition to the Charleston conflict, we were also involved in labor disputes in Montgomery, Alabama, and in Macon, Georgia. (The garbage workers on strike in Macon were predominantly black, but the meat cutters in Montgomery were white.)

According to the newspapers, when I came to Charleston and announced the involvement of the SCLC in the problems of the hospital workers, Gov. Robert McNair took note of my arrival by alerting the South Carolina National Guard. In preparation for my visit, they spent an entire day practicing riot control, bayonets affixed to the ends of their rifles. The governor must have remembered that first day in Memphis, when the Invaders had dogged our steps. But there were no Invaders this time. They had lost interest, as too many young people do after the novelty of the initial experience wears off and there's nothing left but hard work.

I spoke at Morris Brown AME Church and told a crowd of over fifteen hundred that I was in Charleston because of a commitment to fight war, racism, and poverty. At the end of my speech, I made a pledge to them: "If you need me I'll come back. . . . I've been in jail twenty-three times, and I'm itching to make it twenty-four." The crowd came to its feet, cheering, while a nearby white policeman told a reporter: "I won't say that it will blow, but I think it could very easily. It has all the earmarks of a real ugly thing."

We had already decided that in order to attract the kind of national media attention necessary to force federal intervention, I would have to go to jail. The next time I spoke at Morris Brown AME Church, I found more than two thousand people waiting, shouting, singing, ready to hear the word. I brought down the house when I stepped into the pulpit and said "I came to sock it to Charleston." After a speech in which I told them of my commitment to their cause, we began singing "We Shall Overcome" and marched out of the church and down the street to the hospital complex. But no one arrested us.

So the next day, April 22, we tried again. Flanked by Mary Moultrie, president of Local 1199B, and Cleveland Robinson, president of the Negro American Labor Council, I walked down the streets of Charleston with a Bible in one hand and a toothbrush and toothpaste in the other, inviting arrest as soon as we arrived at Charleston County Hospital. At that spot, more than seven hundred of us—many more than the limit of ten set by Judge Singletary—knelt down in front of the hospital while I led the group in a prayer for equal justice and human rights.

Still no one arrested us. "You couldn't get arrested today if you stood on your head," one black woman complained as the police stood by without expression and watched our demonstration. I was beginning to think that the leadership in the South was becoming too wise, that sooner or later they would gain so much wisdom that they would give up our just demands without even resisting.

As we marched back, we passed the entrance to the hospital and saw some of the nonstriking workers staring out the window at us. Some people shouted "scabs," but I smiled and waved for them to join us.

"We're marching for you," I shouted up to them. "Come on down and join us."

After the march, I went back to the rooming house where I was staying in order to huddle with Andy Young, Stoney Cooks, and our lawyers. As we talked over our problems it became clear that Governor McNair and local authorities would be able to hide behind the law indefinitely; technically, state statutes did indeed prohibit state agencies like hospitals from entering into collective bargaining with unions.

"What are our chances of getting the law declared unconstitutional?" I asked.

"Slim to none," our lawyers agreed. "This is not a law passed to discriminate against blacks. It falls under an entirely separate category of law, and we would not be in a strong position if we attempted to challenge it."

"But we can't just pull up stakes and go home," I said. "Either we have to challenge this particular law or else find something else to challenge. I have no intention of leaving these poor people to fight the battle by themselves. If I did, it would be the end of the SCLC."

The lawyers pondered the matter for a while. "Do you suppose they would be content if their organization were not affiliated with a national union?"

"How would that help?" I asked.

"If we could get away from that word 'union' then we might be able to work out something that would accomplish the same thing as a union, yet avoid the term."

"Like what?" somebody asked.

"Like an employees' organization that would be able to speak for the workers in such matters as pay and job security."

"In other words a union," I said.

"Not a union in the strictest definition. At least we could *argue* that it wasn't, and that would put them on the defensive."

I shook my head. I didn't like the idea of making our

position depend on such an obvious manipulation of words, but I was finally convinced we had to try something.

"If you can get Mary Moultrie and the Concerned Clergy to go along, then I guess it's worth a try."

That evening they came back with the word: The others would accept that solution, provided they could ensure that everyone was rehired and that the "non-union" could bargain for the employees. I still wanted no part of it, and the lawyers went to the city officials with the offer. The mayor and his associates said they would discuss the offer with their legal advisors, but they promised nothing. I am certain they thought they could weather the storm and send us packing in a few days.

That was Tuesday. Friday, Juanita flew over from Atlanta and marched with us. I was pleased to have her there beside me, and the local leaders said her presence lent additional authority to the mission of the SCLC, and we felt that we were gaining support locally—at least from the black community. But the white community had yet to give any ground.

When I kissed Juanita at the airport, I prepared her for the inevitable.

"You're probably just in time to see me get arrested. I don't think they can ignore us much longer. But don't worry. I'll be safer in jail than in the streets."

Sure enough, the next day, Saturday, I went to jail for the twenty-fourth time in my career as a civil rights leader for "illegal picketing." We began the day with a morning march from Morris Brown AME Church to the Medical College Hospital and back to the church again. We had about three thousand marchers with us, including Juanita, and at the church I reaffirmed our commitment to them: "We are here to stay, and there's more of us where we came from, and we're going to see this thing through."

That afternoon sixty of us were arrested. We had marched down to where police, state troopers, and national guardsmen were standing in a line, defining the perimeter of hospital property. Without halting, we crossed the line, singing. I was immediately taken into custody and, with about ten others, hauled off in a paddywagon to the Charleston jailhouse. Eventually all sixty were jailed.

Dave Livingston had been right. As jails went, this one was luxurious. Everything was brand new—clean cot, spotless lavatory, and toilet. I remembered the Birmingham jail and considered myself fortunate.

Later I sent word to the press that I would not allow myself to be bailed out of jail, but would remain inside in order to dramatize the plight of the hospital workers. We made it clear that my arrest was "a prelude to a civil rights struggle that will make Birmingham and Selma look like picnics."

It was what I had been seeking, of course, in order to highlight the plight of the hospital workers, but I was somewhat surprised to find myself in a court presided over by Judge Singletary himself.

Since our defense had always been to question the legality of state and local courts in limiting our First Amendment rights to freedom of assembly and freedom of speech, we were less than happy about presenting such an argument to the judge who had issued the injunction, and my lawyers said as much to Judge Singletary and asked him to disqualify himself. After hearing their arguments Judge Singletary refused to step down.

At that point my lawyers asked for immediate dismissal on the grounds that neither I nor the others had been informed of the true nature of the injunction before marching—an argument that happened to be true, though had we been so informed we would certainly have marched anyway. Judge Singletary also denied that motion, and I went to jail.

The day after, a large group of our supporters, mostly young people, lined up after a church rally and prepared to march down historic King Street in protest against my arrest. They were met by a contingent of policemen and state troopers, ready with gas masks and bayonets, and were told they couldn't make the march, that they had to disperse immediately. When they refused to do so, the police arrested a hundred of the demonstrators, which brought to two hundred the total number rounded up.

The following Tuesday Coretta King came to Charleston and led a rally and a march. It was a poignant moment when she came before this group, just a little over a year from the day Martin had been shot. She took the opportunity to point out the similarities between the strike in Charleston and the one in Memphis that had cost her husband his life.

I had expected to stay in jail until the conscience of the nation was aroused, but outside things began to deteriorate rapidly. Instead of continuing our program of nonviolent demonstrations, some of the younger blacks began to retaliate against the harsh and repressive measures of the Charleston police by throwing rocks and bottles. They also began heaving firebombs at houses, and it appeared as if the city might erupt in bloody warfare.

Then, too, the governor was still insisting that the state could not negotiate with the union, that state law prohibited such action, and that he would not violate the law in order to end the strike. Instead, he activated the National Guard, ostensibly to enforce the judge's injunction and to keep the peace.

So with all the legal trappings favoring the state, and with our own people beginning to slip into lawlessness, I finally concluded that for the moment I could do more good outside than inside, so I allowed myself to be bailed out of jail, along with others who had been arrested. Judge Singletary set bail at five hundred dollars and we paid it.

As soon as I got out, I called a press conference to see if I could stir the conscience of President Richard Nixon, who had been in office only a few months. Since I had supported John F. Kennedy in 1960 and Hubert Humphrey in 1968, I knew very little about President Nixon's stance on civil rights and hoped he might be sympathetic to our cause. (He was not the last Republican who would disappoint me in this regard.)

I had heard that the president was coming to South Carolina the next day to pay his respects to former Supreme Court Justice James Byrnes, a well-known segregationist; and I hoped that perhaps he would speak with us, if only to show his impartiality. He was scheduled to see Byrnes in Columbia, only ninety miles away. We made inquiries to see if I could meet with him, but we were told that he would not be available for such a meeting. Still I thought he might make some last-minute gesture in our direction, and so I called a meeting with the press in order to prod him.

At the news conference I first explained why I had allowed myself to be bailed out.

"I posted bond," I said, "because it is crystal clear that the state intends to kill this movement by legal manipulation. . . . I reluctantly left jail with the understanding that I will not forsake Charleston and these brave workers."

Then I called on the president to intervene in Charleston to ensure the constitutional rights of the strikers.

"Will you try to see President Nixon in Columbia?" one of the reporters asked.

"No," I said, "but we will send a group of demonstrators there to remind him of what's going on in Charleston."

We did and they were arrested.

We had heard nothing from our compromise proposal, so Andy had announced the terms of our offer, hoping that the more moderate elements in the community would put pressure on their elected officials to give us what we wanted. But as best we could tell, there were no moderate elements. Led by the *Charleston News and Courier,* the most conservative newspaper in the South, the city seemed as monolithic in its belief as the Soviet Union.

Nor did the State of South Carolina respond any differently. Indeed, Governor McNair's administration did not respond at all. But we were not finished yet. Our numbers and our enthusiasm were building. We had seen intransigence before and I told the hospital workers of Charleston not to lose hope.

On Mother's Day, May 11, our numbers and enthusiasm peaked: twelve thousand people paraded through Charleston in a dramatic demonstration that our momentum was growing, that we would not be turned away. We began in a local auditorium with a giant rally in which a number of visiting dignitaries spoke.

These included Walter Reuther, president of the United Auto Workers, and five Democratic congressmen: William F. Ryan and Ed Koch of New York City; Allard Lowenstein of New York; and John Conyers and Charles Diggs of Michigan.

Walter Reuther gave the union a check for ten thousand dollars to continue their fight and pledged five hundred dollars a week to us for as long as we were in Charleston in support of Local 1199B. "The people who have always been against a living wage," he said, "are the people who have a living wage and don't want to share it with others."

I spoke at the end of the rally and called the people to renewed dedication: "We do not intend to leave Charleston until our job is done. Tonight thousands will be marching with us. Next month, if they don't give us what we want, it may be tens of thousands."

Clearly I had underestimated the number who would come together with us after we left the church. As always, we marched out singing, and suddenly others began to join us from every street and neighborhood. They were like tributaries coming into a large river until it becomes swollen and overruns its banks. By the time we got to Calhoun Street we were twelve thousand strong—an irresistible force had we chosen to flood the grounds of any one of the hospitals.

Most of the marchers were black people from Charleston and the surrounding towns and cities of the South Carolina Low Country. Some of them were union workers, wearing their Local 1199 caps. But there were also black leaders from around the country, white congressmen, and a fair representation of white people, some clergy, but some simply citizens who were marching in support of social justice. With the strike a little less than two months old, we had made considerable progress, and the city leaders were clearly worried, as succeeding events were to prove.

Two days later I flew to Washington to meet with President Nixon and his advisors to discuss poverty in the United States. It was ironic that I should be invited there to consider the plight of the poor only a few days after I had unsuccessfully appealed to this same president for help in securing higher wages for the Charleston hospital workers. Had he really cared about the poor, he might have used the prestige of his office to help settle the strike. I certainly didn't expect him to initiate national legislation, but a few supportive words would have meant a great deal at that moment. Instead he ignored my pleas, then welcomed me at the White House later as if I had never asked for his help.

He had only been president for four months, and the country had high hopes that after the final war-ravaged, riot-torn years of the Johnson administration, Nixon would bring peace and return dignity and respect to the presidency. His advisors—Robert Finch, Daniel Moynihan, and others—were full of earnest resolve and high-blown rhetoric. They had a handle on poverty, they were trying to tell us, and soon, very soon everything would be better. Other leaders—black and white—seemed charmed by the rhetoric and the optimistic glow that hung over the room. But I sat there feeling more and more frustrated, knowing that while they were spinning tales for us, the people in Charleston were preparing to make yet one more march that afternoon in an effort to get their wages up to something higher than $1.30 an hour.

After we left I was angrier than I had been in a long time, and I could not contain my disappointment when reporters outside asked me how the meeting had gone.

"It was the most fruitless and the most disappointing of all the meetings we have had up to this time," I said.

"What about the president?" somebody asked.

I told them that he was very charming and gracious and an astute politician, but nothing constructive had occurred. Later, when they heard what I had said, Moynihan and the others seemed surprised. They had been so certain that their economic double-talk had mesmerized all of us.

When I got back to Charleston, negotiations were still at an impasse, and we continued to march and to confront the local establishment. Our constant disruption of the city was beginning to drive the tourists away, just as it had done in St. Augustine many years earlier; and like St. Augustine, Charleston's chief commercial product was its antique appeal to summer vacationers. Charleston also had its slave market, where a number of shops and restaurants did a thriving business as people in slacks and sunglasses walked around the narrow cobblestone streets and bought photographs and souvenirs. We had spoiled all that with our nightly marches and persistent demands. Merchants counted their receipts and began to long for a settlement and the departure of enemy troops.

Yet even as we began to put economic pressure on the Holy City, our own morale problems increased. The crowds of young blacks were becoming more and more unruly. There were times when we weren't quite in control.

I must say here that the sporadic violence that was beginning to break out during our marches was a sign of the times more than a deliberate change in style on the part of the SCLC. We had continued to "work-shop" our people in Charleston, just as we had always done. But the country as a whole had gone mad, largely because of the war in Vietnam, and the television networks were showing footage of riots on every evening broadcast. Most of these demonstrations were on college campuses and the participants were both white and black youngsters. Many of these protests began peaceably and remained so, but too many got out of hand. And there were also black militants who were determined to provoke more of the kind of rioting that occurred during the nights immediately after Martin's death. They too were getting TV and newspaper coverage, and young people in Charleston were watching this kind of chaos every night before joining us for what was supposed to be a peaceful and nonviolent demonstration.

Unfortunately, when the police and guardsmen confronted us, sometimes with fixed bayonets, our own people followed the examples they had seen on television rather than the examples we had presented to them during our workshop sessions. The results were predictable: Increasingly a few youngsters were hurling stones and bottles over the heads of the marchers and into the ranks of the police. People were getting hurt and the violence was escalating. We tried to remind our demonstrators that they could win only if they followed the path of peaceful nonviolence but a few refused to listen.

The result of this unruly activity was extremely damaging to our cause. Not only were we beginning to give the *Charleston News and Courier* fodder for their cannons, but we also gave Governor McNair a reason (or an excuse) to impose a curfew on the city that extended from 9:00 P.M. to 5:00 A.M., thereby effectively banning our night marches, which produced the greatest crowds.

I don't think I made a speech in Charleston that wasn't punctuated with a plea for nonviolence; yet in the end it was the ignoring of that plea by a few people—none of them SCLC personnel—that got me thrown in jail for the twenty-fifth time and for a period that set a record for the civil rights movement—a record that, as far as I know, still stands.

The day I went to jail began with a rally downtown during which ten people were arrested. When they were slow to move into the paddywagons, the police beat them with billy clubs, an action that infuriated the younger blacks who largely made up the crowd of eighty people. Some rocks and other missiles were thrown at the police. As a result, after consultation with Mayor Gaillard of Charleston, Governor McNair again declared a curfew for the city of Charleston.

With a curfew staring us in the face, we had to determine whether or not we would march that night. We had already defied an injunction by a circuit court judge. In this case we would be defying a curfew imposed by the governor of South Carolina. The question was: "Is it worse to defy a judge or a governor?"

We didn't debate the issue too long. We had always had greater respect for the judiciary, even at the state level, than we had for elected officials like governors, mayors, and city councilmen. We disobeyed courts only after careful consideration. We disobeyed politicians regularly—and as a matter of principle.

Governor McNair's curfew was supposed to prevent violence. Yet, as he well knew, violence continued in Charleston whether or not we staged a night march. So we figured he was simply trying to mask the growing popularity of our campaign to unionize the hospitals. Having come to that conclusion, we decided to defy his curfew. We expected to be arrested. We would accept the sentence, stay in jail long enough to rally additional support, and then bail ourselves out.

So we scheduled a rally at the Memorial Baptist Church in order to teach nonviolent attitudes and techniques before we marched to the hospitals. I was feeling bad that night and had just about decided to remain at the house where I was staying and rock on the front porch. I had been driving myself to the breaking point and had begun to sense that if I didn't rest I might end up in bed. The rumor went around town that I was sick and under the care of a doctor, but such was not the case. I was just trying to take a night off.

Hosea Williams had arrived from Mississippi and intended to address the rally. He had come to Charleston because he had heard I was in trouble; loyal as always, he wanted to share my danger. We talked for a while on the front porch of the house where we were both staying, and then he left for the church, agreeing that we would have to defy whatever curfew had been set by the governor, otherwise we could just pack up and go back to Atlanta.

I sat on the porch for a while, enjoying a small breeze that had sprung up. But my conscience got the better of me, and when I heard singing from the church, I was like an old boxer answering a distant bell. I got up, went into my room, put on blue jeans and a denim shirt, my "arrest outfit," and struck out for the church in a slow trot. When I entered the crowd cheered.

"If anybody is going to march in Charleston tonight," I told them, "it's going to be Ralph Abernathy."

Hosea and I and others spent a good deal of time whipping up the crowd while at the same time reminding them that only with the right kind of protest could we gain what we wanted. After singing, praying, and preaching the gospel of nonviolence, we moved out into the street shortly before midnight.

The police, state troopers, and national guardsmen were already there waiting for us, the ends of their rifles gleaming with bayonets. Chief Conroy came forward and told us in a courteous voice that we would have to disperse, that we could not hold a night march in view of the curfew. Something about his manner led me to understand that he intended to arrest us if we gave him the slightest provocation, and I nodded to let him know that I appreciated the position he was in. We understood each other, and I remember him as one of the most capable and fair-minded of all the chief law officers we faced.

Hosea and I conferred for a moment and finally agreed that instead of leading a march we might just stay where we were and refuse to disperse. So Hosea and I knelt down in the middle of the street and I began to pray, much as I had done at the head of the line at Selma. The crowd turned quiet, and then I heard someone cry out, "All right, grab him." I recognized the voice. It was Mayor Gaillard.

Suddenly two policemen appeared on either side of me, and I felt myself being borne through the air, my knees still bent in an attitude of prayer.

"Don't hurt him," someone ordered. Chief Conroy, I thought.

They hoisted me a little higher and I glided through the hot, damp night toward the paddywagon. They lifted me gently up and inside and Hosea followed me by a few seconds. At this point we were the only ones arrested, but as the doors shut behind us I heard the crowd screaming and shouting, and I figured others were not far behind.

The next day I learned that the night had turned into chaos and near-riot. Blacks had thrown rocks, bottles, and boards at the police; and the confrontation had resulted in six injuries among our marchers. I had hoped to hear that the demonstrations after we left had been nonviolent; but I could hardly have expected as much after the way things had been going. I soon learned, however, that the behavior of the crowd would weigh heavily against us in court and would severely limit my options for the next two weeks.

When we were being booked at the police station, I was surprised to hear the nature of the charge against us. This time we were not accused of violating an injunction or a curfew—both misdemeanors. We were charged with a felony—inciting to riot.

Hosea and I both chuckled when we heard this charge read

out. We had of course done no such thing. We had encouraged
the people in the church to violate the governor's curfew, but we
had repeatedly told them that whatever they did must be done
nonviolently. We had a thousand witnesses to our pleas that no
resistance be offered to arrest, that no one jeopardize the safety of
the police.

But the charge was nothing to chuckle over, as we found
out later that night, when our lawyer came back to our separate
cells to talk to us.

"They've charged you with inciting to riot," he said grimly.

I smiled. "What does that mean?"

"It means," he said, "that your bail is fifty thousand dollars."

"It will take fifty thousand dollars to get us out of here?" I
asked incredulous.

"Not 'us' " he said. "You. It will take one hundred thousand
dollars to get 'us' out."

I couldn't believe my ears. We could no more get one
hundred thousand dollars than we could get one million dollars.
Never in the twenty-four times I had been arrested had the bond
been more than a few hundred dollars. Clearly the judge was
using his power to set bail as a means of restricting our freedom
to protest unfair labor conditions; and while I had intended to
remain in jail for a long time in order to make a point, I was
suddenly distressed at the idea that I had no choice. I conferred
with local lawyers and they were as outraged as I was.

"It's clearly an abuse of judicial power," they said. "We'll
take it into federal court and get the charges dropped or at the
very least allow you to leave jail on your own recognizance."

"That's fine," I said. "And I hope it works. But I'm going to
approach the problem using my own tactics."

They seemed puzzled and a little alarmed.

"What can you do except challenge the ruling through the
courts?"

Clearly they thought I was going to stir up violence.

"I'm going to go on a hunger strike until justice is done, and
that means the settlement of the strike as well as the dropping of
these charges and this ridiculous bail."

"OK," they said, "you pursue your avenue and we'll pursue ours."

So the next time the jailer came down the hall with a tray of food, I waved him off. "You can tell the chef to skip me. I won't be eating while I'm in here."

He seemed surprised, but took the tray back. I hoped by this stratagem to speak not only to the authorities but to my own people as well. I wanted to remind the local and state governments that the power they held could not keep a man, or for that matter a people, from taking positive action in the face of injustice. They could put me in jail, but they couldn't stop me from making my witness in this familiar way.

But I also wanted to remind those outside—and particularly the young blacks—that we were dedicated to nonviolent strategies, that just because I was behind bars didn't mean that I couldn't act in their behalf. I hoped that enough of them had heard of Gandhi to realize what I was up to and give my gesture a chance to make an impact on the public at large, not only in Charleston but in the entire nation.

My attorneys came back in a few hours with what they regarded as good news. First they stopped in to see Hosea Williams, who was occupying the cell next door to me. I heard one of the lawyers say, "Hosea, sign right here."

"What's going on?" I heard Hosea ask.

"You're getting out."

A minute later they came around to my cell.

"They've backed down," they told me. "The solicitor of the Ninth Judicial Circuit has made us an offer. He says they will reduce bail to five thousand dollars. Hosea has already been signed out."

I thought about it for a moment. "I didn't sign anything to get in," I said, "and I'm not signing anything to get out."

"Why not?" they asked, a little confused.

"That's too much money," I said. "The principle hasn't changed. They are still imposing an excessive bond for a crime they know I didn't commit."

"That's right," my lawyers said.

"In which case," I said, "I think we should refuse the bond and go for broke. We should make them do what's right."

"Of course five thousand dollars is only a tenth of fifty thousand dollars," they reminded me.

"Yes," I said, "but it's still ten times more than it should be, and a hundred times more than most blacks could afford to pay. I think we should stick to our guns."

At that moment Hosea's voice came from the next cell.

"Mr. President," he called, "are you going to stay in?"

"That's right," I said. "Until the strike is settled."

"Then I'm going to stay too," he said and he made the lawyers tear up his release papers.

The next day my lawyers announced that a reduction of the bail would not serve justice because the charges were patently false. Any bail, they said, would be a denial of civil rights.

Before they left the lawyers seemed worried about us and anxious to help.

"Is there anything we can get you?" they asked. "Just anything. You name it."

"Yes," I said, "you can get me a radio."

I had never before minded being in jail because always before it had been a stratagem, a way of dramatizing our case to the press, and through them to the people of the nation. Usually we were in one day and out the next. We posted bail. We got out and paused to have our pictures taken on the jailhouse steps. Then later the charges would be dropped in the wake of our final victory or else we would come back, stand trial, be convicted, and pay a small fine. Evan as late as the Poor People's Campaign, being arrested was always something of an adventure.

In Charleston, however, it was an entirely different story. I began to understand how those arrested for other crimes must have felt—men and women who didn't have enough money for bail and weren't certain when they would see the outside again. In my heart I knew I would get out somehow but I was by no means certain when. After a week went by without any alteration in my status, I began to wonder if this might not prove to be a much more serious situation than I had originally thought. Indeed, it occurred to me that I might end up having to serve a genuine prison sentence, maybe for as long as a year or two.

The jailor, a white man, was friendly. Except for a few visitors each day who were allowed to stay only a short time, I had no one else to talk to. I listened to the local radio stations—some of which featured black preachers—and I read the Bible and less often the newspapers. But other than those activities, I tended to lie on my back and think random thoughts.

About the fourth day it occurred to me that with so much time on my hands I should begin to make some plans, work on a project, do something with my mind to spend these days more fruitfully. I thought of all the times I had complained because I couldn't stop, put down what I was doing, and carefully think out some problem or project. Now the Good Lord had made available all the time I could possibly have hoped for and I wasn't taking advantage of it.

My brothers and sisters had lived through the era we were emerging from, and they told me how much they feared for my life at places like Montgomery and Selma and Chicago. I thought of them all, pictured their faces, and tried to remember when we had last been together. We never saw enough of each other, never got together the way we used to when our parents were alive. Why was that? Certainly we enjoyed one another and looked forward to our infrequent reunions. I thought about it and realized why: Because nobody had taken the time to organize a reunion. Well, I certainly had the time. When the jailor came through in a few minutes I asked him for a favor.

"I'd like some paper, preferably a notebook, and a pen or a sharp pencil."

"What are you going to do, write letters?"

"No," I said, "I'm going to plan a family reunion."

For the next few days I worked on a plan for the first annual W. L. and Louivery Abernathy Family Reunion. I worked out everything to the smallest detail: It would take place at the old home place in Linden; it would begin on Saturday with a discussion of our roots; next we would have lunch; then we would rest and after that play softball followed by a pit barbecue, the kind where the hog is turned on a spit all night long. The evening would close with a family caucus to decide whether or not we wanted the reunion to be an annual affair. The next morning, like our mother and father before us, we would rise early and hold family devotions. Then we would eat a full country breakfast of eggs, bacon, biscuits, grits, juice, and coffee. Afterward we would go to the McKinney Cemetery where all of our ancestors were buried, including our parents. Then we would go to Sunday School at Hopewell Baptist Church, followed by the morning service.

Remembering how our grandmother Manerva had prepared the communion service, I intended to propose to my brothers and sisters that we give a communion set to the church in her honor, to be presented on that Sunday morning. But I also wanted to honor Grandpa George on this occasion, and wondered how that could be most appropriately done. Then I recalled how the old man, though unable to read, had nonetheless begun the service each Sunday by opening the Bible and reciting the appropriate scriptural passage. (He would always corral one of us during the week and make us read the verses to him over and over again until he had memorized them.) So it seemed to me quite appropriate that we dedicate a pulpit Bible engraved with his name, despite the fact that had he still been alive he could not have read it.

I planned no gift in memory of my maternal grandparents, not because I didn't revere their memory, but because I never knew either one of them. Had my older brothers and sisters been in jail along with me, we might have also made gifts in memory of the Bells.

As I made these plans, I remembered that years earlier, before I joined the army, I had given a piano to my younger sister, Susie Ellen, and one to the Hopewell Baptist Church. I knew that the congregation still used the old piano, and it occurred to me that it would be fitting if Juanita and I could replace it with a Hammond organ. I even thought about how the organ might be transported to Marengo County.

I hoped to preach the sermon that morning. (And as it

turned out, I did, because our only surviving uncle, Clarence, in the tradition of Grandpa George, took over and, ignoring the existence of the pastor, said: "David, my deceased brother's son, fresh from the jails of Charleston, is here and Reverend, if you have any sense, you will let him preach today.")

Then we would invite the whole congregation down to the home place for a family meal of baked chicken, turkey, roast beef, green beans, rolls, potato salad, cake, pie, peach cobbler, tea, and lemonade. Juanita would join my five sisters and six sisters-in-law to make sure enough food was cooked to serve everybody.

After the long luncheon, we would hold several seminars concerning the family's future (but to which all would be invited). The first would be led by the Reverend L. L. Anderson, pastor of the Tabernacle Baptist Church of Selma, Alabama; the title: "What the Abernathys Should Be Doing in the Field of Religion." The second would be led by SCLC staff member, the Reverend Andrew Young; the title: "What the Abernathys Should Be Doing in Politics." The third would be led by SCLC staff member, Reverend Hosea Williams; the title: "What the Abernathys Should Be Doing in the Field of Economics." With these seminars, the reunion would come to its end.

Had I tackled this task in the middle of a busy schedule I would have dashed off a quick list of steps to be taken and fired it out to the rest of the family with little or no thought.

But with all day, every day, to contemplate and figure, I was amazed at how many problems I could raise and solve. By the time I had the entire plan down on paper, it was as complicated as an automobile engine and as well coordinated. I carefully made copies of the entire document for each of my brothers and sisters and for my wife, while the jailor walked past time and again, stopping to stare through the bars at what I was writing, trying to see what I was up to, because I'm sure he didn't believe me when I told him about the reunion.

So carefully had I worked out the details of this annual reunion that we haven't missed one in almost twenty years now. The events during the three-day celebration follow the same pattern every year just as I laid it out in the Charleston jail in the summer of 1969. Sometimes when we're in the middle of the family baseball game, I remember that we are playing because on those hot humid afternoons I lay on my cot and listened to the Game of the Day blaring on the radio and thought how much fun it might be for the whole family to play together.

But that wasn't all I did during this period. Once the jailor had come to the conclusion that I was harmless and reasonably good natured, he began chatting with me. We talked about the weather, baseball, world affairs, even about politics, though we didn't talk about the events that had led up to my arrest, since neither one of us thought the topic would prove too fruitful. We also discussed religion, and I found out soon enough that he was a churchgoing man. These conversations led him to ask for my help one day.

"Reverend," he said, grasping the bars with both hands and sticking his face in between, "I have a fellow down here who's in need of some spiritual guidance. He won't tell me his name because he's afraid of his parents finding out what happened. Do you suppose you could come down and talk to him."

Surprised, I readily agreed, and he took me to a cell where a young black man about seventeen years old was huddled in a corner, staring at the ceiling.

"This is Reverend Abernathy, son," he said. "He thought you might like to visit with him for a while."

The young man looked at me, his eyes widened, and he nodded.

The jailor unlocked the door and I stepped inside. For a second he hesitated, then locked the door behind be.

"Call me when you're finished."

I don't remember the young man's name, but he was in jail for snatching a woman's purse, a crime of impulse rather than something he had planned. Certainly, he was no hardened criminal.

"Is that the first time you ever did anything like that?" I asked.

"Yes, sir," he said and I believed him. He was well mannered, and after I had talked to him for a few minutes I knew that he had been brought up by good parents and that he was a churchgoer.

"What's your name?" I asked him.

He shook his head, and I thought I understood.

"You don't want your family to know about this, do you?"

He nodded, and the tears welled up in his eyes.

"You know they'll have to find out sooner or later, don't you?"

He hesitated, thought a minute, and then in a barely audible voice, said "Yes, sir."

"The sooner they know the sooner they'll stop worrying about where you are and what's happened to you. Don't you think your pastor can help tell them?"

He was hesitant, but finally, after a few more minutes of conversation, he was ready for the pastor of his church to come down, talk to him, and then tell his parents. I told him I was sure he would be released, though I qualified what I said to some degree because I had thought the same thing about myself.

Within an hour and a half he was released into the custody of his parents, who were more understanding than he had anticipated, which is often the case. The jailor was also grateful for my intervention, and came to me with a proposition.

"Most of the people in here are colored," he said, "and it seems to me that a lot of them are religious folks, though I really don't know for sure. Maybe you could help them the way you've helped that boy and his family. Most of the ones in here don't have a pastor, so you could be their pastor while you're here. That is, if you wanted to. You don't have to do it, of course. It's strictly up to you."

"I think that would be fine," I said. "If I can help, then I would be happy to take on the job."

"There's only one condition," he said, narrowing his eyes.

"What's that?" I asked.

"'You're not to plot with anybody.'"

I laughed so hard that I had to wipe my eyes with my handkerchief.

From then until I was released, I went from cell to cell—white as well as black—and I would spend a few minutes with each of those who seemed receptive, talking with them about their personal problems, giving them advice on how to contact their families or their lawyers, praying with them. I saw mostly drunks, brawlers, and disturbers of the peace; but there were also some thieves and armed robbers among the group, most of whom seemed happy to see me and willing to be helped.

Of course, the knowledge of who I was probably made my job easier, as well as the fact that I was not an outsider at all, but a fellow prisoner, someone under the same authority they were. Naturally, many of them wanted to know how the movement was progressing and what I planned to do when I got out.

As the days went by, I continued my fast, eating nothing and drinking nothing but water and a little juice. Then my stomach began to ache—only a gnawing pain at first, and then I began to feel sharper pangs. At first I thought it was hunger, but toward the end I knew it was something far worse.

The jailor came by and found me doubled up with pain, so he made arrangements for me to go to the hospital the next day for an examination—the very same hospital we had been picketing. The doctor ran a series of tests, including an upper GI, and then called me into the office.

"I think you've got the beginnings of an ulcer," he said. "What have you been eating?"

I smiled. "For the last several days, nothing," I said.

He nodded gravely. "Well, that's the problem," he said. "You can't go without food if you're getting an ulcer. Your gastric juices will eat through the lining of your stomach. They have to have food to absorb them."

I argued with him, but finally compromised. I would eat an egg each morning. But that was all. He shook his head in disapproval, saying that my stomach might get much worse. Then he released me to the policeman, who escorted me back to the jailhouse, where for the next few days I survived on one egg each morning. My stomach continued to hurt, but the pain was bearable.

At that point the AFL-CIO entered the picture when William Kircher, a national director, announced that if the strike continued, the longshoremen would strike in sympathy and shut down the port of Charleston.

"We are marshaling every source of strength and support," he said, "and we will not be reluctant to use these kinds of trade union strengths. We have reached the position reluctantly; we have reached it only after exhausting every avenue of conciliation and mediation."

This particular economic challenge came at a crucial moment in the history of the strike. We had already severely damaged the city's tourist trade, and local merchants were arguing behind the scenes for some kind of settlement that would send us packing. The strike had already been in progress for more than three months, and the momentum seemed tohave shifted in our direction. Now the AFL-CIO was threatening Charleston's other great source of revenue—its busy harbor.

Charleston was the fifth largest port on the East Coast and in 1968 it had done over five hundred million dollars' worth of trade. The import and export business was crucial to both local and state interests. The closing of the port would ensure a recession of even greater proportions than they were already suffering. There would be new economic victims, many of whom were already calling Mayor Gaillard's office, telling him that the time had come for a quick and permanent settlement.

They didn't like the sound of William Kircher's thinly veiled warning: "Perhaps Charleston has not suffered enough economically."

There was something else they didn't like and neither did I: Violence was increasing, despite our constant pleas for peaceful protests. The police and firemen were becoming the targets of attacks—mostly from rocks and bottles, though in one case an officer was shot in the leg with a pellet gun. Vandals were breaking and entering cars, in much the same spirit they had looted stores immediately after Martin's assassination.

Also, there were nightly cases of arson. In fact, an antebellum house, recently restored by the Historic Charleston Foundation, was torched according to Fire Chief Wilmot Guthke by "a flambeau taken from a road barrier and thrown through a window." After three months of stalemate, frustrations were erupting into aggressive acts. The city, known for its old-fashioned civility, had discovered something about its capacity for violence and hatred. The authorities were worried, and so were we.

The president of the United States was also worried. I was told that representatives for President Nixon, who had been bombarded with letters and phone calls, were even then in contact with local and state officials and with representatives of our coalition. As we had so often seen, the power of the federal government, while not always decisive, could be formidable; and Mr. Nixon was beginning to learn its uses only a little more than five months into his first term. Had he been a man of greater courage, he might have entered the picture earlier, when he had been in South Carolina. Now, though he was involved belatedly, we were still happy to have his help.

With all of this pressure on state and local authorities, they finally gave in. A delegation of several of our leaders came to see me in my cell to tell me the news. One of the hospitals had agreed to accept our demands and the other had almost come to terms.

I assumed that the county hospital had been the first to surrender, since it was controlled locally; but I was wrong.

"No," Andy Young told me. "It's the Medical College Hospital. They've agreed to everything."

"Good," I said, overjoyed.

"Sort of agreed," somebody said.

"What do you mean 'sort of'?"

Then they explained. The Medical College agreed that all

employees who had been on the rolls at the time the strike began would be rehired.

"Including the twelve they fired?" I asked.

Yes, they told me, these would be rehired along with all the rest. Also, the wages of all workers now being paid $1.30 per hour would automatically be raised to $1.60 an hour. In fact, to avoid the appearance of responding to the pressures of this strike, the State of South Carolina was raising the minimum wage of *all* state employees.

"What about recognition of the union?" I asked.

"The Medical College Hospital says it will allow employees to negotiate with management," I was told.

"What about South Carolina state law?" I asked. "I thought collective bargaining by a state or local agency was illegal."

"They got around that. They agreed that, when settling a grievance, the complaining employee could bring along any other employee or employees at any stage of the grievance process."

"In other words, 'collective bargaining,' " I said.

"Collective bargaining without ever using the phrase," the lawyers said, smiling.

"What about the AFL-CIO?" I asked. "Will they be happy with this?"

"Sure," said the lawyers. "They said they would allow a union grievance committee to aid employees in the grievance process, and they also approved an employees' credit union."

"Why is that important?" I asked.

"Because the credit union would allow the union to have a dues checkoff—which means the union would get its dues automatically. That's always a big issue with them."

I shook my head in wonder. "These South Carolina officials are the best I've ever seen at changing the meaning of the law. One week it means one thing, and the next week it means another."

But I still wasn't satisfied—not until I knew how the negotiators themselves felt about all this and how it would affect the people at the county hospital.

"I'd like to talk to everybody in here and see how they feel about all this. If I leave jail and they aren't completely satisfied then I will have let them down."

They agreed to bring in the leaders so I could make sure they weren't being stampeded into a settlement just because a few people were getting what they wanted. Meanwhile, Juanita had arrived and when the leaders from the various groups came back to see me, she greeted them too, along with Andy and a few of the other staff members. The cell was crowded with people, but I was able to talk to each one separately in order to receive assurances.

Finally one of the Charleston County Hospital workers came back to see me.

"Have you people gotten everything you wanted?" I asked.

"Almost," said the woman, a little hesitantly. She was clearly holding something back.

"What didn't they give you?" I asked. "Why haven't you settled with the county officials?"

"Because they won't hire back all the strikers," she said.

"How many strikers were there?"

"Sixty-five," she said, "but they've filled about thirty of their jobs. So they say they won't hire back those thirty."

Juanita turned to me, eyes flashing with anger.

"Ralph, you can't go!" she said, and she was right. It would not be fair to build this victory on the defeat of those thirty. We would have to gain a final settlement that would include jobs for everybody who had been at work on March 15—the same terms accorded to the workers from the medical college.

"The county officials claim they can't afford to hire thirty additional people," said one of the lawyers.

"Then they will have to rehire the strikers and get rid of the others," I said. "I hate to see anyone out of a job, but these strikers were there first and they will have to be taken care of first. After all, they originally quit their jobs in support of the Medical College workers, so it would be the height of injustice if they were the ones to end up unemployed. You tell the county officials I won't allow myself to be freed until they have come to terms with the county strikers as well."

It was a statement I meant at the time I made it, and Andy Young and the lawyers carried that message to the community at large. Thinking that I was coming out and that the crisis was over, Governor McNair lifted his curfew, and it appeared as if things would settle back to normal.

But that night Andy made it clear to the city, black as well as white, that the strike was still on.

"Now it's not settled," he told a church rally.

"That's right," the congregation responded.

"You remember when you all walked out of the Medical College Hospital, those people at the county hospital said 'we'll help you' and they walked out too."

"That's right!" they called out.

"Well, then, it wouldn't be right for us to go back to work and just forget about them."

"That's right!" they shouted.

By this time, I had spent over two weeks in jail. The media had forgotten me and I started to feel like the Count of Monte Cristo. I tried to imitate Martin and wrote a letter from a Charleston jail, but no words of indignation came from the national newspapers, no marching crowds poured into Charleston.

One day as the jailor walked by, I stopped him. "I wonder if I might have some more paper. I seem to have run out."

He nodded, brought me another notepad, and watched as I curled up on my cot and began to write. I made it a point to spend hours at a time writing in the notebook, just as I had done with the family reunion. Every so often he would try to peer at the page, but I would always tilt it away from him so he couldn't see the words. Finally, he could stand it no longer.

"Reverend," he said, "are you planning another family reunion?"

"Not this time," I replied cryptically.

He went on down the row, but in a minute or two he returned and leaned against the bars. "Then what *are* you doing?" he asked.

"I'm using my time in jail to devise a plan for the complete elimination of poverty in the United States."

"You want to completely eliminate poverty?" he said incredulously.

"That's right," I said, "and if I have enough time, I'm going to work it all out. Every single detail."

I could see the panic in his eyes as he looked around to see if anybody else had heard. "You want to use this jail to launch a plan to eliminate poverty?"

I nodded and concentrated on what I was writing, while he watched me in silence.

"I've got to get you out of here," he said, and disappeared through the door at the end of the row.

I talked to my lawyers and staff members and learned that the authorities were arranging my release.

"It will be settled anytime now," they said. "They are going to make arrangements to place these other workers elsewhere, but it will take them a while."

"Will it move things forward if I stay in jail?" I asked.

"It might actually help if you allowed them to set you free," they said. "There's worry that until you leave jail the rock throwing and firebombing will continue. You could accept release as an act of faith. That might quiet things down and put the monkey on their backs."

I looked at Juanita, who was sitting beside me in that hot, damp cell, perspiration beading her forehead. I was ready to go, but I didn't want to do anything she wouldn't approve. "What do you think, Juanita?" I asked.

She thought a moment. "I think it might be all right," she said. "After all, if they don't settle the strike, you can always come back."

I turned to the others. "OK," I said, "tell them I'll come out. But I want to read a statement to the press, just so they will understand precisely what's going on. And you can tell them we won't hesitate to march again if they don't settle quickly."

I sat down in my cell and wrote a statement, while Juanita looked over my shoulder. After I had read it to the assembled group and made minor changes, I stood up.

"All right," I called to the jailor. "I'm ready to go."

He came back to the cell and stood there, a huge grin on his face, obviously relieved that I would not draw up the ultimate plan to end poverty while a guest in his jail. Just before I left the cell for the last time, I unplugged my radio, wrapped the cord around it, and started to leave.

"If you don't mind," said the jailor, "I wonder if I could keep the radio—as a souvenir."

He had been kind and thoughtful, one of the best jailors I had known, so I gave it to him gladly.

"Take it," I said, "as a house present."

He took it with both hands, his grin widening. He didn't know quite what to say, so he said nothing, but he nodded his head and continued to grin as I walked down the hall, through the waiting room, and out the front door. For a moment my eyes hurt from the glare of the sun, but they soon adjusted to the outdoor light. No matter how long you've been locked up, you find that you can get used to freedom very quickly, probably because it is a natural state.

I was met by several reporters and a television crew, and they began asking me questions.

I told them I was glad to be out after almost two weeks behind bars, and I pointed out that this stay had been the longest of my career as a jailbird. Then I read my statement.

> Although no agreement has been reached at County Hospital, I have decided, as a further display of good faith [we had suspended our demonstrations], to place my trust in the people of Charleston County and to call upon them to reach a satisfactory settlement at the County Hospital. I am convinced that leaders in this community can find a prompt, fair, and reasonable solution to this problem.
>
> Accordingly, I have accepted my release from jail, and ordered my staff to continue the suspension of nonviolent activities through the weekend.

I have been assured that the people of Charleston County want a settlement and that they can use this time to reach a just conclusion of this strike.

"What are you planning to do now?" one of the reporters asked, after I had finished the statement.

"I plan to go back to Atlanta to take up my responsibilities as pastor of West Hunter Church," I said and walked toward a waiting car.

"Will you be back to Charleston?" another called after me.

I really hadn't thought that far ahead, but I called over my shoulder, "Next week."

"Why?"

I didn't answer, but one of the staff said, "He's coming back to do one of two things—celebrate or demonstrate."

We all came back to celebrate in the middle of August. In fact, the SCLC held its annual meeting there, partly to punctuate the victory we had won by showing the world that we could convene in this old Confederate city in peace and brotherhood. In many ways the Charleston victory had been the most unambiguous we had achieved since Selma, though it by no means had such far-reaching implications. The positive gains we made in Washington at Resurrection City were a long time in coming, though eventually the Congress enacted virtually everything we wanted. But in Charleston we had settled a strike and made a point about all the poor who were working under such unconscionable conditions.

In addition, I had won a personal victory. The Poor People's Campaign had been conceived and planned under Martin's leadership, and whatever positive gains we made were attributed to him, while the failures were attributed to me. But the Charleston campaign had been planned and executed under my leadership, and some of the remaining doubters had been silenced. For the first time people were beginning to believe that the SCLC would have a life and a purpose beyond completing the projects already begun by Martin.

In an effort to point the organization toward the future, I announced to the one thousand assembled delegates at the annual meeting that our "sixteen months of wandering in the wilderness of mourning for Martin" were over. We were now leaving the desert.

"I'm going," I told them, "I'm going through to the promised land."

Wyatt Tee Walker, who also spoke, picked up the allusion and extended it, explicitly comparing my role to that of Joshua.

"Joshua was entirely different from Moses," he said to the cheering audience. "He didn't try to do Moses's job; he just did Joshua's job."

I took the occasion to outline the battles that still remained before us and to try to give the movement a new thrust, in just the way Joshua had done after the Israelites had crossed into the promised land. I acknowledged that we had many enemies still to conquer, that Jericho still lay before us. But I let them know that we were going to press on until the walls came tumbling down.

One of the chief tasks, I told them, was to rally the poor people and organize them into a working force that could speak for itself in the marketplace. It was time for people working for minimum wage or less to band together and seek fair compensation for a day's work. I saw the immediate future as one in which we would intervene in behalf of poor people in their struggle for economic justice. We would concentrate on the black population of course, but our efforts would also benefit poor whites, just as they had in the Poor People's Campaign.

At that moment we all thought we could accomplish anything we set out to do. We had regained the strength of spirit we had lost when Martin had been killed. We saw the future so clearly that August that we forgot about the past.

We were now confronting problems that were older and more deeply rooted than even racial injustice. The gulf between the haves and have nots was present in biblical times, and we soon found out that the victory in Charleston was not even the beginning of a campaign against poverty, but only a skirmish in a neverending war.

As a matter of fact, even as we were holding our convention, a labor dispute broke out in Charleston and two hundred local sanitation workers went out on strike. We cheered them on in our meeting, and pledged our support, not only to them but to our brothers in Chicago who were protesting the discriminatory hiring practices of trade unions in the city. So even as we were celebrating our rebirth that day, we were also beginning to take some measure of the problems we would face in the coming years.

Epilogue

THE STORY I AM ABOUT TO TELL is one I have never told anyone before, not even my wife, Juanita. When she reads it, it will undoubtedly shock her and cause her great pain, as it caused me. But it needs to be told in order to round out the history of the Southern Christian Leadership Conference (SCLC). My pride or vanity matters little at this point when measured against the demand of history to have the whole truth.

In the summer of 1976, I received a letter from Chauncey Eskridge, who at that time was serving as chief fund raiser for the SCLC. The tone of what he had to say was somber, even grim. The organization was in financial difficulties. It had been a long time since we had won a dramatic victory on the national scene or attracted the attention of the national press. The civil rights movement was no longer as fashionable as it once had been. The battles still to be fought were smaller, more complicated, and did not play so well on the evening news. Watergate had been a better show than anything we had managed to stage.

So I wasn't really surprised to read what Chauncey was saying: We could not continue to operate unless we did something to generate funds. We had always been in that situation. In fact, he said he wanted to come to Atlanta and meet with me and members of the board to discuss the future of the organization. He seemed serious, so I called him to ask what he had in mind.

"Just a group who loves the SCLC. We'd like to meet with you."

"Who is 'we?'" I asked.

Eskridge seemed casual about the meeting and the people involved, but he was quick to put forth the names.

"Me. Dr. Claude Young. Joe Lowery. A couple of others."

"I'll be happy to meet with you," I said. "Just tell me when and where."

"I thought maybe we could meet this coming Sunday evening. Maybe at the Hilton Inn, out by the airport. That way everybody from out of town could fly in, make the meeting, then fly out again."

"That sounds fine with me," I said. "I'll look forward to seeing you there."

After I'd hung up I didn't give the meeting more than a passing thought, but at the time I did note that none of my close friends on the board was included. Still, I looked forward to seeing all of these people and I hoped we could come up with some campaign to revitalize our people. Much had been accomplished, but much still remained to be done; and the nation as a whole had lost interest. I had been unable to think of anything dramatic enough to refocus the attention of the nation on our plight, but perhaps a group of us could do better.

When I walked into the suite they were all waiting. I remember how warm and friendly they were, shaking hands, asking about my family. Joe Lowery in particular seemed especially friendly. He had moved to Atlanta a few months after Martin's assassination as pastor of the Central United Methodist Church. For a number of years he had been chairman of the SCLC board, though neither he nor the others present had ever been full time in their commitment to the organization. (I was full time and on-call for whatever emergency arose in the region, but, like Martin, I received no salary.)

After we had talked for a few minutes, Chauncey suggested that we all sit down; when we did, everyone suddenly became quiet. Seated on one end of a padded sofa, I turned, like everyone else, to Chauncey, who sat in a chair that commanded the room.

He began, as I expected, by reciting the financial woes of the organization, a litany I had heard all too often. From the beginning we had been without funds; and though there had been times when we'd almost had enough to do everything we planned, more often than not we were pinching pennies and wondering how we'd pay the next bill. So I was worried, but not really alarmed.

Then, after completing his accounting, he turned to me.

"Mr. President," he said, "we appreciate everything you've done for the organization and the movement, but, well, we feel you've outlived your usefulness. We feel we have to have a change."

As he said this I remained expressionless, but I felt a sudden stab of pain. I hadn't anticipated this move. It had never occurred to me that this was the reason for the meeting. My mind raced back to the recent Indianapolis convention, where I had tried to resign and had been shouted down by everyone present. So why beg me to stay on and then humiliate me only a short time later? I tried to grasp precisely what was going on.

"We need new blood," Chauncey was saying, in a speech that I now realized had been rehearsed. "We need new life."

The others joined in, always framing what they had to say with praise for everything I had done in the past and assurances that my counsel and participation would always be valued in the future. No one could have been more thoughtful than these four men, who told me in the briefest possible speeches that I had failed in my role as leader of the SCLC.

As I listened, I looked around me at the sleek furniture, the porcelain lamps, the thick carpet, and at these gentlemen who had joined the organization after we had begun to meet in fancy places like this instead of in black churches or in the wooden frame houses of Pullman porters and chauffeurs. I remembered the Gaston Motel in Birmingham, a black-only establishment with its cheap curtains and plastic-framed pictures, where our "suite," a bedroom and a sitting room, was blown to bits by a bomb, minutes after Martin and I had left. And I remembered the Lorraine Motel, with only one room for Martin and me, with two narrow beds. We might not have enough money to continue under present circumstances, but we were certainly going under in style.

As Chauncey talked on, in quiet control of the meeting, I felt a growing sense of my own inadequacy that was physically painful. I had given my best. I was certain of that. I didn't know whether that "best" had been outstanding or adequate. I had always assumed the latter, but they were now telling me I had performed poorly.

What hurt was my growing awareness that I had failed the SCLC, an organization that I helped to found, that I had nurtured over the years, that had been left in my keeping by my dear friend, who had somehow known he would soon be dead. I had loved the organization from the very beginning, before it had even come into being, when its only existence was in my mind and in Martin's, a shared dream waiting to be fully conceptualized.

I thought of Juanita and how she would react to this humiliation, and I was glad she thought I was visiting the sick, which I usually did on Sunday nights. I hadn't told her where I was going, and I was certain that if I said nothing when I came in, she would assume I was simply returning from the hospital as usual. I wondered if perhaps I could avoid telling her altogether.

Meanwhile, Claude Young was seconding what Chauncey had said, reviewing the history of the organization over the past two or three years, commenting on our lack of substantial achievements, our falling revenues, our diminished reputation. He too believed we needed "new blood," "fresh ideas." I tried to concentrate on what he was saying, but it was difficult to do so, given the matter-of-fact way he was cataloging my failures.

Finally he finished his speech, and everyone looked at me expectantly. I believe they thought I would offer my resignation immediately, but I knew better than to do so in my present frame of mind. I was hurt and confused. I knew I was in no shape to make such an important decision.

"Gentlemen," I said, "I thank you for what you've said. I'll think about it and let you know."

I thought I saw disappointment in a couple of faces, but they were in no position to ask that I act immediately. When I rose to leave, we all shook hands and they gave me warm and friendly smiles. We left the motel as if we had just had a card game in which everyone had been a winner.

On the way home I was overcome by a sense of shame and dread, shame because my best was not good enough, dread because I knew that I would have to resign and that no explanation could fully hide the reason. Driving along those winding back roads I felt less at home in Atlanta than I did the first day I moved here. When I got home, I walked in with as much bounce in my step as I could manage, determined that Juanita would not know—at least not yet.

"How were things at the hospital?" she asked, without looking up from her book.

"Fine," I said, asking forgiveness for the deception.

Over the next weeks I brooded over the problem, trying to find some way of retiring gracefully, without arousing the suspicion of the rank-and-file members of the organization, flung all over the country, many of whom I knew and often heard from. Most of them were personally loyal to me, and they might be discouraged or angry if they thought I had been kicked out of office. I was resolved that I would find an excuse for leaving that everyone believed—even Juanita.

Our conversation at the Hilton had taken place in late summer, just when the 1976 political campaign was beginning. We were backing Jimmy Carter, because we had known him to be fair to blacks as governor of Georgia and because he was a Democrat—and at that time blacks always voted Democratic. Andy Young, who was serving in Congress, was particularly active in support of Carter; and the rest of us followed his lead in our public statements, though we had found Gerald Ford to be sympathetic and cordial to the black leadership.

In November we were pleased and a little surprised to see Carter win, to become the first Deep South candidate to be elected to the presidency in the twentieth century (unless you count Woodrow Wilson). We were equally surprised to hear that Andrew Young would be appointed ambassador to the United Nations and that he would resign his position in Congress to take that position. Since Young had just been reelected, the governor declared his seat open and called for a special election to fill his position.

Several people suggested I run to replace Andy, and the first couple of times I brushed the idea aside. Then it hit me. If I ran for Congress I could resign my position as president of the SCLC and everyone would understand perfectly. So the next time someone of importance asked me, I replied, "You know. I've actually been giving that idea serious consideration."

Shortly thereafter, I formally announced my candidacy and also my resignation. A number of people called or wrote to tell me that I didn't have to resign my position with the SCLC, that I could either take a formal leave of absence or, since I wasn't drawing a salary, just take the time off. But I was adamant. I couldn't do both things and do them equally well, and the SCLC was too important to leave leaderless, even for a short period of time.

Needless to say, the board accepted my resignation with regret and with many thanks. Juanita may have been a little puzzled by my insistence on handling the matter this way, but in the end she accepted the apparent logic of my reasoning and was perhaps relieved that either way I would not be bearing the burdens of the organization on my shoulders.

Don't misunderstand my motives in running for Congress. I did not simply use the race as a way of bowing out, with never a thought of winning. I *wanted* to win. I wanted to go to Congress—not only because it would have partially vindicated me in my own eyes, but also because it was an opportunity to render greater service to our people. There were very few blacks in Congress and Andy's resignation made one less. My chief opponent in the race, Wyche Fowler, was a white man; and though he lived in the district, often visited black churches, and had consistently supported black causes, it still seemed proper for a black to represent a predominantly black district in the U.S. Congress.

Unfortunately, I wasn't a very good politician. In the first place, I had spent most of my time out on the road, stamping out brush fires in the region, neglecting to build up a strong network of political allies in Atlanta. I was well known, but only at a distance, whereas Wyche Fowler and the other candidates had been shaking hands and meeting voters for years.

Then, too, I couldn't bear to ask anybody for money. I soon learned that it costs a small fortune to run for Congress, and a candidate must be either wealthy in his own right or else be willing to go to people who have money and beg. From time to time I had begged contributions for the SCLC, but I didn't feel comfortable doing so and begging for myself was beyond my poor abilities as a fund-raiser.

So when it became obvious that I was either going to have to raise a large sum of money or else disappear from public sight, I did the only thing I could think of: I mortgaged my house and borrowed $50,000, an enormous amount of money to me, but barely enough to be visible in the field.

I worked hard, spent every waking hour campaigning, and gave it my best effort; but with eight black candidates in the field, Wyche Fowler came in first and I came in third, behind John Lewis, who now holds the seat. The loss was hard for me to bear, but it was not without its uses. I had, after all, been able to withdraw gracefully from the presidency of the SCLC.

Predictably, Joseph Lowery was appointed acting president, with a vow that he would neither seek nor accept the position permanently. But at the next convention, with Hosea Williams seemingly scheduled for election, Joseph Lowery promised that if Hosea would step aside and allow Lowery to be made permanent president, Lowery would immediately appoint Williams executive director, a paid position. Williams withdrew, Lowery was elected, and indeed Williams became executive director—for a few months. Before the year was over, Lowery had fired him.

In retrospect, with such friendly folks surrounding me at that time, I believe my decision to resign from the presidency of SCLC has added years to my life.

Of course, I have kept up with the activities of the SCLC over the years and I am still listed as president emeritus. But my life has been by no means empty since I relinquished my active leadership of the organization. No pastor of a large urban church ever has time on his hands. He is always busy counseling the members of his congregation, visiting the sick, baptizing the newcomers to the faith, marrying the young (as well as the middle-aged and elderly), and burying the dead.

During all the years I was active in the SCLC, I sandwiched these routine duties between marches and jail sentences, or else asked someone else to stand in for me when I was out of town. But when I came home for good, I simply took up the responsibilities of my pastorate and filled my life with them, so there was really no time to look backward, to be bitter about failures, or to grieve for lost opportunities.

Then, too, by that time my last child—my son Kwame Luthuli—was a small boy, and I had more time to spend with him than I had with the other three. I was grateful for this late opportunity to be a better father, though Juanita had done such a fine job with Juandalynn, Ralph III, and Donzaleigh that I had no reason to believe my constant presence was necessary.

But even though I did devote more time to my church and my family after my resignation, I didn't turn my back on the civil rights movement—at least, not entirely. I have continued to make speeches. I have consulted with leaders around the country. When asked, I have never failed to participate in a civil rights demonstration. Indeed, I have concluded that in many ways the struggle for black people in America has just begun.

In the first place, our economic problems are as pressing in 1989 as they were ten or twenty years ago—perhaps more so. While it is certainly true that there are more affluent blacks in the 1980s than in the 1950s or 1960s, the poor also seem to be growing in number, and their poverty is all the more painful when contrasted with the increased affluence of the black middle class.

In the fifties and sixties, we all but won the battle for equal rights under the law, and in so doing we freed black college graduates, black professional people, and black business entrepreneurs to achieve a status never before dreamed of by our people (despite the inequalities that still exist). But in the seventies and eighties we have done little to bring freedom to the uneducated and unskilled people of our community. It was for that segment of our population—the least fortunate of our brothers and sisters—that Martin gave his life and I worked during my tenure as SCLC president.

As for the future, I believe it will be in a commitment to these people that our real strength of character will finally be measured, not only the strength of the black people but of the American people as well. It is one thing for an entire race to rise up and demand what is rightfully theirs, both as human beings and as citizens of the United States—it is another thing for those who have already moved down the road of success to remember those who have been left behind and turn to lend a helping hand.

I am particularly distressed when I hear successful adults look at children living in the inner cities and say, "Nothing can be done for them, because they are incapable of imagining anything other than the circumstances into which they were born and in which they have thus far grown up." No one knows what great things the young black child can accomplish, the one who watches you as you speed by in your car. No one can measure the loss of vision and achievement and wealth when you multiply that one child by the millions you don't see.

As I encounter these tragic young faces all over the country, I remember the faces of my brothers and sisters and cousins a half century ago, working in the fields of rural Alabama, glistening in the hot summer sun. The faces I recall are not as bitter and hopeless as the ones I see today, if only because my father and the other adults in my family understood that economic independence, our ultimate freedom and salvation, was achievable.

Late in life I have begun to think about that proposition and to believe that my father was a wiser man than even I had realized, for he understood the future as well as his own present. He envisioned a time when black people would have an opportunity to move into the mainstream of American life, when, as he put it, the bottom rung would become the top. That time has arrived, but as a people we have not yet taken full advantage of the opportunity.

With this in mind, I came to the conclusion after my defeat in the 1977 congressional race that I would try to do something in the private sector to revitalize our black communities—particularly in the cities—and to teach as many people as possible the lesson my father had taught his family so long ago in Marengo County, Alabama: Education and hard work can transform communities as well as individual lives and can eventually bring to blacks the fullest realization of their potential as human beings, a potential that is much greater than our society has thus far been willing to recognize.

I decided to develop a model program to help black people break the chains of welfare and find a new freedom in self-sufficiency. I knew that the development of such a program and its replication throughout the country would cost money—more money that I personally could supply. So I decided to find support either from the private sector or from some enlightened branch of government that wanted to attack the root cause of poverty rather than merely treat its symptoms.

First I tried the private sector. I talked to several longtime benefactors of black causes, but I soon discovered that no one had the inclination any more to put large sums of money into untried projects; the glamor had gone out of funding black movements, particularly those that wanted to work within the system.

So I decided to turn to the public sector. Given the seemingly hopeless situation among welfare families, it occurred to me (and to a good many other people, I might add) that the government should be more than willing to pay for training designed to free large numbers of able-bodied people from the welfare rolls and turn them into productive taxpayers. The economics of such a proposition seemed irresistible, given the change in the mood of the nation.

But as soon as I began to investigate the prospects for government funding, I discovered a curious thing: A good many people in government were quite happy with the status quo. They *liked* the idea of a huge, economically dependent population. The fact that there were third-generation welfare families pleased them.

I was a lifelong Democrat, but many Democrats I knew were satisfied with the welfare system and saw it as a benign thing rather than as a millstone around the neck of the black population. They too readily accepted the unchallenged assumption that the people on welfare were unwilling and/or unable to support themselves and that the situation in our urban centers was insoluble. So as long as our people continued to support the Democratic party, its leaders would make no attempt to change the system. For them, it was working all too well.

At about this time, I began to hear stories from the state of California about a work program that was designed to remove people from the welfare rolls and turn them into productive, self-sufficient citizens. Some people criticized the program, claiming it was cruel and insensitive, that it "robbed people of their dignity." But others said that, to the contrary, it conferred new dignity on people by providing work for them and teaching them valuable skills in the process.

The architect of this program was not a Democrat but a Republican, and there were those who said that sometime in the near future he would be a candidate for president. His name was Ronald Reagan.

Of course, at that time it was a foregone conclusion that all blacks would vote the straight Democratic ticket, as they had done since the days of Franklin Delano Roosevelt. But by the late 1970s, after worrying about the welfare problem, I had begun to question the wisdom of our perennial and automatic support of the same party—regardless of the nominee or the platform. It seemed increasingly obvious to me that because our voting patterns were so predictable, blacks were being neglected by both parties. The Republicans had long since given up any hope of attracting black voters in significant numbers, so they looked in other directions for their support and devised their plans and platforms accordingly. By the same token, Democrats assumed that we were in their hip pocket and consequently shifted their attention to the groups the Republicans were courting. So both parties were neglecting us, mainly because they thought they knew in advance how we would behave on election day.

Juanita and I talked over the political future of black America at great length and concluded that there should be blacks in both major parties, and that neither party should be able to take the black vote for granted. That way, both conventions would have to listen to us and both would have to make concessions in order to gain our favor.

We tried to convince others of the wisdom of "playing the field," but at the time no one would listen. The Democratic party, they said, was our traditional home. Republicans cared only for big business and the banks. In this respect black southerners and white southerners had something in common: There were a lot of "yellow-dog Democrats" among them.

In the 1960s, however, white Southerners had begun to move into the Republican party; and for the first time since Reconstruction, the GOP was beginning to elect southern congressmen and senators. So when Nixon adopted what was called his "southern strategy," everyone knew it really meant "southern *white* strategy"; I came to understand that this focus was not so much the fault of Republicans as the fault of blacks.

So in 1980, when Ronald Reagan was nominated as the Republican candidate for president, I had two good reasons to consider supporting him. First, he had advocated and initiated job-training programs to remove people from welfare. Second, I believed it was time for blacks to show some openness toward the Republican Party, provided the party showed an openness toward us.

So when I was approached in the summer of 1980 by Governor Reagan's campaign organization, I was willing to talk. Now, I told myself, I could sell someone on my plan to establish a model program.

The man who finally convinced me was Art Teele, a black attorney from Tallahassee, a Republican activist, and the son-in-law of W. C. Patton, the NAACP director for Alabama. After talking with him and outlining my chief concerns, I was pleased to hear that the Reagan administration was indeed planning to initiate job programs for poor people, that unlike previous administrations they would make a genuine effort to bring blacks into the inner circle of those making important decisions, and that I would be one of those who would help to plan a better future for my people.

So I agreed to endorse Ronald Reagan at some point in the campaign—under one condition: "I want to go to the man and hear the commitment from his own mouth," I said. "I want to look him straight in the eye when he says it."

"That can be arranged," Art told me.

Shortly after Reagan's nomination I was in Norfolk, Virginia, preaching a revival for my old friend, the Reverend Charles Hart, when Art called me to tell me the time had come for my face-to-face meeting.

"Governor Reagan is going to be in Detroit tomorrow evening. We want you to fly up and join us there. We'll have a private meeting with the governor in his hotel room, then go to a rally where you can come out publicly."

So the next day I got on a plane and flew to Detroit. Once on the aircraft, I saw my old friend the Reverend Milton Reed, editor of the black newspaper, the *Norfolk Journal and Guide*. We exchanged pleasantries, never imagining that each of us was on his way to the same occasion.

At the Detroit airport, Teele escorted me to a limousine that whisked me off to one of the more fashionable suburbs, where Reagan was staying in a brand-new hotel that was so tall it disappeared in the clouds.

We went shooting up to the top in an elevator and walked down thick-carpeted hallways to the governor's suite, where a Secret Service agent was manning the door. We were immediately cleared inside and I found Governor Reagan waiting with a winning smile on his face. From a distance of ten feet, he looked no different from the man I had watched in the movies years ago, but when I drew close enough to shake hands with him, his face was a network of deep wrinkles. It was something of a shock to see a man age so in a matter of a few strides.

We sat down, and he thanked me for my willingness to endorse his candidacy. He wanted me to know, he said, that he hoped to attract a number of disillusioned blacks into the Republican party during the 1980 campaign, that he thought his party had more to offer us in the coming decade than did the Democrats.

"I'm particularly interested in jobs," I told him. "I want to start a foundation to help jobless people learn new skills and get themselves off welfare."

"That's exactly what we want too," he said, with what seemed like genuine enthusiasm. "That's what we did in California."

We talked for ten minutes or so about the problems my people were facing—about jobs and housing and education—and Reagan promised me that he would make a jobs program a top priority in his administration. Then there was a knock on the door and Art Teele stuck his head inside.

"I think we better have the photographic session now," he said. "We'll be leaving for the rally in a few minutes."

A parade of people marched into the room—a photographer, his assistant, a couple of Secret Service men, Milton Reed (who must have followed me from the airport), Charles Evers (up from Mississippi), and a smiling Hosea Williams. I hadn't known that any of the others would be there.

We posed for pictures with Governor Reagan, individually and then collectively, and after the last flash, we all went down on the elevator, piled into the waiting limousines, and were whisked off to the Christian Methodist Episcopal Church, where the rally was to take place.

With lights glaring and cameras trained on us, Governor Reagan made a speech—one of the few I ever heard that was tailored to a black audience—and then I stepped into the pulpit and made a brief speech endorsing him and urging other blacks to follow my lead. When I had finished, Governor Reagan stepped forward, shook my hand, and then we raised our joined hands in the air. I regarded that act as his public commitment to help black people in America, though my old friend Jo Ann Robinson wrote from California to say that I had made a mistake and that in the Associated Press photograph of the event Ronald Reagan had looked desperately unhappy.

After I had finished, some of the others then spoke; and following the rally I was driven to the airport in order to catch a late flight back to Norfolk to preach a final revival sermon. In Norfolk people were merely curious about what had happened in Detroit. But on my return to Atlanta I received a far less enthusiastic reception than I had left behind in either Detroit or Norfolk.

Already the word of my defection from the Democratic party had preceded me, and some of my old friends treated me with cool and distant disdain. Until then it never occurred to me that political disagreements could mar the close relationships of many years. But Andy Young, Joe Lowery, and Coretta King were clearly disturbed at what I had done and were apparently unforgiving. It was years before I felt that the matter had begun to fade in their minds, and I am not sure that it doesn't linger still.

I also began to get letters and phone calls that attacked me with vicious and at times unspeakable names for having endorsed a "rightwing extremist" like Reagan, "a man who had been the enemy of blacks for his entire political career." The other members of my family suffered similar abuse—particularly Juanita; and I am certain that had I known how much bitterness and resentment I was going to generate, I would never have become involved in the first place.

But having committed myself, I was not going to go back on my word. And the members of my family joined in the campaign with me. As a matter of fact, Donzaleigh traveled all over the country, working with Art Teele, acting as my "advance person" when I made appearances in behalf of the ticket.

We didn't have an easy time. While I had many supporters throughout the country, often black audiences booed us and shouted insults. Sometimes they became more raucous. In Harlem, where Lionel Hampton and I were appearing together on the back of a flatbed truck, a gang of young blacks surrounded the vehicle and attempted to push it over on its side. I never felt that I was in danger of being killed, but I could have ended up with a bloody nose or a broken bone.

On election eve I was in New York working for the Reagan campaign. At the end of the day I got a telephone call from Atlanta. It was Hosea Williams.

"I've got an idea," he said. "Why don't we all fly out to California tomorrow and go to the victory party with Reagan?"

"I can't do that," I said. "I've got to come back to Atlanta and vote."

"No, the man doesn't need your vote. He's going to win hands down," he said. "You and Donzaleigh fly straight out to California. I'll bring the two Juanitas, yours and mine, and we'll meet in Los Angeles. We need to be there at the moment he is elected. Then we'll be able to remind him of his promises."

"But we don't have any clothes," I said. "I don't have a change of shorts, and Donzaleigh doesn't have a dress to wear to a victory party."

"You can wear the same shorts you campaigned in, and I personally will buy Donzaleigh a dress when she gets to California."

The more he talked about it, the more I thought it would be something worth doing. After all, when would we ever again have the opportunity to attend a victory party with a man elected to the nation's highest office? That would be some party.

"I'll call Juanita," I said, "and then call you back." Juanita thought it was a great idea too, so we decided to go to Los Angeles. But as a consequence, though I endorsed him, I can honestly say that I didn't vote for Ronald Reagan.

The party was indeed spectacular; and from the first returns we knew we were going to win. I must say that I had a twinge of sadness when I saw clips of Jimmy Carter campaigning in the last hours. He was a good man, but somehow he had never struck a responsive chord in the American people.

When the networks confirmed Ronald Reagan's victory and he came down to make a victory statement, Juanita and I and Hosea and his Juanita were there on the platform, standing somewhat in the background. Suddenly, I felt someone pushing me from behind, and I found myself being shoved through the crowd on the stage toward the candidate, who was waving to the crowd. I tried to apologize to those being nudged aside, and when

I finally turned around to see who was responsible, I found it was Hosea, a big grin on his face, determined to see that I got maximum credit. By then, however, I was almost upstaging Mrs. Reagan, and the president-elect acknowledged our help, in part because he had no other choice.

Indeed, during the entire evening we were treated with respect and affection by all present. When we went back to the hotel that night, it was with the feeling that we had done something for black people as well as for Ronald Reagan. At last we would see a jobs program at the federal level.

The next morning the phone rang fairly early and I answered it. It was Hosea Williams. He was still in there pushing. "Let's go over and see our man," he said.

"Let the poor man rest," I said, not wanting to be too pushy. I am essentially a shy person, unwilling to intrude on anyone's privacy. My wife, Juanita, is even shyer, and Hosea's wife Juanita is the shyest of all. But Hosea had enough brass to compensate for the rest of us.

"Call him up and ask if we can see him for a few minutes right now," Hosea said. "We need to pin him down on some things right now, before he gets in office and forgets who we are."

"I don't think we should go over there this morning," I said. "I think we. . . ."

"Call him up," Hosea said. "Don't be chicken."

So I made the call, and after a few moment's delay, Governor Reagan came on the line. I explained that we would like to come over briefly, that we would be leaving for Atlanta later in the day and wanted to pay our respects.

"I'm leaving myself," he said, "but if you can come over right now, I'll wait, and I'll tell the Secret Service to let you through."

So we all went—both families. The governor was gracious, as was Ed Meese, who was also there. We chatted amiably for about ten minutes, mostly about irrelevant matters; but we did mention the jobs program again and he assured us that he wouldn't forget. Then he said he had to be going.

"But I'll be holding a meeting at the Plaza Hotel next week," he told me, "and I want you to be there."

I assured him I would come.

Then we shook hands and said goodbye. That morning was the highwater mark of my relationship with the Reagan administration. From then on, it was very difficult to talk to him and impossible to pin him down.

In anticipation of establishing a foundation to help train blacks, I hired James Peterson, a young Californian, to be the organization's executive director. Together we made elaborate and detailed plans for setting up training programs. We didn't know precisely what kinds of skills were needed in the marketplace, but we made educated guesses and began to establish contacts for implementing the plans once we were funded. The entire operation was to be non-profit. I was to be non-salaried. The organization would be called the Foundation for Economic Enterprises Development (FEED).

By the time we had accomplished all this, it was time for the inauguration and I took everyone in the family. We were honored guests at all the social events and were treated as important celebrities. We all had a wonderful time, though we were unable to talk to the new president about business matters.

The following week I tried to call the White House to talk to President Reagan, but I didn't get past a third-echelon staff member, who took my message and told me he would pass it along. James Peterson and I waited by the telephone, but no one called us back. The hours became days. The days became weeks. I tried to talk to the president almost daily; and then I tried to talk to Ed Meese or James Baker, but I couldn't get through to them. No one, it seems, knew or cared about the president's promises.

Finally, in desperation, we put a call through to former President Ford, whose phone number we managed to acquire. This time we got some response. Mr. Ford came to the telephone.

"We're having some problems," I said. "Could we possibly come out there and see you?"

"Sure," he said. "I'd be happy to talk to you. Tell me when you want to come."

We agreed on a date and James and I flew to Palm Springs, where President Ford received us at his office. I must say that of all the Republican politicians I have met—and the list is long—

Gerald Ford was by far the most charming and companionable. He had a way of making us feel at ease in his presence, and I was certain that he was sympathetic with our problems and eager to help.

"You understand," I began, "I don't expect any reward for what I've done, but. . . ."

President Ford interrupted me.

"Reverend," he said, "some people think it's wrong to be rewarded for political activities, but they don't understand how our system works. You reward your friends and punish your enemies. That's how you make needed changes in government. So you needn't apologize for asking that the administration do something for you. What do you have in mind?"

I took out the incorporation papers for FEED, handed them to him, and then James and I outlined what we had in mind. He looked the papers over carefully, then nodded his head.

"This looks like a marvelous idea to me. And I think something should be done."

He thought in silence for a moment.

"I'm going to suggest to the president," he said, "that he call a meeting of one hundred people who can easily donate one hundred thousand dollars to this project. You can explain to them what you've explained to me, and then the president can urge them to make the donations. If he chooses the right people, they will all be happy to make a contribution. That will give you ten million dollars to launch the operation, and I will be a part of it. How does that sound?"

James and I nodded our heads and said that what he proposed sounded just fine.

"Then if you have no objections," he said, "I'll make the call to the White House right now."

We assured him that we had no objections.

He picked up the phone, punched out a number, and waited.

"Let me speak to Mr. Meese," he said. "This is Gerald Ford."

In a moment he was put through.

"Ed," he said, "The Reverend Ralph David Abernathy and a

friend are here at the house, and they have established a foundation to help poor people, particularly minorities, learn skills in order to get off the welfare rolls. Reverend Abernathy, as you know, was a big help to us during the campaign, and I think the president ought to help him pick up some financial support from the private sector so they can get their program into high gear."

He paused, listened, and began to frown. "Oh, no," he said. He put his hand over the speaker. "The Pope's been shot," he said. "They don't know yet whether he survived."

He listened to Ed Meese for a few moments more and shook his head.

"Well, I'll let you go. The details can be worked out later on this foundation, but somebody should get in touch with Ralph Abernathy at the earliest possible moment. I hope you'll arrange the meeting and that Reverend Abernathy will be given a chance to explain what he wants."

He hung up and turned to me.

"It was a bad time to call," he said, "but he made a note to get in touch with you. I'm sure you'll be hearing from him in the next day or two."

We sat around and talked for another forty-five minutes, and President Ford was as relaxed and as friendly as any man I have met. I felt we could have been good friends, and when we said goodbye he again assured me that I would be hearing from Mr. Meese.

James and I flew back to Atlanta, convinced that our troubles were over at last. We took up our station beside the telephone again, and the days went by, just as they had done before. No one called. Not the president. Not Ed Meese. Not Ed Meese's staff. Not even the staff of Mr. Meese's staff.

Even as I write these words, I realize how foolish I was to believe the verbal promises, made in hurried meetings at hotel rooms and campaign offices. Politics doesn't work that way. You don't do business with politicians on a handshake—at least not more than once. It isn't that politicians are worse than other men. It's just that the game they are playing has different rules from those followed by ordinary people. You can't expect them to keep their promises unless you have something they want both *before* and *after* they are elected. Once they get into office, they believe they are immortal. And in most instances they are right, particularly if they are serving in Congress.

But if I didn't receive any support from President Reagan for my FEED project, in 1983 I did get a call from Vice President George Bush's office, asking me to do the administration a favor. The vice president was flying down to Atlanta to make a speech on Martin's birthday celebration and they wanted me to appear with him on the platform.

"I'd be happy to be there," I said. "Just give me a time."

"Actually, we'd really like it if you would come to Washington and join Mr. and Mrs. Bush on the flight down. That way the TV would cover you getting off the plane."

"Fine," I said. "I'll be happy to do that."

I was given a time and told to meet Mr. Bush and his party at Andrews Air Force Base just outside the nation's capital. I might add that no one said a word about sending me a plane ticket to Washington, but I was more than happy to pay my expenses, given the nature of the occasion. Clearly, Mr. Bush was willing to devote some time to the black community.

So I bought the ticket and flew up to Washington, where I met the Bush party, which included Lionel Hampton, and joined them on the plane. I must say that George Bush was friendly and thoughtful. He made a short speech to everyone on the plane and then spoke to each of us separately. When he got to me, we talked about the problems blacks were facing, particularly in the inner cities; and I was impressed by the scope of his knowledge and the genuineness of his concern. He agreed that the solution to our problems lay in economic development, and he said he was certain that President Reagan was still committed to a comprehensive jobs program of the sort I had been proposing and that such a bill would be submitted in the future, when the time was ripe. (I have no reason to think that he didn't believe what he was saying.)

We landed in Atlanta and before we got off the plane to face local television cameras and news reporters, the vice president indicated the order in which he wanted us to deplane: He would go first, followed by Mrs. Bush, me, and Lionel Hampton. There was a receiving line of local dignitaries waiting for us, one of whom was Andy Young, and we shook hands solemnly while the cameras were grinding, each of us thinking private thoughts. But I really don't think our traveling party made a big impression on the people of Atlanta, in part because the newspeople gave the event as little coverage as possible and in part because the city was heavily Democratic and loved the memory of former president Jimmy Carter.

I was happy to serve the administration in that way, and I was sorry that they never saw fit to call on me in other ways. Of course, I didn't expect to be a cabinet member or even an assistant secretary or a deputy assistant secretary. But I did expect to be used. For example, President Reagan could easily have put me on the U.S. Civil Rights Commission, where my experience in the movement and my many contacts throughout the country might have proven valuable. I might also have been part of a presidential commission to deal with the problem of minority unemployment. Also, late in the Reagan administration, when I became concerned with the high incidence of AIDS among our people I had some interest in serving on the presidential AIDS commission.

But I was never called to perform such services. They did call on me again in 1988, when someone—a lower echelon presidential staff member—invited me to a White House ceremony honoring Martin. It was an afterthought by a young man who knew his history and saw the appropriateness of my being there. But, unlike others in the group, I was not allowed to bring my son with me, so he had to remain in the audience during the proceedings.

At that time Mr. Reagan shook hands and said, "Reverend, it's been too long since I've seen you."

I tried to tell the president that I still wanted to talk to him about jobs programs, that I felt something could be salvaged in this area. He listened politely and seemed surprised that I hadn't gotten through.

"I've been told that the way to get in to see you is to go through Mrs. Reagan," I said. "Do you think that might help?"

He laughed, but didn't answer my question; and I never heard from him or from the White House again. My feelings weren't hurt, because I didn't want anything for myself. But I must confess that I am still unhappy with the Reagan administration over its failure to make an effort to solve the problems of urban blacks. Not only did Mr. Reagan fail to sponsor any innovative legislation to promote jobs among minorities, but he didn't even speak specifically to black people during his term as president.

If he had any quality that made him an outstanding leader, it was his ability to rally the support of the American people and to make them feel good about themselves and their future. I am convinced that the resurgence of the general economy during his eight years in office and the upbeat mood of the country as a whole were the result of his speeches and public gestures. People liked him, responded to his inherent optimism, and in turn became bolder and more decisive in the marketplace.

But he never spoke directly and exclusively to blacks, who had special needs and required special encouragement. Would it have alienated his own constituents so much if he had made just one speech to black Americans on the occasion of Martin's death, showing his concern for their welfare and encouraging them to believe in the nation's capacity to help them help themselves? Would it have damaged his Soviet peace initiative had he also extended the hand of friendship to the black community, encouraging cultural exchange between his world and theirs?

He knew very well that blacks believed he had no interest in their plight, that he was preoccupied with the concerns of upper income white people and had no sympathy for the poor. So why didn't he do something to correct that perception? If, as he so often said, he believed his administration had helped lower income Americans in general and blacks in particular, then why didn't he make an effort to communicate directly with us?

One thing is certain, to black people he was not the Great Communicator but the Great Stone Face, the man who never had a soft word or a smile for the minorities of this country. And if behind that seemingly cold exterior there really burned a heart filled with compassion, then whose fault was it that black people never understood him?

As for FEED, in eight years we received two very small government contracts for training programs, both of which we competed for without White House assistance and both of which we successfully completed—one for the Department of Labor and one for the Department of Transportation. Time and time again, we were passed over while we saw other, whiter organizations awarded the bids. When we made inquiries we were told that our proposal "did not concur with the specifications of the job" or that we were somehow asking for grants when the programs we proposed "were not funded under current legislation."

Perhaps these reasons were valid, according to the strictest interpretation of federal regulations. But why didn't somebody in the administration help us to prepare more acceptable proposals? And why didn't they make an effort to show us precisely what funding was available? Heaven knows we asked for help on enough occasions. We were by no means proud or unreasonable in our demands. We were eager to be instructed in the skills of obtaining federal funds from the bureaucracy for the sake of our people.

At the time we didn't believe the Reagan administration was deliberately ignoring us. We concluded that they didn't even know we existed, that my name and Peterson's meant nothing to the people who were running the White House staff. But toward the end I began to think the matter over and to note the degree to which the president's people paid homage to those black leaders who had opposed him—and who continued to do so. Indeed, the more I thought about it, the more I began to understand what had happened.

I believe it went something like this: I had announced my backing of President Reagan in 1980 and had campaigned in his behalf. As a consequence of my commitment to his candidacy, I had lost credibility among other black leaders and to some degree among black Americans as a whole. Because of this loss of credibility, I was no longer useful to them. Therefore, they made certain that I received no public recognition and no administrative support.

On the other hand, most of the other black leaders had supported the Democrats and had continued to attack the Republicans in general and the president in particular throughout the administration. As a consequence, they retained their credibility in the black community and were repeatedly honored at the White House. For all I know, they probably got federal funding because they were people to be won over.

So I learned a lesson from watching the Reagan administration and it is this: If you want to be treated with respect and generosity by the Republicans, the worst thing you can do is support them and campaign openly for their candidates. At least, that's true if you're black.

This was a lesson I had learned well, and in both 1984 and 1988 I backed Jesse Jackson. Not only have people been greeting me in a warm and friendly fashion since that time, but my telephone has not once rung in the dead of night with some disgruntled Democrat on the other end of the line, ready to curse me for my treason. So in the last few years I have slept better at night, and for more reasons than one.

On the other hand, while my public life has become simpler and less confrontational, other problems have come along to trouble my life—some of them the natural result of growing older. At the beginning of 1983 I had a particularly strenuous speaking schedule, and the years finally caught up with me. It was near the middle of January, during the period when Martin's birthday (January 15) was celebrated all over the country and I had scheduled about twenty lectures over a ten-day period. I finally got back to Atlanta on the night of the seventeenth, exhausted, but with a lot of work piled up at the office.

So the next day I went down to the church and dictated some letters to my secretary. In the middle of a sentence, I suddenly found myself stumbling over the word "obstruction," and only after three or four tries was I able to enunciate it properly.

"I guess I need some rest," I told her, and after finishing the letter, we called it a day and I drove home.

It was a good thing we had knocked off when we did. An ice storm swept into Atlanta that afternoon, and everything was covered with crystal—the streets, the trees, the cars, the houses. The streets were impassable, branches were down in the roads, and all the businesses were closed. I remembered worrying all day because I couldn't deposit the checks from my speaking tour. So I lay around, watching a little television, and feeling strangely enervated. That night, however, I revived a little when Juanita told me about supper.

My older daughter had been home for Christmas and had done a lot of cooking while I was away on my speaking tour and Juanita surprised me with the results.

"The day before Juandalynn left she cooked some shrimp gumbo, and I saved you a big serving. Do you want it tonight?"

"That and some of her chitlins," I said.

So Juanita thawed the meal and set it before me.

"I believe I'd like a little. . . ."

I intended to say "bread," but the word wouldn't come out. It was as if it were stalled somewhere between my brain and my mouth. I tried to form the word and then force the sound between my teeth—but nothing happened.

"I'd like some. . . ."

It wouldn't come. I couldn't say that one, simple word.

"What's wrong, Ralph?" Juanita said, alarm in her voice.

Carefully I told her about my speech problem, recalling the experience at the office that day.

"Ralph," she said, "somebody has to look at you right now. We can't take you to the hospital because the roads are too icy, but I'm going next door and get Mrs. Wright."

I started to protest but thought better of it. Something was clearly wrong with me and Mrs. Wright was a nurse. Juanita was right. We needed a diagnosis.

I nodded, feeling just a little groggy.

I lay down on the sofa and waited while Juanita put on a coat and disappeared through the door. They were back in a couple of minutes, Mrs. Wright with her blood pressure gauge. She squeezed the band around my arm and then peered into my eyes. Then she turned to Juanita.

"It wouldn't hurt to take him to the hospital," she said quietly.

Juanita drove me, slipping and sliding all the way on the sheet of ice the road had become, and I was met at the hospital by my doctor, Bernard Bridges. After he examined me thoroughly in the emergency room, I was taken upstairs, but not before he said he thought I had suffered a small stroke.

"We won't know for sure unless you have an angiogram—that is, if you want us to run one."

"Why wouldn't we?" asked Juanita, who was standing beside me holding my hand as I lay on the examining table.

"Well," he said, "there's a slight risk. Occasionally we lose a patient during the procedure."

I didn't like the sound of that, and I brooded over the decision as they wheeled me down the hallway and into an elevator. As soon as I got into the room I picked up the telephone and sought the advice of Dr. Isaac Willis, a good friend and an excellent physician. I knew he was both skilled enough and concerned enough to give me the best possible medical advice.

"'It sounds like a stroke," he said, "but you'll never know for sure until you have an angiogram."

"I understand there's a risk," I said.

"A small one," he said.

"What would you do in my position?" I asked him.

"Have the angiogram," he said. "Otherwise you'll never know."

When Dr. Bridges came up to my room after signing me in, I told him that I would be willing to run the risk and, after thinking about it, he ordered the procedure for 10:00 the next morning. Afterward he came to my room to tell us the results: I had had a stroke.

"There's a blockage in the carotid artery, the one that carries blood to the brain. It wasn't a massive stroke, but you'll suffer some impairment of speech."

"Is there anything to be done?" I asked.

"There's a new operation," he said. "You might want to look into it."

At that point I knew whom to consult. I called Dr. Levi

Watkins, whom I had baptized years ago when he was a boy. Levi was now at Johns Hopkins—perhaps the best hospital in the world—and if the operation was available anywhere, someone at Hopkins could do it.

"I would advise Dr. Mel Epstein," he said. "He's the best there is, and I will make sure that you get the best possible people on your team."

It took a month to make all the preparations, and I made one abortive trip to Johns Hopkins before they scheduled the surgery; but finally the preparations were completed, and Dr. Epstein performed the operation—building me a new carotid artery. I was the fifty-first person to undergo this surgical procedure at Johns Hopkins.

Just before I went under the anesthesia, they told me, "Now when you come out of the anesthetic we're going to ask you who the President of the United States is, and we want you to say 'Ronald Reagan.' "

I nodded and suddenly the world lurched and I didn't know anything until I saw faces swimming around in the air above me and heard faraway voices.

"Dr. A. Dr. A. Are you awake?"

"I love Jesus," I said. "I love Jesus. I love Jesus."

That's all they needed to hear. No one asked me about the president, which is just as well. Given the heavy dose of Pentothal I had taken, heaven knows what I might have said about Ronald Reagan.

I stayed in the Intensive Care Unit overnight and then was taken back to my room, even though most people who have had this five-hour operation generally remain in ICU for over two weeks. The next morning I called Juanita at the Hopkins Sheraton, where she had been staying.

"Ralph," she said, "what in the world are you doing?"

"I'm just finishing up a breakfast of bacon, eggs, and coffee," I said. "Let's go home."

For most of my adult life I had preached the integration of American society and the unity of the races of the world. We were one people, I had always said—brothers and sisters under the fatherhood of God. But it never occurred to me that my own family would be one of the starting points for the process. I knew that Donzaleigh was seeing a young white man named George Bosley, from Baltimore, Maryland; but it still came as a surprise when she called and told me they wanted to get married on May 1, 1986—and in my church.

So I had two adjustments to make—one as a father, the other as pastor of West Hunter Street Baptist Church. To my knowledge there had never before been an interracial marriage in the Abernathy family, and the old-timers in the congregation said that nothing of the sort had ever occurred in the church. Juanita and I talked about it at some length and finally concluded that it was a fine thing. We were happy for the young people, and their wedding would make a point to members of the congregation, to Atlanta, and to the world. It was a point for blacks as well as whites to heed, since some members of both races still held serious reservations concerning such unions.

We spent many weeks planning the ceremony and the reception afterward. The ceremony posed some problems, because I had a dual role to perform, and I couldn't be both father and minister at the same time. To facilitate the service and underline the nature of this biracial union, I invited Father Jamnicky to help officiate at the wedding. Father Jamnicky, a white Roman Catholic priest from Chicago, would take the first part of the service, while I brought my daughter down the aisle. Then I would replace him and perform the rest of the ceremony, finally pronouncing them man and wife. The team of black Baptist preacher and white Roman Catholic priest would break whatever barriers still remained in Atlanta and scandalize anyone left who genuinely needed scandalizing. On paper it sounded like a perfect plan.

But things didn't go according to plan. When the time came for the service to begin, there was no groom. Donzaleigh asked for the time every second, and I kept reassuring her that she had nothing to worry about, that most weddings started just a little late. But even as I was trying to soothe her anxieties, mine were building up inside.

What if George had suddenly changed his mind? What if this racial business had begun to gnaw at him? What if he had no intention of showing up? The church was jammed. People were practically sitting on each other's laps. The photographer was there. The reception was even at that moment being set up next door. And my precious child was down in the bridal quarters, waiting.

And still no George. Ten minutes passed. Twenty minutes passed. Thirty minutes passed. George did not arrive, and Juanita looked at me and frowned when Donzaleigh wasn't looking. In all the years of police, dogs, and would-be assassins I had never contemplated violence, but I was contemplating violence that afternoon. No one—NO ONE—was going to humiliate my daughter in this way. Not MY daughter.

Then, forty-five minutes after the announced time, a car screeched into the parking lot and George jumped out and made a dash for the church. By then I was trembling.

His explanation, blurted out, calmed us all somewhat. His mother had been rushed to the hospital with some kind of seizure—perhaps a heart attack. He had gone to the hospital to see if she was all right before he came to the church—and to show her how he looked in his tails. In the midst of all this turmoil, he had not thought to call and tell us what was happening.

Donzaleigh was all smiles, but I was still a cauldron of conflicting emotions. However, the most evident emotion was relief. As I led her down the aisle, I managed to smile and wave at everyone as if nothing unusual had happened.

After I had given her in marriage, the congregation sang "Joyful, Joyful, We Adore Thee," while I changed into my clericals and returned to pronounce them man and wife. They kissed. I breathed a sigh of relief.

But my official duties had not yet ended. Another interracial couple—a black man and a white woman—had also asked me to marry them that afternoon, so we held that ceremony immediately after Donzaleigh and George were securely united. There was some overlapping of guests, but most people attended both ceremonies.

Afterward we went back into the pastor's study to sign the marriage papers, but I couldn't see the writing on the page. I even held the pen upside down. At that point I realized how much the events of the afternoon had affected me.

Then we all went next door for the reception. Ironically, "next door" was the "Wren's Nest," the home of Joel Chandler Harris, author of the Uncle Remus stories. Wren's Nest is usually presided over by a white woman wearing an antebellum hoop skirt, but that day it was filled with blacks and whites who had come to toast the marriage, to eat a wedding supper, and to dance to the orchestra I had engaged.

Frankly, Juanita and I had been surprised when Donzaleigh chose Wren's Nest for the reception. Years earlier, when she had been the only black student in her class, the teacher had taken them all to visit the home of Harris, and Donzaleigh had been turned back at the door. The teacher, outraged by such an action, had terminated the visit; but Juanita and I had never forgotten the incident. Donzaleigh, however, held no grudge against Harris or Wren's Nest; and we engaged the place for the reception at her request.

I had even hired a noted Italian chef to serve a continental meal to the hundreds of guests present. It was to be in seven courses, served on the patio by experienced European waiters, with an exotic fish dish as the final entree. Shortly after the meal had begun I realized we had made a terrible mistake in not advising the guests about the nature of the meal, because when they finished the first course, most of them began drifting away from the table.

After the meal was over, the patio was cleared, the orchestra began playing, and everyone began to dance. I even danced with the bride, despite the fact that the Baptist preacher doesn't usually dance with anyone. It was my daughter's wedding, and after a great deal of trouble we had finally brought it off. All's well that ends well, I told myself.

But all had not ended—at least not for me.

I had rented a Cadillac for the occasion, and driving home the parked cars on both sides of the road seemed to be crowding in on me, rushing by like speeding traffic. I found it difficult to steer a course between them, and I was relieved when we got home without banging the fender of the car. I immediately fell into bed, and when I awoke, my eyes were still out of focus.

The next morning was Sunday, and Father Jamnicky volunteered to take my place in the pulpit, an offer I gladly accepted. In fact, he also went with me to Second Mt. Vernon Baptist Church that afternoon and again gave the sermon I was supposed to give. I suppose he thought I was just worn out, but I was beginning to suspect that something else was wrong. As we were leaving Second Mt. Vernon Church in separate cars, we agreed that he would lead me back to my house.

When I got inside, I kept my worries to myself—at least for a while. We had a house full of guests, including Juanita's brother Herman, Donzaleigh's favorite uncle. Finally, when Herman noticed that something was wrong, I told him about my symptoms, including what had happened in my study. He told Juanita and she immediately called the doctor.

As I suspected, it was another stroke—again nothing too serious. But this time, though they gave me another angiogram, I had no operation. The doctors at Johns Hopkins had told me I might have another stroke of the same sort, but that these were small incidents and would probably not lead to further impairment, nor, in all likelihood, would they prove fatal.

Since I was already suffering from glaucoma, a consequence of the first stroke, I had to give up any hope of being able to read books or even short articles, and I have to be very careful to take my medication. I also drive as little as possible, since my peripheral vision has been affected. All of these restrictions are annoying, but they are a small price to pay in return for the great gift of life that God continues to grant me.

Also, I find that as pastor of West Hunter Street Baptist Church I can still do a lot to help my people—particularly those in great need. Our church did manage to get a grant from the federal government to build a six million dollar senior citizens home, Ralph David Abernathy Tower, which contains one hundred units. In addition, we sleep three hundred men each night in our gymnasium and feed that number every day. There is no reason why each Christian church could not feed, clothe, and shelter the poor and homeless of this nation. If they did so, the problem could be considerably alleviated, if not solved.

While I have not really involved myself in national politics since 1980, I am still trying to develop job-training programs for blacks, and I have also continued to speak in churches and at universities around the country. In fact, I probably average two speeches a week, sometimes three thousand miles apart, so in a way I am still fighting the same battles, still demonstrating in my own way for the same old cause.

Often when I walk out of an airport a cab driver or fellow traveler will say, "Aren't you Ralph Abernathy?" and I will stop and chat a while. I have always tried to speak to those who remember the old days. I am touched by their gratitude and by their memories—particularly of Martin.

On rare occasions I will run across somebody who knew him and can tell me an anecdote about something he did, or else can recall some words he spoke that I didn't hear. When I come across stories of this sort I find myself longing for those earlier times, when we were all together, young, alive, and ready to take on any challenge. In my own recollections, I sometimes even forget just how hard life was for all our people and how bitter the struggle was, particularly near the end, when we finally began to realize that we would never mend every flaw in America, no matter how brave we were and no matter how often we were beaten or jailed or killed.

It's all right in a way for those of us who lived through it to feel a certain nostalgia for the struggle, for old friends and for distant places, even though the times were hard; but I worry about the younger people, who never entered doors marked "colored," never were forbidden to use public libraries, never went to Jim Crow schools or ate in Jim Crow restaurants or slept in Jim Crow motels.

They take the past too much for granted. Do they understand what the older members of their families suffered under such a system, what constant faith they maintained? Will they try to understand? Whatever their burdens, young blacks enjoy the benefits of the great sacrifices made by those who came before them. Humble, usually uneducated, these earlier blacks lived for the most part without the smallest luxuries, maintained a spare dignity in their often brief lives, and went to graves in segregated cemeteries, their deaths unreported by the local newspapers. Had it not been for the character and courage of these simple people, we would not have raised up a generation of leaders and nothing would have changed. We would still be looking from afar at the high walls of an impregnable city. So these are the first great heroes and heroines of our struggle. Yet today they are remembered only in the Book of Life and in the hearts of a few old soldiers, the ones of us who still remain.

Soon we too will be gone, the last of us who shouted down the walls of Jericho. Of course, I grieve for those who were killed in the struggle, and most of all for my dear friend Martin. I wish he had lived to see his fine children and the better land in which they live. Yet in the growing twilight my heart also aches for those anonymous generations who never saw the Promised Land, even from the mountaintop.

And it is for them as well as for all the others that I have written this book.

Appendix

MY LAST LETTER TO MARTIN

A sermon delivered April 7, 1968
at the West Hunter Street Baptist Church, Atlanta, GA

MARTIN,

I miss you and it has been just a few days. I thought I would write you a short letter. It is probably more for my good than it is for yours. I hope it will not be too long before you read it. In Heaven I know you have so much to do, so many people to see. And I know many of them have already been looking and waiting for you. It wouldn't surprise me Martin, if God didn't have a special affair just to introduce his special activist black son to so many others like you that have gone on ahead. I know you wouldn't believe that could happen but then you did not understand how wonderful you are.

But look up these black friends and talk to the ones you and I have talked about; and the ones that you and I led; and the ones who so gallantly followed your leadership. Say thanks to those prophets we quoted all over America and everywhere else that they asked for us. Give a special word from me to Peter, the man who was once sand, but Jesus made him a rock. Give my warmest felicitations to my favorite apostle, John, who loved my Master so much until he stood with his mother at the foot of the Cross. Pass my greetings on to Isaiah, who had the prophetic vision to see the coming of a Saviour whose name would be Wonderful, a Mighty Counselor, an Everlasting Father, and a Prince of Peace. Stop by and chat with Hosea. And find Mahatma K. Gandhi, the man who inspired us so much in our struggle to free black people through the philosophy and techniques of nonviolence. And in the midst of your conversations, Martin, mention me. Look up Bartholomew. For some strange reason I always liked him.

But, above all, I want you to see Jesus. Go to the throne and tell how thankful we are. Yes, go see Jesus, and tell Him about us down here, all of us, and all of our families, and how we have sustained ourselves in the many battles all through our lives. Tell Him how much we love Him. Tell Him how His name is music in our ears. Tell Him how at His name our knees will forever bow and our tongues will always confess. Tell Him that we follow not only His words but we follow His life, for His footprints lead to Bethany, for that's where He stayed; but they lead to Gethsemane, for it was there He prayed. They lead to Calvary where salvation was complete. There we were saved by His grace.

Then, Martin, go from the throne and find the Rev. George Lee, that stalwart hero who could barely read and write, who was shot down on the streets of Belzoni, Miss., simply because he wanted to vote. Check with Medgar Evers, who was shot down by mean and cruel white men, who thought they could turn us around by taking the life of this young man. Check with William Moore, another casualty in Alabama. And then Jimmy Lee Jackson, who died on the battlefield of Alabama. Oh, I wish you would look up Mrs. Viola Liuzzo, a white woman who was killed, you remember, on Highway 80; and then check with Jonathan Daniels, a young theological Catholic student who died in Haynesville, Ala., down in Lowndes County, standing up for the rights of black people. James Reeb should be seen also, Martin. For James Reeb, a Unitarian minister, was beaten to death when he came to march for us in Selma. And don't forget Michael Schwerner and Andrew Goodman and James Chaney. You remember those three freedom fighters that they killed in Mississippi and buried their bodies beneath an earthen dam. Express our thanks to them. And then, Martin, don't forget the four little innocent girls who died in a Sunday School class in the 16th Street Baptist Church in Birmingham. They've been waiting to hear from us. Give them a good and complete report. And tell them that you left your people on your way. And we're determined that we ain't gonna let nobody turn us around.

And then, Martin, find Frederick Douglass, that great and marvelous human personality who lived in even more difficult times than we live today. Check with Nat Turner, and Marcus Garvey, for they, too, are heroes in our crusade. And oh, I wish that you would pause long enough at the mansion that is occupied by Abraham Lincoln, the man who freed us from physical bondage here in this country. Then, Martin, we owe a great debt of gratitude to John Fitzgerald Kennedy who less than five years ago, young as you were, brilliant as you were, filled with new ideas as you were, was shot down and killed as you were in cold blood by a mean, vicious and angry society. And don't forget Malcolm X. Look for Malcolm X, Martin. Remember our God is a loving God and he understands things we don't think that he understands. Malcolm may not have believed what we believe and he may not have preached but he was a child of God and he was concerned about the welfare of his people. And then, Martin, please do not forget about all of those who died across Alabama, Mississippi, Louisiana, Chicago, and New York, and all other places where men have died for the liberty and justice of other men. Martin, it may seem like a big order, but if you find one of them, he will know where the rest are. And he will take you to them. I know that they have founded the grand international company of freedom fighters, and can't wait to introduce you to take over the final hours.

A man on Hunter Street said, "I envy the way that he died. He will be with so many who have died like he did."

I know that you have a lot to talk about and you will have a wonderful time, but, remember, your brother, Ralph, will be coming along one day. One thing, we won't have any critics up there, Martin. I don't think they will make it, that they will be there. Every day will be Sunday. None but the righteous will see God.

The day after I last saw you in Memphis, I remembered you from the first time I saw you. It was in Montgomery, Ala. This was a very jovial memory. In fact I first saw you in church. You were still a student at Crozier Theological Seminary. You were preaching at the Ebenezer Baptist Church. Even then you moved me. You remember that you were preaching that Sunday on the subject of *The Christian and Faith*. Afterwards when everybody was shaking hands with you, I shook your hand, also. And I remembered your handshake. It was warm and strong. It was soft and tender. I liked you even then.

Strangely enough, Martin, the second time I saw you was at Spelman's Sisters Chapel. You were well-dressed and you were giving your attention to a very pretty lady. You escorted her there in the prime of your life. I need not remind you that it wasn't Coretta, for this was long before she came into your life. You were young, then. You were a student and you were just playing the field. How different now, dear friend. You had come there to see others. Now others are coming to see you. I know you can hardly believe it as you look down on us and see those long silent lines of people waiting in the cool evening, the early mornings, the springtime noon, and even in the weary midnight hours, passing under the budding green trees past your silent bier. Well, Martin, if you ever had any moments of doubt about whether people loved you, now in the time of death, you no longer have to doubt. You kept the faith with them, and you brought us through the dark and difficult days and nights of our movement. Now they keep it with you throughout the night, around the clock. Today so much is happening in Sisters Chapel, the second place where I saw you. And even more will happen in the Ebenezer Baptist Church and the Morehouse Quadrangle and all across the world in the days and the years to come.

It was after that third time, Martin, that I met you when we really became fast friends. You will remember this meeting. It was in my home, the parsonage of the First Baptist Church in Montgomery. We were never separated until the other day, as you know. I was right behind you there as I have always been. I don't know why they got you and left me. I can't help but talk about it. I ran to you as quickly as I could and I said, "It's me,

Ralph." You rolled your eyes around in your head, and, even with your jaw shot out and your vocal chords gone, you still tried to talk to me. Those were some of the last thoughts. You who had been our spokesman couldn't speak any more. But don't worry, Martin, for they're playing your words all around the world and this will continue for a few days. But you may be assured that we won't ever let your words die. Like the words of our Master, Jesus Christ, they will live in our minds and our hearts and in the souls of black men and white men, brown men and yellow men as long as time shall last.

Let me go back to our third meeting. It was so different in that third meeting. You had arrived to become the new pastor of the Dexter Avenue Baptist Church in Montgomery. I left the parsonage and came over to greet you. You remember you had picked up that great preacher, Vernon Johns, by accident, and brought him back to preach at the First Baptist Church. He had preceded you at Dexter and everyone was happy to see you two together. The great old preacher, Vernon Johns, with his quick wit and pervading wisdom, served as a softening force to our personal thoughts and feelings. We became real friends and true companions that afternoon. Thank God we have remained so through the years. That was the beginning. Our families spend many nights and days together. We were at one house and then the other house, discussing the great issues and ideals, simply because there were no restaurants or motels or hotels that we could go in on a non-discriminatory basis. Those were fighting times for thought and for planning. We got to know each other very well and we got to know the souls of each other in those moments. As I write, I realize that God made us good friends so that he could later make us a working team. As a man in the Movement says, God knows what he is doing. That stays on my mind these days. But I wish so very much that it were the other way. Looking back, things seem clearer now than ever before. Dates come to me. How people looked is clearer, and the meaning of some events that have come to me with greater emphasis.

It was early in the morning on December 2nd when I received a telephone call from E. D. Nixon, a Pullman porter, who told me how Mrs. (Rosa) Parks had been jailed, fingerprinted and mugged like a common criminal. He said to me that something ought to be done because this woman only wanted to sit down on the bus. And she refused to give her seat to a white man. But, before doing anything, I checked with you, Martin. Upon your suggestion, I went into action, began organizing the ministers, calling meetings. And from that day until now, our lives have been in action together. I remember how we talked together about who should be the leader of the new movement. You had not been in Montgomery very long. You were just out of the seminary and some people wanted me because they knew me. And I was president of many organizations in Montgomery. And I could have forced myself to be the leader. But I never, as you know, Martin, wanted to be the leader. I only wanted to stand with you, as Caleb stood with Moses.

From the grand action of the Montgomery movement, our lives were filled with the action of doing God's will in village, hamlet and city. We used to talk theology and then we learned to do theology. It was great. It has been great, Martin. Remember Gee's Bend down in Wilcox County, Ala.? Remember that day we stopped at a little filling station and bought jars of pickled pig's feet and some skins in Mississippi because they would not serve us at a restaurant. Remember, Martin, they wouldn't let us eat downtown? But our staff in that little crowded black man's country store had a fellowship, a *kononia*, together. We had a purpose and we had a universal sense of love that they did not have downtown. Some of my experiences with you will never be forgotten. You will recall how we went to Greensboro, N.C., when the sit-ins broke out, and how we sat in, in order that black men might stand up all over the world. You remember the Freedom Rides and how we were incarcerated and how we were forced to spend the night in the First Baptist Church in Montgomery with thousands of our followers while angry mobs stood on the outside. You remember the Albany movement and how Police Chief [Laurie] Pritchett and his forces tried to turn us around, and a divided Negro community became disgusted and despondent? You said to me, "Ralph, we must go on, anyhow." You remember Bull Connor brought out his vicious dogs, his fire engines and his water hoses and tried to stop us in Birmingham.

But it was you, Martin, who said to me, "Ralph, don't worry about the water, because we've started a fire in Birmingham that water can't put out."

You will recall Savannah, Ga., and how we went there to the aid and rescue of Hosea Williams. Hosea is still with me and he has promised to be to me, Martin, what I tried to be to you. You remember the March of Washington, when more than 250,000 Americans and people from all over the world came to hear you talk about "I Have a Dream?" You remember Danville, Va., and how they put us in jail? You remember St. Augustine, Fla., and Hoss Manuei when he said that he did not have any evil vices whatever? He did not drink liquor, he did not chase after women, he did not smoke. His only hobby was beating and killing niggers. But we knew how to deal with Hoss and we changed him from a Hoss into a mule. You remember how we worked on Bull Connor and changed him from a bull into a steer? You remember how we marched across Edmund Pettis Bridge in Selma and the state troopers lined across upon the orders of Gov. George Wallace and said that we could not pass. But we kept on marching. And when we got there, it opened up, like the Red Sea opened up for Moses and his army. You remember how Mayor [Richard] Daley tried to stop us in Chicago. But we would not let him turn us around.

My dear friend, Martin, now that you have gone, there are some special thoughts that come to me during this Lenten season. There are so many parallels. You were our leader and we were your disciples. Those who killed you did not know that you loved them and that you worked for them as well. For, so often, you said to us: "Love your enemies. Bless them that curse you and pray for them that despitefully use you." They did not know, Martin, that you were a good man, that you hated nobody. But you loved everybody. They did not know that you loved them with a love that would not let you go. They thought that they could kill our movement by killing you, Martin.

But Martin, I want you to know that black people loved you. Some people say that they were just burning and looting in the cities of the nation at this time. But you and I know that just folk, poor people, have had a hard time during these difficult days in which we have lived on this earth. And, in spite of the burning,

I think they are saying: "He died for us." It may seem that they are denying our nonviolence for they are acting our their frustrations. And even a man of good, as you were, was killed in such an evil world as we live in today. And they are merely seeking to express their frustrations. They do not see a way out.

But I want you to know, Martin, that we're going to point to them a way. That was the frustration of Jerusalem during this same season nearly 2,000 years ago. But we know, Martin, because we love people, that, after the venting of frustration, there will be the need for reconciliation. There you will be invisible but real. Black and white will need you to take them from their shame and reconcile them unto you and unto our Master, Jesus Christ. Your words of love are there and we will be there to follow your leadership. There has been a crucifixion in our nation, but here in this spring season as we see the blossoms and smell the fresh air we know that the Resurrection will shortly appear.

When the Master left the disciples, they felt gloom at first. Then they gathered themselves together in a fellowship. They must. . . . Many grew up overnight. They were covered with their ancient words and with despair. We promise you, Martin, just as the disciples tarried in that upper room, that we're going to wait until the power comes from on high. We're going to wait until the Holy Ghost speaks and when the Holy ghost comes and when the Holy Ghost speaks, we're going to speak as Peter spoke. And others will be converted and added to the movement and God's kingdom will come. We promise you, Martin, that we will tighten our fellowship and cover our word. Don't worry, my friend. We will pull our load. We will do our best. With the help of our friends and above all with the help of God. The Poor People's March will be our first attempt to properly do your will for the poor people of this nation. Just a few lines from your friend and your fellow freedom fighter.

Sincerely,
Ralph

Proclamation

by Dr. Ralph David Abernathy

Making Each January 15th a National People's Holiday

in Honor of

Dr. Martin Luther King, Jr.

WHEREAS, the late Dr. Martin Luther King, Jr. lived, worked and died for the cause of freedom, justice, equality and peace for all people; and

WHEREAS, Dr. King and the principles for which he stood should be suitably honored, commemorated, and carried out; and

WHEREAS, Black People, Poor People, and People of Good Will have a right to observe and celebrate Dr. King and his work;

THEREFORE, I, Ralph David Abernathy, do hereby proclaim and designate each January 15th, the Birthday Anniversary of Dr. Martin Luther King, Jr., as a National People's Holiday in honor and in memory of Dr. King; and

I also encourage all Black People, Poor People, and People of Good Will to observe this National People's Holiday by taking the time they need each January 15th to engage in commemorative services, memorial and study assemblies, nonviolent demonstrations, and other activities which are consistent with Dr. King's philosophy and which will make life better for Poor People and all Mankind.

I issue this Proclamation through the powers vested in me as President of the Southern Christian Leadership Conference and leader of the Poor People's Campaign.

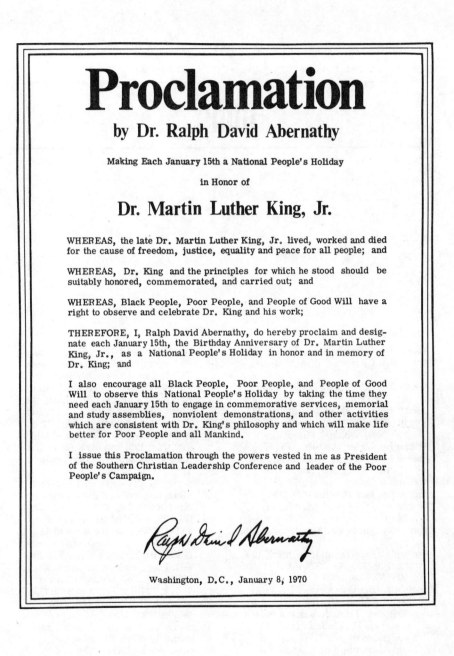

Washington, D.C., January 8, 1970

Index

Finch, Robert, 554
First Baptist Church
(Montgomery): Abernathy invited to
preach at, 82–83; Abernathy resigns
as pastor of, 188, 198–99;
Abernathy's early days as pastor of,
101–2; Abernathy selected as pastor
of, 95–99; bombing of the, 179–86;
Bratcher resigns from, 95–96; Dex-
ter Avenue Baptist Church
compared with, 118–19; Jackson
(Joseph) speaks at the, 171; Johns
preaches at the, 123, 127, 617; and
the Montgomery bus boycott, 161,
171, 179–86; restoration of the,
186–88
First Mt. Pleasant District Baptist Associ-
ation, 7
Fisher, Franklin, 192, 193, 194
Fitzgerald, Ella, 354
Food stamps, 414, 502–3, 518, 522,
529
Ford, Gerald, 85, 583–84, 596–98
Forman, James, 301
Fort Benning, Georgia, 34–37
Fort Devens, Massachusetts, 40–49
Foundation for Economic Enterprises
Development (FEED), 596–98, 602
Fountain, Stanley, 340–41
Fowler, Wyche, 584–85
Franklin, Ruth, 91–92
Freedom Rides, 618
French, Edgar N., 143–45, 147, 148
Fund raising: and Abernathy as the bag-
man, 482–84; for Abernathy's con-
gressional campaign, 585; for
Birmingham, 236, 244–45, 261,
266; for Charleston, 544; and the
Chicago protest, 373; and King's
personal funds, 481; for the March
on Washington, 275–76; for the
Montgomery bus boycott, 159–60,
165–66, 482; and the Poor People's
Campaign, 505–6, 522; and the St.
Augustine protest, 286; and SCLC
general needs, 236; and SCLC's decline, 497, 498; and violence, 286

Gage Park (Chicago, Illinois), 380–82,
383, 389, 393, 396, 492
Gandhi, Mahatma K., 156, 614
Garrow, David, 287, 292, 392
Garvey, Marcus, 615
Gaston, A. G., 239–40, 248, 265, 267
Gaston Motel (Birmingham), 239–40,
248, 270, 299, 581–82
Gay, Richard, 284
GI insurance, 53–54

Goldberg, Arthur, 460
Goldwater, Barry, 295, 322, 326
Good Friday march (Birmingham), 246–
52, 258
Goodman, Andrew, 614–15
Grafman, Hilton, 247–48
Grant, Inez, 199, 206
Gray, Earl, 460
Gray, Fred, 142, 165–66, 175
Greenberg, Jack, 339
Greensboro, North Carolina, 451, 618
Greenwood Baptist Church (Tuskegee),
96, 97
Gregory, Dick, 350, 354
Guaranteed annual income, 368, 512,
528
Guaranteed minimum wage, 414
Gurley, Mary, 462

Hall, David and Rosa Belle, 353
Hall Street Baptist Church (Montgom-
ery), 96–99
Hampton, Lionel, 593, 599, 600
Hanes, Arthur J., 231–32, 234, 259, 271
Hardy, G. Garrett, 64
Hare, James, 298–99, 307–8
Harrington, Cornelius J., 389
Harris, Joel Chandler, 609
Hart, Charles, 591
Hart, Mrs. Phillip, 511
Harvey, Francis, 97
Hatchet, Jack, 43–44, 49–50, 51–52, 58,
59
Hayling, Robert B., 283, 284, 285
Health care, 528
Height, Dorothy, 523
Helicon, Alabama, 107
Heston, Charlton, 278
Hill, Minnie Lee, 512
Hilliard Chapel AME Zion Church
(Montgomery), 137–39
Hobson, Julius, 452
Hogan, Joe (Papa Joe), 99–101
Holt Street Baptist Church (Montgom-
ery), 139, 149–53
Hooks, Benjamin, 433–34, 447, 448
Hoover, J. Edgar, 310–12, 361, 453,
472–75
Hopewell Baptist Church, 7, 13, 26, 80–
82, 83, 563
Hoses: used in Birmingham, 159, 257,
259–60, 261, 263, 618–19
Hotel Detwiler (Birmingham), 242
Housing: in Chicago, 368–71, 374–75,
378–79, 383, 386, 396–98; as a de-
mand of the Poor People's
Campaign, 503, 528
Howard, Emma Payne, 63–64